THE KOVELS'
OFFICIAL BOTTLE
PRICE LIST

BOOKS BY RALPH AND TERRY KOVEL

The Complete Antiques Price List

Know Your Antiques

American Country Furniture 1780–1875

Dictionary of Marks — Pottery and Porcelain

The Official Bottle Price List

The Kovels' Collector's Guide to Limited Editions

The Kovels' Collector's Guide to American Art Pottery

THE KOVELS' OFFICIAL BOTTLE PRICE LIST

Third Edition

by Ralph M. and Terry H. Kovel

Illustrated

Crown Publishers, Inc., New York

To C. "Tiny" Kennedy, one of the most memorable of
the huge family of bottle collectors

and, of course, to Lee and Kim

Library of Congress Cataloging in Publication Data

Kovel, Ralph M
    The Kovels' official bottle price list.

    First-2d ed. published under title: The official bottle price list.
    Bibliography: p.
    1.   Bottles, American—Catalogs.   I.   Kovel, Terry H., joint author.
II.   Title.   III.   Title: Official bottle price list.
NK5440.B6K6 1973   666'.19   75-12542
ISBN 0-517-52189-X

ACKNOWLEDGMENTS

To the following companies and collectors, our special thanks for their help in obtaining pictures of bottles used in this book. Many of the bottles pictured in color were photographed at bottle shows and special exhibits.

Dick Abott; Allan Allerding; Annette's Antiques; Charles and Jane Aprill; Austin Nichols and Co. Inc. (Mac Taub); Avon Products (Art Goodwin, Marion Mann, D. B. Smith, Sherry Van Orten); Paul and Mary Ballentine; Doug Bedore; Edmund and Jayne Blaske; Ralph Bond; Gene Bradberry; Bill Buker, Jr.; Bill Buker, Sr.; Bruce Burwell; Carter's Ink (J. F. McKey); Russell and Lois Cassity; James Conley; Donald Coulter; Jack Daniel Distillery; Jim Davis; Richard Davis; Double Springs (Gerald Marco); Bill and Wanda Dudley; Sandy and Don Duquid; Roger Durflinger; Jane and Scott Edsall; Engle's Antiques & Bottles; Eppinger's Bottle; Ezra Brooks Distilling Company (Joseph P. Tremont); Famous Firsts (Richard Magid); Bob Faville; Dave O. Geduhn; Larry Gerstner; Goffinet's Glass Works; Paul and Eve Gordon; Charles W. Griffin, Jr.; George Hansen; Christopher Hartz; Haviland's Antiques; Gene Heisey; Larry and Janet Heller; Chuck Henigin; Heritage Shop; Holly City Bottle (Ed Johnson); Jim Huey; Gene Jenkins; Desert John; G. Judy; Steve Keith; Gary Kothera; Mark Larrick; James Beam Distilling Company (Martin Lewin); Lionstone Distilleries, Ltd.; Mark Miller; Elvin and Cherie Moody; Bob Morrison; Tony Natelli; John Odell; George Odom; Ray Priebe; Ed Provine; Bob and Jo Pyne; Jim Reid; Marvin L. Roop; Signal the Fruit Jar; Austin Smith; David M. Spaid; Burt Spiller; Jack Sprow; Bill Stankard; Bob Stern; Aubrick Stevenson; Stitzel Weller — Old Fitzgerald & Cabin Still; Mike Stuckey; Paul and Pat Van Vactor; Al Waller; Joe Weiss; Don Welscher; Bob and Hope West; Wheaton Commemoratives (William Jackson); Jim Whetzel; Don Wicks; Duncan Wolcott; Tom Wolfe; B. W. Yarbrough.

Our special thanks go to the Federation of Historical Bottle Clubs of Memphis, Tennessee, and the Louisville Bottle Show of Louisville, Kentucky, for their courtesy in allowing us to photograph their bottles.

For a job well done, a thank you to our staff, especially Debby Herman and Eleanor Dion.

AN IMPORTANT ANNOUNCEMENT TO COLLECTORS AND DEALERS

Every second year, THE KOVELS' OFFICIAL BOTTLE PRICE LIST is completely rewritten. Every entry and every picture is new because of the rapidly changing antiques market. The only way so complete a revision can be accomplished is by using a computer, making it possible to publish the bound book two months after the last price is received.

Yet many price changes occur between editions of THE KOVELS' OFFICIAL BOTTLE PRICE LIST. Important sales produce new record prices each day. Inflation, the changing price of silver and gold, and the international demand for some types of antiques influence sales in the United States.

The serious collector will want to keep up with developments from month to month rather than from year to year. Therefore, we call your attention to a new service to provide price information almost instantaneously: "Ralph and Terry Kovel on Antiques," a nationally distributed illustrated newsletter, published monthly.

This new monthly newsletter covers prices, special interest antiques, what to buy now, how to save and make money on antiques, forums and classes to attend, refinishing and first aid for your possessions, marks, decorating and displaying antiques, book reviews and other pertinent antique news.

Additional information about the newsletter and a complimentary copy are available from the authors at P.O. Box 957, Des Moines, Iowa 50304.

INTRODUCTION

Bottle collecting has become one of the top hobbies in the United States. Not only early historical flasks and figural bottles are collected, but also many types of modern bottles and reproductions. Bottle clubs and bottle shows have set the rules for this *Official Bottle Price List.* We have taken the terms from those in common usage and tried to organize the thousands of listings in easy-to-use form. Many abbreviations have been included that are part of the bottle collector's language. The Tibbits' abbreviations appear throughout the book.

ABM means automatic bottle machine.

BIMAL means blown in mold, applied lip.

BIMALOP means blown in mold, applied lip, open pontil.

FB means free blown.

SC means sun colored.

SCA means sun colored amethyst.

OP means open pontil.

To make the descriptions of the bottles as complete as possible, in some categories, an identification number has been added to the description. The serious collector knows the important books about his specialty and these books have numbered lists of styles of bottles. Included in this book are identification numbers for milk glass from Belknap, flasks from Van Rensselaer and McKearin, candy containers from Eikelberner, figurals from Umberger, bitters from Watson, and ink bottles from Covill. The full titles of the books used are included in the bibliography and listed in the introductory paragraph for each category.

Medicine bottles include all medicine or drugstore bottles, except those under the more specific headings of bitters or sarsaparilla. Modern liquor bottles are listed under the brand name if more than five of the bottles are in the collectible series. If you are not a regular at bottle shows, it may take a few tries to become accustomed to the method of listing. If you cannot find a bottle, try several related headings. For instance, hair dye is found under "household" bottles; many named bottles are found under "medicine," "food," "fruit jar," etc. If your fruit jar has several names, such as "Ball, Mason," look under "fruit jar, ball," or "fruit jar, mason."

The prices shown are in most cases the actual prices asked for bottles during the past year. A few bottles have been included to complete a listing. When this has been done, the prices are estimates based on known prices of the past two years. The estimated prices appear only for modern bottles in a series. Pre-World War I bottles are all listed at actual sale price.

Prices may vary in different parts of the country, so a range is given. Because of the idiosyncrasies of the computer, it was impossible to place a range of price on bottles that are illustrated. The price listed is an average.

Spelling is meant to help the collector. If the original bottle spelled the word "catsup" or "ketchup," that is the spelling that appears. If the period was omitted from "Dr." or the apostrophe from "Jones' sarsaparilla," that is the way it appears. A few bottles are included that had errors in the original spelling and that error is used in the list. "Whiskey" is used even if the bottle held Scotch or Canadian and should be spelled "whisky."

Every bottle illustrated in black and white is indicated by the word "illus." in the text. Every bottle pictured in color is indicated by the word "color" in the listing.

There are a very limited number of the color illustrated bottles shown without prices. They are so rare that no accurate prices are available. We thought the pictures should show the best ones to be an incentive to the collector. To guess at the price would be unfair to everyone. These bottles have a price listing of "XX.XX."

We welcome any information about clubs, prices, or content for future books, but cannot give appraisals by mail. We have tried to be accurate, but we cannot be responsible if any errors in pricing appear.

Ralph and Terry Kovel
(American Society of Appraisers)

1974 LIST OF

DISCONTINUED DECANTERS

The following decanters are no longer offered for sale. In keeping with Avon policy, should any of these decanters be reintroduced in the future, one of the following differentiations will occur: 1) In almost every case, the container or the closure (cap) will be different in color from the original issue; 2) In some cases the decanter will appear identical to the original but will be identified with the letter "R" to mark it as a reissue. Please note that this policy applies to *containers* only. *Product names* may be reused in the future without notification.

Year of Introduction	Product
1969	A MAN'S WORLD AFTER SHAVE (globe)
1968	AFTER SHAVE CADDY
1965	AFTER SHAVE LOTION STEIN (8 oz. — silver)
1966	ALPINE DECANTER (flask)
1969	AVON CLASSICS (books)
1966	AVON DEFENDER (cannon)
1967	AVON GAVEL DECANTER
1971	AVON PONY EXPRESS AFTER SHAVE
1968	AVON PUMP DECANTER
1965	AVON ROYAL ORB
1967	BATH SEASONS
1968	BATH SEASONS
1969	BATH SEASONS
1963	BATH URN
1971	BABY GRAND PERFUME GLACÉ
1962	BAY RUM
1965	BAY RUM GIFT DECANTER
1967	BIRDFEEDER
1968	BUD VASE COLOGNE
1964	CAPTAIN'S CHOICE
1966	CASEY'S LANTERN
1970	CHIEF SCRUBBEM LIQUID SOAP
1969	CHRISTMAS COLOGNE
1967	CHRISTMAS ORNAMENT
1968	CHRISTMAS SPARKLER
1968	CHRISTMAS TREE
1963	CLOSE HARMONY
1967	COLOGNE CLASSIC
1968	COLOGNE RIVIERA
1966	COLOGNE TRILOGY
1968	DAYLIGHT SHAVING TIME

1968	PONY DECANTER
1966	PONY POST
1964	PRETTY PEACH COLOGNE MIST
	(ice cream soda)
1971	PUFFER-CHUGGER BUBBLE BATH
1969	PYRAMID OF FRAGRANCE
1967	RÉGENCE PERFUMED CANDLE
	(green and gold)
1968	RÉGENCE PERFUMED CANDLE
	(frosted glass)
1970	RUBY BUD VASE COLOGNE
1968	SCHOOLHOUSE (Bubble Bath)
1968	SCIMITAR
1968	SCRUB MUG
1971	SEA MAIDEN
1972	SEA TROPHY AFTER SHAVE
1970	SILK 'N HONEY MILK BATH (milk can)
1964	SKIN-SO-SOFT DELUXE DECANTER (fluted)
1966	SKIN-SO-SOFT DECANTER
1965	SKIN-SO-SOFT URN
1962	SKIN-SO-SOFT VASE
1972	SMALL WONDER (caterpillar perfume)
1970	SMALL WORLD COLOGNE
1971	SMALL WORLD COLOGNE MIST
1971	SMALL WORLD CREAM SACHET
1971	SNOOPY'S BUBBLE TUB
1968	SPACE ACE (rocket)
1970	STAMP DECANTER
1968	STEIN (silvery redesign — 6 oz.)
1969	STRUCTURED FOR MAN (3 colognes:
	wood, glass, steel)
1970	THE ANGLER
1968	THE WOLF
1968	TIC TOC TURTLE
1968	TOUCH OF BEAUTY (soap dish and soaps)
1968	TRIBUTE COLOGNE (frosted warrior)
1967	TRIBUTE DECANTER (blue and silver
	warrior — After Shave)
1967	TWENTY PACES (dueling pistols)
1966	VIKING HORN
1967	WESTERN CHOICE (steer horns)
1969	WISE CHOICE (owl)

BIBLIOGRAPHY

Authors' Note

Most of the books not published privately and listed in the bibliography can be obtained at local bookstores. We list below the specialized shops that carry many books not normally stocked.

WHERE TO BUY BOOKS ABOUT BOTTLES

Antique Publications
Emmitsburg, Maryland 21727

Collector Books
P.O. Box 3009
Paducah, Kentucky 42001

Hotchkiss House
89 Sagamore Drive
Rochester, New York 14617

Mid-America Book Company
Leon, Iowa 50144

Old Time Bottle Publishing Co.
611 Lancaster Drive N.E.
Salem, Oregon 97301

Ole Empty Bottle House
Box 136
Amador City, California 95601

The Little Glass Shack
3161 57th Street
Sacramento, California 95820

GENERAL

Adams, John P. *Bottle Collecting in New England.* New Hampshire Publishing Company, Somersworth, New Hampshire 03878, 1969. $3.95.

_____. John P. *Adams' Third Bottle Book.* New Hampshire Publishing Company, Somersworth, New Hampshire 03878, 1972. $3.95.

Bailey, Shirley R. *Bottle Town.* Privately printed, 1968. $3.50. (Order from author, 24 Westwood Terrace, Millville, New Jersey.)

Bates, Virginia T., and Chamberlain, Beverly. *Antique Bottle Finds in New England.* Privately printed, 1968. $3.95. (Order from William L. Bauhan, Inc., Noone House, Peterborough, New Hampshire.)

Belknap, E. M. *Milk Glass.* New York: Crown Publishers, Inc., 1959. $6.00.

Blumenstein, Lynn. *Bottle Rush U.S.A.* Salem, Oregon: Old Time Bottle Publishing Company, 1966. $4.25.

_____. *Old Time Bottles Found in Ghost Towns.* Privately printed, 1966. $2.50.

_____. *"Redigging the West" for Old Time Bottles.* Privately printed, 1966. $4.25.

Colcleaser, Donald E. *Bottles of Bygone Days, Part II.* Privately printed, 1966. $2.00.

_____. *Bottles Yesterday's Trash Today's Treasures.* Privately printed, 1967. $3.75.

Davis, Marvin and Helen. *Antique Bottles.* Privately printed, 1967. $3.00. (Order from author, 2320 Highway 66, Ashland, Oregon 97520.)

_____. *Bottles and Relics.* Privately printed, 1970. $4.50.

_____. *Pocket Field Guide for the Bottle Digger.* Privately printed, 1967. $2.00.

Devner, Kay. *At the Sign of the Mortar.* Privately printed, 1970. $2.75. (Order from author, 8945 E. 20th, Tucson, Arizona 85710.)

Ferraro, Pat and Bob. *A Bottle Collector's Book.* Privately printed, 1966. $3.00. (Order from author, Box 239, Lovelock, Nevada 89419.)

Foster, John Morrill. *Old Bottle Foster and His Glass-Making Descendants.* Fort Wayne, Indiana: Keefer Printing Company, 1972. $4.95.

Freeman, Dr. Larry. *Grand Old American Bottles.* Watkins Glen, New York: Century House, 1964. $25.00.

Hughey, Karen L. *A Price Guide to Infants Nursing Bottles. Book 1.* Privately printed, 1972. (Order from The Ladies of the Lake, P.O. Box 540, Mackinac Island, Michigan 49757.)

Illinois Glass Company. *Old Bottle List Bonanza, Illustrated Catalogue & Price List.* Watkins Glen, New York: Century House, Americana Publishers.

Kaufmann, Don and June. *Dig Those Crazy Bottles: A Handbook of Pioneer Bottles.* Privately printed, 1966. (Order from author, 3520 Laramie Street, Cheyenne, Wyoming.)

Kendrick, Grace. *The Antique Bottle Collector, Including Latest Price Guide.* New York: Pyramid Books, 1971. $2.95.

_____. *"The Mouth-Blown Bottle."* Privately printed, 1968. $6.95.

Kenyon, Harry C. *Jersey Diggins,* Volume 1. Privately printed, 1969. $3.50. (Order from The Old Barn, Newfield, New Jersey.)

Kincade, Steve. *Early American Bottles and Glass.* Privately printed, 1964. $3.00. (Order from Clovis Printing Company, 619 Fifth Street, Clovis, California.)

Klamkin, Marian. *The Collector's Book of Bottles.* New York: Dodd, Mead & Company, 1971. $8.95.

Kovel, Ralph and Terry. *The Kovels' Complete Antiques Price List.* New York: Crown Publishers, Inc., 1974. $6.95.

_____. *Know Your Antiques.* New York: Crown Publishers, Inc., 1967. $7.95.

Lane, Lyman and Sally, and Pappas, Joan. *A Rare Collection of Keene and Stoddard Glass.* New York: Crown Publishers, Inc., 1970. $4.95.

Leahy, Midge and Phil. *The Bottles of Leadville, Colorado.* Privately printed, 1967. $2.00. (Order from author, 4165 Stuart Street, Denver, Colorado.)

Maust, Don. *Bottle and Glass Handbook.* Uniontown, Pennsylvania: E. G. Warman Publishing Company, 1956. $3.00.

McConnell, Walter E. *Tri-State Bottles.* Privately printed, 1969. $3.00. (Order from author, RD #2, Box 116, Newton, New Jersey 07860.)

McKearin, George L. and Helen. *Two Hundred Years of American Blown Glass.* New York: Crown Publishers, Inc., 1950. $15.00.

Motter, Faye. *Stories in Bottles.* Privately printed, 1966. (Order from author, P.O. Box 37, Edina, Missouri.)

Munsey, Cecil. *The Illustrated Guide to Collecting Bottles.* New York: Hawthorn Books, Inc., 1970. $9.95.

Paul, John R., and Parmalee, Paul W. *Soft Drink Bottling, A History with Special Reference to Illinois.* Springfield, Illinois: Illinois State Museum Society, Illinois State Museum, 1973. $5.00.

Phillips, Helen V. *400 Old Bottles, Book #1.* Privately printed, 1967. (Order from author, 528 W. 5th Street, Cheyenne, Wyoming.)

Putnam, P. A. *Bottled Before 1865.* Privately printed, 1968. $2.75. (Order from House of Putnam, P.O. Box 578, Fontana, California 92325.)

Rawlinson, Fred. *Old Bottles of the Virginia Peninsula, 1885–1941.* Privately printed, 1968. $4.30. (Order from FAR Publications, P.O. Box 5456, Newport News, Virginia 23605.)

Reed, Adele. *Bottle Talk.* Privately printed, 1966. $2.00. (Order from author, 272 Shepard Lane, Bishop, California 93514.)

Sellari, Carlo and Dot. *Eastern Bottles Price Guide, Volume 1.* Privately printed, 1969. $4.50.

_____. *Eastern Bottles Price Guide, Volume 2.* Privately printed. 1970. $4.50.

Tibbits, John C. *How to Collect Antique Bottles.* Privately printed, 1969. $4.00.

_____. *John Doe, Bottle Collector.* Privately printed, 1967. $4.00.

_____. *1200 Bottles Priced.* Privately printed, 1970. $4.50. (Order from The Little Glass Shack, 3161 56th Street, Sacramento, California 95820.)

Toulouse, Julian Harrison. *Bottle Makers and Their Marks.* Camden, New Jersey: Thomas Nelson, Inc., 1971. $15.00.

Tufts, James W. *The Manufacture and Bottling of Carbonated Beverages.* Frontier Book Company, Publisher, Fort Davis, Texas 79734, 1969. $3.50.

Umberger, Art and Jewel. *It's a Corker!* Privately printed, 1966. $3.00. (Order from author, 819 W. Wilson, Tyler, Texas 75701.)

_____. *Top Bottles, U.S.A.* Privately printed, 1971. $4.50. (Order from author, 819 West Wilson, Tyler, Texas 75701.)

Unitt, Doris and Peter. *Bottles in Canada.* Peterborough, Ontario, Canada: Clock House Publications, 1972.

Walbridge, William S. *American Bottles Old & New, 1607 to 1920.* Frontier Book Company, Publisher, Fort Davis, Texas 79734, 1969. $4.00.

Watson, George, and Skrill, Robert. *Western Canadian Bottle Collecting.* Privately printed, 1971. $3.50.

Wood, Serry. *The Old Apothecary Shop.* Watkins Glen, New York: Century House, 1956. $2.00.

Yount, John T. *Bottle Collector's Handbook & Pricing Guide.* Educator Books, Inc., Drawer 32, San Angelo, Texas 76901, 1970. $3.95.

ENGLISH — GENERAL

Beck, Doreen. *The Book of Bottle Collecting.* Feltham, Middlesex, England: The Hamlyn Publishing Group Limited, 1973.

Davis, Derek C. *English Bottles & Decanters 1650–1900.* New York: The World Publishing Company, 1972. $5.95.

Fletcher, Edward. *Bottle Collecting: Finding, Collecting and Displaying Antique Bottles.* London, England: Blandford Press Ltd., 1972.

MODERN

Pictorial Bottle Review. *Collectors Edition Presents Beams, Avons, Ezra Brooks, Luxards, Garniers, Fancy and Figural Bottles.* B & K Enterprises, P.O. Box 42558, Los Angeles, California 90050, 1969.

Avon

Ahrendt, L. *Avon Bottle Collector's Guide.* Privately printed, $2.00. (Order from author, 5101 Stockton Road, Sacramento, California 95820.)

_____. *Avon Powder Boxes, Plastics & Toys.* Privately printed, 1969. $2.00.

_____. *Avon's California Perfume Company.* Privately printed, 1969. $3.00.

_____. *Mini Miniatures of Avon.* Privately printed, 1969. $2.00.

Flowers, Bryant. *The Flowers Collection. Avon Guide.* Privately printed, 1970. $5.00. (Order from author, P.O. Box 1613, Pampa, Texas 79065.)

Hanson, Hollis, Jr. *Hollis Hanson's Avon Guide on Rare and Fabulous Avons for the Advanced Collector.* Privately printed, 1970. $3.75. (Order from author, 350 E. Vassar, Fresno, California 93704.)

Hastin, Bud. *Avon Bottle Encyclopedia.* Privately printed, 1971. $8.95. (Order from author, Box 9868, Kansas City, Missouri 64134.)

International Avon Collectors Club. *International Avon Collectors Club, 1969–1970 Annual.* Privately printed, 1970. $5.00. (Order from author, P.O. Box 1406, Mesa, Arizona 85201.)

Newson, Ralph W., and Lamalfa, Jean V. *Fun with Avon Old & New: Bottle Collectors Notebook.* Privately printed, 1969. $3.75. (Order from Arjay Specialties, Box 4371, Panorama City, California 91412.)

_____. *Treasures of Avon.* Privately printed, 1969. $3.75.

Stuart, Lynn R. *Stuart's Book on Avon Collectables.* Privately printed, 1971. $4.20. (Order from author, P.O. Box 862, Gilbert, Arizona 85234.)

_____. *Collector's Guide to Avon Glass Figural Bottles, 1972 Edition.* Privately printed, 1972. $2.50. (Order from author, P.O. Box 862, Gilbert, Arizona 85234.)

Texas Collector's. *Texas Collector's Guide.* Privately printed, 1970. $5.00. (Order from author, Box 1479, Pampa, Texas 79065.)

Underwood, Beatrice and Judith Ann. *Pacific Coast Avon Museum Catalogue. 1974 Edition.* 1974. $9.95. (Order from Pacific Coast Avon Museum, 137 Park Way South, Santa Cruz, California 95060.)

Western World. *Avon–3: Western World Handbook & Price Guide to Avon Bottles.* 1973. $9.95. (Order from Western World Publishers, 511 Harrison Street, San Francisco, California 94105.)

Beam

Cembura, Al, and Avery, Constance. *Jim Beam Bottles, 1973/74 Seventh Edition, Identification and Price Guide.* Privately printed, 1973. (Order from author, 139 Arlington Avenue, Berkeley, California 94707.)

Bischoff

Avery, Constance and Leslie, and Cembura, Al. *Bischoff Bottles, Identification and Price Guide.* Privately printed, 1969. $4.75. (Order from Al Cembura, 139 Arlington Avenue, Berkeley, California 94707.)

Ezra Brooks

Western Collector. *Western Collector's Handbook and Price Guide to Ezra Brooks Decanters.* San Francisco, California: Western World Publishers, 1970. $4.95. (Order from Western Collector Books, 511 Harrison Street, San Francisco, California 94105.)

Garnier

Avery, Constance, and Cembura, Al. *Garnier Bottles.* Privately printed, 1970. $4.95. (Order from Al Cembura, 139 Arlington Avenue, Berkeley, California 94707.)

Schwartz, Jeri and Ed. *Just Figurals: A Guide to Garnier.* Privately printed, 1969. $4.25. (Order from author, North Broadway, Yonkers, N.Y. 10701.)

Luxardo

Avery, Constance, and Cembura, Al. *Luxardo Bottles: Identification and Price Guide.* Privately printed, 1968. $4.75. (Order from Al Cembura, 139 Arlington Avenue, Berkeley, California 94707.)

BITTERS

Bartholomew, Ed. *1001 Bitters Bottles.* Bartholomew House, Publishers, Fort Davis, Texas 79734, 1970. $4.95.

Watson, Richard. *Bitters Bottles.* New York: Thomas Nelson & Sons, 1965. $10.00.

_____. *Supplement to Bitters Bottles.* Camden, New Jersey: Thomas Nelson & Sons, 1968. $6.50.

CANDY CONTAINERS

Eikelberner, George, and Agadjanian, Serge. *American Glass Containers.* Privately printed, 1967. $7.50. (Order from Serge Agadjanian, River Road, Belle Mead, New Jersey 08502.)

_____. *More American Glass Candy Containers.* Privately printed, 1970. $6.00.

Matthews, Robert T. *Old Glass Candy Containers Price Guide.* Privately printed, 1966. $3.62. (Order from author, Glenelg, Maryland 21737.)

COCA-COLA

Coca-Cola Company, The. *The Coca-Cola Company . . . An Illustrated Profile.* Atlanta, Georgia: The Coca-Cola Company, 1974. $5.50. (Order from author, P.O. Drawer 1734, Atlanta, Georgia 30301.)

Goldstein, Shelly and Helen. *Coca-Cola Collectibles With Current Prices and Photographs in Full Color* (Vol. 1–111). Privately printed, 1971, 1973, and 1974. Vol. I, $10.00; Vol. II and III, $10.95. (Order from author, P.O. Box 301, Woodland Hills, California 91364.)

Munsey, Cecil. *The Illustrated Guide to the Collectibles of Coca-Cola.* New York: Hawthorn Books, Inc., 1972. $12.95.

FIGURAL

Revi, Albert Christian. *American Pressed Glass and Figure Bottles.* New York: Thomas Nelson & Sons, 1964. $15.00.

Umberger, Jewel and Arthur L. *Collectible Character Bottles.* Privately printed, 1969. $12.50. (Order from Corker Book Company, 819 West Wilson, Tyler, Texas.)

Vincent, Pal. *The Moses Bottle.* Privately printed, 1969. $4.25. (Order from The Palabra Shop, Jct. Rtes. 26 and 122, Poland Spring, Maine 04274.)

Wearin, Otha D. *Statues That Pour: The Story of Character Bottles.* Denver, Colorado: Sage Books, 2679 South York Street, 1965. $6.00.

FLASKS

Barber, Edwin A. *Old American Bottles.* New York: David McKay Co., 1900. $3.50. (Reprint available from Frontier Book Co., Publisher, Fort Davis, Texas 79734.)

McKearin, George L. and Helen. *American Glass.* New York: Crown Publishers, Inc., 1959. $14.95.

Thomas, John L. *Picnics, Coffins, Shoo-Flies.* Privately printed, 1974. $8.25. (Order from author, P.O. Box 446, Weaverville, California 96093.)

Van Rensselaer, Stephen. *Early American Bottles & Flasks.* Southampton, New York: Cracker Barrel Press, 1921. $3.00.

_____. *Early American Bottles & Flasks—Revised.* Stratford, Connecticut, 1969. $15.00. (Order from J. Edmund Edwards, 61 Winton Place, Stratford, Connecticut 06497.)

FRUIT JARS

Bird, Douglas, and Corke, Marion and Charles. *A Century of Antique Canadian Glass Fruit Jars.* Privately printed, 1970. $6.95. (Order from Douglas Bird, 859 Valetta Street, London 74, Ontario, Canada.)

_____. *North American Fruit Jar Index.* Privately printed, 1968. $6.00.

Burris, Ronald B. *An Illustrated Guide for Collecting Fruit Jars with Price Guide.* Privately printed, 1966. $1.75. (Order from author, 2941 Campus Drive, Visalia, California 93277.)

_____. *Collecting Fruit Jars, Book #2, with Price Guide.* Privately printed, 1967. $2.00.

_____. *More Collectable Jars, Book #3, with Price Guide.* Privately printed, 1968. $2.50.

_____. *Rare and Unusual Fruit Jars, Book #4, with Price Guide.* Privately printed, 1970. $2.75.

Creswick, Alice, and Rodrigues, Arleta. *The Cresrod Blue Book of Fruit Jars.* Privately printed, 1969. $4.50. (Order from Cresrod Publishing Company, 0-8525 Kenowa SW, Grand Rapids, Michigan 49504.)

Harvest Publishing Company. *Harvest 2nd Fruit Jar Finders Price Guide.* Privately printed, 1970. $3.95. (Order from Harvest Publishing Company, Box 3015-M, Milwaukee, Wisconsin 53218.)

Hawkins, R. Doug. *For Preserving Fruit.* Privately printed, 1972. $4.00. (Order from author, 1209 S. Brundidge St., Troy, Alabama 36081.)

Rodrigues, Arleta. *Fruit Jars—Canister to Kerr.* Privately printed, 1971. $4.50. (Order from James Publications, P.O. Box 2413, Castro Valley, California 94546.)

Rodrigues, Arleta, and Creswick, Alice. *A Collection of Yesterday's Fruit Jars from Great Aunt May's Cellar.* Privately printed, 1967. $6.50. (Order from Arleta Rodrigues, P.O. Box 2413, Castro Valley, California 94546.)

Schroeder, Bill. *1000 Fruit Jars Priced & Illustrated.* Privately printed, 1970. $3.95. (Order from author, Route 4, Paducah, Kentucky 42001.)

Toulouse, Julian Harrison. *Fruit Jars: A Collector's Manual.* Jointly published by Camden, New Jersey: Thomas Nelson & Sons, and Hanover, Pennsylvania: Everybody's Press, 1969. $15.00.

Umberger, Art and Jewel. *The Kitchen Cupboard: Fruit Jar Price Guide.* Privately printed, 1967. $3.00. (Order from author, 819 West Wilson, Tyler, Texas 75701.)

INKWELLS

Covill, William E., Jr. *Ink Bottles and Inkwells.* Taunton, Massachusetts: William S. Sullwold, Publishing, 1971. $17.50.

McGraw, Vincent. *McGraw's Book of Antique Inkwells, Volume 1.* Privately printed, 1972. (Order from author, P.O. Box 23016, Minneapolis, Minnesota 55423.)

Nelson, Lavinia, and Hurley, Martha. *Old Inks.* Privately printed, 1967. $5.00. (Order from "Old Inks," 22 Bryant Road, Nashua, New Hampshire.)

Walter, Leo G., Jr. *Walter's Inkwells of 1885: Book #1.* Privately printed, 1968. $3.75. (Order from Stagecoach Antiques, 443 West Market Street, Akron, Ohio 44303.)

MEDICINE

Agee, Bill. *Collecting the Cures.* Privately printed, 1969. $3.00. (Order from author, 1200 Melrose, Waco, Texas 76710.)

Baldwin, Joseph K. *A Collector's Guide to Patent and Proprietary Medicine Bottles of the Nineteenth Century.* New York: Thomas Nelson, Inc., 1973. $15.00.

Bartholomew, Ed. *1200 Old Medicine Bottles with Prices Current.* Frontier Book Company, Fort Davis, Texas 79734, 1970. $3.95.

Blasi, Betty. *A Bit About Balsams, A Chapter in the History of Nineteenth Century Medicine.* Privately printed, 1974. $7.50. (Order from author, 5801 River Knolls Drive, Louisville, Kentucky 40222.)

Devner, Day. *Patent Medicine Picture.* Privately printed, 1968. $2.50. (Order from author, 8945 East 20th, Tucson, Arizona 85710.)

Freeman, Dr. Larry. *The Medicine Showman.* Watkins Glen, New York: Century House, 1957. $4.00.

Jensen, Al and Margaret. *Old Owl Drug Bottles & Others.* Privately printed, 1968. $3.50. (Order from author, 783 Alice Avenue, Mountain View, California 94040.)

Penland, Belle. *Bottles, Corks & Cures.* Privately printed, 1963. $2.65. (Order from author, P.O. Box 118, Twain, California 95984.)

Wilson, Bill and Betty. *Nineteenth Century Medicine in Glass.* Amador City, California: 19th Century Hobby & Publishing Company, 1971.

MILK

Rawlinson, Fred. *Make Mine Milk.* Privately printed, 1970. $3.85. (Order from FAR Publications, Box 5456, Newport News, Virginia 23605.)

Roth, Evelyn. *The Milky Way.* Privately printed, 1969. $2.50. (Order from author, 245 Shore Road, Ocean View, New Jersey 08230.)

Taylor, Gordon A. *Milk Bottle Manual: A Collector's Pictorial Primer and Pricing Guide.* Salem, Oregon: Old Time Bottle Publishing Company, 1971. $3.95.

MINIATURES

Cembura, Al, and Avery, Constance. *A Guide to Miniature Bottles* (Volumes 1–3). Privately printed, 1972 and 1973. Vol. I, $3.95; Vol. II and III, $2.95. (Order from author, 139 Arlington Avenue, Berkeley, California 94708.)

Snyder, Robert E. *Bottles in Miniature.* Privately printed, 1969. $4.00. (Order from author, 4235 West 13th, Amarillo, Texas 79106.)

_____. *Bottles in Miniature, Volume II.* Privately printed, 1970. $4.75.

_____. *Bottles in Miniature, Volume III.* Privately printed, 1972. $6.00.

Spaid, David M. *Mini World, 1971–1972 Identification and Price Guide.* Los Angeles, California: B & K Enterprises, 1971. $3.50.

POISON BOTTLES

Durflinger, Roger L. *Poison Bottles Collectors Guide, Vol. 1.* Privately printed, 1972. $3.95. (Order from author, 132 W. Oak Street, Washington C.H., Ohio 43160.)

Stier, Wallis W. *Poison Bottles: A Collectors' Guide*. Privately printed, 1969. $3.50. (Order from author, P.O. Box 243, Rockland, Idaho 83271.)

SARSAPARILLA

Shimko, Phyllis. *Sarsaparilla Bottle Encyclopedia*. Privately printed, 1969. $6.50. (Order from author, Box 117, Aurora, Oregon 97002.)

Umberger, Art and Jewel. *It's a Sarsaparilla! Price Guide*. Privately printed, 1968. $3.00. (Order from author, 819 W. Wilson, Tyler, Texas 75701.)

SODA AND MINERAL WATER

Fountain, John C., and Colcleaser, Donald. *Dictionary of Soda & Mineral Water Bottles*. Amador City, California: "Ole Empty Bottle House Publishing Company," 1968. P.O. Box 136. $3.75.

Jones, J. L. *Soda and Mineral Water Bottles*. Greer, South Carolina: Palmetto Enterprises, 1972. $8.00.

Lincoln, Gerald David. *Antique Blob Top Bottles, Central & Southern New England*. Privately Printed, 1970. $3.25. (Order from author, 700 Berlin Road, Marlboro, Massachusetts 01752.)

Markota, Peck and Audie. *Western Blob Top Soda and Mineral Water Bottles*. Amador City, California: Antique and Hobby Publishing Company, 1971. $5.00.

Schmeiser, Alan. *Have Bottles Will Pop*. Privately printed, 1968. $6.95. (Order from author, 370 E. Mayes Street, Dixon, California 95620.)

_____. *More Pop*. Privately printed, 1970. $10.00. (Order from author, 370 E. Mayes Street, Dixon, California 95620.)

WHISKEY AND BEER

Anderson, Sonja and Will. *Andersons' Turn-of-the-Century Brewery Dictionary*. Privately printed. $15.95. (Order from author, 1 Lindy Street, Carmel, New York 10512.)

_____. *Beers, Breweries & Breweriana*. Privately printed, 1969.

Anderson, Will. *The Beer Book, An Illustrated Guide to American Breweriana*. Princeton, New Jersey: The Pyne Press, 1973. $17.50.

Fountain, John C., and Colcleaser, Donald. *Dictionary of Spirits and Whiskey Bottles*. Amador City, California: "Ole Empty Bottle House Publishing Company," 1969. P.O. Box 136. $3.75.

Howe, John. *A Whiskeyana Guide: Antique Whiskey Bottles*. Privately printed, 1967. $3.00. (Order from author, 4894 Sandy Lane, San Jose, California 95124.)

Kaufmann, Don and June. *The United States Brewers' Guide, 1630–1864*. Privately printed, 1967. $1.75. (Order from author, 3520 Laramie Street, Cheyenne, Wyoming 82001.)

Martin, Byron and Vicky. *Here's to Beers, Blob Top Beer Bottles 1880–1910.* Privately printed, 1973. $5.00. (Order from The Achin Back Saloon, 8400 Darby Avenue, Northridge, California 91324.)

Peewee Valley Press. *Decanter Collector's Guide.* Privately printed, 1970. $2.75. (Order from author, P.O. Box 248, Peewee Valley, Kentucky 40056.)

Silva, Bev and Joe. *Research on San Francisco Whiskey Bottles.* Privately printed, 1967. $2.00. (Order from author, 6829 Mayhews Lndg. Road, Newark, California 94560.)

Wilson, Bill and Betty. *Spirits Bottles of the Old West.* Privately printed, 1968. $10.00. (Order from Antiques & Hobby Publishing Company, Box 136, Amador City, California 95601.)

NEWSPAPERS OF INTEREST TO BOTTLE COLLECTORS

The American Collector
13920 Mt. McClelland Blvd.
Reno, Nevada 89506

Antique Monthly
P.O. Drawer 440
Tuscaloosa,
Alabama 35401

Antique News
P.O. Box B
Marietta,
Pennsylvania 17547

The Antiques Gazette
P.O. Box 776
Merrimack,
New Hampshire 03054

Antique Trader Weekly
P.O. Box 1050
Dubuque, Iowa 52001

The Antiquity
Mt. Hermon Road
Hope, New Jersey 07844

Collector's News
P.O. Box 156
Grundy Center, Iowa 50638

Collector's Weekly
Drawer C
Kermit, Texas 79745

Maine Antique Digest
RFD 3 Box 76—A
Waldoboro, Maine 04572

Tri-State Trader
P.O. Box 90
Knightstown,
Indiana 46148

West Coast Peddler
P.O. Box 4489
Downey, California 90241

NEWSLETTERS OF INTEREST TO BOTTLE COLLECTORS

*Milkbottles Only
Organization (MOO)*
Fred Rawlinson
P.O. Box 5456
Newport News,
Virginia 23605

Miniature Bottle Mart
24 Gertrude Lane
West Haven,
Connecticut 06516

*The Western World
Avon Quarterly*
511 Harrison Street
San Francisco,
California 94105

MAGAZINES OF INTEREST TO BOTTLE COLLECTORS

Antique Bottle World
5888 Executive Boulevard
Dayton, Ohio 45424

Antiques Journal
P.O. Box 1046
Dubuque, Iowa, 52001

Antiques Today
P.O. Box 1034
Kermit, Texas 79745

Bottle News
P.O. Box 1000
Kermit, Texas 79745

Bottles & Relics
P.O. Box 654
Conroe, Texas, 77301

Collector's World
P.O. Box 654
Conroe, Texas 77301

Hobbies
Lightner Publishing
Corporation
1006 South Michigan Ave.
Chicago, Illinois 60605

Journal of the Federation of Historical Bottle Clubs
10118 Schuessler
St. Louis, Missouri 63128

"the miniature bottle collector"
P.O. Box 2161
Palos Verdes Peninsula,
California 90274

Old Bottle Magazine
The Old Bottle Exchange
525 E. Revere
Bend, Oregon 97701

Pictorial Bottle Review
B & K Enterprises, Inc.
P.O. Box 42558
Los Angeles,
California 90050

Relics
P.O. Box 3338
Austin, Texas 78764

Spinning Wheel
Everybody's Press
Hanover,
Pennsylvania 17331

BOTTLE CLUBS

National Clubs

FEDERATION OF
HISTORICAL BOTTLE
CLUBS
c/o Gene Bradberry,
President
4098 Faxon Avenue
Memphis,
Tennessee 38122

INTERNATIONAL AVON
COLLECTORS CLUB (IAAC)
P.O. Box 1406
Mesa, Arizona 85201

LIONSTONE BOTTLE
COLLECTORS OF AMERICA
P.O. Box 75924
Los Angeles,
California 90075

MILKBOTTLES ONLY
ORGANIZATION (MOO)
P.O. Box 5456
Newport News,
Virginia 23605

NATIONAL AVON BOTTLE
& COLLECTABLES CLUB,
U.S.A., INC.
P.O. Box 232
Amador City,
California 95601

NATIONAL AVON CLUB
P.O. Box 5490
Overland Park,
Kansas 66212

NATIONAL EZRA BROOKS
BOTTLE & SPECIALTIES
CLUB
420 West 1st Street
Kewanee, Illinois 61443

NATIONAL JIM BEAM
BOTTLE & SPECIALTIES
CLUB
6702 Stockton Avenue
El Cerrito, California 94530

PIONEER BOTTLE CLUB
OF FAIRHOPE
P.O. Box 294
Battles Wharf,
Alabama 36533

ALABAMA ANTIQUE
BOTTLE COLLECTORS
SOCIETY
Box 2091
Birmingham,
Alabama 35202

ALABAMA BOTTLE
COLLECTORS'
ASSOCIATION
2713 Hanover Circle S.
Birmingham,
Alabama 35205

ALABAMA BOTTLE
COLLECTORS' SOCIETY
1768 Hanover Circle
Birmingham,
Alabama 35205

NORTH ALABAMA BOTTLE
& GLASS CLUB
P.O. Box 109
Decatur, Alabama 35601

HUNTSVILLE HISTORICAL
BOTTLE CLUB
113 Monte Sano Blvd. S.E.
Huntsville, Alabama 35801

HUNTSVILLE HISTORICAL
BOTTLE CLUB
5605 Woodridge S.W.
Huntsville, Alabama 35802

MONTGOMERY BOTTLE &
INSULATOR CLUB
851 Portland Avenue
Montgomery,
Alabama 36111

MOBILE BOTTLE
COLLECTORS CLUB
Rt. #4 Box 28
Theodore, Alabama 36582

TUSCALOOSA ANTIQUE
BOTTLE CLUB
c/o Glenn House
1617 11th Street
Tuscaloosa,
Alabama 35401

ALASKA BOTTLE CLUB
(formerly THE
ANCHORAGE BEAM CLUB)
8510 E. 10th
Anchorage, Alaska 99504

WHITE MOUNTAIN
ANTIQUE BOTTLE
COLLECTORS
ASSOCIATION
P.O. Box 503
Eager, Arizona 85925

AVON COLLECTORS CLUB
P.O. Box 1406
Mesa, Arizona 86201

ARIZONA TREASURES
UNLIMITED
5506 W. McDowell Road
Phoenix, Arizona 85009

KACHINA-EZRA BROOKS
BOTTLE CLUB
4331 North 31st Drive
Phoenix, Arizona 85017

KACHINA-EZRA BROOKS
BOTTLE CLUB
2801 N. 34th Drive
Phoenix, Arizona 85009

PICK & SHOVEL ANTIQUES
BOTTLE CLUB OF ARIZONA
Box 7446
Phoenix, Arizona 85011

VALLEY OF THE SUN
BOTTLE & SPECIALTY
CLUB
3117 West Bethany
Home Road
Phoenix, Arizona 85017

ARIZONA EZRA BROOKS
BOTTLE CLUB
14 Walking Diamond Drive
Prescott, Arizona 86301

VALLEY OF THE SUN
BOTTLE & SPECIALTY
CLUB
212 East Minton
Tempe, Arizona 85281

ARIZONA TERRITORY
ANTIQUE BOTTLE CLUB
P.O. Box 1221
Tucson, Arizona 85715

ARIZONA TERRITORY
ANTIQUE BOTTLE CLUB
P.O. Box 6364
Speedway Station
Tucson, Arizona 85716

SOUTHWEST ARKANSAS
BOTTLE CLUB
c/o Joe Parker
Star Route
Delight, Arkansas 71940

HEMPSTED COUNTY
BOTTLE CLUB
710 So. Hervey
Hope, Arkansas 71801

MADISON COUNTY
BOTTLE COLLECTORS
CLUB
Rt. 2 Box 304
Huntsville, Arkansas 72740

LITTLE ROCK ANTIQUE
BOTTLE COLLECTORS
P.O. Box 5003
Little Rock,
Arkansas 72205

RAZORBACK JIM BEAM
BOTTLE & SPECIALTY
CLUB
7813 Kanis Road
Little Rock,
Arkansas 72204

GOLDEN GATE EZRA
BROOKS BOTTLE &
SPECIALTIES CLUB
Mr. Kenneth Busse,
President
438 Pacific Avenue
Alameda, California 94501

GOLDEN GATE
HISTORICAL BOTTLE
SOCIETY
P.O. Box 129
Alameda, California 94501

CALIFORNIA SKI
COUNTRY BOTTLE CLUB
212 South El Molino Street
Alhambra, California 91801

NATIONAL ASSOCIATION
OF MINIATURE
ENTHUSIASTS
(N.A.M.E.)
P.O. Box 2621
Brookhurst Center
Anaheim, California 92804

QUEEN MARY BEAM &
SPECIALTY CLUB
P.O. Box 2054
Anaheim, California 92804

SHASTA ANTIQUE BOTTLE
COLLECTORS
ASSOCIATION
Route 1 Box 3147-A
Anderson, California 96007

GOLD STATE BOTTLE &
SPECIALTIES CLUB
P.O. Box 463
Aptos, California 95003

KERN COUNTY ANTIQUE
BOTTLE CLUB
P.O. Box 6724
Bakersfield,
California 93306

CHERRY VALLEY BEAM &
SPECIALTIES CLUB
P.O. Box 145
Beaumont,
California 92223

NATIONAL ASSOCIATION
OF JIM BEAM &
SPECIALTY CLUBS
490 El Camino Real
Belmont, California 94002

PENINSULA BOTTLE CLUB
P.O. Box 886
Belmont, California 94002

BENTON BEAMS &
ANTIQUES
MaBelle V. Bramlettle
Benton, California 93512

JIM BEAM BOTTLE CLUB
139 Arlington
Berkeley, California 94707

BISHOP BELLES & BEAUX
BOTTLE CLUB
P.O. Box 1475
Bishop, California 93514

HANGTOWN BOTTLEERS
P.O. Box 208
Camino, California 95709

GOLDEN CADILLAC
BOTTLE & ANTIQUE CLUB
P.O. Box 1088
Cherry Valley,
California 92223

BIDWELL BOTTLE CLUB
Box 546
Chico, California 95926

CHICO ANTIQUE BOTTLE
CLUB
Route 2 Box 474
Chico, California 95926

AVON BOTTLE &
SPECIALTY CLUB
P.O. Box 23
Claremont,
California 91711

PETALUMA BOTTLE &
ANTIQUE CLUB
9773 Minn. Avenue
Cotati, California 94928

ORIGINAL SIPPIN
COUSINS EZRA BROOKS
SPECIALTIES CLUB
5823 Bartmus Street
Downey, California 90040

MT. BOTTLE CLUB
422 Orpheus
Encinitas, California 92024

HUMBOLDT ANTIQUE
BOTTLE CLUB
P.O. Box 6012
Eureka, California 95501

RELIC ACCUMULATORS
P.O. Box 3513
Eureka, California 95501

TEEN BOTTLE CLUB
Route 1 Box 60-T E
Eureka, California 95501

SAN BERNARDINO
COUNTY HISTORICAL
BOTTLE CLUB
c/o Fontana Y.W.C.A.
17366 Merrill Avenue
Fontana, California 92335

NORTHWESTERN BOTTLE
CLUB ASSOCIATION
10190 Martinelli Road
Forestville,
California 95436

MONTEREY BAY BEAM
BOTTLE & SPECIALTY
CLUB
P.O. Box 258
Freedom, California 95019

ANTIQUE BOTTLE CLUB
ASSOCIATION OF FRESNO
P.O. Box 1932
Fresno, California 93718

SAN JOAQUIN VALLEY
JIM BEAM BOTTLE &
SPECIALTIES CLUB
4085 North Wilson Avenue
Fresno, California 93704

SOUTH BAY BOTTLE CLUB
1221 West 186th Street
Gardena, California 90248

SAN DIEGO EZRA BROOKS
BOTTLE & SPEC. CLUB
P.O. Box 16118
Imperial Beach,
California 92032

SAN FRANCISCO BAY AREA
MINIATURE BOTTLE CLUB
c/o Darwin Williams
160 Lower Via Casitas #8
Kentfield, California 94904

MT. WHITNEY
BOTTLE CLUB
P.O. Box 688
Lone Pine,
California 93545

WESTERN WORLD AVON
CLUB — CHAPTER II —
LONG BEACH
c/o Fran Bronn, President
1049 Freeland Street
Long Beach,
California 90807

AMETHYST BOTTLE CLUB
3245 Military Avenue
Los Angeles,
California 90034

EZRA BROOKS
SPECIALTIES CLUB
4908½ Meridian Street
Los Angeles,
California 90042

JIM BEAM BOTTLE CLUB
OF SO. CALIF.
12206 Malone Street
Los Angeles,
California 90066

LOS ANGELES HISTORICAL
BOTTLE CLUB
P.O. Box 60672
Terminal Annex
Los Angeles,
California 90060

MISSION BELLS (BEAMS)
1114 Coronada Terrace
Los Angeles,
California 90026

SOUTH BAY BOTTLE CLUB
8324 Colegio Drive
Los Angeles,
California 90045

SOUTHERN CALIFORNIA
MINIATURE BOTTLE CLUB
5626 Corning Avenue
Los Angeles,
California 90056

LOS BANOS ANTIQUE
BOTTLE CLUB
635 Jefferson Avenue
Los Banos,
California 93635

MODESTO OLD BOTTLE
CLUB (MOBC)
P.O. Box 1791
Modesto, California 95354

AVON BOTTLE &
SPECIALTIES COLLECTORS
Southern California Division
9233 Mills Avenue
Montclair, California 91763

NORTHERN CALIFORNIA
JIM BEAM BOTTLE &
SPECIALTY CLUB
P.O. Box 186
Montgomery Creek,
California 96065

SUNNYVALE ANTIQUE
BOTTLE COLLECTORS
ASSOCIATION
1660 Yale Drive
Mountain View,
California 94040

CURIOSITY BOTTLE
ASSOCIATION
Box 103
Napa, California 94558

JIM BEAM BOTTLE CLUB
P.O. Box 103
Napa, California 94558

CAMELLIA CITY JIM BEAM
BOTTLE CLUB
3734 Lynhurst Way
North Highlands,
California 95660

WESTERN WORLD
COLLECTORS
ASSOCIATION
P.O. Box 409
Ontario, California 91761

JEWELS OF AVON
2297 Maple Avenue
Oroville, California 95965

PARADISE GLASSHOPPERS
6982 Skyway
Paradise, California 95969

SAN LUIS OBISPO BOTTLE
SOCIETY
124 21st Street
Paso Robles,
California 93446

NORTHWESTERN BOTTLE
COLLECTORS
ASSOCIATION
1 Keeler Street
Petaluma, California 94952

PETALUMA BOTTLE &
ANTIQUE CLUB
P.O. Box 1035
Petaluma, California 94952

MT. DIABLO BOTTLE CLUB
4166 Sandra Circle
Pittsburg, California 94565

TEHAMA COUNTY
ANTIQUE BOTTLE CLUB
P.O. Box 541
Red Bluff, California 96080

NORTHERN CALIFORNIA
JIM BEAM BOTTLE &
SPECIALTY CLUB
2110 Elmira Drive
Redding, California 96001

SOUTH BAY ANTIQUE
BOTTLE CLUB
c/o Hillcrest School
200 N. Lucia
Redondo Beach, California

HOLLYWOOD STARS EZRA
BROOKS BOTTLE CLUB
18344 Schoolcraft
Reseda, California 91335

GOLDEN GATE EZRA
BROOKS BOTTLE &
SPECIALTY CLUB OF
NORTHERN CALIFORNIA
12517 San Pablo Avenue
Richmond,
California 94805

LIVERMORE AVON CLUB
6385 Claremont Avenue
Richmond,
California 94805

HIGH DESERT BOTTLE
HUNTERS
P.O. Box 581
Ridgecrest,
California 93555

BEAM BOTTLE CLUB OF
SOUTHERN CALIFORNIA
3221 N. Jackson
Rosemead,
California 91770

SKI-COUNTRY BOTTLE
CLUB OF SOUTHERN
CALIFORNIA
c/o Zee Guidotti
3148 N. Walnut Grove
Rosemead,
California 91770

BRONZE STAGECOACH
EZRA BROOKS BOTTLE &
SPECIALTIES CLUB
P.O. Box 1108
Roseville,
California 95678

CENTRAL CALIFORNIA
AVON BOTTLE CLUB
5101 Stockton Blvd.
Sacramento,
California 95820

GREATER CALIFORNIA
HISTORICAL BOTTLE CLUB
P.O. Box 55
Sacramento,
California 95801

MISSION TRAIL
HISTORICAL BOTTLE CLUB
c/o Bart Parker
45 Penzance
Salinas, California

GOLDEN GATE EZRA
BROOKS BOTTLE &
SPECIALTY CLUB
P.O. Box 5612
San Francisco,
California 94102

MISSION TRAILS EZRA
BROOKS BOTTLES &
SPECIALTIES CLUB, INC.
4923 Bel Canto Drive
San Jose, California 95124

NATIONAL JIM BEAM
BOTTLE & SPEC. CLUB
816 Stanyan Street
San Francisco,
California 94117

SAN DIEGO ANTIQUE
BOTTLE CLUB
P.O. Box 536
San Diego,
California 92112

SAN DIEGO JIM BEAM
CLUB
c/o Dusty Rhodes
4320 Ridgeway
San Diego,
California 92116

GLASS BELLES OF SAN
GABRIEL
518 W. Neuby Avenue
San Gabriel,
California 91776

SAN JOSE ANTIQUE
BOTTLE COLLECTORS
ASSOCIATION
P.O. Box 5432
San Jose, California 95150

LILLIPUTIAN BOTTLE
CLUB
c/o David Spaid
1927 Toscanini
San Pedro,
California 90732

MARIN COUNTY BOTTLE
CLUB
c/o Jean Wyrick
31 Ridge Drive
San Rafael,
California 94901

ANTIQUE BOTTLE CLUB
OF ORANGE COUNTY
P.O. Box 10424
Santa Ana,
California 92711

ANTIQUE BOTTLE
COLLECTORS OF
ORANGE COUNTY
223 E. Ponona
Santa Ana,
California 92707

MINI SPIRITS BOTTLE
CLUB
1230 Genoa Drive
Santa Ana,
California 92704

ORANGE COUNTY
MINIATURE COLLECTORS
1230 Genoa Drive
Santa Ana,
California 92704

SANTA BARBARA BEAM
BOTTLE CLUB
5307 University Drive
Santa Barbara,
California 93111

SANTA BARBARA
BOTTLE CLUB
5381 Paseo Cameo
Santa Barbara,
California 93105

NORTHWESTERN BOTTLE
COLLECTORS
ASSOCIATION
P.O. Box 1121
Santa Rosa,
California 95402

MISSION TRAIL
HISTORICAL BOTTLE CLUB
P.O. Box 721
Seaside, California 93940

HOFFMAN'S MR. LUCKY
BOTTLE CLUB
c/o Mr. Jim Roberts,
President
2104 Rhoda Street
Simi Valley,
California 93065

M. T. BOTTLE CLUB
P.O. Box 608
Solana Beach,
California 92075

STOCKTON HISTORICAL
BOTTLE SOCIETY
748 E. Mayfair Avenue
Stockton, California 95207

CHIEF SOLANO BOTTLE
CLUB
4-D Boynton Avenue
Suisun, California 94585

SUNNYVALE ANTIQUE
BOTTLE COLLECTORS
ASSOCIATION
613 Torrington
Sunnyvale,
California 94087

TAFT ANTIQUE BOTTLE
CLUB
P.O. Box 334
Taft, California 93268

SAN LUIS OBISPO BOTTLE
SOCIETY
Rt. 1 Box 108
Templeton,
California 93465

GLASSHOPPER FIGURAL
BOTTLE ASSOCIATION
P.O. Box 6642
Torrance, California 90504

CALIFORNIA FRUIT JAR
COLLECTORS
Maxine Bush, Secretary
16646 Montego Way
Tustin, California 92680

MOTHERLODE ANTIQUE
BOTTLE CLUB OF
CALAVERAS COUNTY
c/o Sharon Shewpack
P.O. Box 112
Valecto, California 95251

NAPA-SOLANO BOTTLE
CLUB
c/o Ginny Smith
1409 Delwood
Vallejo, California 94590

JUNIPER HILLS
BOTTLE CLUB
Rt. 1 Box 18
Valyerma, California 93563

SEQUOIA ANTIQUE
BOTTLE SOCIETY
2105 S. Court Street
Visalia, California 93277

LOS ANGELES HISTORICAL
BOTTLE CLUB
868 S. Duff Avenue
West Covina,
California 91790

CHERRY VALLEY BEAM
BOTTLE & SPECIALTY
CLUB
6851 Hood Drive
Westminster,
California 92683

FIRST DOUBLE SPRINGS
COLLECTORS CLUB
13311 Illinois Street
Westminster,
California 92683

WILLITS BOTTLE CLUB
c/o John Hathaway
Willits, California 95490

NAPA-SOLANA BOTTLE
CLUB
P.O. Box 554
Yountville,
California 94559

MARYSVILLE-YUBA CITY
ANTIQUE BOTTLE CLUB
475 South Barrett Road
Yuba City, California 95991

CHERRY VALLEY BOTTLE
& SPECIALTIES CLUB
12724 Ninth Street
Yucaipe, California 92399

ALAMOSA BOTTLE
COLLECTORS
c/o Mrs. Robert Russell
Route 2 Box 170
Alamosa, Colorado 81101

HIGH-COUNTRY ANTIQUE
BOTTLE CLUB
311 14th Street
Alamosa, Colorado 81101

MILE HIGH EZRA BROOKS
BOTTLE CLUB
3685 Chase Court
Boulder, Colorado 80303

NORTHEASTERN ANTIQUE
BOTTLE CLUB
513 Curtis
Brush, Colorado 80723

AVON CLUB OF
COLORADO SPRINGS,
COLORADO
707 N. Farragut
Colorado Springs, Colorado
80909

LIONSTONE WESTERN
FIGURAL CLUB
P.O. Box 2275
Colorado Springs, Colorado
80901

PEAKS & PLAINS ANTIQUE
BOTTLE CLUB
P.O. Box 814
Colorado Springs, Colorado
80901

WESTERN FIGURAL & JIM
BEAM SPECIALTY CLUB
P.O. Box 4331
Colorado Springs,
Colorado 80930

FOUR CORNERS BOTTLE
& GLASS CLUB
P.O. Box 45
Cortez, Colorado 81321

ANTIQUE BOTTLE CLUB
OF COLORADO
P.O. Box 63
Denver, Colorado 80201

ROCKY MOUNTAIN JIM
BEAM BOTTLE &
SPECIALTY CLUB
c/o George Hoeper
Alcott Station
P.O. Box 12162
Denver, Colorado 80212

HORSETOOTH ANTIQUE
BOTTLE COLLECTORS
ASSOCIATION
P.O. Box 944
Fort Collins,
Colorado 80521

NORTHEASTERN
COLORADO ANTIQUE
BOTTLE CLUB
Box 634
Ft. Morgan, Colorado 80701

NORTHERN COLORADO
ANTIQUE BOTTLE CLUB
227 W. Beaver Avenue
Ft. Morgan,
Colorado 80701

WESTERN SLOPE
BOTTLE CLUB
P.O. Box 354
Palisade, Colorado 81526

TELLURIDE ANTIQUE
BOTTLE COLLECTORS
P.O. Box 344
Telluride, Colorado 81435

COLORADO MILE-HIGH
EZRA BROOKS BOTTLE
CLUB
Mr. Gil Nation, President
7401 Decatur Street
Westminster,
Colorado 80030

4-in-1 BOTTLE &
DECANTER CLUB
7401 Decatur Street
Westminster,
Colorado 80030

OLE FOXIE
JIM BEAM CLUB
P.O. Box 560
Westminster,
Colorado 80020

CONNECTICUT
SPECIALTIES CLUB
c/o Steve Richardson
1135 Barnum Avenue
Bridgeport,
Connecticut 06610

GREENWICH ANTIQUE
BOTTLE COLLECTORS
CLUB
c/o Wilfred M. Cameron,
President
6 Relay Court
Cos Cob,
Connecticut 06807

HOUSATONIC ANTIQUE
BOTTLE ASSOCIATION
Falls Village,
Connecticut 06031

EAST COAST MINI
BOTTLE CLUB
c/o Jack Pleines
156 Hillfield Road
Hamden, Connecticut

ANTIQUE BOTTLE CLUB
OF MIDDLETOWN, CONN.
P.O. Box 596
Middletown,
Connecticut 06457

NUTMEG STATE BROOKS
& BEAM CLUB
c/o Roy Schmidt
25 Meadowood Drive
Middletown,
Connecticut 06457

SOUTHEASTERN NEW
ENGLAND ANTIQUE
BOTTLE CLUB
656 Noank Road
Mystic, Connecticut 06355

SOUTHERN CONNECTICUT
ANTIQUE BOTTLE
COLLECTORS
ASSOCIATION, INC.
P.O. Box 346
Seymour,
Connecticut 06483

SOMERS ANTIQUE BOTTLE
CLUB, INC.
Box 373
Somers, Connecticut 06071

CONNECTICUT
SPECIALTIES BOTTLE CLUB
P.O. Box 624
Stratford,
Connecticut 06497

EAST COAST CLUB
c/o Art Swearsky
24 Gertrude Lane
West Haven,
Connecticut 06516

MINIATURE BOTTLE MART
24 Gertrude Lane
West Haven,
Connecticut 06516

TRI-STATE BOTTLE
COLLECTORS & DIGGERS
CLUB
Box 9
Hockessin, Delaware 19707

MASON-DIXON BOTTLE
COLLECTORS
ASSOCIATION
P.O. Box 505
Lewes, Delaware 19958

APOLLO BEACH ANTIQUE
BOTTLE COLLECTORS
ASSOCIATION
P.O. Box 3354
Apollo Beach,
Florida 33570

BAY CITY HISTORICAL
BOTTLE COLLECTORS
P.O. Box 3454
Apollo Beach,
Florida 33570

THE ANTIQUE BOTTLE
COLLECTORS OF
SARASOTA
P.O. Box 4082
Cortez Plaza Branch
Bradenton, Florida 33507

M-T BOTTLE COLLECTORS
ASSOCIATION
P.O. Box 1581
Deland, Florida 32720

HARBOR CITY
1232 Causeway
Eau, Florida 32935

ISLAMORADA ORIGINAL
FLORIDA KEYS
COLLECTORS CLUB
c/o Ella Ellis
P.O. Box 386
Islamorada, Florida 33036

ORIGINAL FLORIDA KEYS
COLLECTORS CLUB
P.O. Box 212
Islamorada, Florida 33036

ANTIQUE BOTTLE
COLLECTORS OF
JACKSONVILLE
P.O. Box 1767
Jacksonville, Florida 32201

NORTH FLORIDA BOTTLE
COLLECTORS
ASSOCIATION
13533 Mandarin Road
Jacksonville,
Florida 32223

CENTRAL FLORIDA
ANTIQUE BOTTLE CLUB
1219 Plant Avenue
Lakeland, Florida 33801

ANTIQUE BOTTLE
COLLECTORS
ASSOCIATION OF FLORIDA
P.O. Box 273
Tavernier, Florida 33070

FLORIDA NATIONAL EZRA
BROOKS BOTTLE &
SPECIALTIES CLUB
20706 S. Dixie Highway
Miami, Florida 33157

SOUTH FLORIDA JIM
BEAM BOTTLE &
SPECIALTIES CLUB
9300 S. Dixie Highway
Miami, Florida 33156

WORLD WIDE MINIATURE
BOTTLE CLUB
11120 Killian Park Road
Miami, Florida 33156

MID-STATE ANTIQUE
BOTTLE COLLECTORS INC.
3122 Corrine Drive
Orlando, Florida 32803

ST. ANDREW BAY BOTTLE
CLUB ASSOCIATION
P.O. Box 12082
Panama City,
Florida 32401

PENSACOLA BOTTLE &
RELIC COLLECTORS
ASSOCIATION
1004 Fremont Avenue
Pensacola, Florida 32505

NORTHWEST FLORIDA
REGIONAL BOTTLE CLUB
P.O. Box 282
Port St. Joe, Florida 32456

SUNCOAST ANTIQUE
BOTTLE CLUB
P.O. Box 12712
St. Petersburg,
Florida 33733

SANFORD ANTIQUE
BOTTLE COLLECTORS
CLUB
2656 Grandview Avenue
South
c/o George C. Scott
Sanford, Florida 32771

SUNCOAST JIM BEAM
BOTTLE & SPEC. CLUB
P.O. Box 5067
Sarasota, Florida 33579

WEST COAST FLORIDA
EZRA BROOKS
BOTTLE CLUB
1360 Harbor Drive
Sarasota, Florida 33579

TAMPA ANTIQUE BOTTLE
COLLECTORS
P.O. Box 4232
Tampa, Florida 33607

ANTIQUE BOTTLE
COLLECTORS
ASSOCIATION OF
FLORIDA
P.O. Box 273
Tavernier, Florida 33070

SOUTH FLORIDA JIM
BEAM BOTTLE &
SPECIALTY CLUB
7741 N. W. 35th Street
West Hollywood,
Florida 33024

PEACHSTATE BOTTLE &
SPECIALTY CLUB
5040 Vallo Vista Court
Atlanta, Georgia 30342

BULLDOG DOUBLE
SPRINGS BOTTLE
COLLECTOR CLUB OF
AUGUSTA, GEORGIA
1916 Melrose Drive
Augusta, Georgia 30906

GEORGIA-CAROLINA
EMPTY BOTTLE CLUB
P.O. Box 1184
Augusta, Georgia 30903

FLINT ANTIQUE BOTTLE
& COIN CLUB
c/o Cordele-Crisp Co.
Recreation Department
204 2nd Street North
Cordele, Georgia 31015

GEORGIA BOTTLE CLUB
c/o Tom Zachary
2996 Pangborn Road
Decatur, Georgia 30033

SOUTHEASTERN A.B.C.
Box 657
Decatur, Georgia 30033

MACON ANTIQUE
BOTTLE CLUB
P.O. Box 5395
Macon, Georgia 31208

COASTAL EMPIRE BOTTLE
CLUB
P.O. Box 3714 Station B
Savannah, Georgia 31404

ANTIQUE BOTTLE CLUB
OF HAWAII
P.O. Box 591
Ewa, Hawaii 96706

HAWAII BOTTLE
COLLECTORS CLUB
P.O. Box 8618
Honolulu, Hawaii 96815

HAUOLI BEAM BOTTLE
COLLECTORS' CLUB OF
HAWAII
45-349 Mokulele Drive
Kaneohe, Hawaii 96744

GEM ANTIQUE BOTTLE
CLUB, INC.
P.O. Box 8051
Boise, Idaho 83707

BUHL ANTIQUE BOTTLE
CLUB
500 12th North
Buhl, Idaho 83316

ROCK & BOTTLE CLUB
c/o Mrs. M. E. Boothe
Route 1
Fruitland, Idaho 83619

EAGLE ROCK HISTORICAL
ASSOCIATION
P.O. Box 2321
Idaho Falls, Idaho 83401

PACATELLO ANTIQUE
BOTTLE CLUB
ASSOCIATION
Route 2
Inkon, Idaho 83245

EM TEE BOTTLE CLUB
P.O. Box 62
Jerome, Idaho 83338

INLAND EMPIRE JIM
BEAM BOTTLE &
COLLECTORS' CLUB
1117 10th Street
Lewiston, Idaho 83501

FABULOUS VALLEY
ANTIQUE BOTTLE CLUB
P.O. Box 769
Osburn, Idaho 83849

POCATELLO ANTIQUE
BOTTLE COLLECTORS
ASSOCIATION
915 Yellowstone
Pocatello, Idaho 83201

ALTON AREA BOTTLE
CLUB
1110 Logan Street
Alton, Illinois 62002

GREATER ST. LOUIS AREA
BEAM BOTTLE CLUB
P.O. Box 819
Belleville, Illinois 62223

INTERNATIONAL EZRA
BROOKS BOTTLE CLUB
103 Powder Mill Road
Belleville, Illinois 62223

ILLINI JIM BEAM BOTTLE
& SPECIALTY CLUB
P.O. Box 13
Champaign, Illinois 61820

FIRST CHICAGO BOTTLE
CLUB
P.O. Box 48125
Chicago, Illinois 60648

METRO EAST BOTTLE &
JAR ASSOCIATION
c/o Wyndham Losser
1702 North Keesler
Collinsville, Illinois 62234

LAND OF LINCOLN
BOTTLE CLUB
c/o Mrs. Beverly Taylor
2515 Illinois Circle
Decatur, Illinois 62526

HEART OF ILLINOIS
ANTIQUE BOTTLE CLUB
2010 Bloomington Road
East Peoria, Illinois 61611

SWEET CORN CAPITOL
BOTTLE CLUB
c/o Bill Rankin
1015 W. Orange
Hoopeston, Illinois 60942

CHICAGO EZRA BROOKS
BOTTLE & SPECIALTY
CLUB
1305 W. Marion Street
Joliet, Illinois 60436

CHICAGO JIM BEAM
BOTTLE & SPECIALTY
CLUB
1305 W. Marion Street
Joliet, Illinois 60436

JOLIET BOTTLE CLUB
c/o C. W. Sieber
12 E. Kenmore Avenue
Joliet, Illinois 60431

LOUIS JOLIET BOTTLE
CLUB
12 Kenmore
Joliet, Illinois 60433

EZRA BROOKS BOTTLE &
SPECIALTIES CLUB
420 N. First Street
Kewanee, Illinois 61443

KELLY CLUB
c/o Mary Kelly
147 North Brainard Avenue
La Grange, Illinois 60525

CENTRAL & MIDWESTERN
STATES BEAM &
SPECIALTIES CLUB
c/o Elmer Collins
44 S. Westmore
Lombard, Illinois 60148

METRO EAST BOTTLE &
JAR ASSOCIATION
P.O. Box 185
Mascoutah, Illinois

FIRST CHICAGO BOTTLE
CLUB
P.O. Box 254
Palatine, Illinois 60067

PEKIN BOTTLE
COLLECTORS
ASSOCIATION
P.O. Box 535
Pekin, Illinois 61554

BLACKHAWK JIM BEAM
BOTTLE & SPECIALTIES
CLUB
2003 Kishwaukee Street
Rockford, Illinois 61101

ILLINOIS BOTTLE CLUB
P.O. Box 181
Rushville, Illinois 62681

SAUK VILLAGE BOTTLE
CLUB
21911 Merriell Avenue
Sauk Village, Illinois 60411

METRO-EAST BOTTLE AND
JAR ASSOCIATION
5305 A Hesse Avenue
Scott AFB, Illinois 62225

LEWIS & CLARK JIM BEAM
BOTTLE & SPECIALTY
CLUB
P.O. Box 451
Wood River, Illinois 62095

WE FOUND 'EM BOTTLE
& INSULATOR CLUB
P.O. Box 578
Bunker Hill, Indiana 46914

STEEL CITY EZRA BROOKS
CLUB
3506 Revere Court
East Gary, Indiana 46405

FORT WAYNE BOTTLE
CLUB
c/o Thurman Fuhrman
5622 Arbor Avenue
Fort Wayne, Indiana 46807

FORT WAYNE HISTORICAL
BOTTLE CLUB
5124 Roberta Drive
Fort Wayne, Indiana 46805

THE MIDWEST ANTIQUE
FRUIT JAR & BOTTLE
CLUB
298 N. Washington
Hagerstown,
Indiana 47346

HOOSIER BOTTLE CLUB
c/o Fred Challis
P.O. Box 33126
Indianapolis,
Indiana 46203

HOOSIER JIM BEAM
BOTTLE & SPECIALTIES
CLUB
P.O. Box 24234
Indianapolis
Indiana 46224

INDIANA EZRA BROOKS
BOTTLE CLUB
P.O. Box 24344
Indianapolis,
Indiana 46224

FOUR FLAGS EZRA
BROOKS BOTTLE CLUB
c/o Mr. Peter Groote,
President
P.O. Box 791
Mishawaka, Indiana 46544

STEEL CITY EZRA BROOKS
BOTTLE CLUB
R.R. #2 Box 32A
Valparaiso, Indiana 46383

MICHIANA JIM BEAM
BOTTLE & SPECIALTY
CLUB
58955 Locust Road
South Bend, Indiana 46614

DES MOINES JIM BEAM &
SPECIALTY CLUB
c/o Edward Van Dyke
2417 48th Street
Des Moines, Iowa 50310

HAWKEYE DES MOINES
AVON CLUB
1406 60th
Des Moines, Iowa 50311

IOWA ANTIQUE
BOTTLEERS
1506 Albia Road
Ottumwa, Iowa 52501

LARKIN BOTTLE CLUB
c/o Clarence Larkin
107 W. Grimes
Red Oak, Iowa 51566

CHEROKEE STRIP EZRA
BROOKS BOTTLE &
SPECIALTY CLUB
P.O. Box 631
Arkansas City,
Kansas 67005

SOUTH EAST KANSAS
BOTTLE & RELIC CLUB
c/o Bill Lock
302 So. Western
Chanute, Kansas 66720

FLINT HILLS BEAM &
SPECIALTY CLUB
201 W. Pine
El Dorado, Kansas 67042

JAYHAWK BOTTLE CLUB
7919 Grant
Overland Park,
Kansas 66212

ANTIQUE BOTTLE CLUB
c/o Bob Billamagna
2502 W. 32nd St. South
Apt. "D"
Wichita, Kansas 67217

WICHITA EZRA BROOKS
BOTTLE & SPECIALTIES
CLUB
Mr. Larry Carter, President
8045 Peachtree Street
Wichita, Kansas 67207

LOUISVILLE BOTTLE
COLLECTORS
11819 Garrs Avenue
Anchorage,
Kentucky 40223

KENTUCKY CARDINAL
BEAM BOTTLE CLUB
428 Templin
Bardstown,
Kentucky 41104

DERBY CITY JIM BEAM
BOTTLE CLUB
4105 Spring Hill Road
Louisville, Kentucky 40207

KENTUCKY BLUEGRASS
EZRA BROOKS BOTTLE
CLUB
6202 Tabor Drive
Louisville,
Kentucky 40218

HISTORICAL BOTTLE
ASSOCIATION OF
BATON ROUGE
1843 Tudor Drive
Baton Rouge,
Louisiana 70815

DIXIE DIGGERS BOTTLE
CLUB
P.O. Box 626
Empire, Louisiana 70050

CAJUN COUNTRY
COUSINS EZRA BROOKS
BOTTLE & SPECIALTY
CLUB
P.O. Box 462
Franklin, Louisiana 70538

NEW ORLEANS ANTIQUE
BOTTLE CLUB
1016 Carnation Avenue
Metairie, Louisiana 70001

NORTHEAST LOUISIANA
BOTTLE & INSULATOR
CLUB
P.O. Box 4192
Monroe, Louisiana 71201

BAYOU BOTTLE BUGS
216 Dahlia
New Iberia,
Louisiana 70560

BAYOU TECHE BOTTLE
CLUB
P.O. Box 634
New Iberia,
Louisiana 70560

NEW ALBANY GLASS
WORKS BOTTLE CLUB
732 N. Clark Blvd.
Parksville, Louisiana 47130

Charles Chaudoir
5212 Shreveport Hwy.
Pineville, Louisiana 71360

NORTHEAST LOUISIANA
BOTTLE & INSULATOR
CLUB
112 Pinewood Drive
West Monroe,
Louisiana 71291

KENNEBEC VALLEY
BOTTLE CLUB
9 Glenwood Street
Augusta, Maine 04330

DIRIGO BOTTLE
COLLECTOR'S CLUB
c/o 59 Fruit Street
Bangor, Maine 04401

PAUL BUNYAN BOTTLE
CLUB
c/o Mrs. Francis Kearns
237 14th Street
Bangor, Maine 04401

WALDO COUNTY
BOTTLENECKS CLUB
Head-of-the-Tide
Belfast, Maine 04915

THE GLASS BUBBLE
BOTTLE CLUB
P.O. Box 91
Cape Neddick,
Maine 03902

TRI-COUNTY BOTTLE
COLLECTORS
ASSOCIATION
c/o John E. Irvin
RFD 3
Dexter, Maine 04930

DOVER FOXCROFT
BOTTLE CLUB
c/o Wayne Champion
50 Church Street
Dover Foxcroft,
Maine 04426

NEW ENGLAND BOTTLE
CLUB
c/o Mrs. Ralph L.
Everson, Secretary
45 Bolt Hill Road
Eliot, Maine 03903

JIM BEAM COLLECTORS
CLUB
10 Lunt Road
Falmouth, Maine 04105

NEW ENGLAND BOTTLE
CLUB
Parsonfield, Maine 04047

PINE TREE ANTIQUE
BOTTLE CLUB
Buxton Road
Saco, Maine 04072

MID COAST BOTTLE CLUB
c/o Miriam Winchenbach
Waldoboro, Maine 04572

MASON-DIXON BOTTLE
COLLECTORS
ASSOCIATION
601 Market Street
Denton, Maryland 21629

BLUE & GRAY EZRA
BROOKS BOTTLE CLUB
2106 Sunnybrook Drive
Frederick, Maryland 21201

BALTIMORE ANTIQUE
BOTTLE HOUNDS
c/o Route 2 Box 379
Glenarm, Maryland 21057

CATOCTIN BEAM BOTTLE
CLUB
P.O. Box 325
Greenbelt, Maryland 20770

SOUTH COUNTY BOTTLE
COLLECTOR'S CLUB
Florence Bast, President
Bast Lane
Shady Side,
Maryland 20867

THE BOTTLE
PROSPECTORS CLUB
c/o Brewster Town Hall
Brewster,
Massachusetts 02631

ESSEX COUNTY BOTTLE
CLUB
7c Broad Street
East Lynn,
Massachusetts 01902

NEW ENGLAND BEAM &
SPECIALTIES CLUB
6 Merritt Avenue
Groveland,
Massachusetts 01830

NEW ENGLAND BEAM &
SPECIALTY CLUB
1104 Northampton Street
Holyoke,
Massachusetts 01040

BERKSHIRE ANTIQUE
BOTTLE ASSOCIATION
P.O. Box 294
Lee, Massachusetts 01238

NEW ENGLAND BOTTLE
COLLECTORS
ASSOCIATION
7a Broad Street
Lynn,
Massachusetts 01902

MERRIMACK VALLEY
BOTTLE CLUB
96 Elm Street
North Andover,
Massachusetts 01845

SATUIT ANTIQUE BOTTLE
CLUB
P.O. Box 27
North Scituate,
Massachusetts 02060

THE BOTTLE
PROSPECTOR'S CLUB
143 Main Street
Yarmouth Port,
Massachusetts 02675

TRAVERSE AREA BOTTLE
& INSULATOR CLUB
P.O. Box 205
Acme, Michigan 49610

HURON VALLEY BOTTLE
& INSULATOR CLUB
c/o Richard Havelka
1600 E. Stadium Blvd.
Ann Arbor, Michigan 48104

MICHIANA BOTTLE CLUB
P.O. Box 135
Buchanan, Michigan 49120

AVON BOTTLE
COLLECTOR'S CLUB OF
DETROIT
P.O. Box 8683
Detroit, Michigan 48224

WORLD WIDE AVON
BOTTLE COLLECTORS
CLUB
P.O. Box 8683
Detroit, Michigan 48224

MICHIGAN'S VEHICLE CITY
BEAM BOTTLE &
SPECIALTIES CLUB
907 Root Street
Flint, Michigan 48503

FLINT ANTIQUE BOTTLE
CLUB
1460 Coutant Street
Flushing, Michigan 48433

YE OLD BOTTLE CLUB
Gaastra, Michigan 49027

GRAND VALLEY BOTTLE
CLUB
31 Dickinson S.W.
Grand Rapids,
Michigan 49507

W.M.R.A.C.C.
331 Bellevue S.W.
Grand Rapids,
Michigan 49508

MICHIGAN BOTTLE CLUB
145 Spruce Box 48
Hemlock, Michigan 48626

DICKINSON COUNTY
BOTTLE CLUB
717 Henford Avenue
Iron Mountain,
Michigan 49801

YE OLDE CORKERS
BOTTLE CLUB
c/o Shirley Wodzinski
Route 1
Iron River, Michigan 49935

MICHIGAN BOTTLE
COLLECTORS
ASSOCIATION
144 W. Clark Street
Jackson, Michigan 49203

MANISTEE COIN &
BOTTLE CLUB
207 E. Piney Road
Manistee, Michigan 49660

HURON VALLEY BOTTLE
CLUB
12475 Saline-Milan Road
Milan, Michigan 48160

WOLVERINE BEAM
BOTTLE & SPECIALTY
CLUB OF MICHIGAN
36009 Larchwood
Mt. Clemens,
Michigan 48043

FOUR FLAGS EZRA
BROOKS BOTTLE CLUB
P.O. Box 653
Niles, Michigan 49120

EMMETT HISTORICAL
BOTTLE ASSOCIATION
108 Grove Street
Petoskey, Michigan 49770

NORTHERN MICHIGAN
BOTTLE CLUB
P.O. Box 421
Petoskey, Michigan 49770

CHIEF PONTIAC BOTTLE
CLUB
755 Scottwood
Pontiac, Michigan 48058

METROPOLITAN DETROIT
BOTTLE CLUB
c/o Alice Stephens
17721 Martin Road
Roseville, Michigan 48066

LIONSTONE COLLECTORS
BOTTLE & SPECIALTIES
CLUB OF MICHIGAN
c/o Walter Steck
3089 Grand Blanc Road
Swartz Creek,
Michigan 48473

WORLD WIDE AVON
BOTTLE COLLECTORS
CLUB
22708 Wick Road
Taylor, Michigan 48180

DUMP DIGGERS
P.O. Box 24
Dover, Minnesota 55929

LAKE SUPERIOR ANTIQUE
BOTTLE CLUB
P.O. Box 67
Knife River,
Minnesota 55609

MINNESOTA'S FIRST
ANTIQUE BOTTLE CLUB
5001 Queen Avenue North
Minneapolis,
Minnesota 55430

NORTH STAR HISTORICAL
BOTTLE ASSOCIATION
3308 32nd Avenue South
Minneapolis,
Minnesota 55406

ARNFALT COLLECTORS
BEAM CLUB
c/o Tony Arnfalt
New Richland,
Minnesota 56072

THE MAGNOLIA STATE
BOTTLE CLUB
P.O. Box 6023
Handsboro,
Mississippi 39501

MIDDLE MISSISSIPPI
ANTIQUE BOTTLE CLUB
P.O. Box 233
Jackson, Mississippi 39205

SOUTH MISSISSIPPI
ANTIQUE BOTTLE CLUB
c/o Aaron Rogers
203 S. 4th Avenue
Laurel, Mississippi 39440

OXFORD ANTIQUE
BOTTLERS
Pat Christian
128 Vivian Street
Oxford, Mississippi 38633

MID-WEST ANTIQUE
BOTTLE & HOBBY CLUB
122 Hightower Street
El Dorado Springs,
Missouri 64744

GREATER KANSAS CITY
JIM BEAM BOTTLE &
SPECIALTY CLUB
P.O. Box 6703
Kansas City,
Missouri 64123

KANSAS CITY ANTIQUE
BOTTLE COLLECTORS
ASSOCIATION
1131 East 77 Street
Kansas City,
Missouri 64131

ST. LOUIS ANTIQUE
BOTTLE COLLECTOR
ASSOCIATION
306 N. Woodlawn Avenue
Kirkwood, Missouri 63122

MINERAL AREA BOTTLE
CLUB
Knob Lick, Missouri 63651

HEART OF THE OZARKS
Ozark, Missouri 65721

MOUND CITY JIM BEAM
DECANTER COLLECTORS
42 Webster Acres
Webster Groves,
Missouri 63119

NORTHWEST MISSOURI
BOTTLE & RELIC CLUB
c/o Bob Hale
3006 S. 28th Street
St. Joseph, Missouri 64503

ST. LOUIS ANTIQUE
BOTTLE ASSOCIATION
c/o Joseph Messler
32 W. Jackson
Webster Groves,
Missouri 63119

ST. LOUIS EZRA BROOKS
CERAMICS CLUB
42 Webster Acres
Webster Groves,
Missouri 63119

BOZEMAN BOTTLE BUGS
c/o Mrs. Delmer Self
519½ E. Lamme
Bozeman, Montana 59715

HELLGATE ANTIQUE
BOTTLE CLUB
P.O. Box 411
Missoula, Montana 59801

J. V. GUNN MIDWESTERN
EZRA BROOKS BOTTLE
CLUB
P.O. Box 29198
Lincoln, Nebraska 68529

MINI-SEEKERS
Walter Jackman
"A" Acres, Rt. 8
Lincoln, Nebraska 68506

NEBRASKA BIG RED
BOTTLE & SPECIALTY
CLUB
N. Street Drive-In
200 So. 18th Street
Lincoln, Nebraska 68508

NEBRASKA ANTIQUE
BOTTLE & COLLECTORS
CLUB
Box 37021
Omaha, Nebraska 68137

MINERAL COUNTY
ANTIQUE BOTTLE CLUB
P.O. Box 349
Babbitt, Nevada 89415

EAGLE VALLEY GOPHERS
ANTIQUE BOTTLE CLUB
805 Winnie Lane
Carson City, Nevada 89701

VIRGINIA & TRUCKEE JIM
BEAM BOTTLE &
SPECIALTIES CLUB
P.O. Box 1596
Carson City, Nevada 89701

NEVADA BEAM CLUB
c/o Terry duPont III
The B-Lazy-2
P.O. Box 426
Fallon, Nevada 89406

SO. NEVADA ANTIQUE
BOTTLE COLLECTORS, INC.
884 Lulu
Las Vegas, Nevada 89109

WEE BOTTLE CLUB
INTERNATIONAL
P.O. Box 1195
Las Vegas, Nevada 89101

LINCOLN COUNTY
ANTIQUE BOTTLE CLUB,
INC.
P.O. Box 371
Pioche, Nevada 89043

ANTIQUE BOTTLE CLUB
ASSOCIATION OF RENO-
SPARKS
4965 Mason Road
Reno, Nevada 89500

RENO-SPARKS ANTIQUE
BOTTLE COLLECTORS
ASSOCIATION
P.O. Box 6145
Reno, Nevada 89503

SILVER STATE EZRA
BROOKS CLUB
2030 Clear Acre Lane
Reno, Nevada 89502

TONAPAH ANTIQUE
BOTTLE CLUB
P.O. Box 545
Tonopah, Nevada 89049

GRANITE STATE BOTTLE
CLUB
R.F.D. #1
Belmont,
New Hampshire 03220

BOTTLEERS OF NEW
HAMPSHIRE
125A Central Street
Farmington,
New Hampshire 03835

NEW ENGLAND BEAM &
SPECIALTIES CLUB
P.O. Box 502
Greenville,
New Hampshire 03048

NEW ENGLAND BOTTLE
CLUB
P.O. Box 472
Henniker,
New Hampshire 03242

YANKEE BOTTLE CLUB
P.O. Box 702
Keene,
New Hampshire 03431

GRANITE STATE BOTTLE
CLUB
c/o Alfred Davis
116 Academy Street
Laconia,
New Hampshire 03246

NEW JERSEY EZRA
BROOKS BOTTLE CLUB
Sayers Neck Road
Cederville,
New Jersey 08311

TRENTON JIM BEAM
BOTTLE CLUB, INC.
17 Easy Street
Freehold,
New Jersey 07728

SOUTH JERSEY'S
HERITAGE BOTTLE &
GLASS CLUB
P.O. Box 122
Glassboro,
New Jersey 08028

NORTH JERSEY ANTIQUE
BOTTLE CLUB
ASSOCIATION
14 Birchwood Road
Hawthorne,
New Jersey 07506

JERSEY DEVIL'S BOTTLE
DIGGERS
P.O. Box 131 Main Street
Juliustown,
New Jersey 08042

WEST ESSEX BOTTLE CLUB
76 Beaufort Avenue
Livingston,
New Jersey 07039

SOUTH JERSEY HERITAGE
BOTTLE & GLASS CLUB
c/o Old Bottle & Book Barn
Harmony Road Route 295
Mickleton,
New Jersey 08056

SUSSEX COUNTY
ANTIQUE BOTTLE
COLLECTORS
Division of Sussex County
Historical Society
82 Main Street
Newton, New Jersey 07860

TWIN BRIDGES BEAM
BOTTLE & SPECIALTY
CLUB
P.O. Box 347
Pennsville,
New Jersey 08070

LIONSTONE COLLECTORS
CLUB OF DELAWARE
VALLEY
R.D. #3 Box 93
Sewell, New Jersey 08080

LAKELAND ANTIQUE
BOTTLE CLUB
24 Main Street
Succasunna,
New Jersey 07876

THE JERSEY SHORE
BOTTLE CLUB
c/o RD #1 Box 72V
Toms River,
New Jersey 08753

ARTIFACT HUNTERS
ASSOCIATION INC.
c/o 29 Lake Road
Wayne, New Jersey 07470

NORTH NEW JERSEY
ANTIQUE BOTTLE CLUB
ASSOCIATION
P.O. Box 617
Westwood,
New Jersey 07675

SOUTH JERSEY AVON
COLLECTORS CLUB
Box 315 R.D. #2
Williamstown,
New Jersey 08094

ROADRUNNER BOTTLE
CLUB OF NEW MEXICO
2341 Gay Road S.W.
Albuquerque,
New Mexico 87105

CAVE CITY ANTIQUE
BOTTLE CLUB
Route 1, Box 155
Carlsbad,
New Mexico 88220

NORTHERN NEW YORK
BOTTLE CLUB
ASSOCIATION
P.O. Box 257
Adams Center,
New York 13606

AUBURN BOTTLE CLUB
11 Beach Avenue
Auburn, New York 13021

TRYON BOTTLE BADGERS
R.D. 2 Box 415H
New Progress Road
Gloversville,
New York 12078

FINGER LAKES BOTTLE
CLUB ASSOCIATION
P.O. Box 815
Ithaca, New York 14850

THE GREATER CATSKILL
ANTIQUE BOTTLE CLUB
P.O. Box 411
Liberty, New York 12754

EMPIRE STATE BOTTLE
COLLECTORS
ASSOCIATION
4135 Wetzel Road
Liverpool, New York 13088

WESTERN NEW YORK
BOTTLE COLLECTORS
87 S. Bristol Avenue
Lockport, New York 14094

CATSKILL MOUNTAINS
JIM BEAM BOTTLE CLUB
c/o William Gibbs
Six Gardner Avenue
Middletown,
New York 10940

EMPIRE STATE BOTTLE &
SPECIALTY CLUB
c/o William Bateman
East Main Street
Milford, New York 13807

UPPER SUSQUEHANNA
BOTTLE CLUB
P.O. Box 183
Milford, New York 13807

COLLECTORS GUILD
1925 Pine Avenue
Niagara Falls,
New York 14301

SUFFOLK COUNTY
ANTIQUE BOTTLE
ASSOCIATION
31 Harborview Drive
Northport, New York 11768

SOUTHERN TIER BOTTLE
& INSULATOR
COLLECTORS
ASSOCIATION
47 Dickinson Avenue
Port Dickinson,
New York 13901

ST. LAWRENCE SEAWAY
VALLEY BEAM-BROOKS
SPECIALTY CLUB
R.D. #2
Potsdam, New York 13676

GENESEE VALLEY
BOTTLE COLLECTORS
ASSOCIATION
P.O. Box 7528
West Ridge Station
Rochester, New York 14615

ROCHESTER NEW YORK
BOTTLE CLUB
7908 West Henrietta Road
Rush, New York 14543

CHAUTAUQUA COUNTY
BOTTLE COLLECTORS
CLUB
Morse Hotel
Main Street
Sherman, New York 14781

RENSSELAER COUNTY
ANTIQUE BOTTLE CLUB
Box 792
Troy, New York 12180

EASTERN MONROE
COUNTY BOTTLE CLUB
c/o Bethlehem Lutheran
Church
1767 Plank Road
Webster, New York 14580

WEST VALLEY
BOTTLETIQUE
West Valley,
New York 14171

CAROLINA BOTTLE CLUB
c/o Industrial Piping Co.
Anonwood, Charlotte,
North Carolina 28210

CAROLINA JIM BEAM
BOTTLE CLUB
1014 N. Main Street
Burlington,
North Carolina 27215

ALBERMARLE BOTTLE &
COLLECTORS CLUB
c/o Sam Taylor, Secretary
Rt. 3 Box 687-A
Elizabeth City,
North Carolina 27909

YADKIN VALLEY BOTTLE
CLUB
General Delivery
Gold Hill, North Carolina

GOLDSBORO BOTTLE
CLUB
117 North James Street
Goldsboro,
North Carolina 27530

GREATER GREENSBORO
MOOSE EZRA BROOKS
BOTTLE CLUB
217 S. Elm Street
Greensboro,
North Carolina 27401

KINSTON COLLECTORS
CLUB, INC.
c/o 325 E. Lenoir
Kinston,
North Carolina 28501

CAPITAL CITY BOTTLE
CLUB
1225½ Duplin Road
Raleigh,
North Carolina 27609

RUBBER CAPITOL JIM
BEAM CLUB
151 Stephens Road
Akron, Ohio 44312

OHIO BOTTLE CLUB
P.O. Box 585
Barberton, Ohio 44203

FIRST CAPITAL BOTTLE
CLUB
233 Vine Street
Chillicothe, Ohio 45601

BUCKEYE JIM BEAM
BOTTLE CLUB
1211 Ashland Avenue
Columbus, Ohio 43212

CENTRAL OHIO BOTTLE
CLUB
P.O. Box 19864
Columbus, Ohio 43219

DIAMOND PIN WINNERS
AVON CLUB
5281 Fredonia Avenue
Dayton, Ohio 45431

GEM CITY BEAM BOTTLE
CLUB
1463 E. Stroop Road
Dayton, Ohio 45429

INTERNATIONAL
DECANTERS CLUB
c/o Opal Redman
101 E. Third Street
Dayton, Ohio 45402

TRI-STATE HISTORICAL
BOTTLE CLUB
P.O. Box 609
East Liverpool, Ohio 43920

THE BUCKEYE BOTTLE
CLUB
c/o Gilbert Gill
229 Oakwood Street
Elyria, Ohio 44035

GEM CITY BEAM BOTTLE
CLUB
1463 E. Stroop Road
Kettering, Ohio 45429

OHIO EZRA BROOKS
BOTTLE CLUB
8741 Kirtland Chardon
Road
Kirtland Hills, Ohio 44094

ALLYN BOTTLE CLUB
8501 Freeway-Drive
Macedonia, Ohio 44056

NORTH EASTERN OHIO
BOTTLE CLUB
P.O. Box 57
Madison, Ohio 44057

NORTHWEST OHIO
BOTTLE CLUB
307 Maple Street
Pemberville, Ohio 43450

BUCKEYE BOTTLE
DIGGERS
Route 1, Box 48
Thornville, Ohio 43076

JEFFERSON COUNTY
ANTIQUE BOTTLE CLUB
308 N. 4th Street
Toronto, Ohio 43964

BAR-DEW ANTIQUE
BOTTLE CLUB
817 E. 7th Street
Dewey, Oklahoma 74029

LITTLE DIXIE ANTIQUE
BOTTLE CLUB
P.O. Box 741
Krebs, Oklahoma 74501

SOUTHWEST OKLAHOMA
ANTIQUE BOTTLE CLUB
35 S. 49th Street
Lawton, Oklahoma 73501

SOONER EZRA BROOKS
BOTTLE CLUB
7309 South Klein
Oklahoma City,
Oklahoma 73139

PONCA CITY OLD
BOTTLE CLUB
2408 Juanito
Ponca City,
Oklahoma 74601

McDONNELL DOUGLAS
ANTIQUE CLUB
5752 E. 25th Place
Tulsa, Oklahoma 74114

TULSA ANTIQUE BOTTLE
& RELIC CLUB
P.O. Box 4278
Tulsa, Oklahoma 74104

TULSA OKLAHOMA
BOTTLE CLUB
5752 E. 25th Place
Tulsa, Oklahoma 74114

OREGON BOTTLE CLUB
ASSOCIATION
P.O. Box 175
Aurora, Oregon 97002

CENTRAL OREGON
BOTTLE & RELIC
COLLECTORS
Route 2, Box 185
Bend, Oregon 97701

SOUTHERN OREGON
BOTTLE CLUB, INC.
P.O. Box 335
Canyonville, Oregon 97417

EMERALD EMPIRE
BOTTLE CLUB
P.O. Box 292
Eugene, Oregon 97401

GOLDDIGGERS ANTIQUE
BOTTLE CLUB
P.O. Box 56
Gold Hill, Oregon 97525

PIONEER FRUIT JAR
COLLECTORS
ASSOCIATION
P.O. Box 175
Grand Ronde,
Oregon 97347

CENTRAL SOUTH OREGON
ANTIQUE BOTTLE CLUB
708 South F. Street
Lakeview, Oregon 97630

OREGON BOTTLE
COLLECTORS
ASSOCIATION
4207 S.E. Covell
Milwaukee, Oregon 97222

OREGON ANTIQUE
BOTTLE CLUB
c/o William Blackburn
Route 3 Box 23
Molalla, Oregon 97038

MOLALLA BOTTLE CLUB
Route 1 Box 205
Mulino, Oregon 97042

FRONTIER COLLECTORS
504 N. W. Bailey
Pendleton, Oregon 97801

LEWIS & CLARK BOTTLE
CLUB ASSOCIATION
8435 S.W. 52nd Avenue
Portland, Oregon 97219

LEWIS & CLARK
HISTORICAL BOTTLE
SOCIETY
4104 N.E. 105th
Portland, Oregon 97211

THE OREGON BEAVER
BEAM BOTTLE &
SPECIALTIES
P.O. Box 7
Sheridan, Oregon 97378

OREGON BOTTLE
COLLECTORS
ASSOCIATION
21805 SW Pacific Hwy.
Sherwood, Oregon 97140

EAST COAST DOUBLE
SPRINGS SPECIALTY
BOTTLE CLUB
P.O. Box 419
Carlisle,
Pennsylvania 17013

WASHINGTON COUNTY
BOTTLE & INSULATOR
CLUB
R.D. #1 Box 342
Carmichaels,
Pennsylvania 15320

FRIENDLY JIM'S BEAM
CLUB
c/o James Bradley, Sr.
508 Benjamin Franklin
H.W. East
Douglassville,
Pennsylvania 19518

FORKS OF THE DELAWARE
BOTTLE CLUB
P.O. Box 693
Easton,
Pennsylvania 18042

PENNSYLVANIA DUTCH
JIM BEAM BOTTLE CLUB
812 Pointview Avenue
Ephrata,
Pennsylvania 17522

ERIE BOTTLE CLUB
P.O. Box 373
Erie, Pennsylvania 16512

ENDLESS MOUNTAIN
ANTIQUE BOTTLE CLUB
P.O. Box 75
Granville Summit,
Pennsylvania 16926

INDIANA BOTTLE CLUB
240 Oak Street
Indiana,
Pennsylvania 15701

PITTSBURGH BOTTLE
CLUB
P.O. Box 401
Ingomar,
Pennsylvania 15127

FLOOD CITY BEAM
BOTTLE AND SPEC. CLUB
422 Lincoln Street
Johnstown,
Pennsylvania 15901

EAST COAST EZRA
BROOKS BOTTLE CLUB
2815 Fiddler Green
Lancaster,
Pennsylvania 17601

BEAVER VALLEY JIM
BEAM CLUB
1335 Indiana Avenue
Monaca,
Pennsylvania 15061

DELAWARE VALLEY
BOTTLE CLUB
P.O. Box 19
Revere,
Pennsylvania 18953

PHILADA BOTTLE CLUB
8203 Elberon Avenue
Philadelphia,
Pennsylvania 19111

TRI-COUNTY ANTIQUE
BOTTLE & TREASURE
CLUB
R.D. #2 Box 30
Reynoldsville,
Pennsylvania 15851

PENNSYLVANIA BOTTLE
COLLECTORS
ASSOCIATION
743 Woodberry Road
York, Pennsylvania 17403

LITTLE RHODY BOTTLE
CLUB
67 Roslyn Avenue
Providence,
Rhode Island 02908

UNION BOTTLE CLUB
c/o Russell E. Clark
Linervilla Road
Buffalo,
South Carolina 29321

SOUTH CAROLINA BOTTLE
CLUB
1119 Greenridge Lane
Columbia,
South Carolina 29210

GREER BOTTLE
COLLECTORS CLUB
P.O. Box 384
Greer,
South Carolina 29651

LOW COUNTRY ANTIQUE
BOTTLE COLLECTORS
P.O. Box 274
John's Island,
South Carolina 29455

LEXINGTON COUNTY
COLLECTORS CLUB
Route 2 Box 329-H
Lexington,
South Carolina 29072

THE NATIONAL
GRENADIER BOTTLE CLUB
OF AMERICA
P.O. Box 3343
305 43rd Avenue
N. Cherry Grove,
N. Myrtle Beach,
South Carolina

UNION BOTTLE CLUB
107 Pineneedle Road
Union,
South Carolina 29379

GREATER SMOKY
MOUNTAIN EZRA BROOKS
BOTTLE CLUB
P.O. Box 3351
Knoxville,
Tennessee 37917

GREAT SMOKY MOUNTAIN
BEAM BOTTLE &
SPECIALTY CLUB
Donald Payne
c/o B & T Distributing
Company
P.O. Box 3351
Knoxville,
Tennessee 37917

MEMPHIS ANTIQUE
BOTTLE CLUB
1070 Terry Circle
Memphis,
Tennessee 38107

MEMPHIS BOTTLE
COLLECTORS CLUB
c/o 4083 Wildwood Drive
Memphis,
Tennessee 38111

MIDDLE TENNESSEE
BOTTLE COLLECTORS
CLUB
P.O. Box 12083
Nashville,
Tennessee 37212

THE AUSTIN BOTTLE
COLLECTORS
c/o Russell Barnes
1801 Kingwood Cove
Austin, Texas 78758

GULF COAST BEAM CLUB
128 W. Bayshore Drive
Baytown, Texas 77520

FOARD C. HOBBY CLUB
P.O. Box 625
Crowell, Texas 79227

EL PASO PROSPECTORS
CLUB
P.O. Box 2369
El Paso, Texas 79952

REPUBLIC OF TEXAS
JIM BEAM BOTTLE &
SPECIALTY CLUB
616 Donley Drive
Euless, Texas 76039

AMERICAN ASSOCIATION
OF PERFUME COLLECTORS
P.O. Box 55074
Houston, Texas 77055

TEXAS LONGHORN
BOTTLE CLUB
P.O. Box 5346
Irving, Texas 75060

FOURSOME (Jim Beam)
H. G. Lewis, Sr.
1208 Azalea Drive
Longview, Texas 75601

FORT CONCHO BOTTLE
CLUB
c/o Ave-N-Driv-Up Antique
Bottle Shop
1703 West Avenue
N. San Angelo,
Texas 76901

GULF COAST BOTTLE &
JAR CLUB
P.O. Box 1754
Pasadena, Texas 77501

ALAMO CHAPTER
ANTIQUE BOTTLE CLUB
ASSOCIATION
c/o Robert Duff
701 Castano Avenue
San Antonio, Texas 78209

SAN ANTONIO ANTIQUE
BOTTLE CLUB
c/o 3801 Broadway
Witte Museum -
Auditorium
San Antonio, Texas 78209

UTAH ANTIQUE BOTTLE
CLUB
P.O. Box 15
Ogden, Utah 84402

UTAH ANTIQUE BOTTLE
SOCIETY
4907 S. 2400-A
Roy, Utah 84067

POTOMAC BOTTLE
COLLECTORS
P.O. Box 375
Arlington, Virginia 22210

GREEN MOUNTAIN
BOTTLE CLUB
c/o Fred Brown
P.O. Box 269
Bradford, Vermont 05033

VERMONT BOTTLE CLUB
P.O. Box 767
Springfield,
Vermont 05156

HISTORICAL BOTTLE
DIGGERS
Route 3 Box 204
Broadway, Virginia 22815

DIXIE BEAM BOTTLE CLUB
Forest Hill Avenue
Clarksville, Virginia 23927

YE OLD BOTTLE CLUB
General Delivery
Clarksville, Virginia 23927

HISTORICAL BOTTLE
DIGGERS OF VIRGINIA
c/o Roger Lantz
Route 3 Box 203
Harrisburg, Virginia 22801

RICHMOND AREA BOTTLE
COLLECTORS
ASSOCIATION
5901 Wonderland Lane
Mechanicsville,
Virginia 23111

BOTTLE CLUB OF THE
VIRGINIA PENINSULA
514 Brent Wood Drive
Newport News,
Virginia 23601

OLD DOMINION BOTTLE
CLUB
c/o 8434 Tidewater Drive
Norfolk, Virginia 23518

TIDEWATER BEAM BOTTLE
& SPECIALTY CLUB
P.O. Box 14012
Norfolk, Virginia 23518

HAMPTON ROADS AREA
BOTTLE CLUB
c/o Linda Dennis
1521 White Dogwood Trail
Suffolk, Virginia 23433

HAMPTON ROADS AREA
BOTTLE COLLECTORS
ASSOCIATION
P.O. Box 3061
Portsmouth,
Virginia 23701

RICHMOND AREA BOTTLE
CLUB ASSOCIATION
3064 Forest Hills Avenue
Richmond, Virginia 23225

APPLE VALLEY BOTTLE
COLLECTORS CLUB, INC.
Route 1 Box 410
Winchester, Virginia 22601

WASHINGTON STATE
ANTIQUE BOTTLE CLUB
ASSOCIATION
1200 112 S.W.
Everett, Washington 98201

KLICKITAL BOTTLE CLUB
ASSOCIATION
Goldendale,
Washington 98620

CHINOOK EZRA BROOKS
CLUB
721 Grade Street
Kelso, Washington 98626

EVERGREEN STATE
BEAM BOTTLE CLUB
1540 Maple Lane
Kent, Washington 98031

MT. RAINIER EZRA
BROOKS BOTTLE &
SPECIALTIES CLUB
1540 Maple Lane
Kent, Washington 98031

PACIFIC NORTHWEST
AVON BOTTLE CLUB
c/o Bill & Bette Bouma
25425 68th South
Kent, Washington 98031

WASHINGTON BOTTLE
COLLECTORS
ASSOCIATION
c/o 26020 135th S.E. # 13
Kent, Washington 98031

SO. WHEDLEY BOTTLE
CLUB
c/o Juanita Clyde
Langley, Washington 98260

SKAGIT BOTTLE & GLASS
COLLECTORS
1314 Virginia
Mt. Vernon,
Washington 98273

CAPITOL BOTTLE
COLLECTORS
1636 College Street, N.E.
Olympia,
Washington 98506

WASHINGTON BOTTLE
CLUB ASSOCIATION
8319 49th Street East
Puyallup,
Washington 98371

MT. RAINIER EZRA
BROOKS BOTTLE CLUB
c/o Samuel A. Rose,
President
13320 S.E. 99th Street
Renton, Washington 98055

CASCADE TREASURE CLUB
254 N.E. 45th
Seattle, Washington 98105

EVERGREEN STATE BEAM
BOTTLE & SPECIALTY
CLUB
P.O. Box 99244
Seattle, Washington 98199

SEATTLE JIM BEAM
BOTTLE COLLECTORS
CLUB
8015 15th Avenue N.W.
Seattle, Washington 98107

ANTIQUE BOTTLE & GLASS
COLLECTORS
P.O. Box 163
Snohomich,
Washington 98290

GREATER SPOKANE
BOTTLE & COLLECTORS
ASSOCIATION
P.O. Box 920
Spokane,
Washington 99210

INLAND EMPIRE BOTTLE
& COLLECTORS CLUB
12824 E. 4th
Spokane,
Washington 99216

NORTHWEST BEAM &
SPECIALTIES CLUB
P.O. Box 4365 Station B
Spokane,
Washington 92202

NORTHWEST JIM BEAM
BOTTLE COLLECTORS
ASSOCIATION
P.O. Box 7401
Spokane,
Washington 99207

NORTHWEST TREASURE
HUNTER'S CLUB
c/o Louise Bosh
East 107 Astor Drive
Spokane,
Washington 99208

LEWIS & CLARK
HISTORICAL BOTTLE
SOCIETY
4105 Main Street
Vancouver,
Washington 98663

ANTIQUE ACRES EZRA
BROOKS CLUB
P.O. Box 559
Yelm, Washington 98597

JIM BEAM COLLECTORS
107 Mohawk Drive
Barrackville,
West Virginia 26559

WILD & WONDERFUL
WEST VIRGINIA EZRA
BROOKS BOTTLE &
SPECIALTY CLUB
1924 Pennsylvania Avenue
Weirton,
West Virginia 26062

MILWAUKEE JIM BEAM
BOTTLE & SPECIALTIES
CLUB, LTD.
14215 W. North Avenue
Brookfield,
Wisconsin 53005

CAMERON BOTTLE
DIGGERS
P.O. Box 276
314 South 1st Street
Cameron, Wisconsin 54822

FIGURAL BOTTLE
ASSOCIATION
The Bottle Stopper
Eagle, Wisconsin 53119

BADGER BOTTLE DIGGERS
1420 McKinley Road
Eau Claire,
Wisconsin 54701

BADGER JIM BEAM CLUB
OF MADISON
P.O. Box 5612
Madison, Wisconsin 53705

SOUTH CENTRAL
WISCONSIN BOTTLE CLUB
618 Clemons Avenue
Madison, Wisconsin 53704

CENTRAL WISCONSIN
BOTTLE COLLECTORS
1608 Main Street
Stevens Point,
Wisconsin 54481

MILWAUKEE ANTIQUE
BOTTLE CLUB
2343 Met-To-Wee Lane
Wauwatosa,
Wisconsin 53226

MILWAUKEE JIM BEAM &
ANTIQUE BOTTLE CLUB
120 N. 15th Avenue
West Bend,
Wisconsin 53095

CASPER ANTIQUE &
COLLECTORS CLUB
2555 E. 9th
Casper, Wyoming 82601

CHEYENNE A.B.C.
P.O. Box 1251
Cheyenne, Wyoming 82001

PAUL & FRAN'S - MODERN
FIGURALS
P.O. Box 388
Cheyenne, Wyoming 82001

INSUBOTT BOTTLE CLUB
P.O. Box 34
Lander, Wyoming 82520

SOUTHWESTERN
WYOMING AVON CLUB
P.O. Box 1688
Rock Springs,
Wyoming 82901

Canada

FIRST CANADIAN BOTTLE
& SPECIALTY CLUB
P.O. Box 3232 Station B
Calgary 41, Alberta, Canada

CAMPBELL RIVER
ANTIQUE BOTTLE &
RELIC CLUB
c/o Bill Patterson
#12 2705 (N Island) Hwy.
Campbell River,
British Columbia, Canada

DIGGERS CLUB
c/o Mrs. E. Klimes,
R. R. 2
Ladysmith, British
Columbia, Canada

NANAMINO OLD TIME
BOTTLE ASSOCIATION
c/o Robert Skrill
Parkway Drive R.R. #1
Lantzville, B.C.
VOR 2HO Canada

SKEENA ROCK &
BOTTLE CLUB
c/o Mrs. Rod Miller
4735 Soucie Avenue
Terrace, British Columbia,
Canada

OLD TIME BOTTLE CLUB
OF BRITISH COLUMBIA
P.O. Box 77154
Postal Station 5
Vancouver/6,
British Columbia, Canada

SOOKE ROTO-ROOTERS
13 Maddock
Victoria, British Columbia,
Canada

VICTORIA GLASS & BOTTLE
COLLECTOR'S SOCIETY
4603 W. Saanich Road
Victoria,
British Columbia, Canada

SAINT JOHN ANTIQUE
BOTTLE CLUB
25 Orange Street
Saint John,
New Brunswick, Canada

ARCADIA BOTTLE CLUB
c/o 16 Quarry Road
Halifax, Nova Scotia,
Canada

PICTOU COUNTY
HISTORICAL BOTTLE
CLUB
c/o George C. Dooley
P. 09 Box 408
Westville, Nova Scotia,
Canada

BYTOWN BOTTLE SEEKERS
Box 4099 Station E
Ottawa,
Ontario, Canada KIS 5B1

MONTREAL HISTORICAL
BOTTLE ASSOCIATION
P.O. Box 184
T.M.R. Montreal,
Quebec, Canada

International

AUSTRALIAN BOTTLE
COLLECTORS' CLUB
39 Ellington Street
Ekibin, Queensland, 4121,
Australia

NASSAU INTERNATIONAL
ANTIQUE BOTTLE CLUB
c/o Joanne M. Kelly,
P.O. Box 6191
Nassau, New Providence
Island, Bahamas

CANAL ZONE BOTTLE
CLUB ASSOCIATION
P.O. Box 2232
Balboa, Canal Zone

JIM BEAMS BOTTLE CLUB
DENMARK
Mr. Kurt Vendelbo
Oresundsvej 130
2300 Copenhagen S,
Denmark

BRITISH BOTTLE
COLLECTORS' CLUB
49 Elizabeth Road
Brentwood, Essex, England

RHINELAND FFALZ
BEAM'S BOOZE & BOTTLE
CLUB
295th Avn. Company
A.P.O. New York 09185

JIM BEAM BOTTLE CLUB
Mainzerstr. 60,
6530 Bingen/Rhein,
West Germany

Acid, Liquid Carbonic Mfg.Co., Honey Amber, 8 3/4 In.	8.00
Apothecary, Amber, Gallon	4.50
Apothecary, Aralia Rac On Gold & Red Glass Label, OP, 8 3/4 In.	25.00
Apothecary, Black Amethyst, Gallon	115.00
Apothecary, Blown Stopper, 8 1/2 In.	5.00
Apothecary, Blown Stopper, 9 1/2 In.	6.00
Apothecary, Blown Stopper, 12 1/2 In.	8.00
Apothecary, Bulbous, 12 In.	27.50
Apothecary, Cut Crystal, 5 1/4 In.High	12.00
Apothecary, Cut Glass, Blown, Paneled, Permanent Label, Stopper, 5 1/4 In.	12.00
Apothecary, F.& S., St.Louis, Mo., 1894, Square, Glass Label, 1/2 Gallon	35.00
Apothecary, Fl.Ext.Verat.Vir. On Gold & Red Glass Label, OP, 7 1/2 In.	22.50
Apothecary, Flared Ground Lip, Ground Stopper, OP, Honey Amber, 8 1/2 In.	11.00
Apothecary, Free-Blown, C.1840, Jet Black, 8 In.	40.00
Apothecary, Glass Label, OP, Honey Amber, 8 1/2 In.	11.00
Apothecary, Glycerine, Wide Mouth, 3 Parts, Pouring Mouth, Collar, Quart	32.50
Apothecary, Gossipium On Gold & Red Glass Label, OP, 8 3/4 In.	25.00
Apothecary, Ground Stopper, OP, 8 1/4 In.	4.00
Apothecary, Ground Stopper, OP, 10 In.	4.00
Apothecary, Imbedded Gold Label Outlined In Red, Cobalt Blue, 10 In., Pair	35.00
Apothecary, Ol.Tiglii On Gold & Red Glass Label, OP, 7 1/2 In.	22.50
Apothecary, R.Zingib, Glass Label, Thumbprint Stopper, 1/2 Gallon	42.50
Apothecary, Red Smalts On Gold & Red Glass Label, OP, 8 3/4 In.	25.00
Apothecary, Roof Shouldered, Pat.Apr.21, 1889, 5 In.	4.00
Apothecary, Round Shoulder, Flared Lip, Ground Stopper, Amber, 8 1/2 In.	12.00
Apothecary, Round, Label Under Glass, 7 In.	3.50
Apothecary, Round, Label Under Glass, 10 In.	3.50
Apothecary, Small Mouth, Square, Flat Top Stopper, Glass Label, Amber, Pint	12.50
Apothecary, Small Mouth, Square, Flat Top Stopper, Glass Label, Amber, 8 In.	15.00
Apothecary, Small Mouth, Thumbprint Stopper, Glass Label, Round, Pint	14.50
Apothecary, Small Mouth, Thumbprint Stopper, Glass Label, Round, 1/2 Gallon	32.50
Apothecary, Small Mouth, Thumbprint Stopper, Glass Label, 9 1/2 In.	17.50
Apothecary, Small Neck, Pull Stopper, San Francisco, Amber, 10 1/2 In.	17.50
Apothecary, Square, Label Under Glass, 7 In.	3.50
Apothecary, Square, Label Under Glass, 10 In.	3.50
Apothecary, St.Louis, 1894, Glass Label, Thumbprint Stopper, 1/2 Gallon	55.00
Apothecary, T.C.W.Co., U.S.A., Finger Pull Stopper, Amber, 10 In.	45.00
Apothecary, Theodore Campbell, Overbrook, Cobalt, 5 In.	10.00
Apothecary, Tinct.Zingib, J. On Gold & Red Glass Label, OP, 7 1/2 In.	22.50
Apothecary, Tr.Arnicae, Glass Label, Thumbprint Stopper, 1/2 Gallon	42.50
Apothecary, W.T.Co., U.S.A., Square, Wide Mouth, Flat Stopper, Amber, 1/2 Pint	6.50
Apothecary, W.T.Co., U.S.A., Square, Wide Mouth, Flat Stopper, Amber, 7 In.	8.50
Apothecary, Wheaton Apothecary Products, Embossed, ABM, 12 In.High	50.00
Apothecary, Wide Mouth, Flat Top Stopper, Glass Label, Round, Quart	17.50
Apothecary, Wide Mouth, Flat Top Stopper, Glass Label, 9 1/2 In.	25.00
Apothecary, Wide Mouth, Pull Stopper, San Francisco, Amber, 8 In.	27.50
Apothecary, Wide Mouth, Thumbprint Stopper, Glass Label, Round, Pint	14.50
Apothecary, Wide Mouth, Thumbprint Stopper, Glass Label, Round, Quart	18.50
Apothecary, Wide Mouth, Thumbprint Stopper, Glass Label, 9 In.	17.50
Apothecary, Wide Mouth, Thumbprint Stopper, Glass Label, 10 1/2 In.	25.00
Atomizer, Cut Glass, Paperweight, Tuthill, 10 In.	135.00
Atomizer, De Vez, Cut Brown Floral On Yellow Satin, Signed, 7 1/2 In.	150.00
Atomizer, DeVilbiss, Clear & Opalescent Coin Spot, 4 In.	15.00
Atomizer, Moser, Gold Encrusted, Graphic Flowers & Birds, 9 1/2 In.	85.00
Atomizer, Steuben, Aurene, Blue, 6 In.High	135.00
Austin Nichols, Tom Turkey, 1971	65.00
Austin Nichols, Turkey On A Log, 1972	25.00
Austin Nichols, Turkey On The Wing, 1973	21.50
Austin Nichols, Wild Turkey, 1974 _Color_	29.95

Avon started in 1886 as the California Perfume Company. It was not until 1929 that the name Avon was used. In 1939 it became the Avon Products, Inc. Each year Avon sells many figural bottles filled with cosmetic products. Ceramic, plastic, and glass bottles are made in limited editions.

Avon, A Quilt, 1969	35.00

Avon, Abraham Lincoln Decanter, 1971, 4 Ozs. 2.25
Avon, After Shower Flask, 1959 .... 45.00
    Avon, Airplane, see Avon, Spirit of St.Louis
Avon, Aladdin's Lamp, 1971 ....*Color* 5.00
Avon, All Body Powders, Round Tin 25.00
Avon, Alpine Flask After Shave Lotion, 1966, 8 Ozs. .... 45.00 To 55.00
Avon, American Beauty Fragrance Jar, 1934, Tassel 35.00
Avon, American Eagle Test Bottle, 1971 .... 35.00
Avon, American Eagle, 1971, Dark Amber, 5 Ozs., Full & Boxed 3.50
Avon, Angler, 1970 .... 3.00 To 5.00
Avon, Angler, 1970, Silver Reel Cap & Trim, Blue, 5 Ozs., Full & Boxed 6.50
Avon, Anniversary Diary & Perfume, 1949 .... 95.00
Avon, Anniversary Spoons, Set Of 7, 1969 .... 50.00
Avon, Antique Car Pitcher, 1971 .... 15.00
Avon, Apothecary Jar Soap, 1965 .... 13.00
Avon, Apple Blossom Cologne, 1936, 6 Ozs. 75.00
Avon, Apple Blossom Cologne, 1942 .... 20.00
Avon, Apple, Golden, 1968 .... 8.00
Avon, Attention Cologne, 1947, 6 Ozs. 75.00
Avon, Attention Pink Ribbon Set, 1943 .... 20.00 To 40.00
    Avon, Avon Calling, see Avon, Telephone
Avon, Avon Lady Club Bottle, 1972 .... 75.00
Avon, Baa Baa Black Sheep, 1954 .... 55.00
Avon, Ballad Perfume, 1936 .... 55.00
Avon, Ballad Perfume, 1945, Label, Tassel .... 75.00 To 100.00
Avon, Barber Bottle, 1963, Gold Letters & Neck, White, 8 Ozs. .. 12.00 To 25.00
    Avon, Barometer, see Avon, Weather-Or-Not
    Avon, Baseball Mitt, see Avon, Fielder's Choice
Avon, Bath Seasons, 1967 .... 3.00 To 3.50
Avon, Bath Seasons, 1968, Lavender, Full & Boxed 1.25
Avon, Bath Seasons, 1968, Pink, Full & Boxed 1.25
Avon, Bath Seasons, 1968, Yellow, Full & Boxed 1.25
Avon, Bath Urn, 1963, Milk Glass .... 3.00 To 7.50
Avon, Bath Urn, 1966 .... 12.50
Avon, Bath Urn, 1967 .... 10.00
Avon, Bath Urn, 1971 .... 3.00
Avon, Bay Rum Gift Set, 1964 .... 25.00
Avon, Bay Rum Jug, 1962 .... 12.00
Avon, Bay Rum Jug, 1964, Label, 8 Ozs. .... 4.95 To 6.95
Avon, Bay Rum Jug, 1964, Label, 8 Ozs., Full 7.95
Avon, Bay Rum Keg, 1965, Label, 8 Ozs. .... 12.00 To 14.95
Avon, Bay Rum Keg, 1965, Label, 8 Ozs., Full 15.95
Avon, Bay Rum, 1969 .... 7.00
Avon, Beehive Set, 1951, Full & Boxed .... 60.00 To 100.00
Avon, Bell, 1968, Fragrance 4.00
Avon, Belle, 1965, Fragrance, 4 Ozs. 10.00
Avon, Big Whistle, 1972, 4 Ozs., Full & Boxed 3.00
Avon, Bird Of Paradise Figural Bottle, 1970, 8 In., Full & Boxed 6.00
Avon, Birthday Cake Representative's Gift, 1951 .... 100.00 To 125.00
Avon, Blacksmith Anvil, 1972, 4 Ozs. 4.00
Avon, Blue Blazer Deluxe Set, 1965, Full & Boxed 42.50
Avon, Blue Blazer Hair Dressing Gel, 1964, Full & Boxed 4.99
Avon, Blue Blazer Soap Set, 1964 .... 13.00
Avon, Blue Blazer Tie Tac Deluxe Box, 1965 .... 45.00
Avon, Bonbon Cologne, Poodle, 1972, Full & Boxed 3.50
Avon, Book, Amber, Bay Rum, 1969 .... 6.50 To 7.00
Avon, Book, Blue, 1969 .... 6.50 To 7.00
Avon, Book, Classic, 1969, Amber .... 6.50 To 7.00
Avon, Book, Classic, 1969, Blue .... 6.50 To 7.00
Avon, Book, Classic, 1969, Brown 6.50
Avon, Book, Classic, 1969, Set Of 4 .... 16.00
Avon, Book, First Edition, 1967, 6 Ozs. .... 3.95 To 5.00
Avon, Boot, 1965, Silver Top, Amber, 8 Ozs. .... 5.50 To 6.50
Avon, Boot, 1966, Gold Top, Amber, 8 Ozs. 3.25
Avon, Boot, 1966, Gold Top, Amber, 8 Ozs., Full & Boxed 3.95

Avon, Boot, 1967, Spray Cologne, Black Cap, Tan Plastic, 3 Ozs., Full & Boxed 3.50
    Avon, Bowling Pin, see Avon, King Pin
Avon, Boxing Gloves, 1960 .... 12.50
Avon, Bright Night Cologne, 1/2 Oz. .... 75.00 To 150.00
Avon, Bright Night Perfume, 1954, Full & Boxed 65.00
Avon, Bright Night Powder Sachet, 1954, Full & Boxed 9.00
Avon, Bright Night Toilet Water, 1954, Full & Boxed 14.00
Avon, Bucking Bronco, Copper Cowboy, Amber, Boxed, 1971 .... 5.00
Avon, Bud Vase, 1968 .... 8.00
Avon, Bud Vase, 1968, Full & Boxed 4.50
Avon, Buffalo Nickel, 1971, 5 Ozs., Full & Boxed 3.60
Avon, Bugle, 1965 .... 7.00
Avon, Bulldog Pipe, 1972, 6 Ozs., Full & Boxed 3.60
Avon, Bullet Christmas Gift Perfume, 1964 .... 40.00
Avon, Bunnies Dream Soap On A Rope, 1967 .... 8.00
Avon, Butterfly, 1972, 1 1/2 Ozs. 4.00
Avon, Butterfly Soap Set, 1966 .... 9.95
Avon, Buttons & Bows Bubble Bath, 1962, Full & Boxed 5.00
Avon, Buttons & Bows Cologne Mist, 1961 .... 5.00
Avon, Buttons & Bows Roll On, 1962, Full & Boxed 5.00
Avon, Caddy Set, 1968, Embossed, Set Of 3 .... 12.00
Avon, Cadillac, 1969, Gold, 6 Ozs., Full & Boxed 5.00
Avon, California Perfume Company, Bay Rum, 1908, 4 Ozs. 95.00
Avon, California Perfume Company, Cold Cream, 1908 .... 35.00
Avon, California Perfume Company, Cream Shampoo, 1908 .... 100.00
Avon, California Perfume Company, Elite Powder, 1912, Glass Jar 35.00
Avon, California Perfume Company, Perfection Coloring Set, 1923, Full, Boxed 115.00
Avon, California Perfume Company, Perfection Extract, 1/2 Oz. 15.00
Avon, California Perfume Company, Perfection Extract, 2 Ozs. 20.00
Avon, California Perfume Company, Perfection Extract, 4 Ozs. 40.00
Avon, California Perfume Company, Perfection Food Coloring, 1932, 2 Ozs. 15.00
Avon, California Perfume Company, Smoker's Tooth Powder 65.00
Avon, California Perfume Company, Tooth Tablets, 1906, Contents 55.00
Avon, California Perfume Company, Trailing Arbutus Talcum Powder Tin 45.00
Avon, California Perfume Company, Vernafleur Face Powder 15.00
Avon, Cameo Ring Glace, 1969, Compartmented 6.00
Avon, Cameo Sachet, 1961 .... 4.50
Avon, Candle, 1964, Milk Glass 4.00
Avon, Candle, 1965, Amber 10.00
Avon, Candle, 1965, Red 10.00
Avon, Candle, 1967, Frosted 7.00
Avon, Candle, 1968, Regence, 10 1/2 In. 7.00
Avon, Candlestick Cologne, 1966, 3 Ozs. 5.00
Avon, Candlestick Cologne, 1970, Glass, 4 Ozs. 5.00
Avon, Candlestick Cologne, 1972, 5 Ozs. 5.00
Avon, Cannon, Defender, 1966, 6 Ozs. 15.00
Avon, Capitol Decanter, 1970, 5 Ozs., Full & Boxed .... 2.50 To 3.60
Avon, Captain's Choice, 1964, Label, 8 Ozs., Full 7.95
Avon, Captain's Pride, 1970 .... 3.00
Avon, Car Glasses, 1971, Set Of 8 .... 12.00
Avon, Car, Camper, 1972 .... 8.00
Avon, Car, Duesenberg, Silver, 1970, 5 Ozs. 6.00
Avon, Car, Duesenberg, 1970, Silver, 5 Ozs., Full & Boxed 7.00
Avon, Car, Dune Buggy, 1971 .... 4.00
Avon, Car, Electric Charger, 1970 .... 5.00
Avon, Car, Electric Charger, 1970, Test Bottle 75.00
Avon, Car, Maxwell 23, 1972, 6 Ozs., Full & Boxed 4.50
Avon, Car, MG, 1974, After Shave, White Plastic Top, Red Milk Glass, 7 In. 3.99
Avon, Car, Model A, 1972, Wild Country, Full & Boxed 3.60
Avon, Car, Packard Roadster, 1970, 6 Ozs., Full & Boxed 4.50
Avon, Car, Racing Car 5, 1972, Sure Winner, 5 Ozs., Full & Boxed 2.70
Avon, Car, Reo Depot Wagon, 1972, 5 Ozs., Full & Boxed 4.50
Avon, Car, Rolls Royce, 1972 .... 6.50
Avon, Car, Solid Gold Cadillac, 1970 .... 5.00
Avon, Car, Stanley Steamer Test Bottle, 1971 .... 30.00

Avon, Car, Stanley Steamer, 1971, 5 Ozs., Full & Boxed 3.60
Avon, Car, Station Wagon Test Bottle, 1971 .... 50.00
Avon, Car, Station Wagon, 1971, 6 Ozs., Full & Boxed 4.50
Avon, Car, Sterling Six, 1968, 7 Ozs., Full & Boxed 4.95
Avon, Car, Straight 8, 1969, 5 Ozs., Full & Boxed 4.50
Avon, Car, Touring T Test Bottle, 1969 .... 100.00
Avon, Car, Touring T, 1969, 6 Ozs., Full & Boxed 6.50
Avon, Car, Volkswagen, 1971, Red, 4 Ozs., Full & Boxed 2.70
Avon, Casey Jones, Jr., Soap, 1956, Full & Boxed 32.50
Avon, Casey's Lantern, 1966, Amber, 10 Ozs., Boxed 29.50
Avon, Casey's Lantern, 1966, Green 25.00
Avon, Casey's Lantern, 1966, Red 25.00
Avon, Cat, see Avon, Ming Cat
Avon, Changing Of The Guard, 1956 .... 30.00
Avon, Charisma Jewelry, 1969, Set Of 3 .... 25.00
Avon, Charlie Brown Mug, 1969, Charlie Brown 4.00
Avon, Charlie Brown Mug, 1969, Linis 4.00
Avon, Charlie Brown Mug, 1969, Snoopy 4.00
Avon, Cherub Soap, 1966 .... 10.00
Avon, Chess Piece, 1971, Smart Move, 3 Ozs., Full & Boxed 2.95
Avon, Chess Piece, 1972, The King, 3 Ozs. 2.00
Avon, China Teapot, 1972 .... 12.00
Avon, Christmas Fragrance, 1965, Set Of 3 .... 50.00
Avon, Christmas Ornament, 1959, Stockholder's 50.00
Avon, Christmas Ornament, 1967, Round 5.00
Avon, Christmas Ornament, 1968, Indented 4.00
Avon, Christmas Ornament, 1970, Pointed Tip 3.00
Avon, Christmas Plate, 1972, Rose 7.00
Avon, Christmas Sparkler, 1968, Red 3.00
Avon, Christmas Tree, 1968 .... 4.00
Avon, Circus Wagon Soap 25.00
Avon, Classic Book, see Avon, Book, Classic
Avon, Clock, Daylight Shaving Time, 1968, 6 Ozs. .... 3.50 To 4.50
Avon, Clock, Daylight Shaving Time, 1968, 6 Ozs., Full & Boxed 4.95
Avon, Clock, Grandfather, Fragrance Hours, 1971, 6 Ozs. 5.00
Avon, Clock, Leisure Hours Bath Oil, 1970, 5 Ozs. 3.00
Avon, Coffee Mill, see Avon, Country Store
Avon, Cologne, 1958, 2 Ozs. 10.00
Avon, Cornucopia, 1971, 6 Ozs. 5.00
Avon, Cotillion Beauty Dust, 1959 .... 5.00
Avon, Cotillion Body Powder, 1958, Full & Boxed 8.00
Avon, Cotillion Cologne, 1947, Bubble Sides, Full & Boxed 60.00
Avon, Cotillion Cologne, 1953, 4 Ozs. 6.00
Avon, Cotillion Cologne, 1961, 2 Ozs. 10.00
Avon, Cotillion Cream Lotion, 1954 .... 5.00
Avon, Cotillion Cream Lotion, 1954, Full & Boxed 7.00
Avon, Cotillion Cream Sachet, 1957, Full & Boxed 6.95
Avon, Cotillion Powder Sachet, 1937, Full 13.00
Avon, Cotillion Sachet, 1953, Pink Glass, 1/2 Original Powder 5.00
Avon, Cotillion Soap, 1948 .... 20.00
Avon, Cotillion Toilet Water, 1953, 2 Ozs. 5.00
Avon, Country Kitchen, Roaster, 1973, 6 Ozs. 3.50
Avon, Country Store, Coffee Mill, 1972, 5 Ozs. 6.00
Avon, Courting Lamp, 1970 ....Color 12.00
Avon, Covered Wagon, 1970, 6 Ozs. 3.75
Avon, Covered Wagon, 1970, 6 Ozs., Full & Boxed 3.60
Avon, Cream Hair Lotion, 1949, Full & Boxed 8.00
Avon, Crystal Chandelier 3.50
Avon, Crystal Glory Spray Essence, 1962 .... 8.00 To 20.00
Avon, Cuckoo Clock Bubble Bath, 1965, 10 Ozs. 6.00
Avon, Daisy Chain Gift Set, 1963, Full & Boxed 10.50
Avon, Daisy Won't Tell .... 5.00 To 18.00
Avon, Daylight Shaving Time Clock .... 3.50 To 4.50
Avon, Decanter, Armoire, 1972, 5 Ozs. 4.00
Avon, Decanter, Secretaire, 1972, 5 Ozs. 4.00

Avon, Decisions, 1965 .... 20.00
Avon, Decisions, 1965, Foreign 25.00
Avon, Defender Cannon, 1966 .... 15.00
Avon, Demi Cup, 1968, Gold Band, 3 Ozs. 15.00
Avon, Demi Cup, 1969, Three Colors, 3 Ozs. 4.00
Avon, Demi Cup, 1969, Wild Rose, 3 Ozs. 4.00
Avon, Demi Cup, 1971, Dutch Treat, 3 Ozs. 4.00
Avon, Deodorant For Men, 1961, Stagecoach Embossed, 2 Ozs., Full & Boxed 11.00
Avon, Dew Kiss, 1960 .... 4.50
Avon, Dollar, Liberty 3.60
Avon, Dollars & Scents Soap On A Rope, 1966 .... 20.00
Avon, Dollars & Scents, 1966, 8 Ozs. .... 15.95 To 22.00
Avon, Dollars & Scents, 1966, 8 Ozs., Full & Boxed 22.50
Avon, Dolphin Soap Dish 3.50
Avon, Dolphin, 1968, 8 Ozs. 7.50
Avon, Dovecote Cologne, 1974 .... 3.00
Avon, Duck Organizer, 1971 .... 22.00
Avon, Duck, Frilly, 1960 .... 7.00
Avon, Duck, Mallard, 1967, 6 Ozs. .... 3.50 To 7.50
Avon, Duck, Mallard, 1967, 6 Ozs., Full & Boxed 8.95
Avon, Dueling Pistol, 1760, 1973 ....*Color* 10.00
Avon, Dueling Pistol, 1972, 4 Ozs. 10.00
     Avon, Dueling Pistols, see also Avon, Twenty Paces
     Avon, Duesenberg, see Avon, Car, Duesenberg
     Avon, Dutch Treat Demi Cup, see Avon, Demi Cup
Avon, Eagle, American, 1971 .... 3.50
Avon, Eagle, Bureau Organizer, 1972 .... 16.00 To 25.00
Avon, Eiffel Tower, 1970, 3 Ozs. 5.00
     Avon, Electric Charger, see Avon, Car, Electric Charger
Avon, Elegante, 1956, 1/2 Oz. .... 75.00 To 150.00
Avon, Elephant, 1962 .... 8.00
Avon, Enchanted Hours Cologne, 1972, 5 Ozs. 3.00
Avon, Excalibur Cologne, 1969, 6 Ozs. 2.00
Avon, Excalibur Cologne, 1969, 6 Ozs., Full & Boxed 3.50
Avon, Fair Lady Set, 1945 .... 100.00
Avon, Fashion Figurine, 1971, Victorian, 4 Ozs. 3.50
Avon, Fashion Figurine, 1972, Elizabethan, 4 Ozs. 3.50
Avon, Fashion Figurine, 1972, Roaring Twenties, 3 Ozs. 3.50
Avon, Fielder's Choice, 1971, 5 Ozs., Full & Boxed 2.70
Avon, Fife, 1965 .... 7.00
Avon, Fife, 1965, Full & Boxed 8.50
Avon, Fire Engine, First Volunteer, 1971 .... 5.95
Avon, First Class Male, 1970 .... 5.00
Avon, First Down, 1970, 6 Ozs., Full & Boxed 11.00
Avon, First Down Football, 1965 .... 8.00 To 10.00
     Avon, First Edition, see Avon, Book, First Edition
Avon, First Mate, 1963 .... 9.00
Avon, First Volunteer Fire Engine, 1971, 6 Ozs. 5.95
     Avon, Fish, see Avon, Dolphin, Avon, Sea Spirit
Avon, Fishing Reel, 1970, 5 Ozs. 7.00
Avon, Floral Medley Set, 1967, Boxed 5.99
Avon, Flowertime Cologne, 1949, 2 Ozs. 11.50
Avon, Flowertime Set, 1949 .... 21.00
Avon, Flowertime Set, 1949, Full & Boxed 60.00
Avon, Flowertime Talc, 1949 .... 11.50
Avon, Flowertime Toilet Water, 1949, 2 Ozs. 11.50
     Avon, football, see Avon, First Down
Avon, Football Helmet, 1968, Clear 100.00
Avon, Football Helmet, 1968, Dull Gold, Blue Stripe, 6 Ozs. 7.95
Avon, Football Helmet, 1968, Dull Gold, Blue Stripe, 6 Ozs., Full & Boxed 9.95
Avon, Football Helmet, 1968, Dull Gold, No Stripe, 6 Ozs. 15.00
Avon, Football Helmet, 1968, Dull Gold, White Stripe, 6 Ozs. 9.00
Avon, Football Helmet, 1969, Shiny Gold, 6 Ozs. 20.00
Avon, Football Helmet, 1969, Shiny Gold, 6 Ozs., Full & Boxed .... 20.00 To 22.50
Avon, Forever Spring Body Powder, 1951, Full & Boxed 10.00

Avon, Forever Spring Cologne, 1956 .... 12.00
Avon, Forever Spring Perfume, 1/2 Oz. .... 75.00 To 150.00
Avon, Forever Spring Powder Sachet, 1950 .... 10.00
Avon, Forever Spring Toilet Water, 1950 .... 14.95 To 20.00
Avon, Forever Spring Toilet Water, 1951, Full & Boxed 15.00
Avon, Fox Hunt Set, 1966 .... 28.00
Avon, Fragrance Bell, 1965, Full 7.00
   Avon, Fragrance Hours, see Avon, Clock, Grandfather
Avon, Fragrance Jar Liquid, 1936, Full & Boxed 13.00
Avon, Fragrance Jar, 1934 .... 22.00
Avon, Fragrance Jar, 1952 .... 10.00
Avon, Fragrance Touch Bud Vase, 1969 .... 4.99
Avon, Fragrance Trio, 1964 .... 8.00
Avon, Fragrant Mist Set, 1950, Full & Boxed 27.50
Avon, Frame Cologne 3.50
   Avon, French Telephone, see Avon, Telephone, French
Avon, Futura, 1969, 5 Ozs. 12.50
Avon, Futura, 1969, 5 Ozs., Full & Boxed 14.95
Avon, Gavel, 1967, 5 Ozs. 9.95
Avon, Gavel, 1967, 5 Ozs., Full & Boxed .... 12.50 To 14.50
   Avon, Gay 90's Figurine, see Avon, Victorian Lady
Avon, Gem In Crystal Set, 1957 .... 60.00
Avon, General 4-4-0, 1971, 5 1/2 Ozs., Full & Boxed 4.95
Avon, Gentlemen's Choice, 1969, Set Of 3 .... 7.50
Avon, Gentlemen's Collection, 1968 .... 15.00
Avon, George Washington Decanter, 1970, 4 Ozs., Full & Boxed 2.25
Avon, George Washington Decanter, 1974 .... 5.99
Avon, Glass, 1969, Wood & Steel 15.00
Avon, Globe, 1969, 6 Ozs. 7.00
Avon, Globe Bank, 1966, Full 7.00
Avon, Gold Cadillac 4.75
Avon, Gold Piece, 1971 .... 4.50
Avon, Gold Top Boot, 1966 .... 4.00
Avon, Golden Apple, 1968 .... 8.00
Avon, Golden Heirloom, 1968 .... 35.00
Avon, Golden Moments Necklace, 1971, Full & Boxed 10.00
Avon, Golden Mouse, 1970, 1/2 Oz. 10.00
Avon, Golden Promise, 1/2 Oz. .... 75.00 To 150.00
Avon, Golden Promise Body Powder, 1947, Full & Boxed 10.00
Avon, Golden Promise Cologne, 1947, Full & Boxed 15.00
Avon, Golden Promise Perfume, 1951, 1/8 Oz. 10.00
Avon, Golden Thimble, 1972, 2 Ozs. 2.50
Avon, Golden Vanity & Mirror, 1967 .... 25.00
Avon, Goldilocks Soap, 1966, Full & Boxed 7.00
Avon, Golf Cart, 1972, Avon Open, 5 Ozs. 4.50
Avon, Grecian Pitcher, 1972, 5 Ozs. 3.00
Avon, Greek Goddess, 1969 .... 5.00
Avon, Guard Set, 1958, Full & Boxed 40.00
Avon, Hand Lotion, 1963 .... 5.00
Avon, Hand Lotion, 1963, Full & Boxed 5.95
Avon, Happy Hours Perfume, 1949 .... 35.00
Avon, Happy Hours Set, 1948, Full 55.00
Avon, Hawaiian Delights, 1962, Full & Boxed 12.00
   Avon, Head, see Avon, Warrior Head
Avon, Hearth Lamp, 1973 .... *Color* XXXX.XX
Avon, Heliotrope Powder Sachet, 1886, C.P.C. 35.00
   Avon, Helmet, see Avon, Football Helmet
Avon, Here's My Heart Cream Lotion, 1958 .... 2.50
Avon, Here's My Heart Perfume 150.00
Avon, Here's My Heart Plastic Squeeze, 1957 .... 6.00
Avon, Here's My Heart Soap, 1962, Boxed 7.00
Avon, Hickory Dickory Clock Shampoo, 1971 .... 2.69
Avon, Homestead, Decanter, 1973, 4 Ozs. 2.50
Avon, Horns, Steer, Western Choice .... 15.00 To 16.50
Avon, Hostess Sampler, 1965 .... 15.00

Avon, Hostess Soap Set, 1964 .... 11.95
Avon, Ice Cream Sundae 15.00
Avon, Icicle Perfume, 1967, Full & Boxed 5.00
Avon, Imperial Garden Ceramic Vase 9.00
Avon, Indian Head Penny, 1970, 4 Ozs., Full & Boxed .... 2.00 To 3.00
Avon, Inkwell, 1969, 6 Ozs. 4.95
Avon, Inkwell, 1969, 6 Ozs., Full & Boxed 5.95
Avon, Insect Repellent, 1959 .... 3.50
Avon, Iron Horse Shaving Mug, 1974 .... 5.99
Avon, Island Lime, 1966, Basket Weave, Dark Yellow 7.00
Avon, It's A Blast, Horn, 1970, 5 Ozs., Full & Boxed 5.40
Avon, It's A Blast, 1970, 5 Ozs. 3.50
Avon, Jasmine Soap, 1946 .... 25.00
Avon, Jennifer 22.00
Avon, Jewel Collection, 1964 .... 50.00
Avon, Jolly-Holly-Day Set, 1963 .... 12.50
Avon, Just Two, 1965, Boxed 75.00
Avon, Kanga Winks 2.50
Avon, Keynote Perfume, 1967, Boxed .... 10.00 To 12.50
Avon, King Pin, 1969, White, 4 Ozs. 4.00
Avon, Kitten Little, 1972, 1 1/2 Ozs. 3.50
Avon, Koffee Klatch, 1971 ....*Color* 4.00
Avon, Lady Slippers 2.50
Avon, Lamp, Parlor, 1971, 3 Ozs. 5.00
    Avon, Lantern, see Avon, Casey's Lantern
Avon, Lavender & Lace, 1970 .... 5.00
Avon, Leisure Hours Clock, 1970, Milk Glass .... 3.00 To 5.00
Avon, Leisure House 2.50
Avon, Lemonol Soap Set, 1963 .... 8.99
Avon, Liberty Bell, 1971, 5 Ozs., Full & Boxed 2.70
Avon, Liberty Dollar, 1970, 6 Ozs., Full & Boxed 3.60
Avon, Light Bulb Soap On A Rope, 1967, Full & Boxed 8.00
Avon, L'il Captain, 1963 .... 9.00
Avon, L'il Folk Time Bubble Bath, 1961, 8 Ozs. 7.00
Avon, L'il Mate, 1963 .... 9.00
Avon, Little Folks Time Clock, 1961, Full & Boxed 7.00
Avon, Little Girl Blue, 1972, 3 Ozs. 2.50
Avon, Little Helper Iron, 1962, Full & Boxed 10.00
Avon, Little Helper Iron, 1964 .... 5.00
Avon, Little Missy Rolling Pin, 1966, Boxed 6.00
Avon, Little Slugger, 1962 .... 7.50
Avon, Love Bird, 1969, 1/4 Oz. 5.00
Avon, Lullaby Baby Set, 1964, Full & Boxed 9.00
Avon, Luscious Perfume 100.00
Avon, Luscious Perfume, 1951, 1/8 Oz. 10.00
Avon, Mad Hatter Decanter Bubble Bath, 1970, 6 Ozs. 1.99
Avon, Makeup Ensemble, 1952 .... 16.50
Avon, Mallard Duck, 1967 .... 3.50 To 7.50
Avon, Man's World, 1969 .... 5.00
Avon, Master Organizer, 1970 .... 25.00
Avon, Milk Glass, Greek Figure, Classic Bath Oil, 1969 .... 8.00
Avon, Milk Glass, Hand Holding Bottle, 1969 .... 5.00
Avon, Milk Glass, Nesting Dove, 1970 .... 8.00
Avon, Milk Glass, Urn, 1963 .... 12.50
Avon, Milk Glass, Urn, 1971, 5 Ozs. 4.00
Avon, Ming Cat, 1971, 6 Ozs. 6.00
Avon, Mini Bike, 1972 .... 4.00
Avon, Miss Lollypop Boot 7.50
Avon, Miss Lollypop Cologne Mist, 1967 .... 5.00
Avon, Miss Lollypop Kitten & Ball Jar, 1967 .... 2.00
Avon, Miss Lollypop Powder, 1967 .... 5.00
Avon, Miss Lollypop Powder Mitt, 1967, Boxed 2.00
Avon, Miss Lollypop Spray 7.50
Avon, Moonwind Jewelry Box, 1971 .... 20.00
Avon, Moonwind Tray, 1971 .... 15.00

Avon, Motorcycle, 1971, 4 Ozs., Full & Boxed	4.50
Avon, Mouse, see Avon, Golden Mouse	
Avon, Mr.Many Moods, 1965, Full & Boxed	5.00
Avon, My Pet Ceramic Doll	22.00
Avon, Nearness Body Powder, 1956, Full	8.00
Avon, Nearness Cologne, 1955	14.00
Avon, Nearness Dusting Powder, 1959	10.00
Avon, Nearness Powder Sachet, 1956, Full	6.00
Avon, Nearness Toilet Water, 1956, Full & Boxed	14.00
Avon, Nearness, 1/2 Oz.	75.00 To 150.00
Avon, Nesting Dove, see Avon, Milk Glass	
Avon, Nickel, Buffalo, 1971	3.60
Avon, Old Faithful, 1972, 5 Ozs.	4.50
Avon, Old '99 Soap, 1958, Full & Boxed	17.00
Avon, Open Golf Cart, 1972	Color XXXX.XX
Avon, Opening Play, see Avon, Football Helmet	
Avon, Orchard Blossom Cologne, 1941	50.00
Avon, Owl Fancy Cologne Gelee, 1974, Full & Boxed	3.79
Avon, Owl, Precious, 1972, 1 1/2 Ozs.	4.00
Avon, Owl, Wise Choice, 1969	5.00
Avon, Paddle N Ball, 1963	7.50
Avon, Paid Stamp	3.00
Avon, Pale Fire Pendant	5.00
Avon, Penny, Indian Head	2.00 To 3.00
Avon, Penny Arcade, 1951	40.00
Avon, Perfection Extract, Marked Avon, 1/2 Oz.	13.00
Avon, Perfection Extract, Marked Avon, 2 Ozs.	15.00
Avon, Perfection Liquid Shoe White, 1941, Boxed	10.00
Avon, Perfection Spots Out, 1943, Full & Boxed	12.50
Avon, Perfume Handkerchief Set, 1937	35.00
Avon, Perfume Pendant, 1970, Full & Boxed	3.50
Avon, Perfumed Glace Necklace, 1966, Black, Full & Boxed	12.00
Avon, Perfumed Glace Necklace, 1966, Topaz, Full & Boxed	12.00
Avon, Persian Treasure Set, 1959, Full & Boxed	32.50
Avon, Persian Wood Beauty Dust, 1957	7.00
Avon, Persian Wood Cologne Mist, 1956, Label	12.00
Avon, Persian Wood Cream Lotion, 1961	4.00
Avon, Persian Wood Lotion Sachet, 1957	6.00
Avon, Persian Wood Lotion Sachet, 1958	5.00
Avon, Petal Of Beauty Set, 1945, Orchard Blossoms, Full & Boxed	70.00
Avon, Petit-Point Perfume Glace, Label, Full	8.50
Avon, Petite Mouse Perfume, 1970	10.00
Avon, Petti Fleur, 1969	2.50
Avon, Pheasant, 1972, 5 Ozs.	5.00
Avon, Piano, 1972, 4 Ozs., Full & Boxed	2.70
Avon, Pig, 1964	10.00
Avon, Pin Bottle, see Avon, King Pin	
Avon, Pincushion, 1964	30.00
Avon, Pine Bath Salts, 1936, 9 Ozs., Full	20.00
Avon, Pine Soap, 1940	15.00
Avon, Pineapple Petite, 1973, 1 Oz.	1.50 To 2.00
Avon, Pink Ribbon Set, 1943, Full & Boxed	40.00
Avon, Pipe, Bulldog, 1972, 6 Ozs.	3.60
Avon, Pipe Dream, 1967, 6 Ozs.	13.50 To 15.00
Avon, Pipe Full, 1971, 2 Ozs., Full & Boxed	2.95
Avon, Pipe Full, 1973, 2 Ozs.	2.00
Avon, Pistols, see Avon, Twenty Paces	
Avon, Pony Express Rider, 1971, Full & Boxed	4.50
Avon, Pony Post Test Bottle, 1966	300.00
Avon, Pony Post, 1966, 8 Ozs.	5.95
Avon, Pony Post, 1968, Short, 4 Ozs.	3.00
Avon, Pony Post, 1968, Short, 4 Ozs., Full & Boxed	3.50
Avon, Pony Post, 1972, Bronze, 5 Ozs., Full & Boxed	3.60
Avon, Pool Paddler, 1951	25.00
Avon, Pool Paddler's Soap, 1959, Full & Boxed	17.00

Avon, Potbelly Stove Test Bottle, 1970	50.00
Avon, Potbelly Stove, 1970, 5 Ozs., Full & Boxed	4.50
Avon, Pre-Electric, 1961, Wood Cap, 6 Ozs.	10.00
Avon, Precious Pear Set, 1953, Full & Boxed	45.00
Avon, Pretty Beginner Set, 1960, Full & Boxed	15.00
Avon, Pretty Peach Cologne, 1964	3.00
Avon, Pretty Peach Pop Spray	5.00 To 18.00
Avon, Pretty Peach Soda Cologne Mist, 1964	7.00
Avon, Pretty Peach Talc, 1964	3.00
Avon, Pretty Peach, 1964, Ice Cream Soda, Straws, Flowers	4.00
Avon, Pump, see Avon, Town Pump	
Avon, Pyramid, 1969, Boxed	13.00
Avon, Quaintance Harmony Set, 1952, Full & Boxed	35.00
Avon, Quaintance Harmony Set, 1954, Full & Boxed	35.00
Avon, Quaintance Leisure Hours Set, 1954, Full & Boxed	35.00
Avon, Quaintance Perfume, 1951, 1/8 Oz.	10.00
Avon, Quaintance Silver Wings Set, 1954, Full & Boxed	27.50
Avon, Quaintance, 1/2 Oz.	75.00 To 150.00
Avon, Radio, see Avon, Remember When	
Avon, Rapture Perfumed Skin Softener, 1964, Turquoise Milk Glass, 5 Ozs.	5.00
Avon, Rapture Rhapsody, 1965	25.00
Avon, Regence, Candle Container, 10 1/2 In.	7.00
Avon, Regence Perfume Glace, 1967	6.00
Avon, Regence Perfume, 1966, 1 Oz., Full & Boxed	30.00
Avon, Remember When Radio, Decanter, 1972, 5 Ozs.	2.70
Avon, Remember When School Desk, 1973	4.00
Avon, Rhino, 1972, 4 Ozs., Full & Boxed	3.60
Avon, Riviera Decanter, 1968	12.00
Avon, Rocker Perfume, 1959, 1 Oz., Full & Boxed	47.50
Avon, Rolls Royce, 1972 ....Color	6.50
Avon, Rooster, see Avon, Country Kitchen	
Avon, Rose Fragrance Jar, 1948, Clear Stopper	15.00
Avon, Rose Fragrance, 1956, Frosted Stopper	10.00
Avon, Rosebud Vase, 1963	9.00
Avon, Royal Coach, 1972, 5 Ozs.	4.00
Avon, Royal Orb, 1965, White Letters	75.00
Avon, Royal Orb, 1965, 8 Ozs.	16.50
Avon, Royal Orb, 1965, 8 Ozs., Full & Boxed	19.95
Avon, Royal Orb, 1969, Men's, Set Of 4 Classics	15.00
Avon, Royal Pine Set, 1954, Full & Boxed	19.50
Avon, Royal Swan Cologne, 1974	2.49
Avon, Royal Vase, 1970, Blue	7.00
Avon, Ruff Tuff Muff, 1968, Full & Boxed	3.50
Avon, Sales Award Cream Sachet, 1962	8.00
Avon, Santa & Elves, 1955	20.00
Avon, Satin Sachet, 1942, From Your Friends, 3 X 3 In.	5.00
Avon, Scent With Love, 1971, Full & Boxed	4.00
Avon, School Belle, 1965	13.00
Avon, School Desk, 1973, Remember When	4.00
Avon, Schooner, 1972, 4 1/2 Ozs.	4.00
Avon, Scimitar, 1968, 6 Ozs.	12.00
Avon, Scimitar, 1968, 6 Ozs., Full & Boxed	15.95
Avon, Sea Maiden, 1971, 6 Ozs.	3.00
Avon, Sea Spirit, 1973, 5 Ozs.	4.00
Avon, Sea Treasure, 1971, 1/4 Oz.	5.00
Avon, Sea Trophy, 1972, 5 1/2 Ozs.	6.00
Avon, Seahorse, 1970, 6 Ozs.	3.50
Avon, Seashell, see Avon, Sea Treasure	
Avon, Sharp Shooter, 1961	10.00
Avon, Sheriff's Badge, 1961	10.00
Avon, Side-Wheeler Riverboat, 1971, 5 Ozs., Full & Boxed	3.60
Avon, Silver Top Boot, 1965	10.00
Avon, Sitting Pretty, 1971, 4 Ozs.	3.50
Avon, Skin-So-Soft Cologne, 1965	6.00
Avon, Skin-So-Soft Cologne, 1966	6.00

Avon, Skin-So-Soft Cologne, 1967 .... 6.00
Avon, Skin-So-Soft Decanter, 1964 .... 14.00
Avon, Skin-So-Soft Decanter, 1965 .... 12.50
Avon, Skin-So-Soft Decanter, 1967 .... 5.00
Avon, Skin-So-Soft Glass Bottle, 1962, 8 Ozs., Full & Boxed 5.00
Avon, Skin-So-Soft Soap, 1965, Boxed 5.99
Avon, Skin-So-Soft Urn, 1960, Milk Glass 13.00
Avon, Slugger, 1961 .... 10.00
Avon, Small Wonder Worm 3.00
    Avon, Smart Move, see Avon, Chess Piece
Avon, Snail Perfume, 1968, 1/4 Oz. 6.00
Avon, Snail, 1968, 1/4 Oz., Full & Boxed 5.50
Avon, Snoopy, Ace, 1969 .... 3.00
Avon, Snoopy, Surprise Package, 1969, 5 Ozs., Full & Boxed 3.95
Avon, Soap Dish, 1969, Shell Shape, White Iridescent 1.50
Avon, Soap Jar, 1963, Full 8.00
    Avon, Solid Gold Cadillac, see Avon, Car
Avon, Somewhere Bath Classic, 1962, Full & Boxed 20.00
Avon, Somewhere Perfection Oil For The Bath, 1963 .... 9.95
Avon, Somewhere Perfume, 1961, Full 35.00
Avon, Somewhere Perfume, 1961, 1 Oz. 125.00
Avon, Sonnet Mirror, 1972 .... 20.00
Avon, Sonnet Tray, 1972 .... 10.00
Avon, Special Christmas Award, 1964, Full & Boxed 35.00
Avon, Spirit Of St.Louis Airplane, 1970, 6 Ozs., Full & Boxed 5.95
Avon, Spirit Of St.Louis, 1/2 Inch Protrusions 50.00
Avon, Splash & Spray Set, 1968 .... 19.00
Avon, Splash & Spray Set, 1968, Full & Boxed 17.50
Avon, Sports Rally All Purpose Talk, 1966 .... 3.00
Avon, Spray Boot, 1966 .... 3.00
Avon, Stagecoach, 1970, 5 Ozs. .... 2.50 To 3.00
Avon, Stagecoach, 1970, 5 Ozs., Full & Boxed 3.60
Avon, Stamp Paid, Test Bottle, 1970 .... 50.00
Avon, Stamp Paid, 1970, 4 Ozs. 2.95
Avon, Stamp Paid, 1970, 4 Ozs., Full & Boxed 3.50
Avon, Stein, 1965, Silver, 6 Ozs. .... 5.00 To 7.95
Avon, Stein, 1965, Silver, 8 Ozs., Full & Boxed 9.50
Avon, Stein, 1968, Silver, 6 Ozs. 4.95
Avon, Stein, 1968, Silver, 6 Ozs., Full & Boxed .... 5.25 To 6.50
Avon, Stein, Hunter's, 1972 .... 10.00
Avon, Stockholder's Christmas Ornament, 1959 .... 50.00
    Avon, Straight Eight Car, see Avon, Car
Avon, Strawberry, 1971, 4.5 Ozs. 3.00
Avon, Structured For Men 12.50
Avon, Sunny Hours Parasol Set 50.00
Avon, Super Cycle, 1971 .... Color   6.00
Avon, Super Shaver 3.00
Avon, Surprise Package 3.50
Avon, Sweet As Honey Beehive, 1952 .... 125.00
Avon, Swinger Golf Bag Test Bottle, 1969 .... 75.00
Avon, Swinger Golf Bag, 1969, 5 Ozs. 5.00
Avon, Swinger Golf Bag, 1969, 5 Ozs., Full & Boxed 5.00
    Avon, Sword, see Avon, Scimitar 500
Avon, Tabletop Jewelry, 1971, 4 Piece Set, Full & Boxed 20.00
Avon, Teapot .... 5.00 To 6.95
Avon, Telephone, Avon Calling Set, 1969, 6 & 1 1/4 Ozs. 7.50
Avon, Telephone, Avon Calling Set, 1969, 6 & 1 1/4 Ozs., Full & Boxed 8.95
Avon, Telephone, French, 1971, 6 Ozs. 20.00
Avon, Texas Sheriff Badge Soap Set, 1962, Full & Boxed 22.50
Avon, Three Hearts On Tray, 1964 .... 20.00
Avon, Tic Toc Tiger Bubble Bath, 1967, 8 Ozs. 4.00
Avon, Tic Toc Turtle Bubble Bath, 1968, 8 Ozs. 2.29
Avon, Tiffany Lamp, 1973, 5 Ozs. 5.50
    Avon, To A Wild Rose, see Avon Wild Rose, Avon, Demi Cup
Avon, Topaz Gem Perfume, 1960, 1 Oz. 95.00

Avon, Topaz Perfume Bottle, Amber	55.00
Avon, Tot N Tyke Bar Soap, 1964, Full & Boxed	4.00
Avon, Touring Tee Car, see Avon, Car	
Avon, Town Pump, 1968, 6 Ozs.	5.00
Avon, Town Pump, 1968, 6 Ozs., Full & Boxed	5.50
Avon, Town Pump Test Bottle, 1968, Brown	100.00
Avon, Train, see Avon General 4-4-0	
Avon, Turtle Soap, 1962	5.00 To 8.00
Avon, Tutch Up Twins, 1966, Full & Boxed	12.00
Avon, Twenty Dollar Gold, 1971, 6 Ozs., Full & Boxed	4.50
Avon, Twenty Paces, 1968, Black Lined Box	65.00
Avon, Twenty Paces, 1968, Blue Lined Box	95.00
Avon, Twenty Paces, 1968, Red Lined Box	35.00
Avon, Two Loves, 1955, Full & Boxed	15.00
Avon, Unforgettable Heirloom, 1965	25.00
Avon, Unforgettable Perfume, 1966, 1/2 Oz., Full & Boxed	10.00
Avon, Unforgettable Set, 1962, Full & Boxed	17.50
Avon, Victorian Lady, 1972, 5 Ozs.	4.00
Avon, Victorian Manor, 1972 *Color*	4.00
Avon, Victorian Powder Sachet	4.00
Avon, Victoriana Pitcher & Bowl, 1971 *Color*	6.00
Avon, Vigorate Cylinder, 1959	45.00
Avon, Vigorate, 1959, 8 Ozs., Full	40.00
Avon, Vigorate, 1961, Stagecoach Embossed, Full & Boxed	11.00
Avon, Viking Horn, 1966, 7 Ozs.	12.50 To 14.00
Avon, Viking Horn, 1966, 7 Ozs., Full & Boxed	15.95
Avon, Violet Bouquet Bottle, 1945, Faded Label	100.00
Avon, Volkswagen	2.00
Avon, Warrior Head, 1968, Cobalt	15.00
Avon, Warrior Head, 1968, Frosted, 6 Ozs.	2.95
Avon, Warrior Head, 1968, Frosted, 6 Ozs., Full & Boxed	3.95
Avon, Warrior Head, 1971, Ribbed Top	3.00
Avon, Wassail Bowl	3.50
Avon, Watering Can, 1962	8.00
Avon, Watering Can, 1962, Full & Boxed	10.00
Avon, Weather-Or-Not, 1969, 5 Ozs.	3.95
Avon, Weather-Or-Not, 1969, 5 Ozs., Full & Boxed	4.95
Avon, Western Choice, Steer Horns, 1967, 2 3 Oz. Bottles & Base	15.00 To 16.50
Avon, Western Choice, Steer Horns, 1967, 2 3 Oz. Bottles & Bases, Full	17.50
Avon, Western Saddle Test Bottle, 1971	75.00
Avon, Western Saddle, 1971, Full & Boxed	5.50
Avon, White Moire Cologne, 1947, 6 Ozs.	75.00
Avon, Wild Country Body Powder, 1967	5.00
Avon, Wild Country Saddle Kit, 1970	7.50
Avon, Wild Rose Beauty Dust, 1955	7.50
Avon, Wild Rose Cologne, 1940	15.00
Avon, Wild Rose Cologne, 1950	15.00
Avon, Wild Rose Cologne, 1950, 4 Ozs.	9.95
Avon, Wild Rose Cologne, 1955	9.00
Avon, Wild Rose Cologne, 1960, Pink Ribbon, Full & Boxed	18.00
Avon, Wild Rose Cream Lotion, 1956	15.00
Avon, Wise Choice Owl, 1969	5.00
Avon, Wish Coin Trio Set, 1963	30.00
Avon, Wish Come True Set, 1963, Full & Boxed	11.00
Avon, Wishing Coin Trio Set, 1963	30.00
Avon, Wishing Set, 1958, Full & Boxed	22.50
Avon, World's Greatest Dad Trophy, 1971, 4 Ozs.	2.00
Avon, World's Greatest Dad Trophy, 1971, 4 Ozs., Full & Boxed	2.95
Avon, Worldwide Commemorative Bottle, 1973	35.00
Avon, Worldwide Viking Horn Club, 1972	75.00
Avon, Yo-Yo Soap Set, 1966	10.95
Avon, 54 Hair Lotion, 1953, 1 Oz.	14.00
Baccarat, see also Cologne, Baccarat, Decanter, Baccarat, Dresser, Baccarat, Perfume, Baccarat	
Baccarat, Swirled, 5 3/4 In.	32.50

Baccarat, Swirled, 6 1/4 In.		37.50
Ballantine, Charioteer		5.00
Ballantine, Discus Thrower		5.00
Ballantine, Duck	*Illus*	15.00
Ballantine Fisherman	*Illus*	13.00
Ballantine, Gladiator		5.00
Ballantine, Golf Bag	*Illus*	9.00
Ballantine, Knight, Silver	*Illus*	13.00
Ballantine, Mallard, see Ballantine, Duck		
Ballantine, Mercury		5.00
Ballantine, Zebra	*Illus*	14.00
Banfi, Macaw		8.00
Banfi, Pheasant		8.00
Banfi, Quail		8.00

Ballantine, Duck

Ballantine, Fisherman

Bank, Basket, Bird Finial, Sandwich, Blown, McKearin 58a-2, Clambroth		200.00
Bank, Bear, Snowcrest, Cap, 7 In.		5.00
Bank, Bear, 8 1/2 In.		6.50
Bank, Cat, Grapette		5.00
Bank, Clown, Grapette		2.00 To 2.50
Bank, Ear Of Corn, Earthenware, 10 3/4 In. Long		65.00
Bank, Elephant, Grapette		2.00 To 2.50
Bank, Lincoln's Log Cabin, Ceramic, Van Dyke Teas, 3 3/4 X 2 1/2 In.		35.00
Bar, Cylinder, Fountain Spring, White Enamel Lettering, Quart		18.50
Bar, Cylinder, Woodbury, White Enamel Lettering, Quart		22.50
Bar, Flint, Paneled Lattice & Ovals, Clear		25.00
Bar, Fountain Spring, White Enamel Lettering, Cylindrical, Quart		18.50
Bar, Pittsburgh, 8 Panels, Pewter Stopper, Amethyst, 10 3/4 In.		110.00
Bar, Pittsburgh, 8 Panels, Sapphire Blue, 10 1/2 In.		130.00
Bar, Pressed Glass, Ashburton, Bar Lip		38.00
Bar, Pressed Glass, Diamond Point, Clear		35.00
Bar, Pressed Glass, Flute, Clear, Pair		40.00
Bar, Pressed Glass, Lattice & Oval Panels, Flint, Pint		22.00
Bar, Pressed Glass, Pillar, Small Size		33.50
Bar, Woodbury, White Enamel Lettering, Cylindrical, Quart		22.50

Barber bottles were used at either the barbershop or the home. They held hair tonic. These special, fancy bottles were popular in the last half of the nineteenth century.

Barber, BIMAL, Lady's Leg Neck, Embossed Base, Cobalt Blue, 7 1/2 In.		32.00
Barber, Blown, Silver Deposit, Brass Stopper, Honey Amber		47.50
Barber, Bohemian Glass, Deer & Castle, Ruby		25.00
Barber, Cotton's Fine Bay Rum On Gold & Red Glass Label, 9 In.		20.00
Barber, Enameled Daisies, 6 1/2 In.	*Color*	100.00
Barber, End-Of-Day		92.50
Barber, Gold Incised Lettering Bitters & Absinthe, Amethyst, Pair		60.00

Barber, Hair Tonic & Bay Rum, Black	12.00
Barber, Honeycomb, 6 Petal Flowers, Pewter Shaker Top, Clear, 6 In.High	30.00
Barber, Laureline, Milk Glass, 9 In.	75.00
Barber, Mary Gregory, Girl Playing Tennis, Cobalt Blue, 9 1/2 In.High	75.00
Barber, Milk Glass, Metropolitan Art Co., 9 1/2 In.High	12.00
Barber, Milk Glass, 9 In. *Illus*	35.00
Barber, Milk Glass, 17 In., Set Of 4 *Illus*	400.00
Barber, New England Glass Co., Inverted Thumbprint, Amberina, 8 1/4 In.	350.00
Barber, Oriental Type, Pair	215.00
Barber, Red & White Enameled Decoration, Double Rounded Body, Emerald	22.50
Barber, Rose Cased Satin Glass, Square Base, 7 In.High	35.00
Barber, Showgirl, Shaker Stopper, C.1880, Milk Glass, 11 In.	55.00
Barber, Squared, Spanish Lace, Cranberry With Opalescence	115.00
Barber, Toilet Water, Black	12.00
Barber, White Design, 9 In. *Color*	48.00
Barber, 6 Sided Base, Cranberry Casing, White Opalescent Overlay	85.00
Bardi, Masked Girl & Boy Bookends, Pair	20.00
Bardi, Politicals, Pair	14.95

Ballantine, Knight, Silver
(See Page 12)

Ballantine, Golf Bag
(See Page 12)

Ballantine, Zebra
(See Page 12)

Barber, Milk Glass, 9 In.
(See Page 13)

Barber, Milk Glass, 17 In., Set Of 4
(See Page 13)

Barrel, see Bitters, Greeley's, Bitters, Old Sachem, Bitters,
Roback's Stomach, Barrel, Figural, Barrel

Barsottini, Alpine Pipe	10.00
Barsottini, Antique Auto	7.00
Barsottini, Antique Carriage	7.00
Barsottini, Apollo	13.50
Barsottini, Arch Of Triumph	11.00
Barsottini, Bacchus	10.00
Barsottini, Bagpiper	10.00
Barsottini, Candlestick	9.00
Barsottini, Cannon	12.00
Barsottini, Carriage Lamp	9.00
Barsottini, Clock	15.00
Barsottini, Clock With Cherub	25.00
Barsottini, Clown	9.00
Barsottini, Coliseum	12.00
Barsottini, Donkey	6.00
Barsottini, Eiffel Tower	10.00
Barsottini, Elephant	6.00
Barsottini, Elk's Head	11.00
Barsottini, Father John	12.00
Barsottini, Florentine Steeple	12.00
Barsottini, Fruit Basket	11.00
Barsottini, Giraffe	17.00
Barsottini, Horse Head	11.00
Barsottini, Lamplighter	17.50
Barsottini, Leaning Tower	8.00
Barsottini, Lido Antique Peddler	10.00
Barsottini, Lovebirds	14.00
Barsottini, Lucky Dice	8.00
Barsottini, Mandolin	8.00
Barsottini, Mezzotint	9.00
Barsottini, Monastery Cask	16.00
Barsottini, Monk	10.00
Barsottini, Monk & Drink	16.00
Barsottini, Owl	13.50
Barsottini, Pheasant	12.00 To 20.00
Barsottini, Pillaze	5.00
Barsottini, Pistol, Brown	7.50
Barsottini, Pistol, Green	7.50
Barsottini, Rabbit With Carrot	12.00
Barsottini, Renaissance	10.00
Barsottini, Roman Tribune	13.00
Barsottini, Roman Urn	10.00
Barsottini, Rooster	15.00

Barsottini, Santa Claus	12.00
Barsottini, Space Rocket	11.00
Barsottini, Wagon Barrel	20.00
Barsottini, William Tell	13.00
Barton, Confederate Soldier	9.00
Barton, Mountie	9.00

Beam bottles are made as containers for the Kentucky Straight Bourbon made by the James Beam Distilling Company. The Beam ceramics were first made in 1953. Executive series bottles started in 1955. Regal china specialties were started in 1955 and political figures in 1956. Customer specialties were first made in 1956, trophy series in 1957, state series in 1958.

Beam, Agnew Elephant, 1970

Beam, Arizona, State, 1968, 1969

Beam, Bacchus, Armanetti, 1973
(See Page 16)

Beam, see also Whiskey, Bell's Scotch

Beam, ABC Liquor Stores, 1973	13.00 To 15.00
Beam, Agnew Elephant, 1970	*Illus* 2400.00
Beam, Ahepa, 1972	5.00 To 10.00
Beam, Akron Rubber Club, 1973	20.00 To 37.50
Beam, Alaska Purchase, 1966, Centennial	14.00 To 15.00
Beam, Alaska Star, 1958, State	70.00 To 80.00
Beam, Alaska Star, 1964, State, Reissue	60.00 To 70.00
Beam, American Tobacco Company, 1973	9.00 To 10.95
Beam, Amvets, 1970	5.00 To 7.00
Beam, Antioch, 1967, Centennial	6.00 To 10.00
Beam, Antique Trader, 1968, 11th Anniversary	4.00 To 7.00
Beam, Arizona, State, 1968, 1969	*Illus* 6.00
Beam, Armanetti Award Winner, 1969	6.00 To 12.00
Beam, Armanetti Bacchus, 1970	12.00 To 23.00
Beam, Armanetti Fun Bottle, 1971	8.00 To 18.00
Beam, Armanetti Vase, 1968	6.00 To 10.00
Beam, Art Institute, Chicago, Zimmerman, 1972	10.00 To 14.00
Beam, Ashtray, Ivory, 1955	18.00 To 25.00

Beam, B.P.A.A., 1974 .... 32.00
Beam, B.P.O. Does, 1971 .... 7.00 To 9.00
Beam, Bacchus, Armanetti, 1973 .... *Illus* 23.00
Beam, Bartender's Association, 1973 .... 7.00 To 10.00
Beam, Baseball Centennial, 1969 .... 5.00 To 7.00
Beam, Bass, Small Mouth, 1973, Trophy .... 8.00 To 12.00
Beam, Beatty Burro, 1973 .... 14.00 To 16.00
Beam, Bell, Scotch, 1970 .... 6.00 To 9.00
Beam, Bellringer No.1, Plaid, 1970 .... 6.00 To 8.50
Beam, Bellringer No.2, Coat Of Arms, 1970 .... 6.00 To 8.50
Beam, Bing Crosby, 29th Pro-Am, 1970 .... 5.00 To 8.00
Beam, Bing Crosby, 30th Pro-Am, 1971 .... 4.00 To 6.00
Beam, Bing Crosby, 31st Pro-Am, 1972 .... 17.00 To 20.00
Beam, Bing Crosby, 32nd Pro-Am, 1973 .... 14.00 To 17.00
Beam, Bing Crosby, 33rd Pro-Am, 1974 .... 14.00 To 20.00
Beam, Binion's Horseshoe, 1970 .... 7.00 To 10.00
Beam, Black Katz Cat, 1968 .... 8.00 To 12.95
Beam, Blue Beauty, Zimmerman's, 1973 .... 14.00 To 17.00
Beam, Blue Cherub, Executive, 1960 .... 75.00 To 135.00
Beam, Blue Crystal, 1971 .... 3.00 To 5.00
Beam, Blue Daisy, Zimmerman, 1967 .... 4.00 To 8.00
Beam, Blue Fox, 1967, Club .... 120.00 To 125.00
Beam, Blue Goose, 1971 .... 5.00 To 8.00
Beam, Blue Jay, 1969, Trophy .... 7.00 To 8.50
Beam, Blue Sapphire .... 4.00 To 5.00
Beam, Blue Slot Machine, Harolds Club, 1967 .... 10.00 To 12.00
Beam, Bluegill, 1974, Trophy .... 9.00 To 10.00
Beam, Bob Hope Desert Classic, 1973 .... 15.00 To 20.00
Beam, Bob Hope Desert Classic, 1974 .... 14.00 To 20.00
Beam, Bohemian Girl, 1974 .... 20.00 To 24.00
Beam, Boothill, Dodge City, 1972, Centennial .... 7.00 To 10.00
Beam, Boxer, 1974 .... 11.00 To 13.00
Beam, Boy's Town Of Italy, 1973 .... 5.00 To 9.00
Beam, Broadmoor Hotel, 1968 .... 4.00 To 5.00
Beam, Bronze Shell, Florida, 1968, State .... 4.00 To 5.00
Beam, Buffalo Bill, 1974 .... 6.00 To 7.00
Beam, Burmese Cat, 1967, Trophy .... 10.00 To 11.00
Beam, Burro Race, Beatty, 1973 .... 14.00 To 16.00
Beam, C.P.O., Navy, 1974 .... 10.00 To 12.00
Beam, C.R.L.D.A., 1973 .... 7.00 To 10.00
Beam, Cable Car, 1968, 1969 .... *Illus* 6.00
Beam, California Derby, 1971, Golden Gate Fields .... 18.00 To 21.00
Beam, California Mission Club, 1973 .... 20.00 To 24.00
Beam, Cameo, 1956, Blue .... 2.00 To 5.00
Beam, Cannon, 1973 .... 2.00 To 5.00
Beam, Cardinal, Female, 1973, Trophy .... 15.00 To 20.00
Beam, Cardinal, Male, 1968, Trophy .... *Illus* 49.50
Beam, Cat, Burmese, 1967, Trophy .... 10.00 To 11.00
Beam, Cat, Siamese, 1967, Trophy .... 10.00 To 11.00
Beam, Cat, Tabby, 1967, Trophy .... 10.00 To 11.00
Beam, Cedars Of Lebanon, 1973 .... 4.00 To 8.00
Beam, Centennial, 1960, Santa Fe .... 175.00 To 225.00
Beam, Centennial, 1961, Civil War, North .... 31.00 To 40.00
Beam, Centennial, 1961, Civil War, South .... 31.00 To 40.00
Beam, Centennial, 1964, St.Louis Arch .... 20.00 To 21.00
Beam, Centennial, 1966, Alaska Purchase .... 14.00 To 15.00
Beam, Centennial, 1967, Antioch .... 6.00 To 10.00
Beam, Centennial, 1967, Cheyenne .... 5.00 To 10.00
Beam, Centennial, 1967, St.Louis Arch, Reissue .... 15.00 To 19.00
Beam, Centennial, 1968, Laramie .... 4.00 To 6.00
Beam, Centennial, 1968, Reno .... 5.00 To 9.00
Beam, Centennial, 1968, San Diego .... 3.00 To 5.00
Beam, Centennial, 1969, Baseball .... 5.00 To 7.00
Beam, Centennial, 1969, Lombard Lilac .... 4.00 To 5.00
Beam, Centennial, 1969, Portola Trek .... 4.00 To 6.00

Beam, Centennial, 1969, Powell Expedition .... 5.00 To 10.00
Beam, Centennial, 1970, Preakness .... 4.00 To 8.00
Beam, Centennial, 1970, Riverside .... 10.00 To 15.00
Beam, Centennial, 1971, Chicago Fire .... 8.00 To 10.00
Beam, Centennial, 1971, Indianapolis Sesquicentennial .... 5.00 To 10.00

Beam, Cable Car, 1968, 1969
(See Page 16)

Beam, Cardinal, Male, 1968, Trophy
(See Page 16)

Beam, Centennial, 1972, Colorado Springs .... 5.00 To 8.00
Beam, Centennial, 1972, Dodge City, Boothill .... 7.00 To 10.00
Beam, Centennial, 1972, General Stark .... 9.00 To 15.00
Beam, Centennial, 1973, Cherry Hills Country Club .... 10.00 To 12.00
Beam, Centennial, 1973, Phi Sigma Kappa .... 5.00 To 10.00
Beam, Centennial, 1973, Ralph's Market .... 10.00 To 15.00
Beam, Centennial, 1973, Reidsville, N.C. .... 14.00 To 16.00
Beam, Charisma, Executive, 1970 .... 10.00 To 13.00
Beam, Cherry Hills Country Club, 1973, Centennial .... 10.00 To 12.00
Beam, Cherub, Blue, Executive, 1960 .... 75.00 To 135.00
Beam, Cherub, Gray, Executive, 1958 .... 150.00 To 170.00
Beam, Cherub, Lavender, Zimmerman, 1967 .... 7.00 To 10.00
Beam, Cherub, Salmon, Zimmerman, 1969 .... 4.00 To 10.00
Beam, Cheyenne, Centennial, 1967 .... 5.00 To 10.00
Beam, Chicago Art Institute, 1973 .... 10.00 To 14.00
Beam, Chicago Fire, Centennial, 1971 .... 8.00 To 10.00
Beam, Churchill Downs, 95th, Pink Roses, 1969, 1970 .... 4.00 To 6.00
Beam, Churchill Downs, 95th, Red Roses, 1969, 1970 .... 7.00 To 8.50
Beam, Churchill Downs, 96th, Red Roses, 1970 .... 8.00 To 9.00
Beam, Churchill Downs, 97th, Red Roses, 1974 .... 6.00 To 9.95
Beam, Churchill Downs, 98th, 1972 .... 7.00 To 12.95
Beam, Civil War, North, Centennial, 1961 .... 31.00 To 40.00
Beam, Civil War, South, Centennial, 1961 .... 31.00 To 40.00
Beam, Cleopatra, 1962, Rust .... 4.00 To 5.00
Beam, Cleopatra, 1962, Yellow .... 10.00 To 12.50
Beam, Clint Eastwood, 1973 .... 6.00 To 9.00
Beam, Club, Akron Rubber, 1973 .... 20.00 To 37.50
Beam, Club, Fox, Blue, 1967 .... 120.00 To 125.00
Beam, Club, Fox, Gold, 1969 .... 65.00 To 75.00
Beam, Club, Fox, Green, 1965 .... 40.00 To 45.00
Beam, Club, Fox, Uncle Sam, 1971 .... 10.00 To 15.00
Beam, Club, Fox, White, 1969 .... 32.00 To 36.00
Beam, Coach Devaney, 1973, Nebraska .... 10.00 To 12.95
Beam, Cocktail Shaker, 1953 .... 4.00 To 5.00
Beam, Cocktail Shaker, 1956 .... 4.00 To 5.00
Beam, Coffee Warmer, 1954 .... 7.00 To 9.00
Beam, Collector's Edition, Blue Boy, Vol II, 1967 .... 7.00 To 8.50

Beam, Collector's Edition, On The Terrace, Vol.II, 1967 .... 4.00 To 5.00
Beam, Collector's Edition, Soldier & Girl, Vol. II, 1968 .... 4.00 To 5.50
Beam, Collector's Edition, Whistler's Mother, Vol.IV, 1969 .... 2.00 To 3.00
Beam, Colorado Springs, Centennial, 1972 .... 5.00 To 8.00
Beam, Colorado, 1959, State .... 37.00 To 45.00
Beam, Convention, 1st, Denver, 1971 .... 8.00 To 12.00
Beam, Convention, 3rd, 1973 .... 20.00 To 25.00
Beam, Convention, 4th, Horse & Wagon, 1974 .... 20.00 To 24.50
Beam, Covered Wagon, Harolds Club, 1969 .... 4.00 To 7.00
Beam, Crystal, Blue, 1971 .... 3.00 To 5.00
Beam, Crystal, Clear, Bourbon, 1967 .... 4.00 To 6.00
Beam, Crystal, Clear, Scotch, 1966 .... 5.00 To 8.00
Beam, Crystal, Clear, Vodka, 1967 .... 4.00 To 6.00
Beam, Crystal, Emerald, 1968 .... 4.00 To 6.00
Beam, Crystal, Opaline, 1969 .... 4.00 To 6.00
Beam, Crystal, Ruby, 1967 .... 5.00 To 8.00
Beam, Curved Dash Oldsmobile, 1972 .... 18.00 To 27.50
Beam, Dancing Couple, 1964 .... 70.00 To 75.00
Beam, Dancing Scot, Short, 1963 .... 30.00 To 35.00
Beam, Dancing Scot, Tall, 1964 .... 9.00 To 12.00
Beam, Delaware, 1972, State, Blue Hen .... 8.00 To 11.00
Beam, Delft, 1956, Blue .... 4.00 To 6.00
Beam, Denver Rocky Mountain Club, 1971 .... Illus   25.00

Beam, Denver Rocky Mountain Club, 1971

Beam, Desert Classic, 1973, Bob Hope .... 15.00 To 20.00
Beam, Desert Classic, 1974, Bob Hope .... 14.00 To 20.00
Beam, Dodge City, Boothill, Centennial, 1972 .... 7.00 To 10.00
Beam, Doe, 1963, Trophy .... 28.00 To 35.00
Beam, Doe, 1967, Reissue .... 27.00 To 30.00
Beam, Dog, English Setter, 1959, Trophy .... 55.00 To 60.00
Beam, Duck, 1957, Trophy .... 25.00 To 35.00
Beam, Ducks & Geese, 1955 .... 6.00 To 7.00
Beam, Ducks Unlimited, 1972 .... 9.00 To 10.00
Beam, Eagle, New Hampshire, 1971 .... 33.00 To 40.00
Beam, Eagle, 1966, Trophy .... 12.00 To 15.00
   Beam, Elephant, see Beam Political
Beam, Elks Club, 1968 .... 4.00 To 7.00
Beam, Emmett Kelly, 1973 .... 9.00 To 15.00
Beam, Evergreen State, 1974 .... 20.00 To 22.00
Beam, Executive, 1955, Royal Porcelain .... 180.00 To 265.00
Beam, Executive, 1956, Royal Gold .... 100.00 To 125.00
Beam, Executive, 1957, Royal Di Monte .... 68.00 To 84.00
Beam, Executive, 1958, Gray Cherub .... 150.00 To 170.00
Beam, Executive, 1959, Tavern Scene .... 60.00 To 70.00
Beam, Executive, 1960, Blue Cherub .... 75.00 To 135.00
Beam, Executive, 1961, Golden Chalice .... 65.00 To 75.00
Beam, Executive, 1962, Flower Basket .... 45.00 To 53.00

Beam, Executive, 1963, Royal Rose .... 45.00 To 60.00
Beam, Executive, 1964, Royal Gold Diamond .... 45.00 To 60.00
Beam, Executive, 1965, Marbled Fantasy .... 60.00 To 65.00
Beam, Executive, 1966, Majestic .... 32.00 To 38.00
Beam, Executive, 1967, Prestige .... 15.00 To 19.00
Beam, Executive, 1968, Presidential .... *Illus*   11.00
Beam, Executive, 1969, Sovereign .... 8.00 To 10.00
Beam, Executive, 1970, Charisma .... 10.00 To 13.00
Beam, Executive, 1971, Fantasia .... 10.00 To 12.00
Beam, Executive, 1972, Regency .... 12.00 To 20.00
Beam, Executive, 1973 .... 13.00 To 16.00
Beam, Executive, 1974 .... 15.00 To 18.00
Beam, Expo 74 .... 13.00 To 15.00
Beam, Fantasia, Executive, 1971 .... 10.00 To 12.00
Beam, Fiesta Bowl Football, 1973 .... 10.00 To 16.00
Beam, Fiji Islands, 1971 .... 6.00 To 7.50
Beam, First National Bank Of Chicago, 1964 .... 2250.00 To 3000.00
Beam, Fish, 1957, Trophy .... 29.00 To 35.00
Beam, Florida, Shell, Bronze, 1968, State .... 4.00 To 5.00
Beam, Florida, Shell, White, 1968, State .... 4.00 To 5.00
Beam, Flower Basket, Executive, 1962 .... 45.00 To 53.00
Beam, Football Hall Of Fame, 1972 .... 11.00 To 13.00
Beam, Ford Roadster, 1974 .... 20.00 To 24.50
Beam, Foremost Black & Gold, 1956 .... 130.00 To 195.00
Beam, Foremost Gray & Gold, 1956 .... 130.00 To 150.00
Beam, Foremost Pink Speckled, 1956 .... 380.00 To 600.00
Beam, Fox, Blue, 1967, Club .... 120.00 To 125.00
Beam, Fox, Female .... 12.00 To 14.00
Beam, Fox, Gold, 1969, Club .... 65.00 To 75.00
Beam, Fox, Green, 1965, Club .... 40.00 To 45.00
Beam, Fox, Uncle Sam, 1971 .... 10.00 To 15.00
Beam, Fox, White, 1969, Club .... 32.00 To 36.00
Beam, Franklin Mint, 1970 .... 5.00 To 7.00
Beam, Fun Bottle, Armanetti, 1971 .... 8.00 To 18.00
Beam, General Stark, Centennial, 1972 .... 9.00 To 15.00
Beam, Genie, Smoked Crystal, 1964 .... 6.00 To 8.00
Beam, Germany, Hansel & Gretel, 1971 .... 6.00 To 7.00
Beam, Germany, 1970 .... 5.00 To 8.00
Beam, Germany, 1973 .... 9.00 To 10.00
Beam, Golden Chalice, Executive, 1961 .... 65.00 To 75.00
Beam, Golden Gate Casino, 1973 .... 7.00 To 12.00
Beam, Golden Gate Fields, 1971, California Derby .... 18.00 To 21.00
Beam, Golden Gate, 1969 .... 40.00 To 52.00
Beam, Golden Nugget, 1969 .... 40.00 To 52.00
Beam, Grand Canyon, 1969 .... 11.00 To 15.00
Beam, Gray Cherub, Executive, 1958 .... 150.00 To 170.00
Beam, Grecian, 1956 .... 4.00 To 7.00
Beam, Green China Jug, 1965 .... 5.00 To 10.00

Beam, Harolds Club Slot Machine
(See Page 20)

Beam, Hannah Duston, 1973 .... 17.00 To 20.00
Beam, Hansel & Gretel, 1971, Germany .... 6.00 To 7.00
Beam, Harolds Club, Blue Slot Machine, 1967 .... 10.00 To 12.00
Beam, Harolds Club, Covered Wagon, 1969 .... 4.00 To 7.00
Beam, Harolds Club, Gray Slot Machine, 1967 .... 4.00 To 9.00
Beam, Harolds Club, Gray Slot Machine, 1968 .... *Illus* 9.00
Beam, Harolds Club, Man In Barrel, No.1, 1957 .... 340.00 To 450.00
Beam, Harolds Club, Man In Barrel, No.2, 1958 .... 230.00 To 265.00
Beam, Harolds Club, Nevada, Gray, 1963 .... 145.00 To 160.00
Beam, Harolds Club, Nevada, Silver, 1964 .... 155.00 To 180.00
Beam, Harolds Club, Pinwheel, 1965 .... 50.00 To 75.00
Beam, Harolds Club, Silver, Opal, 1957 .... 20.00 To 22.00
Beam, Harolds Club, V.I.P., 1967 .... 40.00 To 50.00
Beam, Harolds Club, V.I.P., 1968 .... 40.00 To 50.00
Beam, Harolds Club, V.I.P., 1969 .... 75.00 To 120.00
Beam, Harolds Club, V.I.P., 1970 .... 50.00 To 60.00
Beam, Harolds Club, V.I.P., 1971 .... 40.00 To 60.00
Beam, Harolds Club, V.I.P., 1972 .... 30.00 To 40.00
Beam, Harolds Club, V.I.P., 1973 .... 30.00 To 32.00
Beam, Harrah's Nevada, Gray, 1963 .... 450.00 To 500.00
Beam, Harrah's Nevada, Silver, 1963 .... 800.00 To 880.00
Beam, Harry Hoffman, 1969 .... 4.00 To 8.00
Beam, Harvey's Wagonwheel, 1969 .... 5.00 To 10.00
Beam, Hatfield, 1973 .... 18.00 To 22.00
Beam, Hawaii Aloha, 1971 .... 5.00 To 8.00
Beam, Hawaii Club, 1971 .... 8.00 To 10.00
Beam, Hawaii Open Pro-Am, 1972, Pineapple .... 6.00 To 8.00
Beam, Hawaii Open Pro-Am, 1973, Pineapple .... 6.00 To 10.00
Beam, Hawaii Open Pro-Am, 1974 .... 8.00 To 9.00
Beam, Hawaii Tiki, 1974 .... 8.00 To 10.00
Beam, Hawaii, 1959, State .... 55.00 To 70.00
Beam, Hawaii, 1967, State, Reissued .... 50.00 To 57.00
Beam, Hemisfair, 1968 .... 8.00 To 10.00
Beam, Hoffman, Harry, 1969 .... 4.00 To 8.00
Beam, Horse, Black, 1961, Trophy .... 20.00 To 26.00
Beam, Horse, Black, 1967, Reissue, Trophy .... 17.00 To 19.00
Beam, Horse, Brown, 1961, Trophy .... 18.00 To 22.00
Beam, Horse, Brown, 1967, Reissue, Trophy .... 15.00 To 18.00
Beam, Horse, White, 1961, Trophy .... 18.00 To 22.00
Beam, Horse, White, 1967, Reissue, Trophy .... 18.00 To 22.00
Beam, Horseshoe Club, 1969 .... 7.00 To 9.00
Beam, Humboldt County Fair, 1970 .... 17.00 To 20.00
Beam, Hyatt House, 1971 .... 20.00 To 30.00
Beam, Idaho, 1963, State .... 55.00 To 70.00
Beam, Illinois, 1968, State .... 4.00 To 8.00
Beam, Indiana, 1970, Imperial Session .... 5.00 To 6.00
Beam, Indianapolis Sesquicentennial, 1971 .... 5.00 To 10.00
Beam, Indianapolis 500, 1970, 54th Anniversary, 1970 .... 5.00 To 7.00
Beam, International Petroleum, 1971 .... 6.00 To 7.50
Beam, Ivory Ashtray, 1955 .... 18.00 To 25.00
Beam, Jackalope, 1972 .... 8.00 To 10.00
Beam, Jackalope, 1972, Gold .... 22.00 To 30.00
Beam, Jade, 1956 .... 3.00 To 5.00
Beam, Jewel T, Food Store Wagon .... 20.00 To 25.00
Beam, John Henry, 1972 .... 40.00 To 65.00
Beam, Jug, Green, 1965 .... 5.00 To 10.00
Beam, Jug, Oatmeal, 1966 .... 35.00 To 42.00
Beam, Jug, Turquoise, 1966 .... 4.00 To 6.00
Beam, Jug, Two Handled, Zimmerman, 1965 .... 100.00 To 125.00
Beam, Kaiser International, 1971 .... 6.00 To 8.00
Beam, Kansas, 1960, 1961, State .... 54.00 To 70.00
Beam, Katz Cat, Black, 1968 .... 8.00 To 12.95
Beam, Katz Cat, Yellow, 1967 .... 18.00 To 22.00
Beam, Kentucky Colonel, 1970 .... 5.00 To 6.00
Beam, Kentucky Derby, 95th, 1969, Pink Roses .... 4.00 To 5.00

Beam, Kentucky Derby, 95th, 1969, Red Roses .... 5.00 To 6.00
Beam, Kentucky Derby, 96th, 1970, Red Roses .... 6.00 To 7.00
Beam, Kentucky Derby, 97th, Double Roses .... 7.00 To 8.00
Beam, Kentucky Derby, 98th, 1972 .... 7.00 To 8.00
Beam, Kentucky, Black Head, 1967 .... 14.00 To 15.00
Beam, Kentucky, Brown Head, 1967 .... 15.00 To 20.00
Beam, Kentucky, White Head, 1967 .... 15.00 To 20.00
Beam, Key West, Florida, 1973 .... 6.00 To 9.00
Beam, King Kamehameha, 1972 .... 15.00 To 20.00
   Beam, Kitten, see Beam, Cat
Beam, Kiwi Bird, New Zealand, 1973 .... 9.00 To 10.00
Beam, Koala Bear, 1973 .... 9.00 To 10.00
Beam, Laramie, Centennial, 1968 .... 4.00 To 6.00
Beam, Las Vegas Golden Gate, 1969 .... 40.00 To 52.00
Beam, Las Vegas Golden Nugget, 1969 .... 40.00 To 52.00
Beam, Las Vegas, 1969 .... 4.00 To 7.00
Beam, Lombard Lilac, Centennial, 1969 .... 4.00 To 5.00
Beam, London Bridge, 1971 .... 4.00 To 7.00
Beam, Maine, 1970, State .... *Illus*   8.50
Beam, Majestic, Executive, 1966 .... 32.00 To 38.00
Beam, Man In Barrel No.1, Harolds Club, 1957 .... 340.00 To 450.00

Beam, Maine, 1970, State

Beam, Man In Barrel No.2, Harolds Club, 1958 .... 230.00 To 265.00
Beam, Marbled Fantasy, Executive, 1965 .... 60.00 To 65.00
Beam, Marina City, 1962 .... 33.00 To 40.00
Beam, Mark Antony, 1962 .... 20.00 To 24.00
Beam, McCoy, 1973 .... 18.00 To 22.00
Beam, Michigan, 1972, State .... 9.00 To 12.00
Beam, Milwaukee Club Stein, 1972 .... 34.00 To 41.00
Beam, Minnesota Viking, 1973 .... 6.00 To 10.00
Beam, Mint 400, 1970, Ceramic Stopper .... 9.00 To 11.00
Beam, Mint 400, 1970, Metal Stopper .... 8.00 To 9.00
Beam, Mint 400, 1971, Motorcycle Stopper .... 7.00 To 10.00
Beam, Mint 400, 1972, Helmet Stopper .... 9.00 To 12.00
Beam, Mint 400, 1973 .... 11.00 To 17.00
Beam, Mission Club, 1970, California .... 20.00 To 24.00
Beam, Model T Ford, Runabout 32.00
Beam, Moila Shrine, 1972 .... 20.00 To 25.00
Beam, Momence Flower Festival, 1974 .... 9.00 To 10.75
Beam, Montana, 1963, State .... 80.00 To 85.00
Beam, Mr.Richards, 1972 .... 3.00 To 5.00
Beam, Mt.Rushmore, 1972 .... 4.00 To 4.50
Beam, Musicians On Wine Cask, 1964 .... 6.00 To 10.00
Beam, Muskie, Wisconsin, 1971, Trophy .... 9.00 To 11.00
Beam, Muskie, Wisconsin, 1971, Trophy, Gold .... 28.00 To 32.00
Beam, National Bank Of Chicago, 1964 .... 2250.00 To 3000.00
Beam, National Convention, 1st, 1971 .... 8.00 To 12.00

Beam, National Convention, 2nd, 1972 .... 15.00 To 17.00
Beam, National Convention, 3rd, 1973 .... 20.00 To 25.00
Beam, National Convention, 4th, 1974 .... 20.00 To 24.50
Beam, National Tobacco, 1973 .... 13.00 To 15.00
Beam, Navy, C.P.O., 1974 .... 10.00 To 12.00
Beam, Nebraska, Coach Devaney, 1973 .... 10.00 To 12.95
Beam, Nebraska, 1967, State .... 7.00 To 12.00
Beam, Nevada, 1963, 1964, State .... 50.00 To 60.00
Beam, New Germany, 1973 .... 9.00 To 10.00
Beam, New Hampshire, Eagle, 1971 .... 33.00 To 40.00
Beam, New Hampshire, 1967, State .... 6.00 To 8.00
Beam, New Jersey, 1963, 1964, State, Blue .... 66.00 To 75.00
Beam, New Jersey, 1963, 1964, State, Gold .... 57.00 To 65.00
Beam, New Jersey, 1963, 1964, State, Gray .... 70.00 To 75.00
Beam, New Jersey, 1963, 1964, State, Yellow .... 55.00 To 60.00
Beam, New Mexico Vase, 1972 .... 10.00 To 19.00
Beam, New Mexico, 1972, State .... 3.00 To 5.00
Beam, New York World's Fair, 1964 .... 15.00 To 25.00
Beam, New Zealand Bird, Kiwi, 1973 .... 9.00 To 10.00
Beam, Nixon Bottle & Plate Set .... 1700.00 To 1900.00
Beam, North Dakota, 1964, State .... 80.00 To 90.00
Beam, North Shore Club, Smith's, 1972 .... 14.00 To 29.00
Beam, Oatmeal Jug, 1966 .... 35.00 To 42.00
Beam, Odessa Texas Oil Show, 1972 .... 7.00 To 11.00
Beam, Ohio Hall Of Fame, 1972 .... 10.00 To 12.00
Beam, Ohio State Fair, 1973 .... 12.00 To 13.00
Beam, Ohio, 1966, State .... 8.00 To 15.00
Beam, Oldsmobile, Curved Dash, 1972 .... 18.00 To 27.50
Beam, Olympia, 1971 .... 4.00 To 5.00
Beam, Olympian, 1960 .... 4.00 To 5.00
Beam, Opaline Crystal, 1969 .... 4.00 To 6.00
Beam, Oregon, 1959, State .... 30.00 To 40.00
Beam, Oriental Jade, 1956 .... 3.00 To 5.00
Beam, P.G.A., 1971 .... 7.00 To 8.00
Beam, Paul Bunyan, 1970 .... *Illus*   9.00

Beam, Paul Bunyan, 1970

Beam, Pearl Harbor, 1972 .... 7.00 To 10.00
Beam, Peddler, Zimmerman, 1971 .... 14.00 To 17.00
Beam, Pennsylvania, 1967, State .... 5.00 To 7.00
Beam, Petroleum Man .... 5.00 To 6.00
Beam, Pheasant, 1960, Trophy .... 16.00 To 18.00
Beam, Pheasant, 1961, Trophy, Reissue .... 13.00 To 16.00
Beam, Pheasant, 1963, Trophy, Reissue .... 13.00 To 16.00
Beam, Pheasant, 1966, Trophy, Reissue .... 13.00 To 16.00
Beam, Pheasant, 1967, Trophy, Reissue .... 13.00 To 16.00
Beam, Pheasant, 1968, Trophy, Reissue .... 13.00 To 16.00
Beam, Phi Sigma Kappa, Centennial, 1973 .... 5.00 To 10.00

Beam, Pied Piper, 1974	8.00 To 9.00
Beam, Pin, Gold Top	7.00 To 8.00
Beam, Pin, Wood Top, Pint	7.00 To 8.50
Beam, Pink Speckled Beauty, Foremost, 1956	380.00 To 600.00
Beam, Pinwheel, Harold's Club, 1965	50.00 To 75.00
Beam, Political, Agnew Elephant, 1970	1800.00 To 2400.00
Beam, Political, Donkey, 1956, Ashtray	14.00 To 15.00
Beam, Political, Donkey, 1960, Campaigner	14.00 To 15.00
Beam, Political, Donkey, 1964, Boxer	14.00 To 15.00
Beam, Political, Donkey, 1968, Clown	6.00 To 7.00
Beam, Political, Donkey, 1972, Football	6.00 To 7.00
Beam, Political, Elephant, San Diego, 1972	15.00 To 25.00
Beam, Political, Elephant, 1956, Ashtray	14.00 To 15.00
Beam, Political, Elephant, 1960, Campaigner	14.00 To 15.00
Beam, Political, Elephant, 1964, Boxer	14.00 To 15.00
Beam, Political, Elephant, 1968, Clown	6.00 To 7.00
Beam, Political, Elephant, 1972, Football	6.00 To 7.00
Beam, Ponderosa, 1969	7.00 To 18.00
Beam, Ponderosa, 1972	14.00 To 20.00
Beam, Pony Express, 1968	4.00 To 6.00
Beam, Poodle, Gray, 1970, Trophy	5.00 To 8.00
Beam, Poodle, White, 1970, Trophy	Illus 8.00
Beam, Portland Roses, 1972	5.00 To 10.00
Beam, Portola Trek, Centennial, 1969	4.00 To 6.00
Beam, Powell Expedition, Centennial, 1969	5.00 To 10.00
Beam, Preakness, Pimlico, Centennial, 1970	4.00 To 8.00
Beam, Presidential, Executive, 1968	Illus 11.00

Beam, Poodle, White, 1970, Trophy

Beam, Presidential, Executive, 1968

Beam, Prestige, Executive, 1969	15.00 To 19.00
Beam, Prima Donna, 1969	8.00 To 8.50
Beam, Rabbit, Texas, 1971	8.00 To 10.00
Beam, Rabbit, Texas, 1971, Gold	28.00 To 32.00
Beam, Ralph's Market, Centennial, 1973	10.00 To 15.00
Beam, Ram, 1958, Trophy	100.00 To 165.00
Beam, Redfin Submarine, 1970	4.00 To 6.00
Beam, Redheaded Woodpecker, 1969, Trophy	7.00 To 9.00
Beam, Redwood Map, 1967	6.00 To 10.00
Beam, Regency, Executive, 1972	12.00 To 20.00
Beam, Reidsville, N.C., Centennial, 1973	14.00 To 16.00
Beam, Rene, The Fox, 1974	32.00
Beam, Reno, Centennial, 1968	5.00 To 9.00
Beam, Richard's New Mexico, 1967	4.00 To 6.00
Beam, Rifle, Yuma, 1968	20.00 To 30.00

Beam, Riverside, Centennial, 1970 .... 10.00 To 15.00
Beam, Robin, 1969, Trophy .... 6.00 To 8.00
Beam, Rocky Marciano, 1973 .... 6.00 To 9.00
Beam, Royal Crystal, 1956 .... 3.00 To 5.00
Beam, Royal Di Monte, Executive, 1957 .... 68.00 To 84.00
Beam, Royal Emperor, 1969 .... 4.00 To 5.00
Beam, Royal Gold Diamond, Executive, 1964 .... 45.00 To 60.00
Beam, Royal Gold, Executive, 1956 .... 100.00 To 125.00
Beam, Royal Porcelain, Executive, 1955 .... 180.00 To 265.00
Beam, Royal Reserve .... 4.00 To 5.00
Beam, Royal Rose, Executive, 1963 .... 45.00 To 60.00
Beam, Rubber Capitol, 1972, Akron .... 20.00 To 37.50
Beam, Ruidoso, 1968 .... 4.00 To 5.00
Beam, Sahara Invitational, 1971 .... 6.00 To 8.00
Beam, Sailfish .... 30.00 To 35.00
Beam, Salute To The Navy, 1973 .... 9.00 To 11.00
Beam, Samoa, 1973 .... 8.00 To 10.00
Beam, San Diego, Centennial, 1968 .... 3.00 To 5.00
Beam, Santa Fe, Centennial, 1960 .... 175.00 To 225.00
Beam, Seattle Sea Fair, 1972 .... 7.00 To 11.00
Beam, Seattle World's Fair, 1962 .... 18.00 To 25.00
Beam, Shriners, 1970 .... Illus 7.00
Beam, Siamese Cat, 1967, Trophy .... 10.00 To 11.00

Beam, Shriners, 1970

Beam, State, South Carolina, 1970
(See Page 25)

Beam, Slot Machine, 1967, Blue, Harolds Club .... 10.00 To 12.00
Beam, Slot Machine, 1968, Gray, Harolds Club .... 4.00 To 9.00
Beam, Small Mouth Bass, 1973, Trophy .... 8.00 To 12.00
Beam, Smith's North Shore Club, 1972 .... 14.00 To 29.00
Beam, Smoked Crystal, Genie, 1964 .... 6.00 To 8.00
Beam, South Carolina, 1970, State .... Illus 8.50
Beam, South Dakota, 1969, 1970, State .... 6.00 To 7.00
Beam, Sovereign, Executive, 1969 .... 8.00 To 10.00
Beam, St.Louis Arch, Centennial, 1964 .... 20.00 To 21.00
Beam, St.Louis Arch, Centennial, 1967, Reissue .... 15.00 To 19.00
Beam, St.Louis Club, 1972 .... 24.00 To 35.00
Beam, State, Alaska, 1958 .... 70.00 To 80.00
Beam, State, Alaska, 1964, Reissue .... 60.00 To 70.00
Beam, State, Arizona, 1968, 1969 .... 4.00 To 6.00

Beam, State, Colorado, 1959 .... 37.00 To 45.00
Beam, State, Delaware, 1972 .... 8.00 To 11.00
Beam, State, Florida, Bronze Shell, 1968 .... 4.00 To 5.00
Beam, State, Florida, White Shell, 1968 .... 4.00 To 5.00
Beam, State, Hawaii, 1959 .... 55.00 To 70.00
Beam, State, Hawaii, 1967, Reissue .... 50.00 To 57.00
Beam, State, Idaho, 1963 .... 55.00 To 70.00
Beam, State, Illinois, 1968 .... 4.00 To 8.00
Beam, State, Kansas, 1960, 1961 .... 54.00 To 70.00
Beam, State, Kenutcky, Black Head, 1967 .... 14.00 To 15.00
Beam, State, Kentucky, Brown Head, 1967 .... 15.00 To 20.00
Beam, State, Kentucky, White Head, 1967 .... 15.00 To 20.00
Beam, State, Maine, 1970 .... 4.00 To 8.50
Beam, State, Michigan, 1972 .... 9.00 To 12.00
Beam, State, Montana, 1963 .... 80.00 To 85.00
Beam, State, Nebraska, 1967 .... 7.00 To 12.00
Beam, State, Nevada, 1963, 1964 .... 50.00 To 60.00
Beam, State, New Hampshire, 1967 .... 6.00 To 8.00
Beam, State, New Jersey, Blue, 1963 .... 66.00 To 75.00
Beam, State, New Jersey, Gold, 1963 .... 57.00 To 65.00
Beam, State, New Jersey, Gray, 1963 .... 70.00 To 75.00
Beam, State, New Jersey, Yellow, 1963 .... 55.00 To 60.00
Beam, State, New Mexico, 1972 .... 3.00 To 5.00
Beam, State, North Dakota, 1964 .... 80.00 To 90.00
Beam, State, Ohio, 1966 .... 8.00 To 15.00
Beam, State, Oregon, 1959 .... 30.00 To 40.00
Beam, State, Pennsylvania, 1967 .... 5.00 To 7.00
Beam, State, South Carolina, 1970 .... 5.00 To 8.50
Beam, State, South Dakota, 1969, 1970 .... 6.00 To 7.00
Beam, State, West Virginia, 1963 .... 125.00 To 150.00
Beam, State, Wyoming, 1965 .... 55.00 To 70.00
Beam, Submarine, Redfin, 1970 .... 4.00 To 6.00
Beam, Tabby Cat, 1967, Trophy .... 10.00 To 11.00
Beam, Tavern Scene, Executive, 1959 .... 60.00 To 70.00
Beam, Texas Oil Show, 1972, Odessa .... 7.00 To 11.00
Beam, Texas Rabbit, 1971 .... 8.00 To 10.00
Beam, Texas Rabbit, 1971, Gold .... 28.00 To 32.00
Beam, Thailand, 1969 .... 3.00 To 5.00
Beam, Tiffiny, 1973, Trophy .... 9.00 To 11.00
Beam, Tombstone, 1973 .... *Illus* 5.00 To 7.00

Beam, Tombstone, 1973

Beam, Travel Lodge, 1972 .... 6.00 To 9.00
Beam, Trophy, 1957, Duck .... 25.00 To 35.00
Beam, Trophy, 1957, Fish .... 29.00 To 35.00
Beam, Trophy, 1958, Ram .... 100.00 To 165.00
Beam, Trophy, 1959, Dog .... 55.00 To 60.00
Beam, Trophy, 1960, Pheasant .... 16.00 To 18.00
Beam, Trophy, 1961, Horse, Black .... 20.00 To 26.00

Beam, Trophy, 1961, Horse, Brown .... 18.00 To 22.00
Beam, Trophy, 1961, Horse, White .... 18.00 To 22.00
Beam, Trophy, 1961, Pheasant, Reissue .... 13.00 To 16.00
Beam, Trophy, 1963, Doe .... 28.00 To 35.00
Beam, Trophy, 1963, Pheasant, Reissue .... 13.00 To 16.00
Beam, Trophy, 1965, Fox, Green .... 40.00 To 45.00
Beam, Trophy, 1966, Eagle .... 12.00 To 15.00
Beam, Trophy, 1966, Pheasant, Reissue .... 13.00 To 16.00
Beam, Trophy, 1967, Cats, Burmese, Siamese, Tabby .... 10.00 To 11.00
Beam, Trophy, 1967, Doe, Reissue .... 27.00 To 30.00
Beam, Trophy, 1967, Fox, Green, Reissue .... 35.00 To 38.00
Beam, Trophy, 1967, Horse, Black, Reissue .... 17.00 To 19.00
Beam, Trophy, 1967, Horse, Brown, Reissue .... 15.00 To 18.00
Beam, Trophy, 1967, Horse, White, Reissue .... 18.00 To 22.00
Beam, Trophy, 1967, Pheasant, Reissue .... 13.00 To 16.00
Beam, Trophy, 1968, Cardinal, Male .... 40.00 To 49.50
Beam, Trophy, 1968, Pheasant, Reissue .... 13.00 To 16.00
Beam, Trophy, 1969, Blue Jay .... 7.00 To 8.50
Beam, Trophy, 1969, Robin .... 6.00 To 8.00
Beam, Trophy, 1969, Woodpecker .... 7.00 To 9.00
Beam, Trophy, 1970, Poodle, Gray .... 5.00 To 8.00
Beam, Trophy, 1970, Poodle, White .... 5.00 To 8.00
Beam, Trophy, 1971, Wisconsin Muskie .... 9.00 To 11.00
Beam, Trophy, 1973, Cardinal, Female .... 15.00 To 20.00
Beam, Trophy, 1973, Small Mouth Bass .... 8.00 To 12.00
Beam, Trophy, 1973, Tiffiny .... 9.00 To 11.00
Beam, Trophy, 1974, Blue Gill .... 9.00 To 10.00
Beam, Truth Or Consequences, 1973 .... 9.00 To 11.00
Beam, Turquoise China Jug, 1966 .... 4.00 To 6.00
Beam, Twin Bridges, 1971 .... 55.00 To 70.00
Beam, Two Handled Jug, Zimmerman, 1965 .... 100.00 To 125.00
Beam, U.S. Open, 1972 .... 12.00 To 18.00
Beam, Uncle Sam Fox, 1971, Club .... 10.00 To 15.00
Beam, V.F.W., 1971 .... 6.00 To 8.00
Beam, V.I.P., 1967, Harolds Club .... 40.00 To 50.00
Beam, V.I.P., 1968, Harolds Club .... 40.00 To 50.00
Beam, V.I.P., 1969, Harolds Club .... 75.00 To 120.00
Beam, V.I.P., 1970, Harolds Club .... 50.00 To 60.00
Beam, V.I.P., 1971, Harolds Club .... 40.00 To 60.00
Beam, V.I.P., 1972, Harolds Club .... 30.00 To 40.00
Beam, V.I.P., 1973, Harolds Club .... 30.00 To 32.00
Beam, Volkswagen, Blue, 1973 .... 22.00 To 25.00
Beam, Volkswagen, Red, 1973 .... 22.00 To 25.00
Beam, W.G.A., 1971 .... 6.00 To 7.00
Beam, West Virginia, 1963, State .... 125.00 To 150.00
Beam, Wisconsin Muskie, 1971, Trophy .... 9.00 To 11.00
Beam, Woodpecker, 1969, Redheaded, Trophy .... 7.00 To 9.00
Beam, Wyoming, 1965, State .... 55.00 To 70.00
Beam, Yellow Katz, 1967 .... 18.00 To 22.00

Beer, B M B & Co., Brown, 9 1/2 In.
(See Page 27)

Beam, Yellowstone, 1972	5.00 To 12.00
Beam, Yosemite, 1967	4.00 To 6.00
Beam, Yuma Rifle Club, 1968	20.00 To 30.00
Beam, Zimmerman Blue Beauty, 1973	14.00 To 17.00
Beam, Zimmerman Blue Daisy, 1967	4.00 To 8.00
Beam, Zimmerman Cherub, Lavender, 1968	7.00 To 10.00
Beam, Zimmerman Cherub, Salmon, 1969	4.00 To 10.00
Beam, Zimmerman Chicago Art Institute, 1972	10.00 To 14.00
Beam, Zimmerman Glass, 1969	4.00 To 6.00
Beam, Zimmerman Jug, Green, 1965	4.00 To 6.00
Beam, Zimmerman Peddler, 1971	14.00 To 17.00
Beam, Zimmerman Two Handled Jug, 1965	100.00 To 125.00
Beam, Zimmerman Vase, Brown, 1972	5.00 To 7.00
Beam, Zimmerman Vase, Green, 1972	5.00 To 7.00
Beam, Zimmerman Z, 1970	11.00 To 13.00

*Beer was bottled in all parts of the United States by the time of the
Civil War. Stoneware and the standard beer bottle shape of the 1870s are
included in this category.*

Beer, A.Palmthe & Co., Eureka, Cal., Blob Top, Amber, Quart	12.00
Beer, A.W.Kenison Co., Auburn, Cal., Embossed, Bimal, Amber, 9 1/2 In.	5.00
Beer, Acme, Miniature	2.50
Beer, Anheuser-Busch, Eagle-A Monogram, Embossed, ABM, Amber, 9 1/2 In.	5.00
Beer, B M B & Co., Brown, 9 1/2 In.	*Illus* 1.50
Beer, Ballantine's, Red Lettering, Miniature	4.00
Beer, Becker Products Co., Ogden, Utah, Embossed, ABM, Amber, 8 In.	5.00
Beer, Bell Skirt, Amber, 10 Ozs.	2.00
Beer, Blatz, Milwaukee, Embossed, Bimal, Amber, 9 1/2 In.	5.00
Beer, Blatz, Miniature	2.50
Beer, Blob Top, Amber, Quart	2.00
Beer, Born & Co., Columbus, O., Blob Top, Amber, 9 1/2 In.	4.00
Beer, Bosch Brewing Co., Mich., Clyde Glass, Blob, Stain, Amber, Quart	7.00
Beer, Budweiser, C.Conrad & Co., Etched, 24 Ozs.	12.00
Beer, Budweiser, C.Conrad & Co., 32 Ozs.	35.00
Beer, Budweiser, Miniature	2.50
Beer, Buffalo Brewing Co., Cal., Porcelain Stopper, Blob, Amber, Quart	12.00
Beer, Buffalo Brewing Co., Sacramento, Cal., Bimal, Amber, 11 1/2 In.	8.00
Beer, Buffalo Brewing Co., Sacramento, Cal., Bimal, Aqua, 11 1/2 In.	5.00
Beer, Buffalo Brewing Co., San Francisco, Embossed, Bimal, Amber, 7 3/4 In.	8.00
Beer, Burger, Cincinnati, O., Display, Labels, 30 In.	62.00
Beer, Capitol Bottling Works, Petaluma, Cal., Bimal, Amber, 11 3/4 In.	5.00
Beer, Carling's Black Label, Miniature	6.00
Beer, Coronation Ale, June 22nd, 1911, 1/2 Pint	20.00
Beer, Drewry's Ale, Miniature	1.75
Beer, Drexler Immohr & Co., City Brewery, Ky., Blob Top, Amber, Quart	20.00
Beer, Dubuque Brewing & Malting Co., Iowa, D & Hops Monogram, 2 Quart	12.75
Beer, Eastside, Miniature	5.00
Beer, Edelweiss, Miniature	6.00
Beer, Eldorado Brewing Co., Stockton, Cal., Embossed, Bimal, Amber, 11 1/2 In.	5.00
Beer, Embossed, Blob, Amber, 9 In.	4.00
Beer, Ennis Bros., Utica, N.Y., Blob Top, Quart	10.00
Beer, Enterprise Brewing Co., S.F., Blob Top, Amber, 11 3/4 In.	9.00
Beer, Enterprise Brewing Co., San Francisco, Cal., Bimal, Amber, 11 1/4 In.	5.00
Beer, Enterprise Brewing Co., San Francisco, Cal., Blob Top, Amber, Quart	8.95
Beer, Ernst Tosetti Brewing Co., Chicago, C.C.G.Co., Blob, Aqua, Pint	8.00
Beer, Evans Ale, Hudson, N.Y., Embossed, ABM, Amber, 10 In.	3.00
Beer, F.& M.Schaefer, N.Y., Embossed, Aqua, 10 In.High	3.00
Beer, Falstaff, Embossed, Green, 11 1/2 In.	10.00
Beer, Fort Pitt, Miniature	3.00
Beer, Fort Pitt, Salt & Pepper, 3 & 4 In.High	3.00
Beer, Fredericksburg Bottling Co., San Francisco, Blob, Amber, Quart	8.00
Beer, Fredericksburg, San Jose, Whittled, Red Amber, Quart	45.00
Beer, Free-Blown, Pontil, Sand Particles In Glass, C.1820, Amber, Quart	28.00
Beer, Geo.H.Lett & Co.Ltd., Mill Park Brewery, Enniscorthy, 7 3/4 In.	5.00
Beer, George Bechtel Brewing Co., Crown Lip, Bubbles, Seeds, Amber, 9 1/4 In.	12.00

Beer, German Brewing Co., The, Brown, 9 3/4 In. ....*Illus*   3.00
Beer, Gold Edge Bottling Works, J.F.Deininger, 4 Mold, Amber, Quart 8.00
Beer, Grace Bros. Brewing Co., Santa Rosa, Cal., Bimal, Amber, 9 1/2 In. 5.00

Beer, German Brewing Co., The, Brown, 9 3/4 In.

Beer, H.Berghoff, Ft. Wayne, Ind., Quart 10.00
Beer, H.Jackel, Norwich, Conn., Metal Cap, Amber, 9 1/2 In.High 3.00
Beer, Hamm's, Bear, Mini, 1972 ....   8.00
Beer, Hamm's, Bear, Mini, 1973 ....   8.00
Beer, Hamm's, Bear, 1972 ....   25.00
Beer, Hamm's, Bear, 1973 ....   20.00
Beer, Hamm's, Oktoberfest Mug, 1973 ....   4.00
Beer, Hansen & Kahler, Oakland, Cal., Embossed, Bimal, Amber, 11 1/2 In. 5.00
Beer, Honolulu Brewing Co., Round, Aqua, 12 In.High 15.00
Beer, Hoster, Columbus, O., Blob Top, Bimal, Amber, Quart .... 2.45 To 7.00
Beer, Huebner Toledo Breweries Co., The, Toledo, O., Brown, 9 1/2 In. 7.00
Beer, Humboldt Bottling Co., Pint 10.00
Beer, Hyde Park, St.Louis, Crown Top, Bimal, Amber, 12 Ozs. 3.00
Beer, Indianapolis Brewing Co., Dancing Girl, Bimal, Aqua, 9 1/4 In. 8.00
Beer, Indianapolis Brewing, Embossed Dancing Girl, Light Green, 9 1/2 In. 6.00
Beer, J.A.Blaffer, New Orleans, Squat, Amber, 6 1/2 In. 25.00
Beer, J.Gahm & Sons, Boston, JC In Mug, Embossed, Bimal, Amber, 9 1/4 In. 5.00
Beer, Jacob L.Alther & Co., 1881, Boston, Sheared Lip, Red Amber, 9 3/4 In. 12.00
Beer, John A.Lomax, Weiss, Chicago, 8 1/2 In. ....*Color* XXXX.XX
Beer, John Rapp & Son, San Francisco, Blob Top, Amber, Quart, 12 In. 12.00
Beer, John Rapp & Son, San Francisco, Blob Top, 4 Mold, Amber, Quart 8.00
Beer, L.Speidel & Co., Boston, Embossed Hop Leaf & B, Blob Top, 8 1/2 In. 8.00
Beer, Leisy, Peoria, Ill., Crown Top, Bimal, Amber, Quart 2.00
Beer, Lemon, Stoneware, Cobalt Glaze, 10 In. 18.00
Beer, Los Angeles Brewing Co., Embossed, Bimal, Amber, 9 1/4 In. 5.00
    Beer, Miniature, see Miniature, Beer
Beer, Mrs.M.Kinney's Mead Ale, Pottery, Incised, 10 In. 23.50
Beer, National Lager Beer, H.R.Monogram, Blob Top, Amber, Pint, 9 1/2 In. 7.00
Beer, National Lager, H.Rohrbacher, Cal., Blob Top, 4 Mold, Amber, Pint 7.00
Beer, National Lager, H.Rohrbacher, Stockton, Cal., Blob Top, Amber, 1/2 Pint 5.00
Beer, National Lager, H.Rohrbacher, Stockton, Cal., Blob Top, Amber, Pint 6.95
Beer, Olympia Co., San Francisco, Cal., Embossed, Bimal, Aqua, 9 1/4 In. 5.00
Beer, Pabst, Arched, Bimal, Amethyst, 9 1/2 In. 7.00
Beer, Park Brewing Co., Winona, Miss., Picnic, Bubbles, Gold Amber, 1/2 Gallon 25.00
Beer, Peru Co., Peru, Ill., Crown Top, Bimal, Amber, Quart 3.00
Beer, Popel-Giller, Warsaw, Ill., Crown Top, Bimal, Amber, Pint 3.50
Beer, Porter, Black Amethyst, Pint 42.00
Beer, Porter, Black Amethyst, Quart 42.00
Beer, R.Wegener, Alexandria, Minn., Blob Top, Amber, 12 In. 12.00
Beer, Rainier Brewing Co., San Francisco, Cal., Bimal, Green, 9 1/2 In. 5.00
Beer, Reck's Brewing Co., Lady's Leg, 12 Oz. 4.00
Beer, Richmond Bottling Works, Blob, 9 1/2 In. 6.00
Beer, Richmond Bottling Works, Blob, 12 In. 6.00
Beer, Riverside Brewery, Zanesville, Ohio, Quart, Blob Top, Aqua 27.00
Beer, Robert Portner Brewing Co., Blob Top, Amber, 7 In. 15.00
Beer, Royal Ruby, Anchor Glass, ABM, Red, Quart, 9 1/2 In. 5.95

Figural, girl in tights, 13½ in. $50

Flask, overlay on blue, painted center, 7½ in. $150

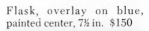

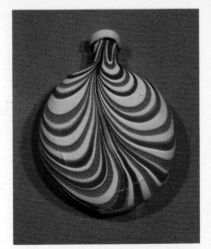

Flask, looped decoration, 7½ in. $150

Milk Glass, pewter top, painted, 10 in.

Medicine, Hopkins' Chalybeate, Baltimore, graphite pontil, 7½ in.

Medicine, Wishart's Pine Tree Tar Cordial, Phila., Patent 1859, 9½ in. $65

Food, Louis Frere's Bordeaux, 8½ in. $47

Candy Container, Tot Telephone, 2½ in. $22.50

Flask, swirled decoration, 5½ in. $115

Bininger, Bininger & Co., clock regulator, 19 Broad St., N.Y., 6 in. $400

Miniature,
Motto Jug, 4½ in. $18

Miniature, Motto Jug,
Old Continental Whiskey,
3½ in. $17.50

Miniature,
Motto Jug, Compliments
James B. Weaver,
2¼ in. $7.50

Whiskey, Durham, 11½ in. $800

Figural, ear of corn, carnival glass, 5 in. $175

Bininger, Bininger & Co., cannon, Broad St. $450

Soda, Frank Nardorff, Louisville, Kentucky, 7½ in.

Whiskey, H F & B, N.Y., 9½ in. $800

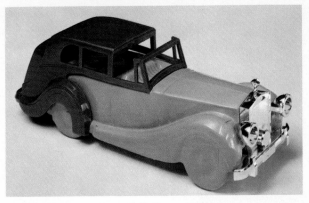

Avon, Rolls Royce, 1972

Avon, Courting Lamp,
1970

Avon, Koffee Klatch,
1971

Avon, Super Cycle, 1971

Mineral Water, Upper
Blue Lick, Jas. W. Pierce,
Prop., Maysville, Ky., 9
in. $250

Medicine, Coke Dandruff
Cure, A. R. Bremer Co., N.Y.,
Chicago, 7½ in. $25

Wheaton Commemoratives — 1972 Campaign Decanters

McGovern-Shriver
(Reversed)

McGovern-Shriver

McGovern-Eagleton
(Reversed)

Nixon-Agnew

McGovern-Eagleton

Drug, Sp. Camph.,
8½ in. $18

Bitters, Angostura Bark,
Eagle Liqueur Distilleries, 7
in. $165

Bitters, Brown's
Iron, 9 in. $27

Whiskey, Old Ken-
tucky Bourbon, 1849
Reserve, Bininger &
Co., 8½ in. $200

Ink, Carter's, Cathe-
dral, C-102, 8 in. $85

Whiskey, Holiday Chimes, 1903–1904, A Merry Christmas and A Happy New Year, 4½ in. $60

Decanter, etched, pink, 6½ in. $40

Bitters, Geo. Benz & Sons Appetine, St. Paul, Minn., 8½ in. $650

Holly City — *Left to right:* Israel's 25th Anniversary, 1973; John F. Kennedy Rocking Chair Memorial, 1973; Watergate, Third Run, 1973; The Jersey Devil, 1974

Beer, Royal Seal Export, Cincinnati, O., Blob Top, Amber, Pint 12.00
Beer, Ruby Red, Quart .... 5.50 To 8.00
Beer, Ruby, 7 Ozs. .... 5.00 To 15.00
Beer, Ruhstaller's Giltedge Lager, Sacramento, Cal., Bimal, Amber, 9 1/4 In. 5.00
Beer, Schlitz, Globe, 1971 .... 14.95
Beer, Schlitz, Red, 12 Ozs. 6.00
Beer, Schlitz, 1950, Ruby Red, Quart 7.00
Beer, Smith's White Root Ale, July 17, 1866, Blob, Pottery, 11 In .... 23.50 To 27.00
Beer, St.Helena Bottling & Cold Storage Co., Cal., Blob, Amber, Quart 10.00
Beer, St.Louis Bottling Co., Embossed, Bimal, Amber, 9 1/4 In. 5.00
Beer, Stars & Stripes, Omaha, Quart 12.00
Beer, Terre Haute Brewing Co., Embossed, Bimal, Amber, 9 1/2 In. 5.00
Beer, Torch Lake Brewery Co., Jos.Bosch & Co., C.G.Co., Blob, Amber, Pint 8.00
Beer, Torch Lake Brewery Co., Jos.Bosch & Co., C.G.Co., Blob, Amber, Quart 8.00
Beer, Union Brewing Co., Cincinnati, O., Crown Top, Bimal, Amber, Quart 3.00
Beer, Victoria-Phoenix Brewing Co., Ltd., Victoria, B.C., Amber, 9 1/8 In. 3.00
Beer, Wm.J.Sackett, Saranac, N.Y., ABM, Ruby Red, Quart 5.00
Beer, Wunder Bottling Co., San Francisco, Calif., Blob Top, Amber, 1/2 Pint 5.00
Beer, 1913 On Bottom, Embossed, ABM, Aqua, 9 1/2 In. 5.00
Beneagles, Bridge 3.00
Beneagles, Deer 3.00
Beneagles, Edinburgh Castle 3.00
Beneagles, Golf Ball 4.00
Beneagles, Loch Ness Monster 4.00
Beneagles, Pheasant 3.00
Beneagles, Tower 3.00
Beneagles, Trout 3.00
    Bininger, see also Bitters, Bininger
Bininger, A.M., Whiskey, Barrel, Pontil, Light Amber, 8 In. 185.00
Bininger, A.M., Whiskey, Barrel, Pontil, Quart .... 225.00 To 350.00
Bininger, Barrel, Dark Amber, 8 In. 150.00
Bininger, Barrel, 19 Broad St., Light Amber, Quart 200.00
Bininger, Bourbon, New York, 1848 ....Illus   90.00

Bininger, Bourbon, New York, 1848

Bininger, Cannon, Bininger & Co., Broad St. ....Color   450.00
Bininger, Clock, Regulator, Bininger & Co., N.Y., 6 In. ....Color   400.00
Bininger, Gin, Old London Dock, Square, Green, Quart 45.00
Bininger, Gin, 19 Broad St., Amber, Pint 48.00
Bininger, Old Kentucky Bourbon, Barrel, Amber, Quart 225.00
Bininger, Old Kentucky Bourbon, Barrel, Amber, 3/4 Quart 140.00
Bininger, Urn & A.M.Bininger & Co., Handled, Amber, Pint 1100.00
Bininger, Whiskey, Barrel, Quart 250.00

*Bischoff Company has made fancy decanters since it was founded in 1777 in
Trieste, Italy. The modern collectible Bischoff bottles have been
imported to the United States since about 1950. Glass, porcelain, and
stoneware decanters and figurals are made.*

Bischoff, African Head, Ceramic, 1962	18.00
Bischoff, Alpine Pitcher, Porcelain, 1969	12.00
Bischoff, Amber Flowers Decanter, Glass, 1952	35.00
Bischoff, Amber Leaves Decanter, 1952	35.00
Bischoff, Amphora, Majolica, 1950	25.00 To 30.00
Bischoff, Aqua & Gold Decanter, Water Scene, 1956	30.00
Bischoff, Aqua & Silver Decanter, Gondola, 1954	35.00
Bischoff, Ashtray, Miniature, Ceramic, 1962	4.50
Bischoff, Bell House, Ceramic, 1960	30.00
Bischoff, Bell Tower, Ceramic, 1959	30.00
Bischoff, Boy, Chinese, Ceramic, 1962	40.00
Bischoff, Boy, Spanish, Ceramic, 1961	30.00 To 45.00
Bischoff, Cameo Pitcher Decanter, Ceramic, 1962	20.00
Bischoff, Candlestick, Antique, Glass, 1958	18.00
Bischoff, Candlestick, Fruit, Ceramic, 1964	25.00
Bischoff, Candlestick, Gold, Glass, 1958	18.00 To 20.00
Bischoff, Cat, Black, 1969	20.00
Bischoff, Chariot Urn, 2 Compartments, Ceramic, 1966	25.00
Bischoff, Christmas Tree Decanter, 1957	65.00
Bischoff, Clown, Black Hair, Ceramic, 1963	40.00
Bischoff, Clown, Red Hair, Ceramic, 1963	40.00
Bischoff, Coach Bottle, 1948	42.00
Bischoff, Cobalt Blue & Gold Decanter, Gondola, 1956	50.00
Bischoff, Cobalt Blue & Silver Decanter, 1954	45.00
Bischoff, Coronet Decanter, Amber Glass, 1952	40.00
Bischoff, Dachshund, Glass, 1966	32.00
Bischoff, Deer, Ceramic, 1969	10.00
Bischoff, Dog, Alabaster Glass, 1969	18.00 To 20.00
Bischoff, Dolphin, Double	18.00
Bischoff, Duck, Glass, 1964	60.00
Bischoff, Egyptian Ashtray, Ceramic, 1961	8.00
Bischoff, Egyptian Decanter, 2 Handles, 2 Compartments, 1960	30.00
Bischoff, Egyptian Man Vase, Ceramic, 1961	30.00
Bischoff, Egyptian Musician Pitcher, 2 Musicians, Ceramic, 1963	19.00
Bischoff, Egyptian Pitcher, 3 Musicians, 1959	25.00
Bischoff, Emerald Decanter, Roses, 1952	45.00
Bischoff, Festival, Jeweled Vase Decanter, 1957	50.00
Bischoff, Fish, Glass, 1969, Ruby	17.00
Bischoff, Fish, Multicolor, 1964	50.00
Bischoff, Floral Canteen, Ceramic, 1969	15.00
Bischoff, Flower Decanter, Gold, Pink, Blue, Green Flowers, 1956	50.00
Bischoff, Flower Decanter, Ruby, 1953	32.00
Bischoff, Flower Jug	4.50
Bischoff, Fruit Canteen, Ceramic, 1969	25.00
Bischoff, Geese Decanter, Amber, 1952	26.00
Bischoff, Geese Decanter, Ruby, 1952	26.00
Bischoff, Girl, Chinese, Ceramic, 1962	35.00
Bischoff, Girl, Spanish, Ceramic, 1961	35.00
Bischoff, Gold Dust & Green Decanter, 1958	40.00
Bischoff, Grapes Decanter, Ruby, 1953	35.00
Bischoff, Grecian Vase Decanter, Ceramic, 1969	13.00
Bischoff, Green & Silver Decanter, 1954	35.00
Bischoff, Green Striped Decanter, 1958	35.00
Bischoff, Horse Head, Amber	15.00
Bischoff, Jungle Scene, Amber Glass, 1952	34.00
Bischoff, Jungle Scene, Ruby Glass, 1952	34.00
Bischoff, Lavender & Gold Decanter, Roses, 1954	20.00
Bischoff, Lavender & Silver Decanter, Daisies, 1954	33.00
Bischoff, Mask, Ceramic, Gray, 1963	20.00
Bischoff, Nigerian Mask, 1963	20.00
Bischoff, Oil & Vinegar Cruets, Ceramic, Black, White, 1959	23.00
Bischoff, Opaline, Aqua Glass Decanter, 1957	50.00
Bischoff, Red Bell Shaped Decanter, 1957	45.00
Bischoff, Red Rose Decanter, Hand-Painted Flowers, 1957	50.00
Bischoff, Rose Decanter, Gold, 1952	25.00

Bischoff, Rose Decanter, Green, 1954	30.00
Bischoff, Rose Decanter, Pink, 1952	27.50
Bischoff, Ruby Etched Decanter, Glass, 1952	40.00
Bischoff, Silver Spotted Decanter, 1958	35.00
Bischoff, Sleigh Bottle, 1949	42.00
Bischoff, Striped Decanter, 1958	35.00 To 40.00
Bischoff, Topaz & Gold Decanter, 1955	26.00
Bischoff, Topaz & Silver Decanter, 1955	40.00
Bischoff, Topaz Basket Decanter, 1958	35.00
Bischoff, Vase, Deer Decoration	4.00
Bischoff, Vase, Gold, Painted Flowers, 1955	16.00
Bischoff, Vase, Modern, Ceramic, Black & Gold, 1959	30.00
Bischoff, Venetian Decanter, Blue, 1953	20.00 To 24.00
Bischoff, Venetian Decanter, Green, 1953	20.00 To 24.00
Bischoff, Venetian Decanter, Violet, 1953	20.00 To 24.00
Bischoff, Watchtower, Ceramic, 1960	10.00
Bischoff, Wedding Procession Vase, Ceramic, 1962	30.00
Bischoff, White & Yellow Vase, 1959	20.00
Bischoff, White Pitcher, Gold Handle, 1960	21.00
Bischoff, White Swags, Jeweled Vase Decanter, 1957	55.00
Bischoff, Wild Geese Decanter, Ruby, Glass, 1952	28.00
Bischoff, Wild Geese Pitcher, Ceramic, 1969	26.00

Bitters bottles held the famous 19th-century medicine called bitters. It was often of such a high alcohol content that the user felt healthier with each sip. The word bitters must be embossed on the glass or a paper label must be affixed for the collector to call the bottle a bitters bottle. Most date from 1840 to 1900. The numbers used in the entries in the form W-0 or W-L-0 refer to the books Bitters Bottles and Supplement to Bitters Bottles by Richard Watson.

Bitters, see also Sarsaparilla

Bitters, Adolpho Wolfe's Aromatic Schnapps, Olive Amber, 9 1/2 In.	13.50
Bitters, African Stomach, Amber, W-0	36.00
Bitters, American Deobstruent, Oval, Applied Lip, Paper Label, 6 1/2 In.	75.00
Bitters, American Life, P.Eiler, Cabin, W-9	750.00
Bitters, American Stomach, Meyer's Remedy Co., C.1905, Label, 9 In.	27.50
Bitters, Angelica Bitter Tonic, Jos.Triner, Chicago, Oval, Amber, 9 In.	55.00
Bitters, Angostura Bark, Eagle Distilleries, 7 In., W-11 ....Color	165.00
Bitters, Angostura, Screw Cap, Green, 5 In.	6.50

Bitters, Appetine, see Geo. Benz & Sons Appetine

Bitters, Aromatic Orange Stomach, Dark Amber, W-384	115.00
Bitters, Aromatic Schnapps, Amber, Quart	20.00
Bitters, Atwood's Genuine, W-15	20.00
Bitters, Atwood's Genuine Physical Jaundice, Blue Aqua, 6 In., W-16	25.00
Bitters, Atwood's Gourdic, Moses Atwood, Md., Round, Aqua	5.00
Bitters, Atwood's Gourdic, Moses Atwood, Md., Round, Clear	5.00
Bitters, Atwood's Jaundice, ABM, Aqua, Sample Size, W-17	6.00 To 10.00
Bitters, Atwood's Jaundice, Moses Atwood, 12 Sided, Aqua, W-17	4.75 To 7.50
Bitters, Augauer, Green, W-21	65.00
Bitters, Baker's Orange Grove, W-23	75.00
Bitters, Baker's Stomach, Lady's Leg, Light Amber	75.00
Bitters, Baxter's Mandrake, W-29	9.00 To 18.00
Bitters, Berkshire, Pig, Olive Amber, Large Size, W-38	140.00
Bitters, Big Bill Best, Amber, W-41	90.00
Bitters, Bininger, Barrel, OP, Quart	225.00
Bitters, Bitters In Silver On Side, Metal Shaker Top, Clear, 6 In.	18.00
Bitters, Boerhave's Holland, Aqua, 8 In., W-48	56.00
Bitters, Boonekamp Aperitif, Labels, Round, Amber, Miniature	25.00
Bitters, Brown's Celebrated Indian Herb, Amber, W-57 ....Illus	320.00
Bitters, Brown's Iron, 9 In., W-399 ....Color	30.00
Bitters, Bryant's Stomach, 1857, 8 Sided, Olive Green, 12 1/2 In.	3000.00
Bitters, Bryant's Stomach, 8 Sided, OP, Dark Olive, 12 1/2 In., W-400	3000.00
Bitters, Buhrer's Gentian, Amber, Quart, W-402	75.00
Bitters, Burand's Stomach, Ohio, 4 Indented Panels, Label, 7 1/2 In.	30.00
Bitters, Burdock Blood, Aqua, 8 1/2 In., W-60	25.00

Bitters, Burdock Blood, Buffalo, N.Y., Embossed, Amethyst, W-60 .... 18.00
Bitters, Burdock Blood, Toronto, Ont., Aqua, 8 1/2 In., W-60 .... 6.00 To 15.00
    Bitters, Byrne, see Bitters, Professor Byrne
Bitters, C.K.Wilson's Wa-Hoo, Ohio, Rectangular, Label, 8 1/2 In. 20.00
    Bitters, C.W.Roback's, see also Bitters, Dr.C.W.Roback's
Bitters, C.W.Roback's, IP, Lemon Yellow, 10 In., W-280 .... 500.00
Bitters, C.W.Roback's, Yellow Amber, 10 In. 250.00
    Bitters, Cabin, see Bitters, American Life, Bitters, Drake's
    Plantation, Bitters, Golden, Bitters, Kelly's, Bitters, Old Homestead
Bitters, Caldwell's Herb, Amber, 12 1/4 In., W-65 .... 100.00
Bitters, Caldwell's Herb, Great Tonic, 3 Sided, IP, Amber, 12 3/4 In., W-65 .... 175.00
Bitters, Carl Snompe, Green, 6 In. .... *Illus* 30.00
Bitters, Caroni, Green Shoulder & Bottom, 5 In., W-72 .... 10.00
Bitters, Caroni, Stain, Sample, 5 1/4 In. 25.00
Bitters, Carter's Aromatic Scotch, Mass., 4 Indented Panels, Aqua, 8 In. 30.00
Bitters, Clarke's Sherry Wine, Aqua, Pint, W-88 .... 45.00
Bitters, Clarke's Sherry Wine, Haze, 8 1/2 In., W-88 .... 55.00
Bitters, Clarke's Sherry Wine, Rockland, Me., Cloudy, Aqua, Gallon, W-88 .... 55.00
Bitters, Clarke's Sherry Wine, Sharon, Mass., Whittled, Aqua, 14 In., W-88 .... 130.00

Bitters, Brown's Celebrated Indian Herb, Amber, W-57
(See Page 31)

Bitters, Carl Snompe, Green, 6 In.

Bitters, Clarke's Vegetable Sherry Wine, Mass., Aqua, 11 1/4 In., W-88 .... 55.00
Bitters, Clarke's Vegetable Sherry Wine, 70 Cents, OP, Aqua, 12 In. 90.00
Bitters, Cole Bros. Vegetable, Aqua, W-413 .... 25.00
Bitters, Columbo Peptic, Amber, W-93 .... 26.00
Bitters, Constitution, Honey Amber, W-95 .... 350.00
Bitters, Corwitz Stomach, On 2 Sides, 4 Indented Panels, Square, 7 1/2 In. 85.00
Bitters, Creswell's, 2 5/8 In. 8.00
Bitters, Curtis & Perkins Wild Cherry, Whittled, Pontil, 7 In., W-102 .... 90.00
Bitters, Damiana, Aqua, W-103 .... 26.00
Bitters, Delhi Kidney & Liver, Los Angeles, Square, Label, Amber, 8 1/2 In. 50.00
Bitters, DeWitt's Stomach, Amber, 9 1/4 In., W-426 .... 50.00
Bitters, Doctor Fisch's, Fish Shape, Amber, Quart, W-124 .... 130.00
Bitters, Doyle's Hop, 1872, Asa T.Soule, Amber, 9 1/2 In., W-110 .... 15.00
Bitters, Doyle's Hop, 1872, L & W, Amber, 9 1/2 In., W-110 .... 30.00
Bitters, Dr.Baker's Restorative Life, Infolded Lip, Label, Teal Blue 60.00
Bitters, Dr.Baxter's Mandrake, Aqua, 6 In. 5.00
Bitters, Dr.Bell's Blood Purifying, The Great Remedy, W-31 .... 100.00
Bitters, Dr.Bell's Golden Tonic, Side Hole, 10 1/2 In. ....*Color* 1750.00
Bitters, Dr.Boyce's Tonic, Embossed, Light Citron, W-53 .... 35.00
Bitters, Dr.Buzzell's Vegetable Bilious, Nathan Wood, Label, Aqua, 7 1/2 In. 35.00
    Bitters, Dr.C.W.Roback's, see also Bitters, C.W.Roback's
Bitters, Dr.C.W.Roback's Stomach, Barrel, Cincinnati, O., Amber, 10 In., W-280 .... 105.00

Bitters, Dr.Carey's Original Mandrake, Elmira, N.Y., Embossed, Aqua, W-407	33.00
Bitters, Dr.Flint's Quaker, W-126	22.50
Bitters, Dr.Geo.Pierce's Indian Restorative, Aqua, W-258	30.00
Bitters, Dr.Geo.Pierce's Indian Restorative, Lowell, W-258	30.00 To 38.00
Bitters, Dr.Geo.Pierce's Indian Restorative, OP, 8 In.	40.00
Bitters, Dr.Gerrish, Lowell, Standard, Jug, Salt Glaze, 2 Quart, 9 In.	500.00
Bitters, Dr.Harter's Wild Cherry, Bimal, Miniature	25.00
Bitters, Dr.Harter's Wild Cherry, Dayton, 4 1/2 In., W-158	25.00
Bitters, Dr.Harter's Wild Cherry, St.Louis, Amber, 4 In., W-158	50.00
Bitters, Dr.Harter's Wild Cherry, St.Louis, Medium Amber, 4 7/8 In.	25.00
Bitters, Dr.Harter's, St.Louis, Embossed, Light Red Amber, 4 In.	27.00
Bitters, Dr.Harter's, St.Louis, Sample, W-158	23.00
Bitters, Dr.Hicks' Stomach & Liver, Fischer Drug Co., Label, 5 In.	35.00
Bitters, Dr.Hoofland's, Philadelphia, Embossed, Etched, Aqua, 7 In., W-174	30.00
Bitters, Dr.Hopkins Union Stomach, W-177	42.00
Bitters, Dr. Hostetter, see Bitters, Dr. J. Hostetter	
Bitters, Dr.J.Hostetter's Stomach, Amber, W-179	4.00
Bitters, Dr.J.Hostetter's Stomach, Black, W-179	60.00
Bitters, Dr.J.Hostetter's Stomach, Brown, 9 In., W-179 .... *Illus*	9.00
Bitters, Dr.J.Hostetter's Stomach, Olive Amber, 8 5/8 X 2 3/4 In., W-179	90.00
Bitters, Dr.J.Hostetter's Stomach, Olive Green, 9 1/2 X 3 In., W-179	80.00
Bitters, Dr.J.Hostetter's Stomach, Yellow, W-179	20.00
Bitters, Dr.Kaufmann's, A.P.Ordway, N.Y., Oval, Label, Light Aqua, 8 In.	20.00
Bitters, Dr.Kaufmann's, Formerly Dr.Kaufmann's Sulphur, Label, Aqua, 8 In.	20.00
Bitters, Dr.Langley's Root & Herb, Aqua, W-206	35.00
Bitters, Dr.Langley's Root & Herb, 99, Bimal, Aqua, 7 In., W-206	25.00
Bitters, Dr.Langley's, Embossed, Aqua, W-206F	20.00
Bitters, Dr.Langley's, 99 Reversed, Dull, 9 In.	35.00
Bitters, Dr.Lawrence's Wild Cherry Family, Newark, N.J., Square, Amber, 5 In.	95.00
Bitters, Dr.Lion's Stomach, Amber, 10 In. .... *Illus*	30.00
Bitters, Dr.Loew's Celebrated Stomach, Emerald Green, 9 1/4 In., W-217	160.00
Bitters, Dr.Loew's Stomach & Nerve Tonic, Free Sample, Green	110.00
Bitters, Dr.M.M.Fenner's Capitol, W-122	35.00
Bitters, Dr.Montgomery's Vegetable, Aqua, 5 1/2 X 3 X 2 In.	10.00
Bitters, Dr.Owen's European Life, Detroit, 8 Panels, OP, Aqua, 3/4 Pint	160.00
Bitters, Dr.S.B.H.& Co., Label, Cork, 9 In.	2.50
Bitters, Dr.Sawens' Life Invigorating, Square, Label, Amber, 9 3/4 In., W-295	35.00
Bitters, Dr.Skinner's Celebrated 25 Cent, 8 Sided, Aqua, 9 1/2 In., W-306	100.00
Bitters, Dr.Stephen Jewett's, Aqua, W-193	30.00
Bitters, Dr.Stewart's Tonic, Labels, W-500	30.00
Bitters, Dr.Van Dyke's Holland, 1896, 4 Indented Panels, Label, 9 3/4 In.	29.50
Bitters, Dr.Van Dyke's Holland, 1896, 4 Indented Panels, 9 3/4 In.	10.00
Bitters, Dr.Von Hopf's Curacao, Amber, 8 In., W-343	48.00

Bitters, Dr.J.Hostetter's, Stomach, Brown, 9 In., W-179

Bitters, Dr.Lion's Stomach, Amber, 10 In.

Bitters, Dr.Warren's Bilious, Boston, Flask, Ring Lip, Aqua, 6 1/2 In. 50.00
Bitters, Dr.Williams, Doolittle & Smith, Boston, Oval, Label, 8 3/4 In. 30.00
Bitters, Drake's Plantation, Green, 10 In. ....Color XXXX.XX
Bitters, Drake's Plantation, 4 Log .... 40.00 To 60.00
Bitters, Drake's Plantation, 4 Log, Amber, W-111 .... 35.00 To 65.00
Bitters, Drake's Plantation, 4 Log, Burst Bubble, Amber 45.00
Bitters, Drake's Plantation, 4 Log, Dark Amber 60.00
Bitters, Drake's Plantation, 4 Log, Honey Amber, W-111 .... 55.00 To 70.00
Bitters, Drake's Plantation, 4 Log, Honey With A Touch Of Yellow, W-111 .... 85.00
Bitters, Drake's Plantation, 4 Log, Light Amber, W-111 .... 55.00 To 75.00
Bitters, Drake's Plantation, 4 Log, Medium Amber, W-111 .... 48.00 To 55.00
Bitters, Drake's Plantation, 4 Log, Yellow, W-111 .... 95.00
Bitters, Drake's Plantation, 5 Log, Amber, W-111 .... 65.00
Bitters, Drake's Plantation, 5 Log, Burst Bubble, W-111 .... 140.00
Bitters, Drake's Plantation, 6 Log .... 50.00 To 60.00
Bitters, Drake's Plantation, 6 Log, Amber, W-111 .... 40.00 To 70.00
Bitters, Drake's Plantation, 6 Log, Burst Bubble, Stain, Yellow, Amber, W-111 .... 75.00
Bitters, Drake's Plantation, 6 Log, Claret, W-111 .... 150.00 To 175.00
Bitters, Drake's Plantation, 6 Log, Dark Amber, W-111 .... 40.00 To 55.00
Bitters, Drake's Plantation, 6 Log, Dark Cherry Red, W-111 .... 140.00
Bitters, Drake's Plantation, 6 Log, Dark Chocolate Amber, W-111 .... 85.00
Bitters, Drake's Plantation, 6 Log, Faint Embossing, Amber, W-111 .... 57.00
Bitters, Drake's Plantation, 6 Log, Golden Amber, W-111 .... 55.00
Bitters, Drake's Plantation, 6 Log, Light Amber, W-111 .... 60.00
Bitters, Drake's Plantation, 6 Log, Light Honey Amber 55.00
Bitters, Drake's Plantation, 6 Log, Light Orange Amber, W-111 .... 75.00
Bitters, Drake's Plantation, 6 Log, Medium Amber 60.00
Bitters, Drake's Plantation, 6 Log, Orange Amber 50.00
Bitters, Drake's Plantation, 6 Log, Puce, W-111 .... 125.00
Bitters, Drake's Plantation, 6 Log, Reddish Amber, W-111 .... 85.00
Bitters, Drake's Plantation, 6 Log, Scroll Design Around Lettering, Red 190.00
Bitters, Drake's Plantation, 6 Log, Whittled, Honey Amber, W-111 .... 48.00
Bitters, Drake's Plantation, 6 Log, 1862, Amber 85.00
Bitters, Durand's Stomach, Ohio, 4 Indented Panels, C.1900, 7 1/2 In. 30.00

Bitters, Fish, American,
19th Century
(See Page 35)

Bitters, Gentiana Root & Herb,
Seth E.Clapp, Aqua, 10 In
(See Page 35)

Bitters, E.A.Smith, M.D., Herb, Vt., Oval, Embossed, Label, Aqua, 9 1/2 In. 35.00
   Bitters, Ear of Corn, see Bitters, National, Ear of Corn
   Bitters, Electric, see Bitters, H.E.Bucklen
Bitters, Erso Anti-Bilious, Pa., C.1906, Rectangular, Label, 8 1/4 In. 30.00
Bitters, Feinster Stuttgarter Magen, 10 1/2 In. ....*Color* 90.00
Bitters, Ferro-China Bisleri, Milano 4.00
   Bitters, Fish, see also Bitters, Dr.Fisch
Bitters, Fish, ABM, Amber, 10 In. 3.00
Bitters, Fish, American, 19th Century ....*Illus* 350.00
Bitters, Fish, Honey Amber, 11 1/2 In., W-125 .... 150.00
Bitters, Fish, W.H.Ware, Amber, 11 1/2 In., W-125 .... 40.00 To 100.00
Bitters, Gentiana Root & Herb, Boston, Litthauer Shape, Stain, Aqua, 10 In. 110.00
Bitters, Gentiana Root & Herb, Seth E.Clapp, Aqua, 10 In ....*Illus* 125.00
Bitters, Geo.Benz & Sons Appetine, Minn., Amber, 8 In., W-383 .... 350.00
Bitters, Geo.Benz & Sons Appetine, Minn., Nov.23, 1897, 3 1/2 In., W-383 .... 250.00
Bitters, Geo.Benz & Sons Appetine, Minn., Scrollwork, Black Amethyst, 8 In. 450.00
Bitters, Geo.Benz & Sons Appetine, Minn., 8 1/2 In. ....*Color* XXXX.XX
Bitters, Germania Peppermint Schnapps, Bimal, 6 Sided, Quart 18.00
Bitters, Gilka, Green, Quart 25.00
Bitters, Goff's Herb, Camden, N.J., Embossed, Aqua, 7 1/2 In., W-137 .... 22.00
Bitters, Gold Lion Celery, Whiskey Shape, Label, 6 In., W-L-54 .... 15.00
Bitters, Golden, Hubbel & Co., Cabin Shape, Aqua, W-L-190 .... 50.00
Bitters, Goofland's German, 9 In. 35.00
Bitters, Greeley's Bourbon Whiskey, Barrel, Dark Amethyst, W-145 .... 525.00
Bitters, Greeley's Bourbon Whiskey, Barrel, Light Olive Green, W-145 .... 425.00
Bitters, Greeley's Bourbon Whiskey, Barrel, Rose Pink, W-145 .... 400.00
Bitters, Greer's Eclipse, Ky., 4 Flat Panels, Embossed, Amber, 9 In., W-147 .... 63.50
Bitters, H.E.Bucklen Electric Brand, ABM, 8 3/4 In., W-115 .... 20.00
Bitters, H.E.Bucklen & Co. Electric, Amber, 8 1/2 In. ....*Illus* 25.00

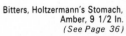

Bitters, H.E.Bucklen & Co. Electric, Amber, 8 1/2 In.

Bitters, Holtzermann's Stomach,
Amber, 9 1/2 In.
(See Page 36)

Bitters, H.E.Bucklen Electric Brand, 10 In. ....*Color* 24.00
Bitters, H.H.Warner & Co., Tippecanoe, Amber, 8 3/4 In. .... 52.50 To 90.00
Bitters, H.P.Herb Wild Cherry, Cabin, Variant, Amber, 9 In., W-148 .... 250.00
Bitters, H.U.A. On Base, Lady's Leg, Amber, 12 1/4 In. .... 12.50 To 15.00
Bitters, H.U.A., Lady's Leg, Crooked Neck, Red Amber, 12 1/4 In. 30.00
Bitters, Hansard's Genuine Hop, Swansea & Llanelly, Pottery, Tan, 8 In. 60.00
Bitters, Hartwig Kantorowicz Nachfolger Berlin, 6 Sided, Amber, 12 In. 50.00

Bitters, Hartwig Kantorowicz, Embossed Pine Trees & Sun, 13 1/2 In. 65.00
Bitters, Hartwig Kantorowicz, Embossed, Labels, Milk Glass, 3 1/4 In. 300.00
Bitters, Hartwig Kantorowicz, Green 165.00
Bitters, Hartwig Kantorowicz, Milk Glass, 4 1/8 In. 275.00
Bitters, Hartwig Kantorowicz, Milk Glass, 9 In. .... 47.50 To 125.00
Bitters, Hentz's Curative, Free Sample, Square, Bimal, Dug, 3 In. 25.00
Bitters, Hentz's Curative, Free Sample, 4 1/4 In. 38.00
Bitters, Holtzermann's Patent Stomach, Log Cabin, Amber, 9 3/4 In., W-172 .... 145.00
Bitters, Holtzermann's Stomach, Amber, 9 1/2 In. ....*Illus* 140.00
Bitters, Holtzermann's Stomach, Labels, Contents, W-172 .... 145.00
Bitters, Holtzermann's, 2 Roofer Cabin, Golden Amber 550.00
   Bitters, Hostetter's, see Bitters, Dr. J. Hostetter
   Bitters, Hubbel & Co., see Bitters, Golden
Bitters, Hufeland Original Swiss Stomach Tonic, Calif., Label, 9 1/2 In. 30.00
Bitters, Imperial Kidney & Liver, 9 1/2 In. ....*Illus* 125.00
   Bitters, Indian Restorative, see Bitters, Dr.Geo.Pierce
Bitters, Indian Sagwa, Embossed Indian, Rectangular, 9 In. 8.50
Bitters, Inspector Braesig Stomach, Adolf Prince, N.Y., 9 3/4 In., W-L-195 .... 50.00
Bitters, J.G.B.Siegert & Sons Angostura, Stain, Green, Miniature 4.00
Bitters, Jackman, Carnival, Pint 16.00
Bitters, Jean Marie Farina, 333 Ruest Honore Embossed, 1865, Barrel, Clear 30.00
Bitters, John Roots, 10 1/2 In. ....*Color* 325.00
Bitters, John Steele's Niagara Star, Amber, 10 In., W-316 .... 185.00
Bitters, Johnson's Calisaya, Vt., 10 1/2 In. ....*Color* 75.00
Bitters, Jos.Triner's, ABM, Sample Size 13.50
Bitters, Kaiser Wilhelm Co., Sanducky, O., Squat, Amber, 10 In., W-197 .... 35.00
Bitters, Kaiser Wilhelm, Pontil, W-197 .... 52.50
Bitters, Kelly's Old Cabin, Patent 1863, 9 In., W-199 ....*Color* 595.00
Bitters, Keystone, Amber, 11 1/2 In., W-201 ....*Illus* 365.00

Bitters, Keystone, Amber, 11 1/2 In., W-201

Bitters, Imperial Kidney & Liver, 9 1/2 In.

Bitters, Kidney Shape, Applied Lip, Brown, 8 1/2 In. 20.00
Bitters, King Solomon's, Amber, 8 1/2 In., W-457 .... 75.00
Bitters, King Solomon's, 7 1/4 In. 60.00
Bitters, Lady's Leg, Amber, 13 In. 35.00
Bitters, Lady's Leg, Inside Stain, Amber, 12 1/2 In. 25.00

Bitters, Lady's Leg, Long Neck, Dark Amber, 12 1/4 In. 40.00
Bitters, Lady's Leg, Unembossed, Amber, 13 In. 35.00
Bitters, Langley's, Embossed Vertically, Bimal, 5 In. 25.00
Bitters, Langley's, 99 Union St., Bimal, 7 In. 27.00
Bitters, Lash's Kidney & Liver, Square, Amber, 9 1/4 In., W-208 .... 7.50
Bitters, Lash's Natural Tonic Laxative, Label, ABM, Amber, 9 1/2 In., W-207 .... 8.65
Bitters, Lash's Natural Tonic Laxative, Sample, 5 In. ....Color 135.00
Bitters, Lash's, Labeled Hill's Irish Moss, Oval, Quart 15.00
Bitters, Litthauer Stomach, Milk Glass 125.00
   Bitters, Litthauer Stomach, see also Bitters, Hartwig Kantorowicz
Bitters, Liver, C M Co., N.Y. In Slug Plate, Oval, Bimal, Amber, 8 1/2 In. 34.95
Bitters, Loew's, Emerald Green, Miniature, W-217 .... 145.00
Bitters, Lynnboro, L.G.Co. On Base, Flask, Light Amber, Pint 27.00
Bitters, Mack's Sarsaparilla, Amber, 9 1/4 In., W-462 .... 300.00
   Bitters, Mandrake, see Bitters, Dr. Baxter's
Bitters, Marshall's, Amber, 8 3/4 In., W-227 .... 25.00 To 32.00
Bitters, Meredith's Celery With Pepsin, East Liverpool, O., Green, 10 In. 200.00
Bitters, Mishler's Herb, Bubbles, Amber, 8 3/4 In., W-229 .... 35.00 To 40.00
Bitters, Moulton's Oloroso, Embossed Pineapple, 5 Star, Aqua, 11 In., W-233 .... 350.00
Bitters, N.K.Brown, Iron & Quinine, Burlington, Vt., Embossed, Aqua 40.00
Bitters, N.K.Brown's Iron & Quinine, 4 Indented Panels, Label, 8 1/2 In. 25.00
Bitters, National, Ear Of Corn, Dark Amber, 12 1/2 In. ....Illus 225.00

Bitters, National, Ear Of Corn, Dark Amber, 12 1/2 In.

Bitters, National, Ear Of Corn, Lemon Color, W-236 .... 700.00
Bitters, New York Hop, Cloudy, Light Green, W-472 .... 200.00
Bitters, O.L.Darling's Indian Herb Zenic, C.1903, 8 1/4 In., W-L-174 .... 35.00
Bitters, Old Dr.Goodhue's Root & Herb, Aqua, 9 In., W-437 .... 55.00
Bitters, Old Home, Amber, 10 In., W-241 .... 175.00
Bitters, Old Homestead Wild Cherry, Amber, 10 In., W-242 .... 165.00
Bitters, Old Homestead Wild Cherry, Olive Green, 10 In., W-242 .... 550.00
Bitters, Old Sachem, Barrel, Honey Amber, 9 1/2 In., W-244 .... 190.00
Bitters, Old Sachem, Barrel, Puce, 9 1/2 In., W-244 .... 325.00
Bitters, Oscoda Herbal, Continental Products Co., Label, Amber, Quart 20.00
Bitters, Oscoda Herbal, Continental Products Co., Label, Amber, 9 1/2 In. 20.00
Bitters, Otto's, 6 In. 7.00
Bitters, Oxygenated For Dyspepsia, Etc., OP, Aqua, 7 1/2 In., W-249 .... 55.00
Bitters, Oxygenated, Rectangular, Aqua, 8 In., W-249 .... 40.00
Bitters, Penn's, For The Liver, Square, Amber, 6 1/2 In. 45.00
Bitters, Peruvian, Amber, 10 In., W-254 .... 25.00
Bitters, Peychaud's Aromatic Cocktail, Applied Top, Amber, 11 In. 35.00
Bitters, Peychaud's Aromatic Cocktail, Plastic Top, Label, Amber, 9 3/4 In. 12.00
Bitters, Peychaud's Bitter Cordial, Cylinder, Amber, Fifth 12.00
   Bitters, Pig, see Bitters, Berkshire, Bitters, Suffolk
Bitters, Pine Tree Tar Cordial, Green, Quart 55.00
Bitters, Pineapple, W.& Co., N.Y., Amber, 9 1/4 In. ....Illus 295.00
Bitters, Pineapple, 9 In. ....Color 250.00
Bitters, Polar Star, 4 In. 5.00
Bitters, Pond's Kidney & Liver, Amber, 9 3/4 In., W-487 .... 25.00
Bitters, Poor Man's Family, Aqua, 6 1/2 In., W-262 .... 25.00

Bitters, Porter's, 5 In. 5.00
Bitters, Porter's, 6 5/8 In. 5.00
Bitters, Professor Byrne Universal, Amber, 10 1/2 In., W-63 .... 600.00
    Bitters, Quaker, see Bitters, Dr. Flint's
Bitters, Ramsey's Trinidad, Embossed, Dark Green, W-268 .... 40.00
Bitters, Renault, Bimal, Sample, 3 3/4 In. 2.50
Bitters, Renault, Est. 1870, ABM, Contents, Amber, W-L-107 .... 5.95
Bitters, Renault, Est. 1870, Pewter Cap, ABM, Amber, W-L-107 .... 5.95 To 9.95
Bitters, Richardson's, S.O., Aqua, 6 1/2 In., W-275 .... 27.00
Bitters, Roback's Stomach, Barrel, IP, Medium Amber, W-280 .... 225.00
Bitters, Roback's Stomach, Barrel, Stain, 9 1/2 In. 50.00
Bitters, Romaine's Crimean, Light Yellow Amber, 10 In., W-282 .... 185.00
Bitters, Rothery's, The Great English Tonic, Rectangular, Amber, 8 In. 90.00
Bitters, Roxana Brand, Amber, 9 1/4 In., W-L-113 .... 30.00
Bitters, Royal Pepsin Stomach, Amber, Quart, 9 In., W-287 .... 75.00
Bitters, Royal Pepsin Stomach, Cork, Glass Stopper, Amber, Pint, W-287 .... 90.00
Bitters, Rush's, Amber, 9 In., W-289 .... 33.00 To 45.00
Bitters, Russ St.Domingo, Bubbly, Citron, W-290 .... 150.00
Bitters, S & S, Der Doktor, Haze, 1/5 Gallon 55.00
Bitters, S.Grover Braham's, 6 5/8 In. 8.00
    Bitters, S.T. Drake's, see Bitters, Drake's
Bitters, Sailing Ship Label Under Glass, Wicker Covered, Amber, Fifth 58.00
Bitters, Sanborn's Kidney & Liver, Amber, W-293 .... *Illus* 75.00

Bitters, Pineapple, W.& Co., N.Y., Amber, 9 1/4 In.
(See Page 37)

Bitters, Sanborn's Kidney & Liver, Amber, W-293

Bitters, Saxlehner's Bitterquelle Hunyadi Janos, Blob Lip, Emerald, 9 In. 2.50
Bitters, Saxlehner's Bitterquelle Hunyadi Janos, Whittled, 9 1/4 In. 2.95
Bitters, Saxlehner's Bitterquelle, Hunyadi Janos, Whittled, Green, 9 1/4 In. 2.95
Bitters, Sazerac, Wide Collar, Crude Lip, Milk Glass, 11 3/4 In., W-296 .... 385.00
Bitters, Schiedam Aromatic Schnapps, Deep Olive, Large Size 35.00
Bitters, Schroeder's, Established 1845, Dug, Amber, 5 1/16 In., W-297 .... 190.00
Bitters, Severa, Red Amber, 10 In., W-321 .... 35.00
Bitters, Shamrock, Round, Paper Label, 16 Ozs., 9 1/2 In. 30.00
Bitters, Similar To Doyle's Hop, Embossed Anchors, Square, Amber, 10 1/2 In. 80.00
Bitters, Sonny Stomach, Paper Label, Amber, Quart, W-L-119 .... 45.00
Bitters, Sonoma Wine, 1867, Applied Lip, Embossed, Amber, 9 1/2 In., W-L-120 .... 37.50
Bitters, Sonoma Wine, 1867, Mass., Embossed, Paper Label, Amber, 9 1/4 In. 37.50
Bitters, St.Goddard Herb, St.Louis, Mo., Stain, Bubbly, Amber 55.00
Bitters, Star Anchor, Portsmouth, Ohio, Embossed, Amber, W-499 .... 80.00
Bitters, Stonsdorfer, W.Koerner & Co., Tapered, Label, 11 In. 50.00
Bitters, Suffolk, Figural, Philbrook & Tucker, 10 In. .... *Color* 750.00
Bitters, Suffolk, Philbrook & Tucker, Boston, Pig, Canary Yellow, W-322 .... 850.00
    Bitters, Tippecanoe, see Bitters, H.H.Warner

Bitters, Toneco, Label, Contents, Pint, 8 Ozs., W-330 .... 35.00
Bitters, Tonic With Bitters On 3 Panels, 12 Panels, Bimal, Green, 7 1/2 In. 39.95
Bitters, Triner's American Elixir Of Bitter Wine, 9 In. ....*Illus* 5.00
Bitters, Tuft's Tonic, Rectangular, 3 Indented Panels, Aqua, 9 In., W-L-134 .... 35.00
Bitters, Turner's Modoc Indian, Calif., Paper Label, Amber, 8 1/2 In. 42.50
Bitters, Udolpho Wolfe's Aromatic Schnapps, Green, 8 In. ....*Illus* 18.00
Bitters, Udolpho Wolfe's Aromatic Schnapps, Purple Amber, Quart 17.00
Bitters, Udolpho Wolfe's Aromatic Schnapps, Square, Light Amber, 9 1/2 In. 5.00
Bitters, Udolpho Wolfe's Aromatic Schnapps, Stain, Olive Green, 8 In. 15.00
Bitters, Udolpho Wolfe's Schiedam Aromatic Schnapps, Green, 7 7/8 In. 35.00
Bitters, Underberg, Germany, Screw Top, Miniature, W-L-134 .... 3.00
Bitters, Underberg, Lady's Leg, Labels, Red Amber, 12 1/2 In. 25.00
Bitters, Underberg, Lady's Leg, Red Amber, 10 In. 8.00
Bitters, Vermont Saxe, Green, Quart 40.00
Bitters, Voldner's Aromatic, Schiedam Applied Lip, Olive, 9 1/2 In. 55.00
Bitters, Wakefield's Strengthening, Thin Glass, Aqua, 7 1/4 In., W-510 .... 75.00
   Bitters, Warner, see Bitters, H.H.Warner

Bitters, Triner's American Elixir Of Bitter Wine,
   9 In.

Bitters, Udolpho Wolfe's Aromatic Schnapps, Green, 8 In.

Bitters, White Enamel Bitters, Pewter Cap & Rim, Red, 6 In. 24.00
Bitters, Yerba Buena, Flask, Amber, W-375 .... 75.00 To 85.00
Bitters, Yerba Buena, San Francisco, No.2, Strap Sided, Amber, 9 1/2 In. 65.00
Bitters, Zadoc Porter Stomach, Label, Contents, Aqua, 5 1/4 In., W-L-101 .... 12.00
Black Amethyst, Cylindrical, Long Neck, Deep Kick Up, OP, 11 In. 40.00
Black Amethyst, Cylindrical, Pontil, Quart 9.00
Black Amethyst, Doneraile House, Blob Seal, 3 Mold, Graphite Pontil, Quart 55.00

Black Amethyst, Graphite Pontil, 8 1/4 In. 7.95
Black Amethyst, Seal, Embossed Ioii Vonpein, Quart 60.00
Black Amethyst, Seal, Quart 75.00
Black Amethyst, Van Denberg & Co., Blob Seal, 10 1/4 In. 40.00
Black Amethyst, 9 1/4 In. 5.95
Blown, Amber, 4 1/4 In.High 6.00
Blown, Barrel, Horizontal, Patent Mark, Aqua, 5 1/2 X 5 In. 105.00
Blown, Barrel, Upright, Threaded Top & Bottom, Blue Flecks, White, 6 In. 60.00
Blown, Bellows, Applied Clear Decoration, Cranberry, 8 1/4 In. 55.00
Blown, Bellows, Cambridge, Applied Rigaree, White Loopings, 5 1/4 In. 40.00
Blown, Bellows, Cambridge, Pink & White Looping, 12 1/2 In. 95.00
Blown, Bellows, New England, Applied Clear Decoration, Cobalt, 8 3/4 In. 45.00
Blown, Bellows, New England, Clear Decoration, Footed, Cranberry, 13 In. 55.00
Blown, Bellows, New England, Threading, Applied Rigaree, Vaseline, 10 In. 45.00
Blown, Bellows, New England, White Feather, Decoration, Burgundy, 9 In. 70.00
Blown, Bellows, New York State, Applied Decoration, Aqua, 8 1/2 In. 55.00
Blown, Bellows, New York State, Applied Rigaree, Aqua, 9 1/2 In. 45.00
Blown, Bimal, Embossed Monks In Each Of 6 Arches, Amber, Quart 60.00
Blown, Carboy, Free-Blown, Aqua, 24 X 17 In. 150.00
Blown, Cylindrical, Applied Amber Lip, Dark Green, 2 3/4 In. 17.00
Blown, Cylindrical, Blue Green, 9 1/2 In. 5.00
Blown, Cylindrical, Golden To Reddish Amber, 6 1/4 In. 12.50
Blown, Cylindrical, Tapering Neck, Deep Amber, 9 3/4 In. 65.00
Blown, Dark Olive Amber, 5 In. 30.00
Blown, Globular, Blue Green, 11 3/4 In. 35.00
Blown, Globular, Club Shape, Broken Swirl, Aqua, 8 3/4 In. 55.00
Blown, Globular, Flanged Lip, Deep Aqua, 6 1/2 In. 35.00
Blown, Globular, Flanged Lip, Yellow Green, 4 1/4 In. 25.00
Blown, Globular, Folded Over Lip, Flat Shoulders, Blue Green, 3 In. 100.00
Blown, Globular, Green, 8 In. 45.00
Blown, Globular, Green, 8 3/4 In. 20.00
Blown, Globular, Light Green, 7 1/2 In. 45.00
Blown, Globular, Yellow Olive, 10 In. 45.00
Blown, Globular, 12 Ribs, Long Neck, Deep Yellow Green, 8 In. 300.00
Blown, Globular, 24 Ribs Swirled To Left, IP, Yellow Green, 7 1/2 In. 700.00
Blown, Globular, 24 Swirled Ribs, Aqua, 7 1/4 In. 65.00
Blown, Globular, 25 Swirled Ribs, Aqua, 8 1/2 In. 75.00
Blown, Globular, 32 Vertical Ribs, Applied Handle, Aqua, 7 In. 150.00
Blown, Hand-Blown, Fancy Design, Ground Top, Cork, 7 Gallon 50.00
Blown, In Mold, Block On Stilts, Threaded Top, 5 1/2 In.High 15.00
Blown, Jar, Keene, Pontil, Olive Green, Gallon 75.00
Blown, Jug, Flattened Chestnut, Amber, 8 In. 50.00
Blown, Jug, Handled, Pontil, Dark Claret Black, Quart 35.00
Blown, Kick-Up, Laid-On Neck Ring, IP, Clear Olive Green, 12 In. 12.00
Blown, Ludlow, Deep Yellow Green, 9 1/2 In. 55.00
Blown, Mantua, Club Shape, 16 Vertical & 16 Swirled Ribs, Aqua, 8 In. 45.00
Blown, Midwestern, Club Shape, 16 Swirled Ribs, Aqua, 8 In. 55.00
Blown, Midwestern, Globular, Aqua, 9 In. 65.00
Blown, Midwestern, Globular, Light Green, 7 1/2 In. 55.00
Blown, Midwestern, 16 Vertical Ribs, Blue Green, 7 3/4 In. 65.00
Blown, New York State, 2 Mold, Rigaree Holds 2 Parts, Aqua, 5 1/2 In. 10.00
Blown, New York, Jar, Cylindrical, Green, 5 3/4 X 5 In. 20.00
Blown, Ohio, Club Shape, Broken Swirl, Aqua, 8 1/4 In. 60.00
Blown, Ohio, Club Shape, Broken Swirl, Aqua, 8 1/2 In. 50.00
Blown, Ohio, Flattened Globular, 24 Swirled Ribs, Aqua, 8 3/4 In. 60.00
Blown, R.Lenoc In Wafer, Round, Deep Olive Amber, 10 3/4 In. 30.00
Blown, Round, Olive Amber, 4 3/4 In. 10.00
Blown, Swirled, Yellow Amber, Pint 20.00
Blown, Taper Shape, C.1818, Translucent Blue, 15 1/2 In.High 85.00
Blown, Water, Bulbous, Polished Pontil, 8 1/2 In. 15.00
Blown, Whitney Glass Works, 3 Mold, Inside Screw, Embossed, Amber, 11 In. 25.00
Blown, 2 Mold, Crown Shape, Dark Amber, 8 In. 10.00
Blown, 2 Mold, Flattened Globular, Jug, Dark Amber, 7 In. 20.00
Blown, 2 Mold, Globular, Jug, IP, Olive Green, 6 In. 130.00
Blown, 2 Mold, 34 Ribs, Light Green, 9 In. 20.00

Blown, 3 Mold, Cylindrical, Patent On Shoulder, Olive Green, Quart	8.00
Blown, 3 Mold, Cylindrical, Patent On Shoulder, Orange Amber, Quart	10.00
Blown, 3 Mold, Pouring Lip, McKearin G II-6, 7 In.	65.00
Blown, 3 Mold, 2 Lip Rings, Bimal, IP, Black Amethyst, 10 In.	8.00
Blown, 3 Mold, 2 Lip Rings, Bimal, IP, Black Amethyst, 12 In.	9.00
Blown, 24 Swirled Ribs, Flaring Lip, Aqua, 6 5/8 In.	55.00
Blown, 1790-1810, Olive Green, Gallon	35.00
Bohemian Glass, Grape Pattern, Stopper, 16 In., Pair	120.00
Bohemian Glass, Red & Clear, 14 1/2 In., Pair	100.00
Bols, Ballerina	8.95
Bols, Delft Type, Blue & White, 8 In.	13.00
Bols, Pewter, 8 In.	20.00

Borghini ceramic containers are filled in Pisa, Italy. The more recent imports are stamped with the words "Borghini Collection Made in Italy, 1969."

Borghini, Alpine House	40.00
Borghini, Amber Hurricane Lamp	3.00
Borghini, Black Cat, 5 1/2 In.	3.25
Borghini, Black Stone	4.00
Borghini, Canary On Vase	3.00
Borghini, Clown	15.00
Borghini, Dog	15.00
Borghini, Firenze Ponte Vecchio Bridge	3.00
Borghini, Fish Scale, Black	3.00
Borghini, Fish Scale, White	3.00
Borghini, Giannotti Electric Lamp	4.00
Borghini, Gondola	3.00
Borghini, Horse's Head	12.00
Borghini, Looking Glass	4.00
Borghini, Masquarage Bookend, Female	2.50
Borghini, Masquarage Bookend, Male	2.50
Borghini, Roadster	3.00
Borghini, Roman Bridge	2.00
Borghini, Roman Bust, Female	2.00
Borghini, Roman Bust, Male	3.00
Borghini, Rooster	5.00
Borghini, Santa Maria	4.00
Borghini, Scotsmen	3.00
Borghini, Sedan Car	3.00
Borghini, Tiger On Vase	3.00
Borghini, Totem Pole	4.00
Borghini, Turtle	1.00
Bottles Beautiful, Bersaglieri, 17 In.	20.00
Bottles Beautiful, Butterflies	12.20
Bottles Beautiful, Centurion, 18 In.	20.00
Bottles Beautiful, Coffee Mill, 13 In.	30.00
Bottles Beautiful, Gardsltd, 17 1/2 In.	20.00
Bottles Beautiful, Gramaphone, 10 In.	13.00
Bottles Beautiful, Hen, 12 In.	20.00
Bottles Beautiful, Hurdy-Gurdy, 13 In.	30.00
Bottles Beautiful, Napoleon, 17 1/4 In.	20.00
Bottles Beautiful, Rooster, 15 In.	20.00
Bottles Beautiful, Scales, 13 In.	30.00
Bottles Beautiful, Sewing Machine, 10 In.	13.00
Bottles Beautiful, Telephone, French, 1969	13.00
Brandy, Apricot, Button Amphora, Silver Metal Trimmed, 5 In.	9.95
Brandy, Blackberry, Back Bar, Paste Mold, Crooked Neck, Enamel, Quart	11.00
Brandy, Cherry, Button Amphora, Silver Metal Trimmed, 5 In.	9.95
Brandy, Crescent, Round, Yellow Brown, 10 In.	17.00
Brandy, Courvoisier, Cannon On Black Plastic Carriage, 2 1/2 In.	4.50
Brandy, Cusenier, Lady's Leg Neck, Whittled, Collared Lip, Olive Green, 7 In.	9.00
Brandy, Peach, Double Collar, Label, Olive Amber, Quart	10.00
Brandy, Savvion, T.F.Freeman & Co., Mass., Straight Sided, Pint	7.00
Bronte, Jug, Large	12.00

Brooks, see Ezra Brooks
Burgermeister, Burgie Man, Ceramic, 10 1/2 In. 60.00
Burgermeister, Ceramic Bottle, 1972 .... 7.00
    C.P.C., California Perfume Company, see Avon
    Cabin Still, see Old Fitzgerald
    Calabash, see Flask
Cameo, Daum Nancy, Berries & Leaves, Gold Enamel, C.1900, Blue, 3 In. 150.00
Cameo, Daum Nancy, Berries & Leaves, Gold Enamel, C.1900, Green, 3 In. 100.00
Cameo, Lalique, Snail Design, Nude Kneeling Girl Stopper, Frosted, 4 In. 235.00
Cameo, Webb, White Floral On Red, Silver Top, 2 In. 215.00
Camphor Glass, Cut Design, 6 In.High 30.00
Canadian Mist, Mounted Policeman 8.00

Candy containers of glass were very popular after World War I. Small
glass figural bottles held dime-store candy. Today many of the same shapes
hold modern candy in plastic bottles.
Candy Container, Airplane 14.00
Candy Container, Airplane, Army Bomber 15-P-7 .... 14.00
Candy Container, Airplane, Spirit Of Good Will, Pilot 36.00
Candy Container, Alarm Clock 1.00
Candy Container, Army Bomber, Embossed, Paper Closure, Candy 17.50
Candy Container, Army Jeep, Embossed, Paper Closure, Candy 17.50
Candy Container, Army Tank 10.50
Candy Container, Automobile 15.00
Candy Container, Baby Carriage, Tin Top Slides Back 19.00
Candy Container, Baby Chick 37.50
Candy Container, Barney Google And Ball 60.00
Candy Container, Barrel 3.00
Candy Container, Battleship 8.00
Candy Container, Bear 4.00
Candy Container, Bear, Labels, Black 60.00
Candy Container, Bell 18.00
Candy Container, Bell, Red Cross, 2 1/4 In. 6.00
Candy Container, Billiken, Patented, Screw Top, 4 In. ....*Color* 45.00
Candy Container, Billy Club 25.00
Candy Container, Bomber, J.H.Millstein Co., 4 In. 18.00
Candy Container, Boot, Large Size 5.00
Candy Container, Boot, Small Size 3.00
Candy Container, Bulldog .... 15.00 To 25.00
Candy Container, Bulldog, Screw Opening In Base 20.00
Candy Container, Bulldog, Sitting, Painted 28.00
Candy Container, Bulldog, Sitting, Tin Cover, Black Paint 14.00
Candy Container, Buster Brown, Hat Shaker 12.00
Candy Container, Car, Chip, Bright Blue, 5 In. ....*Illus* 28.00
Candy Container, Cat, 2 X 4 In. ....*Color* 50.00
Candy Container, Chamberstick 5.50
Candy Container, Charlie Chaplin .... 34.00 To 42.00
Candy Container, Charlie Chaplin, Tin Closure Slotted For Bank 55.00
Candy Container, Chick, 3 1/2 In. ....*Illus* 48.00
Candy Container, Chicken On A Nest, 5 In.Long 8.00
Candy Container, Chicken On Nest, Marked Millstein, 4 1/2 In. .... 8.00 To 9.00
Candy Container, Chicken, Large Size 6.00

Candy Container, Car, Chip, Bright Blue, 5 In.

Candy Container, Clock	15.00
Candy Container, Clown	3.00
Candy Container, Clown Dog	4.25
Candy Container, Country Store, Wide Mouth, Stoppered, 12 In.	10.00
Candy Container, Cruiser	10.50
Candy Container, Dog	4.00 To 6.00
Candy Container, Dog, Brass Top, Manor Frepes, 5 In.	12.50
Candy Container, Dog, Open Top	7.00
Candy Container, Dog, Sitting	6.00
Candy Container, Dog, Sitting, Cobalt	8.50
Candy Container, Duck	20.00
Candy Container, Ducks, Swimming	25.00
Candy Container, Ear Of Corn	15.00
Candy Container, Felix The Cat, 5 In. .... *Illus*	37.50
Candy Container, Fire Engine	10.00 To 30.00
Candy Container, Fire Engine Ladder Truck	12.50
Candy Container, Fire Engine, 5 1/2 In. .... *Illus*	30.00
Candy Container, Fire Truck, Dept.1	9.50
Candy Container, Fire Truck, Victory Glass Co., 5 In.	18.00
Candy Container, Gun, Ground Top, Amber	27.00
Candy Container, Hat, Military	9.00
Candy Container, Hen On Nest	6.50 To 10.00
Candy Container, Hen On Nest, Bottom Opening, 5 In.	12.50
Candy Container, Horn	22.00
Candy Container, Horn, Three Valve With Tin Whistle	75.00
Candy Container, Horse & Cart	7.50 To 12.50
Candy Container, Hot Doggie	100.00
Candy Container, Hound Dog, Screw Top, 2 1/2 In.High	4.00
Candy Container, Iron Horse Train	12.00
Candy Container, Iron, 4 1/2 In. .... *Illus*	25.00

Candy Container, Fire Engine, 5 1/2 In.

Candy Container, Felix The Cat, 5 In.

Candy Container, Chick, 3 1/2 In.
(See Page 42)

Candy Container,
Iron, 4 1/2 In.

Candy Container, Kewpie At Barrel 37.50
Candy Container, Kolt 15.00
Candy Container, Lamp, Miniature 10.00
Candy Container, Lantern .... 8.00 To 12.00
Candy Container, Lantern, Black Tin Top 10.00
Candy Container, Lantern, Electric, Bond Playmate, Jersey City, N.J. 15.00
Candy Container, Lantern, Flint Globe 20.00
Candy Container, Lantern, Green & Red Metal Lid, T.H.Stough, Jeanette, Pa. 12.00
Candy Container, Lantern, Railroad 10.00
Candy Container, Lantern, Ribbed Globe, Marked 14.00
Candy Container, Lantern, Tin Top 18.00
Candy Container, Lantern, Tin Top, Bottom, & Handle .... 4.75 To 9.00
Candy Container, Learned Fox 45.00
Candy Container, Liberty Bell, Pale Green 18.50
Candy Container, Liberty Bell, 3 1/2 In. .... *Illus* 25.00
Candy Container, Lighthouse, 5 1/2 In. 10.00
Candy Container, Locomotive .... 6.00 To 10.00
Candy Container, Locomotive, 5 In. 8.50
Candy Container, Madonna, Handle, Closure, Cobalt 37.50
Candy Container, Monkey 15.00
Candy Container, Monkey, Screw Cap, 5 In. .... *Illus* 50.00

Candy Container, Liberty Bell, 3 1/2 In.

Candy Container, Monkey,
Screw Cap, 5 In.

Candy Container, Moses, Glass Stopper 30.00
Candy Container, Motorboat, Clear 4.95
Candy Container, Mug, Child's 4.50
Candy Container, Mug, Drum 19.00
Candy Container, Mug, Necco Sweets, 2 1/8 X 1 1/2 In. 22.50
Candy Container, Nursing Bottle, Nipple, 3 In.High 4.00
Candy Container, Nursing Bottle, Wooden Nipple 15.00
Candy Container, P.T.Boat 9.50
Candy Container, Peasant, Signed M.G.Husted, Labels 62.00
Candy Container, Piano, Glass Cover 20.00
Candy Container, Pig 4.00
Candy Container, Pistol .... 9.00 To 15.00
Candy Container, Pistol, Amber 20.00
Candy Container, Pistol, 7 1/2 In. 9.95
Candy Container, Pony Pulling Cart 6.50
Candy Container, Queen Elizabeth 8.00
Candy Container, Rabbit 30.00
Candy Container, Rabbit Eating Carrot, 4 1/2 In. .... 7.50 To 12.00
Candy Container, Rabbit Family 27.50

Candy Container, Rabbit In Egg	25.00
Candy Container, Rabbit, J.H.Millstein Co., 6 1/2 In.	18.00
Candy Container, Rabbit, Sitting, Millstein Co., Pa., Patent	6.00 To 9.00
Candy Container, Rabbit, Sitting, 6 1/2 In.	20.00
Candy Container, Railroad Engine, Covered, Clear, 6 In.Long	89.50
Candy Container, Revolver, Amber	11.00
Candy Container, Revolver, Cap, 7 1/2 In.	12.00
Candy Container, Revolver, Checkered Grip, Tin Cap, 8 In.Long	35.00
Candy Container, Revolver, Pair	13.00
Candy Container, Revolver, Round Butt, Tin Cover, 6 1/2 In.	10.00
Candy Container, Sad Dog, Geneva, O.	5.00
Candy Container, Sadiron	20.00
Candy Container, Sailboat, Ground Top	20.00
Candy Container, Santa Claus	15.00 To 25.00
Candy Container, Santa Claus At Chimney, Closure	27.50
Candy Container, Santa Claus Leaving Chimney	55.00
Candy Container, Santa Claus, Labels	62.00
Candy Container, Santa Claus, Screw Closure	28.00
Candy Container, Santa Claus, Screw-On Lid	25.00
Candy Container, Santa Claus, 2 1/2 In. _Illus_	50.00
Candy Container, Santa, Plastic Head	20.00
Candy Container, Santa's Boot	4.00 To 6.00
Candy Container, Scottie Dog _Illus_	18.00
Candy Container, Scottie Dog, Head Opens, 3 1/4 In.	7.00
Candy Container, Scottie Dog, Standing	12.50

Candy Container, Santa Claus, 2 1/2 In.

Candy Container, Scottie Dog

Candy Container, Scottie, 4 In.	8.00
Candy Container, Sedan With 6 Vents, Yellow Paint	40.00
Candy Container, Soldier, Embossed, Glass Hat, Frosted	175.00
Candy Container, Spark Plug, Painted	38.00
Candy Container, Speedboat	6.00 To 9.00
Candy Container, Station Wagon, 4 1/2 In. _Illus_	7.50
Candy Container, Steer's Horn, Ground Top, Tin Screw Cover, 4 1/2 In.	10.00
Candy Container, Suitcase	12.00 To 23.00
Candy Container, Suitcase, Decal Victorian Ladies & Man, Milk Glass	35.00
Candy Container, Suitcase, Milk Glass, Clear & Decal Victorian Scene	40.00
Candy Container, Suitcase, Tin Closure	17.50
Candy Container, Suitcase, Tin Closure, Metal Handle	12.50 To 16.00
Candy Container, Suitcase, 3 1/2 In. _Illus_	30.00

Candy Container, Station Wagon, 4 1/2 In.
(See Page 45)

Candy Container, Suitcase, 3 1/2 In.
(See Page 45)

Candy Container, Tank, Victory Glass Co., 4 In.	18.00
Candy Container, Telephone	1.75
Candy Container, Telephone Base	4.50
Candy Container, Telephone, Desk, Contents	12.50
Candy Container, Telephone, French	6.50
Candy Container, Telephone, Metal Receiver Over Screw Top, 1 3/4 In.High	4.00
Candy Container, Telephone, Upright, 7 In. .... *Illus*	15.00
Candy Container, Telephone, 4 3/4 In. .... *Illus*	8.00
Candy Container, Three Ducks, 6 In. .... *Illus*	42.50
Candy Container, Three Naked Children, Germany	75.00
Candy Container, Tot Telephone, 2 1/2 In. .... *Color*	22.50
Candy Container, Train	40.00
Candy Container, Train, 4 1/2 In.Long .... *Illus*	15.00
Candy Container, Turkey	15.00
Candy Container, Twins On Anchor	12.75
Candy Container, Wash Tub, Mary Louise Stanley	4.50
Candy Container, Washington's Bust, Screw Closure, Cobalt	12.00
Candy Container, Willy's Jeep .... *Illus*	10.00
Candy Container, Windmill, Tin Bottom & Windmill Arms, 4 3/4 In.High	10.00
Canning Jar, see Fruit Jar	
Cartridges, The Cartridge Box, Cobalt, 6 In. .... *Illus*	45.00

*Case bottles are those of the traditional shape known by this name. The
bottles have flat sides and are almost square. Some taper and are narrower
at the bottom. Case bottles can be of any age from the mid-1600s to the
present day.*

Case Gin, AH In Applied Seal, Polished Pontil, Black Amethyst, 11 1/2 In.	65.00
Case Gin, Blankenheym	18.00
Case Gin, Daniel Visser & Zonen Schiedam, Sealed, Bimal, Dark Green	69.00
Case Gin, Deep Olive Green, Quart	4.50
Case Gin, E.Kiderlen, Dark Green, 9 3/4 In.	22.00
Case Gin, Flare Lip, OP, Dark Olive	24.00
Case Gin, Free-Blown, Flared Lip, Light Olive Green, 9 1/2 In.	39.50
Case Gin, HDB & C, Applied Seal, 8 In.	55.00
Case Gin, Knickerbocker Gin Company, N.Y., Dark Teal, 5 3/4 In.	90.00
Case Gin, Meder & Zoon, W.P., Embossed Swan, 9 In.High	50.00
Case Gin, Olive Green, OP, Quart	45.00
Case Gin, Olive Green, 1/2 Pint	12.00
Case Gin, Olive Green, Pint	8.00
Case Gin, P.Hoppe Schiedam, Sealed, Yellow Green	49.50
Case Gin, Pynchon, Boston, Pontil, 4 3/4 In.	12.00
Case Gin, Rolled Flare Lip, Satiny, Green	8.00

Candy Container, Telephone, Upright, 7 In.
(See Page 46)

Candy Container, Telephone, 4 3/4 In.
(See Page 46)

Candy Container, Three Ducks, 6 In.
(See Page 46)

Candy Container, Train, 4 1/2 In.Long
(See Page 46)

Case Gin, Shingle, Green, 8 1/2 In.	8.00
Case Gin, Stain, Olive Green, 4 In.	27.00
Case Gin, V.Marken & Co., Bimal, 10 In.	27.50
Case Gin, Vandenbergh & Co., Flared Lip, Sealed, Olive Green	42.50
Case Gin, Whittled, Dark Olive Green, 11 In.	15.00
Case Gin, Whittled Effect, Green, 11 In.	7.00
Case, Blown, Amelung Type, Flint, Gilt Decoration, Pontil, 7 In.	35.00
Case, Blown, Cut Decoration, 9 3/4 In.	20.00
Case, Gold Decoration, OP, 1/2 Pint	9.00
Case, OP, Quart	5.00

Candy Container, Willy's Jeep
(See Page 46)

Castor, Inverted Thumbprint, Cranberry Glass	6.50
Castor, Inverted Thumbprint, Vaseline	6.50
Castor, Pressed Glass, Etched Grape & Fern Band	4.50
Castor, Pressed, Bellflower, Double Lip	32.50
Chemical, B.F.Goodrich Vulcanizing Solution, Akron, Ohio, Amber, 6 1/2 In.	8.00
Chemical, Bucine, Iron City, Pittsburgh, Bimal, Aqua, 7 In.	4.00
Chemical, C.W.Merchant, Chemist, Lockport, N.Y., Cylindrical, Green, 7 In.	60.00
Chemical, Celery Phos., Fo Gotham Co., N.Y.C., Cobalt, 4 1/4 In.	5.00
Chemical, Chas.H.Phillip's Co., N.Y., Aqua, 4 X 10 In.	5.00
Chemical, E.F.Bacheller Photographic Supplies, 6 Sided, Amber, 5 1/2 In.	5.50
Chemical, Elysian Mfg.Co., Detroit, Rectangular, Cobalt, 5 1/4 In.	8.00
Chemical, G.W.Merchant, Chemist, From The Lab Of, 5 1/2 In.	45.00
Chemical, G.W.Merchant, Chemist, Pint	45.00
Chemical, H.E.Geman Co., Chemists, Aqua, 10 1/2 In.	10.00
Chemical, Hageman & Co., Chemists, New York, Rectangular, Aqua, 10 In.	10.00
Chemical, Keasbey & Mattison, Phila., Rectangular, Cobalt, 5 In.	5.00
Chemical, Maltine Mfg.Co., Chemist, N.Y., Bimal, Amber, 7 1/4 In.	1.25
Chemical, Oval, Corker, 9 In.	.75
Chemical, Rumford Chemical Works, Green, 6 In.	7.50
Chemical, Rumford Chemical Works, Teal Blue, 5 3/4 In.	3.00
Chemical, Rumford Chemical Works, 8 Sided, Teal Green, 5 1/2 In.	5.00
Chemical, Rumford, Embossed Bottom, Patent March 10, 1868, OP, Aqua, 8 In.	15.00
Chemical, Rumford, Turquoise, 8 In.	7.00
Chemical, Rumford, 8 Sided, Blue Green, 7 1/4 In.	7.00
Chemical, Undertaker's Supply, Chicago, Ill., Tin Cap, Measurements, 8 In.	2.00
Chemical, Winchester Hypophosphite Of Manganese, Aqua, 6 3/4 In.	5.00
Chemical, Woodward, Nottingham, Bimal, Cobalt, 6 1/4 In.	18.00
Clevenger Bros.Glass Works, Christmas 1973, St.Nick, 1st Issue	15.00
Clevenger Bros.Glass Works, Christmas 1974	8.00
Clevenger Bros.Glass Works, Jug, Grapes & Eagle, Clayton, N.Y., Green, Quart	15.00
Cobalt Blue, Bottle, Dutch, 9 In.High	3.00

*Coca-Cola was first made in 1886. Since that time the drink has been
sold in all parts of the world in a variety of bottles. The "waisted" bottle
was first used in 1916.*

Coca-Cola, Amber		9.00
Coca-Cola, Amber, 1916, Paper Label	*Illus*	30.00
Coca-Cola, Arabic, 1960s	*Illus*	2.00
Coca-Cola, Avon Park, Fla., Dated Nov.1923		3.75
Coca-Cola, Biedenharn, 1900, Paper Label	*Illus*	30.00
Coca-Cola, Bottle, Seltzer, Etched, Uniontown, Green		45.00
Coca-Cola, Bottle, Square		2.50
Coca-Cola, C On Bottom, Machine Made, Aqua, 2 1/2 In.		5.00
Coca-Cola, Centennial Turkey Trot, 1872-1972		2.50
Coca-Cola, Cleveland, Double Arrow, Bimal, Amber		8.00
Coca-Cola, Dispenser, Fountain, 1920, 10 1/2 In.		15.00
Coca-Cola, Donald Duck, Pictures On Both Sides, 7 Ozs.		3.00
Coca-Cola, Embossed Indian Head Profile, Casco, Pat.12/29/25, Me., Aqua		50.00
Coca-Cola, Embossed On Bottom, 9 1/2 In.		1.00
Coca-Cola, Filled & Capped, 2 1/2 In.		1.50
Coca-Cola, Filled & Capped, 3 In.		1.50
Coca-Cola, Hutchinson, 1899, Birmingham	*Illus*	95.00

Left to Right:
Coca-Cola, Hutchinson, 1899,
Birmingham *(See Page 48)*
Coca-Cola, Biedenharn, 1900,
Paper Label *(See Page 48)*
Coca-Cola, Tampa, Florida,
Paper Label
Coca-Cola, Amber, 1916,
Paper Label *(See Page 48)*

Cartridges, The Cartridge Box, Cobalt, 6 In.
(See Page 46)

Coca-Cola, Arabic, 1960s
(See Page 48)

Cologne, Figural,
Boy, 4 1/2 In.
(See Page 51)

Cologne, Bunker Hill Monument, 6 1/2 In.
(See Page 50)

Coca-Cola, **Made In Mexico,** Script On 2 Sides, Weighs 7 Pounds	20.00
Coca-Cola, **Miniature,** Marked Coca-Cola On 2 Sides, Capped, 3 In.High	.75
Coca-Cola, **Patent Dec.25,** 1923, Covington, Tenn. X-Fine On Bottom, 6 Ozs.	3.50
Coca-Cola, **Patent Nov.16,** 1915, Lexington, Tenn. X-Nice On Bottom, 6 Ozs.	3.00
Coca-Cola, **Perfume,** Glass Top, 3 In.	15.00
Coca-Cola, **Plastic,** 1 1/2 In.	.12
Coca-Cola, **Plastic,** 24 In Red Plastic Case, 1 5/8 In.	5.00
Coca-Cola, **Script,** Straight Sided, Green	2.95
Coca-Cola, **Seltzer,** Winona, Minn. ....*Color*	35.00
Coca-Cola, **Soda Water,** Square	2.00
Coca-Cola, **Soda Water,** 4 Square Panels, 6 Stars, Dated Nov.27, 1923, Green	3.75
Coca-Cola, **St.Louis,** Aqua	4.00
Coca-Cola, **Straight Sided,** Aqua	7.50
Coca-Cola, **Straight Sided,** C.1905, 6 1/2 Ozs.	3.75
Coca-Cola, **Tampa,** Florida, Paper Label ....*Illus*	25.00
Coca-Cola, **To Promote King Size Coke In Mexico,** White Script, 20 In.	20.00
Coca-Cola, **Uncle Sam,** Square, Green, 6 Oz.	10.00
Coca-Cola, **World War I,** Dated Nov.16, 1915	4.50

Coca-Cola, 12 Embossed & 12 White Script, Wooden Case, 24 .... 18.00
Collector's Art, Blue Jay .... 12.95 To 20.00
Collector's Art, Bluebird .... *Illus* 25.00
Collector's Art, Canary .... *Illus* 17.00
Collector's Art, Cardinal .... 11.50 To 17.00
Collector's Art, Chipmunks 12.95
Collector's Art, Goldfinch 12.95
Collector's Art, Hummingbird 17.00
Collector's Art, Koala Bear .... 12.95 To 20.00
Collector's Art, Meadowlark .... *Illus* 25.00

Collector's Art, Bluebird   Collector's Art, Meadowlark   Collector's Art, Canary

Collector's Art, Parakeet .... 11.50 To 17.00
Collector's Art, Rabbits 12.95
Collector's Art, Robin 12.95
   Cologne, see also Perfume, Toilet Water
Cologne, Aurene, Amphora Shape, Peacock Blue Iridescent, Stopper, 2 1/2 In. 450.00
Cologne, Baccarat, Amber Swirl, 5 1/2 In. 18.50
Cologne, Baccarat, Amberina Swirl, Stopper, 5 3/4 In.High 25.00
Cologne, Baccarat, Enameled Floral & Leaf, Clear Swirl, 7 In. 25.00
Cologne, Baccarat, Gold Star On Top, Gold Leaf, Pinecones Center, 9 1/2 In. 49.50
Cologne, Baccarat, Lacy, Pink, 5 In. 12.50
Cologne, Baccarat, Lacy, Pink, 6 In. 15.00
Cologne, Baccarat, Swirled, Ruby To Clear, 6 3/4 In. 25.00
Cologne, Baroque, Flat Lipped Top, McKearin 243-14, 5 In. 40.00
Cologne, Basket Of Flowers, OP, Aqua, 4 1/4 In. 55.00
Cologne, Beaded, Ribbed, 5 3/4 In. 35.00
Cologne, Beaded, Ribbed, 8 In. 40.00
Cologne, Blown In Mold, Floral Compotes In Panels, McKearin 243-14 .... 30.00
Cologne, Blown In Mold, Similar To McKearin 244-3, Aqua, 5 1/2 In. 45.00
Cologne, Blown Stopper, Floral & Bird, Gilt, Black Amethyst, 9 1/2 In. 50.00
Cologne, Blown, Boot Shape, Lace & Tie Front, Cork Stopper, Clear, 3 1/4 In. 25.00
Cologne, Boston & Sandwich Glass Co., Gold Trim, Opaque Jade, 5 3/8 In. 150.00
Cologne, Bristol, Bulbous Base, Thumbprint Stopper, White, 7 In. High, Pair 35.00
Cologne, Bunker Hill Monument, 6 1/2 In. .... *Illus* 37.00
Cologne, Cameo, Silver Fittings, Blue To White To Clear, 4 3/4 In. 40.00
Cologne, Cathedral, Madonna & Child, OP, Aqua, 5 3/4 In. 65.00
Cologne, Cathedral, Pontil, 5 1/2 In. 68.00
Cologne, Cut Glass, Geometrics, 6 In. 25.00
Cologne, Cut Glass, Hawkes, Gravic, Carnation, Sterling Top, 6 1/4 In. 120.00
Cologne, Cut Glass, Hobstar, Fan, & Crosshatching, Hobstar Base, 6 1/2 In. 65.00
Cologne, Cut Pineapple & Fan, Cut Crystal Stopper, Rubina, 7 1/2 In. 25.00
Cologne, Cylindrical, Tapering Neck, Opaque Light Blue, 8 3/4 In. 160.00

Cologne, **Dancing Nudes On 6 Panels,** Ground Stopper, Frosted, 5 1/4 In. 35.00
Cologne, **Diamond Shape,** Embossed Indians, McKearin 244-5, Pale Green 75.00
Cologne, **Diamonds,** Ruby Flashed To Clear, 7 1/4 In. 15.00
Cologne, **Eagle & Columns,** "Juiliet/1830", Fiery Opalescent, 5 1/2 In. 270.00
Cologne, **Eau De Cologne,** W.E.Armstrong, Pewter Lid, Paper Label, Tapered 9.00
Cologne, **Embossed Man In Doorway,** Aqua, 3 In. 35.00
Cologne, **Figural,** Boy, 4 1/2 In. ....*Illus* 65.00
Cologne, **Figural,** Cucumber, Green, 4 1/2 In. 35.00
Cologne, **Figural,** Man, Pontil, 7 3/4 In. 62.00
Cologne, **Figural,** Woman's Shoe, C.1880, 4 1/2 In. 38.00
Cologne, **Flint,** Lions On 4 Corners, Seeing Eyes, OP, 7 1/2 In. 100.00
Cologne, **Floral Tree,** 4 In. 40.00
Cologne, **French Label,** Scrolled Leaf Design, 4 1/8 In. 30.00
Cologne, **French Label,** Violin Shape, Baroque Design, 5 In. 40.00
Cologne, **French Poodle Shape,** Sapphire Blue, 8 In. .... 25.00 To 30.00
Cologne, **Heisey,** Cut Floral & Leaf, Sterling & Pink Enamel Stopper, 1 Oz. 26.00
Cologne, **Hexagonal,** Floriform Stopper, Gold Trim, Honey Amber, 5 5/8 In. 170.00
Cologne, **Hexagonal,** Floriform Stopper, Honey Amber, 6 1/2 In. 225.00
Cologne, **Hexagonal,** Loop Panels, Electric Blue, 4 In. 150.00
Cologne, **Hexagonal,** Squat, Canary Yellow, 7 1/4 In. 275.00
Cologne, **House With Mansard Roof Shape,** Milk Glass, 4 3/4 In. 300.00
Cologne, **J.M.Farina,** 6 Sided, Pontil, 4 3/8 In. 25.00
Cologne, **J.M.Farina,** 6 Sided, 4 1/2 In. 15.00
Cologne, **Johann Maria Farina No.4,** Embossed, Round Flat Shape, 4 In. 12.34
Cologne, **Kaziun,** Yellow Rose Stopper, Square Pedestal, Signed, 9 1/2 In. 485.00
Cologne, **Lalique,** Mauve To Clear, 4 1/4 In.High 80.00
Cologne, **Lalique,** Raised Lacy Spiral Design, Clear, 5 1/2 In., Pair 70.00
Cologne, **Lay Down,** Cut Glass, Harvard, 16 In. 45.00
Cologne, **Made In Italy,** Nailhead, Amber, 10 In.High, Pair 20.00
Cologne, **McKearin 243-9,** Aqua, 5 1/4 In. 60.00
Cologne, **McKearin 243-11,** Aqua, 5 3/4 In. 35.00
Cologne, **Milk Glass,** 9 1/2 In.High 25.00
Cologne, **Molded Corners,** Square, Opaque Marbled Blue, 5 1/2 In. 150.00
Cologne, **Moser,** Bulbous, Floral On Pale Lavender, 6 1/4 In.High 95.00
Cologne, **OP,** Aqua, 6 1/2 In. 35.00
Cologne, **Opalescent,** 6 In. 40.00
Cologne, **Palmer,** Cylindrical, Deep Emerald Green, 6 3/4 In. 11.00

Cologne, Pontil, 4 3/4 In.

Cologne, Ricksecker's Sweet
Clover, 8 3/4 In.
(See Page 52)

Cologne, **Pontil,** 4 3/4 In. ....*Illus* 90.00
Cologne, **Pot Of Flowers,** Pale Green, 4 1/4 In. 35.00
Cologne, **Pressed Glass,** Block & Panel, Stopper, Clear, 7 In.High 8.00
Cologne, **Pressed Glass,** Daisy & Button, Square Sided, Stopper, Clear, 7 In. 25.00
Cologne, **Raised Gold Design,** Black Amethyst, 9 In. 35.00

Cologne, Ribbed Hobnail, Milk Glass, 5 1/2 In.	60.00
Cologne, Ribbed Hobnail, Milk Glass, 8 1/2 In.	90.00
Cologne, Ribbed, Diagonal Strips Of Stars, Milk Glass, 6 1/2 In.	50.00
Cologne, Ricksecker, Flat Sided, Green, 6 In.	9.00
Cologne, Ricksecker, N.Y., Porcelain, Cupid On Ivory, 2 Handles, C.1890, 8 In.	38.00
Cologne, Ricksecker's Sweet Clover, 8 3/4 In. ....Illus	225.00
Cologne, Sabino, Relief Dancing Nudes, Opalescent, 6 In.	115.00
Cologne, Sandwich Glass, Flint, OP, C.1800, McKearin G I-9	50.00
Cologne, Sandwich Glass, McKearin 243, 12 Sided, Tooled Lip, Amethyst	85.00
Cologne, Sandwich Glass, 12 Panels, Amethyst, 4 1/2 In.	55.00
Cologne, Sandwich Glass, 12 Panels, Cobalt, 4 1/2 In.	55.00
Cologne, Sandwich Glass, 12 Panels, Green, 4 1/2 In.	55.00
Cologne, Sandwich, Clear Cut Mirror Pattern, Ruby Flashed, 8 1/2 In.	200.00
Cologne, Sandwich, Fluted Sides, Cut Panels, Electric Blue, 6 7/8 In.	350.00
Cologne, Sandwich, Hexagonal, Incurved Oval Panels, Deep Amethyst, 7 1/2 In.	550.00
Cologne, Sandwich, Octagonal, Paneled, Raised Flowers, Canary, 7 5/8 In.	125.00
Cologne, Sandwich, Pagoda Shape, Gold Trim, Deep Opalescent Blue, 6 1/4 In.	225.00
Cologne, Sandwich, Paneled, Amethyst, 4 5/8 In.	55.00
Cologne, Sandwich, Paneled, Amethyst, 4 3/4 In.	58.00
Cologne, Sandwich, Paneled, Green, 4 3/4 In.	55.00
Cologne, Sandwich, 12 Panel, Amethyst, 4 1/2 In.	55.00
Cologne, Tapered, Square, Cable & Star Design, 5 7/8 In.	20.00
Cologne, Tapered, Square, Molded Corners, 5 1/2 In.	20.00
Cologne, Tappan, N.Y., 6 In. ....Illus	43.00
Cologne, Violin Shape, Similar To McKearin 244-9, Aquamarine, 5 1/2 In.	50.00
Cologne, Waisted, Oblong, Incurved Sides, Deep Amethyst, 4 5/8 In.	120.00
Cologne, Waisted, Oblong, Incurved Sides, Translucent Blue, 4 1/8 In.	190.00
Cologne, Waisted, Octagonal, Ground Inside, Emerald Green, 4 1/2 In.	170.00
Cologne, Waisted, Octagonal, Similar To McKearin 243-11, Amethyst, 6 In.	160.00
Cologne, 10 Sided, Similar To McKearin 243-1-8, Amethyst, 4 1/4 In.	75.00
Cologne, 12 Panels, Pontil, Aqua, 7 3/8 In.	30.00
Cologne, 12 Sided, Label, Similar To McKearin 243-12, 5 1/4 In.	50.00
Cologne, 12 Sided, Similar To McKearin 243-2 & 3, Cobalt, 4 3/4 In.	50.00
Cologne, 12 Sided, Similar To McKearin 243-2 & 3, Dark Emerald, 5 1/2 In.	80.00
Cologne, 12 Sided, Similar To McKearin 243-2 & 3, Dark Emerald, 7 3/8 In.	110.00
Cologne, 12 Sided, Similar To McKearin 243-2 & 3, Deep Emerald, 7 3/4 In.	125.00
Cologne, 12 Sided, Similar To McKearin 243-2 & 3, Emerald Green, 5 In.	60.00
Cologne, 12 Sided, Similar To McKearin 243-2 & 3, Light Green, 4 3/4 In.	100.00
Cologne, 12 Sided, Similar To McKearin 243-2 & 3, Opaque Blue, 5 5/8 In.	170.00
Cologne, 12 Sided, Similar To McKearin 243-2 & 3, Purple Blue, 5 1/2 In.	90.00
Cologne, 12 Sided, Similar To McKearin 243-2 & 3, Sapphire Blue, 4 In.	70.00
Cologne, 12 Sided, Similar To McKearin 243-2, Deep Amethyst, 7 3/8 In.	80.00
Cologne, 12 Sided, Similar To McKearin 243-2, Deep Cobalt, 8 3/4 In.	100.00
Cologne, 12 Sided, Similar To McKearin 243-2, Deep Cobalt, 10 1/4 In.	125.00
Cologne, 12 Sided, Similar To McKearin 243-2, Light Amethyst, 7 3/8 In.	90.00
Cologne, 12 Sided, Similar To McKearin 243-2, Light Emerald, 7 1/2 In.	100.00
Cologne, 12 Sided, Similar To McKearin 243-2, Opalescent Blue, 11 1/4 In.	375.00
Cologne, 12 Sided, Similar To McKearin 243-6, Deep Sapphire, 7 3/4 In.	120.00
Columbian Exposition, Gold Trim, 14 In. ....Illus	50.00
Cosmetic, Batchelor's Liquid Hair Dye No.1, OP, Stain, Aqua, 3 In.	17.00
Cosmetic, Batchelor's Liquid Hair Dye, Open Pontil, Square, Aqua, 3 In.	24.00
Cosmetic, Bath Salts, Tiffany, Glass, Hinged Sterling Top, 3 In.High	47.50
Cosmetic, Buckingham Whisker Dye, Amber, 5 In.	5.00
Cosmetic, C.Damaschinsky Liquid Hair Dye, N.Y., Blue Aqua, 3 1/2 In.	3.00
Cosmetic, C.Damaschinsky Liquid Hair Dye, N.Y., Blue Aqua, 4 In.	3.00
Cosmetic, Camm's Spanish Lustral Or Hair Preservative, Aqua, Pint	150.00
Cosmetic, Cold Cream, Milk Glass, 1906	2.50
Cosmetic, Colgate's Charmis Cold Cream, Jar, Lady In Peignoir	4.00
Cosmetic, DeWitt's Toilet Creams, Rectangular, Cork, Clear, Boxed, 5 In.	1.50
Cosmetic, Elysian Hair Curling Fluid, Rectangular, Cork, Clear, 5 In.High	3.00
Cosmetic, Farr's For Gray Hair, Boston, Mass., ABM, Amber, 5 1/2 In.	4.00
Cosmetic, Farr's Gray Hair Restorer, Boston, Mass., Amber, 6 Ozs.	2.00
Cosmetic, Fine Turtle Hair Oil, Figural Turtle, 5 In.	75.00
Cosmetic, Genuine Essence, Rectangular, 4 1/2 In.	18.00
Cosmetic, Gold Dandruff Cure, Rectangular, 7 1/2 In.	11.00

Cologne, Tappan, N.Y., 6 In.
(See Page 52)

Columbian Exposition, Gold Trim, 14 In.
(See Page 52)

Cosmetic, La Creole Hair Dressing, Amber, 8 1/2 In.

Cosmetic, Helene Curtis, Embossed, Jug, Gallon	1.00
Cosmetic, Imperial Hair Regenerator, Aqua, 4 1/2 In.	10.00
Cosmetic, Jar, Pomade, Bear, Sandwich, Flint, Amethyst	195.00
Cosmetic, Jar, Pomade, Cut Overlay, Silver Top, Blue To White To Clear	30.00
Cosmetic, La Creole Hair Dressing, Amber, 8 1/2 In. ....*Illus*	3.00
Cosmetic, Lyon's Kathairon For The Hair, Open Pontil, Rectangular, 6 In.	20.00
Cosmetic, Mascaro Tonique For The Hair, Embossed Wig, 6 In.	6.00
Cosmetic, McGregor Shaving Lotion, Horse's Head Shape, 4 1/2 In.	2.00
Cosmetic, Mme.F.Robinnaire's Walnut Hair Dye, Atlanta, Ga., 3 3/4 In.	5.00
Cosmetic, Mrs.S.A.Allen's Worlds Hair Restorer, Honey Amber, 7 1/8 In.	12.00
Cosmetic, Noxzema, Embossed Across Base, Cobalt, 1/2 Gallon	100.00
Cosmetic, Pompeian Massage Cream, Embossed, Ground Stopper, Clear, 3 1/2 In.	5.00
Cosmetic, Quinine Hair Tonic, Metal Over Cork Top, Paper Label, Clear, 7 In.	8.00
Cosmetic, Richard Hudnut White Rose Sachet, Gold Metal Cap, 3 1/2 In.	4.50
Cosmetic, S.A.Allen's World's Hair Balsam, Aqua, 6 5/8 In.	15.00
Cosmetic, S-Zalia Hair Tonic, Boston, Blob Lip, Ball Neck, 7 In.	5.00
Cosmetic, Wright Brothers Pond Lily Wash, Aqua, 7 1/2 In.	6.00
Crackle Glass, Amethyst, 7 1/2 In.High	5.00
Cure, see Medicine	
Cut Glass, Cane Pattern, Ornate Silver Top, 4 3/4 In. High	65.00
Cut Glass, Water, Diamond & Fan, 8 In., Pair	150.00
Cyrus Noble, Assayer	59.95
Cyrus Noble, Bartender	39.95 To 50.00
Cyrus Noble, Burro	35.00 To 80.00
Cyrus Noble, Gambler	35.00
Cyrus Noble, Gold Miner	375.00
Cyrus Noble, Snowshoe Thompson	50.00

*Dant figural bottles first were released in 1968 to hold J.W.Dant
alcoholic products. The company has made the Americana series, field
birds, special bottlings, and ceramic bottles.*

Dant, Alamo	5.00
Dant, American Legion	7.00
Dant, Bobwhite	6.00
Dant, Boeing 747	5.00 To 7.50
Dant, Boston Tea Party	4.00 To 5.00
Dant, Eagle, Facing Left	3.00 To 8.00

Dant, Eagle, Facing Right

Dant, Field Bird, Woodcock

Dant, Eagle, Facing Right	*Illus*	6.00
Dant, Field Bird, California Quail		6.50
Dant, Field Bird, Chukar Partridge		6.50
Dant, Field Bird, Mountain Quail		6.50
Dant, Field Bird, Prairie Chicken		6.50
Dant, Field Bird, Ruffed Grouse		6.50
Dant, Field Bird, Woodcock	*Illus*	6.50
Dant, Fort Sill Centennial, 1969	*Illus*	10.00
Dant, Indy 500		4.00
Dant, Mt.Rushmore	*Illus*	10.50
Dant, 1969, Colonial Dueling Scene		2.75
Dant, 1969, Naval Battle Between Sailing Ships		2.75
Dant, 1969, 30th Anniversary Of The American Legion, 1919-1969		2.75

Decanters were first used to hold the alcoholic beverages that had been stored in kegs. At first a necessity, the decanter later was merely an attractive serving vessel.

Dant, Fort Sill Centennial, 1969

Decanter, Austrian Porcelain, Open Web Handles, Lilac To Green, 9 1/2 In.	20.00
Decanter, Baccarat, Round, Bulbous Stopper, Crystal, 13 1/4 In.	32.00
Decanter, Bar, Blown, 5 Rings On Neck, Clear Yellow Green, Quart	45.00
Decanter, Bar, Engraved Kenwood With Gold On Front, Ground Stopper, 11 In.	22.00
Decanter, Bar, Pressed Glass, Flint, Pillar & Bird's-Eye, Collared Lip, Quart	30.00

Dant, Mt.Rushmore
(See Page 54)

Decanter, Bell Shape, Gold Decoration, Deep Amethyst, 9 In.	32.00
Decanter, Blown, Applied Crystal Handle & Steeple Stopper, Vaseline, 10 In.	75.00
Decanter, Blown, Applied Rope At Neck, 4 In.	75.00
Decanter, Blown, Blown Stopper, Dark Blue, 12 In.High	45.00
Decanter, Blown, Clover Lip, White Lilies Of The Valley, Green, 10 1/2 In.	30.00
Decanter, Blown, Engraved Daisies, Faceted Stopper, Clear, 11 1/2 In.High	45.00
Decanter, Blown, Flint, C.1800, Quart	30.00
Decanter, Blown, Flint, Pattern Molded Panels, C.1790, 1/2 Pint	40.00
Decanter, Blown, Flint, Pillar Mold, 8 Rib, Applied Stem & Foot, 10 In.	65.00
Decanter, Blown, Gold Threading, Applied Amber Rigaree, 10 1/2 In.	140.00
Decanter, Blown, Horizontal & Vertical Molding, Quart	45.00
Decanter, Blown, Ribbed Mushroom Stopper, Ribbed Base, Amber, 12 In.	58.00
Decanter, Blown, Thumbprint, Amber, 7 In.	35.00
Decanter, Blown, Vertical Ribs, Amethyst, Pint	60.00
Decanter, Blown, Vertical Ribs, Pint	60.00
Decanter, Blown, Vertical Ribs, Quart	40.00 To 80.00
Decanter, Blown, 3 Mold, Baroque Pattern, Pint, Pair	120.00
Decanter, Blown, 3 Mold, Baroque, Quart	80.00
Decanter, Blown, 3 Mold, Baroque, 1/2 Pint	110.00
Decanter, Blown, 3 Mold, Diamond Point, Quart	75.00
Decanter, Blown, 3 Mold, Geometric, Clear Olive Green, Pint	375.00
Decanter, Blown, 3 Mold, Geometric, Light Amethyst Cast, 1/2 Pint	150.00
Decanter, Blown, 3 Mold, Geometric, Olive Green, Quart	400.00 To 725.00
Decanter, Blown, 3 Mold, Geometric, 1/2 Pint	130.00
Decanter, Blown, 3 Mold, Geometric, Pint	50.00 To 110.00
Decanter, Blown, 3 Mold, Geometric, Quart	60.00 To 80.00
Decanter, Blown, 3 Mold, Geometric, Straight Tapering Sides, Quart	110.00
Decanter, Blown, 3 Mold, Geometric, Word Rum, Quart	220.00
Decanter, Blown, 3 Mold, Sunburst Pattern, Stopper, Pint	85.00
Decanter, Bohemian Glass, Deer & Trees, Cut To Clear, Red 8 In. High	145.00
Decanter, Bohemian Glass, Etched Vintage, Hollow Stopper, Ruby, 11 1/4 In.	70.00
Decanter, Bohemian Glass, Gold Detail, Steeple Stopper, 18 In.	175.00

Decanter, **Bohemian Glass,** Vintage Pattern, Numbered, 14 In.High, Pair	75.00
Decanter, **Brandy,** Cut Glass, Diamond Pattern Bowl, Ground Stopper, Pair	30.00
Decanter, **Brandy,** Cut Glass, Diamonds, Ground Stopper	30.00
Decanter, **Captain's,** Cut Glass, American, Flat Bottom	150.00
Decanter, **Captain's,** Cut Glass, Gorham Ball Stopper, Hobstar, Cane, & Fan	450.00
Decanter, **Captain's,** Cut Glass, Teardrop Stopper, Strawberry Diamond & Fan	175.00
Decanter, **Crystal,** Inverted Thumbprint, Faceted Stopper, 10 In.	12.50
Decanter, **Cut Glass,** Deep Cutting, 3 Ring Neck, 12 In.High	85.00
Decanter, **Cut Glass,** Double Lozenge, Ball Stopper, 12 In.	110.00
Decanter, **Cut Glass,** Faceted Ball Stopper, Double Lozenge, 12 In.	135.00
Decanter, **Cut Glass,** Faceted Stopper, Notched Handle, Shamrock, 13 In.	100.00
Decanter, **Cut Glass,** Geometrics, Cut Stopper, C.1800, 14 In.High, Pair	275.00
Decanter, **Cut Glass,** Honeycomb & Punty, Hollow Stopper, Pint	65.00
Decanter, **Cut Glass,** Nailhead Cut, American, Stopper, 13 3/4 In.High	100.00
Decanter, **Cut Glass,** Square, Geometrics, 16 Point Star Base, 8 1/2 In.	70.00
Decanter, **Cut Glass,** St.Louis, Stepped Shoulder, Stopper, 11 1/2 In.High	165.00
Decanter, **Cut Glass,** Sulfide Bust Of A Man, Cut Stopper, 11 In.	200.00
Decanter, **Cut Glass,** Vertical Panels, Honeycomb Stopper, 13 1/2 In.	45.00
Decanter, **Cut Panels,** Lacy Stopper, 3 Ring, 10 In., Pair	90.00
Decanter, **Cut To Clear Ducks In Water & Cattails,** Honey Amber, 15 In.	45.00
Decanter, **Cut To Clear,** Amber, 18 In.High, Pair	200.00
Decanter, **Cut,** Crosshatched Drape & Swag With Bull's-Eye, Cobalt, 15 In.	250.00
Decanter, **Diamond Pattern,** Vaseline, 11 In.	24.00
Decanter, **Eight Panels Blown In Base,** Cut Top, Deep Amethyst, 13 1/4 In.	95.00
Decanter, **Etched,** Initial W, Stopper, Polished Pontil, 10 3/4 In.High	15.00
Decanter, **Etched,** Pink, 6 1/2 In. ....*Color*	40.00
Decanter, **Faceted Crystal Stopper,** Amethyst, 10 In.	15.00
Decanter, **Flint,** Ashburton, Bar Lip, Quart	32.00
Decanter, **Flint,** Ashburton, Pint	125.00
Decanter, **Flint,** Bar Lip, Diamond Thumbprint, Pint	95.00
Decanter, **Flint,** Diamond Thumbprint, Pewter Cork, Quart	125.00
Decanter, **Flint,** Fairy, Applied Bar Lip, Clear, 10 1/4 In.High	95.00
Decanter, **Flint,** Thumbprint, Bar Lip, 12 In.	70.00
Decanter, **Free-Blown,** Folded Lip, Rough Pontil, Flint, 1/2 Pint	35.00
Decanter, **Galle,** Light & Dark Green Ferns, Pedestal, Cut Stopper, 12 In.	295.00
Decanter, **Galle,** Swirl Rib, Enamel Orchid & Butterflies, Amber, 10 1/2 In.	750.00
Decanter, **Heisey,** Rigley, 11 1/2 In.	70.00
Decanter, **Lalique,** Hexagonal, Paneled, Cut Chevrons, C.1930, 10 1/4 In.	100.00
Decanter, **Mary Gregory,** Boy Holding Bird In Air, Girl Watching, Blue, 15 In.	195.00
Decanter, **McKearin G I-25,** Quart	40.00
Decanter, **McKearin G I-29,** Blown, 3 Mold, Quart	90.00
Decanter, **McKearin G II-7,** 3 Mold, Stopper Green, Pint	250.00
Decanter, **McKearin G II-18,** Blown, Applied Double Neck Rings, Pair	175.00
Decanter, **McKearin G II-18,** Blown, 3 Mold, Rigaree Neck Rings, Quart	90.00
Decanter, **McKearin G II-18,** Mold-Blown, Quart, Pair	165.00
Decanter, **McKearin G II-18,** OP, Quart, Pair	80.00
Decanter, **McKearin G II-18,** Pint	57.00
Decanter, **McKearin G II-18,** Quart, Pair	100.00
Decanter, **McKearin G II-18,** Sandwich, Mold-Blown, Stopper, Quart	125.00
Decanter, **McKearin G II-22,** Blown, 3 Mold, Lacy Stopper, 8 1/2 In.	75.00
Decanter, **McKearin G II-28,** Square, Chamfered Corners, OP	300.00
Decanter, **McKearin G II-34,** OP, Quart	80.00
Decanter, **McKearin G III-2,** Type 2, Blown, 3 Mold, Stain, Quart	180.00
Decanter, **McKearin G III-5,** Molded, 3 Double Rigaree Rings, Quart	100.00
Decanter, **McKearin G III-5,** 3 Mold, Stopper, 5 Quart	95.00
Decanter, **McKearin G III-6,** Geometric, OP, Pair	260.00
Decanter, **McKearin G III-12,** Three Mold, Clear, Miniature	125.00
Decanter, **McKearin G III-14,** Blown, 3 Mold, 1/2 Pint	120.00
Decanter, **McKearin G III-16,** Keene, Geometric, Dark Green, Pint	300.00
Decanter, **McKearin G III-16,** Keene, Geometric, Light Green	275.00
Decanter, **McKearin G III-16,** Keene, Geometric, Olive Amber, Pint	300.00
Decanter, **McKearin G III-16,** Keene, Geometric, Olive Green	300.00
Decanter, **McKearin G III-16,** Keene, OP, Olive Green, Pint	310.00
Decanter, **McKearin G III-24,** Blown, 3 Mold, Blue Sunburst Stopper, Pint	100.00
Decanter, **McKearin G III-26,** Blown, 3 Mold, Stain, Quart	160.00

Decanter, McKearin G V-8, Baroque, OP, Quart 90.00
Decanter, McKearin G V-8, Plate 116, No.2, Baroque Shell & Ribbing, Quart 88.00
Decanter, McKearin G V-10, 3 Mold 55.00
Decanter, McKearin G V-12, 3 Mold 70.00
Decanter, McKearin G V-13, Blown, 3 Mold, Stain In Base, Pint 140.00
Decanter, McKearin 114-17, Blown, 3 Mold, Quart 90.00
Decanter, Ohio Riverboat, 8 Rib, Polished Pontil, Clear, Quart 65.00
Decanter, Peachblow, Wheeling, Flattened Ovoid, Rope Handle, Amber Stopper 1295.00
Decanter, Pressed Glass, Bellflower, Double Vine, Quart 90.00
Decanter, Pressed Glass, Bull's-Eye Variant, Flint, Quart 70.00
Decanter, Pressed Glass, Flint, Ashburton, Pint 125.00
Decanter, Pressed Glass, Flint, Bar, Waffle & Thumbprint, 1/2 Pint 45.00
Decanter, Pressed Glass, Flint, Cable, Clear, Pint 90.00
Decanter, Pressed Glass, Flint, Diamond Point, Quart, Pair 90.00
Decanter, Pressed Glass, New England Pineapple, Stopper, Clear, Pint 150.00
Decanter, Pressed Glass, Triangular, Chrome Screw Cap, 1966, 4 In. 4.00
Decanter, Ringed, OP, 1/2 Pint 15.00
Decanter, Riverboat, Blown, Flint, 8 Rib Pillar Mold, Neck Ring, Quart 65.00
Decanter, Russian Art Glass, Triple Overlay, Cut Floral, C.1750, 20 In. 375.00
Decanter, Sandwich Glass, Flat Diamond & Panel, Quart, Pair 125.00
Decanter, Sandwich Type, Cobalt, Pint 10.00
Decanter, Sandwich, Ribbed, Petticoat Base, Pear Shape Stopper, Quart 90.00
Decanter, Silver Overlay, Green, 9 In.High 17.00
Decanter, Spirit Of '76, General Washington & Eagle, 11 In. 2.00
Decanter, Three Fish With Anchor Between Each, Tails To Neck, 3 Mold, Quart 72.00
Decanter, Whiskey, Carnival Glass, Grape & Cable, Marigold 300.00
Decanter, Whiskey, Carnival Glass, Grape & Cable, Purple 850.00
Decanter, Whiskey, Mold Blown, Pressed Cut Glasslike Pattern 45.00
Decanter, Whiskey, Stiegel Type, Stopper, Etched Tulips & Foliage, Pint 30.00
Decanter, White & Gold Enamel, 1 Handle, Green 35.00
Decanter, Wine, Bohemian Glass, Vintage, Ruby, 15 1/2 In. 47.50
Decanter, Wine, Cut Glass, Floral Sprays, Emerald Flashed, 12 1/2 In. 65.00
Decanter, Wine, Cut Glass, Grape, Leaf, & Thumbprint, Green To Clear, 13 In. 65.00
Decanter, Wine, Cut Glass, Square, Cut Stopper 75.00
Decanter, Wine, Cut Glass, Stopper, 2 In.High 10.00
Decanter, Wine, Embossed In Silver, Stopper, Glass 25.00
Decanter, Wine, Enameled Flowers, Polished Pontil, Cranberry Flashed 75.00
Decanter, Wine, Enameled White Lilies Of The Valley, Stopper, Green 40.00
Decanter, Wine, Lalique, Beaded Rings On Frosted, Cut Crystal Stopper 110.00
Decanter, Wine, Pointed Hobnail, 11 In.High 38.00
Decanter, Wine, Pressed Glass, Currier & Ives, Faceted Stopper 35.00
Decanter, Wine, Pressed Glass, Daisy & Button With Narcissus 50.00
Decanter, Wine, Pressed Glass, Magnet & Grape With Frosted Leaf 500.00
Decanter, Wine, Pressed Glass, Thumbprint, 11 In.High 17.00
Decanter, Wine, Thumbprint, Applied Clear Reeded Handle, Cranberry Glass 65.00
Decanter, World's Fair, 1938, Anchor Signed, Milk Glass, 10 In. 15.00
    Decanter, see also Beam, Bischoff, etc.
Demijohn, Applied Crooked Neck, Amber, 2 Gallon 15.00
Demijohn, Blob Top, Brown, 18 In. 65.00
Demijohn, Blown In 2 Part Mold, Painted Harbor Scene, Olive, 13 1/2 In. 35.00
Demijohn, Blown, Black 31 Painted On Gold, Olive Amber, 13 In. 55.00
Demijohn, Blown, 21 On Gold Paper, Olive, 14 In. 65.00
Demijohn, Graphite Pontil, Bimal, Olive Amber, Gallon 20.00
Demijohn, Graphite Pontil, Blue Green, 12 In. 25.00
Demijohn, Hand-Blown, Impressed Seal, Pontil, C.1700, Green, 36 In. 50.00
Demijohn, OP, Olive Amber, Gallon 7.50
Demijohn, OP, Olive Green, 5 Gallon 40.00
Demijohn, OP, 3 Gallon 55.00
Demijohn, Olive Green, 1/2 Gallon 10.00
Demijohn, Tubular Pontil, Emerald, 16 In. 37.50
Demijohn, Whittled, Bubbles, Amber, 15 In. 16.00
Dickel, Golf Club 5.00
Dickel, Powder Horn, Amber, 12 3/4 In. 5.00
Double Springs, Bull, Red, 1968 .... 9.00
Double Springs, Cadillac, 1913 .... 14.00

Double Springs, Chicago Water Tower	35.00
Double Springs, Coyote, Gold	16.00
Double Springs, Duffer	4.00
Double Springs, Ford, Model T	16.00 To 18.00
Double Springs, Georgia Bulldog	10.00
Double Springs, Hold That Tiger	17.00
Double Springs, Matador	10.00
Double Springs, Mercer	14.00
Double Springs, Milwaukee Buck	10.00
Double Springs, Model T	10.00
Double Springs, Owl, Brown	9.95
Double Springs, Owl, Red	9.95
Double Springs, Peasant Boy	6.00
Double Springs, Peasant Girl	6.00
Double Springs, Pierce Arrow	21.00
Double Springs, Rolls Royce	18.00
Double Springs, Scotsman	10.00
Double Springs, Stanley Steamer	10.00
Double Springs, Stutz Bearcat, 1919	16.00 To 18.00
Double Springs, Tiger On Football	15.00
Double Springs, W.C.Fields	20.00
Double Springs, Wild Catter	5.00
Dresser, Actress, Painted Decoration, Milk Glass, 11 In.	40.00
Dresser, Baccarat, Swirled, Amberina, 5 1/2 In.High	34.50
Dresser, Cut Glass, Hobstar, Crosshatching, & Fan, Hollow Stopper, 6 In.	35.00
Dresser, Mushroom Stopper, Leaf & Vine, Milk Glass, 10 In.	25.00
Dresser, Paneled Fluted, Mushroom Stopper, Cranberry, 7 In., Pair	75.00
Dresser, Pressed & Cut, Strawberry Diamond, Star Base, 8 In.	21.50
Drioli, African Woman	30.00
Drioli, Cherry Log	4.00
Drioli, Gondola	30.00
Drioli, Pitcher, Black	4.00
Drioli, Pitcher, Red	4.00
Drug, Amber, 14 In.	2.00
Drug, American Drug & Press Assn., Decorah, I., Amber, 5 In.	10.00
Drug, Ballagh's Drug Store, Nevada, Mo., Amber, 5 In.	6.50
Drug, Bennett & Abel, Little Falls, N.Y., Jug, Salt Glaze, Bluebird, 2 Gallon	100.00
Drug, Blue, 14 In.	5.00
Drug, Botanic Druggists, Bush & Co., Worcester, Mass., Aqua, 7 In.	2.75
Drug, Bowman's Drug Store, 4 1/2 In.	30.00
Drug, Brown Bros. Chemist's, Glasgow, Scotland, 9 In.	6.00
Drug, C.W.Snow & Co., Syracuse, N.Y., Whittled, Square, Cobalt, 9 1/2 In.	45.00
Drug, Conical, Stain, Pale Aqua, 5 1/2 In.High	3.00
Drug, Emil Cermak, Omaha, Neb., 5 In.	1.00
Drug, F.A.& Co. On Base & Brown Label, Cylindrical, Aqua, 9 In.	2.50
Drug, Geo.H.Fish & Sons, Pharmacists, Saratoga, Cobalt, 6 In.	50.00
Drug, Glyco-Heroin, Smith, Dug, Amber, 8 3/4 In.	4.00
Drug, H.A.Cassebeer, N.Y., Beveled Corners, Cobalt, 2 1/2 X 6 In.	10.00
Drug, J.R.Nichols Co., Boston, Deep Green, 7 In.	7.50
Drug, J.Sullivan Pharmacist, Boston, Rectangular, Milk Glass, 5 1/4 In.	7.50
Drug, Jar, Cobalt, 8 In.	10.00
Drug, Jas.Tarrant, Druggist, New York, Oval, Aqua, 6 3/4 In.	15.00
Drug, John C.Baker & Co., Druggist, Phila., Embossed, Oval, Aqua, 7 In.	22.50
Drug, Krieger's Pharmacy, Poughkeepsie, N.Y., 13 Panels, Amethyst, 5 In.	1.25
Drug, Linn Smith & Co.Wholesale Druggists, Round, Aqua, Gallon	32.00
Drug, London, 4 3/4 In.	1.50
Drug, M.K.Paine, Druggist, Vt., Flattened Oval, Milk Glass, 6 1/2 In.	37.50
Drug, McKesson & Robbins, Maiden Lane, N.Y., Jar, 4 Gallon, 5 In.Mouth	40.00
Drug, Muegge Druggist, Bimal, Emerald Green, 8 1/2 In.	16.00
Drug, New York Pharmaceutical Association, Round Shoulder, Cobalt, 12 In.	25.00
Drug, O'Rourke & Hurley, Druggists, Little Falls, N.Y., Cobalt, 4 In.	16.50
Drug, O'Rourke & Hurley, Druggists, Little Falls, N.Y., Cobalt, 5 In.	18.50
Drug, O'Rourke & Hurley, Little Falls, N.Y., Cobalt, 4 In.	10.50
Drug, O'Rourke & Hurley, Little Falls, N.Y., Cobalt, 5 1/2 In.	13.50
Drug, Owl Co., Rectangular, Embossed, Screw Cap, ABM, Cobalt, 6 1/2 In.	3.00

Drug, Owl Co., Wing Off Center, Poison, Triangular, Cobalt, 4 3/4 In. 25.00
Drug, Owl Drug Co., Embossed Owl, Rectangular, Light Amber, 3 3/4 In. 25.00
Drug, Owl Drug Co., San Francisco, Blob Top, Turquoise, 9 1/2 In. 35.00
Drug, Owl Drug, S.F., Bimal, Green, 16 Oz. 25.00
Drug, Owl, ABM, Stain, Cobalt Blue, 2 3/4 In. 8.00
Drug, Owl, Milk Glass, 3 1/2 In. 8.00
Drug, Owl, Milk Glass, 4 In. 25.00
Drug, Owl, Stain, Cobalt Blue, 4 3/4 In. 20.00
Drug, Owl, 1 Wing, Amber, 5 In. 35.00
Drug, Owl, 2 Wing, Amber, 8 In. 35.00
Drug, Paper Label, Teal, 12 In. 8.00
Drug, Pharmacist's, Corker, 8 In. .... .75
Drug, Poynter's, London, Ky., 5 In. 1.50
Drug, R.A.Robinson & Co.Druggist, Louisville, Square, Cobalt Blue, 6 3/4 In. 25.00
Drug, R.E.Sellers, Pittsburgh, Aqua, 4 3/4 In.High 20.00
Drug, Recessed Label, C.1900, Ground Stopper, Amber, 8 In. 4.00
Drug, Round Shoulders, Knobs On Neck, Stain, Emerald Green, 7 1/2 In. 12.50
Drug, South Carolina Dispensary, Amber, C.1800 .... 22.50
Drug, South Carolina Dispensary, Palmetto Tree, Stain, Aqua, Pint 25.00
Drug, Sp.Camph., 8 1/2 In. ....Color 18.00
Drug, Standard Drug & Sales Co., Phila., 7 In. 1.00

Drug, Taylor & Cutler Druggists, Green, 7 In.

Error, A.Nicholson, Backwards One Side,
Blue, 8 3/4 In.
(See Page 60)

Ezra Brooks, Antique Phonograph, 1970
(See Page 60)

Drug, Stewart & Holms Drug Co., Seattle, Wash., Paneled, Aqua, 6 In. 2.00
Drug, Strong Cobb Wholesale Druggists, Bubbles, Deep Sapphire, 6 3/4 In. 25.00
Drug, Sun, Stain, Green, 4 In. 30.00
Drug, Tarrant Druggist, New York, 8 Sided, SCA, Dug, 4 7/8 In. 15.00
Drug, Taylor & Cutler Druggists, Green, 7 In. ....Illus 125.00
Drug, Thos.L.Desauliniers & Co., Holyoke, Mass., May 15, 88, Amber, 5 1/2 In. 7.50
Drug, U.S.A. Hospital Department, Honey Amber, Quart 38.00
Drug, U.S.A. Hospital Department, Stain, Blue, 9 In. 50.00
Drug, Wing & Sisson, Coxsackie, N.Y., OP, Aqua, 7 In. 20.00

Drug, 12 Sided, Flat Lip, Pale Aqua, 2 1/2 In.High 5.00
Dyottville Glass Works, Cylindrical, IP, Olive Green, Quart 34.00
Dyottville Glass Works, Cylindrical, Marked On Bottom, Citron, 12 In. 15.00
Early American Society, Coach & Tavern 7.95
Early American Society, Delta Queen 7.95
Error, A.Nicholson, Backwards One Side, Blue, 8 3/4 In. .... *Illus* 400.00
Error, Cramer's Kidney Cure, Backward N, Free Sample, Bimal, 4 1/4 In. 5.95
Error, Flask, Keene In Oval Is Spelled Kcckc, Eagle & Masonic, Amber, Pint 250.00
Error, Fruit Jar, Mason's Patent Nov.30, 1858, CFJ, Backward N, Aqua, Quart 15.00
Error, Gargling Oil, Logkport, ABM, Cobalt, Pint 45.00
Error, K.Konishi & Co., Apohercary, Embossed, Blue Green, 8 In. 8.00
Error, Poison, Backward N In Poison, 3 Sided, Amber, 10 1/2 In. 75.00
Error, Stretch Bennet & Co., Phila., Wohlsale Druggists, Aqua, 4 1/2 In. 9.50
Error, Swayzee's Imppover, Fruit Jar, Quart 6.00
Error, Warner's Safe Rheumatic Cure, Backwards S In U.S.A., Amber 55.00
Error, Wheaton Nu-Line, Helen Keller, Born 1880, Died 1868, 1972 Issue 45.00

*Ezra Brooks fancy bottles were first made in 1964. The Ezra Brooks
Distilling Company is from Frankfort, Kentucky.*

Ezra Brooks, Alligator, Florida, No.1, 1972 .... 16.00 To 18.00
Ezra Brooks, Alligator, Florida, No.2, 1973 .... 12.00 To 16.00
Ezra Brooks, American Legion, 1971 .... 20.00 To 22.50
Ezra Brooks, American Legion, 1973, Hawaii .... 30.00 To 35.00
Ezra Brooks, Antique Gold Cannon, 1969 .... 6.00 To 8.00
Ezra Brooks, Antique Phonograph, 1970 .... *Illus*   18.00
Ezra Brooks, Antique Telephone, 1971 .... 9.00 To 12.00
Ezra Brooks, Arizona, 1969 .... 5.00 To 10.00
Ezra Brooks, Arkansas Razorback Hog, 1970 .... 9.00 To 17.50
Ezra Brooks, Asia Elephant, 1973 .... 13.00 To 15.00
Ezra Brooks, Astronaut, Foremost, 1970 .... 5.00 To 11.00
Ezra Brooks, Bagpiper .... 17.00 To 20.00
Ezra Brooks, Balloon Clown .... 12.00 To 15.00
Ezra Brooks, Bare Knuckle Fighter, 1971 .... 6.00 To 11.50
Ezra Brooks, Baseball Player, 1973, Casey .... *Illus*   14.00
Ezra Brooks, Beaver, 1972 .... 9.00 To 14.00
Ezra Brooks, Big Bertha, 1970, Elephant .... 10.00 To 15.00
Ezra Brooks, Big Daddy, 1969 .... 7.00 To 10.00
Ezra Brooks, Big Red No.1, 1970 .... 25.00 To 30.00
Ezra Brooks, Big Red No.2, 1972 .... 10.00 To 15.00
Ezra Brooks, Big Red No.3, 1972 .... 9.00 To 15.00
Ezra Brooks, Bird Dog, 1971 .... *Illus*   11.00

Ezra Brooks, Baseball Player, 1973, Casey

Ezra Brooks, Bird Dog, 1971

Ezra Brooks, Ceremonial Dancer, 1970

Ezra Brooks, Birthday Cake, 1972 .... 6.00 To 16.00
Ezra Brooks, Black Angus, 1973 .... 12.00 To 20.00
Ezra Brooks, Bordertown, 1973 .... 12.00 To 13.00
Ezra Brooks, Bowler, 1973 .... 8.00 To 14.00
Ezra Brooks, Brahma Bull, 1972 .... 12.00 To 14.00
Ezra Brooks, Bucket Of Blood, 1970 .... 5.00 To 13.00
Ezra Brooks, Bucking Bronco, Rough Rider, 1974 .... 11.00 To 13.00
Ezra Brooks, Bucky Badger, 1974, Wisconsin .... 14.00 To 16.00
Ezra Brooks, Buffalo Hunt, 1971 .... 8.00 To 24.00
Ezra Brooks, Cable Cars, San Francisco, 1968 .... 4.00 To 12.00
Ezra Brooks, California Quail, 1970 .... 5.00 To 10.00
Ezra Brooks, Cannon, Antique Gold, 1969 .... 6.00 To 8.00
Ezra Brooks, Cardinal, Virginia, 1973 .... 15.00 To 30.00
Ezra Brooks, Casey At The Bat, Baseball Player, 1973 .... 7.00 To 14.00
Ezra Brooks, Cat, Katz Philharmonic, 1970 .... 6.00 To 11.00
Ezra Brooks, Cat, Katz, 1969 .... 9.00 To 11.00
Ezra Brooks, Ceremonial Dancer, 1970 .... *Illus*   20.00
Ezra Brooks, Charlois, 1973 .... 9.00 To 17.50
Ezra Brooks, Cheyenne Shootout, 1970 .... 5.00 To 10.00
Ezra Brooks, Chicago Water Tower, 1969 .... 8.00 To 14.00
Ezra Brooks, Christmas Decanter, 1964 .... 8.00 To 11.00
Ezra Brooks, Christmas Decanter, 1965 .... 8.00 To 11.00
Ezra Brooks, Christmas Decanter, 1966 .... 8.00 To 11.00
Ezra Brooks, Christmas Decanter, 1967 .... 8.00 To 11.00
Ezra Brooks, Christmas Decanter, 1968 .... 8.00 To 11.00
Ezra Brooks, Churchill, 1969 .... 3.00 To 8.00
Ezra Brooks, Cigar Store Indian, 1968 .... 5.00 To 10.00
Ezra Brooks, Civil War Commemorative .... 6.00 To 8.00
Ezra Brooks, Classic Gun Set, Set Of 4, 1969 .... 17.00 To 22.00
Ezra Brooks, Classic Rooster .... 7.00 To 9.95
Ezra Brooks, Clown, 1972 .... 9.00 To 14.00
Ezra Brooks, Club, Birthday Cake, 1972 .... 6.00 To 16.00
Ezra Brooks, Club, Distillery, 1970 .... 10.00 To 25.00
Ezra Brooks, Club, U.S.Map, 1973 .... 17.00 To 25.00
Ezra Brooks, Clydesdale, 1974 .... 12.00 To 20.00
Ezra Brooks, Conquistadors Drum, 1971 .... 8.00 To 12.00
Ezra Brooks, Court Jester, 1972 .... 10.00 To 15.00
Ezra Brooks, Deadwagon, 1970 .... 6.00 To 10.00
Ezra Brooks, Delta Bell, 1969 .... 9.00 To 15.00
Ezra Brooks, Dice, Harold's, 1968 .... 8.00 To 10.00
Ezra Brooks, Dirt Bike, 1973 .... 10.00 To 12.00
Ezra Brooks, Distillery, Club Bottle, 1970 .... 10.00 To 25.00
Ezra Brooks, Drum & Bugle Corps, 1971 .... 10.00 To 18.00
Ezra Brooks, Dueling Pistol, 1968 .... 7.00 To 10.00
Ezra Brooks, Duesenberg, 1971 .... 10.00 To 11.00
Ezra Brooks, Elephant, 1973, Asian .... 13.00 To 15.00
Ezra Brooks, Elk, 1973 .... 12.00 To 13.00
Ezra Brooks, Fire Engine, 1971 .... 7.00 To 12.00

Ezra Brooks, Foremost Astronaut, 1970

Ezra Brooks, Golden Grizzly Bear, 1968

Ezra Brooks, Florida Big Daddy, 1969 .... 7.00 To 10.00
Ezra Brooks, Florida Gator, No.1, 1972 .... 16.00 To 18.00
Ezra Brooks, Florida Gator, No.2, 1973 .... 12.00 To 14.00
Ezra Brooks, Football Player, 1974 .... 12.00 To 15.00
Ezra Brooks, Fordson Tractor, 1971 .... 15.00 To 17.95
Ezra Brooks, Foremost Astronaut, 1970 ....*Illus*   11.00
Ezra Brooks, Fresno Grape, 1970 .... 6.00 To 12.50
Ezra Brooks, Gamecock, 1970, South Carolina .... 10.00 To 18.00
Ezra Brooks, Georgia Bulldog, 1972 .... 12.00 To 17.00
Ezra Brooks, Go Big Red, No.1, 1970 .... 25.00 To 30.00
Ezra Brooks, Go Big Red, No.2, 1972 .... 10.00 To 15.00
Ezra Brooks, Go Big Red, No.3, 1972 .... 9.00 To 15.00
Ezra Brooks, Go Tiger, 1973 .... 13.00 To 16.00
Ezra Brooks, Gold Cannon, 1969 .... 6.00 To 80.00
Ezra Brooks, Gold Miner, 1970 .... 5.00 To 10.00
Ezra Brooks, Gold Seal, 1972 .... 12.00 To 14.00
Ezra Brooks, Gold Turkey, 1971 .... 37.00 To 42.00
Ezra Brooks, Golden Eagle, 1971 .... 12.00 To 15.00
Ezra Brooks, Golden Grizzly Bear, 1968 ....*Illus*   9.00
Ezra Brooks, Golden Horseshoe, 1970 .... 7.00 To 18.00
Ezra Brooks, Golden Rooster, No.1, 1969 .... 40.00 To 70.00
Ezra Brooks, Grandfather Clock, 1970 .... 6.00 To 8.00
Ezra Brooks, Greensboro, 1972 .... 10.00 To 11.00
Ezra Brooks, Greensboro, 1973 .... 30.00 To 60.00
Ezra Brooks, Grizzly Bear, Golden, 1968 .... 4.00 To 9.00
Ezra Brooks, Hambletonian, 1971 .... 12.00 To 13.00
Ezra Brooks, Harold's Dice, 1968 .... 8.00 To 10.00
Ezra Brooks, Hat, Zimmerman, 1969 .... 8.00 To 15.00
Ezra Brooks, Hereford, 1972 .... 8.00 To 14.00
Ezra Brooks, Historical Flasks, Set Of 4, 1970 .... 15.00 To 20.00
Ezra Brooks, Hockey Player, 1974 .... 12.00 To 15.00
Ezra Brooks, Hog, Razorback, 1970 .... 9.00 To 17.50
Ezra Brooks, Hollywood Cops, 1972 .... 9.00 To 15.00
Ezra Brooks, Horseshoe, Golden, 1970 .... 7.00 To 18.00
Ezra Brooks, Hummingbird Kachina, 1973 .... 30.00 To 40.00
Ezra Brooks, Idaho Potato, 1973, Skier .... 12.00 To 22.50
Ezra Brooks, Indian, Cigar Store, 1968 .... 5.00 To 10.00
Ezra Brooks, Indy 500, 1970 .... 11.00 To 15.00
Ezra Brooks, Iowa Statehouse, 1971 .... 20.00 To 30.00
Ezra Brooks, Iron Horse, 1969 .... 7.00 To 10.00
Ezra Brooks, Jack Of Diamonds, 1969 .... 6.00 To 10.00
Ezra Brooks, Japanese Pistol, 1968 .... 50.00 To 75.00
Ezra Brooks, Jayhawk, Kansas, 1969 .... 8.00 To 14.95
Ezra Brooks, Jester, Court, 1972 .... 10.00 To 15.00
Ezra Brooks, Kachina Doll, 1971 .... 60.00 To 100.00
Ezra Brooks, Kansas Jayhawk, 1969 .... 8.00 To 14.95
Ezra Brooks, Kansas Wheat Shocker, 1971 .... 6.00 To 10.00

Ezra Brooks, Katz Cat, Philharmonic Conductor, 1970

Ezra Brooks, Nugget Classic

Ezra Brooks, Katz Cat, Philharmonic Conductor, 1970	*Illus* 11.00
Ezra Brooks, Katz Cat, 1969	9.00 To 11.00
Ezra Brooks, Killer Whale	21.00 To 27.50
Ezra Brooks, King Of Clubs, 1969	8.00 To 12.00
Ezra Brooks, King Salmon, 1971, Washington	25.00 To 40.00
Ezra Brooks, Legionnaire, 1972	20.00 To 22.50
Ezra Brooks, Liberty Bell, 1970	8.00 To 10.00
Ezra Brooks, Lighthouse, Maine, 1971	16.00 To 18.00
Ezra Brooks, Lion On Rock, 1971	6.00 To 10.00
Ezra Brooks, Liquor Squares, 1972	13.00 To 17.00
Ezra Brooks, Lobster, Maine, 1970	20.00 To 32.00
Ezra Brooks, Longhorn Steer, Texas, 1971	12.00 To 16.00
Ezra Brooks, Maine Lighthouse, 1971	16.00 To 18.00
Ezra Brooks, Maine Lobster, 1970	20.00 To 32.00
Ezra Brooks, Maine Potato, 1974	12.00 To 14.00
Ezra Brooks, Man-O-War, 1969	10.00 To 28.00
Ezra Brooks, Map, U.S., Club Bottle, 1973	17.00 To 25.00
Ezra Brooks, Military Tank, 1971	12.00 To 15.00
Ezra Brooks, Missouri Mule, 1971	6.00 To 12.00
Ezra Brooks, Moose, 1973	12.00 To 15.00
Ezra Brooks, Mortar & Pestle, Walgreen, 1974	20.00 To 25.00
Ezra Brooks, Motorcycle, 1972	7.00 To 14.00
Ezra Brooks, Mountaineer, West Virginia, 1971	80.00 To 120.00
Ezra Brooks, Mr.Foremost, 1969	13.00 To 18.00
Ezra Brooks, Mr.Merchant, 1970	10.00 To 15.00
Ezra Brooks, Mule, Missouri, 1971	6.00 To 12.00
Ezra Brooks, Mule, Tonopah, 1972	15.00 To 19.00
Ezra Brooks, New Hampshire State House, 1970	12.00 To 20.00
Ezra Brooks, Nugget Classic	*Illus* 22.50
Ezra Brooks, Oil Gusher, 1969	6.00 To 12.00
Ezra Brooks, Old Man Of The Mountain, 1970, New Hampshire	16.00 To 20.00
Ezra Brooks, Ontario 500, 1970	6.00 To 10.00
Ezra Brooks, Panda, 1972	10.00 To 14.00
Ezra Brooks, Penguin, 1973	7.00 To 14.00
Ezra Brooks, Penny Farthington, 1973	10.00 To 15.00
Ezra Brooks, Phoenix Bird, 1971	*Illus* 60.00
Ezra Brooks, Phonograph, Antique, 1971	9.00 To 18.00
Ezra Brooks, Pierce Arrow, Sports Phaeton	18.00 To 20.00
Ezra Brooks, Pirate, 1971	8.00 To 10.00
Ezra Brooks, Pistol, Dueling, 1968	7.00 To 10.00
Ezra Brooks, Pistol, Japan, 1968	50.00 To 75.00
Ezra Brooks, Potato, Maine, 1974	12.00 To 14.00
Ezra Brooks, Potbelly Stove, 1968	7.00 To 10.00

Ezra Brooks, Phoenix Bird, 1971
(See Page 63)

Ezra Brooks, Quail, California, 1970 .... 5.00 To 10.00
Ezra Brooks, Queen Of Hearts, 1969 .... 8.00 To 9.00
Ezra Brooks, Race Car, Sprint, 1971 .... 14.00 To 15.00
Ezra Brooks, Ram, 1973 .... 8.00 To 12.00
Ezra Brooks, Razorback Hog, Arkansas, 1970 .... 9.00 To 17.50
Ezra Brooks, Reno Arch, 1968 .... 7.00 To 10.00
Ezra Brooks, Rooster, Classic .... 7.00 To 10.00
Ezra Brooks, Rooster, Golden, No.1 .... 40.00 To 70.00
Ezra Brooks, Rough Rider, Bucking Bronco, 1974 .... 11.00 To 13.00
Ezra Brooks, Sailfish, 1971 .... 8.00 To 12.00
Ezra Brooks, Salmon, Washington, 1971 .... 25.00 To 40.00
Ezra Brooks, San Francisco Cable Car, Brown .... 4.00 To 12.00
Ezra Brooks, San Francisco Cable Car, Gray .... 4.00 To 12.00
Ezra Brooks, San Francisco Cable Car, Green .... 4.00 To 12.00
Ezra Brooks, Sea Captain, 1971 .... 11.00 To 13.00
Ezra Brooks, Senator, 1972 .... 12.00 To 15.00
Ezra Brooks, Sherman Tank, 1971 .... 12.00 To 15.00
Ezra Brooks, Silver Dollar, 1970, Black Bottom .... 12.00 To 16.00
Ezra Brooks, Silver Dollar, 1970, White Bottom .... 10.00 To 13.00
Ezra Brooks, Silver Saddle, 1973 .... 30.00 To 33.00
Ezra Brooks, Silver Spur, 1971 .... 8.00 To 13.00
Ezra Brooks, Ski Boot, 1972 .... 7.00 To 16.00

Ezra Brooks, Tennis Player, 1973
(See Page 65)

Ezra Brooks,
Trout & Fly, 1970
(See Page 65)

West Virginia Mountaineer,
Ezra Brooks, 1971
(See Page 65)

Ezra Brooks, Ski Potato, 1973 .... 12.00 To 22.50
Ezra Brooks, Slot Machine, 1971 .... 16.00 To 20.00
Ezra Brooks, Snowmobile, 1972 .... 8.00 To 11.50
Ezra Brooks, South Carolina Gamecock, 1970 .... 10.00 To 18.00
Ezra Brooks, Sprint Race Car, 1971 .... 14.00 To 15.00
Ezra Brooks, Stagecoach, 1969 .... 7.00 To 9.00
Ezra Brooks, Stove, Potbelly, 1968 .... 7.00 To 10.00
Ezra Brooks, Strongman, 1974 .... 11.00 To 13.00
Ezra Brooks, Tecumseh, 1969 .... 9.00 To 15.00
Ezra Brooks, Telephone, Antique, 1971 .... 9.00 To 12.00
Ezra Brooks, Tennis Player, 1973 .... Illus   14.00
Ezra Brooks, Texas Longhorn Steer, 1971 .... 12.00 To 16.00
Ezra Brooks, Ticker Tape, 1970 .... 7.00 To 10.00
Ezra Brooks, Tonapah Mule, 1972 .... 15.00 To 19.00
Ezra Brooks, Totem Pole, No.1, 1972 .... 15.00 To 17.95
Ezra Brooks, Totem Pole No.2, 1974 .... 14.00 To 16.00
Ezra Brooks, Tractor, Fordson, 1971 .... 15.00 To 17.95
Ezra Brooks, Trail Bike, 1973 .... 7.00 To 12.50
Ezra Brooks, Trojan, U.S.C., 1973 .... 17.00 To 22.00
Ezra Brooks, Trout & Fly, 1970 .... Illus   10.00
Ezra Brooks, Turkey, Gold, 1971 .... 37.00 To 42.00
Ezra Brooks, Turkey, White, 1971 .... 15.00 To 20.00
Ezra Brooks, U.S.C.Trojan, 1973 .... 17.00 To 22.00
Ezra Brooks, U.S.Map, Club Bottle, 1973 .... 17.00 To 25.00
Ezra Brooks, Vermont Skier, 1972 .... 15.00 To 19.00
Ezra Brooks, Virginia Cardinal, 1973 .... 15.00 To 30.00
Ezra Brooks, Washington Salmon, 1970 .... 25.00 To 40.00
Ezra Brooks, Washington Whale, 1972 .... 10.00 To 15.00
Ezra Brooks, Water Tower, Chicago, 1969 .... 8.00 To 14.00
Ezra Brooks, Weirton Steel, W.Virginia, 1974 .... 18.00 To 25.00
Ezra Brooks, West Virginia Mountain Lady, 1972 .... 14.00 To 20.00
Ezra Brooks, West Virginia Mountaineer, 1971 .... Illus   120.00

Famous Firsts,   Famous Firsts,   Famous Firsts,   Famous Firsts,
Animal Pitcher,   Animal Pitcher,   Animal Pitcher,   Animal Pitcher,
Zebra   Leopard   Lion   Tiger

Ezra Brooks, Wheat Shocker, Kansas, 1971 .... 6.00 To 10.00
Ezra Brooks, White Turkey, 1971 .... 15.00 To 20.00
Ezra Brooks, Wichita Centennial, 1970 .... 7.00 To 18.00
Ezra Brooks, Wisconsin Bucky Badger, 1974 .... 14.00 To 16.00
Ezra Brooks, Zimmerman's Hat, 1969 .... 8.00 To 15.00
    Face Cream, see Cosmetic, Medicine
Famous Firsts, Animal Pitcher, Leopard .... Illus   21.00
Famous Firsts, Animal Pitcher, Lion .... Illus   21.00
Famous Firsts, Animal Pitcher, Tiger .... Illus   21.00
Famous Firsts, Animal Pitcher, Zebra .... Illus   21.00
Famous Firsts, Coffee Mill .... 20.00 To 22.50
Famous Firsts, De Witt Clinton Engine, 1969 .... 19.50 To 22.50

Famous Firsts, Honda Motorcycle

Famous Firsts, French Telephone, 1969 .... 20.00 To 26.50
Famous Firsts, Garibaldi .... 15.00 To 17.50
Famous Firsts, Gold Marmon, 1/2 Pint 21.50
Famous Firsts, Gold Racer 12.00
Famous Firsts, Hen .... 11.00 To 13.50
Famous Firsts, Honda Motorcycle .... *Illus*   29.00
Famous Firsts, Napoleon .... 15.00 To 17.50
Famous Firsts, Phonograph 21.50
Famous Firsts, Renault Racer .... 11.00 To 20.00
Famous Firsts, Robert E.Lee Riverboat .... 19.00 To 22.00
Famous Firsts, San Francisco Cable Car, Fifth size .... *Illus*   39.50
Famous Firsts, San Francisco Cable Car, Mini .... *Illus*   13.00

Famous Firsts,
San Francisco Cable Car,
Fifth

Famous Firsts,
San Francisco Cable Car,
Mini

Famous Firsts, Scale .... 19.00 To 22.00
Famous Firsts, Sewing Machine .... 19.00 To 22.00
Famous Firsts, Spirit Of St.Louis 15.00
Famous Firsts, St.Pols Bell .... 7.00 To 9.00
Famous Firsts, Telephone Flora .... *Illus*   26.00
Famous Firsts, Wasp 15.00
Famous Firsts, Winnie Mae, Maxi .... *Illus*   39.50
Famous Firsts, Winnie Mae, Midi .... *Illus*   23.50
Famous Firsts, Winnie Mae, Mini .... *Illus*   11.00

Famous Firsts, Telephone Flora
(See Page 66)

Famous Firsts,
Winnie Mae, Maxi
(See Page 66)

Famous Firsts,
Winnie Mae, Mini
(See Page 66)

Famous Firsts,
Winnie Mae, Midi
(See Page 66)

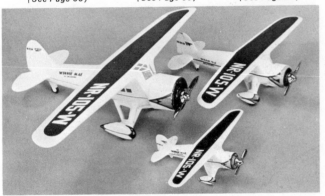

*Figural bottles are specially named by the collectors of bottles. Any
bottle that is of a recognizable shape, such as a human head, or a pretzel, or
a clock, is considered to be a figural. There is no restriction as to date
or material.*

Figural, see also Bitters, Cologne, Perfume

Figural, Accordionist, Bear-A-Tone, Ceramic, Wine, 2 Ozs., 4 1/2 In.	3.00
Figural, Alarm Clock, Embossed Face, 4 1/2 In.	5.00
Figural, Banker, First National Of Great Falls, Mont., 6 In.	5.00
Figural, Barrel O'Kindness, Brodie Tartan Plaid, White, 2 In.	3.25
Figural, Barrel O'Kindness, Gordon Tartan Plaid, 2 In.	3.25
Figural, Barrel O'Kindness, Hamilton Tartan Plaid, White, 2 In.	3.25
Figural, Barrel O'Kindness, MacLeod Tartan Plaid, White, 2 In.	3.25
Figural, Barrel O'Kindness, Stewart Tartan Plaid, White, 2 In.	3.25
Figural, Barrel, Carnival Glass, Marigold, 3 3/4 In.	50.00
Figural, Barrel, Embossed LAM. A & F On Base, Green, 10 In.	24.50
Figural, Barrel, Hoops, Label Space, Flared Mouth, Cobalt, 8 1/2 In.	200.00
Figural, Barrel, Lancaster, N.Y. & Glass Works, Dark Amber, 9 1/2 In.	192.00
Figural, Barrel, Pub, Porcelain, English Cottage Scenes, White, 3 1/4 In.	3.50
Figural, Barrel, Pub, Porcelain, English Maps, White, 3 1/4 In.	3.50

Figural, Barrel, Sewer Tile, 9 1/2 In. .... *Color*   45.00
Figural, Barrel, Theodore Netter, 6 In. 15.00
Figural, Baseball Bat, White Socks, Embossed, 7 Ozs. 12.00
Figural, Bass Viol, Cranberry, 9 1/8 X 5 1/4 X 2 In. 25.00
Figural, Bass Violin, Vetter, Germany, 1955, Liqueur, 5 In. 6.50
Figural, Bear, Bank, Clear, 4 3/4 In. 3.00
Figural, Bear, Partly Frosted, 7 1/4 In. 7.00
Figural, Before & After Faces .... *Illus*   25.00

Figural, Before & After Faces

Figural, Bellboy, Marked Germany, Pink, 8 3/4 In. 8.00
Figural, Betty Boop, 4 In. 20.00
Figural, Big Ben Tower, Black Base, 6 1/2 In. 5.00
Figural, Billiken 30.00
Figural, Billiken, Gold Paint, Screw Cap, 4 In. .... *Illus*   40.00
Figural, Black Man, Frosted Body, 14 In. .... *Illus*   245.00
Figural, Blackpool Tower, Porcelain, Tan, 3 1/2 In. 4.00
Figural, Book, Bikini Clad Girl On Cover, Porcelain, Tan, 3 In. 3.25
Figural, Book, Rutherford, Volume I, Black, 5 In. 2.95
Figural, Book, Rutherford, Volume II, Green, 5 In. 2.95
Figural, Book, Rutherford, Volume III, Blue, 5 In. 2.95
Figural, Book, Rutherford, Volume IV, Red, 5 In. 2.95
Figural, Bull Lying Down, Head Covers Opening 25.00
Figural, Bull-Nosed Morris, Porcelain, Aidess, 1965, Gold, Platinum, 3 1/2 In. 6.00
Figural, Bull, Rutherford, Porcelain, Cork In Head, Brown, 4 1/2 In. 6.50
Figural, Bullfighter, 12 In. 4.00
Figural, Bunch Of Cigars, Amber 30.00
Figural, Bunch Of Grapes, 6 1/4 In. 5.00
Figural, Bust Of Man, Screw Opening, Black Amethyst 15.00
Figural, Car, Amber, 3 In. 15.00
Figural, Carry Nation 10.00
Figural, Carry Nation Carrying Basket Of Pamphlets, Germany, Quart 100.00
Figural, Cat, Smiling, Amethyst, 9 1/4 In. 25.00
Figural, Cat, 11 1/4 In. 25.00
Figural, Cazanove Acrobat, France, Brandy, Molded Glass, 6 In. 10.00
Figural, Cherub Holding Medallion, Bimal 35.00
Figural, Chicken On Nest, 9 1/2 In. 35.00
Figural, Chicken, Molded Glass, Maroon Base, 2 1/2 In. 3.00
Figural, Chicken, 3 Mold, Patented, 9 1/2 In. .... *Color*   45.00
Figural, Chinese Dragon, Rectangular, Cobalt, 2 In. 20.00
Figural, Christmas Tree, Star Stopper, Bimal 125.00
Figural, Cigar 20.00
Figural, Cigar, Amber 20.00
Figural, Cigar, Marshall 35.00
Figural, Claw And Egg, Bimal 28.00
Figural, Clock Face, Kiddie Bottle 5.00
Figural, Corn, Carnival Glass, Green 125.00
Figural, Crinoline Lady, Molded Glass, Black Screw Base, 3 1/2 In. 5.00

Figural, Billiken, Gold Paint, Screw Cap, 4 In.
(See Page 68)

Figural, Black Man, Frosted Body, 14 In.
(See Page 68)

Figural, Dice, Porcelain,
9 In.

Figural, Dog, 11 In.

Figural, Fish, Lilly, Amber
(See Page 70)

Figural, **Crown,** Molded Glass, Gold Plated, 2 1/4 In.	3.00
Figural, **Cucumber,** Green, 4 1/2 In.	25.00
Figural, **Cucumber,** Pottery, Green With Tan, 5 In.	32.50
Figural, **Dagger,** 9 In.	30.00
Figural, **Dice,** Porcelain, 9 In. .... *Illus*	75.00
Figural, **Dickens' Olde Curiosity Shop,** Porcelain, Tan, 2 1/4 In.	5.50
Figural, **Doe's Head,** Porcelain, Tan, 3 3/4 In.	4.50
Figural, **Dog,** Blown, Applied Ears, Legs, & Hollow Tail, Nose Opening, 7 In.	65.00
Figural, **Dog,** Cambridge, Apple Green, 7 3/4 In.	37.50
Figural, **Dog,** Miniature	20.00
Figural, **Dog,** Molded Glass, White Cat, 2 3/4 In.	3.00
Figural, **Dog,** Sham-Poodle, Cobalt, 8 In.	12.00 To 18.00
Figural, **Dog,** Sterling Silver Head, 8 In. ....*Color*	400.00
Figural, **Dog,** 11 In. .... *Illus*	20.00
Figural, **Dreadnaught,** Cloudy	30.00
Figural, **Drunk Cossack,** Vodka, Royal Norfolk Porcelain, 5 In.	6.50
Figural, **Duckling,** Dettling, Molded, White Visor, Switzerland, 2 1/2 In.	4.00
Figural, **Eagle Landing On Rock,** Rutherford, Porcelain, Brown, 5 3/4 In.	8.00

Figural, Ear Of Corn, Blown, Light Amber, 9 1/2 In.	80.00
Figural, Ear Of Corn, Carnival Glass, 5 In. ....*Color*	175.00
Figural, Ear Of Corn, El Kahir Temple, Cedar Rapids, Iowa, 6 1/2 In.	35.00
Figural, Ear Of Corn, Screw Opening	20.00
Figural, Ear Of Corn, 3 Mold, 5 3/4 In.	22.00
Figural, Ear Of Corn, 10 1/2 In. ....*Color* XXXX.XX	
Figural, Eiffel Tower, 14 In.	20.00
Figural, Elephant, Standing With Trunk Wrapped Around A Tree, 3 7/8 In.	60.00
Figural, Elk's Tooth, Embossed Elk & B.P.O.E., Pale Yellow, 4 1/4 In.	60.00
Figural, Fantasia, Clear	20.00
Figural, Fantasia, Frosted	30.00
Figural, Fat Man Holding Glass, 8 1/2 In.	25.00
Figural, Fat Nude	35.00
Figural, Fat Soldier With Sword & Large Hat, 7 1/4 In.	20.00
Figural, Female Nude Holding Urn, Art Deco, Frosted, 14 1/2 In.	24.00
Figural, Fiddle, Pint	5.00
Figural, Fish, Amber, 6 In.	18.00
Figural, Fish, Blue, 11 In.	25.00
Figural, Fish, Cod Liver Oil, Amber	15.00
Figural, Fish, Cork, Amber, 6 1/5 In.	18.00
Figural, Fish, Flared Top, Green	10.00
Figural, Fish, Lilly, Amber ....*Illus*	12.00
Figural, Fish, Pottery, 7 1/2 In. ....*Color*	650.00
Figural, Fish, Screw Cap, 8 3/4 In.	28.50
Figural, Flapper	15.00
Figural, Fox Terrier, Marked Germany, 7 In.	12.00
Figural, French Cavalier	50.00
Figural, French Cavalier, Miniature	25.00
Figural, French Poodle, Cobalt, 8 In.High	15.00
Figural, French Taxi, Frosted & Clear	100.00
Figural, General Electric Refrigerator, Embossed, 1930s, Green	10.00
Figural, George Washington, Clear, 9 1/2 In.High	6.95
Figural, George Washington, Full Figure, Clear, 9 5/8 In.High	6.75
Figural, George Washington, 1732-1932	18.00
Figural, Girl & Biting Dog, "just A Little Nip, " C.1920, Bisque, 4 1/2 In.	5.00
Figural, Girl In Tights Standing On Ball, Depose, Camphor Glass, 13 1/4 In.	32.00
Figural, Girl In Tights, 13 1/2 In. ....*Color*	50.00
Figural, Girl With Umbrella, 5 In. ....*Illus*	3.00
Figural, Golf Ball, On Red Base, Porcelain, White, 1 1/2 In.	3.00
Figural, Golfer Caddy, 12 In.High	35.00
Figural, Good Old Bourbon In A Hogs—, Amber, 3 1/2 In ....*Illus*	200.00

Figural, Girl With Umbrella, 5 In.

Figural, Good Old Bourbon In A Hogs—,
Amber, 3 1/2 In

Figural, Granger's Bust, 6 1/2 In. 40.00
Figural, Hand & Dagger, 15 In. .... *Illus* 20.00
Figural, Hand Holding Vase, Milk Glass, 6 In. 45.00
Figural, Hand, 4 1/2 In. .... *Illus* 12.00
Figural, Happy Jack Toby, Green, 8 3/4 In. 95.00
Figural, Hat, Pontil, Golden Amber, 2 In. 15.00
Figural, Hausdoktor, Military Coat, Blue, 6 1/2 In.High 37.25
Figural, Hemisphere, World's Fair, 1939, Molded, Milk Glass, 9 1/4 In.High 18.00
Figural, Hessian Soldier, Applied Top, 7 1/2 In. 45.00
Figural, Hessian Soldier, Clear, 7 1/4 In. 40.00
Figural, Hessian Soldier, 7 In. 35.00

Figural, Hand & Dagger, 15 In.

Figural, Hand, 4 1/2 In.

Figural, Horn, Pottery, Brown Glaze, 12 In. .... *Illus* 25.00
Figural, Hound, Sad-Eyed, 9 3/4 In. 20.00
Figural, Hound, Sad, Jigger, Green, 8 In. 20.00
Figural, Hull Bros., Detroit, Michigan, 9 In. .... *Color* 375.00
Figural, Husted Santa, Bimal 55.00
Figural, Joan Of Arc On Horseback, Miniature 25.00
Figural, Joan Of Arc On Horseback, 10 In.High 18.00
Figural, Joan Of Arc, Mead Label, Molded Glass, 4 3/4 In. 10.00
Figural, King Arthur, Porcelain, 1965, Tan, 4 3/4 In. 15.00
Figural, Koala Bear Climbing Tree, Molded Glass, Black Base, 3 1/2 In. 5.00
Figural, Lady In Gown, 2 1/2 In. 6.00
Figural, Lady, Frosted, 14 In. .... *Illus* 52.00
Figural, Lady's Leg, Embossed, 3 Mold, Olive, 11 3/4 In. 30.00
Figural, Lamp, Tartan Design On Clear Base, Plastic Shade, 3 In. 3.00
Figural, Lantern, Miner's, Porcelain, Dark Blue, 3 In. 6.00
Figural, Lemon, 'Paul Mangiet Will Hand You One, ' 4 In.High 15.00
Figural, Life Saver, "When Sinking Take Hold, " Porcelain, Gray, 4 3/4 In. 40.00
Figural, Lighthouse, Red Trim, Brown Rock Base, Porcelain, White, 4 1/4 In. 3.50
Figural, Lighthouse, 7 1/2 In. 28.00

Figural, Horn, Pottery,
Brown Glaze, 12 In.

Figural, Lady, Frosted, 14 In.

Figural, Lincoln, Bank, 9 In.

Figural, Log Cabin, Smokine,
Amber, 7 In.

Figural, **Lincoln**, Bank, 9 In.	*Illus*	18.00
Figural, **Little Bopeep**, Cap, 6 In.		7.00
Figural, **Little Girl With Umbrella**, 4 1/2 In.		12.00
Figural, **Loch Ness Monster**, Monarch, 1964, Porcelain, Blue & Green, 2 1/2 In.		5.00
Figural, **Log Cabin**, Smokine, Amber, 7 In.	*Illus*	240.00
Figural, **Madonna**, Handle, Cobalt, 13 In.		15.00
Figural, **Man From The Moon**, Painted, 11 In.	*Illus*	40.00
Figural, **Man In Black Cape**, Royal Doulton, 4 5/8 In.		40.00
Figural, **Man**, 13 1/2 In.		6.00
Figural, **Mermaid On Seaweed Covered Rock**, Porcelain, Tan, 4 In.		6.00
Figural, **Mermaid Sitting On Rock**, Molded Glass, Black Base, 3 1/2 In.		5.00
Figural, **Mermaid**, Pottery, 12 In.	*Illus*	20.00
Figural, **Monkey & Mirror**, German, Porcelain, 4 1/4 In.High		50.00
Figural, **Monkey Wearing Glasses**, Bimal, 4 1/2 In.		25.00
Figural, **Moses**, Amber, Quart		12.00
Figural, **Moses**, Green, Quart		1.50
Figural, **Moses**, Pint		11.00
Figural, **Moses**, Poland Water, Bimal		75.00
Figural, **Moses**, Quart		15.00
Figural, **Moses**, Screw Top, Green, 10 In.High		2.75 To 3.00
Figural, **Mr.Pickwick**, Clear, 9 In.High		6.95

Figural, Man From The Moon, Painted, 11 In.

Figural, Mermaid, Pottery, 12 In.

Figural, Negro Man Servant, Wine, Screw Top, 11 1/2 In. 25.00
Figural, Nude Dancing Girls, Cha.Stenet Freres, 5 1/4 In. 20.00
Figural, Orange, Ceramic, Natural Color, 3 3/4 In. 15.00
Figural, Owl, Amber, 9 1/8 In. 35.00
Figural, Owl, Amber, 9 1/4 In. 40.00
Figural, Owl, Ground Lip, 8 1/2 In. 35.00
Figural, Owl, Milk Glass, 4 In. 22.50
Figural, Owl, Mustard Jar, Milk Glass 50.00
Figural, Owl, Pink, 9 1/2 In. 35.00
Figural, Owl, Round, 8 In. 35.00
Figural, Owl, Square, Stain, Cobalt, 6 1/4 In. 29.00
Figural, Penguin, Syrup, 8 In. 2.50
Figural, Penguin, 11 In. 10.00
Figural, Pig With Embossed "Good Old Bourbon In A Hogs—, "7 In. 50.00
Figural, Pig, Beiser & Fisher, N.Y., Amber, 9 In. .... *Illus* 1000.00

Figural, Pig, Beiser & Fisher, N.Y., Amber, 9 In.

Figural, Pig, Bieler's Ronny Club, Pottery, 5 1/2 In. .... *Color* XXXX.XX
Figural, Pig, Blown, Green, 10 1/2 In. 40.00
Figural, Pig, "Something Good In A Hogs—, " 4 In. 35.00
Figural, Pineapple, Amber, 9 In. 115.00
Figural, Pixie Elf, Porcelain, Red & Green Trim, Tan, 4 In. 3.50
Figural, Poodle, French, Depose, Pontil, Sun Colored, 12 1/2 In. 60.00
Figural, Poodle, Sham-Poodle, Cobalt, 8 In. .... 12.00 To 18.00
Figural, Potato, Paint, 5 1/2 In. 35.00
Figural, Pretzel, Porcelain, 5 1/4 In.High 35.00
Figural, Quahog, Screw Cap 18.00
Figural, Rabbit, Porcelain, Tan, 3 1/4 In. 3.50
Figural, Rebecca At The Well, Pontil, Frosted Body, 8 In. 45.00
Figural, Refrigerator, Wishing Well Patent, 1932, Embossed, Green 7.00
Figural, Robert Burns' Bust, Ceramic, Matte Finish, White, 4 In. 4.95
Figural, Rolling Pin, Child's, Lockport Color, 4 In. 150.00
Figural, Sad Hound With Jigger, Green, 8 In. 20.00
Figural, Sad Hound, Ground Lip, Pink, 10 In. 35.00
Figural, Sad Pup, 2 1/2 In. 3.00
Figural, Santa & Bag Of Toys, Vetter, Christmas Man, Red Plastic Cap, 5 In. 8.50
Figural, Scallop, Screw Cap 18.00
Figural, Scotch Lad, Hispania, Scotch Whiskey Made Here, Porcelain, 13 In. 22.00
Figural, Scotch Thistle, Molded Glass, Plastic Base, 2 3/4 In. 3.00
Figural, Scotch Warrior, Tam & Tartan, Porcelain, 4 In. 4.50
Figural, Scottie, Begging, Porcelain, Tartan Coat, Black, 4 1/4 In. 4.00
Figural, Senorita, Milk Glass, 6 1/4 In. 30.00
Figural, Shakespeare's Birthplace House, Tan & Brown, 2 In. 5.95
Figural, Shamrock, Swirled Rib, Applied Handle, Dark Blue Iridescent, 6 In. 35.00
Figural, Ship's Running Light, Aidees, Molded, Green Lens, 2 1/2 In. 3.00
Figural, Ship's Running Light, Aidees, Molded, Red Lens, 2 1/2 In. 3.00
Figural, Ship's Running Light, Aidees, Molded, Yellow Lens, 2 1/2 In. 3.00
Figural, Ship's Running Light, Porcelain, 1969, Green Lens, Tan, 3 In. 4.50
Figural, Ship's Running Light, Porcelain, 1969, Red Lens, Tan, 3 In. 4.50
Figural, Shoe, Revenue Stamp On Sole, 4 1/2 In.High 22.50
Figural, Shoe, 3 3/4 In. 15.00
Figural, Sitting Bear, Black Milk Glass, Green Base 40.00
Figural, Skeleton Sitting On Barrel, Glass Eyes, Bisque, 9 In. 125.00
Figural, Skeleton With Left Finger Alongside Face, Germany, Quart 100.00
Figural, Slipper, 3 1/2 In. 12.00
Figural, Slipper, 4 1/2 In. 12.00

Figural, Slipper, 5 3/4 In. 22.00
Figural, Smiling Cat, Amethyst, 9 1/4 In. 25.00
Figural, Soccer Ball, Porcelain, 2 In. 3.50
Figural, Spanish Lady, Lace Mantilla, Compania Hollandesa, 12 In.High 55.00
Figural, Standing Owl, Gray, Feathers Outlined In Dark Blue 125.00
Figural, Tam-O'-Shanter, Porcelain, Red Pompon, Blue, 1 1/2 In. 4.00
Figural, Teddy Bear, Green, 13 In.High 15.00
Figural, Teddy Roosevelt, 13 1/2 In. 89.50
Figural, Tennis Ball, Porcelain, White, 2 1/2 In. 4.00
Figural, Three Pinecones, Majolica, Brown & Green, 8 1/4 In. 65.00
Figural, Tin Mine In Cornwall, Ceramic, 1967, Brown & Tan, 4 In. 6.00
Figural, Toby Mug, Porcelain, Red & Green Trim, Tan, 3 1/2 In. 4.00
Figural, Train, Screw Opening 30.00
Figural, Turtle, Fine Turtle Hair Oil, Cork & Glass Head, Amber, 4 3/4 In. 75.00
Figural, Two Men, Depose, 11 In. ....*Illus* 55.00

Figural, Two Men, Depose, 11 In.

Figural, Two Milk Bottles In Basket, Milk Glass, 3 3/4 In. 47.50
Figural, Uncle Sam, Cloudy, 9 1/2 In. 17.50
Figural, Venus Rising From Sea, Screw Opening In Base, Frosted Blue 25.00
Figural, Violin, Amber, Potstone, 9 3/4 In. 18.00
Figural, Violin, Cobalt Blue, 8 In.High 1.25
Figural, Violin, Dark Amethyst, 9 3/4 In. 15.00
Figural, Violin, Emerald Green 20.00
Figural, Violin, Fleur-De-Lis, Aqua, 1/2 Pint, 6 In. 30.00
Figural, Violin, Honey Amber, 8 3/4 In.High 15.00
Figural, Violin, Ice Blue, 7 1/2 In. 10.00
Figural, Violin, Musical Scale, Hanger, 10 In. 10.00
Figural, Violin, Olive Green, 6 1/4 In. 12.00
Figural, Warrior's Head, Screw Opening, Black Amethyst 15.00
Figural, Washington Bust, Whiskey, Bimal, Cobalt, 9 1/2 In.High 25.00
Figural, Washington Standing 10.00
Figural, Washington, Screw Top, 4 In. ....*Color* 12.00
Figural, Welsh Hat, Porcelain, Peaked, Red Band, Black, 2 In. 3.00
Figural, Whiskey Cask, Porcelain, Gold Bands, Tan, 1 3/4 In. 3.25
Figural, Woman & Man, Volendam, Holland, Blue, 3 3/4 & 3 1/2 In., Pair 10.00
Figural, Woman's High Laced Shoe & Stockinged Leg, C.1880, 12 1/2 In. 38.00
Figural, Ye Olde Beer Handle, Hunting Scenes, Gold, Porcelain, 5 3/4 In. 4.00
Figural, Zorro, Royal Doulton .... 40.00 To 47.50
Fire Extinguisher, Blue, 6 1/2 In. ....*Illus* 22.00
Fire Extinguisher, Copper & Brass, 2 1/2 Gallon 25.00
Fire Extinguisher, Embossed Magic Fire Extinguisher Co., 3 Mold, Amber 55.00
Fire Extinguisher, Globe, Aqua, 6 In. 50.00
Fire Extinguisher, Harden's Hand Grenade, Amber, 8 In. ....*Color* 60.00
Fire Extinguisher, Harden's Hand Grenade, Blue, 8 In. ....*Color* 30.00
Fire Extinguisher, Harden's Hand Grenade, Green, 8 In. ....*Color* 100.00
Fire Extinguisher, Harden's, Embossed, Molded Star In Circle, Blue 26.00
Fire Extinguisher, Harden's, No.2, Footed, Hand 45.00
Fire Extinguisher, Mason Clyde, N.Y., Three Lions' Faces, Green, 6 X 6 In. 25.22

Fire Extinguisher, Rockford, Cobalt, 11 1/2 In. .... *Illus*   75.00
     Fitzgerald, see Old Fitzgerald

Fire Extinguisher, Blue, 6 1/2 In.
(See Page 74)

Fire Extinguisher, Rockford,
Cobalt, 11 1/2 In.

Flasks have been made since the 18th century in America. The free blown, mold blown, and decorated flasks are all popular with collectors. The numbers that appear with some of the entries are those used in the McKearin book, American Glass. The numbers used in the entries in the form Van R-0 or Mc Kearin G I-0 refer to the books Early American Bottles & Flasks by Stephen Van Rensselaer and American Glass by George P. and Helen McKearin.

Flask, Almedia Co., Boston, Straight Sided, 1/2 Pint	3.00
Flask, Amber, Pint	4.00
Flask, Amber, Quart	8.00
Flask, Anchor & Baltimore Glass Works & Resurgam & Eagle, Aqua, Pint	68.00
Flask, Anchor & Baltimore Glass Works & Resurgam, Amber, Pint	105.00
Flask, Anchor & Baltimore Glass Works & Resurgam, Aqua, Pint	60.00
Flask, Anchor & Baltimore Glass Works & Sheaf Of Rye, Aqua, 1/2 Pint	40.00
Flask, Anchor & Ravenna Glass Co. & Eagle & 13 Stars, Amber, Pint	95.00
Flask, Anchor & Scrolls & Baltimore Glass Works, Lip Ring, Aqua, 1/2 Pint	65.00
Flask, Anchor & Springgarden Glass Works & Log Cabin, Deep Aqua, Pint	45.00
Flask, Anchor, Amber, Pint	20.00
Flask, Anchor, Amber, Quart	25.00
Flask, Anchor, Strap Sides, Aqua, Pint	12.00
Flask, Applied Crude Lip, Thin Mold Line, Dark Green, 1/2 Pint	18.00
Flask, Ballet Dancer & C.C.Goodale, Rochester, N.Y., Amber, 1/2 Pint	35.00
Flask, Baltimore Glass Works & Phoenix & Resurgam, Pale Aqua, Pint	50.00
Flask, Baltimore Glass Works & Resurgam, Aqua, Pint	40.00 To 80.00
Flask, Baltimore Glass Works & Resurgam, Aqua, Quart	75.00
Flask, Baltimore Glass Works & Resurgam, OP, Aqua, Pint	35.00
Flask, Baltimore Glass Works & Resurgam, Stain, Aqua, Pint	55.00
Flask, Baltimore Monument & Liberty & Union, Pale Aqua, Pint	200.00
Flask, Baltimore Monument & Sailboat, Light Yellow Green, 1/2 Pint	110.00
Flask, Banded, Amber, Quart	5.00
Flask, Blanchard & Farrar, Boston, Strap Sided, Union Oval, Blob Lip, Pint	15.00
Flask, Blown, Ribbed Sides, Drapery & Star Molding, Cobalt, 7 In.	45.00
Flask, Blown, Ribbed, Deep Aqua, 1/2 Pint	32.50
Flask, Blown, Ribbed, Flanged Lip, 6 1/2 In.	25.00
Flask, Bonnie Bros., Louisville, Ky., Sheaf Of Wheat In Slug Plate, 1/2 Pint	6.00
Flask, Bryan-Swell, 1896, United Democratic Ticket, Amber, 5 1/4 In.	275.00
Flask, Cabin & Spring Garden Glass Works, Aqua, Pint	80.00
Flask, Calabash, Clasped Hands & Masonic Emblem, OP, Quart	52.00
Flask, Calabash, Eagle & Banner, IP, Green, 9 In.	135.00
Flask, Calabash, Eagle & Clasped Hands, Amber, Quart	175.00
Flask, Calabash, Hunter Shooting Gun & Fisherman & House, Aqua, 9 1/2 In.	45.00

Flask, Calabash, Hunter Shooting Gun & Fisherman & House, Blue Green, 9 In. 135.00
Flask, Calabash, Jenny Lind & Fislerville Glass Works, Aqua, 9 In. 40.00
Flask, Calabash, Jenny Lind & Glass House, Fislerville, Green, 9 1/2 In. 310.00
Flask, Calabash, Jenny Lind & Glass House, Ravenna, IP, Aqua, 10 In. 135.00
Flask, Calabash, Sheaf Of Rye & Star, Applied Handle, Amber, 9 In. 340.00
Flask, Calabash, Sheaf Of Wheat, Rake, & Fork & Star, Aqua, 9 In. 35.00
Flask, Calabash, Tree In Foliage & Sheaf Of Rye, Rake, & Fork, Aqua, 9 In. 25.00
Flask, Calabash, Union & Clasped Hands & Eagle & 2 Banners, Amber, 9 In. 100.00
Flask, Calabash, Union & Masonic & Eagle & Banners, Aqua, 9 In. 35.00
Flask, Chestnut Type, OP, Olive Green, 8 In. 20.00
Flask, Chestnut, Applied Handle, Ring On Sheared Lip, Red Amber, 8 In. 25.00
Flask, Chestnut, Blown, Amber, 4 3/4 In. 150.00
Flask, Chestnut, Blown, Clear, 4 In. 55.00
Flask, Chestnut, Blown, Clear, 5 5/8 In. 15.00
Flask, Chestnut, Blown, Dark Green, 7 1/4 In.High 68.00
Flask, Chestnut, Blown, Light Green, 4 5/8 In. 50.00
Flask, Chestnut, Blown, Ludlow Type, C.1850, Olive Amber, 7 In.High 48.00
Flask, Chestnut, Blown, Olive Amber, 7 1/2 In. 45.00
Flask, Chestnut, Blown, Olive Yellow, Pint, 6 3/4 In. 45.00
Flask, Chestnut, Blown, Olive Yellow, 1/2 Pint, 5 In. 35.00
Flask, Chestnut, Blown, Olive, Pint, 7 1/4 In. 45.00
Flask, Chestnut, Blown, 4 1/2 In. 20.00
Flask, Chestnut, Blown, 21 Swirled Ribs, Gray Blue, 6 1/2 In. 25.00
Flask, Chestnut, Blown, 25 Swirled Ribs, Aqua, 4 5/8 In. 65.00
Flask, Chestnut, Broken Swirl, C.1950, Puce, 9 In. 45.00
Flask, Chestnut, Bulbous, 14 Vertical Ribs, Sapphire Blue, 5 1/2 In. 450.00
Flask, Chestnut, Burgen Spital Wurzburg & Flying Bird, Red Amber, 6 In. 35.00
Flask, Chestnut, Domed Bottom, Collared Lip, Deep Amber, Quart 50.00
Flask, Chestnut, Elongated, Midwestern, Allover Ogivals, Green, 1/2 Pint 60.00
Flask, Chestnut, Elongated, Midwestern, 12 Expanded Diamonds, Yellow, 7 In. 95.00
Flask, Chestnut, Elongated, Zanesville, 10 Diamond Mold, Amber, 1/2 Pint 600.00
Flask, Chestnut, Flattened, Applied Handle, Amber, 7 1/2 In. 15.00
Flask, Chestnut, Flattened, Applied Handle, Dark Amber, 8 In. 30.00
Flask, Chestnut, Flattened, Applied Handle, Deep Red Amber, 7 In. 25.00
Flask, Chestnut, Flattened, Ohio, 25 Swirled Ribs, Dark Amber, Pint, 6 5/8 In. 200.00
Flask, Chestnut, Flattened, Stiegel Type, Enamel Decoration, 5 1/4 In. 37.50
Flask, Chestnut, Flattened, 12 Ribs, Applied Handle, Green, 5 1/2 In. 85.00
Flask, Chestnut, Flattened, 18 Vertical Ribs, Round Bottom, Blue, 6 1/2 In. 120.00
Flask, Chestnut, Free-Blown, Sheared Lip, OP, C.1750, Olive Green 55.00
Flask, Chestnut, Green, 3/4 Pint 40.00
Flask, Chestnut, Green, 5 In. 45.00
Flask, Chestnut, Green, 8 1/2 In. 35.00
Flask, Chestnut, Green, 9 1/4 In. 88.00
Flask, Chestnut, Kent, Ohio, 20 Broken Swirled Ribs, Yellow, 1/2 Pint 600.00
Flask, Chestnut, Kent, Ohio, 20 Vertical Ribs, Golden Amber, Pint, 6 In. 550.00
Flask, Chestnut, Kent, Ohio, 20 Vertical Ribs, Sea Green, Pint, 6 1/2 In. 125.00
Flask, Chestnut, Larsen, Expanded Diamond, Cranberry, Pint, 6 In. 55.00
Flask, Chestnut, Light Amber, Pint, 8 In. 35.00
Flask, Chestnut, Ludlow, Bubble Seeds, OP, Green, 8 X 4 7/8 In. 85.00
Flask, Chestnut, Ludlow, OP, Aquamarine, 8 1/4 X 5 In. 55.00
Flask, Chestnut, Mantua, 16 Broken Swirled Ribs, Light Green, 1/2 Pint 250.00
Flask, Chestnut, Mantua, 16 Swirled Ribs, Sea Green, 3 1/4 In. 500.00
Flask, Chestnut, Midwestern, Allover Ogivals, Deep Amethyst, 5 5/8 In. 250.00
Flask, Chestnut, Midwestern, Deep Amethyst, 6 1/4 In. 125.00
Flask, Chestnut, Midwestern, Expanded 15 Diamond Mold, Emerald, 5 1/4 In. 1600.00
Flask, Chestnut, Midwestern, 12 Diamond Mold, Light Amethyst, 5 3/4 In. 500.00
Flask, Chestnut, Midwestern, 13 Ribs Swirled To Left, Dark Citron, 6 1/2 In. 500.00
Flask, Chestnut, Midwestern, 14 Vertical Ribs, Aqua, 4 1/4 In. 60.00
Flask, Chestnut, Midwestern, 16 Vertical Ribs, Half Post, 4 1/2 In. 50.00
Flask, Chestnut, Midwestern, 16 Vertical Ribs, Panels, Half Post, 1/2 Pint 90.00
Flask, Chestnut, Midwestern, 18 Ribs Swirled To Right, Green, 6 In. 70.00
Flask, Chestnut, Midwestern, 18 Ribs Swirled To Right, 1/2 Pint 85.00
Flask, Chestnut, Midwestern, 18 Ribs Swirled To Right, 1 1/2 Pint 40.00
Flask, Chestnut, Midwestern, 18 Swirled Ribs, Half Post, Cobalt, 5 In. 950.00
Flask, Chestnut, Midwestern, 18 Vertical Ribs, Half Post, Cobalt, 5 1/2 In. 700.00

Flask, Chestnut, Midwestern, 18 Vertical Ribs, Turned-Over Lip, 6 1/2 In.	55.00
Flask, Chestnut, Midwestern, 20 Ribs, Green, 1/2 Pint, 5 1/2 In.	350.00
Flask, Chestnut, New England, Olive Amber, 8 In.	55.00
Flask, Chestnut, New England, 6 1/4 In.	55.00
Flask, Chestnut, OP, Amber, 5 In.	45.00
Flask, Chestnut, OP, Amber, 11 In.	35.00
Flask, Chestnut, OP, Broken Bubble, Amber, 11 In.	15.00
Flask, Chestnut, OP, C.1800, 3 1/2 In.	75.00
Flask, Chestnut, OP, C.1800, 8 In.	75.00
Flask, Chestnut, OP, Clear Olive Green, 8 In.	50.00
Flask, Chestnut, OP, Dug, Burst Bubble, Aquamarine, 2 1/2 In.	20.00
Flask, Chestnut, OP, Light Green, 4 In.	40.00
Flask, Chestnut, OP, Olive Amber, 7 In.	35.00
Flask, Chestnut, OP, Olive Amber, 8 1/2 In.	40.00
Flask, Chestnut, OP, Olive Amber, 9 1/2 In.	40.00
Flask, Chestnut, OP, Olive Amber, 11 In.	40.00
Flask, Chestnut, OP, Olive Green, 5 In.	30.00 To 50.00
Flask, Chestnut, OP, Olive Green, 5 1/2 In.	40.00
Flask, Chestnut, OP, Olive Green, 6 In.	40.00 To 50.00
Flask, Chestnut, OP, Olive Green, 7 In.	20.00
Flask, Chestnut, OP, Olive Green, 8 1/2 In.	30.00 To 55.00
Flask, Chestnut, OP, Olive Green, 10 1/2 In.	30.00
Flask, Chestnut, OP, Olive Green, 11 In.	40.00
Flask, Chestnut, OP, Olive Green, 11 1/2 In.	70.00
Flask, Chestnut, Ohio, 16 Broken Swirled Ribs, Half Post Method, Green, Pint	125.00
Flask, Chestnut, Ohio, 16 Ribs, Deep Yellow Green, 1/2 Pint	650.00
Flask, Chestnut, Ohio, 18 Vertical Ribs, Aqua, 3 7/8 In.	120.00
Flask, Chestnut, Ohio, 20 Swirled Ribs, Aqua, Pint	200.00
Flask, Chestnut, Olive Green, 6 1/2 In.	45.00
Flask, Chestnut, Pinched, Aqua, 2 1/2 In.	45.00
Flask, Chestnut, Red Amber, 8 1/4 In.	25.00
Flask, Chestnut, Sloping Collar, OP, C.1800, 10 1/2 In.	35.00
Flask, Chestnut, Stiegel Type, Allover Ogivals, Deep Amethyst, Pint	125.00
Flask, Chestnut, Tooled Collar, OP, Light Apple Green, Quart	60.00
Flask, Chestnut, Zanesville, 10 Diamond Mold, Amber, 1/2 Pint	450.00
Flask, Chestnut, Zanesville, 10 Diamond Mold, Aqua, 1/2 Pint, 5 In.	250.00
Flask, Chestnut, Zanesville, 12 Diamond Mold, Citron, 5 In.	1400.00
Flask, Chestnut, Zanesville, 10 Diamond, Blue Green, 5 3/5 In.	200.00 To 250.00
Flask, Chestnut, Zanesville, 24 Ribs Swirled To Left, Aqua, 1/2 Pint	200.00
Flask, Chestnut, Zanesville, 24 Ribs Swirled To Left, Dark Amber, 1/2 Pint	250.00
Flask, Chestnut, Zanesville, 24 Ribs Swirled To Right, Yellow Green, Pint	1100.00
Flask, Chestnut, Zanesville, 24 Ribs, Amber, Larger Than 1/2 Pint, 5 1/4 In.	225.00
Flask, Chestnut, Zanesville, 24 Vertical Ribs, Amber, Pint, 7 In.	375.00
Flask, Chestnut, Zanesville, 24 Vertical Ribs, Dark Amber, 5 In.	145.00
Flask, Chestnut, Zanesville, 24 Vertical Ribs, Dark Amber, 6 3/4 In.	300.00
Flask, Chestnut, Zanesville, 24 Vertical Ribs, Golden Amber, 1/2 Pint	300.00
Flask, Chestnut, 12 Ribs, Half Post, Pint, 6 1/2 In.	45.00
Flask, Chestnut, 12 Vertical Ribs, Cobalt Blue, Pint, 6 3/4 In.	35.00
Flask, Chestnut, 19 Swirled Ribs, Amethystine, 4 1/2 In.	195.00
Flask, Clasped Hands & Eagle & Banner, Aqua, 1/2 Pint, 6 1/4 In.	12.00
Flask, Clasped Hands & Eagle & Flying Banner, Aqua, 1/2 Pint, 6 1/4 In.	12.50
Flask, Clasped Hands & Eagle & Shield, Aqua, Quart	30.00
Flask, Clasped Hands & Wreath, Aqua, 1/2 Pint	30.00
Flask, Coffin, Embossed A.& W. On Side, Aqua, Quart	12.50
Flask, Coffin, Embossed Crown, Aqua, Imperial Pint	9.00
Flask, Coffin, Embossed Key On Front, Aqua, Pint	30.00
Flask, Coffin, Letters On Base, Aqua, Pint	2.00
Flask, Coffin, S.F.On Bottom, Sheared Lip, Ball Neck, Oval Sides, 1/4 Pint	6.00
Flask, Columbus, Embossed, Medallion Shape, Screw Cap, 6 1/4 In.	17.50
Flask, Cornucopia & Urn, Olive Amber, 1/2 Pint	65.00
Flask, Cornucopia & Urn, Olive Green, 1/2 Pint, 5 1/4 In.	45.00
Flask, Cornucopia & Urn, OP, Olive Green, Pint	70.00 To 75.00
Flask, D.B.Lester, Savannah, Ga., Embossed, Banded, Dug, Amber, 1/2 Pint	12.00
Flask, Double Eagle & Cunningham, Aqua, 1/2 Pint	75.00
Flask, Double Eagle & Cunningham, Pittsburgh In Oval, Aqua, Pint	30.00

Flask, Double Eagle & Dot In Ovals, Amber, 1/2 Pint 60.00
Flask, Double Eagle & Dot In Ovals, OP, Amber, 1/2 Pint 50.00
Flask, Double Eagle & Dot In Ovals, Stoddard Type, Olive Amber, 1/2 Pint 70.00
Flask, Double Eagle & Dot In Ovals, Stoddard Type, Olive Green, 1/2 Pint 60.00
Flask, Double Eagle & Geo.A.Berry & Co., Aqua, Quart 45.00
Flask, Double Eagle & Granite Glass Co., Stoddard, N.H., Amber, Pint 100.00
Flask, Double Eagle & Granite Glass Co., Stoddard, N.H., Golden Amber, Pint 90.00
Flask, Double Eagle & Granite Glass Co., Stoddard, N.H., Green, Pint 160.00
Flask, Double Eagle & Granite Glass Co., Stoddard, N.H., OP, Amber, Pint 70.00
Flask, Double Eagle & Louisville, Aqua, 1/2 Pint 310.00
Flask, Double Eagle & Ovals, Amber, Pint 65.00
Flask, Double Eagle & Ovals, Amber, Quart 25.00
Flask, Double Eagle & Ovals, OP, Amber, 1/2 Pint 50.00
Flask, Double Eagle & Ovals, OP, Amber, Pint 40.00
Flask, Double Eagle & Pittsburgh, Aqua, 1/2 Pint 38.50
Flask, Double Eagle & Pittsburgh, Blue Aqua, Pint 50.00
Flask, Double Eagle & Pittsburgh, Honey Amber, 1/2 Pint 75.00
Flask, Double Eagle & Pittsburgh, Pa. In Oval, Amber, Pint 60.00
Flask, Double Eagle & Pittsburgh, Pa. In Oval, Aqua, Quart, 9 In. 35.00
Flask, Double Eagle & Pittsburgh, Pa., Amber, Pint 120.00
Flask, Double Eagle & Pittsburgh, Pa., Cornflower Blue, 1/2 Pint 125.00
Flask, Double Eagle & Pittsburgh, Pa., Dark Green, Pint 145.00
Flask, Double Eagle & Pittsburgh, Pa., Quart 48.00
Flask, Double Eagle & Pittsburgh, Pa., Smooth Base, Olive Green, Pint 100.00
Flask, Double Eagle & Pittsburgh, Pa., Yellow Green, Pint 80.00
Flask, Double Eagle & Ribbon & Oval, Keene Type, Amber, 1/2 Pint 85.00
Flask, Double Eagle & Ribbon & Oval, Keene Type, Olive Green, Pint 85.00
Flask, Double Eagle & Ribbon & Stoddard, OP, Amber, 1/2 Pint 80.00
Flask, Double Eagle & Ribbon, OP, Olive Amber, Pint 85.00
Flask, Double Eagle & Ribbon, Stoddard Type, OP, Amber, 1/2 Pint 85.00
Flask, Double Eagle & Ribbon, Stoddard Type, OP, Olive, Pint 90.00
Flask, Double Eagle & Stoddard, Glob Of Glass In Bottom, Amber, 1/2 Pint 85.00
Flask, Double Eagle & Stoddard, N.H. In Oval, Pontil, Olive Amber, Pint 150.00
Flask, Double Eagle & Stoddard, N.H., Amber, 1/2 Pint 90.00
Flask, Double Eagle & Stoddard, N.H., Olive Amber, Pint .... 70.00 To 80.00
Flask, Double Eagle & Stoddard, N.H., Olive Green, Pint 100.00
Flask, Double Eagle & Stoddard, N.H., OP, Amber, Pint .... 10.00 To 90.00
Flask, Double Eagle & Stoddard, N.H., Sand Check, Olive Amber, Pint 60.00
Flask, Double Eagle & Stoddard, OP, Smoky Amber, 1/2 Pint 85.00
Flask, Double Eagle & Wreath & Pittsburgh, Amber, 1/2 Pint 95.00
Flask, Double Eagle & Wreath, Cloudy, Aqua, 1/2 Pint 12.00
Flask, Double Eagle Over Oval & Pittsburgh, Deep Green, Quart 125.00
Flask, Double Eagle Over Oval & Pittsburgh, Green, Quart 117.00
Flask, Double Eagle Over Oval, Aqua, Pint .... 40.00 To 42.50
Flask, Double Eagle Over Oval, IP, Deep Aqua, Pint .... 47.50 To 49.50
Flask, Double Eagle Over Oval, Pontil, Olive Amber, 1/2 Pint 79.50
Flask, Double Eagle, Amber, Pint .... 50.00 To 100.00
Flask, Double Eagle, Aqua, 1/2 Pint .... 17.50 To 95.00
Flask, Double Eagle, Aqua, Pint .... 32.00 To 95.00
Flask, Double Eagle, Haze, Aqua, Pint .... 30.00 To 38.75
Flask, Double Eagle, Light Amber, 7 In. 810.00
Flask, Double Eagle, OP, Amber, 1/2 Pint .... 85.00 To 90.00
Flask, Double Eagle, OP, Light Amber, 1/2 Pint 125.00
Flask, Double Eagle, OP, Olive Amber, 1/2 Pint 95.00
Flask, Double Eagle, OP, Olive Green, 1/2 Pint 115.00
Flask, Double Eagle, Olive Amber, 1/2 Pint, 6 In. .... 45.00 To 75.00
Flask, Double Eagle, Olive Green, 2 Quart 105.00
Flask, Double Eagle, Pint, Amber 50.00
Flask, Double Eagle, Pittsburgh Type, Aqua, Pint .... 30.00 To 40.00
Flask, Double Eagle, Pittsburgh Type, Stain, Burst Bubble, Amber, Pint 60.00
Flask, Double Eagle, Sheared Top, OP, Golden Citron, 1/2 Pint 150.00
Flask, Double Eagle, Sick, Aqua, Pint, 7 1/4 In. 20.00
Flask, Double Eagle, Slight Cloud, Pint 30.00
Flask, Double Eagle, Stain, Aqua, Pint 20.00
Flask, Double Eagle, Stoddard Type, Olive Amber, 1/2 Pint .... 60.00 To 70.00

Flask, Double Eagle, Stoddard Type, Olive Amber, Pint .... 50.00 To 130.00
Flask, Double Eagle, Stoddard Type, Olive Amber, Quart 120.00
Flask, Double Eagle, Stoddard Type, Olive Green, Pint 60.00
Flask, Double Eagle, 1/2 Pint 50.00
Flask, Double Sheaf Of Rye, Aqua, Pint 40.00
Flask, Double Sheaf Of Wheat & Westford Glass Co., Dark Amber, 1/2 Pint 55.00
Flask, Double Sheaf Of Wheat & Westford Glass Co., Dark Amber, Pint 60.00
Flask, Double Sheaf Of Wheat, Pint 75.00
Flask, Double Union & Clasped Hands, Aqua, Quart 35.00
Flask, Eagle & A & DH, C In Oval & Girl On Bicycle, Light Blue, Pint 80.00
Flask, Eagle & Banner & Clasped Hands, Pint 60.00
Flask, Eagle & Clasped Hands, Amber, 1/2 Pint 100.00
Flask, Eagle & Clasped Hands, Aqua, 1/2 Pint, 6 1/4 In. 20.00
Flask, Eagle & Clasped Hands, Aqua, Pint 50.00
Flask, Eagle & Clasped Hands, Wormser, Aqua, 9 In. .... *Illus* 90.00

Flask, Eagle & Clasped Hands, Wormser, Aqua, 9 In.

Flask, Eagle & Cornucopia, OP, Olive Green, Pint .... 80.00 To 90.00
Flask, Eagle & Cornucopia, Olive Green, Pint 120.00
Flask, Eagle & Credo & For Pike's Peak, Aqua, 1/2 Pint, 6 1/4 In. 40.00
Flask, Eagle & Cunningham & Pittsburgh Glass Manufacturers, Aqua, Pint 40.00
Flask, Eagle & For Pike's Peak, Aqua, 1/2 Pint 30.00
Flask, Eagle & Girl On Bicycle, Light Blue, Pint 100.00
Flask, Eagle & Granite Glass Co. & Eagle & Stoddard, Amber, Pint 195.00
Flask, Eagle & Liberty & Willington Glass Co., Dark Amber, Pint 125.00
Flask, Eagle & Oval & Eagle & Pittsburgh, Pa., Green, Pint 80.00
Flask, Eagle & Pittsburgh, Dark Green, 7 1/2 In. .... *Illus* 165.00

Flask, Eagle, Pittsburgh, Dark Green, 7 1/2 In.

Flask, Eagle & Pittsburgh, Pa. In Oval & Eagle & Oval, Yellow Green, Quart 75.00
Flask, Eagle & Stars & Ravenna Glass Co. & Anchor, Aqua, Pint, 7 3/4 In. 90.00
Flask, Eagle & Traveler & Arsenal Glass Works, Pittsburgh, Pa., Green, Pint 300.00
Flask, Eagle & Willington, Amber, Quart 130.00
Flask, Eagle & 13 Stars & Ravenna Glass Co. & Anchor, Golden Amber, Pint 250.00
Flask, Eagle, Double Collar, Amber, Pint 85.00
Flask, Eagle, Embossed, Amber 25.00
Flask, Eagle, Embossed, Short Neck, Clear Amber, 5 3/4 In. 30.00
Flask, Etched Pennsylvania Tulip, C.1790, 1/2 Pint 135.00
Flask, Etched Picture Of Hunter, 7 In. ....*Color* 60.00
Flask, Fells Point & Sailboat & Washington Monument, 1/2 Pint 200.00
Flask, Flora Temple, Amber, Pint 250.00
Flask, Flora Temple, Amber, Quart 290.00
Flask, Flora Temple, Dark Red Amber, Quart 90.00
Flask, Flora Temple, Handled, Red Amber, Quart 250.00
Flask, Flora Temple, Puce, Quart 400.00
Flask, Flora Temple, Smoky Yellow, Pint 425.00
Flask, For Pike's Peak & Eagle & Banner, Aqua, Pint 15.00
Flask, For Pike's Peak & Eagle & Credo, Aqua, Pint 25.00
Flask, For Pike's Peak & Eagle & Prospector, Aqua, Pint 50.00
Flask, For Pike's Peak & Eagle & Prospector, Aqua, Quart 45.00
Flask, For Pike's Peak & Eagle Over Mirror & Prospector, Haze, Aqua, Quart 45.00
Flask, For Pike's Peak & Eagle Over Oval, Haze, Aqua, Quart 38.50
Flask, For Pike's Peak & Eagle, Applied Lip Ring, Aqua, Pint 60.00
Flask, For Pike's Peak & Eagle, Aqua, 1/2 Pint 35.00
Flask, For Pike's Peak & Eagle, Aqua, Pint .... 38.50 To 60.00
Flask, For Pike's Peak & Eagle, Banner, & Oval, Sick, Aqua, Pint 15.00
Flask, For Pike's Peak & Eagle, Pint 57.00
Flask, For Pike's Peak & Eagle, Shield, & Streamer, Aqua, Pint 40.00
Flask, For Pike's Peak & Hunter Shooting Deer, IP, Aqua, 1/2 Pint 110.00
Flask, For Pike's Peak & Old Rye, Aqua, Pint 75.00
Flask, For Pike's Peak & Prospector & Hunter & Deer, Deep Aqua, 1/2 Pint 110.00
Flask, For Pike's Peak & Spread Winged Eagle & Traveler, Aqua, Quart 50.00
Flask, For Pike's Peak, Aqua, 1/2 Pint 38.00
Flask, For Pike's Peak, Aqua, Pint 75.00
Flask, For Pike's Peak, Aqua, Quart .... 40.00 To 45.00
Flask, For Pike's Peak, Graphite Pontil, Aqua, Pint 55.00
Flask, For Pike's Peak, Green, Pint 90.00
Flask, Franklin & Dr.Dyott, Pint 50.00
Flask, Free-Blown, Quart 40.00
Flask, Free-Blown, 2 Quart 40.00
Flask, French, Blown, Molded Ribs, Diamond & Daisy, 7 1/4 In. 20.00
Flask, GAR-We Drank From The Same Canteen 1861-66, Tin, Felt, Miniature 20.00
Flask, Gen.Taylor Never Surrenders, Aqua, 8 1/2 In. ....*Illus* 65.00

Flask, Gen. Taylor Never Surrenders, Aqua, 8 1/2 In.

Flask, **Geo.W.Robinson,** Main St., W.Va., Embossed, Blue Aqua, Pint	50.00
Flask, **German Porcelain,** Girl In Champagne Glass, 6 1/4 In.	45.00
Flask, **German Porcelain,** Monkey & Mirror, 4 1/4 In.	50.00
Flask, **Ginter Co. Importers,** Collared Lip, Straight Sided, Green, 8 1/2 In.	5.00
Flask, **Girl On Bicycle & On Steamer & Not For Joe,** Aqua, Pint	100.00
Flask, **Granite Glass Co. & Stoddard,** N.H., Amber, Pint	60.00 To 80.00
Flask, **Granite Glass Co. & Stoddard,** N.H., Burst Base Bubble, Amber, Quart	75.00
Flask, **Granite Glass Co. & Stoddard,** N.H., Amber, Pint	60.00
Flask, **Granite Glass Co. & Stoddard,** N.H., Burst Bubble, Olive Amber, Pint	60.00
Flask, **Granite Glass Co. & Stoddard,** N.H., Deep Red Amber, Pint	122.00
Flask, **Granite Glass Co. & Stoddard,** N.H., Pontil, Olive Green, Pint	200.00
Flask, **Granite Glass Co. & Stoddard,** N.H., Stain On Inside, Amber, Pint	100.00
Flask, **Green Aqua,** 6 1/4 In.	15.00
Flask, **GRJA-AD,** OP, Olive Green, Pint	175.00
Flask, **H.D.Fowle,** Boston, 2 Mold, Applied Lip, Oval, Aqua, 5 3/4 In.	5.00
Flask, **Hip,** Latticed Metal Cover & Cap, C.1920, 1/2 Pint	8.00
Flask, **Honest Measure & Wortmann Bros.,** N.Y., Bimal, Dug, Stain, Quart	5.00
Flask, **Honest Measure In Banner,** Strap Sided, Lip Ring, Collared, 4 1/2 In.	5.50
Flask, **Honest Measure In Banner,** Strap Sided, Tapered, Lip Ring, 4 3/4 In.	6.00
Flask, **Hunter & Running Dog,** Olive Yellow, Pint	320.00
Flask, **Isabella Glass Works & Anchor & Glass House,** Aqua, Quar	55.00 To 70.00
Flask, **Isabella Glass Works & Sheaf Of Wheat,** Aqua, Pint	27.50
Flask, **Isabella Glass Works,** OP, Aqua, Pint	120.00
Flask, **J.F.Callahan & Co.,** Boston In Script, Straight Sided, Pint	5.00
Flask, **Jackman,** Carnival, Pint	8.00
Flask, **Jenny Lind & Fislerville Glass Works,** Light Green, Quart	85.00 ←
Flask, **Jo Jo,** Amber, 1/2 Pint	12.50
Flask, **Keene,** Melon Ribbed, Aqua, Pint	35.00
Flask, **L.G.Co. On Base,** Sand Check, Amber, 1/2 Pint	35.00
Flask, **L.G.Co.,** Double Ring Lip, Bubbles, Honey Amber, Pint	19.00
Flask, **L.G.Co.,** Whittled Base, Amber, Pint	20.00
Flask, **Lady On Bicycle & A & DHC In Oval & Eagle,** Aqua, Pint	80.00
Flask, **Lady Pictured Under Glass,** 5 1/2 In. ....Color	40.00
Flask, **Lady's,** Cut Glass, Stopper & Cap, 1/2 Pint	75.00
Flask, **Lady's,** Cut Glass, 1/2 Pint	75.00
Flask, **Liberty & Eagle & Willington Glass,** Green, 8 In. ....Illus	160.00

Flask, Liberty & Eagle, Willington Glass,
Green, 8 In.

Flask, **Light Yellow Amber,** 6 3/4 In.	7.50
Flask, **Log Cabin & Anchor & Spring Garden Glass Works,** Aqua, Pint	67.55
Flask, **Looped Decoration,** 7 1/2 In. ....Color	150.00
Flask, **Lynnboro,** L.G.Co.On Base, Amber, Pint	27.00
Flask, **Mantua,** Pitkin Type, 16 Broken Swirled Ribs, Green, 6 1/2 In.	400.00
Flask, **Mantua,** Traveling, 16 Broken Swirled Ribs, Medium Yellow Green, 6 In.	225.00
Flask, **Masonic & Seeing Eye,** OP, Amber, Pint	140.00
Flask, **Masonic & Steubenville,** O., Ceramic, 3 In.	29.00
Flask, **McKearin G I-2,** General Washington & Eagle, Green, Pint	110.00
Flask, **McKearin G I-2,** Washington	500.00

Flask, McKearin G I-2, Washington & Eagle & Beaded Oval, Green, Pint 235.00
Flask, McKearin G I-2, Washington & Eagle, Light Green, Pint 235.00
Flask, McKearin G I-3, General Washington & Eagle & Shield, Aqua, Pint 500.00
Flask, McKearin G I-6, Washington & Eagle & J.R. In Oval, & Laird, Pint 800.00
Flask, McKearin G I-6, Washington & Eagle & J.R. In Oval, Amethyst, Pint 800.00
Flask, McKearin G I-10, Washington .... 300.00 To 500.00
Flask, McKearin G I-10, Washington & Eagle & Oval & 15 Pearls, Aqua, Pint 310.00
Flask, McKearin G I-14, Firecracker, OP, Stain, Aqua, Pint 170.00
Flask, McKearin G I-14, Washington & Eagle & T.W.D. In Oval, Aqua, Pint 130.00
Flask, McKearin G I-16, Washington & Eagle & T.W.D. In Oval, Aqua, Pint 110.00
Flask, McKearin G I-16, Washington & Eagle & T.W.D. In Oval, Green, Pint 75.00
Flask, McKearin G I-18, Washington & Monument & Baltimore, Green, Pint 85.00
Flask, McKearin G I-22, Washington & Baltimore & Bust, Aqua, Quart 35.00
Flask, McKearin G I-24, Washington & Taylor & Bridgetown, N.J., Aqua, Pint 95.00
Flask, McKearin G I-25, Washington & Bridgetown, N.J. & Bust, Green, Quart 100.00
Flask, McKearin G I-25, Washington & Clay & Bridgetown Works, Aqua, Quart 50.00
Flask, McKearin G I-31, Olive Amber 160.00
Flask, McKearin G I-31, Washington & Jackson, Burst Bubble, Amber, Pint 80.00
Flask, McKearin G I-31, Washington & Jackson, Light Olive Amber, Pint 160.00
Flask, McKearin G I-31, Washington & Jackson, Olive Amber, Pint 190.00
Flask, McKearin G I-31, Washington & Jackson, Olive Green, Pint 160.00
Flask, McKearin G I-31, Washington & Jackson, OP, Olive Amber 105.00
Flask, McKearin G I-32, Light Olive Green 195.00
Flask, McKearin G I-32, Washington & Jackson, Aquamarine, Pint 175.00
Flask, McKearin G I-33, Washington & Jackson, Olive Amber, Pint 150.00
Flask, McKearin G I-34, Washington & Jackson, Amber, 1/2 Pint 130.00
Flask, McKearin G I-34, Washington & Jackson, Olive Amber, 1/2 Pint 190.00
Flask, McKearin G I-35, Calabash, Washington & Tree, Stain, Aqua 30.00
Flask, McKearin G I-35, Washington & Tree, OP, Aqua 40.00
Flask, McKearin G I-37, Washington & Taylor & Dyottville, Green, Quart 150.00
Flask, McKearin G I-37, Washington & Taylor, Amber, Pint 110.00
Flask, McKearin G I-38, Father Of His Country & Dyottville, Green, Pint 70.00
Flask, McKearin G I-38, Father Of His Country & Taylor, Blue, Pint 45.00
Flask, McKearin G I-38, OP, Aqua, Pint 35.00
Flask, McKearin G I-38, Washington & Taylor & Dyottville, Aqua, Pint 45.00
Flask, McKearin G I-38, Washington & Taylor, Aqua, Pint 55.00
Flask, McKearin G I-39, OP, Aqua, Pint 25.00
Flask, McKearin G I-39, Washington & Taylor, Aqua, Quart 45.00
Flask, McKearin G I-39, Washington & Taylor, Blue Green, Quart 230.00
Flask, McKearin G I-39, Washington & Taylor, OP, Aqua, Pint 30.00
Flask, McKearin G I-39, Washington & Taylor, OP, Aqua, Quart .... 10.00 To 59.75
Flask, McKearin G I-40a, Aqua 65.00
Flask, McKearin G I-40a, Washington & Taylor, Light Aqua, Pint 20.00
Flask, McKearin G I-41, Father Of His Country & Taylor, Aqua, 1/2 Pint 40.00
Flask, McKearin G I-41, Washington & Taylor, Aqua, 1/2 Pint .... 45.00 To 50.00
Flask, McKearin G I-41, Washington & Taylor, Blob Top, Aqua, Pint 115.00
Flask, McKearin G I-42, Aqua 65.00
Flask, McKearin G I-42, Aqua, Quart 35.00
Flask, McKearin G I-42, Captain Bragg, Aqua, 9 In. .... *Illus* 175.00
Flask, McKearin G I-44, Washington, OP, Aqua, Pint 40.00
Flask, McKearin G I-47, Father Of His Country & Taylor, Aqua, Quart 35.00
Flask, McKearin G I-47, Single Rounded Collar Lip, OP, Green, Quart 275.00
Flask, McKearin G I-49, Washington & Gen.Z.Taylor, Aqua, Pint 30.00
Flask, McKearin G I-49, Washington & Gen.Z.Taylor, Pale Aqua, Pint 30.00
Flask, McKearin G I-50, Washington & G.Z.Taylor, Pale Aqua, Pint 35.00
Flask, McKearin G I-50, Washington & G.Z.Taylor, Smoke Color, Pint 125.00
Flask, McKearin G I-51, Washington & Taylor, Yellow Green, Quart 310.00
Flask, McKearin G I-55, Washington & Taylor, OP, Aqua, Pint .... 35.00 To 100.00
Flask, McKearin G I-56, OP, Aqua, 1/2 Pint 35.00
Flask, McKearin G I-57, OP, Cloudy, Aqua, Quart 15.00
Flask, McKearin G I-57, Washington & Wheat, Aqua, 9 In. .... *Illus* 135.00
Flask, McKearin G I-58, Bust Of Washington & Sheaf Of Rye, Aqua, Pint 35.00
Flask, McKearin G I-59, Washington & Sheaf Of Rye, Crooked, Aqua, 1/2 Pint 65.00
Flask, McKearin G I-59, Washington & Sheaf Of Wheat, Cloudy, Aqua 25.00
Flask, McKearin G I-59, Washington & Sheaf, Aqua, 1/2 Pint .... 50.00 To 60.00

Flask, McKearin GI-42, Captain
Bragg, Aqua, 9 In.
(See Page 82)

Flask, McKearin GI-57, Washington,
Wheat, Aqua, 9 In.
(See Page 82)

Flask, McKearin G I-59, Washington & Taylor's Bust, Green, Quart	55.00
Flask, McKearin G I-66, Jackson & Eagle & J.R. In Oval, & Laird, Pint	1200.00
Flask, McKearin G I-66, Jackson & Eagle & J.R., Amethyst Tint, Pint	1200.00
Flask, McKearin G I-68, General Jackson & Floral Medallion, Green, Pint	900.00
Flask, McKearin G I-71, Aqua, Pint	80.00
Flask, McKearin G I-71, Double Eagle, Olive Amber, 1/2 Pint	180.00
Flask, McKearin G I-71, Rough & Ready Major Ringgold, Aqua, Pint	85.00
Flask, McKearin G I-71, Taylor & Major Ringgold, Aqua, Pint	85.00
Flask, McKearin G I-71, Taylor & Major Ringgold, Light Aqua, Pint	45.00
Flask, McKearin G I-72, Rough & Ready & Major Ringgold, Rolled Lip, Aqua	135.00
Flask, McKearin G I-73, Taylor & Baltimore, Aqua	135.00
Flask, McKearin G I-73, Taylor & Monument & Fells Point, Green, Pint	110.00
Flask, McKearin G I-79, Eagle & Union & Grant's Bust & Wreath, Aqua, Pint	165.00
Flask, McKearin G I-79, Grant's Bust & Eagle Over Union, Aqua, Pint	210.00
Flask, McKearin G I-80, Lafayette & DeWitt Clinton, Olive Amber, Pint	625.00
Flask, McKearin G I-81, Lafayette & DeWitt Clinton, Amber, 1/2 Pint	350.00
Flask, McKearin G I-85, Lafayette & Liberty Cap, Olive Amber, Pint	600.00
Flask, McKearin G I-86, Lafayette & Liberty Cap, Olive Amber, 1/2 Pint	500.00
Flask, McKearin G I-86, Lafayette, OP, Neck Bubble, Amber, 1/2 Pint	450.00
Flask, McKearin G I-86, Lafayette, OP, Olive Amber, 1/2 Pint	450.00
Flask, McKearin G I-90, Lafayette & Republican Gratitude, Aqua, Pint	130.00
Flask, McKearin G I-94, Dyott & Franklin, Stain, Aqua, Pint	120.00
Flask, McKearin G I-94, Franklin & T.W.Dyott, M.D. & Bust, Green, Pint	150.00
Flask, McKearin G I-96, Dr.Dyott & Franklin, Aqua, Quart	325.00
Flask, McKearin G I-97, Double Franklin, Aqua, Quart	150.00

Flask, McKearin G I-99, Calabash, Jenny Lind & S.Huffsey, Aqua, 10 In. 65.00
Flask, McKearin G I-99, Jenny Lind, Aqua, Pint 68.50
Flask, McKearin G I-99, Jenny Lind, Deep Blue Green 120.00
Flask, McKearin G I-100, Calabash, Jenny Lind & Kossuth, OP, Stain, Aqua 40.00
Flask, McKearin G I-100, OP, Aqua 190.00
Flask, McKearin G I-101, Calabash, Jenny Lind, Pontil, Stain, Aqua 30.00
Flask, McKearin G I-102, Calabash, Jenny Lind, OP, Aqua 45.00
Flask, McKearin G I-103, Calabash, Jenny Lind, OP, Stain, Aqua & Yellow 50.00
Flask, McKearin G I-103, Calabash, Jenny Lind, Pontil, Stain, Aqua 30.00
Flask, McKearin G I-107, Calabash, Jenny Lind & Fislerville, Aqua 45.00
Flask, McKearin G I-107, Calabash, Jenny Lind & Fislerville, Aqua, 10 In. 55.00
Flask, McKearin G I-107, Calabash, Jenny Lind, Aqua, Quart Plu .... 30.00 To 40.00
Flask, McKearin G I-107, Jenny Lind, Aqua 30.00
Flask, McKearin G I-107, Jenny Lind, OP, Aqua 30.00
Flask, McKearin G I-111, Kossuth, Bridgeton, N.J. & Sloop, Aqua, Pint 125.00
Flask, McKearin G I-113, Calabash, Kossuth & Tree, Pontil, Stain, Aqua 35.00
Flask, McKearin G I-114, Amber 185.00
Flask, McKearin G I-114, Byron & Scott, Gold Amber, 1/2 Pint 185.00
Flask, McKearin G I-114, Byron & Scott, Honey Amber, 1/2 Pint 125.00
Flask, McKearin G I-114, Byron & Scott, Light Amber 200.00
Flask, McKearin G I-114, Byron & Scott, Olive Green, 1/2 Pint 180.00
Flask, McKearin G I-114, Byron & Scott, OP, Amber, 1/2 Pint .... 120.00 To 130.00
Flask, McKearin G I-114, Byron & Scott, OP, Olive Green, 1/2 Pint 50.00
Flask, McKearin G I-114, Classical Busts, Amber, 1/2 Pint 130.00
Flask, McKearin G I-124, Eagle & Waterford, Aqua, Quart 75.00
Flask, McKearin G II-2, Double Eagle, Aqua, Pint 130.00
Flask, McKearin G II-3, Sheaf Of Rye & Bunch Of Grapes, Green, 1/2 Pint 130.00
Flask, McKearin G II-6, Liberty & Eagle & Willington, Amber, Quart 90.00
Flask, McKearin G II-7, Eagle & 32 Ray Sunburst, Yellow Tint, Pint 725.00
Flask, McKearin G II-11, Eagle & Inverted Cornucopia, Aqua, 1/2 Pint 175.00
Flask, McKearin G II-11, Eagle & Inverted Cornucopia, Green, 1/2 Pint 150.00
Flask, McKearin G II-11, Eagle & Inverted Cornucopia, 1/2 Pint 300.00
Flask, McKearín G II-12, Eagle & Inverted Cornucopia, Aqua, 1/2 Pint 265.00
Flask, McKearin G II-16, Eagle & Cornucopia, Aqua, 1/2 Pint 20.00
Flask, McKearin G II-18, Zanesville Eagle & Cornucopia, Amber, 1/2 Pint 250.00
Flask, McKearin G II-19, Eagle & Morning Glory & Vine, Aqua, Pint 275.00
Flask, McKearin G II-20, Eagle, Deep Aqua, Pint 1275.00
Flask, McKearin G II-21, For Pike's Peak & Eagle & Country, Aqua, Pint 80.00
Flask, McKearin G II-24, Double Eagle, Louisville Type, Aqua, Pint 150.00
Flask, McKearin G II-26, Double Eagle, Dark Blue Green, Quart 80.00
Flask, McKearin G II-26, Louisville & Double Eagle, Aqua, Quart 100.00
Flask, McKearin G II-33, Eagle & Louisville, Ribbed, Amber, 1/2 Pint 160.00
Flask, McKearin G II-33, Louisville, Ribbed, Amber, Pint 500.00
Flask, McKearin G II-35, Eagle In Oval & Louisville, Ky., Green, Quart 90.00
Flask, McKearin G II-36, Eagle, Aqua, 7 1/2 In. .... *Illus* 165.00

Flask, McKearin GII-36, Eagle, Ribbed, Aqua, 7 1/2 In

Flask, McKearin G II-38, Dyottville & Eagle, Aqua, Pint 120.00
Flask, McKearin G II-40, Double Eagle, Aqua, Pint .... 25.00 To 85.00
Flask, McKearin G II-41, Eagle & Tree, Aqua, 6 1/2 In. 105.00
Flask, McKearin G II-43, Eagle & T.W.D. & Cornucopia, Green, 1/2 Pint 65.00
Flask, McKearin G II-43, OP, Cloudy, Aqua, 1/2 Pint 105.00
Flask, McKearin G II-47, Eagle & Tree In Foliage, Light Aqua, Quart 250.00
Flask, McKearin G II-48, Eagle & Coffin & Hay, Hammonton, Aqua, Quart 160.00
Flask, McKearin G II-49, Eagle & Stag & Coffin & Hay, Aqua, 1/2 Pint 205.00
Flask, McKearin G II-52, Eagle & Flag & For Our Country, Aqua, Pint 85.00
Flask, McKearin G II-53, Eagle & For Our Country, Aqua, 6 1/2 In. 85.00
Flask, McKearin G II-54, Eagle & Flag & For Our Country, Aqua, Pint 70.00
Flask, McKearin G II-54, Eagle & Flag, Aqua, Pint .... 90.00 To 225.00
Flask, McKearin G II-55, Eagle & Grapes, Aqua 135.00
Flask, McKearin G II-56, Eagle & Grapes, Stain, Aqua, 1/2 Pint 100.00
Flask, McKearin G II-60, Charter Oak, Aqua, 1/2 Pint 210.00
Flask, McKearin G II-60, Charter Oak, Round Bottom, Green, 1/2 Pint 200.00
Flask, McKearin G II-60, Eagle & Liberty Tree, Aqua, 1/2 Pint 250.00
Flask, McKearin G II-60, Eagle & Liberty Tree, Light Green, 1/2 Pint 270.00
Flask, McKearin G II-61, Willington & Eagle, Amber, Quart 65.00
Flask, McKearin G II-61, Willington & Eagle, Olive Green, Quart 90.00
Flask, McKearin G II-61, Willington, Whittle Mold, Olive Green, Quart 115.00
Flask, McKearin G II-62, Collared, Emerald Green, Pint 125.00
Flask, McKearin G II-62, Collared, Red Amber, Pint 110.00
Flask, McKearin G II-62, Eagle & Liberty & Willington, Amber, Pint 75.00
Flask, McKearin G II-62, Eagle & Willington Glass, Olive Green, Pint 120.00
Flask, McKearin G II-62, Willington & Eagle Over Liberty, Olive, Pint 126.00
Flask, McKearin G II-63, Collared, Amber, 1/2 Pint 125.00
Flask, McKearin G II-63, Eagle & Liberty & Willington, Olive, 1/2 Pint 75.00
Flask, McKearin G II-63, Eagle & Liberty & Willington, Olive, Pint 150.00
Flask, McKearin G II-63, Eagle & Willington Glass Co., Green, 1/2 Pint 110.00
Flask, McKearin G II-63, Eagle & Willington, Olive Green, 1/2 Pint 144.00
Flask, McKearin G II-64, Eagle & Liberty & Willington, Olive, Pint 145.00
Flask, McKearin G II-64, Eagle & Willington Glass Co., Green, Pint 140.00
Flask, McKearin G II-64, Eagle & Willington, Olive Amber, Pint 70.00
Flask, McKearin G II-64, Eagle & Willington, Olive Green, Pint 70.00
Flask, McKearin G II-65, Eagle & Liberty & Westford, Amber, 1/2 Pint 158.00
Flask, McKearin G II-65, Eagle & Liberty, Olive Green, 1/2 Pint 85.00
Flask, McKearin G II-65, Eagle & Westford Glass Co., Amber, 1/2 Pint 90.00
Flask, McKearin G II-66, Eagle & New London, Yellow Streak, Aqua, Quart 400.00
Flask, McKearin G II-67, Eagle & New London Glass Works, Aqua, 1/2 Pint 275.00
Flask, McKearin G II-67, Eagle & New London, Yellow Green, 1/2 Pint 550.00
Flask, McKearin G II-68, Anchor & New London Glass Works, Amber, Pint 225.00
Flask, McKearin G II-68, Eagle & New London Glass Works, Green, Pint 325.00
Flask, McKearin G II-69, Eagle & Inverted Cornucopia, Green, 1/2 Pint 375.00
Flask, McKearin G II-70, Double Eagle, OP, Olive Amber, Pint 225.00
Flask, McKearin G II-70, Eagle Sideways, OP, Amber, Pint 160.00
Flask, McKearin G II-71, Double Eagle, Olive Green, 1/2 Pint 160.00
Flask, McKearin G II-71, Double Horizontal Eagle, Amber, 1/2 Pint 160.00
Flask, McKearin G II-71, Eagle & Cornucopia & Keene, OP, Aqua, Pint 85.00
Flask, McKearin G II-72, Eagle & Cornucopia, Golden Amber, Pint 60.00
Flask, McKearin G II-72, Eagle & Cornucopia, Olive Amber, Pint 100.00
Flask, McKearin G II-72, Eagle & Cornucopia, OP, Olive Green, Pint 65.00
Flask, McKearin G II-72, Eagle, Keene, Pint 100.00
Flask, McKearin G II-73, Aqua 140.00
Flask, McKearin G II-73, Eagle & Cornucopia & Keene, Olive Green, Pint 93.00
Flask, McKearin G II-73, Eagle & Cornucopia, Light Blue Green, Pint 180.00
Flask, McKearin G II-73, Eagle & Cornucopia, Olive Amber, Pint 110.00
Flask, McKearin G II-73, Eagle & Cornucopia, Olive Green, Pint 85.00
Flask, McKearin G II-73, Eagle & Cornucopia, OP, Golden Amber, Pint 60.00
Flask, McKearin G II-73, Eagle & Cornucopia, OP, Olive Green, Pint 60.00
Flask, McKearin G II-73, Eagle & Horn Of Plenty, Dark Amber, Pint 100.00
Flask, McKearin G II-74, Eagle & Shield & Cornucopia, Green, Pint 70.00
Flask, McKearin G III-2, Double Cornucopia, Aqua, 1/2 Pint 55.00
Flask, McKearin G III-2, Double Cornucopia, Light Aqua, 1/2 Pint 50.00
Flask, McKearin G III-4, Cornucopia & Urn, Amber, Pint 35.00

Flask, McKearin G III-4, Cornucopia & Urn, Green, Pint 100.00
Flask, McKearin G III-4, Cornucopia & Urn, Olive Green, Pint 50.00
Flask, McKearin G III-4, Cornucopia & Urn, OP, Olive Amber, Pint 75.00
Flask, McKearin G III-4, Cornucopia & Urn, OP, Olive Green, Pint 73.00
Flask, McKearin G III-4, Cornucopia, Amber, 6 3/4 In. .... *Illus* 50.00

Flask, McKearin G III-4, Cornucopia, Amber, 6 3/4 In.

Flask, McKearin G III-7, Cornucopia & Urn Of Produce, Aqua, 1/2 Pint 60.00
Flask, McKearin G III-7, Cornucopia & Urn, Green, 1/2 Pint... 95.00
Flask, McKearin G III-7, Cornucopia & Urn, Light Green, 1/2 Pint 40.00
Flask, McKearin G III-7, Cornucopia & Urn, Light Olive, 1/2 Pint 50.00
Flask, McKearin G III-7, Cornucopia & Urn, Olive Amber, 1/2 Pint 75.00
Flask, McKearin G III-7, Cornucopia & Urn, Olive Green, 1/2 Pint 70.00
Flask, McKearin G III-7, Cornucopia & Urn, Olive Yellow, 1/2 Pint 35.00
Flask, McKearin G III-8, Cornucopia & Urn, Light Green, 1/2 Pint 60.00
Flask, McKearin G III-8, Cornucopia & Urn, Olive Amber, 1/2 Pint 60.00
Flask, McKearin G III-8, Cornucopia & Urn, Olive Green, 1/2 Pint 60.00
Flask, McKearin G III-8, Cornucopia & Urn, Olive Yellow, 1/2 Pint 45.00
Flask, McKearin G III-10, Cornucopia & Urn, OP, Amber, 1/2 Pint 50.00
Flask, McKearin G III-10, Cornucopia & Urn, OP, Olive Amber, 1/2 Pint 60.00
Flask, McKearin G III-10, Cornucopia & Urn, OP, Olive Green, 1/2 Pint 79.00
Flask, McKearin G III-10, Cornucopia, Light Golden Amber, 1/2 Pint 60.00
Flask, McKearin G III-11, Olive Amber 80.00
Flask, McKearin G III-12, Cornucopia & Urn, Olive Amber, 1/2 Pint 75.00
Flask, McKearin G III-12, Eagle & Cornucopia, OP, Amber, 1/2 Pint 85.00
Flask, McKearin G III-14, Cornucopia & Urn, Olive Green, Pint 65.00
Flask, McKearin G III-15, Cornucopia & Urn, Aqua, 1/2 Pint 100.00
Flask, McKearin G III-15, Cornucopia & Urn, Deep Yellow Green, 1/2 Pint 95.00
Flask, McKearin G III-16, Cornucopia & Urn & Lancaster, Blue, Pint 725.00
Flask, McKearin G III-16, 3 Mold, Olive Green, 7 1/2 In. 325.00
Flask, McKearin G III-53, For Our Country, Pontil, Aqua 130.00
Flask, McKearin G III-72, Eagle & Cornucopia, Olive Green, Pint 70.00
Flask, McKearin G IV-1, Masonic & Eagle, Blue Green, 7 1/2 In. 280.00
Flask, McKearin G IV-1, Masonic & Eagle, Pint 525.00
Flask, McKearin G IV-1, Masonic & JP, OP, Deep Aqua, Pint 300.00
Flask, McKearin G IV-7, Masonic & Eagle & Shield, Emerald, Pint 350.00
Flask, McKearin G IV-9, Masonic & Eagle & Keene, Light Amber, 7 1/2 In. 150.00
Flask, McKearin G IV-11, Masonic, Aqua, 7 In. 350.00
Flask, McKearin G IV-11, Masonic, Pint 320.00
Flask, McKearin G IV-14, Masonic & Eagle, Blue Green, 5 3/4 In. 320.00
Flask, McKearin G IV-14, Masonic & Eagle, Deep Blue Green, 5 3/4 In. 320.00
Flask, McKearin G IV-17, Masonic & Eagle & Keene In Oval, Green, Pint 130.00
Flask, McKearin G IV-17, Masonic & Eagle & Keene, Amber, Pint 175.00
Flask, McKearin G IV-17, Masonic & Eagle & Keene, Yellow Amber, Pint 175.00
Flask, McKearin G IV-17, Masonic & Eagle, Olive Amber, Pint 160.00
Flask, McKearin G IV-17, Masonic & Keene, OP, Amber, Pint .... 110.00 To 170.00
Flask, McKearin G IV-17, Masonic & Keene, OP, Potstone, Amber, Pint 70.00
Flask, McKearin G IV-17, Masonic, Olive Green 225.00
Flask, McKearin G IV-17, Masonic, Olive, Pint 200.00
Flask, McKearin G IV-18, Masonic & Eagle, Olive Amber, Pint .... 140.00 To 180.00
Flask, McKearin G IV-18, Masonic & Keene, Olive Amber 160.00

Flask, McKearin G IV-19, Masonic & Eagle & KCCNC In Oval, Amber, Pint 150.00
Flask, McKearin G IV-19, Masonic & Eagle, Olive Amber, Pint .... 140.00 To 190.00
Flask, McKearin G IV-19, Masonic & Keene, Olive Green, Pint 130.00
Flask, McKearin G IV-19, Masonic & Keene, OP, Amber, Pint 140.00
Flask, McKearin G IV-19, Masonic & Keene, Pontil, Olive Amber, Pint 120.00
Flask, McKearin G IV-19, Masonic, Amber, Pint 120.00
Flask, McKearin G IV-19, Masonic, Olive Green 225.00
Flask, McKearin G IV-20, Keene & Masonic, OP, Amber, Pint 150.00
Flask, McKearin G IV-20, Keene & Masonic, Pontil, Olive Green, Pint 100.00
Flask, McKearin G IV-21, Masonic & Eagle, Olive Amber, Pint 190.00
Flask, McKearin G IV-21, Masonic & Eagle, Olive Green, Pint 230.00
Flask, McKearin G IV-21, Masonic & Keene, Olive Green 245.00
Flask, McKearin G IV-24, Masonic & Eagle & Oval, Olive Amber, 1/2 Pint 250.00
Flask, McKearin G IV-24, Masonic & Eagle, Burst Bubble, Amber, 1/2 Pint 110.00
Flask, McKearin G IV-24, Masonic & Eagle, Olive Amber, 1/2 Pint 220.00
Flask, McKearin G IV-24, Masonic & Eagle, Olive Amber, Pint 150.00
Flask, McKearin G IV-24, Masonic & Eagle, Olive Green, 1/2 Pint 170.00
Flask, McKearin G IV-24, Masonic & Eagle, OP, Dark Green, 1/2 Pint 150.00
Flask, McKearin G IV-24, Masonic, OP, Olive Green, 1/2 Pint 150.00
Flask, McKearin G IV-27, Masonic & Eagle & N.E.G.Co., Green, Pint 235.00
Flask, McKearin G IV-28, Double Dotted Masonic, Stain, Green, 1/2 Pint 250.00
Flask, McKearin G IV-28, Double Masonic Arch, Blue Green, 1/2 Pint 400.00
Flask, McKearin G IV-28, Double Masonic, Deep Blue Green, 1/2 Pint 250.00
Flask, McKearin G IV-28, Masonic, OP, Deep Aqua, 1/2 Pint 390.00
Flask, McKearin G IV-30, Crossed Keys 2000.00
Flask, McKearin G IV-31, Masonic & Eagle, Yellow Green, Pint 900.00
Flask, McKearin G IV-32, Golden Amber 425.00
Flask, McKearin G IV-32, Shepherd & Eagle & Zanesville, Amber, Pint 400.00
Flask, McKearin G IV-32, Shepherd & Eagle, Dark Amber, Pint 450.00
Flask, McKearin G IV-32, Shepherd & Masonic, Aqua, Pint .... 130.00 To 190.00
Flask, McKearin G IV-34, Masonic & Ship Franklin, Aqua, Pint 180.00
Flask, McKearin G IV-41, OP, Aqua, 1/2 Pint 40.00
Flask, McKearin G IV-42, Calabash, Aqua, Pint .... 25.00 To 30.00
Flask, McKearin G IV-42, Calabash, Masonic, Graphite Pontil, Aqua 30.00
Flask, McKearin G V-1, Double Success To The Railroad, Sapphire, Pint 1950.00
Flask, McKearin G V-3, Double Success To The Railroad, Olive Amber, Pint 190.00
Flask, McKearin G V-3, Olive Amber 195.00
Flask, McKearin G V-3, OP, Amber, Pint 150.00
Flask, McKearin G V-3, Success To The Railroad, Dark Olive, 6 3/4 In. 175.00
Flask, McKearin G V-3, Success To The Railroad, Golden Amber 250.00
Flask, McKearin G V-3, Success To The Railroad, Olive Green, Pint 150.00
Flask, McKearin G V-3, Union & Clasped Hands, Aqua, 1/2 Pint 45.00
Flask, McKearin G V-4, Double Success To The Railroad, Olive Amber, Pint 550.00
Flask, McKearin G V-4, Green 210.00
Flask, McKearin G V-4, Success To The Railroad, Light Amber, 6 3/4 In. 225.00
Flask, McKearin G V-4, Success To The Railroad, Olive Green, 6 3/4 In. 190.00
Flask, McKearin G V-5, Double Success To The Railroad, Olive Amber, Pint 160.00
Flask, McKearin G V-5, Railroad, OP, Olive Green, Pint 10.00
Flask, McKearin G V-5, RR, OP, Amber, Pint 150.00
Flask, McKearin G V-5, Success To The Railroad, Deep Green, Pint 200.00
Flask, McKearin G V-5, Success To The Railroad, Deep Olive Green, Pint 30.00
Flask, McKearin G V-6, Double Success To The Railroad, Amber, Pint 190.00
Flask, McKearin G V-6, Double Success To The Railroad, Olive Green, Pint 180.00
Flask, McKearin G V-6, Railroad, OP, Olive Amber, Pint 160.00
Flask, McKearin G V-8, Railroad & Eagle, Olive Amber, Pint 215.00
Flask, McKearin G V-8, Success To The Railroad & Eagle, Green, Pint 175.00
Flask, McKearin G V-9, Railroad, OP, Olive Amber, Pint 150.00
Flask, McKearin G V-9, Success To The Railroad & Eagle, Olive Green, Pint 200.00
Flask, McKearin G V-10, Lowell Railroad & Eagle & Stars, Olive, 5 1/2 In. 240.00
Flask, McKearin G V-10, Lowell Railroad, Olive Green, 1/2 Pint 175.00
Flask, McKearin G V-10, Lowell Railroad, OP, Light Amber, 1/2 Pint 225.00
Flask, McKearin G V-10, Railroad, Light Olive Green, 1/2 Pint 230.00
Flask, McKearin G V-10, Railroad, OP, Amber, 1/2 Pint 180.00
Flask, McKearin G VI-4, Corn For The World & Baltimore, Amber, Quart 200.00
Flask, McKearin G VI-4, Corn For The World & Baltimore, Green, Quart 150.00

Flask, McKearin G VI-7, Corn For The World & Baltimore, Green, 1/2 Pint 95.00
Flask, McKearin G VIII-1, Sunburst, Green, Pint, 8 1/2 In. 225.00
Flask, McKearin G VIII-2, Sunburst, Green, Pint .... 450.00 To 500.00
Flask, McKearin G VIII-3, Sunburst, Olive Amber, Pint .... 400.00 To 450.00
Flask, McKearin G VIII-5, Sunburst, Golden Amber, Pint 460.00
Flask, McKearin G VIII-5A, Sunburst, Olive Amber, Pint 775.00
Flask, McKearin G VIII-8, Keene & P & W, OP, Olive Green 325.00
Flask, McKearin G VIII-8, Sunburst & Keene, Light Olive Amber, Pint 325.00
Flask, McKearin G VIII-8, Sunburst, Olive Amber, Pint .... 400.00 To 425.00
Flask, McKearin G VIII-9, Keene In Sunburst & P.& W., Olive, 1/2 Pint 170.00
Flask, McKearin G VIII-9, OP, Amber, 1/2 Pint 280.00
Flask, McKearin G VIII-9, Sunburst, Olive Amber, 1/2 Pint .... 250.00 To 330.00
Flask, McKearin G VIII-10, Keene In Sunburst & P.& W., Olive, 1/2 Pint 475.00
Flask, McKearin G VIII-16, OP, Olive Green, 1/2 Pint 300.00
Flask, McKearin G VIII-16, Sunburst, Olive Amber, 1/2 Pint .... 300.00 To 310.00
Flask, McKearin G VIII-16, Sunburst, Olive, 1/2 Pint, 6 In. 435.00
Flask, McKearin G VIII-16, Sunburst, OP, Yellow Green, 1/2 Pint 320.00
Flask, McKearin G VIII-16, Sunburst, Yellow Olive 350.00
Flask, McKearin G VIII-17, Sunburst & Coventry, Light Olive, 1/2 Pint 375.00
Flask, McKearin G VIII-18, Sunburst, Olive Amber, 1/2 Pint 425.00
Flask, McKearin G VIII-18, Sunburst, OP, Olive Green, 1/2 Pint 375.00
Flask, McKearin G VIII-18, Sunburst, Yellow Amber, 1/2 Pint 250.00
Flask, McKearin G VIII-25, Sunburst, Clear With Tint, 1/2 Pint 300.00
Flask, McKearin G VIII-27, Sunburst, OP, Aqua, 1/2 Pint 270.00
Flask, McKearin G VIII-27, Sunburst, Pale Aqua, Pint 175.00
Flask, McKearin G VIII-27, Sunburst, Stain, Green Tint, 1/2 Pint 100.00
Flask, McKearin G VIII-29, Deep Aqua, Pint 260.00
Flask, McKearin G VIII-29, Double Sunburst, Ribbed, Blue Green, 3/4 Pint 250.00
Flask, McKearin G VIII-29, Sunburst, Clear Medium Green, Pint 175.00
Flask, McKearin G VIII-29, Sunburst, Light Blue Green, 1/2 Pint 275.00
Flask, McKearin G VIII-29, Sunburst, OP, Light Green, Pint 300.00
Flask, McKearin G VIII-54, Sunburst, Olive Amber, Pint 775.00
Flask, McKearin G IX-1, Scroll, Aqua, Pint, 7 In. 35.00
Flask, McKearin G IX-2, Graphite Pontil, Stain, Aqua, Quart 60.00
Flask, McKearin G IX-2, OP, Stain, Aqua, 2 Quart 60.00
Flask, McKearin G IX-2, Scroll, Burst Bubble, Aqua, Quart 45.00
Flask, McKearin G IX-2, Scroll, IP, Blue Aqua, Quart .... 70.00 To 75.00
Flask, McKearin G IX-3, Scroll, Aqua, Quart 80.00
Flask, McKearin G IX-3, Scroll, Dark Olive Amber, Quart 150.00
Flask, McKearin G IX-6, Scroll, Aqua, 8 1/2 In. .... Illus 155.00

Flask, McKearin GIX-6, Scroll,
Aqua, 8 1/2 In.

Flask, McKearin GX-15, Summer & Winter, Aqua, Pint

Flask, McKearin G IX-10, Double Eagle, Light Blue, 1/2 Pint	70.00
Flask, McKearin G IX-10, Scroll, Bluish Green, Pint	45.00
Flask, McKearin G IX-11, Scroll, Applied Ring, IP, Aqua	45.00
Flask, McKearin G IX-11, Scroll, Aqua, Pint	35.00
Flask, McKearin G IX-11, Scroll, Blue Green, Pint	100.00
Flask, McKearin G IX-11, Scroll, OP, Strong Aqua, Pint	65.00
Flask, McKearin G IX-11A, Scroll, Light Green, Pint	95.00
Flask, McKearin G IX-12, Scroll, Amber, Pint	375.00
Flask, McKearin G IX-14, Scroll, Pontil, Aqua, Pint	55.00
Flask, McKearin G IX-15, Summer & Winter, Stain, Aqua, Pint	20.00
Flask, McKearin G IX-16, Scroll, Aqua, Pint	45.00
Flask, McKearin G IX-26, Scroll, Marked S.McKee, Aqua, Pint	400.00
Flask, McKearin G IX-31, Scroll, Aqua, 1/2 Pint	60.00
Flask, McKearin G IX-34, Scroll, Aqua, 1/2 Pint	75.00
Flask, McKearin G IX-36, Scroll, IP, Uneven Lip, Aqua, 1/2 Pint	59.00
Flask, McKearin G IX-37, Scroll, Aqua, 1/2 Pint	70.00
Flask, McKearin G IX-38, Scroll & B.P.& B., Stain, Aqua, 1/2 Pint	110.00
Flask, McKearin G X-1, Stag & Good Game & Weeping Willow, Aqua, Pint	145.00
Flask, McKearin G X-3, Sheaf Of Wheat & Grapes, Light Aqua, 1/2 Pint	135.00
Flask, McKearin G X-5, Grapevine	295.00
Flask, McKearin G X-8, Ship & Star, Aqua, 1/2 Pint	50.00
Flask, McKearin G X-9, Sloop & Star, Green, 1/2 Pint	100.00
Flask, McKearin G X-11, Liberty & Sheaf Of Wheat & Star, Aqua, 1/2 Pint	130.00
Flask, McKearin G X-12, Men Arguing & Grotesque Head, Green, 1/2 Pint	55.00
Flask, McKearin G X-15, Summer & Winter, Aqua, Pint *Illus*	100.00
Flask, McKearin G X-15, Summer & Winter, OP, Aqua, Pint	25.00
Flask, McKearin G X-16, Summer & Winter Tree, Pale Aqua, 1/2 Pint	55.00
Flask, McKearin G X-16, Summer & Winter, Aqua, 1/2 Pint	65.00
Flask, McKearin G X-17, Tree In Circle, Aquamarine, 6 3/4 In.	375.00
Flask, McKinley & Hobart, 1/2 Pint	110.00
Flask, Mechanic Glass Works, Phila. & Sheaf Of Wheat & Tools, Aqua, Quart	80.00
Flask, Midwestern, 16 Swirled Ribs, Aqua, 6 1/8 In.	50.00
Flask, Midwestern, 16 Swirled Ribs, Aqua, 6 1/2 In.	55.00
Flask, Midwestern, 18 Swirled Ribs, Aqua, 7 In.	55.00
Flask, Midwestern, 18 Swirled Ribs, Light Green, 6 1/4 In.	35.00
Flask, Midwestern, 18 Swirled Ribs, 6 1/2 In.	55.00
Flask, Midwestern, 25 Swirled Ribs, Blue Green, 7 1/4 In.	85.00
Flask, Nailsea, Double, Light Blue & Opalescent, 8 In.	90.00
Flask, Nailsea, Rough Pontil, White Loopings, Cranberry, 6 In.	125.00
Flask, Nailsea, White Loops, OP, Green, 1/2 Pint	95.00
Flask, Not For Joe & Eagle & Lady Riding Bicycle, Aqua, Pint	95.00
Flask, Not For Joe & Lady Riding Bicycle, Aqua, Pint	100.00
Flask, Ohio Type, Ribbed, OP, Light Green, 1/2 Pint	35.00
Flask, Ohio Type, 12 Ribs, OP, Blue, Pair	90.00

Flask, Ohio, Flattened Globular, 16 Ribs, Dark Claret, 5 1/2 In. 60.00
Flask, Ohio, Globular, Swirled, Aqua, Quart 50.00
Flask, Ohio, Stiegel Type, OP, Aqua, 1/2 Pint .... 15.00 To 30.00
Flask, Ohio, 16 Swirled Ribs, Amber, Pint, 6 3/4 In. 200.00
Flask, Ohio, 16 Swirled Ribs, Amethystine Tint, Pint, 6 In. 65.00
Flask, Ohio, 16 Swirled Ribs, Aqua Green, Pint, 6 1/4 In. 145.00
Flask, Ohio, 18 Swirled Ribs, Yellow Green, Pint, 6 1/4 In. 175.00
Flask, Ohio, 20 Broken Swirled Ribs, Yellow Green, Pint, 7 In. 200.00
Flask, Ohio, 24 Swirled Ribs, OP, Aqua 40.00
Flask, Ohio, 24 Swirled Ribs, 16 Vertical Ribs, Light Green, Pint, 7 In. 160.00
Flask, Onion, Squat, Pontil, Olive Green, Quart 22.00
Flask, Oval Eagle Medallion & Louisville Glass Works, Ribbed, Aqua, Pint 140.00
Flask, Overlay On Blue, Painted Center, 7 1/2 In. .... Color 150.00
Flask, Patent On Shoulder, Amber, 1/2 Pint 35.00
Flask, Patent 1907, Tin Over Glass, Screw Cap, 8 In. .... Illus 35.00

Flask, Patent 1907, Tin Over Glass, Screw Cap, 8 In.

Flask, Patent, Amber, 1/2 Pint 15.00
Flask, Patent, Amber, Pint 15.00
Flask, Patent, Amber, Quart 25.00
Flask, Patent, Stone In Glass, Amber, Pint 20.00
Flask, Pewter Top, Amber, 1/2 Pint 22.50
Flask, Picnic, Amber, 1/2 Pint 35.00
Flask, Picnic, Boar's Head, Deer, 1/2 Pint 65.00
Flask, Picnic, Crooked Neck, 3 1/2 In. 3.00
Flask, Picnic, Embossed Star, 3 In. 9.00
Flask, Picnic, Embossed Try It, Golden Amber, 4 1/2 In. 32.00
Flask, Picnic, Embossed 5 Pointed Star, Blob Lip With Skirt, 3 1/2 In. 5.00
Flask, Picnic, Spider Web, Bimal, Pint .... 3.50 To 6.00
Flask, Picnic, Stars & Sunburst, Fluted Sides, Pedestal, Ball Neck, 4 In. 9.00
Flask, Picnic, "Try It, " Amber, 1/4 Pint 22.00
Flask, Picnic, 5 Pointed Star On Front, Blob Lip With Ring, 3 1/2 In. 5.50
Flask, Picnic, 5 Pointed Star On Front, Blob Lip With Skirt, 3 1/2 In. 6.00
Flask, Picnic, 5 Pointed Star, Blob Lip With Skirt, Long Neck, 3 3/4 In. 6.00
Flask, Pink Loopings On Opaque White, Pint 50.00
Flask, Pitkin, Connecticut, 36 Broken Swirled Ribs, Yellow Olive, Pint 150.00
Flask, Pitkin, Connecticut, 36 Ribs, Blown, Light Olive Amber, 6 1/2 In. 170.00
Flask, Pitkin, Connecticut, 36 Swirled Ribs, Olive Amber, 1/2 Pint 195.00
Flask, Pitkin, Eastern, Swirled, Light Olive Amber, 1/2 Pint 215.00
Flask, Pitkin, Eastern, 32 Swirled Ribs, Olive, Pint, 7 In. 185.00
Flask, Pitkin, Eastern, 36 Broken Swirled Ribs, Yellow Olive, Pint 150.00
Flask, Pitkin, Flat, Broken Swirl, Olive Green, Pint 225.00
Flask, Pitkin, Green, Pint 185.00
Flask, Pitkin, Midwestern, Swirled, Green, 1/2 Pint 290.00
Flask, Pitkin, Midwestern, 20 Broken Swirled Ribs, Yellow Green, 5 In. 750.00
Flask, Pitkin, Midwestern, 20 Swirled Ribs, OP, Pint 80.00
Flask, Pitkin, Midwestern, 32 Broken Swirled Ribs, Amber, 6 1/2 In. 225.00
Flask, Pitkin, Midwestern, 32 Broken Swirled Ribs, Green, Pint, 7 1/4 In. 175.00
Flask, Pitkin, Midwestern, 32 Broken Swirled Ribs, Light Green, Pint 150.00
Flask, Pitkin, Midwestern, 32 Broken Swirled Ribs, Olive, 5 In. 200.00
Flask, Pitkin, Midwestern, 32 Broken Swirled Ribs, Yellow Green, Pint 550.00

Flask, Pitkin, Midwestern, 36 Broken Swirled Ribs, Yellow Olive, 5 In.	180.00
Flask, Pitkin, New England, Blown, Applied Handle, Amber, 7 3/4 In.	70.00
Flask, Pitkin, New England, 24 Broken Swirled Ribs, Olive, 5 1/4 In.	195.00
Flask, Pitkin, New England, 36 Ribs Swirled To Right, Olive Green	230.00
Flask, Pitkin, OP, Green, Pint	190.00
Flask, Pitkin, OP, Olive Amber, 1/2 Pint	170.00
Flask, Pitkin, Pennsylvania, 36 Broken Swirled Ribs, Dark Olive, Pint, 6 In.	200.00
Flask, Pitkin, Pontil, Green, Pint	125.00
Flask, Pitkin, Popcorn, OP, Light Olive Green, Pint	210.00
Flask, Pitkin, Popcorn, OP, Olive Green, Pint	190.00
Flask, Pitkin, Round, Broken Swirl, Amber, 1/2 Pint	80.00
Flask, Pitkin, Swirled Ribs, Deep Green, Pint	175.00
Flask, Pitkin, Swirled Ribs, Green, Pint	200.00
Flask, Pitkin, Swirled Ribs, Olive Amber, 1/2 Pint	35.00 To 200.00
Flask, Pitkin, Swirled Ribs, Olive Amber, Pint	55.00 To 230.00
Flask, Pitkin, Swirled Ribs, Olive Yellow To Amber, 5 1/4 In.	205.00
Flask, Pitkin, 18 Ribs, Olive Green, Pint	170.00
Flask, Pitkin, 32 Ribs, Broken Swirl At Bottom, Olive, Pint	170.00
Flask, Pittsburgh & Double Eagle, Aqua, 1/2 Pint	30.00
Flask, Pittsburgh & For Pike's Peak, Aqua, Pint	40.00
Flask, Pittsburgh & For Pike's Peak, Graphite Pontil, Aqua, Quart	75.00
Flask, Pocket, Silver Plate, Bust Of Man In Relief, Floral, Round	24.00
Flask, Pocket, Webb, Ovoid, Hinged Lock Top, White Floral, Citron, 5 1/4 In.	725.00
Flask, Pocket, White Enamel Decoration, Pint	35.00
Flask, Powder, Ellenville, N.Y., Dark Amber, 13 1/2 In.	75.00
Flask, Pumpkinseed, A.F.Benard, Larkin & Fulton St. In Circle, 5 1/2 In.	22.00
Flask, Pumpkinseed, Amber, Pint	19.00 To 25.00
Flask, Pumpkinseed, Aqua, 9 Ozs.	19.00
Flask, Pumpkinseed, Blob Lip With Ring, 4 1/2 In.	4.50
Flask, Pumpkinseed, Blob Lip With Skirt, Blue Aqua, 4 1/2 In.	6.00
Flask, Pumpkinseed, Blob Lip With Skirt, Light Yellow Green, 4 3/4 In.	7.00
Flask, Pumpkinseed, Blob Lip With Skirt, 4 1/2 In.	6.00
Flask, Pumpkinseed, Blonde Girl On Glass Label, 1/2 Pint	65.00
Flask, Pumpkinseed, Clock Face, Pint	22.00
Flask, Pumpkinseed, Hotel Statler, Monogram, 3 1/4 In.	14.00
Flask, Pumpkinseed, Leaf & Fruit Center, Dated 1870, 5 1/4 In.	14.00
Flask, Pumpkinseed, Merry Christmas & Happy New Year, 4 1/2 X 3 1/4 In.	20.00
Flask, Pumpkinseed, Spider Web, Bent Neck, Dug, Aqua, Pint	10.00
Flask, Pumpkinseed, Spider Web, Stain, Aqua, 4 1/2 X 3 1/4 In.	10.00
Flask, Pumpkinseed, Spider Web, 4 1/2 X 3 1/4 In.	12.00
Flask, Pumpkinseed, Spider Web, 5 1/4 X 3 3/4 In.	12.00
Flask, Pumpkinseed, Stopper, Amber, 9 Ozs.	26.00
Flask, Pumpkinseed, "try It, " 4 1/2 In.	28.00
Flask, Quilt Edge, Clipper Ship On Glass Label, Wicker Cover, Amber, Quart	50.00
Flask, Quilted, Aqua, 1/4 Pint	40.00

Flask, Resurgam Eagle,
Baltimore Works, Amber, 8 In.
(See Page 92)

Flask, Ravenna Glass Co. & Anchor & Eagle & 13 Stars, Amber, Pint, 8 In. 250.00
Flask, Ravenna Glass Works & Anchor & Star, Yellow Green, Pint, 7 3/4 In. 145.00
Flask, Ravenna Glass Works & 5 Pointed Star, Aqua, Pint 75.00
Flask, Ravenna Glass Works, Aqua, Pint, 7 3/4 In. 75.00
Flask, Ravenna Traveler's Companion, Applied Neck Ring, IP, Aqua, Quart 85.00
Flask, Resurgam & Baltimore Glass Works, Smooth Base, Pint 58.00
Flask, Resurgam Eagle, Baltimore Works, Amber, 8 In. .... *Illus* 175.00
Flask, Resurgam Eagle, Baltimore Works, Ocher, 7 1/2 In. .... *Illus* 75.00

Flask, Resurgam Eagle, Baltimore Works, Ocher, 7 1/2 In.

Flask, Ribbed, OP, Aqua, 1/2 Pint 35.00
Flask, Rolled Lip, Ribs Swirled To Left, Vertical Ribs Lower, Aqua, Quart 120.00
Flask, S.S.P. Embossed On Bottom, Strap Sided, Bubbles, Emerald, 1/2 Pint 9.00
Flask, S.S.P. Embossed On Bottom, Strap Sided, Green, Quart 5.00
Flask, S.S.P. Embossed On Bottom, Strap Sided, Olive Green, 1/2 Pint 9.00
Flask, S.S.P. Embossed On Bottom, Strap Sided, Olive Green, Quart 10.00
Flask, Saddle, Amber, 10 In.High 65.00
Flask, Saddle, Aqua, 6 1/4 In. 3.50
Flask, Saddle, Blob Top, Amber, 10 In. 65.00
Flask, Saddle, London, 1892, Silver Collar & Hinged Lid, 9 3/4 In. 28.00
Flask, Saddle, Persian, OP, Dark Green, 9 In. 10.00
Flask, Scroll, Applied Ring Lip, Quart 75.00
Flask, Scroll, Aqua Green, 1/2 Pint, 6 1/4 In. 22.50
Flask, Scroll, Aqua, 1/2 Pint 25.00
Flask, Scroll, Aqua, Pint, 7 In. 30.00
Flask, Scroll, Aqua, Quart, 8 3/4 In. 35.00
Flask, Scroll, Aqua, 2 Quart 175.00
Flask, Scroll, Blue Green, 7 1/4 In. 50.00
Flask, Scroll, Clambroth, Quart 110.00
Flask, Scroll, Cobalt, Pint 200.00
Flask, Scroll, Fleur-De-Lis In Panel, Sheared Lip, Pontil, Aqua, 1/2 Pint 49.00
Flask, Scroll, Graphite Pontil, Aqua, Pint .... 35.00 To 55.00
Flask, Scroll, Graphite Pontil, Aqua, Quart 35.00
Flask, Scroll, Gunmetal Blue, Pint, 5 3/4 In. 505.00
Flask, Scroll, IP, Aqua, 1/2 Pint, 5 3/4 In. 40.00
Flask, Scroll, IP, Aqua, Pint 53.00
Flask, Scroll, IP, Aqua, Quart, 7 1/4 In. 35.00
Flask, Scroll, IP, Blue Aqua, Quart 45.00
Flask, Scroll, IP, Pint 48.00
Flask, Scroll, Light Green, Gallon 400.00
Flask, Scroll, OP, Aqua, 1/2 Pint 65.00
Flask, Scroll, OP, Aqua, Pint .... 30.00 To 45.50

Fire Extinguisher, Harden's
Hand Grenade, Blue, 8 in.
$30
 Green, 8 in. $100
 Amber, 7½ in. $35–60

Fruit Jar, Johnson's 2
Patent Jan. 7th, 1868,
9½ in. $350

Flask, etched picture of
hunter, 7 in. $60

Medicine, E. A. Buckhout,
Dutch liniment, pontil, 7 in.

Nursing, Greetings to the
New Baby, 4¾ in. $5

Figural, chicken,
three mold, pat-
ented, 9½ in. $45

Poison, Pat. Applied for,
4 in. $300

Whiskey, The Dew
Drop, Hotchkiss,
Fenner & Bennett,
8½ in. $150

Bitters, Dr. Bell's Golden
Tonic, hole in side, pontil,
10½ in. $1,750

Whiskey, R. B. Cutter,
Louisville, Ky., 9 in. $275

Milk Glass, painted, 7½
in. $47.50

Bitters, Drake's Plan-
tation, Green, 10 in.

Coca-Cola, Seltzer,
Winona, Minn. $35

Fruit Jar, Webster's Patented
Feb. 16, 1864, 7½ in. $850

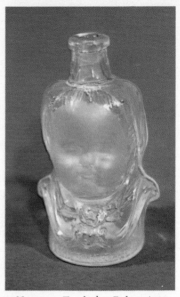

Nursing, Feed the Baby, 4 in.
$125

Soda, J.A. Lomax, Charles Place,
Chicago, cobalt, 7 in. $40

Figural, pottery pig, Bieler's Ronny
Club, 10½ in. long, 5½ in. high

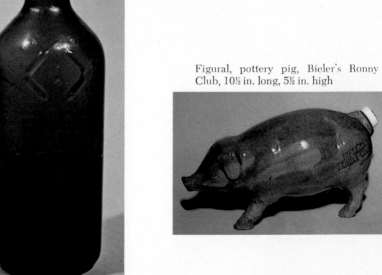

Bitters, Dr. Johnson's Calisaya, Burlington, Vt., 10½ in. $75

Bitters, John Roots, 10½ in.

Bitters, H. E. Bucklen Electric Brand, 10 in. $24

Medicine, Dr. Kilmer's Female Compound, 9 in. $20

Avon, Hearth
Lamp, 1973

Avon, Victoriana
Pitcher & Bowl,
1971

Avon, Aladdin's Lamp, 1971

Avon, Golf Cart, 1972

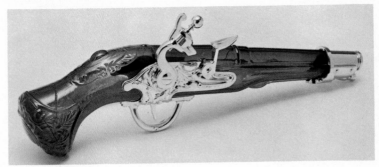

Avon, Dueling Pistol 1760, 1973

Austin Nichols, Wild Turkey, 1974

Avon, Victorian Manor, 1972

Figural, Hull Bros., Detroit, Michigan, 9 in. $375

Beer, John A. Lomax, Famous Weiss Beer, No. 18 Charles Place, Chicago, Ill., 8½ in.

Medicine, Alka Seltzer, with dispenser. $35

Figural, Dog, sterling silver head, 8 in. $400

Miniature, R. E. Garner, Fine Liquors, Anniston, Ala., 3 in. $15

Flask, Scroll, OP, Aqua, Quart .... 40.00 To 50.00
Flask, Scroll, OP, Deep Aqua, Pint 35.00
Flask, Scroll, OP, Pint 60.00
Flask, Scroll, Rough Pontil, Blue Aqua, Pint 50.00
Flask, Scroll, Sheared Lip, Graphite Pontil, Dark Aqua, Quart 50.00
Flask, Scroll, Sheared Lip, IP, Aqua, Pint 45.00
Flask, Scroll, Sheared Lip, OP, Aqua, 1/2 Pint 49.00
Flask, Scroll, Sheared Lip, OP, Aqua, Quart 48.00
Flask, Scroll, Sheared Lip, OP, Dug, Aqua, Pint 25.00
Flask, Scroll, Sheared Lip, Pontil, Aqua, Pint 45.00
Flask, Scroll, Yellow Green, Pint, 6 In. 380.00
Flask, Seated Monkey & Banjo & Dancing Monkey, Amber, 1/2 Pint 130.00
Flask, Seeing Eye & GRJA, Olive Yellow, Pint 195.00
Flask, Seeing Eye, OP, Amber, Pint 150.00
Flask, Seeing Eye, OP, Olive Amber, Pint 170.00
Flask, Seeing Eye, Olive Amber, Pint .... 180.00 To 220.00
Flask, Sheaf Of Rye & Tools & 5 Pointed Star, Dark Olive Amber, 1/2 Pint 165.00
Flask, Sheaf Of Rye & Tools & 5 Pointed Star, Green, Pint 185.00
Flask, Sheaf Of Rye, Scythe, & Rake & Westford Glass Co., Yellow, 1/2 Pint 70.00
Flask, Sheaf Of Rye, Scythe, & Rake & Westford Glass, Olive Yellow, 1/2 Pint 70.00
Flask, Sheaf Of Wheat & Star & Westford Glass, Conn., Amber, Pint 110.00
Flask, Sheaf Of Wheat & Tools & Westford Glass Co., Dark Amber, Pint 50.00
Flask, Sheaf Of Wheat & Traveler's Companion, Westford Type, Amber, Quart 110.00
Flask, Sheaf Of Wheat & Westford Conn., Olive Amber, Pint 80.00
Flask, Sheaf Of Wheat & Westford Glass Co., Amber, Pint .... 70.00 To 80.00
Flask, Sheaf Of Wheat & Westford Glass Co., Olive Amber, 1/2 Pint 70.00
Flask, Sheaf Of Wheat & Westford Glass Co., Olive Green, Pint 60.00
Flask, Sheaf Of Wheat & Westford Glass Company, Amber, 1/2 Pint 75.00
Flask, Sheaf Of Wheat, Tibby Bros., Pitts., Pa.On Base, Clear, 1/2 Pint 20.00
Flask, Shield With Rampant Lion & Grapes, European, Cobalt, 6 1/2 In. 32.50
Flask, Shield With Rampant Lion, European, Swirled, Cobalt, 6 1/2 In. 35.00
Flask, Shield With Rampant Lion, European, Swirled, Yellow Green, 6 1/2 In. 10.00
Flask, Soldier & Balt., Md. & Dancing Girl & Chapman, Pale Green, Pint 65.00
Flask, Soldier & Dancer & Chapman & Baltimore, Md., OP, Pint 95.00
Flask, Soldier Riding Horse & Dog, Aqua, Quart 32.00
Flask, Soldier Riding Horse & Dog, Cloudy, Aqua, Quart 25.00
Flask, South Carolina Dispensary With Monogram, Pint 9.75
Flask, Spring Garden Glass Works, Aqua, Pint 30.00
Flask, Sterling Silver, International Silver Co., 1/2 Pint 30.00
Flask, Stiegel Type, Aqua, 1/2 Pint 80.00
Flask, Stiegel Type, Enameled, Pewter Top, 5 1/2 In. 150.00
Flask, Stiegel Type, Graphite Pontil, Light Green, 1/2 Pint 55.00
Flask, Stiegel Type, Half Post, Pewter Cap, Painted Red, Blue, & Green, 10 In. 145.00
Flask, Stiegel Type, OP, Pale Green, 1/2 Pint 40.00
Flask, Stiegel Type, Ribbed, Enamel Polychrome Lady, Flower, & Words, 6 In. 35.00
Flask, Stiegel Type, Swirled Ribs, OP, Sapphire Blue, 4 1/4 In. 150.00
Flask, Stiegel Type, Traveling, Blown, Allover Ogivals, 5 3/4 In. 35.00
Flask, Stoddard & Double & X In Oval, Amber, 1/2 Pint 40.00
Flask, Stoddard & Double Eagle, Amber, 1/2 Pint 55.00
Flask, Stoddard & Double Eagle, Amber, Pint 60.00
Flask, Stoddard & Double Eagle, Dot In Oval, Amber, 1/2 Pint 55.00
Flask, Stoddard & Double Eagle, Olive Amber, Pint 125.00
Flask, Stoddard & Double Eagle, Olive Green, Pint 55.00
Flask, Stoddard & Double Eagle, OP, Quart 125.00
Flask, Stoddard & Granite Glass Co., Stoddard, N.H., Amber, Pint 120.00
Flask, Stoddard Patent, Red Amber, Pint 15.00
Flask, Stoddard Type, Blob Lip With Skirt, Bubbles, Red Amber, 1/2 Pint 15.00
Flask, Stoddard Type, Double Ring Top, Whittled, Amber, 1/2 Pint 12.00
Flask, Stoddard Type, Double Ring Top, Whittled, Amber, Pint 12.00
Flask, Stoddard, Bubbles, Red Amber, 1/2 Pint 25.00
Flask, Stoddard, Embossed Patent, Red Amber, Pint 30.00
Flask, Stoddard, Patent, Pint 25.00
Flask, Stoddard, Whittled, Patent, Pint 30.00
Flask, Stoddard, Whittled, Red Amber, 1/2 Pint 18.00
Flask, Stoneware, Ovoid, Gray, Brown Glaze, 7 1/2 In. 55.00
Flask, Strap Sided, Amber, 1/2 Pint 5.00

Flask, Strap Sided, Amber, Pint 6.00
Flask, Strap Sided, Anchor On Bottom, Applied Top, Aqua, 1/2 Pint 8.00
Flask, Strap Sided, Citron, Pint .... 10.00 To 16.00
Flask, Strap Sided, Emerald Green, Quart 16.00
Flask, Straus Bros.Co., Chicago, Ribbed, Olive, 1/2 Pint 12.00
Flask, Success To The Railroad, Clear Deep Olive Green, Pint 190.00
Flask, Summer & Winter Tree, Medium Blue Green, Quart 65.00
Flask, Swirled Decoration, 5 1/2 In. ....Color 115.00
Flask, Swirled, Ribbed, Sheared Lip, Vaseline Opalescent, Quart 130.00
Flask, T.J.Carty, Port Jervis, N.Y., Warranted, 1/2 Pint 10.00
Flask, T.Roosevelt, On Gold Ground, Metal Cap, Glass Label, Pint 90.00
Flask, Taylor & Dyottville Glass Works, Light Blue, Quart 145.00
Flask, Taylor Never Surrenders, Sheared Lip, Haze, Aqua, Quart 45.00
Flask, Tea, Porcelain, Oriental, Scenes, Brass Neck, White, 6 1/2 In. 70.00
Flask, Teardrop, Applied Thread, Ground Lip, Amber, 1/2 Pint 25.00
Flask, Threaded Neck, Ground Lip, Metal Cap, Amber, Pint 6.75
Flask, Tippecanoe, Cabin, Pinhole, Deep Olive Green 0100.00
Flask, Tracer Co., Cincinnati, Amber, 1/2 Pint 5.00
Flask, Traveler's Companion & Ravenna Glass Co., Aqua, Pint 65.00
Flask, Traveler's Companion & Ravenna Glass Works, Aqua, Pint 85.00
Flask, Traveler's Companion & Sheaf Of Wheat & Sun, Olive Amber, Quart 80.00
Flask, Traveler's Companion & Sheaf Of Wheat, Amber, Quart 100.00
Flask, Traveler's Companion & Sheaf, Fork, & Rake, Red Amber, Quart 150.00
Flask, Traveler's Companion, Dark Olive Green, Quart 120.00
Flask, Traveler's Companion, Whittled, Red Amber, Quart 125.00
Flask, Traveling, Blown, 18 Vertical Ribs, Green, 8 3/4 In. 32.50
Flask, Traveling, Cobalt Blue, 8 1/4 In. 25.00
Flask, Traveling, 18 Ribs, Light Green, 5 3/4 In. 65.00
Flask, Union & A.& D.H.Chambers, Aqua, Quart 52.00
Flask, Union & Cannon & Flag, Aqua, Pint 40.00
Flask, Union & Clasped Hands & Cannon, Aqua, Pint, 7 1/2 In. 35.00
Flask, Union & Clasped Hands & Eagle & Banner, Aqua, 1/2 Pint, 6 In. 17.50
Flask, Union & Clasped Hands & Eagle & Banner, Aqua, 7 1/2 In. 40.00
Flask, Union & Clasped Hands & Eagle & L.F.& Co., Aqua, 7 1/2 In. 30.00
Flask, Union & Clasped Hands & Eagle & Pittsburgh, A.& D.H.C., Aqua, Pint 35.00
Flask, Union & Clasped Hands & Eagle & 2 Banners, Light Green, 1/2 Pint 45.00
Flask, Union & Clasped Hands & Eagle, Aqua, Pint 40.00
Flask, Union & Clasped Hands & Eagle, Aqua, 7 1/2 In. ....Illus 70.00

Flask, Union & Clasped Hands & Eagle, Aqua, 7 1/2 In.

Flask, Union & Clasped Hands & Eagle, Ground Top, Amber, 1/2 Pint 25.00
Flask, Union & Clasped Hands & Eagle, Shield, & Cl & Sons, Aqua, Pint 30.00
Flask, Union & Clasped Hands & Eagle, 1/2 Pint 38.00
Flask, Union & Clasped Hands & Eagle, 2 Banners, & A & Co., Aqua, Quart 35.00
Flask, Union & Clasped Hands & Fa & Co. & Cannon, Aqua, Pint 20.00
Flask, Union & Clasped Hands & Flying Eagle & Banner, Aqua, 1/2 Pint 30.00
Flask, Union & Clasped Hands & Wm.Frank & Sons, Pittsburgh, Aqua, Pint 80.00
Flask, Union & Clasped Hands & Wreath, Aqua, 1/2 Pint 35.00
Flask, Union & Clasped Hands In Shield & Eagle & Banners, Amber, 1/2 Pint 55.00
Flask, Union & Clasped Hands & L.F.& Co., Eagle, & Pittsburgh, Aqua, Pint 49.50
Flask, Union & Clasped Hands, Aqua, 1/2 Pint .... 43.50 To 50.00
Flask, Union & Clasped Hands, Aqua, Pint 43.50
Flask, Union & Clasped Hands, Aqua, Quart 40.00
Flask, Union & Clasped Hands, 1/2 Pint 45.00
Flask, Union & Clasped Hands, Pint 35.00
Flask, Union & Clasped Hands, Quart 39.50
Flask, Union & Eagle & Banner, Aqua, 1/2 Pint, 6 In. 17.50
Flask, Union & Eagle & Pittsburgh, Pa. In Oval, Aqua, Pint 45.00
Flask, Union & Eagle & 11 Stars On Shoulder, Neck Ring, Aqua, 1/2 Pint 45.00
Flask, Union & Eagle & Shield, Amber, 1/2 Pint 60.00
Flask, Union & Eagle, Collared, Amber, 1/2 Pint 65.00
Flask, Union & Flying Eagle & L.F.& Co., Pittsburgh, Pa., Aqua, 7 1/2 In. 30.00
Flask, Union & Wm.Frank & Sons, Pitt. & Cannon & Flag, Light Blue, Pint 65.00
Flask, Union Oval, Blanchard & Farrar, Boston, Oval Slug Plate, Aqua, Quart 11.00
Flask, Union Oval, C.J.T.Co.In Shield, 1847, Strap Sided, Aqua, Quart 6.00
Flask, Union Oval, Embossed Anchor On Front, Banded, Amber, Pint 16.00
Flask, Union Oval, F On Bottom, Strap Sided, Whittled, Blob Lip, 1/2 Pint 6.00
Flask, Union Oval, F On Bottom, Strap Sided, Whittled, Ice Blue, 1/2 Pint 7.00
Flask, Union Oval, Strap Sided, Blob Lip, Honey Amber, Pint 3.00
Flask, Union Oval, Strap Sided, Blob Lip, Honey Amber, 1/2 Pint 3.00
Flask, Union Oval, Strap Sided, Blob Lip, Red Amber, Pint 3.00
Flask, Union Oval, Strap Sided, Full Quart In Script, Aqua, 9 1/2 In. 5.00
Flask, Union Oval, Strap Sided, Honey Amber, Pint 6.00
Flask, Union Oval, Strap Sided, Light Amber, 1/2 Pint 5.00
Flask, Union Oval, Strap Sided, Whittled, Bimal, Golden Amber, Pint 6.00
Flask, Union, Aqua, Pint 25.00
Flask, Union, Aqua, Quart 25.00
Flask, Urn & Cornucopia & Twig & Whitney Glass Works, Olive Green, Quart 26.50
Flask, Vertical Ribs, Aqua, Pint .... 35.00 To 40.00
  Flask, Violin, see Flask, Scroll
Flask, Warranted, Strap Sided, Amber, Pint 37.50
Flask, Washington & Eagle & Shield, 1932, 9 In. 3.95
Flask, Washington & Lockport Glass Works, Aqua, Pint 49.00
Flask, Washington & Taylor, Dyottville Glass Works, Phila., OP, Aqua, Pint 60.00
Flask, Washington & Taylor, G.Z., Sheared Lip, Pontil, Aqua, Pint 48.00
Flask, Washington & Taylor, Reproduction, 20th Century, Cobalt, Pint 15.00
Flask, Washington & Taylor, Sheared Lip, Pontil, Cloudy Base, Aqua, Quart 50.00
Flask, Waterford & Clasped Hands, Graphite Pontil, Aqua, Quart 35.00
Flask, Westford & Sheaf Of Wheat, Amber, Pint 25.00
Flask, Westford & Sheaf Of Wheat, Deep Red Amber, 1/2 Pint 95.00
Flask, Westford & Sheaf Of Wheat, Olive Green, 1/2 Pint 70.00
Flask, Westford & Sheaf Of Wheat, Tools, & Star, Pint 115.00
Flask, Westford & Star Under Sheaf Of Wheat, Blood Amber, Pint 100.00
Flask, Whiskey, Belt Hanger, Round, 5 In. Diameter 28.00
Flask, Whiskey, Civil War Officer's Field, Pewter Cover Is Cup 12.50
Flask, Whiskey, Cut Glass, Sterling Silver Top 68.00
Flask, Whiskey, Flat Oval, Sterling Silver 72.00
Flask, Whiskey, Lady's, Art Deco, 4 Shot Capacity 85.00
Flask, Whiskey, Lady's, English Silver 18.00
Flask, Whiskey, Leather Covered, A Century Of Progress, 1933 .... 8.00
Flask, Whiskey, Silver Plate, Art Deco, Embossed & Engraved Golf Scene 150.00
Flask, White Loopings On Clear, Pint 30.00
Flask, Whitney Glass Works Embossed On Base, Amber, 1/2 Pint 25.00
Flask, Whitney Glass Works Embossed On Base, Dark Amber, 1/2 Pint 30.00
Flask, Whitney Glass Works, OP, Aqua, Pint 18.00

Flask, Whitney Glass Works, Pat.1861, Screw Type, Pressed, Amber, 6 3/4 In. 50.00
Flask, Will You Take A Drink, Will A Duck Swim, Aqua, Pint 75.00
Flask, William Jennings Bryan, Aqua, 1/2 Pint 125.00
Flask, Willington & Liberty Eagle, Amber, Quart 90.00
Flask, XX & Eagle & Cunningham & Co., Pittsburgh, Light Blue, Quart 75.00
Flask, XX & Eagle, IP, Pint 50.00
Flask, XX & Eagle, Pontil, Quart 65.00
Flask, Zanesville City Glass Works, Aqua, Pint .... 42.50 To 45.00
Flask, Zanesville, Grandfather's, 24 Broken Swirled Ribs, Amber, 8 1/4 In. 900.00
Flask, Zanesville, Grandmother's, 24 Broken Swirled Ribs, Honey Amber, 5 In. ... 870.00
Flask, Zanesville, Mellon Ribbed, Amber, Quart 800.00
Flask, Zanesville, Swirled, Golden Amber, 1/2 Pint 150.00
Flask, Zanesville, Vertical Ribbing, Deep Reddish Amber, 1/2 Pint 200.00
Flask, Zanesville, 24 Broken Swirled Ribs, Honey Amber, 7 In. 550.00
Flask, Zanesville, 24 Vertical Ribs, Yellow Green, 7 1/4 In. 220.00
    Flask, Zanesville, see also Flask, Chestnut, Zanesville
Flask, 3 Dots At Front Bottom, Straight Sided, Sheared Lip, Aqua, 1/2 Pint 9.00
Flask, 16 Coarse Ribs, Medium Yellow Green, 1/2 Pint 25.00
Flask, 16 Vertical Ribs Swirled To Left At Bottom, Aqua, Quart 85.00
Flask, 16 Vertical Ribs, Half Post Neck, 7 1/4 In. 45.00
Flask, 20 Coarse Vertical Ribs, Medium Olive Green, Pint 30.00

    Food bottles include all of the many grocery store containers, such as
    catsup, horseradish, jelly, and other foodstuffs. A few special items, such
    as vinegar, are listed under their own headings.

Food, AJC Tomato Sauce, Embossed, Dark Purple, 9 3/4 In. 25.00
Food, A.L.Murdock Liquid Food, 12 Sided, Amber, 7 In. 6.50
Food, As You Like It Horseradish, Pottery, 1/2 Pint 10.00
Food, Bierley's Juice, Wide Mouth, 6 1/2 In. 3.00
Food, Brandy Peaches, Free-Blown, Aqua, 1/2 Gallon 60.00
Food, Brooke's Lemos Sweetened Diluted Lemon Juice, 1906, Label 6.00
Food, Buster Brown Mustard, 2 1/2 In.High 3.50
Food, California Fig Syrup Co., 7 In. 1.50
    Food, California Perfume Co., see Avon, California Perfume Co.
Food, Candy Bros. Confectioneries, St.Louis, Aqua, 2 Quart 15.00
Food, Capers, Emerald Green, 6 In. 3.00
Food, Capers, 8 Concave Sides, Ball Neck, Roof Shoulder, Green, 9 1/4 In. 6.00
Food, Champion Syrup Refining Co., Indianapolis, Aqua, Quart 13.50
Food, Cherry Syrup, Recessed Glass Covered Label, 12 In.High 35.00
Food, Chocolate Syrup, Decal Label, 12 In.High 18.00
Food, Columbia Catsup, Embossed, Sample Size 3.00
Food, Condiment, 8 In. 1.00
Food, Cork Seal, Seal On Shoulder, Bubbles, Amber, 1/2 Gallon 50.00
Food, Curtis & Moore Fruit Syrups, 10 In. 3.00
Food, Derby Mustard, London, England, Embossed, Round, Milk Glass, 4 In. ... 12.00
Food, Dexter's Syrup, Square, IP, Aqua, 9 1/2 In. 70.00
Food, Embossed Birds & Palm Trees, Ground Screw Thread, Tin Top, Aqua, 4 In. 37.00
Food, Eskay's Albumenized Food, Pat.1893, Amber, 3 1/2 In. 3.00
Food, Eskay's Albumenized Food, Pat.1893, Tin Clamp Cover, Amber, 7 1/4 In. ... 5.95
Food, Extract Of Lemon, Label, 4 In. 4.00
Food, French's Mustard, 14 Ozs. 1.00
Food, Gilt Edge Dressing, Round, Aqua, 3 3/4 In. 6.00
Food, Gilt Edge Dressing, 7 Pointed Star, 30, & Maltese Crosses, Aqua, 4 In. ... 5.00
Food, Glenrosa, Paneled, 6 1/2 In. 3.00
Food, Golden West Peanut Butter, Embossed Peanuts, Pint 5.00
Food, Good Value Extract, Peppermint, 6 In. .... *Illus* 2.00
Food, Grape Juice, Benton Myers & Co., Cleveland, Crock, 1/2 Pint 17.50
Food, Heinz, Patent June 9, 1891, 5 In. 2.50
Food, Honey, Pure, Embossed, Aqua, 2 Lbs. 4.00
Food, Horlick's Malted Milk, 6 Quart 8.50
Food, Horlick's, Amethyst, 10 In. 7.00
Food, Horlick's, 1/2 Pint 2.00
Food, Horlick's, Pint 2.00
Food, Horseradish, Seville Packing Co., N.Y., Emerald Green, 7 1/4 In. 8.00
Food, Huckleberry, Aqua, 11 1/4 In. 25.00

Food, Good Value Extract, Peppermint, 6 In.
(See Page 96)

Food, Indian Root Beer Extract, Blob Lip, Oval Front Panel, Aqua, 4 1/2 In.	5.00
Food, Jam Ginger, Calabash, Fluted Neck, White Enamel, Pint	9.75
Food, Jamaican Ginger, Decanter, White Enamel Letters, Pint	10.00
Food, Jumbo Brand Peanut Butter, Frank Tea & Spice Co., O., Pint	2.00
Food, Jumbo Peanut Butter, Embossed Elephant, ABM, Pint	2.25
Food, Jumbo Peanut Butter, Embossed Elephant's Head, 5 Ozs.	4.00
Food, Jumbo Peanut Butter, Embossed Elephant's Head, 7 Ozs.	3.50
Food, Jumbo Peanut Butter, Embossed Elephant's Head, 10 Ozs.	3.50
Food, Jumbo Peanut Butter, Embossed Elephant's Head, 16 Ozs.	3.50
Food, Jumbo Peanut Butter, 4 Ozs.	5.00
Food, L.G. Yoe & Co. Maple Syrup, Turning Amethyst, 8 1/4 In.	25.00
Food, Lemon Syrup, Decal Label, 12 In.High	18.00
Food, Log Cabin Syrup, Bank, Clear	35.00
Food, Louis Frere's Bordeaux, 8 1/2 In. ....Color	47.00
Food, Lucky Joe Mustard, Bank	4.00

Food, McMechen's Always The Best, Old Virginia, 5 In.

Food, Mellin's Infant's Food,
Large Letters

Food, McIlhenny Co., Sauce, Avery Island, La., Spiral, Amethyst, 7 In.	10.00
Food, McLaughlin's Manor House Coffee, Quart	2.50
Food, McMechen's Always The Best, Old Virginia, 5 In. ....*Illus*	45.00
Food, Mellin's Food Co., Round, Embossed, Aqua & Clear, 6 In.High	1.00
Food, Mellin's Food For Infants, Embossed Sample, Screw Cap, Aqua, 3 1/4 In.	3.50
Food, Mellin's Infant's Food, Large Letters ....*Illus*	9.00
Food, Mellin's, Free Sample, Blob Top, Aqua, 3 1/2 In.	1.00 To 4.50
Food, Missouri Ozark Made Country Sorghum, Cottage, Brown	5.00
Food, Mustard, E.C.Flaccus & Co., Elk's Head, Honey Amber	185.00
Food, Nash's Happy Time Mustard, 4 1/2 In. ....*Illus*	5.00
Food, New England Maple Syrup Co., Boston, Aqua, Pint	12.00
Food, New England Maple Syrup Co., Boston, Pint	12.00

Food, Nash's Happy Time Mustard, 4 1/2 In.
(See Page 97)

Food, Superior Grated Horseradish, 7 In.

Food, Rose's Lime Juice, 9 In.

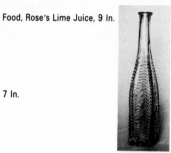

Food, **Ohio Valley Ketchup,** Applied Screw Thread, Fluted, Label, 8 3/4 In.	8.00
Food, **Oil & Vinegar,** Cut Glass, Hawkes, 1916, Sterling Cap, 7 3/8 In.	59.95
Food, **Oil & Vinegar,** Hawkes, Copper Wheel Engraved Floral, Sterling Stopper	35.00
Food, **Olive Oil,** OP, Stain, 10 1/2 In.	2.95
Food, **Oyster,** Light Purple, Pint	10.00
Food, **Paskola,** The Predigested Food Co., Embossed Pineapple, Amber, Pint	55.00
Food, **Penguin Syrup,** 8 In.	2.50
Pepper Sauce, see Pepper Sauce	
Food, **Pickle, see Pickle**	
Food, **Pineapple Syrup,** Recessed Glass Covered Label, 12 In.High	35.00
Food, **Planter's Peanuts,** Octagonal, Peanut Finial, 8 In.	45.00
Food, **Planter's Peanuts,** Signed Leap Year 1940	16.00 To 22.00
Food, **Planter's Peanuts,** Square Peanut On Top, 7 1/2 In.	65.00
Food, **Professor Horsford's Baking Powder,** Round, Label, Embossed, Cork, Clear	3.00
Food, **Prune Juice,** Green, Large Size	3.98
Food, **Raspberry,** Gold & Black Label, 12 In.High	18.00
Food, **Rawleigh's Compound Extract Of Vanilla,** Embossed, Rectangular, Aqua	3.00
Food, **Rope's Lemon New York,** Rectangular, Clear, 5 In.High	1.50
Food, **Rose's Lime Juice,** 9 In. *Illus*	30.00
Food, **Rose's Lime Juice,** 11 In.	8.00
Food, **Rose's West India Lime Juice,** Embossed, Glass Stopper, Aqua, 5 In.	6.00
Food, **Royal Mint Sauce,** Detroit, Calabash, Fluted Neck, Emerald, 1/2 Pint	6.75
Food, **Royal Mint Sauce,** HC Mfg. Co., Detroit, Green, 7 1/2 In.	5.00
Food, **Sauce,** Honeywell Type, Concave Panels, Rolled Lip, OP, Aqua, 6 In.	5.95
Food, **Spice,** Square, Rolled Lip, Pontil, Aqua, 7 X 3 In.	9.50
Food, **Squirrel Brand Peanut,** Finial Lid	55.00
Food, **Strittmatter Pure Honey,** Embossed Bee, Blue Aqua, Pint	7.50
Food, **Sunshine Coffee,** Embossed, Pound	2.50
Food, **Superior Grated Horseradish,** 7 In. *Illus*	65.00

Food, The 3 Millers Orangeade Syrup, Recessed Glass Label	50.00
Food, Valentine's Meat Juice, Blown, Amber, 3 1/8 In.	17.50
Food, Wan-Eta Cocoa, Aqua, Quart	6.00
Food, Wine Cocoa Syrup, Metal Top, Blue & White Paper Label, 11 In. High	50.00
Food, Worcestershire, Cut Glass, Strawberry Diamond & Fan, Flat Stopper	60.00
Food, Yogurt, Embossed, Quart	6.00
Food, 400 Fruit Drink, 7 Ozs.	1.50

Fruit jars made of glass have been used in the United States since the 1850s. Over one thousand different jars have been found with varieties of closures, embossing, and colors. The date 1858 on many jars refers to a patent, not the age of the bottle. Be sure to look in this listing under any name or initial that appears on your jar. If not otherwise indicated, the jar is clear glass, quart size. The numbers used in the entries in the form T-0 refer to the book A Collectors' Manual of Fruit Jars by Julian Harrison Toulouse.

Fruit Jar, A & C, Aqua, 1/2 Gallon	35.00
Fruit Jar, ABC, Aqua, Quart	165.00
Fruit Jar, ABC, Pint	175.00
Fruit Jar, ABC, Quart	165.00 To 175.00
Fruit Jar, A.Conrad, New Geneva, Pa., Stoneware, Quart	30.00
Fruit Jar, A.Conrad, New Geneva, Pa., Stoneware, 1/2 Gallon	30.00
Fruit Jar, A.Conrad, New Geneva, Pa., Stoneware, Gallon	30.00
Fruit Jar, A.P.Donaghho, Parkersburg, W.Va., Stoneware, Quart	18.00
Fruit Jar, A.P.Donaghho, Parkersburg, W.Va., Stoneware, 1/2 Gallon	18.00
Fruit Jar, A.P.Donaghho, Parkersburg, W.Va., Stoneware, Gallon	18.00
Fruit Jar, Acme In Shield, Pint	1.00
Fruit Jar, Acme In Shield, Quart	1.00
Fruit Jar, Acme, Pint	1.00 To 3.00
Fruit Jar, Acme, Quart	1.00
Fruit Jar, Acme, Stars & Stripes In Shield, Glass Lid, Wire Bail, Quart	3.00
Fruit Jar, Airtight, Barrel, Potter & Bodine, Pontil, Turquoise, Quart	60.00
Fruit Jar, Airtight, Barrel, Potter & Bodine, Pushed-Up, IP, Aqua, Quart	500.00
Fruit Jar, Almy, Quart	20.00
Fruit Jar, American Soda Co., 1/2 Gallon	7.00
Fruit Jar, American, Quart	55.00
Fruit Jar, American, 1/2 Gallon	60.00
Fruit Jar, Anchor Hocking Lightning, Pint	3.00
Fruit Jar, Anchor Hocking Mason, Aqua, 1/2 Pint	1.00
Fruit Jar, Anchor Hocking Mason, Aqua, Pint	1.00
Fruit Jar, Anchor Hocking Mason, Aqua, Quart	1.00
Fruit Jar, Anchor Hocking Mason, Aqua, 1/2 Gallon	1.00
Fruit Jar, Anchor Hocking Mason, 1/2 Pint	1.00
Fruit Jar, Anchor Hocking Mason, Pint	1.00 To 1.50
Fruit Jar, Anchor Hocking Mason, Quart	1.00
Fruit Jar, Anchor Hocking Mason, 1/2 Gallon	1.00
Fruit Jar, Anchor Hocking, Embossed Anchor On 2 Sides, Pint	3.50
Fruit Jar, Atlas E-Z Seal, Amber, Quart	22.50 To 25.00
Fruit Jar, Atlas E-Z Seal, Amber, 1/2 Gallon	22.50
Fruit Jar, Atlas E-Z Seal, Aqua, 1/2 Pint	1.00 To 5.00
Fruit Jar, Atlas E-Z Seal, Aqua, Pint	.60 To 1.00
Fruit Jar, Atlas E-Z Seal, Aqua, Quart	.60 To 1.00
Fruit Jar, Atlas E-Z Seal, Aqua, 1/2 Gallon	1.00
Fruit Jar, Atlas E-Z Seal, Blue, 1/2 Pint	25.00
Fruit Jar, Atlas E-Z Seal, Blue, Pint	1.00
Fruit Jar, Atlas E-Z Seal, Blue, Quart	1.00 To 4.50
Fruit Jar, Atlas E-Z Seal, Cornflower Blue, Quart	7.00 To 15.00
Fruit Jar, Atlas E-Z Seal, Embossed Bottom, Quart	.75
Fruit Jar, Atlas E-Z Seal, Glass Lid, Wire Bail, Amber Tint, Quart	4.00
Fruit Jar, Atlas E-Z Seal, Glass Lid, Wire Bail, Aqua, Pint	2.75
Fruit Jar, Atlas E-Z Seal, Glass Lid, Wire Bail, Aqua, Quart	2.50
Fruit Jar, Atlas E-Z Seal, Glass Lid, Wire Bail, Aqua, 1/2 Gallon	2.00
Fruit Jar, Atlas E-Z Seal, Glass Lid, Wire Bail, Blue, Quart	5.00
Fruit Jar, Atlas E-Z Seal, Glass Lid, Wire Bail, Green Tint, Quart	2.00
Fruit Jar, Atlas E-Z Seal, Glass Lid, Wire Bail, Light Blue, Quart	2.00

Fruit Jar, **Atlas E-Z Seal,** Glass Lid, Wire Bail, Orange Amber, Quart	35.00
Fruit Jar, **Atlas E-Z Seal,** Glass Lid, Wire Bail, 1/2 Pint	4.00
Fruit Jar, **Atlas E-Z Seal,** Glass Lid, Wire Bail, Pint	2.50
Fruit Jar, **Atlas E-Z Seal,** Glass Lid, Wire Bail, Quart	2.00
Fruit Jar, **Atlas E-Z Seal,** Light Olive, Quart	8.00
Fruit Jar, **Atlas E-Z Seal,** Light Olive, 1/2 Gallon	8.00
Fruit Jar, **Atlas E-Z Seal,** Milk Glass Lid, Amber, Quart	30.00
Fruit Jar, **Atlas E-Z Seal,** Pint	1.00
Fruit Jar, **Atlas E-Z Seal,** Quart	1.00
Fruit Jar, **Atlas E-Z Seal,** Squat Bell Shape, Glass Lid, Blue, Pint	2.75
Fruit Jar, **Atlas E-Z Seal,** Squatty, Aqua, Pint	1.25
Fruit Jar, **Atlas E-Z Seal,** Squatty, Blue, Quart	2.00
Fruit Jar, **Atlas E-Z Seal,** 1/2 Pint	1.00 To 2.00
Fruit Jar, **Atlas E-Z Seal,** 1/2 Gallon	1.00
Fruit Jar, **Atlas E-Z Seal,** 48 Ozs.	7.00
Fruit Jar, **Atlas E-Z Seal,** 58 Ozs.	7.00
Fruit Jar, **Atlas Good Luck Mason,** Glass Lid, Wire Bail, Quart	2.50
Fruit Jar, **Atlas Good Luck,** 1/2 Pint	6.00
Fruit Jar, **Atlas Good Luck,** Pint	1.00 To 8.00
Fruit Jar, **Atlas Good Luck,** Quart	2.25 To 3.00
Fruit Jar, **Atlas H-A Mason,** 1/2 Pint	3.00
Fruit Jar, **Atlas H-A Mason,** Pint	1.50
Fruit Jar, **Atlas H-A Mason,** Quart	1.50
Fruit Jar, **Atlas Mason Improved Pat'd,** Aqua, Pint	3.50
Fruit Jar, **Atlas Mason Improved Pat'd,** Aqua, Quart	3.00
Fruit Jar, **Atlas Mason,** Green, Pint	1.00
Fruit Jar, **Atlas Mason,** Green, Quart	1.00
Fruit Jar, **Atlas Mason,** Improved Patent, Aqua, Pint	4.00
Fruit Jar, **Atlas Mason,** Improved Patent, Aqua, Quart	4.00
Fruit Jar, **Atlas Mason,** Improved Patent, Knowlton Vacuum Lid, Pint	4.00
Fruit Jar, **Atlas Mason,** Improved Patent, Pint	4.00
Fruit Jar, **Atlas Mason,** Pint	2.00
Fruit Jar, **Atlas Mason,** Quart	1.50
Fruit Jar, **Atlas Mason,** Square, Pint	2.00
Fruit Jar, **Atlas Mason,** Square, Quart	1.50
Fruit Jar, **Atlas Mason,** Square, 1/2 Gallon	3.50
Fruit Jar, **Atlas Mason,** Zinc Lid, Bank, 3 1/2 In.	3.00
Fruit Jar, **Atlas Mason,** 1/2 Gallon	2.75
Fruit Jar, **Atlas Mason,** 10 X 4 1/2 In.	5.98
Fruit Jar, **Atlas Special Mason,** Quart	3.75
Fruit Jar, **Atlas Special Mason,** Wide Mouth, Aqua, Quart	4.00
Fruit Jar, **Atlas Special Mason,** Wide Mouth, Aqua, 1/2 Gallon	6.00
Fruit Jar, **Atlas Strong Shoulder Mason,** Blue, Pint	3.00
Fruit Jar, **Atlas Strong Shoulder Mason,** Blue, Quart	2.00
Fruit Jar, **Atlas Strong Shoulder Mason,** Blue, 1/2 Gallon	3.00
Fruit Jar, **Atlas Strong Shoulder Mason,** Cornflower Blue, Pint	23.50
Fruit Jar, **Atlas Strong Shoulder Mason,** Pint	1.00
Fruit Jar, **Atlas Strong Shoulder Mason,** Porcelain Top, Blue, Pint	3.00
Fruit Jar, **Atlas Strong Shoulder Mason,** Porcelain Top, Blue, Quart	3.00
Fruit Jar, **Atlas Strong Shoulder Mason,** Porcelain Top, Blue, 1/2 Gallon	3.50
Fruit Jar, **Atlas Strong Shoulder Mason,** Porcelain Top, Quart	3.00
Fruit Jar, **Atlas Strong Shoulder Mason,** Porcelain Top, 1/2 Gallon	3.50
Fruit Jar, **Atlas Strong Shoulder Mason,** Quart	1.00
Fruit Jar, **Atlas Wholefruit Jar,** Quart	1.50 To 2.50
Fruit Jar, **Atlas,** Amber, 1/2 Gallon	25.00
Fruit Jar, **Atlas,** Cornflower Blue, Pint	12.75
Fruit Jar, **Atlas,** Cornflower Blue, Quart	12.75
Fruit Jar, **Atlas,** Mason's Patent Nov.30th, 1858, Aqua, 1/2 Gallon	6.50
Fruit Jar, **Atlas,** Mason's Patent Nov.30th, 1858, Deep Blue, Quart	3.00
Fruit Jar, **Atlas,** Mason's Patent, Quart	3.00
Fruit Jar, **Atlas,** Olive Green, Pint	4.50
Fruit Jar, **Atlas,** Olive Green, Quart	6.50
Fruit Jar, **Atlas,** 1/2 Pint	1.25
Fruit Jar, **Automatic Sealer,** The, Aqua, Pint	175.00
Fruit Jar, **B.& B.,** Embossed on Base, Johnson & Johnson Type, Amber, 1/2 Pint	6.00

Fruit Jar, **BBGMco. Monogram**, Aqua, Quart	22.50
Fruit Jar, **BBGMco. Monogram**, Aqua, 1/2 Gallon	25.00
Fruit Jar, **BBGMco. Monogram**, Quart	12.00
Fruit Jar, **Ball Deluxe Jar**, Quart	6.00
Fruit Jar, **Ball Eclipse Wide Mouth**, Glass Lid, Wire Bail, Pint	2.50
Fruit Jar, **Ball Eclipse Wide Mouth**, Glass Lid, Wire Bail, Quart	2.00
Fruit Jar, **Ball Eclipse**, Quart	1.50
Fruit Jar, **Ball Freezer Jar**, Pint	1.00
Fruit Jar, **Ball Freezer Jar**, Quart	1.00
Fruit Jar, **Ball Ideal**, Blue Green, Wire Clamp, 1/3 Pint	15.00
Fruit Jar, **Ball Ideal**, Blue Green, 1/2 Pint	12.00
Fruit Jar, **Ball Ideal**, Blue, 1/2 Pint	1.50 To 15.00
Fruit Jar, **Ball Ideal**, Blue, Pint	.60 To 15.00
Fruit Jar, **Ball Ideal**, Blue, Quart	.60 To 1.50
Fruit Jar, **Ball Ideal**, Blue, 1/2 Gallon	1.50 To 2.50
Fruit Jar, **Ball Ideal**, Glass Lid, Blue, Pint	4.50 To 5.00
Fruit Jar, **Ball Ideal**, Glass Lid, Blue, Quart	3.50 To 4.50
Fruit Jar, **Ball Ideal**, Glass Lid, Pint	2.50 To 3.50
Fruit Jar, **Ball Ideal**, Glass Lid, Quart	2.50
Fruit Jar, **Ball Ideal**, Glass Lid, Wire Clamp, 1/2 Pint	3.00
Fruit Jar, **Ball Ideal**, Light Blue, Pint	1.00
Fruit Jar, **Ball Ideal**, Light Blue, Quart	1.00
Fruit Jar, **Ball Ideal**, Patent July 14, 1908, Aqua, 1/2 Pint	12.00
Fruit Jar, **Ball Ideal**, Patent July 14, 1908, Aqua, Pint	12.00
Fruit Jar, **Ball Ideal**, Patent July 14, 1908, Aqua, Quart	6.50
Fruit Jar, **Ball Ideal**, Patent July 14, 1908, Blue, Pint	1.00 To 3.00
Fruit Jar, **Ball Ideal**, Patent July 14, 1908, Blue, Quart	1.00
Fruit Jar, **Ball Ideal**, Patent July 14, 1908, Glass Lid, Aqua Tint, Quart	3.00
Fruit Jar, **Ball Ideal**, Patent July 14, 1908, Glass Lid, Aqua, Pint	2.00
Fruit Jar, **Ball Ideal**, Patent July 14, 1908, Glass Lid, Blue, Pint	1.50
Fruit Jar, **Ball Ideal**, Patent July 14, 1908, Glass Lid, Blue, Quart	1.50
Fruit Jar, **Ball Ideal**, Patent July 14, 1908, Glass Lid, Blue, 1/2 Gallon	3.00
Fruit Jar, **Ball Ideal**, Patent July 14, 1908, Glass Lid, Wire Bail, Blue, Pint	2.50
Fruit Jar, **Ball Ideal**, Patent July 14, 1908, Glass Lid, Wire Bail, Blue, Quart	2.00
Fruit Jar, **Ball Ideal**, Patent July 14, 1908, Glass Lid, 1/2 Pint	4.00
Fruit Jar, **Ball Ideal**, Patent July 14, 1908, 1/2 Pint	2.00 To 2.50
Fruit Jar, **Ball Ideal**, Patent July 14, 1908, Pint	1.50
Fruit Jar, **Ball Ideal**, Patent July 14, 1908, Quart	1.50
Fruit Jar, **Ball Ideal**, 1/3 Pint	1.50 To 1.80
Fruit Jar, **Ball Ideal**, 1/2 Pint	1.50 To 3.00
Fruit Jar, **Ball Ideal**, Pint	1.50
Fruit Jar, **Ball Ideal**, Quart	1.50
Fruit Jar, **Ball Ideal**, Square, Glass Lid, Pint	2.00
Fruit Jar, **Ball Ideal**, Square, Glass Lid, Quart	2.00
Fruit Jar, **Ball Improved**, Glass Lid, Dark Aqua, Quart	3.00
Fruit Jar, **Ball Improved**, Porcelain Lid, Blue, Quart	5.50
Fruit Jar, **Ball Improved**, Quart	.50 To 4.00
Fruit Jar, **Ball Improved**, 1/2 Gallon	2.25
Fruit Jar, **Ball Jar**, Mason's Patent Nov.30th, 1858, Aqua, Quart	5.00
Fruit Jar, **Ball Jar**, Mason's Patent Nov.30th, 1858, Aqua, 1/2 Gallon	6.00
Fruit Jar, **Ball Mason**, Aqua, Pint	2.00
Fruit Jar, **Ball Mason**, Aqua, Quart	1.00
Fruit Jar, **Ball Mason**, Aqua, 1/2 Gallon	2.00
Fruit Jar, **Ball Mason**, Deep Olive Green, Pint	30.00
Fruit Jar, **Ball Mason**, Deep Olive Green, Quart	15.00 To 30.00
Fruit Jar, **Ball Mason**, Deep Olive Green, 1/2 Gallon	30.00
Fruit Jar, **Ball Mason**, Embossed, Green, 1/2 Gallon	3.00
Fruit Jar, **Ball Mason**, Green, Pint	1.00
Fruit Jar, **Ball Mason**, Green, Quart	1.00
Fruit Jar, **Ball Mason**, Olive Amber, Pint	35.00
Fruit Jar, **Ball Mason**, Olive Amber, 1/2 Gallon	30.00
Fruit Jar, **Ball Mason**, Porcelain Lid, 1/2 Gallon	4.00
Fruit Jar, **Ball Mason**, Porcelain Lined Zinc Lid, Aqua, Pint	1.25
Fruit Jar, **Ball Mason**, Porcelain Lined Zinc Lid, Aqua, 1/2 Gallon	1.50
Fruit Jar, **Ball Mason**, Porcelain Lined Zinc Lid, Green Tint, Quart	3.00

Fruit Jar, Ball Mason, Salt & Pepper Shakers, 3 In., Pair 1.25
Fruit Jar, Ball Mason, 1/2 Gallon .... .75 To 2.75
Fruit Jar, Ball Perfect Mason In Block Letters, Green, Pint 5.00
Fruit Jar, Ball Perfect Mason, Amber, 1/2 Gallon .... 17.00 To 35.00
Fruit Jar, Ball Perfect Mason, Dark Amber, 1/2 Gallon 20.00
Fruit Jar, Ball Perfect Mason, Deep Olive Green, Pint 30.00
Fruit Jar, Ball Perfect Mason, Deep Olive Green, Quart 30.00
Fruit Jar, Ball Perfect Mason, Deep Olive Green, 1/2 Gallon 30.00
Fruit Jar, Ball Perfect Mason, Glass Top, White, Quart 1.00
Fruit Jar, Ball Perfect Mason, Green, Pint 1.00
Fruit Jar, Ball Perfect Mason, Green, Quart 1.00
Fruit Jar, Ball Perfect Mason, Made In U.S.A., Deep Blue, Quart 1.00
Fruit Jar, Ball Perfect Mason, Olive Amber, Quart 30.00
Fruit Jar, Ball Perfect Mason, Pint 1.00
Fruit Jar, Ball Perfect Mason, Quart .... 1.00 To 1.50
Fruit Jar, Ball Perfect Mason, Salt & Pepper Shakers, Zinc Lids, C.1930 .... 10.00
Fruit Jar, Ball Perfect Mason, Salt & Pepper, Dome Lids .... 2.00 To 5.00
Fruit Jar, Ball Perfect Mason, Seven-Up Green, Quart 20.00
Fruit Jar, Ball Perfect Mason, Square, Aqua, Pint 5.00
Fruit Jar, Ball Perfect Mason, Zinc Top, Aqua, Quart .... .50
Fruit Jar, Ball Perfect Mason, Zinc Top, 1/3 Pint 2.00
Fruit Jar, Ball Perfect Mason, 1/2 Pint 1.75
Fruit Jar, Ball Perfect Mason, 1/2 Gallon .... *Illus* 20.00

Fruit Jar, Ball Perfect Mason, 1/2 Gallon

Fruit Jar, Ball Perfect Seal, Amber, 1/2 Gallon 17.00
Fruit Jar, Ball Perfection, Pint 15.00
Fruit Jar, Ball Sanitary Sure Seal, Patent 1908, Lid, Wire Bail, Quart 3.00
Fruit Jar, Ball Special Wide Mouth Mason, Quart .... .50
Fruit Jar, Ball Special, Aqua, Pint 4.00
Fruit Jar, Ball Special, Aqua, 1/2 Gallon 5.00
Fruit Jar, Ball Standard, Script, Aqua, Quart .... 2.00 To 4.50
Fruit Jar, Ball Standard, Script, Aqua, 1/2 Gallon 2.00
Fruit Jar, Ball Standard, Script, Blue, Quart 3.50
Fruit Jar, Ball Standard, Script, Blue, 1/2 Gallon 3.50
Fruit Jar, Ball Standard, Wax Sealer, Blue, Quart 6.50
Fruit Jar, Ball Standard, Wax Sealer, Quart 4.75
Fruit Jar, Ball Sure Seal, Aqua, Pint 2.00
Fruit Jar, Ball Sure Seal, Aqua, Quart 2.00
Fruit Jar, Ball Sure Seal, Blue, Pint 1.50
Fruit Jar, Ball Sure Seal, Blue, Quart 1.50
Fruit Jar, Ball Sure Seal, Lid, Wire Bail, Blue, Pint 1.75
Fruit Jar, Ball Sure Seal, Lid, Wire Bail, Blue, Quart 1.75
Fruit Jar, Ball Sure Seal, Pint 2.00
Fruit Jar, Ball Sure Seal, 1/2 Gallon .... 4.40 To 4.50
Fruit Jar, Ball, Aqua, 1/2 Pint 1.00
Fruit Jar, Ball, Aqua, Pint .... 1.00 To 2.00
Fruit Jar, Ball, Aqua, Quart 1.00
Fruit Jar, Ball, Aqua, 1/2 Gallon 1.00
Fruit Jar, Ball, Blue, 1/2 Pint 10.00
Fruit Jar, Ball, Mason's Patent Nov.30th, 1858, Ball In Script, Aqua, Pint 4.00
Fruit Jar, Ball, Mason's Patent Nov.30th, 1858, Ball In Script, Aqua, Quart 3.00

Fruit Jar, **Ball**, Mason's Patent 1858 Underlined, Aqua, Quart 5.00
Fruit Jar, **Ball**, Olive Amber, 1/2 Gallon 28.00
Fruit Jar, **Ball**, Pint 1.00
Fruit Jar, **Ball**, Porcelain Lid, 1/2 Gallon 4.00
Fruit Jar, **Ball**, Porcelain Lined Zinc Lid, Aqua, Pint 1.25
Fruit Jar, **Ball**, Porcelain Lined Zinc Lid, Aqua, Quart 1.25
Fruit Jar, **Ball**, Porcelain Lined Zinc Lid, Aqua, 1/2 Gallon 1.25
Fruit Jar, **Ball**, Quart 1.00
Fruit Jar, **Ball**, The, 1858, Aqua, 1/2 Gallon 5.00
Fruit Jar, **Ball**, 1/2 Pint .... 1.00 To 3.00
Fruit Jar, **Ball**, 1/2 Gallon 1.00
Fruit Jar, **Bamberger Mason**, Quart 8.00
Fruit Jar, **Bamberger's**, Sure Seal, Pint 8.00
Fruit Jar, **Banner**, Glass Lid, Blue, Quart 8.00
Fruit Jar, **Banner**, Patent Feb.9, 1864, Haze, Quart 35.00
Fruit Jar, **Banner**, Press Down Lid, Stain, Quart 45.00
Fruit Jar, **Banner**, Quart 6.00
Fruit Jar, **Banner**, Trademark Registered, Quart 12.00
Fruit Jar, **Beaver**, Amber, Quart 300.00
Fruit Jar, **Beaver**, Aqua, Quart 20.00
Fruit Jar, **Beaver**, Aqua, 1/2 Gallon 28.00
Fruit Jar, **Beaver**, Ground Mouth, Glass Lid, Zinc Band, Aqua, Pint 40.00
Fruit Jar, **Beaver**, Ground Mouth, Glass Lid, Zinc Band, Light Aqua, Pint 35.00
Fruit Jar, **Beaver**, Ground Mouth, Glass Lid, Zinc Band, Pint 25.00
Fruit Jar, **Beaver**, Light Embossing, Aqua, Quart 12.00
Fruit Jar, **Beaver**, Quart .... 15.00 To 20.00
Fruit Jar, **Beaver**, 1/2 Gallon .... 18.00 To 18.75
Fruit Jar, **Best Fruit Keeper**, The, Aqua, Quart 32.00
Fruit Jar, **Best Fruit Keeper**, The, Quart 32.50
Fruit Jar, **Best**, Embossed On Side, Glass Lid, Zinc Band, 1/2 Gallon 15.00
Fruit Jar, **Best**, Pint 8.00
Fruit Jar, **Best**, Quart .... 20.00 To 21.50
Fruit Jar, **Best**, 1/2 Gallon .... 20.00 To 21.50
Fruit Jar, **Blown**, Folded Over Rim, Iron Top, Quart, 6 3/8 In. 75.00
Fruit Jar, **Blown**, Whittles, Sealing Wax Lip, IP, Aqua, 10 In. 265.00
Fruit Jar, **Blue Ribbon Coffee**, Quart 3.00
Fruit Jar, **Blue Ribbon**, Pint 10.00
Fruit Jar, **Blue Ribbon**, Quart 4.00
Fruit Jar, **Blueberry**, Ribbed, Olive Amber, 8 In. 150.00
Fruit Jar, **Blueberry**, Vertical Ribs, Amber, 8 In. 100.00
Fruit Jar, **Boldt Mason**, Aqua, Quart 8.50
Fruit Jar, **Boldt Mason**, Blue, 1/2 Gallon 20.00
Fruit Jar, **Boldt Mason**, Zinc Lid, Aqua, Quart 10.00
Fruit Jar, **Boldt Mason**, 1/2 Gallon 15.00
Fruit Jar, **Boyd Mason**, Aqua, Quart 3.50
Fruit Jar, **Boyd Mason**, Pint 5.00
Fruit Jar, **Boyd Perfect Mason**, Block Letters, Green, Pint 5.00
Fruit Jar, **Boyd Perfect Mason**, Block Letters, Green, Quart 4.00
Fruit Jar, **Boyd Perfect Mason**, Blue, 1/2 Gallon 2.50
Fruit Jar, **Boyd's Genuine Mason**, Green, Pint 4.50
Fruit Jar, **Boyd's Genuine Mason**, Green, Quart 4.00
Fruit Jar, **Boyd's Genuine Mason**, Pint 3.00
Fruit Jar, **Brockway Clear-Vu**, Pint .... 1.00 To 2.50
Fruit Jar, **Brockway Clear-Vu**, Quart .... 1.00 To 2.00
Fruit Jar, **Brockway Sur-Grip**, Quart 2.50
Fruit Jar, **Buck County Glass Co.**, Embossed, 3 Metal Clamps, Quart 10.00
Fruit Jar, **Buckeye**, Aqua, Quart 150.00
Fruit Jar, **Burlington**, The, 1876, 1/2 Gallon 32.00
Fruit Jar, **C F J Co.**, Mason's Improved, Amber, 1/2 Gallon 65.00
Fruit Jar, **C F J Co.**, Mason's Improved, Aqua, Midget .... 6.00 To 10.50
Fruit Jar, **C F J Co.**, Mason's Improved, Aqua, Quart 3.00
Fruit Jar, **C F J Co.**, Mason's Improved, Butter, 1/2 Gallon 45.00
Fruit Jar, **C F J Co.**, Mason's Improved, Clyde N.Y. On Reverse, Midget 12.75
Fruit Jar, **C F J Co.**, Mason's Improved, Clyde N.Y. On Reverse, Quart 2.00
Fruit Jar, **C F J Co.**, Mason's Improved, Clyde, N.Y., Aqua, Midget .... 5.00 To 7.00

Fruit Jar, **C F J Co.**, Mason's Improved, Clyde, N.Y., Aqua, Quart	6.00
Fruit Jar, **C F J Co.**, Mason's Improved, Clyde, N.Y., Aqua, 1/2 Gallon	8.00
Fruit Jar, **C F J Co.**, Mason's Improved, Cross On Reverse, Aqua, Midget	10.50
Fruit Jar, **C F J Co.**, Mason's Improved, Midget	4.00 To 10.00
Fruit Jar, **C F J Co.**, Mason's Improved, Nov.30th, 1858 & C F J, Midget	12.00
Fruit Jar, **C F J Co.**, Mason's Improved, Nov.30th, 1858, Apple Green, Quart	25.00
Fruit Jar, **C F J Co.**, Mason's Improved, Nov.30th, 1858, Lime Green, Quart	20.00
Fruit Jar, **C F J Co.**, Mason's Improved, Patent Nov.30th, 1858, Aqua, Pint	16.00
Fruit Jar, **C F J Co.**, Mason's Improved, Patent Nov.30th, 1858, Midget	7.00
Fruit Jar, **C F J Co.**, Mason's Improved, Quart	1.25
Fruit Jar, **C F J Co.**, Mason's Improved, Stain, Aqua, 1/2 Gallon	5.00
Fruit Jar, **C F J Co.**, Mason's Improved, Whittled, Midget	6.00
Fruit Jar, **C F J Co.**, Mason's Improved, 1/2 Gallon	4.00
Fruit Jar, **C F J Co.**, Mason's Improved, 1858, Dug, Yellow, Midget	150.00
Fruit Jar, **C F J Co.**, Mason's Midget	6.00 To 7.25
Fruit Jar, **C F J Co.**, Mason's Monogram Improved, Zinc Band, Midget	6.00
Fruit Jar, **C F J Co.**, Mason's Patent Nov.30th, 1858, Aqua, Quart	4.00
Fruit Jar, **C G Co.**, Crystal, Quart	22.50
Fruit Jar, **C G Co.**, Pint	5.00
Fruit Jar, **Calcutt's**, Quart	18.00
Fruit Jar, **Calcutt's**, 1893, Quart	35.00
Fruit Jar, **Canadian Jewel**, Pint	3.00
Fruit Jar, **Canton Domestic**, The, Pint	60.00
Fruit Jar, **Canton Domestic**, The, Quart	45.00 To 65.00
Fruit Jar, **Carroll True Seal**, Pint	5.50
Fruit Jar, **Carroll True Seal**, 1/2 Gallon	10.00
Fruit Jar, **Case Gin Shape**, Wide Mouth, OP, Olive Green, 10 In.	310.00
Fruit Jar, **Chambers Union Fruit Jar**, Waxsealer, Aqua	15.00
Fruit Jar, **Champion Syrup Refining Co.**, Aqua, Quart	12.00 To 14.75
Fruit Jar, **Chef**, Picture, Dated, Quart	6.00
Fruit Jar, **Chef**, Picture, Pint	8.00
Fruit Jar, **Chef**, Picture, Quart	2.75
Fruit Jar, **Chef**, Quart	6.00
Fruit Jar, **Christmas Mason**, Aqua, Quart	5.00
Fruit Jar, **Clark's Peerless**, Aqua, Pint	5.00 To 10.00
Fruit Jar, **Clark's Peerless**, Aqua, Quart	4.00 To 7.00
Fruit Jar, **Clark's Peerless**, Aqua, 1/2 Gallon	39.00
Fruit Jar, **Clark's Peerless**, Pint	6.00
Fruit Jar, **Clark's Peerless**, 1/2 Gallon	9.00
Fruit Jar, **Clarke Fruit Jar Co.**, Cleveland, O., Aqua, Quart	35.00
Fruit Jar, **Cleveland Fruit Juice Co.**, Glass Lid, Wire Bail, 1/2 Gallon	1.50
Fruit Jar, **Climax**, Blue, Pint	10.00
Fruit Jar, **Climax**, Blue, Quart	4.00
Fruit Jar, **Clown**, Pint	2.00
Fruit Jar, **Clown**, Quart	1.50
Fruit Jar, **Clown**, 1/2 Gallon	2.00
Fruit Jar, **Clyde Improved Mason**, Pint	15.00
Fruit Jar, **Clyde Improved Mason**, Quart	6.00
Fruit Jar, **Clyde**, The, Pint	6.00 To 15.00
Fruit Jar, **Clyde**, The, Quart	6.00 To 15.00
Fruit Jar, **Clyde**, The, Script, Hazy, Quart	4.00
Fruit Jar, **Cohansey**, Aqua, Quart	12.00 To 19.00
Fruit Jar, **Cohansey**, Barrel, Quart	50.00
Fruit Jar, **Cohansey**, Haze, Amber, Quart	15.00
Fruit Jar, **Cohansey**, 1/2 Pint	50.00
Fruit Jar, **Cohansey**, Pint	22.00 To 50.00
Fruit Jar, **Cohansey**, Quart	10.00 To 20.00
Fruit Jar, **Cohansey**, Whittled, Aqua, 1/2 Gallon	25.00
Fruit Jar, **Cohansey**, Whittled, 1/2 Gallon	28.00
Fruit Jar, **Cohansey**, 1/2 Gallon	10.00 To 20.00
Fruit Jar, **Columbia**, Cg Monogram	29.00
Fruit Jar, **Columbia**, Light Aqua, Pint	12.00
Fruit Jar, **Columbia**, Pint	16.00 To 30.00
Fruit Jar, **Conserve**, Aqua, Pint	6.00
Fruit Jar, **Conserve**, Pint	3.00 To 6.00

Fruit Jar, **Cork Type,** Aqua, 9 In. 90.00
Fruit Jar, **Crockery Jug,** Blue Writing, 7 1/2 In.High 25.00
Fruit Jar, **Crown Imperial,** Quart 3.00
Fruit Jar, **Crown Mason,** Pint 3.00
Fruit Jar, **Crown Mason,** Quart 2.50
Fruit Jar, **Crown Mason,** Square, Pint 2.50
Fruit Jar, **Crown Mason,** Square, Quart 2.00
Fruit Jar, **Crown,** Aqua, Midget .... 8.00 To 10.00
Fruit Jar, **Crown,** Blue, Quart 3.00
Fruit Jar, **Crown,** Blue, 1/2 Gallon 4.00
Fruit Jar, **Crown,** Cordial, 1/2 Gallon 5.00
Fruit Jar, **Crown,** Heart Shape, Quart 35.00
Fruit Jar, **Crown,** Improved, Script, Quart 6.00
Fruit Jar, **Crown,** Midget .... 7.00 To 12.00
Fruit Jar, **Crown,** Pint 3.00
Fruit Jar, **Crown,** Porcelain Top, Pint 1.75
Fruit Jar, **Crown,** Porcelain Top, Quart 1.75
Fruit Jar, **Crown,** Quart 2.00
Fruit Jar, **Crown,** T.Eaton Co., Quart 6.00
Fruit Jar, **Crown,** 1/2 Pint 4.00
Fruit Jar, **Crystal Jar,** 1/2 Gallon 31.00
Fruit Jar, **Crystal Mason,** Quart 22.00
Fruit Jar, **Crystal,** C G, Quart .... 19.50 To 28.00
Fruit Jar, **Crystal,** C G, 1/2 Gallon 25.00
Fruit Jar, **Crystal,** Quart .... 22.00 To 27.50
Fruit Jar, **Crystal,** 1/2 Gallon 17.50
Fruit Jar, **Crystal,** 6 In. .... *Illus* 45.00
Fruit Jar, **Cunninghams & Co.,** Blue, Quart 275.00
Fruit Jar, **Cunninghams & Co.,** Green, Quart 275.00
Fruit Jar, **Cunninghams & Co.,** Pittsburgh, IP, Quart 142.00
Fruit Jar, **Curtis & Moore,** 1/2 Gallon 20.00
Fruit Jar, **Daisy,** The, F.E.Ward & Co., Aqua, Pint .... 6.00 To 8.00
Fruit Jar, **Daisy,** The, F.E.Ward & Co., Quart .... 4.00 To 9.00
Fruit Jar, **Daisy,** The, Handmade, Quart 90.00
Fruit Jar, **Daisy,** The, Machine Made, Quart 10.00
Fruit Jar, **Dandy,** The, Golden Amber, Quart 70.00
Fruit Jar, **Dandy,** The, Quart 18.00
Fruit Jar, **Dandy,** The, Trademark, Amber, Quart 55.00
Fruit Jar, **Dandy,** The, Trademark, Aqua, Pint 26.00
Fruit Jar, **Darling,** The, ADM Monogram, Aqua, 1/2 Gallon 35.00
Fruit Jar, **Darling,** The, ADM Monogram, Quart 37.50
Fruit Jar, **Darling,** The, Quart 3.00
Fruit Jar, **Darling,** The, 1/2 Gallon 30.00
Fruit Jar, **Dexter,** Aqua, 8 In. .... *Illus* 51.00
Fruit Jar, **Diamond,** Pint 4.00
Fruit Jar, **Diamond,** Quart 5.00

Fruit Jar, Crystal, 6 In.

Fruit Jar, Dexter, Aqua, 8 In.

Fruit Jar, Dictator, D.I.Holcomb & Date, Wax Sealer, Tin Lid, Aqua, Quart	60.00
Fruit Jar, Dillon, Aqua, 1/2 Gallon	12.00
Fruit Jar, Dillon, Fairmont, Ind., Green, 1/2 Gallon	10.00
Fruit Jar, Dillon, Green, Quart	10.00
Fruit Jar, Doolittle Self Sealer, Aqua, Quart	18.00
Fruit Jar, Doolittle, Quart	20.00 To 23.00
Fruit Jar, Doolittle, Sun Colored Amethyst, Quart	25.00
Fruit Jar, Double Safety, Lightning Closure, 1/2 Pint	3.00 To 5.00
Fruit Jar, Double Safety, Lightning Closure, Pint	.50 To 3.00
Fruit Jar, Double Safety, Lightning Closure, Quart	.50 To 2.00
Fruit Jar, Double Safety, Lightning Closure, 1/2 Gallon	4.00
Fruit Jar, Double Safety, S.K.& O., Pint	7.00
Fruit Jar, Double Safety, Script, Glass Lid, Wire Bail, Pint	4.00
Fruit Jar, Double Safety, 1/2 Pint	5.00
Fruit Jar, Drey Improved Everseal, Glass Lid, Pint	2.50 To 4.50
Fruit Jar, Drey Improved Everseal, Glass Lid, Quart	2.50 To 3.50
Fruit Jar, Drey Improved Everseal, Glass Lid, Wire Bail, Pint	2.50
Fruit Jar, Drey Improved Everseal, Glass Lid, Wire Bail, Quart	2.00
Fruit Jar, Drey Improved Everseal, Pint	1.00
Fruit Jar, Drey Improved Everseal, Quart	1.00
Fruit Jar, Drey Mason, Pint	2.00
Fruit Jar, Drey Mason, Porcelain Lined Zinc Lid, Green Tint, Quart	3.00
Fruit Jar, Drey Mason, Turning Amethyst, Quart	1.50
Fruit Jar, Drey Perfect Mason, Pint	3.00
Fruit Jar, Drey Perfect Mason, Quart	2.50
Fruit Jar, Drey Perfect Mason, 1/2 Gallon	4.50
Fruit Jar, Drey Square Mason, Carpenter's Square, Quart	1.25
Fruit Jar, Drey Square Mason, Pint	3.00
Fruit Jar, Drey, Aqua, 1/2 Pint	1.00
Fruit Jar, Drey, Aqua, Pint	1.00
Fruit Jar, Drey, Aqua, Quart	1.00
Fruit Jar, Drey, Aqua, 1/2 Gallon	1.00
Fruit Jar, Drey, 1/2 Pint	1.00
Fruit Jar, Drey, Pint	1.00 To 3.00
Fruit Jar, Drey, Porcelain Top, Pint	4.50
Fruit Jar, Drey, Porcelain Top, Quart	3.50
Fruit Jar, Drey, Quart	1.00 To 3.00
Fruit Jar, Drey, 1/2 Gallon	1.00
Fruit Jar, E G Co., Quart	12.00
Fruit Jar, E G Co., Midget	18.50 To 22.00
Fruit Jar, E H E Co., Embossed On Side, Wax Sealer, Quart	15.00
Fruit Jar, E.C.Hazard, Quart	7.50 To 8.00
Fruit Jar, E.C.Hazard, 1 1/2 Quart	5.00
Fruit Jar, E-Z Seal, 1/2 Pint	2.00
Fruit Jar, Eagle, Aqua, 1/2 Gallon	45.00 To 55.00
Fruit Jar, Eagle, Whittled, Aqua, Quart	70.00
Fruit Jar, Eclipse, The, Aqua, Quart	12.00
Fruit Jar, Eclipse, The, Embossed Side, Wax Sealer, Amber, Quart	600.00
Fruit Jar, Economy Wax Sealer, Patent Sept.13, 1858, Aqua, Quart	60.00
Fruit Jar, Economy, Pint	1.00 To 3.50
Fruit Jar, Economy, Quart	1.00 To 5.00
Fruit Jar, Economy, Trademark, Kerr Glass Co. On Base, Quart	3.00
Fruit Jar, Economy, 1/2 Gallon	1.00
Fruit Jar, Electric, Aqua, 7 1/2 In. _Illus_	35.00
Fruit Jar, Electric, Pint	6.00
Fruit Jar, Electric, World Globe, Pint	55.00
Fruit Jar, Electric, World Globe, Quart	45.00
Fruit Jar, Electroglas, N.W., Quart	2.00 To 5.00
Fruit Jar, Empire, Bail Type, 1/2 Pint	7.00
Fruit Jar, Empire, Stippled Cross, 1/2 Pint	8.00
Fruit Jar, Empire, Stippled Cross, Pint	6.50
Fruit Jar, Empire, Stippled Cross, Quart	4.00
Fruit Jar, Empire, The, Aqua, Quart	44.00
Fruit Jar, Empire, The, Pint	10.00
Fruit Jar, Empire, The, Quart	9.00

Fruit Jar, Electric, Aqua, 7 1/2 In.
(See Page 106)

Fruit Jar, **Empire,** Unembossed, Pint 10.00
Fruit Jar, **Empire,** Unembossed, Quart 10.00
Fruit Jar, **Erie Lightning,** Aqua, Quart 8.00
Fruit Jar, **Eureka I,** Pat'd. Dec.27th, 1864, Aqua, Quart 45.00
Fruit Jar, **Eureka I,** Pat'd. Dec.27th, 1864, Quart 30.00
Fruit Jar, **Eureka I,** Pat'd. Dec.27th, 1864, 1/2 Gallon .... 45.00 To 125.00
Fruit Jar, **Eureka,** Aqua, Quart 15.00
Fruit Jar, **Eureka,** 1/2 Pint .... 8.50 To 12.00
Fruit Jar, **Eureka,** Pint 12.00
Fruit Jar, **Eureka,** 1/2 Gallon 55.00
Fruit Jar, **Everlasting Improved,** 14 Panel, Quart 20.00
Fruit Jar, **Everlasting Jar,** Aqua, Pint 5.00
Fruit Jar, **Everlasting Jar,** Purpled, 1/2 Gallon 15.00
Fruit Jar, **F & S,** Pint 8.00
Fruit Jar, **F A & Co.,** Base Bubble Burst, Blue Aqua, Pint 125.00
Fruit Jar, **F A & Co.,** Embossed On Base, IP, Aqua, 1/2 Gallon 124.00
Fruit Jar, **F A & Co.,** IP, Blue Aqua, 1 1/2 Pint 115.00
Fruit Jar, **F A & Co.,** IP, Burst Bubble, Pint 125.00
Fruit Jar, **F,** On Base, Glass Lid, Wire Bail, Quart 1.00
Fruit Jar, **F,** On Base, Glass Lid, Wire Bail, 1/2 Gallon 1.00
Fruit Jar, **FCG Co.,** Wax Sealer, Aqua, 1/2 Gallon .... 6.00 To 12.00
Fruit Jar, **Federal,** Quart 55.00
Fruit Jar, **Federal,** 1/2 Gallon 60.00
Fruit Jar, **Finney Isles,** Quart 25.00
Fruit Jar, **Finney Isles,** 1/2 Gallon 35.00
Fruit Jar, **Flaccus Bros.,** E.C., Steer's Head, 7 In. ....*Illus* 57.00
Fruit Jar, **Flaccus Co.,** E.C., Milk Glass, Pint 103.00
Fruit Jar, **Flaccus Co.,** E.C., Steer's Head, Pint 50.00
Fruit Jar, **Flaccus Co.,** E.C., Steer's Head, Quart 30.00
Fruit Jar, **Flaccus Co.,** E.C., Steer's Head, Square, Stain, Pint 25.00

Fruit Jar, Flaccus Bros., Steer's Head, 7 In.

Fruit Jar, **Flaccus Co.,** E.C., 1/2 Pint 28.00
Fruit Jar, **Flaccus Type,** Milk Glass, 1/2 Pint 20.00
Fruit Jar, **Flared Mouth,** Olive Green, 12 1/2 In. 70.00
Fruit Jar, **Folded-In Lip,** IP, Aqua, 8 In. 85.00
    Fruit Jar, **Foster, see Fruit Jar, Sealfast, Foster**
Fruit Jar, **Frank & Sons,** Wm., Pittsburgh, Wax Sealer, Aqua, Quart 15.00

Fruit Jar, **Franklin-Dexter,** Aqua, Quart .... 9.00 To 29.00
Fruit Jar, **Franklin-Dexter,** Aqua, 1/2 Gallon .... 18.50 To 20.50
Fruit Jar, **Franklin-Dexter,** Haze, Aqua, Quart 20.00
Fruit Jar, **Franklin-Dexter,** Whittled, Quart 25.00
Fruit Jar, **Franklin-Dexter,** Zinc Top, 1/2 Gallon 25.00
Fruit Jar, **Franklin-Dexter,** 1/2 Gallon 25.00
Fruit Jar, **Free-Blown,** Applied Neck, Tinted Purple, Pint 8.00
Fruit Jar, **Freeman Pasteurized,** J.T.Dougherty, Quart 35.00
Fruit Jar, **French's Mustard,** Pint 2.00
Fruit Jar, **Fruit-Keeper,** Aqua, Quart 25.00
Fruit Jar, **Fruit-Keeper,** C.G.Co., 1/2 Gallon 20.00
Fruit Jar, **Fruit-Keeper,** Clamp, Pint 16.00
Fruit Jar, **G J Co. Monogram,** Domed Zinc Insert Lid, Aqua, Quart 12.00
Fruit Jar, **G J Co.,** Aqua, Pint 25.00
Fruit Jar, **G J Co.,** Aqua, Quart 32.00
Fruit Jar, **G J Co.,** Pint 27.00
Fruit Jar, **Gaynor,** The, Glass Top, Pint .... 7.00 To 9.00
Fruit Jar, **Gaynor,** The, Glass Top, Quart .... 5.50 To 9.00
Fruit Jar, **Gem Cross,** Quart 10.00
Fruit Jar, **Gem Improved,** Made In Canada, Glass Lid, Wire Bail, Pint 2.50
Fruit Jar, **Gem Mason,** Improved Cross, Aqua, Quart 4.00
Fruit Jar, **Gem Mason,** Improved Cross, Aqua, 1/2 Gallon 5.00
Fruit Jar, **Gem,** Mason's Improved Cross, Glass Insert & Band, 1/2 Gallon ... 4.00
Fruit Jar, **Gem,** Mason's Improved Cross, Quart 1.25
Fruit Jar, **Gem,** Mason's Patent Nov.30th, 1858, Cross, Aqua, Quart 3.50
Fruit Jar, **Gem,** Mason's Patent Nov.30th, 1858, Cross, Aqua, 1/2 Gallon 5.00
Fruit Jar, **Gem,** New Wallaceburg, Pint 5.00
Fruit Jar, **Gem,** New Wallaceburg, Quart 3.50
Fruit Jar, **Gem,** The, Aqua, Quart .... 4.00 To 8.00
Fruit Jar, **Gem,** The, Aqua, 1/2 Gallon .... 6.00 To 9.00
Fruit Jar, **Gem,** The, C.F.J.Co., 1/2 Gallon 9.00
Fruit Jar, **Gem,** The, Cross, Aqua, Midget 5.00
Fruit Jar, **Gem,** The, Cross, Quart 5.00
Fruit Jar, **Gem,** The, Faint Letters, 1 1/2 Pint 18.50
Fruit Jar, **Gem,** The, Pat.Nov.26, 67, Shield, Aqua, Quart 17.00
Fruit Jar, **Gem,** The, Quart .... 4.00 To 4.75
Fruit Jar, **Gem,** The, 1/2 Gallon 12.50
Fruit Jar, **Gem,** The, Rutherford, Quart 12.00
Fruit Jar, **Genuine Mason,** Blue, Pint 8.00
Fruit Jar, **Genuine Mason,** Pint 2.00
Fruit Jar, **Genuine Mason,** Porcelain Top, Pint 1.50
Fruit Jar, **Genuine Mason,** Porcelain Top, Quart 1.00
Fruit Jar, **Genuine Mason,** Porcelain Top, 1/2 Gallon 2.50
Fruit Jar, **Genuine Mason,** Quart 1.50
Fruit Jar, **Genuine Mason,** Whittled, Square Shoulders, Pint 5.50
Fruit Jar, **Genuine Mason,** Zinc Lid, Aqua, Pint 10.00
Fruit Jar, **Genuine Mason,** 1/2 Gallon 2.00
Fruit Jar, **Gilberds Improved Jar,** Star, Quart .... 85.00 To 95.00
Fruit Jar, **Gilberds Jar,** Star, Pint .... 175.00 To 200.00
    Fruit Jar, **Gilchrist, see Fruit Jar, G J Co.**
Fruit Jar, **Gimbel Bros.,** Quart 26.00
Fruit Jar, **Glassboro Improved,** Aqua, Pint .... 12.50 To 21.50
Fruit Jar, **Glassboro Improved,** Aqua, Quart 11.00
Fruit Jar, **Glassboro Trademark,** Aqua, Quart 15.00
Fruit Jar, **Globe,** Amber, Pint .... 32.50 To 38.00
Fruit Jar, **Globe,** Amber, Quart .... *Illus* 35.00
Fruit Jar, **Globe,** Amber, 1/2 Gallon .... 26.00 To 32.50
Fruit Jar, **Globe,** Aqua, Pint 12.00
Fruit Jar, **Globe,** Aqua, Quart .... 10.00 To 18.00
Fruit Jar, **Globe,** Aqua, 1/2 Gallon .... 14.00 To 15.00
Fruit Jar, **Globe,** Clamp, Dated Lid, Quart 8.00
Fruit Jar, **Globe,** Honey Amber, Quart 28.00
Fruit Jar, **Globe,** Honey Amber, 1/2 Gallon 35.00
Fruit Jar, **Globe,** Metal Neck Band, Wire & Iron Clamp 15.00
Fruit Jar, **Globe,** Orange Amber, Quart 25.00

Fruit Jar, Globe, Amber, Quart
(See Page 108)

Fruit Jar, Hero Cross, Mason's
Pat. Nov. 30th, 1858, Aqua

Fruit Jar, Globe, Pint	8.50 To 15.00
Fruit Jar, Globe, Quart	11.00
Fruit Jar, Globe, 1/2 Gallon	15.00
Fruit Jar, Globe, Swirls Through Glass, Honey Amber, Quart	40.00
Fruit Jar, Globe, Wide Mouth, Aqua, Quart	30.00
Fruit Jar, Globe, Yellow, Quart	35.00
Fruit Jar, Golden State, Pint	12.00
Fruit Jar, Golden State, Quart	12.00
Fruit Jar, Golden State, 1/2 Gallon	12.00
Fruit Jar, Good House Keeper Regular Mason, Pint	2.00
Fruit Jar, Good House Keeper Regular Mason, Quart	1.50
Fruit Jar, Good House Keeper, Porcelain Lid, Quart	2.00
Fruit Jar, Good Luck, 1/2 Gallon	7.50
Fruit Jar, Green Mountain, G A.Co., Aqua, Quart	9.00
Fruit Jar, Green Mountain, G.A.Co., Pint	4.00 To 6.00
Fruit Jar, Green Mountain, G.A.Co., Quart	4.00 To 6.00
Fruit Jar, Griffin, Aqua, Quart	75.00 To 85.00
Fruit Jar, Griffin, Aqua, 1/2 Gallon	100.00
Fruit Jar, Griffin, 1 1/2 Quart	110.00
Fruit Jar, Griffin, 1/2 Gallon	115.00
Fruit Jar, H & R, Bubbles, Quart	9.00
Fruit Jar, H & R, Whittled, Aqua, 1/2 Gallon	12.00
Fruit Jar, Haines, 1/2 Gallon	60.00
Fruit Jar, Haines' Ne Plus Ultra, 1/2 Gallon	225.00
Fruit Jar, Haines' Patent March 1st, 1870, Tin Lid, Wire Clamp, Quart	100.00
Fruit Jar, Hamilton & Jones, Greensboro, Pa., Stoneware, Quart	30.00
Fruit Jar, Hamilton & Jones, Greensboro, Pa., Stoneware, 1/2 Gallon	30.00
Fruit Jar, Hamilton & Jones, Greensboro, Pa., Stoneware, Gallon	30.00
Fruit Jar, Hamilton, Quart	35.00
Fruit Jar, Hansee's, see Fruit Jar, Palace Home Jar, Hansee's	
Fruit Jar, Hartell & Letchworth Type, Quart	32.00
Fruit Jar, Hartell's, Dated Lid, Aqua, Quart	45.00
Fruit Jar, Hartell's, Quart	35.00
Fruit Jar, Harvest Mason, Quart	8.00 To 10.00
Fruit Jar, Harvest Mason, 1/2 Gallon	20.00
Fruit Jar, Hazel Atlas E-Z Seal, Aqua, Quart	8.00
Fruit Jar, Hazel Atlas E-Z Seal, Pint	8.00
Fruit Jar, Hazel Atlas Lightning Seal, Glass Lid, Wire, Aqua, 1 1/2 Pint	10.00
Fruit Jar, Hazel HA Preserve, Pint	4.50 To 6.00
Fruit Jar, Hazel HA Preserve, Quart	5.00
Fruit Jar, Helme's, see Fruit Jar, Rail Road Mills, Helme's	
Fruit Jar, Hero Cross, Mason's Improved Patent Nov.30th, 1858, Quart	1.25
Fruit Jar, Hero Cross, Mason's Improved, Aqua, Midget	5.00
Fruit Jar, Hero Cross, Mason's Improved, Blue Aqua, Quart	5.00
Fruit Jar, Hero Cross, Mason's Improved, Dated Lid, Zinc Band, 1/2 Gallon	4.00
Fruit Jar, Hero Cross, Mason's Improved, Quart	2.95
Fruit Jar, Hero Cross, Mason's Improved, 1/2 Gallon	2.95
Fruit Jar, Hero Cross, Mason's Pat. Nov.30th, 1858, Aqua *Illus*	8.00

Fruit Jar, Hero Cross, Mason's Patent Nov.30th, 1858, Amber, Quart 70.00
Fruit Jar, Hero Cross, Mason's Patent Nov.30th, 1858, Aqua, Quart 3.50
Fruit Jar, Hero Cross, Mason's Patent Nov.30th, 1858, Midget 10.00
Fruit Jar, Hero Improved, Aqua, Quart 10.00
Fruit Jar, Hero Improved, Quart 16.00
Fruit Jar, Hero, The, Aqua, 1/2 Gallon .... 14.00 To 18.00
Fruit Jar, Hero, The, Cross, Mason's Patent Nov.30th, 1858, Puce, Quart 65.00
Fruit Jar, Hero, The, Cross, Quart 28.00
Fruit Jar, Hero, The, Quart 16.00
Fruit Jar, Hero, The, 1/2 Gallon 10.00
Fruit Jar, Hero, The, Gallon 285.00
Fruit Jar, Hero, The, Tin Lid, Screw Band, Over Glass Lid, Aqua, Quart 25.00
Fruit Jar, Hero, The, Whittled, Gallon 300.00
Fruit Jar, Heroine, The, Glass Lid, Bubbles, Aqua, Quart 25.00
Fruit Jar, Heroine, Top, Aqua, 1/2 Gallon 21.00
Fruit Jar, Honest Mason, Patent 1858, Quart 12.00
Fruit Jar, Honest Mason, Pint 20.00
Fruit Jar, Hormel Fine Food, Pint 2.00
Fruit Jar, Howe, Aqua, 1/2 Gallon 45.00
Fruit Jar, Howe, Scranton, Pa., Weak Embossing, Quart 35.00
Fruit Jar, Howe, The, Aqua, Pint 45.00
Fruit Jar, Howe, The, Aqua, 1/2 Gallon 45.00
Fruit Jar, Howe, The, Pint .... 60.00 To 75.00
Fruit Jar, Howe, The, Quart .... 60.00 To 65.00
Fruit Jar, Howe, The, 1/2 Gallon 45.00
Fruit Jar, Howe, The, Scranton, Pa., Quart 35.00
Fruit Jar, I G Co., Pint 12.50
Fruit Jar, Ideal, The, 1/2 Gallon 15.00
Fruit Jar, Imperial Brand, True's, Pint 6.00
Fruit Jar, Imperial, The, Blue, Quart 4.00
Fruit Jar, Imperial, The, E.G.Co., Aqua, Quart 10.00
Fruit Jar, Imperial, The, E.G.Co., Quart 15.00
Fruit Jar, Independent, Quart 30.00
Fruit Jar, Ivanhoe, On Bottom, Pint .... 1.00 To 2.00
Fruit Jar, Ivanhoe, On Bottom, Quart 10.00
Fruit Jar, J & B, Aqua, Pint 40.00
Fruit Jar, J & B, Aqua, Quart 19.00
Fruit Jar, Jaud J., Squatty, Amber, Quart 25.00
Fruit Jar, Jeanette, Home Packer Mason, Quart 2.50
Fruit Jar, Jeanette, Home Packer, J In Square Mason, Glass Lid, Quart 3.00
Fruit Jar, Johnson & Johnson, Amber, 1/2 Pint .... 3.00 To 12.00
Fruit Jar, Johnson & Johnson, Amber, Quart 9.00
Fruit Jar, Johnson & Johnson, Label & Contents, Amber, 1/2 Pint 15.00
Fruit Jar, Johnson & Johnson, Wax Sealer, Amber, 1/2 Pint 20.00
Fruit Jar, Johnson's 2 Patent Jan.7th 1868, 9 1/2 In. .... Color 350.00
Fruit Jar, Joshua Wright, Phila., Barrel, Aqua, 1/2 Gallon .... 290.00 To 375.00
Fruit Jar, Jumbo, Pint 2.00
Fruit Jar, K.C. Mason, Finest Quality, Square Spacesaver Style, Quart 3.00
Fruit Jar, Kentucky, Wax Sealer, Aqua, 1/2 Gallon 8.50
Fruit Jar, Kerr Golden Anniversary, Quart 15.50
Fruit Jar, Kerr Glass Top Mason, Amber, Quart 7.50
Fruit Jar, Kerr Glass Top Mason, 1/2 Pint 10.00
Fruit Jar, Kerr Self Sealing Mason, Amber, Quart 9.00
Fruit Jar, Kerr Self Sealing Mason, 1/2 Pint 1.75
Fruit Jar, Kerr Self Sealing, Trademark Reg. Widemouth Mason, Pint 3.00
Fruit Jar, Kerr Self Sealing, Trademark Reg. Widemouth Mason, Quart 2.00
Fruit Jar, Kerr Self Sealing, Trademark Reg. Widemouth Mason, 1/2 Gallon 3.00
Fruit Jar, Kerr Self Sealing, Trademark Reg., 1/2 Pint 1.50
Fruit Jar, Kerr Self Sealing, 1915 On Base, Quart 2.50
Fruit Jar, Kerr Self Sealing, 1915 On Front, Quart 2.50
Fruit Jar, Kerr, Economy, Amber, Quart 7.50
Fruit Jar, Kerr, Economy, Cobalt Blue Streak, Quart 12.00
Fruit Jar, Kerr, Economy, 1/2 Pint 3.00
Fruit Jar, Keystone, Trademark Registered, Quart .... 3.00 To 4.00
Fruit Jar, Kilner, K B G Co., Mason's Patent Nov.30th, 1858, Purpled, Pint 12.00

Fruit Jar, Kilner, K B G Co., Mason's Patent Nov.30th, 1858, Quart 7.00
Fruit Jar, King, Crown & Wreath, Pint 10.00
Fruit Jar, King, Flags & Head, Quart 15.00
Fruit Jar, King, Oval, 1/2 Pint 18.00
Fruit Jar, King, Stippled Barrel, Oval Base, Clear, 1/2 Pint 12.50
Fruit Jar, King, Twin Wire Clips, Quart 7.00
Fruit Jar, King, Wire Bail, 1/2 Pint 14.00
Fruit Jar, King, Wire Bail, Pint .... 7.00 To 10.00
Fruit Jar, King, Wire Bail, Quart .... 6.00 To 11.00
Fruit Jar, King, Wire Bail, 7 1/4 In. .... *Illus*   15.00
Fruit Jar, Kinsella 1874 True Mason, Quart 5.00
Fruit Jar, Kivlan & Onthank, Pat'd June 28, '21, Boston, Side Clamps, Quart 4.00
Fruit Jar, Kline, A.R., Patent Oct.27, '68, Stopper .... *Illus*   130.00
Fruit Jar, Kline, Aqua, Quart .... 18.00 To 23.00
Fruit Jar, Kline, Inkwell Stopper, Haze, Quart 100.00
Fruit Jar, Knowlton Vacuum, Pint 20.00

Fruit Jar, King, Wire Bail, 7 1/4 In.

Fruit Jar, Kline, A.R., Patent Oct.27, '68, Stopper

Fruit Jar, Knowlton Vacuum, Quart .... 12.50 To 16.00
Fruit Jar, Knowlton Vacuum, 1/2 Gallon .... 19.00 To 30.00
Fruit Jar, Knox K Mason, Square, Pint 2.50
Fruit Jar, Knox K Mason, Square, Quart 2.00
Fruit Jar, Knox K Mason, 1/2 Gallon .... 2.50 To 5.50
Fruit Jar, L G W, Mason's Improved, Imperial Pint 10.00
Fruit Jar, L G W, Mason's Improved, Pint 6.00
Fruit Jar, L G W, Mason's Improved, Quart 6.00
Fruit Jar, Lafayette, Amber, Pint 165.00
Fruit Jar, Lafayette, Amber, Quart 85.00
Fruit Jar, Lafayette, Aqua, Quart 85.00
Fruit Jar, Lafayette, Aqua, 1/2 Gallon 95.00
Fruit Jar, Lafayette, Quart .... 65.00 To 75.00
Fruit Jar, Lafayette, Round Type Closure, Aqua, 1/2 Gallon 89.00
Fruit Jar, Lamb Mason, Pint 3.00
Fruit Jar, Lamb Mason, Quart .... 2.00 To 2.50
Fruit Jar, Lamb Mason, Porcelain Lid, Pint 3.00
Fruit Jar, Lamb Mason, Porcelain Lid, Quart 3.25
Fruit Jar, Lamb Mason, Porcelain Lid, 1/2 Gallon 3.25
Fruit Jar, Lamb, Rainbow Colored, Pint 15.00
Fruit Jar, Leader, The, Amber, Pint 110.00
Fruit Jar, Leader, The, Amber, Quart .... 70.00 To 80.00
Fruit Jar, Leader, The, Amber, 1/2 Gallon .... 75.00 To 85.00
Fruit Jar, Leader, The, 1/2 Gallon 30.00

Fruit Jar, **Leotric,** Aqua, Pint .... 3.00 To 3.50
Fruit Jar, **Leotric,** Aqua, Quart 9.00
Fruit Jar, **Leotric,** Glass Lid, Wire Bail, Aqua, Pint 8.50
Fruit Jar, **Leotric,** Pint .... 4.00 To 6.00
Fruit Jar, **Leotric,** Quart 4.00
Fruit Jar, **Leotric,** 1/2 Gallon .... 6.00 To 8.00
Fruit Jar, **Leotric,** Whittled, Apple Green, Quart 12.50
Fruit Jar, **Lightning Trademark,** Amber, Pint .... *Illus* 37.50
Fruit Jar, **Lightning Trademark,** Amber, Quart .... 22.50 To 35.00
Fruit Jar, **Lightning Trademark,** Amber, 1/2 Gallon .... 35.00 To 37.50
Fruit Jar, **Lightning Trademark,** Aqua, 1/2 Pint .... 1.00 To 5.00
Fruit Jar, **Lightning Trademark,** Aqua, Pint .... 1.00 To 6.00
Fruit Jar, **Lightning Trademark,** Aqua, Quart .... 1.00 To 1.30
Fruit Jar, **Lightning Trademark,** Aqua, 1/2 Gallon .... 1.00 To 3.50
Fruit Jar, **Lightning Trademark,** Cornflower Blue, Pint .... 2.50 To 30.00
Fruit Jar, **Lightning Trademark,** Cornflower Blue, Quart .... 20.00 To 25.00
Fruit Jar, **Lightning Trademark,** Embossed On Side, Aqua, 1/2 Pint 45.00

Fruit Jar, Lightning Trademark, Amber, Pint

Fruit Jar, **Lightning Trademark,** Honey Amber, Quart 27.00
Fruit Jar, **Lightning Trademark,** Honey Amber, 1/2 Gallon 28.00
Fruit Jar, **Lightning Trademark,** Inside Haze, Amber, Pint 27.00
Fruit Jar, **Lightning Trademark,** Pint .... 1.00 To 1.50
Fruit Jar, **Lightning Trademark,** Quart 1.00
Fruit Jar, **Lightning Trademark,** Putnam On Base, Widemouth, Pint 3.00
Fruit Jar, **Lightning Trademark,** Putnam On Base, Widemouth, Quart 2.50
Fruit Jar, **Lightning Trademark,** Quart 1.50
Fruit Jar, **Lightning Trademark,** 1/2 Gallon 2.50
Fruit Jar, **Lightning Trademark,** Registered, Aqua, Pint 1.00
Fruit Jar, **Lightning Trademark,** Registered, Aqua, Quart 1.00
Fruit Jar, **Lightning Trademark,** Registered, Putnam On Base, Pint 2.50
Fruit Jar, **Lightning With Anchor,** Pint .... 1.00 To 6.00
Fruit Jar, **Lightning With Anchor,** Quart .... 1.00 To 1.30
Fruit Jar, **Lightning,** Anchor Hocking, Pint 1.00
Fruit Jar, **Lightning,** Anchor Hocking, Quart 1.00
Fruit Jar, **Lightning,** On Base, Aqua, 1/2 Pint 5.00
Fruit Jar, **Lightning,** On Base, 1/2 Pint 3.00
Fruit Jar, **Lightning,** Putnam, Aqua, Pint 10.00
Fruit Jar, **Lightning,** Registered, Aqua, Pint 3.00
Fruit Jar, **Lightning,** Weak Embossing, Amber, Quart 15.00
Fruit Jar, **Lightning,** Whittled, Amber, Pint 35.00
Fruit Jar, **Lightning,** Whittled, Amber, Quart 25.00
Fruit Jar, **Lightning,** Whittled, Amber, 1/2 Gallon 35.00
Fruit Jar, **Liquid Carbonic Co.,** Quart 2.50
Fruit Jar, **Lockport Mason,** Aqua, Pint 5.00
Fruit Jar, **Lockport Mason,** Aqua, Quart 4.00
Fruit Jar, **Lockport Mason,** Improved, Quart 3.50
Fruit Jar, **Lockport Mason,** Quart .... 3.00 To 5.00
Fruit Jar, **Lockport,** Quart 4.00
Fruit Jar, **Lorillard & Co.,** P., Amber, Quart 12.00
Fruit Jar, **Lorillard & Co.,** P., Geo.W.Helmes 1872 On Lid, Amber, Quart 6.50

Fruit Jar, **Lorillard & Co.,** P., Ground Mouth, Amber, Quart 12.50
Fruit Jar, **Lorillard,** Amber, Quart .... 7.00 To 12.50
Fruit Jar, **Ludlow,** 1 1/2 Quart 95.00
Fruit Jar, **Ludlow's Patent,** Quart .... 95.00 To 100.00
Fruit Jar, **Lustre,** In Circle, Quart 4.00
Fruit Jar, **Lustre,** R.E.Tongue & Bros. Co., Inc., Phila., Pint .... 4.00 To 5.00
Fruit Jar, **Lustre,** R.E.Tongue & Bros. Co., Inc., Phila., Quart 3.00
Fruit Jar, **Lustre,** R.E.Tongue & Bros. Co., Inc., Phila., Blue, Pint 5.00
Fruit Jar, **Lustre,** R.E.Tongue & Bros. Co., Inc., Phila., Blue, Quart 7.00
Fruit Jar, **Lustre,** 1/2 Gallon 8.00
Fruit Jar, **Lyman,** W.W., Aqua, Quart .... 17.00 To 20.00
Fruit Jar, **Lyman,** W.W., Circled 2 Dated, Pint 48.00
Fruit Jar, **Lyman,** W.W., Patent Feb.9, 1864, Tin Cover, Aqua, 1/2 Gallon 50.00
Fruit Jar, **Lyman,** W.W., Pint 35.00
Fruit Jar, **Lyman,** W.W., Quart .... 35.00 To 40.00
Fruit Jar, **Lyman,** W.W., 1/2 Gallon 17.50
Fruit Jar, **Lyman,** W.W., 1864, Quart 16.50
Fruit Jar, **M F J Co.,** Amber, Quart 15.00
Fruit Jar, **Macomb,** Pottery, Quart 12.00
Fruit Jar, **Macomb,** Pottery, White, Quart 10.00
Fruit Jar, **Magic Star,** Amber, 1/2 Gallon 450.00
Fruit Jar, **Magic Star,** Whittled, Honey Amber, 1/2 Gallon 400.00
Fruit Jar, **Magic,** The, Lid & Clamp, Amber, 1/2 Gallon 250.00
Fruit Jar, **Mansfield Improved Mason,** Pint 6.00
Fruit Jar, **Mansfield Improved Mason,** Quart .... 6.00 To 10.00
Fruit Jar, **Marion,** The, Aqua, Quart .... 6.50 To 8.00
Fruit Jar, **Marion,** The, Aqua, 1/2 Gallon 6.50
Fruit Jar, **Marion,** The, Mason's Patent Nov.30th, 1858, Aqua, Quart 8.00
Fruit Jar, **Marion,** The, Pint .... 9.00 To 12.50
Fruit Jar, **Marion,** The, Quart 9.50
Fruit Jar, **Marion,** The, 1/2 Gallon 9.00
Fruit Jar, **Mason Jar Of 1872,** Aqua, Quart 20.00
Fruit Jar, **Mason Jar Of 1872,** Quart .... 15.00 To 22.00
Fruit Jar, **Mason Jar,** Quart 6.00
Fruit Jar, **Mason Snowflake,** Aqua, Quart 40.00
Fruit Jar, **Mason,** Amber, Pint 35.00
Fruit Jar, **Mason,** Block Letters, Dark Green, Quart 4.00
Fruit Jar, **Mason,** Block Letters, Machine Made, Amber, Pint 29.00
  Fruit Jar, **Mason, Cross, see Fruit Jar, Hero Cross**
Fruit Jar, **Mason,** Light Blue, Pint 15.00
Fruit Jar, **Mason,** Midget 7.00
Fruit Jar, **Mason,** Midget, 1/2 Pint 10.00
Fruit Jar, **Mason,** Patent, Letter N, Quart 7.00
Fruit Jar, **Mason,** Script With Flourish Below, Amethyst, Quart 4.50
Fruit Jar, **Mason,** Snowflake, Quart 12.00
Fruit Jar, **Mason,** Star, Moon, & Sun, Quart 2.00
Fruit Jar, **Mason,** The, Aqua, 1/2 Gallon 3.50
Fruit Jar, **Mason,** The, Bubbles, 1/2 Gallon 6.00
Fruit Jar, **Mason,** The, Pint .... 2.50 To 4.50
Fruit Jar, **Mason,** The, Quart 2.00
Fruit Jar, **Mason,** Underlined, 1/2 Gallon 3.50
Fruit Jar, **Mason,** 1951, Zinc Top, Amber, Gallon 3.00
  Fruit Jar, **Mason's C F J Co., see Fruit Jar, C F J Co.**
Fruit Jar, **Mason's Imperial Cross,** Aqua, Quart 4.50
Fruit Jar, **Mason's Improved Patent Jan.19, 1869,** Midget 12.00
Fruit Jar, **Mason's Improved,** May 1870 On Base, Midget 60.00
Fruit Jar, **Mason's Improved,** 1/2 Gallon 3.50
Fruit Jar, **Mason's K.B.S.Co.,** Monogram, Aqua 6.00
Fruit Jar, **Mason's,** Keystone In Circle, Patent Nov.30, 1858, Amber, Quart 125.00
Fruit Jar, **Mason's Keystone,** Zinc Lid, Midget 10.75
Fruit Jar, **Mason's Keystone,** 1/2 Gallon 15.00
Fruit Jar, **Mason's,** Keystone, 1858, Zinc Lid, Aqua, Midget 9.00
Fruit Jar, **Mason's Midget,** Aqua 6.25
Fruit Jar, **Mason's Monogram Improved,** Clyde, 1/2 Gallon 4.50
Fruit Jar, **Mason's Patent Nov.30th,** 1858, Amber, Quart .... 55.00 To 65.00

Fruit Jar, **Mason's Patent Nov.30th**, 1858, Amber, 1/2 Gallon .... 10.00 To 60.00
Fruit Jar, **Mason's Patent Nov.30th**, 1858, Amethyst, 1/2 Gallon 10.00
Fruit Jar, **Mason's Patent Nov.30th**, 1858, Apple Green, Quart 9.75
Fruit Jar, **Mason's Patent Nov.30th**, 1858, Aqua, Midget 5.00
Fruit Jar, **Mason's Patent Nov.30th**, 1858, Aqua, Pint 4.00
Fruit Jar, **Mason's Patent Nov.30th**, 1858, Aqua, Quart 2.00
Fruit Jar, **Mason's Patent Nov.30th**, 1858, Aqua, 1/2 Gallon .... 2.00 To 3.50
Fruit Jar, **Mason's Patent Nov.30th**, 1858, Ball On Reverse, Aqua, Pint 5.00
Fruit Jar, **Mason's Patent Nov.30th**, 1858, Bottom Nov.26 67, Aqua, Midget 20.00
Fruit Jar, **Mason's Patent Nov.30th**, 1858, Bottom Nov.26 67, Midget 20.00
Fruit Jar, **Mason's Patent Nov.30th**, 1858, Circled Keystone, 1/2 Gallon 8.00
Fruit Jar, **Mason's Patent Nov.30th**, 1858, Cobalt Blue, 1/2 Gallon 10.00
Fruit Jar, **Mason's Patent Nov.30th**, 1858, Deep Green, Quart 5.00
Fruit Jar, **Mason's Patent Nov.30th**, 1858, Green, 1/2 Gallon 10.00
Fruit Jar, **Mason's Patent Nov.30th**, 1858, Honey Amber, Pint 175.00
Fruit Jar, **Mason's Patent Nov.30th**, 1858, Improved Type Band, Midget 15.00
Fruit Jar, **Mason's Patent Nov.30th**, 1858, Keystone, Quart 5.00
Fruit Jar, **Mason's Patent Nov.30th**, 1858, Light Green, Quart 18.75
Fruit Jar, **Mason's Patent Nov.30th**, 1858, Pint 3.00
Fruit Jar, **Mason's Patent Nov.30th**, 1858, Quart .... 1.00 To 3.50
Fruit Jar, **Mason's Patent Nov.30th**, 1858, Porcelain Lid, Blue, Quart 5.00
Fruit Jar, **Mason's Patent Nov.30th**, 1858, Porcelain Lid, Blue, 1/2 Gallon 5.00
Fruit Jar, **Mason's Patent Nov.30th**, 1858, Shield On Reverse, Stain, Midget 30.00
Fruit Jar, **Mason's Patent Nov.30th**, 1858, Snowflake On Back, Blue, Quart 20.00
Fruit Jar, **Mason's Patent Nov.30th**, 1858, Snowflake On Back, Midget 40.00
Fruit Jar, **Mason's Patent Nov.30th**, 1858, Whittled, Bubbles, Vaseline, Pint 90.00
Fruit Jar, **Mason's Patent Nov.30th**, 1858, Whittled, Light Green, 1/2 Gallon 8.00
Fruit Jar, **Mason's Patent Nov.30th**, 1858, 1/2 Gallon 5.00
Fruit Jar, **Mason's Patent 1858 With C**, Aqua, Pint 12.50
Fruit Jar, **Mason's Patent 1858 With S**, Quart 6.00
Fruit Jar, **Mason's Patent 1858**, Tudor Rose, Stain, Aqua, Quart 25.00
Fruit Jar, **Mason's Patent**, Aqua, Pint 4.00
Fruit Jar, **Mason's Patent**, Aqua, Quart 1.50
Fruit Jar, **Mason's Patent**, Blue, Quart 3.00
Fruit Jar, **Mason's Patent**, Blue, 1/2 Gallon 5.00
Fruit Jar, **Mason's Patent**, Golden Amber, Quart 58.00
Fruit Jar, **Mason's Patent**, Porcelain Lid, Blue, Quart 5.50
Fruit Jar, **Mason's Patent**, Porcelain Lined Zinc Lid, Aqua, 1/2 Gallon 3.00
Fruit Jar, **Mason's Patent**, 1880, Midget 17.00
Fruit Jar, **Mason's**, Vaseline, 2 Quart 15.00
Fruit Jar, **Mason's**, 2, 1858, Quart 5.00
Fruit Jar, **Mason's**, 2, 1858, 1/2 Gallon 4.50
Fruit Jar, **Mason's**, 4, 1858, Midget 38.00
Fruit Jar, **Mason's**, 11, 1858, Quart 5.00
Fruit Jar, **McDonald New Perfect Seal**, Pint .... 2.50 To 6.00
Fruit Jar, **McDonald New Perfect Seal**, Quart 2.50
Fruit Jar, **McDonald New Perfect Seal**, 1/2 Gallon 5.00
Fruit Jar, **McDonald New Perfect Seal**, Wire Bail, Blue, Pint .... 2.00 To 3.00
Fruit Jar, **McDonald New Perfect Seal**, Wire Bail, Blue, Quart .... 2.00 To 3.00
Fruit Jar, **McDonald New Perfect Seal**, Wire Bail, Blue, 1/2 Gallon 3.00
Fruit Jar, **McKee & Co.**, S., Wax Seal, Quart 10.00
Fruit Jar, **Michigan Mason**, Pint 22.00
Fruit Jar, **Middleby**, Jr. Inc., Jos., Embossed, 1/2 Gallon 10.00
Fruit Jar, **Middleby**, Jr. Inc., Jos., 1/2 Gallon 5.50
Fruit Jar, **Midwest**, Quart 4.00
Fruit Jar, **Millville Atmospheric**, Aqua, 1/2 Pint 55.00
Fruit Jar, **Millville Atmospheric**, Aqua, Quart 17.00
Fruit Jar, **Millville Atmospheric**, Aqua, 1 1/2 Quart 65.00
Fruit Jar, **Millville Atmospheric**, 1/2 Pint 50.00
Fruit Jar, **Millville Atmospheric**, Pint 25.00
Fruit Jar, **Millville Atmospheric**, Quart .... 140.00 To 250.00
Fruit Jar, **Millville Atmospheric**, 1/2 Gallon 25.00
Fruit Jar, **Millville Atmospheric**, 1861, 1/2 Gallon .... *Illus* 27.50
Fruit Jar, **Millville**, Amber, 1/2 Pint 50.00
Fruit Jar, **Millville**, 1/2 Pint .... 25.00 To 50.00

Fruit Jar, **Millville,** Pint 35.00
Fruit Jar, **Millville,** Quart .... 20.00 To 29.00
Fruit Jar, **Millville,** Square Shoulder, Quart 30.00
Fruit Jar, **Millville,** 1/2 Gallon .... 17.50 To 20.00
Fruit Jar, **Mission Mason,** Aqua, 1/2 Pint 25.00
Fruit Jar, **Mission Mason,** Aqua, Pint 6.00
Fruit Jar, **Mission Mason,** Made In California, Embossed Bell, Quart 2.00
Fruit Jar, **Mission Mason,** 1/2 Pint 25.00
Fruit Jar, **Mission Mason,** Pint .... 4.00 To 5.00
Fruit Jar, **Mission Mason,** Quart .... 3.00 To 6.00
Fruit Jar, **Model Mason,** Quart 11.00
Fruit Jar, **Model Mason,** 1/2 Gallon 200.00
Fruit Jar, **Monarch Finer Foods,** Embossed Lion's Head, Square, Gallon 4.00
Fruit Jar, **Monarch Finer Foods,** Embossed Lion's Head, Zinc Lid, Quart 2.50
Fruit Jar, **Monarch Finer Foods,** 3 1/2 Quart 7.50
Fruit Jar, **Moore's Patent,** Aqua, Quart .... 22.50 To 22.50
Fruit Jar, **Moore's Patent,** Aqua, 1 1/2 Quart 45.00
Fruit Jar, **Moore's Patent,** Fislerville, Dec.3rd, 1861, 1/2 Gallon 135.00
Fruit Jar, **Moore's Patent,** Fislerville, 1/2 Gallon 150.00
Fruit Jar, **Moore's Patent,** Pint 60.00
Fruit Jar, **Moore's Patent,** Quart 25.00
Fruit Jar, **Moore's Patent,** Whittled, Aqua, 1 1/2 Quart 80.00
Fruit Jar, **Mother's,** Aqua, Pint 25.00
Fruit Jar, **Mountain Mason,** Pint 10.00
Fruit Jar, **Myers Test Jar,** Aqua, 7 1/2 In. .... *Illus* 115.00
Fruit Jar, **Myers Test Jar,** Brass Clamp, Quart 90.00
Fruit Jar, **Myers Test Jar,** Quart 125.00
Fruit Jar, **Myers Test Jar,** 1/2 Gallon 85.00
Fruit Jar, **Myers Test Jar,** Whittled, Aqua, 1/2 Gallon 200.00
Fruit Jar, **N.& J.Fleet,** Liverpool, Canadian, Quart .... *Illus* 35.00
Fruit Jar, **N.A.,** Porcelain, Quart 18.00
Fruit Jar, **N.C.L.Co.,** Mason's Patent Nov.30th, 1858, Pint 7.00
Fruit Jar, **N.C.L.Co.,** Mason's Patent Nov.30th, 1858, 1/2 Gallon 7.00

Fruit Jar, Myers Test Jar, Aqua, 7 1/2 In.

Fruit Jar, N.& J.Fleet,
Liverpool, Canadian,
Quart

Fruit Jar, Millville Atmospheric,
1861, 1/2 Gallon
(See Page 114)

Fruit Jar, **National Super Mason,** 1/2 Gallon 8.00
Fruit Jar, **Ne Plus Ultra Airtight,** Olive Green, 10 In. 100.00
Fruit Jar, **Ne Plus Ultra Airtight,** Quart 500.00
Fruit Jar, **Newmark Special Extra Mason,** Pint 8.00
Fruit Jar, **Newmark,** Fleur-De-Lis, Quart 10.00
Fruit Jar, **North American,** Porcelain Lined, 1/2 Gallon 18.00
Fruit Jar, **O G Monogram,** Stain, Aqua, Quart 12.00
Fruit Jar, **Ohio Quality Mason,** Embossed, Pint 6.00
Fruit Jar, **Old Judge Coffee,** Quart 2.50
Fruit Jar, **Old Judge,** Embossed Owl, Quart 1.00
Fruit Jar, **Old Judge,** Embossed Owl, Gallon 3.50
Fruit Jar, **Oval King,** Clear, Quart 8.00
Fruit Jar, **Oval Wears,** Clear, Quart 5.00
Fruit Jar, **Palace Home Jar,** Hansee's, Pint 39.00
Fruit Jar, **Palace Home Jar,** Hansee's, Quart .... 31.00 To 50.00
Fruit Jar, **Pansy,** Aqua Insert, Amber, Quart 310.00
Fruit Jar, **Patent Dec.17th,** 1872 On Bottom, Ground Lip, 1/2 Pint 25.00
Fruit Jar, **Patent Dec.17th,** 1872 On Bottom, Ground Lip, 1/2 Gallon 15.00
Fruit Jar, **Patent Oct.19,** 1858 On Lid, Aqua, 2 Quart 50.00
Fruit Jar, **Patent Sept.18,** 1860, 2 Quart .... *Illus*   80.00

Fruit Jar, Patent Sept.18, 1860, 2 Quart

Fruit Jar, **Patent 1808,** Stain, Aqua, Quart 12.00
Fruit Jar, **Patent 1903,** Aqua, Quart 10.00
Fruit Jar, **Pearl,** The, Aqua, Quart 20.00
Fruit Jar, **Pearl,** The, Quart 18.00
Fruit Jar, **Peerless,** Aqua, 1/2 Gallon 79.00
Fruit Jar, **Perfect Seal,** In Circle, Quart 10.00
Fruit Jar, **Perfect Seal,** 1/2 Pint 10.00
Fruit Jar, **Perfect Seal,** Pint 1.00
Fruit Jar, **Perfect Seal,** Quart 1.00
Fruit Jar, **Perfection,** Aqua, Pint 14.00
Fruit Jar, **Perfection,** Mar.29, 1887, Blue 35.00
Fruit Jar, **Perfection,** Pint 27.50
Fruit Jar, **Perfection,** 1/2 Gallon 25.00
Fruit Jar, **Pet,** Aqua, Quart 35.00
Fruit Jar, **Petal,** 6 Petals, IP, Light Green, Quart 450.00
Fruit Jar, **Petal,** 10 Petals, IP, Emerald Green, Quart 1200.00
Fruit Jar, **Peters,** 1559, 1/2 Pint 9.00
Fruit Jar, **Peters,** 1559, Pint 9.00
Fruit Jar, **Pettit,** Aqua, 3 Quart 15.00
Fruit Jar, **Pettit,** H.W., Light Cobalt, Pint 65.00
Fruit Jar, **Pettit,** H.W., Quart 6.00
Fruit Jar, **Pettit,** Pint 14.00
Fruit Jar, **Pettit,** Quart 10.00
Fruit Jar, **Pine Deluxe,** Clear Glass Lid, Pint 2.25
Fruit Jar, **Pine Deluxe,** Clear Glass Lid, Quart 2.25
Fruit Jar, **Pine Mason,** P, Pint 2.50
Fruit Jar, **Pine Mason,** P, 1/2 Gallon 6.00
Fruit Jar, **Porcelain Lid,** Blue, Quart 5.00

Fruit Jar, Porcelain Lid, Quart	7.50
Fruit Jar, Porcelain Lined, Aqua, Quart	8.00 To 15.00
Fruit Jar, Porcelain Lined, Quart	17.50
Fruit Jar, Porcelain Lined, 1/2 Gallon	9.75 To 11.00
Fruit Jar, Port, Mason's Patent Nov.30th, 1858, 1/2 Gallon	4.00
Fruit Jar, Port, Mason's Patent 1858, Port In Script, Aqua, Pint	4.00
Fruit Jar, Port, Mason's Patent 1858, Port In Script, Aqua, Quart	3.00
Fruit Jar, Potter & Bodine, Barrel, Large Letters, Pontil, 1/2 Gallon	600.00
Fruit Jar, Potter & Bodine, Straight Sides, Quart	215.00
Fruit Jar, Potter & Bodine, see also Fruit Jar, Airtight	
Fruit Jar, Presto Glass Top, Glass Lid, Wire Bail, Quart	1.50
Fruit Jar, Presto Glass Top, Owens, Illinois, Quart	1.50
Fruit Jar, Presto Glass Top, Pint	6.00
Fruit Jar, Presto Supreme Mason, Pint	1.50
Fruit Jar, Protector, Aqua, 1/2 Gallon	22.00
Fruit Jar, Protector, Panels Not Recessed, Aqua, 1/2 Gallon	45.00
Fruit Jar, Protector, Quart	15.00
Fruit Jar, Protector, Recessed Panels, Quart	27.00
Fruit Jar, Puritan, Ship, Quart	95.00
Fruit Jar, Putnam Glass Works, Zanesville, O., Wax Seal, Embossed, Aqua, Quart	35.00
Fruit Jar, Putnam Glass Works, Zanesville, O., 1/2 Gallon	25.00
Fruit Jar, Putnam, Embossed On Bottom, Midget	10.00
Fruit Jar, Putnam, On Bottom, This Is Not A Full Quart	3.00
Fruit Jar, Putnam, Pint	3.00
Fruit Jar, Putnam, Plain, Amber, Quart	20.00
Fruit Jar, Queen, Aqua, 1/2 Pint	1.00
Fruit Jar, Queen, Aqua, Pint	10.00
Fruit Jar, Queen, Aqua, Quart	1.00
Fruit Jar, Queen, Aqua, 1/2 Gallon	1.00
Fruit Jar, Queen, Kant Krack Lid, 1/2 Pint	6.00
Fruit Jar, Queen, Lid, Wire Bail, Quart	3.25
Fruit Jar, Queen, Quick Seal, Quart	3.00
Fruit Jar, Queen, S.K.O. Trademark Widemouth, Glass Lid, Wire Bail, Quart	2.50
Fruit Jar, Queen, S.K.O., Pint	1.00
Fruit Jar, Queen, S.K.O., Quart	1.00 To 1.25
Fruit Jar, Queen, Side Clamps, 1/2 Pint	6.00
Fruit Jar, Queen, The, Aqua, Quart	9.50 To 15.50
Fruit Jar, Queen, The, Aqua, 1/2 Gallon	16.50
Fruit Jar, Queen, The, Whittled, Aqua, Quart	18.50
Fruit Jar, Queen, Tight Seal, Pint	3.00
Fruit Jar, Queen, Tight Seal, Quart	3.00
Fruit Jar, Queen, Trademark, Wide Mouth, Adjustable, Pint	1.00
Fruit Jar, Queen, Trademark, Wide Mouth, Adjustable, Quart	1.00
Fruit Jar, Queen, Trademark, 1/2 Gallon	7.00
Fruit Jar, Queen, 1/2 Pint	1.00 To 8.00
Fruit Jar, Queen, Pint	1.00 To 6.00
Fruit Jar, Queen, Quart	1.00 To 2.00
Fruit Jar, Queen, 1/2 Gallon	1.00
Fruit Jar, Queen, Widemouth, Pint	1.50

Fruit Jar, Quilted, 6 In.
(See Page 118)

Fruit Jar, **Queen,** Widemouth, Quart 1.50
Fruit Jar, **Quick Seal,** Aqua, Quart .... 1.50 To 2.00
Fruit Jar, **Quick Seal,** In Circle, Aqua, Quart 3.50
Fruit Jar, **Quick Seal,** In Circle, Blue, Quart 3.00
Fruit Jar, **Quick Seal,** In Circle, July 14, 1908, Blue, Pint 4.00
Fruit Jar, **Quick Seal,** In Circle, Quart 3.50
Fruit Jar, **Quick Seal,** Light Blue, Pint 1.00
Fruit Jar, **Quick Seal,** Light Blue, Quart 1.00
Fruit Jar, **Quick Seal,** Pint .... 1.00 To 3.00
Fruit Jar, **Quick Seal,** Quart .... 1.00 To 3.00
Fruit Jar, **Quick Seal,** 1908 On Back, Pint 2.50
Fruit Jar, **Quilted,** 6 In. .... *Illus* 12.00
Fruit Jar, **Rail Road Mills,** Helme's, Amber, Quart .... 8.00 To 12.00
Fruit Jar, **Rail Road Mills,** Helme's, Glass & Metal Top, Ground, Amber, Quart 12.00
Fruit Jar, **Rau's Groove Ring,** Quart 35.00
Fruit Jar, **Rau's Improved Groove Ring,** Amethyst, 1/2 Gallon 22.50
Fruit Jar, **Rau's Improved Groove Ring,** Light Amethyst, 1/2 Gallon 28.50
Fruit Jar, **Rau's Improved Groove Ring,** Quart 25.00
Fruit Jar, **Ravenna Glass Works,** Airtight, IP, Pint 1200.00
Fruit Jar, **Red Key Mason,** Aqua, Quart .... 7.00 To 9.50
Fruit Jar, **Red Key Mason,** Aqua, 1/2 Gallon .... 6.50 To 8.50
Fruit Jar, **Red Key Mason,** Pint 9.00
Fruit Jar, **Reed's Patties,** Wire Toggle Clamps Closure, 1/2 Gallon 16.00
Fruit Jar, **Reliable Home Canning Mason,** Quart 2.50
Fruit Jar, **Reservoir,** Quart 200.00
Fruit Jar, **Reservoir,** 1/2 Gallon 160.00
Fruit Jar, **Rolled Lip,** Green, 13 In. 90.00
Fruit Jar, **Root Mason,** Aqua, Pint .... 3.00 To 4.00
Fruit Jar, **Root Mason,** Aqua, Quart .... 2.50 To 3.00
Fruit Jar, **Root Mason,** Aqua, 1/2 Gallon .... 3.50 To 5.50
Fruit Jar, **Root Mason,** Embossed, Blue, 1/2 Gallon 5.00
Fruit Jar, **Root Mason,** Pint 2.00
Fruit Jar, **Root Mason,** Quart 4.00
Fruit Jar, **Root,** Quart 4.00
Fruit Jar, **Royal Trademark Full Measure Reg.,** Amber, Quart 45.00
Fruit Jar, **Royal Trademark Full Measure Reg.,** Glass Lid, Wire Bail, Pint 6.00
Fruit Jar, **Royal Trademark Full Measure,** Reg., Glass Lid, Wire Bail, Quart 5.00
Fruit Jar, **Royal,** A.G.Smalley, Quart 35.00
Fruit Jar, **Royal,** A.G.Smalley, 1/2 Gallon 60.00
Fruit Jar, **Royal,** Aqua, 1/2 Pint 1.00
Fruit Jar, **Royal,** Aqua, Pint 1.00
Fruit Jar, **Royal,** Aqua, Quart 1.00
Fruit Jar, **Royal,** Aqua, 1/2 Gallon .... 1.00 To 9.50
Fruit Jar, **Royal,** Embossed Over Crown, Amber, Quart 65.00
Fruit Jar, **Royal,** Full Measure, Ground Top, Pint 1.50
Fruit Jar, **Royal Full Measure,** Ground Top, Quart 1.50
Fruit Jar, **Royal,** Full Measure, 1/2 Gallon 7.00
Fruit Jar, **Royal,** 1/2 Pint 1.00
Fruit Jar, **Royal,** Pint .... 1.00 To 7.00
Fruit Jar, **Royal,** Quart .... 1.00 To 1.50
Fruit Jar, **S G Co Monogram,** Mason's Patent Nov.30th, 1858, Aqua, Pint 7.00
Fruit Jar, **S G Co Monogram,** Mason's Patent Nov.30th, 1858, Aqua, Quart 8.00
Fruit Jar, **S G Co Monogram,** Mason's Patent Nov.30th, 1858, Light Blue, Quart 18.50
Fruit Jar, **S G Co,** 1858, Pint 5.00
Fruit Jar, **Safety Valve,** Aqua, Pint 10.00
Fruit Jar, **Safety Valve,** Greek Key Border, 1/2 Gallon 20.00
Fruit Jar, **Safety Valve,** Greek Key, Carrying Handle, Aqua, 1/2 Gallon 25.00
Fruit Jar, **Safety Valve,** Greek Key, Carrying Handle, 1/2 Gallon 25.00
Fruit Jar, **Safety Valve,** Greek Key, Pat.May 21, 1895, Aqua, 1/2 Gallon 45.00
Fruit Jar, **Safety Valve,** Greek Key, 1/2 Gallon 29.00
Fruit Jar, **Safety Valve,** No Embossing, Sun Colored, 1/2 Pint 6.00
Fruit Jar, **Safety Valve,** 1/4 Pint 20.00
Fruit Jar, **Safety Valve,** 1/2 Pint .... 10.00 To 11.00
Fruit Jar, **Safety Valve,** Pint 6.95
Fruit Jar, **Safety Valve,** Quart .... 6.95 To 15.00

Fruit Jar, **Safety Valve**, 1895, 1/2 Pint	10.00
Fruit Jar, **Safety**, Amber, Quart	45.00 To 75.00
Fruit Jar, **Safety**, Amber, 1/2 Gallon	75.00
Fruit Jar, **Safety**, Honey Amber, 1/2 Gallon	90.00
Fruit Jar, **Safety**, W.Metl, Quart	12.00
Fruit Jar, **Samco Genuine Mason**, Square, Pint	1.50
Fruit Jar, **Samco Genuine Mason**, Square, Quart	1.00
Fruit Jar, **Sanety**, Quart	12.00
Fruit Jar, **Sanford**, July 10, 1900, Quart	12.50 To 15.00
Fruit Jar, **Sanitary Freezer**, The, On Lid, Porcelain Stopper, Wire Bail, Quart	27.00
Fruit Jar, **Schram Automatic Sealer**, Aqua, Quart	3.00
Fruit Jar, **Schram Automatic Sealer**, Pint	3.00 To 4.50
Fruit Jar, **Schram Automatic Sealer**, Quart	5.00
Fruit Jar, **Scranton**, The, Quart	375.00
Fruit Jar, **Sealfast**, Foster, Embossed, Bail, Pint	1.50
Fruit Jar, **Sealfast**, Foster, Glass Lid, Purple, Pint	4.00
Fruit Jar, **Sealfast**, Foster, Glass Lid, Quart	2.50
Fruit Jar, **Sealfast**, Foster, Glass Lid, Wire Bail, Amber Tint, Quart	4.00
Fruit Jar, **Sealfast**, Foster, Glass Lid, Wire Bail, Pint	3.00
Fruit Jar, **Sealfast**, Foster, Glass Lid, Wire Bail, Quart	2.50
Fruit Jar, **Sealfast**, Foster, Pint	3.00 To 5.00
Fruit Jar, **Sealfast**, Foster, Quart	3.00
Fruit Jar, **Sealfast**, Foster, Wire Snap, 1/2 Pint	3.00
Fruit Jar, **Sealfast**, Foster, 1/2 Gallon	7.50
Fruit Jar, **Sealfast**, 1/2 Pint	5.00
Fruit Jar, **Sealfast**, Pint	2.00 To 8.00
Fruit Jar, **Sealfast**, Quart	2.50
Fruit Jar, **Security Seal**, Aqua, 1/2 Pint	1.00
Fruit Jar, **Security Seal**, Aqua, Pint	1.00
Fruit Jar, **Security Seal**, Aqua, Quart	1.00
Fruit Jar, **Security Seal**, Aqua, 1/2 Gallon	1.00
Fruit Jar, **Security Seal**, F.G.Co. In Triangle, Glass Lid, Wire Bail, Quart	4.00
Fruit Jar, **Security Seal**, 1/2 Pint	1.00
Fruit Jar, **Security Seal**, Pint	1.00
Fruit Jar, **Security Seal**, Quart	1.00 To 6.00
Fruit Jar, **Security Seal**, 1/2 Gallon	1.00
Fruit Jar, **Selco Surety Seal**, Aqua, 1/2 Gallon	5.00
Fruit Jar, **Selco Surety Seal**, Pint	5.00
Fruit Jar, **Selco Surety Seal**, 1/2 Gallon	7.00
Fruit Jar, **Sherwood Pottery**, Quart	12.00
Fruit Jar, **Silicon**, Aqua, Pint	11.00
Fruit Jar, **Silicon**, Aqua, 5 Quart	12.50
Fruit Jar, **Silicon**, Quart	6.00
Fruit Jar, **Simplex**, Pint	4.00 To 10.00
Fruit Jar, **Skotch Thero Jug**, 1/2 Gallon	5.00
Fruit Jar, **Smalley Self Sealer**, The, W.M., Quart	2.50
Fruit Jar, **Smalley**, Cathedral, 1895, 1/2 Pint	8.00
Fruit Jar, **Smalley**, Full Measure, Amber, Quart	35.00
Fruit Jar, **Smalley**, Full Measure, Amber, 1/2 Gallon	28.00
Fruit Jar, **Smalley**, Full Measure, Pint	5.00
Fruit Jar, **Smalley**, Milk Glass Top, Amber, Quart	32.50
Fruit Jar, **Smalley**, On Base, Side Clamps, 1/2 Pint	5.00
Fruit Jar, **Smalley**, Widemouth, Pint	3.00
Fruit Jar, **Smalley**, Widemouth, Quart	3.00
Fruit Jar, **Smalley's Nu-Seal**, Pint	5.00
Fruit Jar, **Smalley's Nu-Seal**, Quart	3.00
Fruit Jar, **Smalley's Royal**, 1/2 Pint	6.00 To 10.00
Fruit Jar, **Smalley's Royal**, Quart	4.00
Fruit Jar, **Smith Son & Co.**, J.P., Pittsburgh, Wax Sealer, Aqua, Quart	20.00
Fruit Jar, **Spencer**, Quart	45.00
Fruit Jar, **Spencer's Improved**, Quart	175.00
Fruit Jar, **Spencer's**, C.F., Rochester, Aqua, Quart	50.00
Fruit Jar, **Spencer's**, C.F., Rochester, Quart	68.00
Fruit Jar, **Standard Mason**, Light Aqua, 1/2 Gallon	4.00
Fruit Jar, **Standard Mason**, Quart	6.00

Fruit Jar, **Standard Mason,** 1/2 Gallon 7.00
Fruit Jar, **Standard,** Quart 4.00
Fruit Jar, **Standard,** Wax Sealer, Aqua, Pint 55.00
Fruit Jar, **Standard,** W.Mc C & Co., Reverse, Aqua, Quart 9.00
Fruit Jar, **Standard,** W.Mc C & Co., Reverse, Aqua, 1/2 Gallon 17.00
Fruit Jar, **Standard,** W.Mc C & Co., Whittled, 1/2 Gallon 25.00
Fruit Jar, **Star Below Star Below Band,** Glass Lid, Quart 22.00
Fruit Jar, **Star Below Star Below Band,** Glass Lid, 1/2 Gallon 25.00
Fruit Jar, **Star Glass Co.,** New Albany, Ind., Bubbles, Quart 20.00
Fruit Jar, **Star,** Quart 35.00
    Fruit Jar, **Steer's Head,** see Fruit Jar, Flaccus
Fruit Jar, **Sterling Mason,** Quart 2.50
Fruit Jar, **Stoddard Preserve Jar,** Medium Green, 13 3/4 In. 135.00
Fruit Jar, **Stoddard Preserve Jar,** OP, C.1800, Light Green, 6 In. 60.00
Fruit Jar, **Stoneware,** Gray Glaze, Wavy Red & Green Band, 8 3/4 In. 35.00
Fruit Jar, **Sun,** Amber, Quart 45.00
Fruit Jar, **Sun,** Aqua, Pint .... 42.00 To 60.00
Fruit Jar, **Sun,** Aqua, Quart 37.00
Fruit Jar, **Sun,** Haze, Quart 44.00
Fruit Jar, **Sun,** Lid & Clamp, Pint 40.00
Fruit Jar, **Sun,** Pint .... 25.00 To 60.00
Fruit Jar, **Sun,** Quart .... 25.00 To 37.50
Fruit Jar, **Sun,** Safety Valve Closure, Quart 25.00
Fruit Jar, **Sun,** 1/2 Gallon 65.00
Fruit Jar, **Sure Seal,** Blue, Pint 4.50
Fruit Jar, **Sure Seal,** Light Blue, Pint 1.00
Fruit Jar, **Sure Seal,** Pint 5.00
Fruit Jar, **Sure Seal,** Quart 2.50
Fruit Jar, **Swayzee's Double Safety,** In Frame, Pint .... 10.00 To 15.00
Fruit Jar, **Swayzee's Double Safety,** In Frame, Quart 10.00
Fruit Jar, **Swayzee's Improved Mason,** Aqua, 1/2 Gallon 6.00
Fruit Jar, **Swayzee's Improved Mason,** Dark Blue Aqua, Quart 2.50
Fruit Jar, **Swayzee's Improved Mason,** Quart 3.50
Fruit Jar, **Swayzee's Improved Mason,** 1/2 Gallon .... 4.00 To 5.00
Fruit Jar, **T.M.Lightning,** Amber, Quart 22.00
Fruit Jar, **Telephone Jar,** Aqua, Pint .... 4.00 To 10.00
Fruit Jar, **Telephone Jar,** Aqua, Quart 6.50
Fruit Jar, **Telephone Jar,** Pint .... 6.00 To 7.50
Fruit Jar, **Telephone Jar,** Quart 6.00
Fruit Jar, **Telephone Jar,** Widemouth, Pint 7.00
Fruit Jar, **Telephone Jar,** Widemouth, Quart .... 5.00 To 7.00
Fruit Jar, **Texas Mason,** Pint .... 10.00 To 12.00
Fruit Jar, **Texas Mason,** Quart 9.00
Fruit Jar, **Tight Seal,** Glass Lid, Blue, Pint 5.50
Fruit Jar, **Tight Seal,** Pint .... 1.00 To 4.50
Fruit Jar, **Tight Seal,** Quart .... 1.00 To 2.50
Fruit Jar, **T'ght Seal,** 1908, Blue, Pint 2.00
Fruit Jar, **True Fruit,** Clamp, 1/2 Gallon 12.00
Fruit Jar, **True Fruit,** 1/2 Gallon 14.00
Fruit Jar, **Unembossed,** 1/2 Pint .... 1.00 To 1.50
Fruit Jar, **Unembossed,** Pint 1.50
Fruit Jar, **Union,** Mason's, Aqua, Quart .... *Illus* 60.00
Fruit Jar, **Union,** Mason's, 1/2 Gallon 35.00
Fruit Jar, **Vacuum Jar,** S.F., Quart 12.00
Fruit Jar, **Vacuum,** Notch In Lip For Pump, Pint 19.50
Fruit Jar, **Vacuum,** Notch In Lip For Pump, Quart 12.00
Fruit Jar, **Vacuum,** Pint 14.00
Fruit Jar, **Valve Jar Co.,** The, Phila., Aqua, Quart 450.00
Fruit Jar, **Valve,** Aqua, Quart 130.00
Fruit Jar, **Valve,** Inlay, Stain, Aqua, Quart 135.00
Fruit Jar, **Van Vliet,** Improved, Quart .... 275.00 To 325.00
Fruit Jar, **Van Vliet,** 1881, Aqua, Quart 275.00
Fruit Jar, **Van Vliet,** 1881, Aqua, 1/2 Gallon 350.00
Fruit Jar, **Van Vliet,** 1881, Quart .... 275.00 To 280.00
Fruit Jar, **Van Vliet,** 1881, Stain, Aqua, Quart 250.00

Fruit Jar, Van Vliet, 1881, 9 In.

Fruit Jar, Mason's Union, Aqua, Quart
(See Page 120)

Fruit Jar, Van Vliet, 1881, Stain, Quart 250.00
Fruit Jar, Van Vliet, 1881, 9 In. ....*Illus* 375.00
Fruit Jar, Van Vliet, 1881, 1/2 Gallon .... 260.00 To 300.00
Fruit Jar, Veteran, Bust In Circle, Quart .... 10.00 To 15.00
Fruit Jar, Victory, On Lid, Side Clamps, 1/2 Pint 6.00
Fruit Jar, Victory, Pint .... 6.00 To 10.00
Fruit Jar, Victory, Quart 6.00
Fruit Jar, Victory, San Francisco Glass Works, Aqua, 1/2 Gallon 28.00
Fruit Jar, Victory, San Francisco Glass Works, Circle Of Dates, 1/2 Gallon 20.00
Fruit Jar, Victory, 1925, 1/2 Pint 4.00
Fruit Jar, W.L.& XI, Aqua 20.00
Fruit Jar, Wan-Eta Cocoa, Amber, 1/2 Pint 8.00
Fruit Jar, Wan-Eta Cocoa, Amber, Quart .... 5.00 To 8.00
Fruit Jar, Wan-Eta Cocoa, Boston, Amber, Quart 5.50
Fruit Jar, Wan-Eta Cocoa, Boston, Blue, Pint 10.00
Fruit Jar, Wan-Eta Cocoa, Pint 10.00
Fruit Jar, Wan-Eta Cocoa, Quart 7.00
Fruit Jar, Wax Sealer, Golden Green, 1/2 Gallon 40.00
Fruit Jar, Wax Sealer, Light Cobalt, 1/2 Gallon 250.00
Fruit Jar, Wax Sealer, Stoneware, Blue Stripes, Quart 18.00
Fruit Jar, Wax Sealer, Stoneware, Blue Stripes, 1/2 Gallon 18.00
Fruit Jar, Wax Sealer, Stoneware, Blue Stripes, Gallon 18.00
Fruit Jar, Wears, On Banner Below Crown, Pint 7.00
Fruit Jar, Wears, On Banner Below Crown, Quart 6.00
Fruit Jar, Wears, Oval, Pint 5.00
Fruit Jar, Wears, Oval, Quart 5.00
Fruit Jar, Wears, 1/2 Pint 6.00
Fruit Jar, Wears, Pint 5.00
Fruit Jar, Wears, 1909 Patent, Quart 8.00
Fruit Jar, Webster's Patent Feb.16, 1864, 7 1/2 In. ....*Color* 850.00
Fruit Jar, Weideman, Quart .... 4.00 To 5.00
Fruit Jar, Weir, Amber Lid, Pint 12.00
Fruit Jar, Weir, Brown & White, Gallon 8.00
Fruit Jar, Weir, Crockery, 1/2 Pint 12.50
Fruit Jar, Weir, Paper Food Label, 2 Tone, 1/2 Gallon 15.00
Fruit Jar, Weir, 1901, Crock, Quart 10.75
Fruit Jar, Western Stoneware, White, 1/2 Gallon 16.00
Fruit Jar, Whitall-Tatum, Blown, Quart 20.00

Fruit Jar, Whitmore's Patent, Rochester, N.Y., 8 1/2 In.

Fruit Jar, Whitall-Tatum, OP, 1/2 Pint	30.00 To 35.00
Fruit Jar, Whitall-Tatum, OP, Pint	25.00
Fruit Jar, Whitall-Tatum, OP, Quart	27.00
Fruit Jar, Whitall-Tatum, OP, 1/2 Gallon	40.00
Fruit Jar, White Crown Mason, Aqua, 1/2 Gallon	5.00 To 9.50
Fruit Jar, Whitmore's Patent, Rochester, N.Y., 8 1/2 In.	*Illus* 140.00
Fruit Jar, Whitney, Mason, Aqua, Quart	6.50
Fruit Jar, Whitney, Mason, Patent 1858, Embossed, Aqua, Pint	8.00
Fruit Jar, Whitney, Mason, Patent 1858, Quart	5.00
Fruit Jar, Wide Mouth, Green, Pint	55.00
Fruit Jar, Williams & Reppert, Greensboro, Pa., Stoneware, Quart	30.00
Fruit Jar, Williams & Reppert, Greensboro, Pa., Stoneware, 1/2 Gallon	30.00
Fruit Jar, Williams & Reppert, Greensboro, Pa., Stoneware, Gallon	30.00
Fruit Jar, Willoughby, J.D., Patent January 4, 1859, Aqua, Quart	50.00
Fruit Jar, Winslow, Open Bubble, Quart	35.00
Fruit Jar, Winslow, Wide Mouth, Quart	35.00
Fruit Jar, Woodbury Improved, Pint	20.00
Fruit Jar, Woodbury Improved, Quart	19.50 To 50.00
Fruit Jar, Woodbury, Aqua, Quart	15.00 To 20.00
Fruit Jar, Woodbury, Monogram, Aqua, Quart	18.00 To 20.00
Fruit Jar, Woodbury, Monogram, Aqua, 1 1/2 Gallon	14.00
Fruit Jar, Woodbury, Pint	22.00 To 35.00
Fruit Jar, Woodbury, Quart	11.00 To 22.50
Fruit Jar, Woodbury, White Enamel, Cylindrical, Haze, Quart	24.00
Fruit Jar, Yeoman Type, Cloudy, 1/2 Gallon	10.00
Fruit Jar, Yeoman's Fruit Bottle, Aqua, 9 1/2 X 4 In.	75.00
Fruit Jar, Yeoman's Fruit Bottle, Quart	40.00
Galliano, Soldier, Sword, Labels, 19 1/2 In.	9.00

Garnier bottles were first made in 1899 to hold Garnier Liqueurs. The firm was founded in 1859 in France. Figurals have been made through the twentieth century, except for the years of Prohibition and World War II.

Garnier, Accordion Player	20.00
Garnier, Alguiere, Pitcher	17.00
Garnier, Aztec, 1965	15.00
Garnier, Basket Of Flowers	17.00
Garnier, Bellhop	20.00
Garnier, Betty Boop	22.50
Garnier, Bluebird, 1970	6.50
Garnier, Bullfighter	6.95
Garnier, Butterfly	6.50
Garnier, California Quail	6.50
Garnier, Car, Alfa Romeo, 1913	12.00
Garnier, Car, Alfa Romeo, 1924	12.00
Garnier, Car, Alfa Romeo, 1929	12.00
Garnier, Car, Citroen	12.00
Garnier, Car, Fiat 500	12.00

Garnier, Car, Ford, 1913	12.00
Garnier, Car, MG 1933	12.00
Garnier, Car, Renault	12.00
Garnier, Car, Stanley Steamer	12.00
Garnier, Card	6.50
Garnier, Cardinal, 1969	6.50
Garnier, Cat, Gray	6.95
Garnier, Chalet, 1955	15.50
Garnier, Chick	20.00
Garnier, Chinese Dog	4.75
Garnier, Christmas Tree, 1956 .... *Illus*	50.00

Garnier, Christmas Tree, 1956

Garnier, Collie	14.00
Garnier, Drunk On Lamppost	20.00
Garnier, Eiffel Tower	11.75
Garnier, Elephant & Rider, 1961	22.00
Garnier, Franesa, Rabbit With Accordion, Pressed Glass	15.00
Garnier, German Shepherd	14.50
Garnier, Hen & Chicks	22.50
Garnier, Indian, 1958	10.00
Garnier, Jockey On Horse	6.95
Garnier, Lady, Full Dress, Southern Sales	15.00
Garnier, Lady, Heart On Dress	8.00
Garnier, Liqueur, 1939, Tapered	7.00
Garnier, Man, Bowler Hat	17.50
Garnier, Man, Brown Cap	17.50
Garnier, Manhattan, Man, Cane, Blue Coat, Pressed Glass	20.00
Garnier, Meadowlark	6.50
Garnier, Milord, Drunk	6.50
Garnier, Native Girl & Palm Tree	6.95
Garnier, New Mexico Roadrunner, 1969	10.00
Garnier, Owl	20.00
Garnier, Parrot	10.00
Garnier, Partridge	6.50
Garnier, Road Runner, 1969	6.50
Garnier, Round Log, 1958	10.00
Garnier, Saint Tropez, 1961	8.00
Garnier, Scarecrow, 1960	13.50
Garnier, Sheriff, 1958	10.00
Garnier, Skier	20.00
Garnier, Soldier, Faceless	35.00
Garnier, Spaniel	16.00
Garnier, Taxicab, Yellow, 1960	16.00
Garnier, Three Monkeys	20.00
Garnier, Trout	5.00
Garnier, Turk	17.50
Garnier, Valley Quail, 1969	6.50
Garnier, Vase .... *Illus*	15.00

Gemel, Blown, 8 1/2 In.	17.50
Gemel, Milk Glass, Free Blown, Applied Stem & Foot, McKearin No.229	65.00
Gemel, New England, Cranberry, 7 1/2 In.	50.00
Gemel, Opaque White Lips, Pink & White Loopings On Clear, 9 1/2 In.High	70.00
Gemel, South Jersey, Opalescent Looping, Ground Neck, Aqua, 7 In.	30.00
Gemel, 7 1/2 In.	10.00

Gin was first made in the 1600s and gin bottles have been made ever since.
Gin has always been an inexpensive drink, that is why so many of these
bottles were made. Many were of a type called case bottles today.

Gin, A.Van Hoboken & Co., Green, 10 In. .... *Illus*	9.00

Garnier, Vase
(See Page 123)

Gin, A.Van Hoboken & Co.,
Green, 10 In.

Gin, Bininger, see Bininger

Gin, Blown, Amber, 9 1/4 In.	45.00
Gin, Blown, Dark Olive, 9 1/2 In.	15.00
Gin, Blown, Olive Amber, Pair	75.00
Gin, Blown, Olive Green, Pair	75.00
Gin, Blown, Olive, 10 In.	30.00
Gin, Case, see Case Gin	
Gin, Charles, London, Cordial, Square, Burst Bubble, Blue Green, 8 In.	31.00
Gin, Cordial, Booth & Sedgwick's London, Olive Green	25.00
Gin, Cosmopoliet Schiedam, Man, 11 In. .... *Color*	98.00
Gin, Cosmopoliet, Embossed Man, Dark Green, 9 1/2 In.	75.00
Gin, Cosmopoliet, J.J.Melcher's, Olive Green, 9 1/2 In. .... *Illus*	75.00
Gin, Daniel Visser, Zonen Schiedam, Seal, Label, Green	45.00
Gin, Devil's Island Endurance, Haze, 1/2 Pint	5.00
Gin, Embossed, Olive Green, 4 In.	40.00
Gin, Free-Blown, Squashed Lip, Pontil, 10 In.	35.00
Gin, Gilbey, Spey Royal	45.00
Gin, Gordon's Dry, London, England, Boar's Head	8.00
Gin, I.A.I.Nolet Scheidam, Black Glass, 8 1/2 In.	25.00
Gin, Iler's Eagle, Willow Springs Distilling Co., Neb., Amethyst, Miniature	25.00
Gin, J.J.Vogt & Co., Druggists, 9 In. .... *Illus*	6.00
Gin, J.T.Daly Club House, Case, Haze, Dug, Olive Green, Quart	45.00
Gin, Juniper Leaf, Amber	60.00
Gin, Kiderlen's Pure Holland, Geneva, Man In Shield, Acid Etched, 9 In.	25.00
Gin, Olive, 11 In.	25.00

Gin, Cosmopoliet, J.J.Melcher's, Olive Green, 9 1/2 In.
(See Page 124)

Gin, J.J.Vogt & Co., Druggists, 9 In.
(See Page 124)

Gin, Pelican, Case, Holland

Gin, Pelican, Case, Holland .... *Illus*	10.00
Gin, R.E.Messenger & Son, London, Cordial, OP, Olive Green, 7 In.	100.00
Gin, Silver Leaf Holland, Basket, Paper Label, Green, 14 In.High	10.00
Gin, Square, Olive Green, Tall	17.00
Gin, Vandenbergh & Co., Three Mold, Blob Seal, Black Glass, 11 In.	40.00
Gin, Vandenburgh, Bell, Blob Seal, Quart	35.00
Gin, Very Old Gin, Handled, Round, Olive, 10 1/2 In.	110.00
Gin, Woolner & Co., Distillers, Peoria, Aqua, Lion's Head	7.50
Gin, 1765, Short Blob Neck, Deep Pontil, Olive, Quart	45.00
Glenmore, Amaretto Di Saronno, Siena Tower Guard, 1970 .... *Illus*	12.00
Glenmore, Yellowstone	15.00

Glenmore, Amaretto Di Saronno,
Siena Tower Guard, 1970

Glue bottles are often included with information about ink bottles. The numbers in the form C-O refer to the book Ink Bottles and Inkwells by William E. Covill, Jr.

Glue, Bell Mucilage, Sheared Lip, Bimal, 3 In.	3.00
Glue, Bell Mucilage, Sheared Lip, Neck Ring, Bubbles, Blue Aqua, 3 1/4 In. ...	5.00
Glue, Egyptian Tenexine, Pyramid Shape, Sheared Lip, Ice Blue, 2 3/4 In. ...	7.00

Glue, **Major's Cement**, Embossed On 4 Sides, Square, Pale Green, 4 In.	3.75
Glue, **Sanford's Library Paste**, Amber, Quart	5.50
Glue, **Sanford's Mucilage**, Rubber Top, 3 1/2 In.	1.00
Glue, **Sanford's Mucilage**, 4 In. *Illus*	12.00
Glue, **Spalding's**, Cylindrical, Pontil, Stain, Aqua, 3 1/4 In.	8.75
Goofus Glass, Embossed Statue Of Liberty & Eagle, Gold Green Paint, 12 In.	49.50

Glue, Sanford's Mucilage, 4 In.

Grant, Scotsman, Drummond   Grant, Lady Scot, Lamond

Grant, Lady Scot, Lamond *Illus*	8.00
Grant, Scotsman, Drummond *Illus*	8.00
Grenadier, Official Scots Fusileer	9.00
Grenadier, Official 3rd Guards Regiment	8.00
Grenadier, Soldier, Captain U.S.Infantry Union	9.95
Grenadier, Soldier, Continental Marines	18.00
Grenadier, Soldier, Corporal Grenadier	8.95
Grenadier, Soldier, Eugene	11.00
Grenadier, Soldier, George S.Custer	9.95
Grenadier, Soldier, Jeb Stuart	9.95
Grenadier, Soldier, Joan Of Arc Club	22.00
Grenadier, Soldier, King's African Rifle Corps	9.00 To 10.00
Grenadier, Soldier, King's African Rifle Corps, Quart	14.00
Grenadier, Soldier, Lannes	11.00
Grenadier, Soldier, Lassal	30.00
Grenadier, Soldier, Major Coldstream	8.95
Grenadier, Soldier, Murat	14.00
Grenadier, Soldier, Napoleon	45.00
Grenadier, Soldier, Ney	11.00

Grenadier, Soldier, Official Scots Fusileer	9.00
Grenadier, Soldier, 1st Official Guard 17th Dragoon	9.00
Grenadier, Soldier, 1st Pennsylvania	22.00
Grenadier, Soldier, 2nd Maryland	30.00
Grenadier, Soldier, 3rd Guards Regiment	5.95
Grenadier, Soldier, 3rd New York	14.00
Grenadier, Soldier, 18th Continental	14.00
Grenadier, Soldier, 1821 British Guards	9.95
Hair Products, see Cosmetics, Medicine	
Hamm, Bear, 1972	15.00 To 2.00
Hamm, Bear, 1973	12.00
Hamm, Burgie Man, 1971	21.00
Hand Lotion, see Medicine	
Heisey, Water, Fancy Loop, 9 1/2 In.	35.00
Historical Bottle Collectors Guild, Jacob's Cabin Tonic Bitters, 1974	27.50
Historical Replica, Girl Riding Boneshaker	8.00
Hoffman, A.J.Foyt Car	20.00
Hoffman, A.J.Foyt Racer	22.00

Hoffman, A.J.Foyt Car

Hoffman, A.J.Foyt Racer

Hoffman, A.J.Foyt, No.2	*Illus*	21.50
Hoffman, Big Red Machine, Baseball Glove		45.00
Hoffman, Gordon Johncock	*Illus*	25.50
Hoffman, Lady Godiva		30.00
Hoffman, Mark Donohue's 66 Sunoco McLaren		22.00
Hoffman, Mr.Cobbler		28.50
Hoffman, Mr.Doctor	22.00 To	30.00
Hoffman, Mr.Harpist	*Illus*	30.00
Hoffman, Mr.Lucky		30.00
Hoffman, Mr.Lucky, Musical		35.00
Hoffman, Mr.Sandman		25.00
Hoffman, Mr.Shoe Cobbler	22.00 To	30.00
Hoffman, Mrs.Lucky	*Illus*	27.00
Holly City, Connecticut		8.00
Holly City, Delaware, Light Amethyst	*Illus*	8.00

Holly City, Georgia, Light Yellow	8.00
Holly City, Gerald R.Ford	5.00
Holly City, Israel's 25th Anniversary, 1973 ....*Color*	8.00
Holly City, The Jersey Devil, 1974 ....*Color*	8.00
Holly City, John F.Kennedy Rocking Chair Memorial, 197 ....*Color*	8.00
Holly City, New Jersey, Light Blue	8.00
Holly City, Pennsylvania, Green	8.00
Holly City, Richard M.Nixon	15.00
Holly City, Senator Howard Baker	15.00
Holly City, Senator Sam Ervin	15.00
Holly City, South Carolina	8.00
Holly City, St.Nick Christmas, 1971	8.00
Holly City, St.Nick Christmas, 1973, Topaz Illus.	15.00

Hoffman, Mrs.Lucky
(See Page 127)

Hoffman, Mr.Harpist
(See Page 127)

Holly City, Delaware, Light Amethyst
(See Page 127)

Holly City, The Jersey Devil, 1974 ....*Color*	8.00
Holly City, Watergate, Amethyst	75.00
Holly City, Watergate, Third Run, 1973 ....*Color*	8.00
Holly City, Watergate, Topaz	8.00
Holly City, Welcome Home, P.O.W.'s, Blue	25.00
Holly City, Welcome Home, P.O.W.'s, Topaz	75.00

Hot Water, Tin, Curved For Stomach Or Back	18.00
House Of Bottles, Elephant On A Drum	37.00
House Of Koshu, Apple Wine	1.00
House Of Koshu, Cherry Wine	1.00
House Of Koshu, Darby	6.00
House Of Koshu, Geisha Girl	4.00
House Of Koshu, Gold Temple	6.00
House Of Koshu, Hiro	2.00
House Of Koshu, Honey Bucket, Large	4.00
House Of Koshu, Honey Bucket, Small	1.00
House Of Koshu, Hotei	8.00
House Of Koshu, Joan	6.00
House Of Koshu, Kamot Suru Sedan Chair	6.00
House Of Koshu, Lion Man, Red	12.00
House Of Koshu, Lion Man, White	12.00
House Of Koshu, Maiden	10.00
House Of Koshu, Noh Mask	14.00
House Of Koshu, Okame Mask	14.00
House Of Koshu, Pagoda, Golden	6.00
House Of Koshu, Pagoda, White	8.00
House Of Koshu, Playboy	10.00
House Of Koshu, Plum Wine	1.00
House Of Koshu, Princess	10.00
House Of Koshu, Sake God, Painted	6.00
House Of Koshu, Sake God, White	50.00
House Of Koshu, Seven Gods, Each	6.00
House Of Koshu, Smokisan	9.00
House Of Koshu, Three Monkeys	6.00
House Of Koshu, Two Lovers	4.00
Household, Ammonia, Parsons, 1882, Aqua, Label ...... Illus	15.00

Household, Ammonia, Parson, 1882, Aqua, Label

Household, Blacking, Whittled, Rolled Lip, Rectangular, Aqua, Blue, 4 1/4 In.	6.00
Household, Camp Minnow Trap, Chicotah, Okla., Whittled, Ground Lip, 10 In.	28.50
Household, Chain Lightning Bug Killer, Flask, Whittled, 9 In.	6.50
Household, Clorox, Amber, Gallon	1.00
Household, Clorox, Amber, Quart	.50
Household, Clorox, Amber, 1/2 Gallon	3.00
Household, Clorox, Cork Type, Amber, Pint	1.50
Household, Clorox, Cork Type, Amber, Quart	1.50
Household, Clorox, Corker, Amber, 16 Ozs., 7 3/4 In.	1.50
Household, Clorox, Corker, Stain, Amber, Quart	5.00
Household, Clorox, Old Sol, Elephant, Figural	25.00
Household, Dead Stuck For Bugs, 9 In. ...... Illus	8.00
Household, Elisha Waters Liquid Mirror Blacking, Troy, N.Y., Olive, 6 In.	75.00
Household, Fly-Tox, 6 In.	1.00
Household, Larkin Soap Co., Emerald Green, 3 In.	2.00
Household, Larkin Soap Co., Green, Stopper	4.00

Household, Liquid Veneer, Corker, 7 In. .... .75
Household, Oxol, Corker, Amber, 16 Ozs., 7 1/2 In. 1.50
Household, Price's Patent Candle Co., Eng., Blue, 7 In. .... *Illus* 65.00
Household, Shoe Polish, see Shoe Polish
Household, Soap Co., Tippecanoe City, O., Rectangular, Bimal, 6 In. 2.45
Household, Use Whitine For Kid, Albion Mfg.Co., N.Y., Aqua, 5 1/4 In. 2.00
Household, Vapo-Cresoline Co., Pat.1894, Square, Aqua, 5 1/4 In.High 3.75
Household, Wycoff & Co., Union Bluing, Aqua 3.50
I.W.Harper, Black Lettering, 2 Medallions, Jug, Handled, Quart 32.75
I.W.Harper, Blue 6.00
I.W.Harper, Compliments, Nelson Co., Ky., Jug, 1/4 Pint 17.50
I.W.Harper, Figural, No Stick, White, 16 1/2 In. 20.00
I.W.Harper, Gray 6.00

Household, Dead Stuck For Bugs, 9 In.
(See Page 129)

Household, Price's Patent Candle Co.,
Eng., Blue, 7 In.

I.W.Harper, Man, White 30.00
I.W.Harper, Nelson Co., Ky., Embossed, Ground Lip, Metal Screw Cap, 1/2 Pint 10.50
I.W.Harper, Nelson Co., Ky., Incised, Jug, 1/4 Pint 17.50
I.W.Harper, Nelson Co., Ky., Pottery, Jug, White, Brown Neck, Black, Quart 45.00
I.W.Harper, Pottery, White Glaze, Brown Neck, Quart 45.00
I.W.Harper, Sample Jug 15.00
I.W.Harper, Whiskey, Amber, Quart 10.00
I.W.Harper, White, Original 55.00
I.W.Harper, Wicker Case, Label, Embossed, Amber, Quart 13.50
I.W.Harper, 100 Percent, Medicinal, Flask, Pint 20.00

Ink bottles were first used in the United States in 1819. Early ink
bottles were of ceramic and were often imported. Inks can be identified by
their shape. They were made to be hard to tip over. The numbers used in
entries in the form C-0 or Mc Kearin G I-0 refer to the books
Ink Bottles and Inkwells by William E. Covill, Jr., and
American Glass by George P. and Helen McKearin.

Ink, Alling's, C-386 .... 20.00
Ink, Alling's Pat'd Apl 25, 1871, Bimal, Light Green, C-704 .... 75.00
Ink, Angus & Co., Schoolhouse Type, Pen Rest, Sheared Collar, Blue, 2 In. 10.95
Ink, B.Heller & Co. Indelible, Cobalt, 6 In. .... *Illus* 15.00
Ink, Barometer, Inkstand, Pat.June 4, 1861, C-1309 .... 42.00
Ink, Barrel, Part Label, 2 X 2 In. 15.00
Ink, Bell Shape, Light Green 36.00
Ink, Bell Shape, Pontil, Light Blue 25.00
Ink, Billing's Mauve Ink, Aqua, Bimal, C-588 .... 49.50
Ink, Billing's Mauve, Beehive Shape, Rolled Flared Lip, Aqua, 1 1/2 In. 15.00
Ink, Billing's Mauve, Beehive Shape, Rolled Lip, Bubbles, Aqua, 1 1/2 In. 25.00

Ink, B.Heller & Co. Indelible, Cobalt, 6 In.
(See Page 130)

Ink, **Bixby Cone,** Aqua 10.00
Ink, **Bixby Embossed On Base,** Cylindrical, Aqua, 2 5/8 In. 25.00
Ink, **Bixby Son & Co.,** N.Y., Aqua, Bimal, 9 Sided, C-590 .... 45.00
Ink, **Blown,** 3 Mold, McKearin G III-18, Olive Amber 135.00
Ink, **Boat Shape,** Green 32.00
Ink, **Bonney,** W.E., So.Hanover, Mass.Clear, Bimal, C-393 .... 10.00
Ink, **Bristol Recorder,** ABM, Amber, 2 1/2 In., C-394 .... 5.00 To 12.00
Ink, **Cabin,** Green 17.00
Ink, **Cane Pattern,** Square, 2 In. 12.00
Ink, **Carmine,** 2 1/4 In. 2.00
Ink, **Carter's,** Aqua, 1/2 Pint 6.00
Ink, **Carter's,** Aqua, Pint 7.50
Ink, **Carter's,** Bimal, Aqua, Quart 18.00
Ink, **Carter's,** Bimal, Cobalt, 1 11/16 In., C-554 .... 10.00
Ink, **Carter's,** Bimal, Teal Blue, 2 1/2 In., C-43 .... 20.00
Ink, **Carter's,** Cathedral, ABM, Cobalt, 1/2 Pint 100.00
Ink, **Carter's,** Cathedral, ABM, Cobalt, Quart .... 37.50 To 45.00
Ink, **Carter's,** Cathedral, Cobalt, 1/2 Pint .... 85.00 To 95.00
Ink, **Carter's,** Cathedral, Cobalt, Pint .... 35.00 To 60.00
Ink, **Carter's,** Cathedral, Cobalt, Quart .... 34.00 To 55.00
Ink, **Carter's,** Cathedral, Cobalt, 2 3/4 In. 70.00
Ink, **Carter's,** Cathedral, Desk Bottle, Cobalt, 4 Ozs., C-555 .... 100.00
Ink, **Carter's,** Cathedral, Label, Cobalt, 8 In. .... *Illus* 115.00

Ink, Carter's, Cathedral, 8 In.

Ink, **Carter's,** Cathedral, Labels, Pint 68.00
Ink, **Carter's,** Cathedral, Labels, Quart 45.00
Ink, **Carter's,** Cathedral, OP, Aqua, Quart 50.00
Innal, Labels, Quart 45.00
Ink, **Carter's,** Cathedral, OP, Aqua, Quart 50.00
Ink, **Carter's,** Cathedral, 1/2 Pint 70.00
Ink, **Carter's,** Cathedral, Pint .... 55.00 To 60.00
Ink, **Carter's,** Cathedral, Quart 45.00
Ink, **Carter's,** Cathedral, Pouring Spout, Label, Cobalt, Quart 45.00
Ink, **Carter's,** Cathedral, 8 In. .... *Color* 85.00
Ink, **Carter's,** Cobalt, Pint 15.00
Ink, **Carter's,** Cobalt, Quart, 9 3/4 In. .... 30.00 To 40.00
Ink, **Carter's,** Cone, Amber, 2 1/2 In. .... 5.00 To 6.50

Ink, **Carter's**, Cylindrical, V Band, Bimal, Aqua, 8 1/4 In. 6.95
Ink, **Carter's**, Embossed, Amber, 10 1/4 In. 16.00
Ink, **Carter's**, Impressed On Bottom & Around Base, Cobalt, 9 3/4 In. 45.00
Ink, **Carter's**, Indelible, Paper Label, Cork, 2 In. 3.00
Ink, **Carter's**, Indelible, 8 Sided, 1 3/4 In. 6.00
Ink, **Carter's**, M On Base, Conical, Double Ring Lip, Bubbles, 2 1/2 In. 7.00
Ink, **Carter's**, Ma & Pa Carter, Heavy Moustache .... 50.00 To 60.00
Ink, **Carter's**, Ma & Pa Carter, Made In Germany, C-1619 .... 69.00
Ink, **Carter's**, Master, Cathedral Windows At Base, Ice Blue, Full Quart 16.00
Ink, **Carter's**, Master, Flared Lip With Ring, Bimal, Blue Aqua, 1/2 Pint 6.00
Ink, **Carter's**, Master, Patent Feb.14, '99, Neck Ring, Sheared Lip, Aqua, 6 In. 10.00
Ink, **Carter's**, Medium Cobalt, Pint 55.00
Ink, **Carter's**, Metal Collar, Cobalt, 8 1/4 In. 20.00
Ink, **Carter's**, No.1, Bimal, Cobalt, 32 Ozs. 11.00
Ink, **Carter's**, No.63, Cone, Blue Aqua, 2 1/2 In. 5.00
Ink, **Carter's**, Pat.Feb.14 - 99, Amethyst, 1/2 Pint 10.00
Ink, **Carter's**, Pencraft, Office & Pen, 10 1/2 In., C-1 ....*Color* 10.00
Ink, **Carter's**, Pouring Spout, ABM, Cobalt, 32 Ozs. 10.00
Ink, **Carter's**, Red Fountain Pen, Cube Shape, Wood Cork, 2 1/2 In. 8.50
Ink, **Carter's**, Stoneware, Embossed, C-996 .... 20.00
Ink, **Carter's**, 1882 ....*Illus* 10.00
Ink, **Carter's**, 1896 ....*Illus* 8.00
Ink, **Carter's**, 1897 ....*Illus* 8.00

Ink, Carter's, 1882

Ink, Carter's, 1897

Ink, Carter's, 1896

Ink, **Carter's**, 1897, Made In U.S.A., Cone, Burst Bubble, Aqua, 2 1/2 In. 5.00
Ink, **Carter's**, 1897, Made In U.S.A., Cone, Seeds, Emerald Green, 2 1/2 In. 12.00
Ink, **Carter's**, 1916 ....*Illus* 6.00
Ink, **Caw's**, Master, Sheared Lip, Neck Ring, Bubbles, Teal Blue Green, Pint 45.00
Ink, **Caw's**, N.Y., Square, Aqua, 2 1/4 In. 8.00
Ink, **Caw's**, Square, 2 1/2 In. 5.00
Ink, **Cone**, Aqua, 2 1/2 In. .... 1.00 To 2.75
Ink, **Cone**, Light Olive Amber, Similar To C-18 .... 125.00
Ink, **Cone**, Octagonal, Pontil, Deep Amber, 2 1/4 X 2 1/2 In. 85.00
Ink, **Cone**, Octagonal, Sapphire Blue, 2 1/2 X 2 1/2 In. 190.00
Ink, **Cone**, 12 Sided, Pontil, Light Green, C-149 .... 95.00
Ink, **Conqueror Red**, 2 1/2 In. ....*Illus* 18.50
Ink, **Coventry Type**, McKearin G VIII-2, Clear Green, Pint 500.00
Ink, **Coventry**, 3 Mold, McKearin G II-18, Deep Amber 110.00
Ink, **CPC**, 12 Panels, Bimal, C-156 .... 10.00
Ink, **Cut Glass**, Cube Shape, Ground Lip, Pewter Cap, 1 1/2 In. 8.00
Ink, **D.& J.J.Arnold**, London, Blob Top, Pottery, 7 In. 7.00
Ink, **Davids & Black**, N.Y., Embossed On Shoulder, Cylindrical, Aqua, 5 In. 65.00
Ink, **Denby Pottery**, England, 3 Sunstreaks, Brown, 9 1/2 In. 16.00
Ink, **Denby Pottery**, Label, Quart 15.00
Ink, **Derby All British**, Embossed, Pyramid Shape, Sealed, C-709 .... 15.00
Ink, **Diamond Co.**, Milwaukee, Square, Straw Color, 1 3/4 In. 5.00
Ink, **Diamond Co.**, Patent 12-1-03, Double Lip Ring, Sun Coloring, 2 3/8 In. 6.00
Ink, **Draper's**, Dublin, Paper Label, Pottery, Pint 22.00

Ink, Carter's, 1916
(See Page 132)

Ink, Farley, Repaired, Amber, 2 In.

Ink, Conqueror Red, 2 1/2 In.
(See Page 132)

Ink, **Dunbar**, Pint	10.00
Ink, **E.S.Curtis**, Pontil, Olive Green, Pint	45.00
Ink, **E.S.Curtis**, Pottery, Eagle, Red, White, & Blue, Label, C-934	30.00
Ink, **E.S.Curtis**, Pottery, Eagle, Red, White, & Blue, 2 Labels, C-934	45.00
Ink, **E.S.Curtis**, Stoddard, 3 Mold, Sloped Collar, IP, Olive Green, 7 In.	60.00
Ink, **E.S.Curtis**, Warranted Superior, Blue Black, 8 In.	*Color* XXXX.XX
Ink, **Eastern**, Fine Swirled Ribs, McKearin 47-6, Deep Olive Green	205.00
Ink, **Eastern**, Threaded, Aqua, 2 In.	105.00
Ink, **Egyptian Tenexine**, Pyramid Shape, Embossed, Sheared Lip, Blue, 2 3/4 In.	16.00
Ink, **Embossed 5**, Aqua, C-506	10.00
Ink, **Embossed 5**, Two Pen Ledges, Cobalt, C-506	15.00
Ink, **Embossed 5**, Two Pen Ledges, Green, C-506	20.00
Ink, **Emerald Green**, C-704	98.00
Ink, **Estes**, N.Y., C-756, Aqua, 8 X 3 1/4 In.	130.00
Ink, **F.W.Styles**, Springfield, Vt., Pair	14.00
Ink, **Farley**, Repaired, Amber, 2 In.	*Illus* 125.00
Ink, **Figural Dog**, Hinged Cover, Clear, 4 In.	15.00
Ink, **Flint**, 3 Mold, McKearin G II-18, Olive Green	135.00
Ink, **Flowers**, Milk Glass, 2 3/4 In.	*Color* XXXX.XX
Ink, **For Fountain Pens**, Peacock, Tin, Blue, 6 In.	*Illus* 12.00
Ink, **Fred D.Alling**, Rochester, N.Y., C-386	25.00
Ink, **Fred D.Alling**, Rochester, N.Y., Master, Label, Green Aqua, 5 In.	65.00
Ink, **Gate's**, Label, Pouring Spout, 8 Ozs.	3.00
Ink, **Geometric**, Olive Green, McKearin G II-18	100.00
Ink, **German**, Gold On Black, 3 1/2 In.	*Illus* 40.00
Ink, **Hand**, Milk Glass, 4 1/4 In.	*Color* XXXX.XX
Ink, **Harrison's Columbian Perfumery**, 8 Sided, Pewter Cap, Aqua, 2 7/8 In.	25.00
Ink, **Harrison's Columbian**, Applied Lip, Cobalt Blue, 4 1/2 In.	140.00
Ink, **Harrison's Columbian**, Label, Open Pontil, Octagon, Blue Aqua, 1 1/2 In.	85.00
Ink, **Harrison's Columbian**, OP, Cloudy, Pint	57.50
Ink, **Harrison's Columbian**, OP, Dug, Cloudy, Pint	46.00 To 52.50
Ink, **Harrison's Columbian**, OP, Pint	64.00

Ink, For Fountain Pens,
Peacock, Tin, Blue,
6 In.

Ink, German, Gold On Black,
3 1/2 In.

Ink, **Harrison's Columbian,** OP, Stain, Pint 39.50
Ink, **Harrison's Columbian,** Pontil, Cobalt, C-194 .... 225.00
Ink, **Harrison's Columbian,** Pontil, Pint 53.50
Ink, **Harrison's Columbian,** Pontil, 5 1/2 In. ....*Illus* 95.00
Ink, **Harrison's Columbian,** Squashed Lip, OP, Pint 59.00
Ink, **Harrison's Columbian,** Whittled, Pontil, Deep Cobalt, 1 7/8 In. 250.00
Ink, **Harrison's Columbian,** 8 Sided, Pontil, 2 1/2 X 1 1/2 In. 65.00
Ink, **Harrison's Columbian,** 8 Sided, 3 3/4 In. 65.00
Ink, **Harrison's Columbian,** 12 Sided, OP, Stain, 2 1/2 X 4 1/2 In. 55.00
Ink, **Harrison's Columbian,** 12 Sided, Pontil, Aqua, 4 3/4 In. 75.00
Ink, **Harrison's,** 1 In. 31.50
Ink, **Hollidge,** Pen Ledge, Olive Green, C-506 .... 30.00
Ink, **Hoyt's Indelible,** Paper Label, Cork, 2 X 1/2 In. 3.00
Ink, **Improved Non-Conducting Metallic Inkstand Registered,** C-1674 .... 60.00
Ink, **J.& I.E.M.,** Aqua 14.00
Ink, **J.& I.E.M.,** Embossed, Dome Offset, Bimal, Aqua, C-627 .... 15.00
Ink, **J.& I.E.M.,** Turtle, 6 Panels, Sheared Lip, Light Blue Aqua, 1 1/4 In. 17.00
Ink, **J.Bourne & Son,** London, Eng., Denby Pottery, Spout, Brown, 7 1/2 In. 24.00
Ink, **J.Bourne,** Pottery, 4 3/4 In. 7.00
Ink, **J.R.Nichols & Co.,** Master, Lip Ring, Whittled, Bubbles, Green, 7 In. 13.00
Ink, **J.T.Billings & Co.,** Lowell, Mass., Perfumed Violet, Cobalt, C-391 .... 20.00
Ink, **John Holland Cincinnati,** Embossed On Front, Aqua, 2 X 2 In. 25.00
Ink, **Jonson's Japan,** 6 Panels, Pottery, 2 1/2 In. ....*Illus* 110.00
Ink, **Keene,** 3 Mold, McKearin G II-18, Deep Amber 150.00
Ink, **Keller's Inks,** Pottery, Pouring Spout, Handle, Blue & Gray, Gallon 65.00
Ink, **L.H.Thomas,** 2 Labels, 9 1/2 In., C-906 .... 26.00
Ink, **Lovatt & Lovatt,** Pottery, Stamp, 4 1/2 In. 5.00
Ink, **Man's Head,** Pottery, Brown, 3 1/2 In. ....*Illus* 15.00
Ink, **Man's Head,** Pottery, Purple, 3 1/2 In. ....*Illus* 15.00
Ink, **Mantua,** OP, Olive Green, 1/2 In. Deep 225.00

Ink, Harrison's Columbian,
Pontil, 5 1/2 In.

Ink, Man's Head, Pottery,
Purple, 3 1/2 In.

Ink, Man's Head, Pottery,
Brown, 3 1/2 In.

Ink, Jonson's Japan, 6 Panels, Pottery, 2 1/2 In.

Ink, **Massachusetts Standard Record,** 6 1/2 In. 2.75
Ink, **Master,** Deep Blue Green 15.00
Ink, **Master,** Draftsman, Handle, Spout, Daisy & Button, Gold Amber 100.00
Ink, **Master,** Edward's, Aqua 15.00
Ink, **Master,** International 15.00
Ink, **Master,** Pottery, Pour Spout, White Glaze, Pint 6.00
Ink, **Master,** 3 Mold, Collared Cone Lip, Skirt, Whittled, Emerald, 9 1/2 In. 18.00
Ink, **Master,** 3 Mold, Pinch Pour Spout, Emerald Green, Pint 15.00
Ink, **Millville,** Footed, Red, Green, Yellow, & Pink, Stopper, 9 1/4 In. 110.00
Ink, **New York State,** Aqua, 1 1/2 X 1 In. 100.00
Ink, **New York State,** Footed, Medium Clear Green, 3 1/4 X 3 In. 100.00
Ink, **New York State,** Stopper, Clear Green, 6 3/4 In. 425.00

Ink, P.& J.Arnold, London, Pottery, Pint	5.00
Ink, P.& J.Arnold, London, Pottery, Quart	29.00
Ink, P.& J.Arnold, London, Pottery, 7 In.	10.00
Ink, P.& J.Arnold, Master, Pour Spout, Crockery, 9 1/2 In.	5.00
Ink, P.& J.Arnold, Pouring Spout, 5 In.	6.75
Ink, Paul's Safety, Patent July 8, 1895, Squat, Light Yellow Green, 1 3/4 In.	6.00
Ink, Paul's, Bimal, Cobalt, 7 1/2 In., C-881	25.00
Ink, Pennell, J.W., Bimal, Aqua, C-560	35.00
Ink, Pontil, Olive Amber, 2 1/4 In., C-18	125.00
Ink, Porcelain, Hinged Brass Collar, Floral On Black, C.1860, Square, 3 In.	35.00
Ink, Pottery, Flared Lip, Brown Glaze, 5 In.	6.00
Ink, Pottery, Label, 8 1/2 In.	13.00
Ink, Pottery, Spout, 5 1/2 In.	4.50
Ink, Pottery, Wide Mouth, 7 1/4 In.	8.50
Ink, Pottery, 1 7/8 In.	3.00
Ink, Pottery, 3 Quill Holes, Gray, C-1556	75.00
Ink, S.O.Dunbar, Pint	12.50
Ink, S.O.Dunbar, Taunton, Mass., Whittled, Aqua, 6 In.	10.00
Ink, S.O.Dunbar, Umbrella, Pontil, Aqua, C-115	1100.00
Ink, S.S.Stafford's, Blue, Quart	16.00
Ink, S.S.Stafford's, Cobalt, Pint	12.00 To 24.00
Ink, S.S.Stafford's, Commercial, Embossed, Pour Spout Lip, Label, 9 1/2 In.	16.00
Ink, S.S.Stafford's, Label, 9 1/2 In.	18.00
Ink, S.S.Stafford's, Made In U.S.A., Eye Pour Spout, Stain, Cobalt, 8 In.	7.00
Ink, S.S.Stafford's, Master, Pour Spout, Cobalt, Pint	10.00
Ink, S.S.Stafford's, Master, Pour Spout, Double Rings, Cobalt, 6 In.	18.00
Ink, S.S.Stafford's, Pour Lip, Cobalt, Quart	30.00
Ink, S.S.Stafford's, Pour Spout, Cobalt, 16 Oz.	8.50
Ink, S.S.Stafford's, Pour Spout, Stain, Cobalt, 16 Oz.	8.50
Ink, Sand Stone, Round, Roof Shoulder, Blob Lip, 1 3/4 In.	15.00
Ink, Sanford's Indelible, Sample	10.00
Ink, Sanford's Patent, 2 In. *Illus*	17.50
Ink, Sanford's, Amber, Quart	5.50
Ink, Sanford's, Flattened Star Bottom, S.Y.Co.On Side, Square, 2 In.	10.00
Ink, Sanford's, Ground Top, Amber, Quart	2.00
Ink, Sanford's, Labels, Amber, 5 Gallon	17.00
Ink, Sanford's, Metal Pour Spout, Ground Lip, Amber, 7 In.	8.50
Ink, Sanford's, Patent Oct.21, 1890, Bimal, C-504	10.00
Ink, Schoolhouse Type, Tin On Shoulder, Sheared Collar, Aqua, 2 X 1 1/2 In.	8.95
Ink, Sheared Collar, 8 Vertical Sides, Aqua, 2 1/4 X 1 3/4 In.	7.95
Ink, Shoe, Screw Cap, 4 In. *Illus*	70.00
Ink, Signet Permanent Fluid, Lepages, Cobalt *Illus*	15.00
Ink, Signet, Cobalt, Pint	6.00
Ink, Signet, Cobalt, Quart	12.00
Ink, Square, Cobalt, 2 Oz.	4.00
Ink, Stoddard, Cylindrical, OP, Olive Green, 3 7/8 In.	55.00

Ink, Sanford's Patent, 2 In.

Ink, Signet Permanent Fluid, Lepages, Cobalt

Ink, Shoe, Screw Cap, 4 In.

Ink, Stoneware, Brown, Pint 7.50
Ink, Stoneware, Brown, Quart .... 7.50 To 8.50
Ink, Stoneware, Gray, C-1556 .... 75.00
Ink, Stoneware, White, Pint 7.50
Ink, Stoneware, White, Quart 7.50
Ink, Strawberry, 8 Sided, Pontil, Deep Green, C-129 .... 60.00
Ink, T On Bottom, Cone, Aqua, 2 1/2 In. 3.50
Ink, T. & M. On 2 Sides, Rectangular, Pontil, Aqua, 1 1/2 In. 40.00
Ink, Try Field's Non-Corrosive, Pottery, 2 1/2 In. ....*Color* XXXX.XX
Ink, Turtle, Embossed Bird In Tree On Dome, Whittled, Blue Aqua, 1 3/8 In. 35.00
Ink, Turtle, Pewter Top, Bimal, Aqua, C-641 .... 15.00
Ink, Umbrella, OP, Aqua, 3 1/2 In., C-136 .... 125.00
Ink, Underwood's, Bimal, Aqua, C-330 .... 25.00
Ink, Underwood's, C-78 .... 15.00
Ink, Underwood's, Cobalt, 32 Ozs. 28.00
Ink, Underwood's, Master, Pour Lip, Bimal, Cobalt, 9 11/16 In., C-914 .... 45.00
Ink, Underwood's, Pouring Spout, Cobalt, 5 In. 25.00
Ink, Waterman's, Cork, 2 1/2 In. .... 3.50 To 4.50
Ink, Wide Flared Lip, Whittled, OP, Green, 6 In. 28.00
Ink, Williams & Carlton, Aqua, C-345 .... 20.00
Ink, Williams', N.Y., Rolled Lip, Bulbous, Squat, Light Green, 2 1/4 In. 20.00
Ink, Wood's Black, Portland, Aqua, C-12 .... 140.00
Ink, Zanesville, 12 Diamond Mold, Green, 2 3/4 X 2 1/4 In. 1350.00
Ink, 3 Mold, Master, Pour Spout, Bubbles & Seeds, Teal Green Blue, 3/4 Quart 15.00
Ink, 3 Mold, McKearin G II-18, Olive Amber 135.00
Ink, 12 Sided, Pontil, Aqua, 3 In. 18.00
Inkstand, Sanford On Base, Bimal, Aqua, 2 1/2 In. 5.00
Inkwell, Cast Iron Frame, Bimal, Similar To C-1457 .... 42.50

Inkwell, Head, Sewer Pipe, 2 1/2 In.

Inkwell, Shotholder, Wooden Heads,
4 1/2 In.

Inkwell, Head, Sewer Pipe, 2 1/2 In. .... *Illus*   65.00
Inkwell, Shotholder, Wooden Heads, 4 1/2 In. .... *Illus*   100.00
Irish Ceramics, Blarney Stone, 1970 .... 8.00
Irish Ceramics, Counties Of Ireland, 1973 .... 10.00
Irish Ceramics, Irish Luck, 1972 .... 12.00
Irish Ceramics, Irish Patriot, 1971 .... 10.00
Irish Ceramics, Leprechaun, With Gold 22.00
Irish Ceramics, Leprechaun, 1968 .... 18.00
Irish Ceramics, Son's Erin, 1969 .... 12.00
Irish Ceramics, Songs Of Ireland, 1971 .... 10.00
Irish Mist, Soldier 9.00
Jack Daniel, Corn Whiskey No.7 .... 18.00
Jack Daniel, Gold Medal, Old No.7 .... *Illus*   15.00
Jack Daniel, Leather Flask .... *Illus*   10.00
Jack Daniel, Old No.7, Battleship Maine 60.00
Jack Daniel, No.7, Square, Quart 6.00
Jack Daniel, Peach Brandy, Lem Motlow .... *Illus*   20.00
Jack Daniel, Tennessee Whiskey, Screw Top .... *Illus*   6.00
Jar, Battery, Porcelain Cover, 10 In. 11.00
Jar, Blown, Cylindrical, Aqua, 5 1/8 In. 6.00
Jar, Measuring, Rochester Tumbler Co., Patent 1880, Clear, Quart 4.95
Jar, Milk Glass, Metal Lid, Dated 1880, 2 1/2 In.High 12.00

Jar, Milk Glass, Owl, Atterbury, White, B-182	145.00
Jar, Ointment, Covered, Octagonal, Milk Glass, 4 In.	12.00
Jar, Powder, Imitation Cut Pattern, Metal Top	6.00
Jar, Pressed Glass, Etched Greek Key, Hinged Silver & Glass Top, Miniature	15.00
Jar, Pressed Glass, Statue Of Liberty, 12 1/2 In.	85.00
Jar, Tobacco Spit, Glazed Pottery	19.00
Jar, Tobacco, Teddy Bear, 5 In.	22.50
Jug, Applied Handle, Amber, 8 1/2 In.	10.00
Jug, Bennington, Blue Slip, 3 Gallon	52.00
Jug, Ceramic, Embossed Eagle On Front, Handled, Brown, 9 In.	125.00
Jug, Globular, Flat, Black Amber, 9 In.	55.00
Jug, Globular, Flat, Deep Amber, 8 In.	30.00
Jug, Globular, Hollow Handle, Medium Blue Green, 10 1/2 In.	50.00
Jug, Globular, 32 Vertical Ribs, Footed, Aqua, 5 In.	150.00
Jug, New York State, Globular, Footed, Aqua, 6 1/4 In.	135.00

Jack Daniel, Gold Medal, Old No.7
(See Page 136)

Jack Daniel, Tennessee Whiskey, Screw Top
(See Page 136)

Jack Daniel, Leather Flask
(See Page 136)

Jack Daniel, Peach Brandy, Lem Motlow
(See Page 136)

Jug, Old Governor Sour Mash, Graf & Co., 1879, 7 1/2 In.

Jug, New York State, Light Green, 8 1/2 In.	95.00
Jug, Ohio, 32 Ribs, Aqua, 6 In.	110.00
Jug, Old Governor Sour Mash, Graf & Co., 1879, 7 1/2 In. .... *Illus*	50.00
Jug, Pickard, Signed Keene, Gold Grapes & Leaves, 6 1/2 In.	130.00
Kentucky Gentleman, Confederate	5.95

Kentucky Gentleman, Frontiersman, Daniel Boone	13.00
Kentucky Gentleman, Kentucky Colonel	12.00
Kentucky Gentleman, Kentucky Tavern, Captain's Quart	10.00
Kentucky Gentleman, Revolutionary	5.95
Kentucky Gentleman, Union	5.95
Kummel Bear, see Figural	
Lestoil, Flask, Franklin, Blue *Illus*	5.00
Lestoil, Flask, Liberty, Green *Illus*	5.00
Lestoil, Flask, Washington *Illus*	5.00
Lewis & Clark, Captain Meriwether Lewis	75.00
Lewis & Clark, Captain William Clark	75.00
Lewis & Clark, Charbonneau	55.00
Lewis & Clark, Charbonneau, 1/5 Size	35.00
Lewis & Clark, Sacajewea With Papoose	65.00
Lewis & Clark, York	50.00
Lewis & Clark, York, 1/5 Size	4.00
Lionstone, Al Unser No.1*	26.00
Lionstone, Annie Christmas	16.00 To 20.00
Lionstone, Annie Oakley	16.00 To 29.00
Lionstone, Arizona Quail	22.00
Lionstone, Bar Scene, Set Of 4	325.00 To 450.00
Lionstone, Bar Scene, Set Of 4 With Nude	500.00
Lionstone, Bartender	18.00 To 45.00
Lionstone, Baseball	32.00
Lionstone, Baseball Players, 1974	32.50
Lionstone, Basket Weaver	32.00
Lionstone, Basketball	35.00
Lionstone, Belly Robber	19.00 To 35.00

Lestoil, Flask,   Lestoil, Flask,   Lestoil, Flask,
Franklin, Blue   Liberty, Green   Washington

Lionstone, Blacksmith, 1974	31.50
Lionstone, Blue Jay, Missouri	32.00
Lionstone, Bluebird, Wisconsin	15.00 To 20.00
Lionstone, Boxer	35.00
Lionstone, Boxing	32.00
Lionstone, Buffalo Bill	34.00
Lionstone, Buffalo Hunter	32.00
Lionstone, Calamity Jane, 1971	31.50 To 32.00
Lionstone, Call House Madam	18.00 To 22.00
Lionstone, Cavalry Scout	9.00 To 14.00
Lionstone, Camp Cook	18.00 To 39.00
Lionstone, Camp Follower *Illus*	29.00
Lionstone, Capistrano Cardinal	26.00
Lionstone, Capistrano Swallow, Gold	49.00
Lionstone, Capistrano Swallow, Silver	69.00
Lionstone, Cardinal, Indiana	26.00 To 32.50
Lionstone, Casual Indian	8.00 To 19.00
Lionstone, Cavalry Scout	8.00 To 19.00
Lionstone, Cherry Valley Club, Gold	35.00
Lionstone, Cherry Valley Club, Silver	42.00

Lionstone, Chinese Laundryman	14.50 To 29.00
Lionstone, Circuit Judge	16.00 To 24.00
Lionstone, Country Doctor	16.50 To 24.00
Lionstone, Cowboy	9.00 To 19.00
Lionstone, Cowgirl	32.00
Lionstone, Dancehall Girl	32.50
Lionstone, Eastern Bluebird	24.00 To 32.00
Lionstone, Egg Merchant	32.00
Lionstone, Falcon	26.00 To 36.00
Lionstone, Firefighter Hat, No.1	30.00 To 34.00
Lionstone, Firefighter Hat, No.7	30.00
Lionstone, Football	35.00
Lionstone, Frontiersman	19.00 To 38.00
Lionstone, Gambels Quail	18.00
Lionstone, Gardener	32.00
Lionstone, Gentleman Gambler	8.00 To 14.00
Lionstone, Gold Panner	45.00 To 53.00
Lionstone, Goldfinch	24.00 To 31.00
Lionstone, Golf	35.00
Lionstone, Highway Robber	14.50 To 18.50
Lionstone, Hockey Players, 1974	32.00 To 35.00
Lionstone, Indiana Cardinal	26.00 To 32.50
Lionstone, Japanese Art Series, Set Of 6	200.00
Lionstone, Jesse James	16.50 To 24.00
Lionstone, Johnny Lightning	*Illus* 22.00
Lionstone, Judge Roy Bean	16.50 To 32.00
Lionstone, Lonely Luke, 1971	32.00 To 32.50
Lionstone, Lucy Buck	24.95
Lionstone, Madame	18.00 To 22.00
Lionstone, Meadowlark	18.00 To 25.00
Lionstone, Miniature, see Miniature, Lionstone	
Lionstone, Mint Bar Scene	325.00 To 450.00
Lionstone, Mint Bar Scene With Nude	500.00
Lionstone, Missouri Blue Jay	34.00
Lionstone, Molly Brown	32.00
Lionstone, Moose	14.95
Lionstone, Mountain Man	*Illus* 28.00
Lionstone, Olsonite Eagle	20.00 To 25.00
Lionstone, Owls	28.00
Lionstone, Perfessor	32.50

Lionstone, Camp Follower
(See Page 138)

Lionstone, Johnny Lightning

Lionstone, Mountain Man

Lionstone, Proud Indian .... 9.00 To 12.00
Lionstone, Quail, Gambels 18.00
Lionstone, Railroad Engineer .... 16.00 To 16.50
Lionstone, Renegade Trader .... *Illus* 35.00
Lionstone, Riverboat Captain .... 14.50 To 19.00
Lionstone, Roadrunner .... 28.00 To 35.00
Lionstone, Roses On Parade .... 39.95 To 54.00
Lionstone, STP Turbo Car .... 12.00 To 15.00
Lionstone, STP Turbo Car, Gold & Platinum, Pair .... 65.00 To 70.00
Lionstone, Screech Owl .... 31.00 To 36.00
Lionstone, Sheepherder .... 47.50 To 60.00
Lionstone, Sheriff .... 8.00 To 14.00
Lionstone, Shoot Out At OK Corral 32.00
Lionstone, Sodbuster .... 16.50 To 24.00
Lionstone, Squaw & Papoose 34.00
Lionstone, Squaw Man .... 18.00 To 20.00
Lionstone, Stagecoach Driver .... 19.00 To 29.00
Lionstone, Telegraph Operator .... 16.00 To 19.00
Lionstone, The Tinker 32.50
Lionstone, Timekeeper 32.00
Lionstone, Tribal Chief, 1974 .... 32.00 To 32.50
Lionstone, Tropical Birds, Miniature, Set Of 6 .... 75.00
Lionstone, Vigilante .... 16.00 To 22.00
Lionstone, Wells Fargo Man .... *Illus* 25.00
Lionstone, Wisconsin Bluebird .... 15.00 To 20.00
Lionstone, Woodhawk .... *Illus* 40.00
Liqueur, A.Bauer, Pineapple Rock & Rye, Paneled Neck, S.C.A., 10 In. 15.00
Liqueur, B.& B., Benedictine, Label, Sealed, Amber, 1/2 Pint 3.00
Liqueur, Benedictine, Haze, Quart 6.00
Liqueur, Bols, Ballerina 8.00
Liqueur, Bulbous, Blown Teardrop Stopper, Gold & Forget-Me-Nots, 8 3/4 In. 18.00
Liqueur, D.O.M. Benedictine, Neck Ring, ABM, Olive Green, 3 1/4 In. 4.00
Liqueur, D.O.M. Benedictine, Sheared Lip With Part Ring, Green, 3 1/4 In. 5.50
Liqueur, Field, Son & Co.Sloe Gin .... *Illus* 8.00
Liqueur, Grand Marnier, Art Glass, Gold, Green, 7 In. .... *Illus* 150.00
Ludlow, Eastern, Globular, Thin Metal, Clear Green, 9 In. 25.00
Ludlow, Globular, Olive, 8 1/4 In. 75.00
Ludlow, New England, Globular, Deep Green, 10 1/2 In. 30.00

Lionstone, Renegade Trader

Lionstone, Woodhawk

Lionstone, Wells Fargo Man

Liqueur, Field, Son & Co.Sloe Gin
(See Page 140)

Luxardo, Alabaster Fish, 1960

Liqueur, Grand Marnier,
Art Glass,
Gold, Green, 7 In.
(See Page 140)

Luxardo, Pheasant,
Black Venetian
Glass

Ludlow, New England, Globular, Green, 10 1/2 In. 40.00

*Luxardo bottles were first used in the 1930s to bottle the italian liqueurs.
The firm was founded in 1821. Most of the Luxardo bottles found today
date after 1943. The dates given are the first year the bottle was made.*

Luxardo, African Heads, Pair 40.00
Luxardo, Alabaster Candlestick, Rose 20.00
Luxardo, Alabaster Fish 25.00
Luxardo, Alabaster Fish, 1960 .... *Illus* 35.00
Luxardo, Alabaster Goose 28.00
Luxardo, Apothecary Jar 6.00
Luxardo, Candlestick, Green 20.00
Luxardo, Ceramic Barrel 8.00
Luxardo, Chess Horse 33.95
Luxardo, Cucciolo Puppy 21.00
Luxardo, Eagle 40.00
Luxardo, Gold & Green Fish 29.00
Luxardo, Gold Vase, Blue Top 14.00
Luxardo, Green Dolphin 35.00
Luxardo, Green Duck 28.00
Luxardo, Modern Pheasant 25.00
Luxardo, Onyx Eagle .... 36.00 To 65.00
Luxardo, Onyx Owl 35.00
Luxardo, Owl 40.00
Luxardo, Penguin 25.00
Luxardo, Penguin, Murano 40.00
Luxardo, Pheasant, Black Venetian Glass .... *Illus* 100.00
Luxardo, Quartz Fish 33.95
Luxardo, Sitting Puppy 25.00
Luxardo, Squirrel 24.00
Luxardo, Venus Di Milo 5.00
Luxardo, Wobble Bottle, 3 Mold 8.00
Luxardo, Zodiac 20.00
Maloney, Hippie 3.00
Maloney, Villain 3.00
Mantua, Globular, 16 Ribs, Aqua, 3 In. 350.00

Marcialla, Donkey & Elephant In Chairs, Large, Pair 27.00
MBC,Laurel & Hardy In Car 14.50
MBC,Laurel & Hardy, Pair 30.00
McCormick, Air Race Decanter 6.50
McCormick, Angelica Globe 24.00
McCormick, Barrel, Aging, 1968 .... 12.00
McCormick, Bat Masterson .... 21.50 To 22.50
McCormick, Billy The Kid .... 21.50 To 22.50
McCormick, Black Bart 21.50
McCormick, Bluebird .... 11.50 To 14.00
McCormick, Calamity Jane 22.00
McCormick, Clock, Queen Anne 22.00
McCormick, Coal Miner 11.00
McCormick, Coffee Mill, Orange 28.50
McCormick, Doc Holiday 21.50
McCormick, Hereford Bull 39.00
McCormick, Jesse James 21.95
McCormick, Joplin Coal Miner .... 11.00 To 12.95
McCormick, Jupiter, Wood Tender, 1960 .... 23.00
McCormick, Kansas City Chief .... 39.00 To 45.00
McCormick, Kansas City Royals 13.00
McCormick, Lobo, New Mexico 32.50
McCormick, Locomotive, Jupiter 17.50
McCormick, Missouri .... 12.00 To 14.50
McCormick, Pirates, Each 9.00
McCormick, Robert E.Lee 25.00
McCormick, Ski Bod 9.00
McCormick, Spirit Of St.Louis 45.00
McCormick, Train, Engine & Cars 125.00
McCormick, Wild Bill Hickok 21.50
McCormick, Wyatt Earp .... 21.95 To 25.00
McCormick, Yacht America .... 23.00 To 25.00

*Medicine bottles held all of the many types of medications used in past
centuries. Most of those collected today date from the 1850-1930 period.
Bitters, sarsaparilla, poison, and a few other types of medicine are listed
under their own headings.*

Medicine, A.A.Cooley, Hartford, Conn., Olive Green, Pint 95.00
Medicine, A.D.Elmer's, It Cures Like A Charm, Bimal, Aqua, 5 In. 3.00
Medicine, Acker's Elixir, W.H.Hooker & Co., Rectangular, Amber, 7 1/2 In. ... 15.00
Medicine, Acker's English Remedy For The Throat & Lungs, Cobalt, 4 3/4 In. ... 7.00
Medicine, Acker's English Remedy For The Throat & Lungs, Cobalt, 5 1/2 In. ... 7.00
Medicine, Acker's English Remedy, Stain, Cobalt Blue, 5 1/2 In.High 10.00
Medicine, Acker's English Remedy, Stain, Cobalt Blue, 6 3/4 In. 15.00
Medicine, Alexander's Liver & Kidney Tonic, Akron, O., Amber, 8 In. 20.00
Medicine, Alka Seltzer, With Dispenser ....*Color* 35.00
Medicine, Allen's Lung Balsam, J.N.Harris & Co., O., Oval, Haze, Aqua, 8 In. ... 3.00
Medicine, Alvas Brazilian Specific Co., Star Shape, Light Aqua, 9 1/2 In. 7.50
Medicine, Ambrosial, B.M.& E.A.W.& Co., Handled Jug, Amber, Pint 100.00
Medicine, American Compound Coventry, Rectangular, Aqua, 7 3/4 In. 24.00
Medicine, Amethyst, 3 1/2 In. 25.00
Medicine, Analgic Liniment, Baker, Keokuk, Iowa, 8 3/4 In. 4.00
Medicine, Apoplexy Preventive & Paralysis Cure, Aqua, 8 1/2 In. 30.00
Medicine, Applied Handle, Prescription Lip, Round, Milk Glass, 7 5/8 In. 37.50
Medicine, Applied Top, 8 Sided, Crude Neck, OP, Olive Amber, 6 1/2 In. 130.00
Medicine, Aqua, 7 1/2 In. 1.50
Medicine, Archibald's Pain Balsam, Blue Tinged, 5 1/2 X 1 3/4 In. 10.00
Medicine, Arnica & Oil Liniment, Aqua, 4 3/4 In. 2.00
Medicine, Arnica & Oil Liniment, Aqua, 6 3/4 In. 3.00
Medicine, Atlas Aconic Oil, Bimal, Aqua, 5 1/2 In. 2.65
Medicine, Atlas Diarrhea Curative, Bimal, Sunk Oval Panel, Aqua, 5 1/2 In. ... 6.95
Medicine, Atlas Liver Pellets, Bimal, Amber, 5 3/4 In. 1.85
Medicine, Atlas Vegetable Tonic Syrup, Bimal, Aqua, 5 1/2 In. 2.65
Medicine, Atwood's, L.F.Monogram, H.H.Hayes Co., ABM, 6 5/8 In. 99.00
Medicine, Australian Dry Air Cure, Wood Tube, Label, 5 In. 7.00

Medicine, Ayer's Cherry Pectoral, Light Green, 7 1/2 In.	8.00
Medicine, Ayer's Cherry Pectoral, Rectangular, OP, Haze, Aqua, 7 In.	16.00
Medicine, Ayer's Cherry Pectoral, Rectangular, Pontil, Aqua, 7 In.	17.50
Medicine, Ayer's Hair Vigor, Blob Lip, Sweated Paper Label, 7 1/2 In.	30.00
Medicine, Ayer's Pectoral, OP, Aqua, 7 In.	14.00
Medicine, Ayer's Senopos, Lowell, Mass., Blob Lip, Skirt, 6 In.	7.00
Medicine, B.Fosgate's Anodyne Cordial, Light Aqua, 4 3/4 In.High	15.00
Medicine, B.P.& Co., Pill, Cobalt, 1 1/2 In.	2.00
Medicine, Baker's Specific, Embossed Uncle Sam Figure, 6 In.	7.00
Medicine, Barry's Canker Cure, 6 In.	8.50
Medicine, Barry's Tricopherous For Skin & Hair, OP, Aqua, 6 In.	22.00
Medicine, Barry's Tricopherous For The Skin & Hair, Aqua, 6 1/4 In.	9.00
Medicine, Barry's Tricopherous For The Skin & Hair, Blue Aqua, 6 1/4 In.	8.00
Medicine, Bauer's Instant Cough Cure, Sample Size	4.50
Medicine, Bears Oil, Pontil, 3 In. .... *Illus*	30.00
Medicine, Bell & Tossler-Prevost, A Paris, IP, Dark Blue Green, 7 1/2 In.	35.00
Medicine, Berry's Tricopherous For Skin & Hair, OP, 6 In.	19.00
Medicine, Blown, Flat, Aqua, 4 In.	12.50
Medicine, Blown, Green, 4 1/4 In.	6.00
Medicine, Blown, 6 Panels, Light Yellow Green Tint, 4 3/4 In.	5.00
Medicine, Brant's Indian Pulmonary Balsam, M.T.Wallace, Light Green, 7 In.	25.00
Medicine, Brant's Indian Pulmonary Balsam, Octagonal, Whittled, Aqua, 7 In.	45.00
Medicine, Bromo Seltzer, Embossed, Cobalt, 4 In.	2.00
Medicine, Bromo Seltzer, Emerson Drug Co., Aqua, 4 In.	10.50
Medicine, Bromo Seltzer, Teal Blue, 2 5/8 In.	2.00
Medicine, Brown's Teething Cordial, Aqua, 5 In.	5.00
Medicine, Buchu Gin, 8 Sided, Emerald Green, 10 In.	95.00
Medicine, Buhrer's Gentian Bitters, Deep Amber, 6 Star	97.00
Medicine, Bull's Cough Syrup, Aqua, 5 1/2 In.	4.50
Medicine, Burnett's Cocaine, Aqua, 6 1/8 In.	3.00
Medicine, Burnett's Cocaine, 7 In.	5.00
Medicine, Burnett's Cocaine, 8 Panel, Aqua, 7 In.	5.50
Medicine, C.C.Clark & Co., New Haven, Conn., 12 Sided, Aqua, 7 1/4 In.	4.00
Medicine, C.W.Davis Inflamatory Extirpator & Cleanser, Aqua, 2 1/2 In.	25.00
Medicine, C.W.Merchant, Lockport, N.Y., Rectangular, Emerald Green, 5 In.	27.50
Medicine, C.Whitcomb's C.L.D. Indian Liniment, Bimal, Aqua, 5 1/2 In.	10.00
Medicine, Cabler's, W.P., Uze-It Pain Oil, 5 1/4 In. .... *Illus*	3.00

Medicine, Bears Oil, Pontil, 3 In.

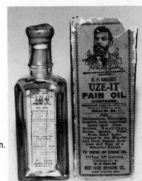

Medicine, Cabler's, W.P., Uze-It Pain Oil, 5 1/4 In.

Medicine, Calder's Dentine, 4 In.	1.00
Medicine, Caldwell's Cough Syrup, Aquamarine Blue, 7 In.	4.00
Medicine, Caldwell's Laxative Senna, 6 3/4 In.	2.50
Medicine, Camuslynie Still, Dark Green, 10 3/4 In.	18.50
Medicine, Cardui, The Woman's Tonic, Blue, 8 1/4 In.	4.00
Medicine, Cardui, The Woman's Tonic, 8 1/2 In.	3.50
Medicine, Cardwell's Syrup Pepsin, Blue, 6 1/2 In.	3.00
Medicine, Carter's No.2, Cobalt	7.00
Medicine, Castor Oil, Dull, Cobalt, 8 In.	5.00

Medicine, Castoria, 5 In.	.50
Medicine, Castoria, 5 3/4 In.	1.50
Medicine, Chamberlain's Cough Remedy, Blue, 5 3/4 In.	3.00
Medicine, Chamberlain's Cough Syrup, Aquamarine Blue, 5 3/4 In.	3.00
Medicine, Chamberlain's Pain Balm, Rectangular, Aqua, 7 In.	5.00
Medicine, Chappelear's Preparations, Zanesville, O., Aqua, Sample Size	12.00
Medicine, Chase Mfg.Co., Newburgh, N.Y., Round Bottom, Oval, Bimal, 1 1/2 In.	5.00
Medicine, Chattanooga, Tin Cap, Amber, 7 1/2 In.	2.50
Medicine, Cherry Malt Phosphite, Lady's Leg Shape, Haze, Amber, 9 In.	15.00
Medicine, Clarke's World Famed Blood Mixture, Cobalt, 7 1/4 In.	18.00
Medicine, Clarke's World Famed Blood Mixture, Lincoln, Rectangular, 7 In.	22.00
Medicine, Clement's Tonic, Rectangular, Amber, 6 3/4 In.	13.00
Medicine, Cod Liver Oil, Fish Shape, Amber, 6 1/4 In.	8.50
Medicine, Cod Liver Oil, Fish Shape, Label, Amber, 3 In.	100.00
Medicine, Cod Liver Oil, Fish Shape, Light Amber, 10 In.	12.50
Medicine, Coffeen's Liniment No.2, OP, Aqua, 4 In.	10.50
Medicine, Coke Dandruff Cure, A.R.Bremer Co., 7 1/2 In. _____Color_	25.00
Medicine, Colac Pile Pills, Amber, 3 In. _____Illus_	.50
Medicine, Compound A Diuretic, Remedies Co., Label, ABM, 12 1/2 Ozs.	15.00
Medicine, Comstock's Vermifuge, Cylindrical, Aqua, 4 In.	12.00
Medicine, Comstock's Vermifuge, OP, Aqua, 3 3/4 X 3/4 In.	14.00
Medicine, Cough & Cold Cure, Chas.A.Barby, N.Y., Rectangular, Aqua, 5 5/8 In.	5.95
Medicine, Cough Cure In Sunken Panel, Square Collar, Bimal, Aqua, 6 1/4 In.	9.95
Medicine, Coventry, Pill, Olive Amber, 2 1/2 In.	50.00
Medicine, Coventry, Pill, Rolled Over Lip, OP, 12 Sided, 2 1/2 In.	60.00
Medicine, Cramer's, Aqua, Sample Size	7.00
Medicine, Cramer's, Sample Size	7.00
Medicine, Cure For The Throat & Lungs, B.H.Bacon, Bimal, Aqua, 6 In.	6.95
Medicine, Cut Glass, Tumbler Insert, Stopper, 8 1/2 In.	350.00
Medicine, Cut Glass, 3 Pint	195.00
Medicine, Cuticura System Of Curing Constitutional Humors, Aqua, 9 1/4 In.	7.00
Medicine, Cuticura System Of Curing Constitutional Humors, Small Size	10.00

Medicine, Colac Pile Pills, Amber, 3 In.

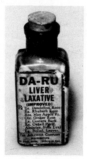

Medicine, Da-Ru Liver Laxative, Amber, 3 In.
(See Page 145)

Medicine, Digestit, 2 1/2 In.
(See Page 145)

Medicine, Dare's Elixir Mentha
Pepsin, 7 1/2 In.
(See Page 145)

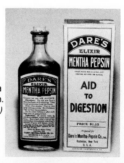

Medicine, Diuretic 1000, Reese Chemical, Green, 6 In.

Medicine, Cylindrical, Cobalt, 12 In.	13.50
Medicine, Cylindrical, Flanged Lip, Deep OP, Deep Aqua, 4 1/2 In.	2.75
Medicine, D.Jayne's Tonic Vermifuge In Sunken Panel, Bimal, Aqua, 5 5/8 In.	1.65
Medicine, Da-Ru Liver Laxative, Amber, 3 In. .... *Illus*	.75
Medicine, Dare's Elixir Mentha Pepsin, 7 1/2 In. .... *Illus*	5.00
Medicine, Davis Vegetable Pain Killer, Aqua, 4 3/4 In.	3.50
Medicine, Davis Vegetable Pain Killer, OP, Aqua, Large Size	20.00
Medicine, Davis Vegetable Pain Killer, OP, Sample, 1 Oz.	22.00
Medicine, DeWitt's Eye Bath, Eyecup, Contents, Box, Brochure	8.50
Medicine, Dean's Barb Wire Remedy, Embossed House & Still, Bimal, 6 1/2 In.	50.00
Medicine, Dean's Barb Wire Remedy, Embossed House & Still, Bimal, 9 1/2 In.	100.00
Medicine, Delights Spanish Lustral, Open Pontil, Aqua, 5 In.	32.00
Medicine, Diabetes Remedy, Remedies Co., Label & Contents, 12 1/2 Ozs.	18.00
Medicine, Digestit, 2 1/2 In. .... *Illus*	.50
Medicine, Diuretic 1000, Reese Chemical, Green, 6 In. .... *Illus*	2.00
Medicine, Doct.Fowler's Anti Epicholic, Canton, N.Y.Aqua, 6 In.High	45.00
Medicine, Doctor C.McLane's American Worm Specific, Aqua, 3 1/2 In.	5.50
Medicine, Donnell's Rheumatic Liniment, Aqua, 6 1/4 In.	2.00
Medicine, Donnell's Rheumatic Liniment, Bimal, Aqua, 6 1/4 In. .... 1.85 To 2.00
Medicine, Donnell's Rheumatic Liniment, Bimal, Boxed, Aqua, 6 1/4 In.	1.85
Medicine, Donnell's Rheumatic Liniment, Contents, Aqua, 6 1/4 In.	1.85
Medicine, Donnell's Rheumatic Liniment, Contents, Bimal, Aqua, 6 1/4 In.	1.85
Medicine, Dr.Agnew's Cure For The Heart, Rectangular, Contents, 9 In.	29.00
Medicine, Dr.August Loenig's Hamburger Tropfen, Aqua, 4 In.	2.00
Medicine, Dr.B.J.Kendall's Quick Relief, Stain, Amethyst, 4 1/2 In.	1.00
Medicine, Dr.Baker's Pain Panacea, Whittled, Aqua, 4 In.	5.00
Medicine, Dr.Bedortha's Blood Purifier, Saratoga Springs, N.Y., Aqua, 9 In.	34.00
Medicine, Dr.Bosanko's Pile Remedy, Aqua, 2 1/2 In.	3.00
Medicine, Dr.Bosanko's Pile Remedy, Phila., Sun Colored Green, 5 1/2 In.	6.00
Medicine, Dr.C.McLane's American Worm Specific, Aqua, 3 1/2 In.	5.50
Medicine, Dr.C.W.Roback's Scandinavian Blood Purifier, Aqua, 7 3/4 In.	60.00
Medicine, Dr.C.W.Roback's Scandinavian Blood Purifier, Aqua, 8 1/2 In.	17.50
Medicine, Dr.Claris Colic Medicine, 7 1/2 In. .... *Illus*	15.00
Medicine, Dr.Coles' Catarrh Cure, Ring Collar, Bimal, Aqua, 2 3/8 In.	7.95
Medicine, Dr.Coles' Catarrh Cure, Ring Collar, Bimal, 2 3/8 In.	7.95

Medicine, Dr.Claris Colic Medicine, 7 1/2 In.

Medicine, Dr.Cumming's Vegetine, Oval, Aqua, 9 1/2 In. .... 3.00 To 6.50
Medicine, Dr.Cumming's Vegetine, Oval, Aqua, 9 3/4 In. 3.95
Medicine, Dr.Cumming's Vegetine, Paper Label, Blue Aqua, 9 1/2 In. 8.00
Medicine, Dr.D.Janye & Co., Boston, Round Bottom, Screw Top, Bimal, 3 1/4 In. 5.00
Medicine, Dr.D.Jayne's Carminative Balsam, Phila., Stain, Aqua, 4 1/2 In. 4.75
Medicine, Dr.D.Jayne's Expectorant, Rectangular, Aqua, 6 In. 2.00
Medicine, Dr.D.Jayne's Tonic Vermifuge, Cork, Aqua, 5 1/2 In. 4.25
Medicine, Dr.Davis Compound Syrup Of Wild Cherry, 8 Panel, Aqua, 6 3/4 In. 23.00
Medicine, Dr.Edwards Tar Of Wild Cherry Cough Syrup, Label, 5 1/4 In. 5.00
Medicine, Dr.Edwards Tar Of Wild Cherry Cough Syrup, 5 1/4 In. 4.00
Medicine, Dr.Evan's Camomile Pills, Square, OP, Cloud On Neck, 3 In. 13.50
Medicine, Dr.Fowler's Anti Epicholic, Canton, N.Y., Aqua, 6 In. 45.00
Medicine, Dr.G.H.Zimmerman's Easy To Take Castor Oil, Pa., Cobalt, 5 In. 10.00
Medicine, Dr.Goerss Chaulmoogra, The East India Cure, Amber, 6 In. 8.00
Medicine, Dr.Greene's Nervura, Blob Lip, 4 Panels, Ice Blue, 9 In. 6.00
Medicine, Dr.H.A.Ingham's Nervine Pain Extract, OP, Aqua, 4 1/2 In. 14.00
Medicine, Dr.H.A.Tucker Diaphoretic Compound, N.Y., Aqua, 5 3/4 In. 6.00
Medicine, Dr.H.G.Dree's Bentheim, Liquor Ferrialbuminati, Amber, 9 1/4 In. 5.00
Medicine, Dr.H.Kelsey, Lowell, Mass., Oval, Aqua, 6 In. 22.00
Medicine, Dr.Hand's General Tonic, 2 Oz. .... Illus   7.00
Medicine, Dr.Hardman's Digestine, 7 In. .... Illus   5.00
Medicine, Dr.Hartshorn's Family, Bull's-Eye, Oval, Aqua, 9 1/2 In. 10.22
Medicine, Dr.Hay's Hair Health, Sunken Panels, Rectangular, Amber, 6 3/4 In. 2.45
Medicine, Dr.Hayne's Arabian Balsam, R.I., 12 Sided, Aqua, 4 In. 2.50
Medicine, Dr.Hayne's Arabian Balsam, R.I., 12 Sided, Aqua 4 1/4 In. 2.75
Medicine, Dr.Hayne's Arabian Balsam, R.I., 12 Sided, 3 1/4 In. 3.00
Medicine, Dr.Hayne's Arabian Balsam, R.I., 12 Sided, 4 1/4 In. .... 2.75 To 3.00
Medicine, Dr.Herrick's German Liniment, 6 1/2 In. .... Illus   4.00
Medicine, Dr.Hobson's Vegetable Prescription .... Illus   4.50
Medicine, Dr.J.Blackman's Genuine Healing Balsam, Open Pontil, 4 1/2 In. 43.50

Medicine, Dr.Hand's
General Tonic, 2 Oz.

Medicine, Dr.Hardman's Digestine, 7 In.

Medicine, Dr.Hobson's Vegetable
Prescription

Medicine, Dr.Herrick's
German Liniment,
6 1/2 In.

Item	Price
Medicine, Dr.J.Clawson Kelley's Vegetable Rob, N.Y., Aqua, Quart	250.00
Medicine, Dr.J.F.Churchill's Specific Remedy For Consumption, Aqua, 9 In.	6.00
Medicine, Dr.J.O.Keller's Family, Ind., Rectangular, Aqua, 6 1/2 In.	8.00
Medicine, Dr.J.Pettit's Canker Balsam, 3 1/8 In.	3.50
Medicine, Dr.James Craigue's Indian Liniment, OP, Label, 1/2 Pint	18.00
Medicine, Dr.Jones' Liniment, Embossed Beaver, 4 Ozs.	5.00
Medicine, Dr.Kennedy's Diarrhea Cordial, Roxbury, Mass., Aqua, 5 1/2 In.	5.00
Medicine, Dr.Kennedy's Medical Discovery, Mass., OP, Aqua, 8 3/4 In.	32.00
Medicine, Dr.Kennedy's Prairie Weed, Rectangular, Aqua, 8 In.	14.00
Medicine, Dr.Kilmer's Cough Cure & Consumption Oil, Aqua, 9 In.	110.00
Medicine, Dr.Kilmer's Cure, 7 In.	4.00
Medicine, Dr.Kilmer's Female Compound, 9 In. ...Color	20.00
Medicine, Dr.Kilmer's Kidney Cure, 3 In.	3.00
Medicine, Dr.Kilmer's Kidney, Liver, & Bladder Cure, Aqua, 7 In.	3.00
Medicine, Dr.Kilmer's Remedy, Bimal, 7 In.	2.00
Medicine, Dr.Kilmer's Swamp Root Kidney Cure, Aqua, Sample Size	3.00
Medicine, Dr.Kilmer's Swamp Root Kidney Cure, Binghamton, N.Y., Sample Size	5.00
Medicine, Dr.Kilmer's Swamp Root Kidney Cure, Sample, Blue Aqua, 3 In.	4.00
Medicine, Dr.Kilmer's Swamp Root Kidney Remedy, Sample Size	5.00
Medicine, Dr.Kilmer's Swamp Root Kidney, Liver, & Bladder Cure, Aqua, 8 In.	6.00
Medicine, Dr.Kilmer's Swamp Root Kidney, Liver, & Bladder Cure, SC, 7 In.	6.00
Medicine, Dr.Kilmer's Swamp Root Kidney, Liver, & Bladder Cure, 8 In.	5.00
Medicine, Dr.Kilmer's, Label, 7 In.	5.00
Medicine, Dr.Kilmer's, Sample Size, 3 In.	2.50
Medicine, Dr.Kilmer's, Sample Size, 4 In.	2.50
Medicine, Dr.Larookah's Vegetable Pulmonic Syrup, Stain, Large Size	25.00
Medicine, Dr.M.M.Fenner's Kidney & Backache Cure, Amber, 11 In.	23.00
Medicine, Dr.M.M.Fenner's Kidney & Backache Remedy, OP, Amber, Large Size	16.00
Medicine, Dr.M.M.Fenner's Kidney & Backache Remedy, OP, Amber, Small Size	13.00
Medicine, Dr.M.M.Fenner's Peoples Remedies, Amber, 10 In.	25.00
Medicine, Dr.M.M.Fenner's Peoples Remedies, Fredonia, N.Y., Amber, 10 In.	20.00
Medicine, Dr.M.M.Fenner's Peoples Remedies, Label, Amber, 11 In.	20.00
Medicine, Dr.M.M.Fenner's, Fredonia, N.Y., Oval, Amber, 5 In.	2.00
Medicine, Dr.MacKenzie's Catarrh Cure, Green, 2 1/2 In.	50.00
Medicine, Dr.McLane's American Worm Specific, Aqua, 3 1/2 In.	4.50
Medicine, Dr.McLane's American Worm Specific, Blue, 3 1/2 In.	6.00
Medicine, Dr.McMunn, Elixir Of Opium, Round, Aqua, 4 1/2 In.	3.75
Medicine, Dr.McMunn, Elixir Of Opium, 4 In. ...Illus	12.00
Medicine, Dr.McMunn, Elixir Of Opium, 4 1/2 In.	12.00
Medicine, Dr.Miles Heart Treatment, 8 1/4 In.	4.00
Medicine, Dr.Miles New Heart Cure, Free Sample	10.00
Medicine, Dr.Miles New Heart Cure, Rectangular, Haze, Aqua, 8 In.	2.75
Medicine, Dr.Miles' Medical Co., Green, 8 1/2 In.	1.50
Medicine, Dr.Miles' Restorative Nervine, Aqua, 4 In.	10.00
Medicine, Dr.Owen's London Horse Liniment, Clarkston, Mich., Deep Aqua	40.00
Medicine, Dr.Peter Fahrney & Sons Forni's Magolo Cough Syrup, 5 1/2 In.	3.50
Medicine, Dr.Peter Fahrney & Sons, Rectangular, ABM, 9 In.	3.00
Medicine, Dr.Peter Fahrney & Sons, 8 3/4 In.	3.50
Medicine, Dr.Pierce's Anuric Tablets For Kidneys, Aqua, 3 1/2 In.	3.00
Medicine, Dr.Pierce's Golden Medical Discovery, 9 In. ...Illus	300.00
Medicine, Dr.Pierce's Smartweed Extract, 5 In.	9.00
Medicine, Dr.Pinkham's Emmenagogue, Aqua, 5 In.	43.50
Medicine, Dr.Pinkham's Emmenagogue, Pontil, Aqua, 6 In. ...Illus	33.00
Medicine, Dr.Pinkham's Emmenagogue, Square, OP, Aqua, 6 In.	35.00
Medicine, Dr.Pinkham's Emmenagogue, Square, OP, Deep Aqua, 6 In.	42.75
Medicine, Dr.Porter's, N.Y., OP, Aqua, 5 In.	20.00
Medicine, Dr.Rose's Tonic Mixture, 6 In. ...Illus	22.00
Medicine, Dr.S.F.Stowe's Ambrosial Nectar, May 22, 1866, Amber, 7 3/4 In.	20.00
Medicine, Dr.S.Hart's Vegetable Compound, Aqua, 7 X 3 1/2 X 2 1/2 In.	23.50
Medicine, Dr.S.S.Fitch, N.Y., Oval, Aqua, 8 In.	4.00
Medicine, Dr.S.S.Fitch, 714 Broadway, N.Y., Oval, Stain, Aqua, 6 In.	2.00
Medicine, Dr.Sawen's Celebrated Oil Liniment, Aqua, 5 1/2 In.	2.00
Medicine, Dr.Schoenfeld, Dusseldorf, Stopper, Milk Glass, 2 3/4 In.	40.00
Medicine, Dr.Seth Arnold's Balsam, Gilman Bros., Boston, Aqua, 3 3/4 In.	4.00
Medicine, Dr.Seth Arnold's Cough Killer, Aqua, 4 3/4 In.	3.50

Medicine, Dr.McMunn, Elixir Of Opium, 4 In.
(See Page 147)

Medicine, Dr.Pierce's Golden Medical Discovery, 9 In.
(See Page 147)

Medicine, Dr.Pinkham's Emmenagogue,
Pontil, Aqua, 6 In.
(See Page 147)

Medicine, Dr.Rose's Tonic Mixture, 6 In.
(See Page 147)

Medicine, Dr.Seth Arnold's Cough Killer, Blob Lip, Aqua, 5 In.	3.50
Medicine, Dr.Seth Arnold's Cough Killer, Blue Aqua, 5 In.	3.00
Medicine, Dr.Shoop's Cough Cure, Rectangular, Aqua, 5 1/2 In.	6.00
Medicine, Dr.Simmon's Liver, Man's Picture, Square, 2 In.	1.00
Medicine, Dr.Slocum's Colt's-Foot Expectorant, Aqua, 6 1/4 In.	4.00
Medicine, Dr.Swayne's Panacea, Round, 8 In.	15.00
Medicine, Dr.Thompson's Eye Water, New London, Conn., ABM, 3 3/4 In.	.25
Medicine, Dr.Townsend's Aromatic Hollands Tonic, Amber, 9 In.	220.00
Medicine, Dr.W.B.Caldwell's Syrup Pepsin, Green, 7 In.	2.75
Medicine, Dr.W.B.Caldwell's, see also Medicine, Caldwell's	
Medicine, Dr.Weaver's Canker Syrup, IP, 9 1/4 In.	50.00
Medicine, Dr.Wilson's British Cough Balsam, Square, Aqua, 5 1/4 In.	10.00
Medicine, Dr.Wistar's Balsam Of Wild Cherry, Aqua, 6 1/2 In.	15.00
Medicine, Dr.Wistar's Balsam Of Wild Cherry, Blob Lip, Ice Blue, 6 1/4 In.	9.00
Medicine, Dr.Wistar's Balsam Of Wild Cherry, Miniature	4.00
Medicine, Dr.Wistar's Balsam Of Wild Cherry, Sample, 1 Oz.	10.00
Medicine, Dr.Wistar's Balsam Of Wild Cherry, Sample, 2 Ozs.	8.00
Medicine, Dr.Wistar's Balsam Of Wild Cherry, 8 Sided, Aqua, 4 In.	3.50
Medicine, Dr.Wistar's Balsam Of Wild Cherry, 8 Sided, Aqua, 5 In.	6.50
Medicine, Dr.Wistar's Balsam Of Wild Cherry, 12 Sided, Aqua, 3 1/2 In.	4.50
Medicine, Dr.Wood's Aromatic Spirit, Bellows Falls, Vt., IP, Aqua, 8 In.	55.00
Medicine, Dunbar Cordial Schnapps, Square, Applied Lip, Green, 8 In.	35.00
Medicine, E.A.Buckhout, Dutch Liniment, Pontil, 7 In.	*Color* XXXX.XX
Medicine, E.Querus Cod Liver Oil Jelly, Test Tube Shape, Whittled, 6 In.	150.00

Medicine, Elixir Alimentaire, Ducro A Paris, Aqua, 8 In. 5.00
Medicine, Elixir De Gullie, Seal, String Lip, Dug, Olive Amber, Miniature 85.00
Medicine, Elliman's Royal Embrocation For Horses 15.00
Medicine, Ely's Cream Balm For Hayfever, Catarrh, N.Y., Amber, 2 1/2 In. 2.00
Medicine, Ely's Cream Balm, Honey Amber, 2 1/2 In. 3.00
Medicine, Embossed Anchors, 4 Roofed Panels, Square, Amber, 10 1/2 In. 90.00
Medicine, Epilecticide, Stain, Amber, 8 In. 5.00
Medicine, F.A.Richter & Co. Pain Expeller, Rectangular, Aqua, 6 In. 5.00
Medicine, Fahnestock's Vermifuge, Cylinder, Light Blue, 3 7/8 In. 15.00
Medicine, Fahnestock's Vermifuge, Cylindrical, Aqua, 4 In. 12.00
Medicine, Fahrney's Panacea, Aqua, 9 1/2 In. 12.00
    Medicine, Fahrney's, see also Medicine, Dr.Peter Fahrney
Medicine, Felix Kruse's Fluid Magnesia, Rectangular, Aqua, 7 1/2 In. 18.00
    Medicine, Fenner's, see Dr.M.M.Fenner's
Medicine, Fink's Magic Oil, 25 Cents, Pa., Rectangular, Aqua, 4 In. 4.00
Medicine, Flagg's Good Samaritan Immediate Relief, OP, Aqua, 6 1/2 In. 110.00
Medicine, Flagg's Good Samaritan Immediate Relief, 5 Sided, Aqua, 3 1/2 In. 60.00
Medicine, Flared Lip, Ground Stopper, Oval Shoulders, OP, Amber, 8 1/4 In. 8.00
Medicine, Fleming's, 3 3/4 In. ....*Illus* 1.00
Medicine, Fletcher's Vege-Tonic, Amber, 8 1/2 In. 15.00
Medicine, Fluid Magnesia Prepared By S.O.Dunbar, Mass., OP, Aqua, 7 In. 30.00

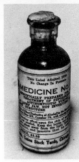

Medicine, Fleming's, 3 3/4 In.

Medicine, Georgian Catarrh Cure, 2 1/4 In.

Medicine, Foley's Cream, Chicago, Square, Bimal, Amethyst, 4 In. .... .75
Medicine, Foley's Honey & Tar, Chicago, Blue Aqua, 5 1/4 In. 3.50
Medicine, Foley's Kidney & Bladder Cure, Contents, Amber, 9 1/2 In. 12.00
Medicine, Foley's Kidney & Bladder Cure, 6 3/8 In. 5.00
Medicine, Four Fold Liver Tonic, Simmons Co., Rectangular, Label, 8 In. 3.50
Medicine, Free-Blown, Cylinder, Short Neck, Wide Mouth, Olive Green, Quart 30.00
Medicine, Free-Blown, Flared Lip, Stopper, OP, Honey Amber, 8 1/4 In. 9.00
Medicine, Drey's Vermifuge, Baltimore, Square, Aqua, 4 1/2 In. 16.00
    Medicine, Friedenwald's, see Medicine, Buchu Gin
Medicine, Fruitcura Woman's Tonic, Madame M.Vale, Blob Lip, Ring, 8 1/2 In. 8.00
Medicine, Gargling Oil, Lockport N.Y., Emerald Green, 5 In. 6.50
Medicine, Gargling Oil, Lockport, N.Y., Green, 5 1/2 In. 10.00
Medicine, Gargling Oil, Lockport, N.Y., Haze, 2 1/4 X 1 1/2 In. 16.00
Medicine, Gargling Oil, Lockport, N.Y., Rectangular, Emerald Green, 7 1/2 In. 20.00
Medicine, Gargling Oil, Lockport, N.Y., Teal Blue, 5 1/2 In. .... 6.00 To 10.50
Medicine, Gargling Oil, Lockport, N.Y., 7 1/2 In. 22.00
Medicine, Genuine Essence, Rectangular, OP, Aqua, 4 1/4 In. 15.00
Medicine, Georgian Catarrh Cure, 2 1/4 In. ....*Illus* 12.00

Medicine, Gibson's Lemon Tablets, E.C.Rich, N.Y., ABM, Aqua, 13 In. 12.00
  Medicine, Gin, see Gin
Medicine, Glover's Imperial Distemper Cure, Amber, 5 In. 5.00
Medicine, Glover's Imperial Mange Cure, Amber, 7 In. .... 4.50 To 5.00
Medicine, Glyco Thymoline, 5 In. 2.00
Medicine, Gold Dandruff Cure, Rectangular, Bimal, 7 1/2 In. 10.95
Medicine, Goodwin's Grand Grease Juice Quintessence Of Fat, 6 1/4 In. 35.00
Medicine, Granitonic, Hair & Scalp Food, Rectangular, Long Neck, Stain, 5 In. 8.00
Medicine, Granitonic, Hair Food, 12 Sided, Cylindrical, Stain, 3 In. 8.00
Medicine, Great American Specific, Bimal, Free Sample, Aqua, 3 In. 9.00
Medicine, Great Indian Mo-Ka-Wa Stomach Treatment, Label, 8 In. 14.00
Medicine, Grove's Tasteless Chill Tonic, 5 3/4 In. 2.75
  Medicine, H.H.Warner's, see Medicine, Warner's
Medicine, H.N.Down's Vegetable Balsamic Elixir, 8 Sided, Aqua, 4 1/2 In. 5.00
Medicine, H.T.Helmbold Genuine Fluid Extracts, Rectangular, Aqua, 6 1/2 In. 16.00
Medicine, Hagan's Magnolia Balm, Oval Shoulders, Ring Lip, Milk Glass, 5 In. 11.00
Medicine, Hagan's Magnolia Balm, Rectangular, Milk Glass, 5 1/8 In. 7.95
Medicine, Hagan's Magnolia Balm, Rectangular, Milk Glass, 5 1/4 In. 9.00
Medicine, Hagan's Magnolia Balm, Rectangular, Milk Glass, 5 1/2 In. 8.95
Medicine, Hagee's Cordial Cod Liver Oil Compound, 8 In. 2.00
Medicine, Hall's Catarrh Cure, Bimal, Ice Blue, 4 1/2 In. 3.50
Medicine, Hall's Catarrh Cure, Bimal, 4 1/2 In. 1.99
Medicine, Hall's Catarrh Cure, Cylindrical, Aqua, 4 1/2 In. 2.00
Medicine, Hansi's Cough Remedy, Rectangular, Cork, Aqua, 6 3/4 In.High 3.00
Medicine, Harper's Brain Food, Washington, D.C., Rectangular, Aqua, 5 In. 3.90
Medicine, Harper's Cephaicine For Headache, Rectangular, Aqua, 5 In. 1.90
Medicine, Hay's Hair Health, Bimal, Amber, 6 3/4 In. 2.35
Medicine, Hay's Hair Health, Golden Amber, 6 1/2 In. 4.00
Medicine, Haywood's Balm Of Savannah, Dandruff, Oval, Aqua, 6 In. 40.00
Medicine, Haywood's Balm Of Savannah, Dandruff, Oval, Aqua, 8 In. 40.00
Medicine, Haywood's Balm Of Savannah, Dandruff, Rectangular, Aqua, 8 In. 35.00
Medicine, Healy & Bigelow Indian Sagwa, Embossed, Aqua, 8 1/2 In. 6.00
Medicine, Healy & Bigelow Kickapoo Indian Oil, Blob Lip, Aqua, 3 In. 11.00
Medicine, Healy & Bigelow Kickapoo Oil, Aqua, 5 1/2 In. 3.00
Medicine, Hemoquinine, Scheffelin & Co., N.Y., Bimal, Amber, 8 In. 6.00
Medicine, Henry, Johnson & Lord, Burlington, Vt., Aqua, 7 1/4 In. 4.95
Medicine, Henry's Calcined Magnesia, Manchester, Square, Haze, 4 In. 7.00
Medicine, Henry's Calcined Magnesia, Manchester, Square, OP, 4 1/2 In. 8.00
Medicine, Hicks' Capudine For Headaches, Miniature 4.00
Medicine, Higby & Stearns, Rectangular, Sun Colored Amethyst, 5 1/2 In. 3.75
Medicine, Hollis' Balm Of America, Lip Ring, Roof Shoulder, Blue, 5 In. 6.50
Medicine, Hollis' Balm Of America, Rolled Lip, Roof Shoulder, Aqua, 5 In. 6.00
Medicine, Hollis' Balm Of America, Rolled Lip, Roof Shoulder, Blue, 5 In. 6.00
Medicine, Hollis' Balm Of America, Vertically Embossed, Bimal, Aqua, 5 In. 6.00
Medicine, Honnewell's Tulu Anodyne, Boston, Mass., Aqua, 4 In. 4.50
Medicine, Hood's Blood & Nerve Tonic, 9 In. 12.00
Medicine, Hood's Pills Cure Liver Ills, Aqua, 2 In. 10.00
Medicine, Hood's Pills, Dose 2 To 6, Aqua, Miniature 2.50
Medicine, Hopkins' Chalybeate, Baltimore, Green, Pint 45.00
Medicine, Hopkins' Chalybeate, Baltimore, 7 1/2 In. ....Color XXXX.XX
Medicine, Household Panacea & Family Liniment, Bimal, Aqua, 5 1/8 In. 2.25
Medicine, Humphrey's Homeopathic Veterinary Specifics, Bimal, 3 1/2 In. 5.00
Medicine, Hunt's Liniment, G.E.Stanton, N.Y., Deep Aqua, 4 1/2 In. 22.00
Medicine, Hunt's Liniment, G.E.Stanton, N.Y., Paneled, Oval, Aqua, 4 1/2 In. 18.00
Medicine, Hunt's Remedy, Providence, R.I., Arched Panel, 7 In. 5.00
Medicine, Hyatt's Infallible Life Balsam, Concave Panels, Green, 9 3/4 In. 9.00
Medicine, Hyatt's Infallible Life Balsam, N.Y., Aqua, 9 1/2 In. 12.00
Medicine, Hyposulph, Part Label, Whittled, Pontil, Aqua, Pound 10.00
Medicine, Indian Sagwa, Embossed Indian's Head, Aqua, 8 1/2 In. 15.00
  Medicine, Indian Sagwa, see also Medicine, Healy & Bigelow
Medicine, Instant Cough Cure, Mt.Morris, N.Y., Rectangular, Aqua, 7 In. 6.95
Medicine, J.B.Wheatley's Compound Syrup, Dallasburgh, Ky., Aqua, 6 In. 52.00
Medicine, J.B.Wilder & Co., Louisville, Rectangular, Aqua, 6 1/2 In. 35.00
Medicine, J.R.Nichols & Co., Boston, Round, Three Mold, Grass Green, 7 In. 10.50
Medicine, J.W.Bull's Cough Syrup, Baltimore, Aqua, 5 1/2 In. 4.00

Medicine, J.W.Bull's Cough Syrup, Bimal, Ice Blue, 5 1/2 In. 6.00
Medicine, John C.Baker Cod Liver Oil, Oval, Aqua, 9 1/2 In. 10.00
Medicine, Johnson & Johnson Aseptic Products Co., Amber, 4 1/2 In. 9.00
Medicine, Johnson & Johnson Gauze, Embossed, Label, Amber, 4 1/2 In. 10.00
Medicine, Johnson's American Anodyne, Round, Aqua, 4 1/4 In. 12.00
Medicine, KKK Cures Brights Disease & Cystitis, Rectangular, 7 In. 17.00
Medicine, Kargon Compound, 3 1/2 In. .... Illus .50
Medicine, Kathairon For The Hair, OP, 6 In. 17.00
Medicine, Katonka Great Indian Remedy, Aqua, 8 In. 6.50
Medicine, Keeley's Gold Cure For Drunkenness 60.00
Medicine, Keene Type, Flange Lip, Pontil, Dark Olive Green, 4 1/2 In. 35.00
Medicine, Kemp's Balsam For Throat & Lungs, Aqua, 5 1/4 In. 1.50
Medicine, Kemp's Balsam, Labeled Sample, Bimal, 2 3/4 In. 3.00
Medicine, Kemp's Balsam, Sample, 3 In. .... .50
Medicine, Kemp's Cough Balsam, Sample Size 5.00
Medicine, Kendall's Spavin Cure For Human Flesh, 10 Panels, Aqua, 5 1/4 In. 5.00
Medicine, Kendall's Spavin Cure, Cover & Closure, Amber, 1/2 Pint 6.00
Medicine, Kendall's Spavin Cure, Vt., 12 Panels, Amber, 5 In. 4.00
Medicine, Kendall's Spavin Cure, Vt., 12 Panels, Amber, 5 1/2 In. 3.95
Medicine, Kendall's Spavin Cure, 5 1/4 In. .... Illus 2.00
Medicine, Kendall's Spavin Cure, 12 Sided, Honey Amber, 5 3/4 In. 6.00
Medicine, Kickapoo Oil, C.I.Hood Co., 5 1/2 In. .... Illus 7.00

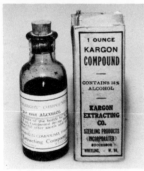

Medicine, Kargon Compound,
3 1/2 In.

Medicine, Kickapoo Oil,
C.I.Hood Co., 5 1/2 In.

Medicine, Kendall's Spavin Cure, 5 1/4 In.

Medicine, Kickapoo Oil, see also Medicine, Healy & Bigelow
Medicine, Kidney & Liver Remedy, Light Olive Green, 16 Ozs. 75.00
Medicine, Kitchel's Wind Puff Cure, Oval, Aqua, Sample Size 19.00
Medicine, Kodol Dyspepsia Cure, Small Size 6.00
Medicine, La Grande's Arabian Catarrh Remedy, N.Y., Oval, Aqua, 9 In. 6.00
Medicine, La Grande's Arabian Catarrh Remedy, Oval, Aqua, Sample Size 4.00
Medicine, Lactopeptine For All Digestive Ailments, Emerald Green, 2 In. 9.00
Medicine, Lactopeptine, Embossed, 3 Sunk Panels, Cobalt Blue, 7 3/4 In. 25.00
Medicine, Lawrence's, W.F., Genuine Preparation, N.H., OP, Aqua, 5 1/2 In. 15.00
Medicine, Laxol, A.J.White, N.Y., Indented Panels, Cobalt, 7 In. 7.00
Medicine, Laxol, Cobalt 8.00
Medicine, Laxol, Green 15.00
Medicine, Laxol, Olive Green 20.00
Medicine, Laxol, Teal Green 15.00
Medicine, Lightning Hot Drops, Aquamarine Blue, 5 1/2 In. 4.00
Medicine, Lightning Hot Drops, Blue, 4 3/4 In. 3.50

Medicine, **Lindsey's Blood Searcher,** Embossed, Paneled, Blue Aqua, 9 In. 40.00
Medicine, **Lindsey's Blood Searcher,** Rectangular, Light Green, 8 1/2 In. 33.75
Medicine, **Linonine,** Kerr's Flax-Seed Emulsion, 9 In. .... *Illus* 3.00
Medicine, **Liquid Opodeldoc,** Cylindrical, OP, Aqua, 4 3/4 In. 15.00
Medicine, **Liquid Opodeldoc,** Cylindrical, OP, 4 1/2 In. 20.00
Medicine, **Log Cabin Cough & Consumption Remedy,** Amber, Small Size 95.00
Medicine, **Log Cabin Cough & Consumption Remedy,** Dark Amber, 6 3/4 In. 97.00
Medicine, **Log Cabin Cough & Consumption Remedy,** Label, OP, Small Size 100.00
Medicine, **Log Cabin Extract,** Rochester, N.Y., Amber, Small Size 59.00
Medicine, **Long's Tar Honey,** Chlorinated, Rectangular, Aqua, 6 3/4 In. 2.00
Medicine, **Lovell's Pain Killing Magic Compound,** Aqua, 5 In. 4.00
Medicine, **Lucky Tiger For Dandruff,** 7 1/2 In. .... *Illus* 25.00
Medicine, **Lydia E.Pinkham's Vegetable Compound,** Blue, 8 1/2 In. 4.00
Medicine, **Lydia E.Pinkham's,** Aquamarine Blue, 8 1/2 In. 4.00
Medicine, **Lydia Pinkham's Vegetable Compound,** 8 1/2 In. 3.00

Medicine, Lucky Tiger For Dandruff, 7 1/2 In.

Medicine, Linonine, Kerr's Flax-Seed Emulsion, 9 In.

Medicine, **Lydia Pinkham's,** Embossed, 14 1/2 Ozs. 3.00
Medicine, **Lyon's Drops,** 5 In. .... *Illus* 1.50
Medicine, **Lyon's Kathairon For The Hair,** N.Y., Double Collar, Aqua, 6 In. 20.00
Medicine, **Lyon's Kathairon For The Hair,** Rectangular, Aqua, 6 1/2 In. 3.50
Medicine, **Lyon's Powder,** B.& P., N.Y., OP, Puce, 4 1/4 In. 130.00
Medicine, **Lyon's Powder,** OP, Puce 84.00
Medicine, **Mackenzie's Tonic Febrifuge,** Cleveland, OP, Aqua, 7 In. 35.00
Medicine, **Maslobralia,** Rectangular, Pontil, Haze, 5 1/2 In. 45.00
Medicine, **Maxi Nerve Food,** Cylindrical, Stain, Aqua, Quart 7.50
Medicine, **Medical Smith's Wonder Worker,** Tiffin, O., Amber, Pint 10.00
Medicine, **Mexican Hair Renewer,** Whiskey Flask Shape, Cobalt, 7 1/8 In. 45.00
Medicine, **Mexican Mustang Liniment,** D.S.Barnes, N.Y., Cylindrical, 4 In. 9.00
Medicine, **Milk's Emulsion,** Bimal, Amber, Large Size 3.00
Medicine, **Milk's Emulsion,** Bimal, Amber, Small Size 2.00
Medicine, **Miller's Genuine Arabian Balsam,** R.I., 12 Sided, Aqua, 4 1/4 In. 2.75
Medicine, **Mitchell's Eye Salve,** Pale Aqua, 1 7/8 In.High 17.00
Medicine, **Mixer's Cancer & Scrotula,** Embossed, Label, Contents, 8 In. 45.00
Medicine, **Moone's Emerald Oil,** 5 In. .... *Illus* 4.00
Medicine, **Morse's Indian Root Pills,** Rectangular, Amber, 2 1/2 In. 3.00
Medicine, **Mother's Worm Syrup,** Wilder & Co., 5 Story Building, 4 1/2 In. 16.50
Medicine, **Moxie Nerve Food,** Quart, 10 In. 8.00
Medicine, **Mrs.Bush Specific Cure For Burns & Scalds,** Aqua, 6 In. 6.50
Medicine, **Mrs.Dinsmore's Cough & Croup Balsam,** Aqua, 6 In. 5.50
Medicine, **Mrs.Winslow's Cough Remedy,** Aqua, 6 1/2 In. 5.00
Medicine, **Mrs.Winslow's Soothing Syrup,** Aqua, 5 In. 3.00
Medicine, **Mrs.Winslow's Soothing Syrup,** Curtis & Perkins, Aqua, 5 In. 12.00
Medicine, **Mrs.Winslow's Soothing Syrup,** Cylindrical, OP, 5 In. 18.00

Medicine, Mrs.Winslow's Soothing Syrup, Cylindrical, Aqua, 5 In.	1.00
Medicine, Mrs.Winslow's Soothing Syrup, Round, Aqua, 5 In.	7.00
Medicine, Mrs.Winslow's Syrup, Anglo American Drug Co., Aqua, 5 In.	8.00
Medicine, Mulford's Laxative Salts Of Fruit, Cylindrical, Cobalt, 3 In.	5.00
Medicine, Mull's Grape Tonic, Rock Island, Ill., Rectangular, 7 1/2 In.	25.00
Medicine, Musterole, Cleveland, Embossed, Milk Glass	2.00
Medicine, N.L.Clark, Peruvian Syrup, Sunken Panels, Blob Lip, Aqua, 8 1/4 In.	9.00
Medicine, National Remedy Co., N.Y., Aqua, 5 1/2 In.	2.00
Medicine, National Remedy Co., N.Y., Blue, 5 1/4 In.	2.50
Medicine, Nerve & Bone Liniment, Cylindrical, Pontil, Stain, Aqua, 4 In.	9.75
Medicine, Newbro's Herpicide For The Scalp, 4 Oz.	6.00
Medicine, OGR 1900 On Bottom, Screw Top, Zinc Cap, Ice Blue, 3 1/4 In.	4.00
Medicine, Ocean-O, Cobalt, 7 In. *Illus*	3.00
Medicine, Old Indian Liver & Kidney Tonic, Label, Blue Aqua, 8 In.	15.00
Medicine, Oldridge's Balm Of Columbia For Hair, Stain, Aqua, 5 In.	60.00
Medicine, One Minute Cough Cure, Rectangular, Aqua, 4 1/4 In.	3.00 To 3.50
Medicine, One Minute Cough Cure, Rectangular, Aqua, 5 1/2 In.	3.00 To 3.50
Medicine, Opium, 3 Mold, OP, Aqua, 6 1/2 In.	6.00

Medicine, Lyon's Drops, 5 In.
(See Page 152)

Medicine, Ocean-O, Cobalt, 7 In.

Medicine, Moone's Emerald Oil, 5 In.
(See Page 152)

Medicine, Opodeldoc Liquid, Round, Aqua, 4 1/2 In.	8.00
Medicine, Oriental, Tear Shape, Label & Contents, 1 1/2 In.	7.50
Medicine, Oval, Whittled, OP, Aqua, 8 In.	15.00
Medicine, Owl, Rectangular, Milk Glass, 5 In.	28.00
Medicine, Oxien Pills, Augusta, Me., Witch Doctor Front, 1 1/2 In.	10.00
Medicine, Paine's Celery Compound, Amber *Illus*	12.00
Medicine, Paine's Celery Compound, Amber, 9 1/2 In.	6.00
Medicine, Paine's Celery Compound, Aqua, 9 In.	15.00
Medicine, Paine's Celery Compound, Aqua, 10 In.	4.00
Medicine, Paine's Celery Compound, Square, Deep Amber, 10 In.	18.00 To 25.00
Medicine, Parker's Ginger Tonic, Amber, 7 1/2 In.	8.00
Medicine, Parker's Hair Balsam, Amber, 7 In.	4.00
Medicine, Parmacia D.Alga Rudak Fime, Aqua, 6 1/4 In.	5.00
Medicine, Pawnee Too-Re, Stomach, Liver & Kidney, Label, Amber, 8 1/4 In.	60.00
Medicine, Peptenzyme, Reed & Carnrick, N.Y., Cobalt, 2 1/4 In.	15.00
Medicine, Peptenzyme, Reed & Carnrick, N.Y., Cobalt, 3 1/8 In.	2.50
Medicine, Peptenzyme, Reed & Carnrick, N.Y., Cobalt, 4 1/2 In.	3.00
Medicine, Peptenzyme, Reed & Carnrick, N.Y., Ground Lip, Cobalt, 2 1/2 In.	9.00
Medicine, Peptenzyme, Reed & Carnrick, N.Y., Threads, Cobalt, 2 1/4 In.	6.00
Medicine, Peruna Cure All, Applied Top, Label, 9 1/2 In.	8.50

Medicine, Paine's Celery Compound, Amber
(See Page 153)

Medicine, Radam's Microbe Killer, Brown, 6 1/2 In.
(See Page 155)

Medicine, Phillips' Phospho-Muriate Of
Quinine, 8 In

Medicine, Peruvian Bark Elixir, Cone Lip, Rectangular, Aqua, 10 1/4 In.	12.50
Medicine, Peruvian Syrup, N.L.Clark & Co., Rectangular, Aqua, 8 1/2 In.	4.00
Medicine, Pestieruxs Pill, Rolled Lip, 1 3/4 In.	1.50
Medicine, Phillips' Emulsion Cod Liver Oil, Rectangular, Amber, 9 In.	7.50
Medicine, Phillips' Magnesia, Cork, Dug, ABM, Cobalt, 7 In.	4.00
Medicine, Phillips' Magnesia, Embossed, Stain, Cobalt, 3 1/2 In.	3.00
Medicine, Phillips' Magnesia, Embossed, Stain, Cobalt, 7 In.	2.50
Medicine, Phillips' Phospho-Muriate Of Quinine, 8 In. .... *Illus*	5.00
Medicine, Pill, Stopper, Canary Yellow, 3 3/4 In.	80.00
Medicine, Pill, Wooden Turned, 2 X 3/4 In.	1.50
Medicine, Pills Cure Liver Ills, Oval, Bimal, 1 3/4 In.	5.95
Medicine, Pine Tree Tar Cordial, see Medicine, Wishart's	
Medicine, Piso's Cure For Consumption, Aqua, 5 In.	4.00 To 4.50
Medicine, Piso's Cure For Consumption, Bimal, Aqua, 5 1/4 In.	2.95
Medicine, Piso's Cure For Consumption, Hazeltine & Co., Green, 5 1/4 In.	4.00
Medicine, Piso's Cure For Consumption, Olive Green, 5 In.	6.00
Medicine, Piso's Cure For Consumption, Yellow Olive Green, 5 In.	6.00
Medicine, Polar Star Cough Cure With Star, Bimal, Sample, 3 7/8 In.	4.95
Medicine, Polar Star Cough Cure, Bimal, Aqua, Large Size	3.00
Medicine, Polar Star Cough Cure, Bimal, Aqua, Small Size	2.00
Medicine, Polar Star Cough Cure, 4 In.	2.50
Medicine, Pond's Extract, 1846, Aqua, Quart	6.00
Medicine, Pond's Ginger Gin, Aqua	6.00
Medicine, Porter's Pain King, Blob Top, Bimal, Dug, Stain, 7 3/4 In.	3.00
Medicine, Porter's Pain King, 6 1/2 In.	2.50
Medicine, Pratt & Butcher Magic Oil, Brooklyn, N.Y., Flask, Aqua, 4 In.	22.00
Medicine, Pratt's Distemper & Pinkeye Cure, Amber, 6 1/2 In.	6.50
Medicine, Primley's Iron & Wahoo Tonic, Ind., Square, Amber, 9 In.	15.00
Medicine, Professor DeGrath's Electric Oil, Phila., OP, Aqua, 2 In.	12.00
Medicine, Professor Dean's King Cactus Oil, 6 1/2 In.	80.00
Medicine, Professor Dean's King Cactus Oil, 9 1/2 In.	85.00
Medicine, Psychine For Consumption & Lung Troubles, Aqua, 9 1/2 In.	20.00
Medicine, Pumley's Iron & Wahoo Tonic, Square, Amber, 9 In.	15.00
Medicine, Pure Family Nectar, Rectangular Paneled, 9 In.	70.00

Medicine, Purifier, Oval, Aqua, 9 In. 12.00
Medicine, R.E.Stieraux's Pills, Round Bottom, Bimal, 1 3/4 In. .... .65
Medicine, Radam's Microbe Cure, Jug, Amber, Gallon 20.00
Medicine, Radam's Microbe Killer No.1, Porcelain, Jug, White Gallon 20.00
Medicine, Radam's Microbe Killer, Brown, 6 1/2 In. .... *Illus* 300.00
Medicine, Radam's Microbe Killer, Square, Amber, 10 In. 68.00
Medicine, Remedies Co., ABM, 6 Oz. 10.00
Medicine, Remedies Co., 60 Percent Label & Contents, 12 1/2 Ozs. 15.00
Medicine, Rennie's Magic Oil, Slogan Bottle, Stain, Sample Size 12.00
Medicine, Rev.N.H.Downe's Vegetable Balsamic Elixir, Aqua, 4 1/2 In. 2.00
Medicine, Rhodes' Fever & Ague Cure, 9 In. .... *Illus* 30.00

Medicine, Rhodes' Fever & Ague Cure, 9 In.

Medicine, Rub-My-Tism, Clear

Medicine, Richter & Co. Pain Expeller For Rheumatism, Gout, Ice Blue, 5 In. 7.00
Medicine, Robt.E.Seller's Vermifuge, Cylindrical, Aqua, 4 1/4 In. 20.00
Medicine, Robt.E.Seller's Vermifuge, Stain, Aqua, 4 3/8 In. 5.00
Medicine, Rock's Cough & Cold Cure, Chas.A.Darby, N.Y., Aqua, 5 5/8 In. 5.95
Medicine, Rock's Cough & Cold Cure, Chas.A.Darby, N.Y., 5 5/8 In. 9.95
Medicine, Rock's Cough & Cold Cure, 5 1/2 In. 7.00
Medicine, Rohrer's Expectoral Wild Cherry Tonic, Golden Amber, 10 1/2 In. 150.00
Medicine, Rohrer's Expectoral Wild Cherry Tonic, IP, Amber, 10 1/2 In. 125.00
Medicine, Rosewood Dandruff Cure, J.R.Reeves Co., Stain, Amethyst, 6 1/2 In. 8.95
Medicine, Royal Pepsin Tonic, 7 1/2 In. 75.00
Medicine, Rub-My-Tism, Clear .... *Illus* 8.00
Medicine, Rupturine, Cures Rupture, Hernia Cure Co., 8 Sided, 6 In. 10.00
Medicine, Rushton Clark & Co., N.Y., Cod Liver Oil, Rectangular, Aqua, 10 In. 35.00
Medicine, Rushton Clark & Co., N.Y., Cod Liver Oil, Rectangular, OP, 10 1/4 In. 35.00
Medicine, Rushton's Cod Liver Oil, N.Y., Rectangular, Aqua, 10 In. 12.00
Medicine, S.A.Chevalier's Life For The Hair, 1/2 Pint 12.00
Medicine, S.A.Richmond Samaritan Nervine, Embossed Bearded Man, 8 In. 6.75
Medicine, Sanford's Extract Of Hamamelis, Cobalt, 11 1/2 In. 105.00
Medicine, Sanford's Ginger Genuine, 1876, Rectangular, Aqua, 6 5/8 In. 3.75
Medicine, Sanford's Radical Cure, Rectangular, Cobalt, 7 1/2 In. 20.00
Medicine, Sanitol For The Teeth, 8 Sided, Milk Glass, 5 In. 10.00
Medicine, Sauer's Liniment, Paper Label, Round, Contents, 5 1/4 In.High 2.00
Medicine, Save The Horse Spavin Cure, Aqua, 6 1/2 In. 10.00
Medicine, Schenck's Pulmonic Syrup, Phila., 8 Sided, Aqua, Small Size 8.00
Medicine, Schenck's Seaweed Tonic, Square, Aqua, 8 1/2 In. 10.00
Medicine, Schenck's Seaweed Tonic, 7 In. 8.00
Medicine, Scott's Emulsion, Aqua, 9 In. 1.00
Medicine, Scott's Emulsion, Fisherman, Light Aqua, 9 1/4 In. 3.50

Medicine, Seng, Sultan Drug Co.,
Amber, 7 In.

Medicine, Shaker Syrup
No.1, Canterbury, N.H.,
Aqua, 8 In.

Medicine, Shiloh For Coughs,
S.C.Wells & Co., 4 1/2 In.

Medicine, Siegel Curative Syrup, 5 In.

Medicine, Sit-I-Cide, 5 In.

Medicine, Scott's Emulsion, Sample Size, 3 In.		3.00
Medicine, Seng, Sultan Drug Co., Amber, 7 In.	*Illus*	5.00
Medicine, Shaker Digestive Cordial, J.White, Rectangular, Aqua, 5 3/4 In.		3.00
Medicine, Shaker Digestive Cordial, J.White, Rectangular, Aqua, 6 7/8 In.		3.00
Medicine, Shaker Digestive Cordial, 11 In.		25.00
Medicine, Shaker Fluid, Square, Aqua, 3 3/4 In.		8.00
Medicine, Shaker Syrup No.1, Canterbury, N.H., Aqua, 8 In	*Illus*	135.00
Medicine, Sharp & Dohme, Labeled, Boxed, Cobalt, 3 3/4 In.		12.50
Medicine, Shiloh For Coughs, S.C.Wells & Co., 4 1/2 In.	*Illus*	150.00
Medicine, Shiloh's Consumption Cure, 5 1/2 In.		3.25
Medicine, Shirley Universal Renovator, OP, Aqua		35.00
Medicine, Siegel Curative Syrup, 5 In.	*Illus*	16.00
Medicine, Sims' Tonic Elixir Of Pyrophosphate Of Iron, N.Y., Amber, 7 In.		8.75
Medicine, Sit-I-Cide, 5 In.	*Illus*	1.00
Medicine, Sloan's Liniment For Man Or Beast, Stain, Aqua, 9 1/2 In.		15.00
Medicine, Sloan's Liniment, 6 1/4 In.		2.50
Medicine, Sloan's Ointment, Square, Aqua, 2 1/2 In.		13.50
Medicine, Smelling Salts, Cut Glass, Cane, Tiffany Sterling Screw Cap, 7 In.		37.50
Medicine, Smelling Salts, Emerald Green, 3 In.		35.00
Medicine, Smith's Green Mountain Renovator, Dose Glass, 2 In.		8.00
Medicine, Smith's Potassium Compound, 4 1/2 In.	*Illus*	1.00

Figural, Washington, screw top, 4 in. $12

Whiskey, Old Dexter Distilling Co., Butler, Ky., Aug. 1891, 7½ in. $62.50

Ink, milk glass, hand, 4¼ in.
Ink, milk glass, flowers, 2¾ in.

Bitters, pineapple, 9 in. $250

Sarsaparilla, Wynkoop's Atharismichonduras, New York, pontil, 10 in.

Whiskey, A Merry Christmas
and A Happy New Year, John
Schuldt, 1½ in. $35

Ink, E. S. Curtis, War-
ranted Superior, Blue
Black, 8 in.

Ink, Carter's, Pen-
craft, Office &
Fountain Pen Ink,
2-K No. 1, 10½ in.
$10

Wine, face un-
der glass, 14 in.
$250

Whiskey, Paul Jones Pure
Rye, 9½ in. $15

Pottery, Lotus Club Hand Made Sour Mash, 8 in. $32

Pottery, T. Kerr & Co., Buffalo, N.Y., 8 in. $37

Barber, enameled daisies, 6½ in. $100

Soda, Cedar Point Pleasure Resort, 5½ in.
Soda, Cedar Point Pleasure Resort, 7 in. $70

Figural, Suffolk Bitters, Philbrook & Tucker, Boston, 10 in. $750

Bitters, Kelly's Old Cabin, Pat. 1863, 9 in. $595

Figural, ear of corn, 10½ in.

Seltzer, Dr. Pepper, 12½ in. $15

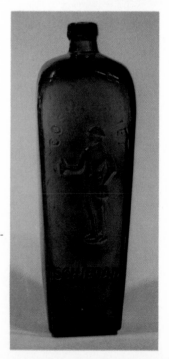

Gin, Cosmopoliet Schiedam, man, 11 in. $98

Candy Container, Billiken, patented, screw top, 4 in. $45

Bitters, Lash's, Natural Tonic Laxative, Sample, 5 in. $135

Figural, barrel, sewer tile, 9½ in. $45

Whiskey, Montezuma Rye, James Maguire, Phila. From United States Hotel, Boston, Mass., 12 in.

Ink, miniature, pottery, Try Field's Non-Corrosive Inks, 2½ in.

Whiskey, Hub Punch, C. H. Graves & Sons, 35 Hawkins St., Boston, Mass., 9 in. $36

Bitters, Feinster Stuttgarter Magen, 10½ in. $90

Flask, lady pictured under glass, 5½ in. $40

Figural, pottery fish, 7½ in. $650

Perfume, nudes, 7¾
in.

Nailsea, looped, 11
in. $140

Candy Container, cat, 2 in. high, 4 in. wide. $50

Barber, white design, 9 in.

Snuff, E. Room, Troy, N.Y. 4½ in. $98

Milk Glass, S. B. Rothenberg
Sole Agent. $133
Variant, pat. applied on front.
$200

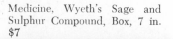

Medicine, Wyeth's Sage and
Sulphur Compound, Box, 7 in.
$7

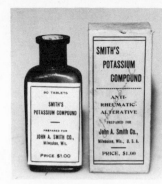

Medicine, Smith's Potassium Compound, 4 1/2 In.
(See Page 156)

Medicine, Sparks, For Kidney & Liver Disease, Camden, N.J., Amber, 9 1/2 In.	63.00
Medicine, Specific A No.1, A Self Cure, Aqua, 5 In.	6.00
Medicine, Square, Olive Green, 4 3/4 In.	20.00
Medicine, St.Andrew's Wine Of Life Root, Label, Amber, 9 In.	20.00
Medicine, St.Jakob's Oil, Charles A.Vogeler Co., Lip Ring, Aqua, 6 1/2 In.	5.00
Medicine, Stella Vitae, Thatcher Co., Rectangular, ABM, Aqua, 8 1/2 In.	4.00
Medicine, Stephen Sweet's Infallible Liniment, Applied Lip, Aqua, 5 In.	6.00
Medicine, Sterling's Ambrosia For The Hair, Rectangular, Aqua, 6 In.	4.50
Medicine, Stoddard Type, Pontil, Olive Green, 7 In.	18.00
Medicine, Sulphate Of Quinine, Paper Label, Cork, Wide Mouth, 6 1/2 In.	8.00
Medicine, Supertah 5 Ointment, Cobalt, 2 1/2 In. *Illus*	3.00
Medicine, Swaim's Panacea, Cloudy, Aqua, Quart	15.00
Medicine, Swaim's Panacea, Green, 8 In. *Illus*	80.00
Medicine, Swaim's Panacea, OP, Aqua, 8 In.	75.00

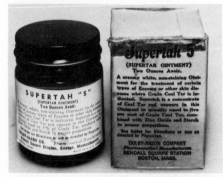

Medicine, Swaim's Panacea,
Green, 8 In.

Medicine, Supertah 5 Ointment, Cobalt, 2 1/2 In.

Medicine, Thompson's Compound Syrup Of Tar, 6 1/4 In.
(See Page 158)

Medicine, Swaim's Panacea, Phila., Aqua With Green Hue, 7 1/2 In. 40.00
Medicine, Swayne's Compound Syrup Of Wild Cherry, Phila., Aqua, 6 3/4 In. 28.00
Medicine, T.B.Smith Kidney Tonic Synthiana, Rectangular, Aqua, 10 1/2 In. 20.00
Medicine, Thatcher's Liver Pills, Chattanooga, Square, Bimal, Aqua, 2 1/2 In. 3.75
Medicine, Thatcher's Liver Pills, Square, Bimal, Amber, 2 1/2 In. 3.75
Medicine, Thompson's Compound Syrup Of Tar, 6 1/4 In. ....*Illus* 60.00
Medicine, Thysolol Antiseptic For The Mouth & Teeth, 3 1/2 In. 1.00
Medicine, Tincture Of Iodine, Poison, Skull & Crossbones, Amber, 2 1/4 In. 3.00
Medicine, Tincture Of Iodine, Poison, Skull & Crossbones, Amber, 2 3/4 In. 3.00
Medicine, Tincture Of Iodine, Poison, Skull & Crossbones, Amber, 3 3/8 In. 3.00
Medicine, Tincture Of Iodine, Rubber Stopper, ABM, Amber, 2 3/4 In. 3.95
Medicine, Tincture Of Iodine, Rubber Stopper, ABM, Amber, 3 3/8 In. 3.95
Medicine, Tincture Of Iodine, Rubber Stopper, ABM, Light Amber, 2 3/4 In. 3.95
Medicine, Tincture Of Iodine, Rubber Stopper, ABM, Light Amber, 3 3/8 In. 3.95
Medicine, Tonic Extract Of Cod Livers, Nation Remedy Co., Amber, 7 1/2 In. 22.00
Medicine, Trafton's Buckthorn Syrup For Scrofula, 8 Sided, Aqua, 7 In. 32.00
Medicine, Tricopherous For The Skin & Hair, Aqua, 6 1/4 In. 2.00
Medicine, Trommer Extract Of Malt Co., Freemont, O., Oval, Amber, 8 In. 3.00
Medicine, True Daffy's Elixir, Dicey & Co., London, Green, 4 1/2 In. 95.00
Medicine, Turlington's Balsam, OP, Aqua, 2 1/2 In. 8.50
Medicine, Turlington's Balsam, The King's Patent, Aqua, 2 1/2 In. 20.00
Medicine, Turner's Essence Of Jamaica Ginger, N.Y., Aqua, 5 3/4 In. 12.00
Medicine, Umatilla Indian Hogan, Aqua, Stained, 9 In. 20.00
Medicine, Universal Cough Remedy, Aqua, Small Size 18.00
Medicine, Vaughn's Vegetable Lithontriptic Mixture, Blue Green, 8 In. 50.00
Medicine, Vaughn's Vegetable Lithontriptic Mixture, Buffalo, Aqua, Quart 30.00
Medicine, Vegetable Pulmonary Balsam, Rectangular, Opalescent, 7 In. 4.00
Medicine, Vegetable Tonic Syrup, Embossed, Bimal, Label, Aqua, 5 1/2 In. 2.65
Medicine, Veno's Lightning Cough Cure, Rectangular, Aqua, 7 1/4 In. 20.00
Medicine, Vernal Remedy Company, Square, 9 In. 5.00
Medicine, Vicks, Sample, Cobalt, 1 3/4 In. 2.00
Medicine, Vigorine Remedy, Bimal, OP, Amber, Quart 20.00
Medicine, Vilane Powder, 4 In. ....*Illus* 1.00
Medicine, Vin-Tone, The Food Tonic, Amber, 9 In. 10.00

Medicine, Vilane Powder, 4 In.

Medicine, Warner's Safe Kidney & Liver,
Brown, 9 1/2 In
(See Page 159)

Medicine, W.T.& Co., Embossed, Acorn Stopper, Milk Glass, 8 In. 37.50
Medicine, Waite's Cough Mixture For The Throat & Lungs, Light Green, 6 In. 1.00
Medicine, Warner's & Co. Ingluvin Powder, Label & Contents, Abm, 1 Oz. 12.00
Medicine, Warner's & Co., Ltd., Melbourne, 5 1/2 In. 47.00
Medicine, Warner's Diabetes Remedy, Label & Contents, 16 Ozs. 40.00
Medicine, Warner's Kidney & Liver Cure, 16 Ozs. 21.00
Medicine, Warner's Kidney & Liver Remedy, Large Size 20.00
Medicine, Warner's Kidney & Liver Remedy, Small Size 25.00

Medicine, Warner's Log Cabin Extract, Box, Label, Cobalt, Small Size	85.00
Medicine, Warner's Log Cabin Extract, Label, Boxed, 8 In.	90.00
Medicine, Warner's Log Cabin Extract, 8 In.	75.00
Medicine, Warner's Nervine, Embossed Safe Remedies Co., Label, Contents	35.00
Medicine, Warner's Nervine, Large Size	28.00
Medicine, Warner's Nervine, Small Size	25.00 To 30.00
Medicine, Warner's Nervine, 1/2 Pint	25.00
Medicine, Warner's Phila., Cobalt, 6 In.	4.00
Medicine, Warner's Safe Cure, Amber, Small Size	21.00
Medicine, Warner's Safe Cure, Canadian Variant, Amber, 9 1/4 In.	60.00
Medicine, Warner's Safe Cure, Concentrated, Oval, Amber, 5 1/2 In.	22.00
Medicine, Warner's Safe Cure, Label & Contents, Small Size	35.00
Medicine, Warner's Safe Cure, London, Red Amber, 9 1/2 In.	125.00
Medicine, Warner's Safe Cure, Medium Stain, Small Size	23.00
Medicine, Warner's Safe Cure, Melbourne, Bimal, 9 1/2 In.	27.00 To 55.00
Medicine, Warner's Safe Cure, Melbourne, Oval, Amber, 9 1/4 In.	27.00 To 35.00
Medicine, Warner's Safe Cure, Rochester, Free Sample, Amber, 4 1/4 In.	15.75
Medicine, Warner's Safe Cure, U.S.A., Canada, England, Amber, 9 1/2 In.	15.00
Medicine, Warner's Safe Cure, 7 1/4 In.	24.00
Medicine, Warner's Safe Cure, 7 1/2 In.	20.00 To 25.00
Medicine, Warner's Safe Kidney & Liver Cure, Amber, 9 1/2 In.	8.00
Medicine, Warner's Safe Kidney & Liver Cure, Dark Amber, 9 1/2 In.	15.00
Medicine, Warner's Safe Kidney & Liver Cure, Embossed Safe, 9 1/2 In.	13.00
Medicine, Warner's Safe Kidney & Liver Cure, Honey Amber, 9 1/4 In.	14.00
Medicine, Warner's Safe Kidney & Liver Cure, N.Y., Amber, 9 1/2 In.	10.00
Medicine, Warner's Safe Kidney & Liver Cure, N.Y., Dark Amber, 9 1/2 In.	5.00
Medicine, Warner's Safe Kidney & Liver Cure, N.Y., Oval, Amber, 9 1/2 In.	6.00
Medicine, Warner's Safe Kidney & Liver Remedy, Amber, 16 Ozs.	70.00
Medicine, Warner's Safe Kidney & Liver, Brown, 9 1/2 In. *Illus*	28.00
Medicine, Warner's Safe Nervine, Boxed, Small Size	50.00
Medicine, Warner's Safe Nervine, Canadian Variant, Amber, 9 1/2 In.	60.00
Medicine, Warner's Safe Nervine, Golden Amber, 7 1/4 In.	45.00
Medicine, Warner's Safe Nervine, Light Stain, 7 1/4 In.	22.00
Medicine, Warner's Safe Nervine, 7 1/4 In.	30.00
Medicine, Warner's Safe Nervine, 9 1/2 In.	18.00
Medicine, Warner's Safe Remedies Co., ABM, Amber, 12 1/2 Ozs., 9 1/4 In.	9.00
Medicine, Warner's Safe Remedies Co., ABM, Aqua, 12 1/2 Ozs., 9 1/4 In.	7.00
Medicine, Warner's Safe Remedies Co., Bimal, Label, Amber, 9 1/4 In.	40.00
Medicine, Warner's Safe Remedies Co., Dug, ABM, Light Amber, 12 1/2 Ozs.	14.00
Medicine, Warner's Safe Remedies Co., Dug, Amber, 12 1/2 Ozs., 9 1/4 In.	12.00
Medicine, Warner's Safe Remedies Co., Label, Contents, ABM, Amber, 6 Ozs.	28.00
Medicine, Warner's Safe Remedies Co., Nervine, Label, Amber, 12 1/2 Ozs.	35.00
Medicine, Warner's Safe Remedies Co., Rochester, N.Y., Bimal, Amber, 9 In.	40.00
Medicine, Warner's Safe Remedies, Label, Contents & Box, 6 Ozs.	25.00
Medicine, Warner's Safe Remedies, Rochester, N.Y., Amber, 6 Ozs., 7 1/4 In.	20.00
Medicine, Warner's Safe Remedies, 6 Ozs.	20.00
Medicine, Warner's Safe Remedies, 12 1/2 Ozs.	20.00
Medicine, Warner's Safe Remedy, Amber, 8 Ozs.	20.00
Medicine, Warner's Safe Remedy, 8 Ozs.	20.00
Medicine, Warners Safe Cure, Animal	300.00
Medicine, Wavenlock For Hair & Scalp, 8 In. *Illus*	8.00
Medicine, Wayne's Diuretic Elixir, Cincinnati, Cobalt, 7 1/2 In.	38.50
Medicine, Weaver's Canker & Salt Rheum, Haze, Oval, Quart	40.00
Medicine, Westerman's Opodel Liniment, Ky., C.1880, Rectangular, 6 1/2 In.	6.00
Medicine, Westlake's Vegetable Ointment, Square, Inrolled Lip, Aqua, 3 In.	30.00
Medicine, Wheeler's Tissue Phosphates, Aqua, 8 3/4 In.	6.00
Medicine, Wheeler's Tissue Phosphates, Collared Lip, Square, Aqua, 8 1/2 In.	6.00
Medicine, Wheeler's Tissue Phosphates, Monogrammed Base, 8 3/4 In.Square	8.50
Medicine, Wheeler's Tissue Phosphates, Square, 8 3/4 In.	9.00
Medicine, White Clover Cream, L.A.Gould, Portland, Me., Labels, 4 3/4 In.	5.50
Medicine, White Eagle's Indian Senna-Tone, 8 In. *Illus*	3.50
Medicine, Wigwam Indian Herb Tonic	7.50
Medicine, William R.Warner Co., Embossed, Square, Amber, 7 1/2 In.	15.00
Medicine, Wilson's Pulmonary Cherry Balsam, 12 Sided, Aqua, 4 3/4 In.	8.00
Medicine, Winan's Bros. Indian Liniment For Man Or Beast, Aqua, 7 In.	17.00

Medicine, Wishart's Pine Tree Tar Cordial, Blue Green, 10 1/4 In. 65.00
Medicine, Wishart's Pine Tree Tar Cordial, Bubbles, Pint 50.00
Medicine, Wishart's Pine Tree Tar Cordial, Emerald Green, Quart 60.00
Medicine, Wishart's Pine Tree Tar Cordial, Green, Pint 55.00
Medicine, Wishart's Pine Tree Tar Cordial, Square, Stain, Green, 9 1/2 In. 65.00
Medicine, Wishart's Pine Tree Tar Cordial, Whittled, Dark Green, 7 1/2 In. 60.00
Medicine, Wishart's Pine Tree Tar Cordial, 9 1/2 In. ....*Color* 65.00
Medicine, Wishart's Pine Tree Tar Cordial, 1859, Emerald Green, 7 3/4 In. 45.00
Medicine, Wishart's Pine Tree Tar Cordial, 1859, Green, 9 1/2 In. 50.00
Medicine, Wolfstirn's Rheumatic Gout Remedy, Hoboken, N.J., Aqua, 5 In. 2.00
Medicine, Wood's Great Peppermint Cure For Coughs & Colds, Amethyst, 5 In. 15.00
Medicine, Wood's Great Peppermint Cure For Coughs & Colds, Aqua, 5 In. 10.00
Medicine, Wood's Great Peppermint Cure For Coughs & Colds, Aqua, 7 In. 15.00
Medicine, Woolford's Sanitary Lotion, 7 In. ....*Illus* 3.00
Medicine, Wyeth & Bro.'s, John, Fluid Extracts, Phila., Amber, 5 In. 6.00

Medicine, Wavenlock For Hair & Scalp, 8 In.
(See Page 159)

Medicine, White Eagle's Indian
Senna-Tone, 8 In.
(See Page 159)

Medicine, Woolford's Sanitary Lotion, 7 In.

Medicine, Wyeth & Bro.'s, John, May 16th, 1899, Dose Cap, Cobalt, 6 In. 6.00
Medicine, Wyeth & Bro.'s, John, May 16th, 1899, Dose Cap, Cobalt, 6 1/4 In. 6.00
Medicine, Wyeth & Bro.'s, John, May 16th, 1899, Dose Cap, Cobalt, 6 1/2 In. 6.00
Medicine, Wyeth & Bro.'s, John, Phila., Oval, Cobalt, 2 3/4 In. 2.00
Medicine, Wyeth, Cobalt, 6 3/4 In. ....*Illus* 15.00
Medicine, Wyeth, Dose Bottle, 5 1/2 In. 6.00
Medicine, Wyeth's Phosphate, Timer & Measurer Top, Label, Cobalt, 6 1/2 In. 10.00
Medicine, Wyeth's Sage And Sulphur Compound, Box, 7 In. ....*Color* 7.00
Milk Glass, Armour Co., 5 1/2 In. 15.00
Milk Glass, Bottle, Actress Head In Panels, 11 In. 75.00
Milk Glass, Embossed Metcalfe Co., Boston, Rectangular, 4 1/4 In. 7.00
Milk Glass, Embossed Swift & Co., Chicago, Round, 6 In. 7.50
Milk Glass, Embossed, Newton, London, Square Sloped Shoulders, 2 3/4 In. 25.00
Milk Glass, Painted, 7 1/2 In. ....*Color* 47.50
Milk Glass, Pewter Top, Painted, 10 In. ....*Color* 28.00
Milk Glass, S.B.Rothenberg Sole Agent ....*Color* 135.00

Medicine, Wyeth, Cobalt, 6 3/4 In.
(See Page 160)

Milk, Brookfield, Double Baby Face, Quart

Milk Glass, S.B.Rothenberg Sole Agent, Patent On Front .... *Color*   200.00
Milk Glass, World's Fair, 1939, 9 In. .... 7.00 To 25.00
    Milk Glass, see also Cologne, Cosmetic, Dresser, Drug, Ink, Medicine

    Milk bottles were first used in the 1880s. The characteristic shape and
    printed or embossed wording identify these bottles for collectors.
Milk, AGS & Co., Boston, Patent April 5, 1898, Quart .... 20.00 To 22.00
Milk, Aber Brothers, Pa., Large A, Round, Embossed, Quart 1.50
Milk, Aiea Dairy, Hawaii, Embossed, 1/2 Pint 2.00
Milk, Alden Bros.Co., Heavy Cream, Bulbous, Tin Screw Top, 1/2 Pint 7.00
Milk, Alden Bros.Co., Heavy Cream, Bulbous, Wide Mouth, 1/2 Pint 5.00
Milk, Alea Dairy, Hawaii, Embossed, Round, 1/2 Pint 2.00
Milk, Alford Lake Jersey Farm, Maine, Squat, Painted Cow & Child, Quart 2.00
Milk, Aoot Milk Co., Pittsburgh, Pa., Round, Embossed, Cream Top, Quart 3.00
Milk, Arlington Dairy, Jeannette, Pa., Round, Embossed, Cream Top, Quart 4.00
Milk, B.L.Sour Cream, Round, Embossed, Pint 2.50
Milk, Baby Face, Quart 5.00
Milk, Badger Farms Creameries, N.H., 5 Cent Store, 1934, Fluted Lip, Quart 3.00
Milk, Badger Farms Creameries, Portsmouth, N.H., 5 Cent Store, 1/2 Pint 5.00
Milk, Bancroft Farm, Reading, Ma., Embossed Indian's Head, 10 Ozs. 4.50
Milk, Bard's Dairy Stores, Inc., Pittsburgh, Pa., Round, Embossed, 1/2 Pint 1.25
Milk, Bartlett Farms, Wichita, Embossed, Quart 2.50
Milk, Belle Vernon Milk, 1928, Round, Embossed, Bars At Neck, 1/2 Pint 1.75
Milk, Bellview Dairy, Syracuse, N.Y., 1/3 Quart 1.50
Milk, Better Dairy Products Co., Round, Embossed, Cream Top, Quart 3.00
Milk, Bill's, Pawhuska, Okla., Painted, Quart 2.00
Milk, Borden's Condensed Milk Co., Eagle Brand, Pint 10.00
Milk, Borden's Malted Milk, 1/2 Pint 3.00
Milk, Borden's, Eagle Emblem, Tin Top, Quart 15.00
Milk, Borden's, Embossed Eagle, Pint 15.00
Milk, Borden's, Whipper, Dated 1915, Pint 10.00
Milk, Boy Riding Tricycle, Enameled Safety Slogan, 1/2 Gallon 2.50
Milk, Brookemaker, Tin Top, Pint 20.00
Milk, Brookfield Dairy, Baby Face Cream Top, 1/2 Pint 6.00
Milk, Brookfield, Double Baby Face, Quart .... *Illus*   12.00
Milk, Brookfield, Single Baby Face, Embossed Town & State, 1/2 Pint 4.50
Milk, Brookville Ice Cream & Dairy Co., Round, Embossed, 1/2 Pint 1.50
Milk, Camp Aiyukpa, Golden Guernsey Products, N.Y., 1/3 Quart 3.00
Milk, Capitol Dairy Co., Sour Cream, Chicago, Ill., Round, Embossed, 16 Ozs. 2.50

Milk, Carlton Hall Dairy, Coffeyville, Kans., Painted, Quart 2.00
Milk, Cast Iron, Pint 30.00
Milk, Castles, Lockport, N.Y., Embossed, 1/2 Pint 2.50
Milk, Chautauqua Lake Creamery, Jamestown, N.Y., Round, Painted, 1/2 Pint 1.00
Milk, Chestnut Farms, Washington, D.C., Embossed, 1/2 Pint 1.75
Milk, City View Dairy, Sour Cream, Cleveland, O., Store Bottle, Pint 2.50
Milk, Clarence A.Alley, Large A, Maine Seal, 1931, Round, Embossed, Quart 2.50
Milk, Clark Weed, T.Mfg.Co., Embossed, Squat, 1/2 Pint 2.50
Milk, Clarkarohen Farm Pure Milk, 1927, Round, Embossed, Quart 1.50
Milk, Cop-The-Cream, Quart 12.00
Milk, Cream, Hayner Lock, Box 290, Dayton, Ohio, Jug, Blue, Quart Plus 25.00
Milk, Crystal Dairy, J.W.Trube, Round, Embossed, Fluted Neck, Quart 1.50
Milk, Dairylee, Double Baby Face, Cream Top, Quart 6.00
Milk, Dairylee, Embossed Deposit, Ring At Neck, Painted Scene, Quart 2.50
Milk, Dairylee, Square, Baby Face, Quart 11.50
Milk, Dairymen's Milk Co., Pittsburgh, Pa., Round, Embossed, 1/2 Pint 1.25
Milk, Davis Products, Newark, Ohio, Embossed, Pint 2.50
Milk, Deerfoot Farm Heavy Cream, Plum Shape, Screw Top, 1/2 Pint 1.50
Milk, Deerfoot Farm, Bulbous, Wide Mouth, 1/2 Pint 5.00
Milk, Deneen's Superior Products, Sour Cream, Sharon, Pa., Painted, 8 Ozs. 2.00
Milk, Deneen's, Sharon, Pa., Embossed, Squat, Quart 1.25
Milk, Deneen's, Sour Cream, Sharon, Pa., Round, Embossed, Pint 2.50
Milk, Dyke's Sour Cream, Warren, Pa., Round, Painted, Pint 2.50
Milk, Echo Farm Dairy Co., Framingham, Round, Painted Sailboat, Quart 3.00
Milk, Elm Farm Sour Cream, Wide Mouth, 1/2 Pint 3.00
Milk, Elmview Jersey Farm, Pa., Round, Embossed, Quart 2.50
Milk, Embossed, Cream Top, Quart 3.50
Milk, Embossed, Store, 3 Cents, Quart 3.00
Milk, Fark's Dairy, Pa., 1936, Round, Embossed, Quart 2.50
Milk, Footman's Dairy, Brewer, Maine Seal, Round, Painted, Quart 1.50
Milk, Fox Dairy, Fostoria, Ohio, Black Script, Baby Face, Cream Top, Quart 3.00
Milk, Fox Dairy, Fostoria, Ohio, Cream Top, Baby Face Type, 1/2 Pint 7.50
Milk, Frank Bratt & Son, Stillwater, N.Y., Large B, Round, Embossed, 1/2 Pint 1.50
Milk, Gail Bordon, Cream, Ribbed, 1/2 Pint .... *Illus* 12.50
Milk, Gail Bordon, Ribbed, Pint .... *Illus* 15.00
Milk, George Washington, Pint 28.00
Milk, Grant's Dairy, Bangor, Maine, Round, Painted, 1/2 Pint 1.50
Milk, H.C.Bonner, Pa., Large B, Round, Embossed, Quart 2.50
Milk, H.C.Hewitt Gen'l Agent Maine Cream, Newburyport, Tin Top, 1/2 Pint 12.00
Milk, H.C.Hewitt, Maine Cream, Newburyport, Embossed, Tin Top, 1/2 Pint 12.00
Milk, H.S.Uhl, Mars, Pa., Round, Embossed, Quart 1.50
Milk, H.W.Gray, Jacksonville, Fla., G In Triangle, Round, Embossed, 1/2 Pint 2.00
Milk, Haleakala Dairy, Hawaii, Embossed, Round, 1/2 Pint 2.00
Milk, Hammond's Creamcrest Dairy Products, O., Round, Embossed, 1/2 Pint 1.25
Milk, Hampden Creamery, Embossed Cow, Tin Top, 1/2 Pint .... 8.50 To 10.00
Milk, Harmony Creamery Co., Pittsburgh, Embossed, Fluted Neck, Purple, Quart 4.00
Milk, Hayward Farms, Mass., Store, Seal, Diagonal Lines On Neck, Quart 3.00

Milk, Gail Bordon, Ribbed, Pint

Milk, Gail Bordon, Cream, Ribbed, 1/2 Pint

Milk, **Hisco,** Haskell Implement & Seed Co., Maine Seal, Round, Embossed, Quart 1.50
Milk, **Holbrook's Poplar Springs Farm Dairy,** Round, Embossed, 1/2 Pint 1.25
Milk, **Home Dairy Co.,** Embossed Cow, Tin Lightning Top, 1/2 Pint .... 7.00 To 18.00
Milk, **Hood's Cream,** Painted White Inside, 1/2 Pint 1.98
Milk, **Horlick's Malted,** Racine, Embossed, Metal Screw Cap, Aqua, 6 3/4 In. 5.00
Milk, **Horlick's Malted,** Racine, Wisc., Gallon 4.00
Milk, **Horn & Farris,** Muskogee, Okla., Painted, Quart 2.00
Milk, **How Good Can Eggs Be–Try Martin's & You'll See,** Square, Quart 1.00
Milk, **Howard R.Baker,** Pasteurized, Round, Painted, Bars At Neck, 1/2 Pint 2.00
Milk, **Hutt's Dairy,** Round, Painted, 1/3 Quart 2.50
Milk, **Ideal,** New Bedford, Square, Painted, Quart 11.50
Milk, **Isaly's,** Baby Face, Quart .... *Illus* 6.00
Milk, **Isaly's,** Youngstown, Ohio, Round, Embossed, Quart 1.25
Milk, **J.Chappo Dairy,** TMC, 1919, Bars At Neck, Round, Embossed, Cloudy, Quart 2.00
Milk, **J.D.Biggins & Son,** Co., Pa., 1931, Round, Embossed, Quart 1.50
Milk, **John Anderson,** Cow's Milk, Maine, Round, Embossed, Quart 2.00
Milk, **Kuehn's Dairy,** Monroeville, Pa., Round, Painted, 1/2 Pint 1.00
Milk, **L.S.Kyte,** Laboratory, Pint .... *Illus* 3.00
Milk, **L.S.Kyte,** Metal Cap, Pint .... *Illus* 3.00

Milk, Isaly's, Baby Face, Quart

Milk, L.S.Kyte, Laboratory, Pint

Milk, L.S.Kyte, Metal Cap, Pint

Milk, **Lang's Creamery,** Inc., Buffalo, N.Y., Round, Embossed, 1/2 Pint 1.50
Milk, **Ligonier Dairy Products Co.,** Pa., Round, Fluted Neck, Embossed, Quart 1.75
Milk, **Lily Brook Farms,** Buffalo, N.Y., Round, Embossed, Bars At Neck, 1/2 Pint 1.50
Milk, **Linger Light Dairy,** New Castle, Pa., 1935, Round, Painted, Quart 1.50
Milk, **Locust Valley Dairy,** Guernsey Products, Pa., Round, Embossed, Quart 2.00
Milk, **Maine Condensed Milk Co.,** 6 Panel, Baby Tin Closure, 1/2 Pint 8.00
Milk, **Maine Dairy,** Portland, Embossed Flag, Quart 10.00
Milk, **Meadow Gold Cottage Cheese,** Embossed, 12 Ozs. 3.00
Milk, **Meadow Gold,** Square, Embossed On Bulb, Cream Top, Quart 1.50
Milk, **Mellow Gold Grade A,** Imprinted, Square, 1/2 Pint 4.00
Milk, **Mellow Gold,** Taste Tells, Imprinted, Square, 1/2 Pint 4.00
Milk, **Merry's Dairy,** Round, Embossed, Quart 1.50
Milk, **Metal Closure,** Lock, 1/2 Pint 6.00
Milk, **Middleton Creamy Rich Milk,** Round, Painted, Quart 1.50
Milk, **Missouri Pacific Railroad,** Embossed, 1/2 Pint .... 2.00 To 3.00
Milk, **Missouri Pacific Railroad,** Embossed, Quart .... 2.00 To 3.00
Milk, **Mong Dairy,** Oil City, Pa., Round, Embossed, 1/2 Pint 1.50
Milk, **Ninth St.Dairy,** Pa., 9 On Front & Bottom, 1925, Round, Embossed, Quart 3.00

Milk, North Hills Dairy, Glenshaw, Pa., Embossed, Fluted Sides, 1/2 Pint 2.00
Milk, O.L.Lozier, Conneaut Lake, Pa., Round, Embossed, Quart 1.50
Milk, Oakmont & Verona Dairy & Ice Co., OVD Monogram, Round, Quart 2.00
Milk, Olin Hill, Applied Neck, 1877, Pint 35.00
Milk, Otto Milk Co., Pittsburgh, Pa., Patent Mar.3, 1925, Cream Top, Pint 5.00
Milk, Otto Milk Dairy, Pittsburgh, Fluted Sided, Embossed, Quart 2.00
Milk, Otto Suburban Dairy, Round, Embossed, Quart 1.50
Milk, Painted, Cream Top, Quart 2.00
Milk, Parker's, Erie, Pa., Embossed, 1/2 Pint 2.50
Milk, Pine State Dairy, Bangor, Maine, Round, Painted, 1/2 Pint 1.25
Milk, Portland Creamery, Tin Top, Ribbed, 1/2 Pint 10.00
Milk, Purity Milk Co., Oil City, Pa., Round, Embossed, Bars At Neck, Quart 1.75
Milk, Puunene Dairy, Hawaii, Embossed, Round, 1/2 Pint 2.00
Milk, Pyroglazed Rojeck's Sour Cream, Tonawanda, N.Y., Pint 2.00
Milk, Quality Dairy, Hannibal, Mo., War Slogan, Cream Top, Round, Quart 3.50
Milk, R.R.Dauphinee, Maine, 1930, Round, Embossed, Quart 2.00
Milk, Rieck's Pure Milk & Cream, Round, Embossed, Flared Lip, Purple, Quart 4.00
Milk, Round Top Farms, Maine, Squat, Painted, Quart 1.25
Milk, Royal Crest Farm Dairy, Sour Cream, Strongsville, O., Painted, 12 Ozs. 2.50
Milk, S.S.P.Pierce Pure Cream, Ground Top, Screw On Tin Lid, 1/2 Pint 15.00
Milk, S.S.Pierce, Boston, Brookline, Pure Cream, Embossed, Tin Top, 1/2 Pint 10.00
Milk, Salisbury Farms Dairy, Conn., Store, Round, Painted Farm Scene, Quart 2.50
Milk, Sangamon, Painted, Gallon 9.50
Milk, Sanitary Dairy, Punxsutawney, Pa., Round, Painted, Quart 1.50
Milk, Sanitary Milk Co., The, Canton, O., Embossed, Bars At Neck, 1/2 Pint 1.50
Milk, Sawyer's Clover Hill Farm, Embossed Four-Leaf Clover, 1/2 Pint 3.00
Milk, Schwab's Dairy, Peoria, Ill., Pint 3.00
Milk, Seegert's Dairy, Silver Creek, N.Y., Embossed, Swirled Neck, 1/2 Pint 1.75
Milk, Shaker Grove Dairy, Cleveland, O., Round, Embossed, Quart 2.50
Milk, Shaker Grove Dairy, Sour Cream, Round, Painted Shaker Woman, 16 Ozs. 2.50
Milk, Shaw's Ridge Farm, Maine, Round, Painted, Quart 1.50
Milk, Sheffield, Embossed On Side, Quart 1.50
Milk, Shelbyville Pure Milk Co., Tenn., Round, Embossed, Quart 1.50
Milk, Silver Seal Meadow Gold, Round, Embossed, 1/2 Pint 1.50
Milk, Silver Seal Meadow Gold, Round, Embossed, Quart 1.50
Milk, Smalley, Tin Cap & Handle, Quart 18.00
Milk, Smalley, Tin Cap & Handle, 1/2 Gallon 35.00
Milk, Smith Dairy Co., The, Boardman, O., Round, Painted, Quart 1.25
Milk, Smith Dairy, Laboratory, 1/2 Pint .... *Illus* 2.00
Milk, Smith Dairy, 5 1/2 In. .... *Illus* 1.00
Milk, Somerset, Dairy, Somerset, Ky., Painted, Quart 2.00
Milk, Speedwell Farms, Embossed Cow, Tin Top, 1/2 Pint .... 8.50 To 10.00
Milk, Steven's Dairy, Fayette City, Round, Painted, Quart 1.50
Milk, Store, Detroit, Michigan, 3 Cents, 1/2 Pint 3.00

Milk, Smith Dairy, Laboratory, 1/2 Pint

Milk, Smith Dairy, 5 1/2 In.

Milk, Store, N.C., 5 Cents, Pint 3.00
Milk, Store, N.C., 5 Cents, Quart 3.00
Milk, Strittmatter Dairy, North Side, Pittsburgh, Fluted Sides, Quart 3.00
Milk, Supple Wills, Jones, S On Back, Round, Embossed, Fluted Neck, Quart ... 1.50
Milk, Sweet Cream, White Paint On Inside, Cow On Outside, Quart 4.50
Milk, Texas Dairy, Enamel Label, Amber, Quart 2.75
Milk, Thatcher, Man Milking Cow, H.D.T.& Co., Potsdam, N.Y., Pint 145.00
Milk, Thatcher, Man Milking Cow, H.D.T.& Co., Potsdam, N.Y., Quart 110.00
Milk, Try Our Delicious Buttermilk, Dutch Girl & Buckets, 1/2 Gallon 2.75
Milk, Twin City Dairy, Hurley, Wis., Pint .... .50
Milk, Union Dairy, Embossed Flag With 10 Stars, Tin Top, Quart 45.00
Milk, Upton's Farm, Bridgewater, Mass., Baby Face, Pint 2.75
Milk, Urbana, Illinois, Pyroglaze Label, 1/2 Pint .... .50
Milk, V.M.& I.C.Co., Amber, 1/2 Pint 28.00
Milk, Valley Dairy Co., Round, Embossed, 1/2 Pint 1.50
Milk, Vinal's Dairy, Maine, Round, Painted, Quart 1.50
Milk, Vine City Dairy, Westfield, N.Y., Round, Embossed, 1/2 Pint 1.00
Milk, Warren County Dairy Assn., Pa., Round, Embossed, 1/2 Pint 1.50
Milk, Whites Farm Dairy, Square, Baby Face, Painted, 1/2 Pint 11.50
Milk, Wilson's Mello-D, Detroit, Mich., Embossed, Chain At Neck, 1/2 Pint 1.50
Milk, Wm.Colteryahn & Sons Co., Sour Cream, Round, Painted, Pint 2.00
Milk, Wm.Evans Dairy Co., Brooklyn, Haze, Pint 2.00
Milk, Wood's Petersburg Dairy, Inc., Va., Round, Embossed, Fluted Lip, Quart 2.00
Milk, Wray's Dairy, Ford City, Pa., Round, Painted Farm Scene, Quart 2.00
Milk, Young's, Grove City, Pa., Round, Painted, 1/2 Pint 1.25
Milk, 5 Cent Universal Store Bottle, Ribbed, 1/2 Pint 2.00

Mineral Water, Buffalo Lithia, Aqua, 1/2 Gallon

Mineral Water, C.Clark, Dark Olive, 7 In.

Mineral water bottles held the fresh natural spring waters favored for health and taste. Most of the bottles collected today date from the 1850-1900 period. Many of these bottles have blob tops.

Mineral Water, see also Pottery

Mineral Water, Acid Springs, Lockport, Whittled, Green, Quart 45.00
Mineral Water, Adirondack Spring, Green, Pint 38.00
Mineral Water, Adirondack Spring, Westport, N.Y., Emerald Green, Quart 60.00
Mineral Water, Aluminum, Rock Bridge, Va., Graphite Pontil, Green, 1/2 Gallon 120.00
Mineral Water, Artesian Spring, Ballston Spa, N.Y., Green, Pint .... 32.00 To 37.00
Mineral Water, Benscot Natural Springs Lithia, Ga., Aqua, 1/2 Gallon 11.00
Mineral Water, Blout Springs Sulphur, Cobalt, 7 1/2 In. 25.00
Mineral Water, Boothbay Medicinal Spring, Edward E.Race, Teal Blue, Quart 35.00
Mineral Water, Buffalo Lithia, Aqua, 1/2 Gallon .... *Illus* 7.50
Mineral Water, Buffalo Sprint, Label, 1/2 Gallon 8.00
Mineral Water, Byron Acid Spring, Round, IP, Emerald Green, 7 3/4 In. 85.00
Mineral Water, C.& E.Hotchkiss & Son, Open Bubble On Base, Green, Quart 22.00
Mineral Water, C.Clark, Dark Olive, 7 In. .... *Illus* 75.00
Mineral Water, C.Ebberwein, Aqua, 8 In. 6.00

Mineral Water, Caledonia Springs, Wheelock, Vt., Amber, Quart 155.00
Mineral Water, Castalian, California Natural, Amber, 8 In. 5.00
Mineral Water, Castalian, Embossed At Shoulder, Amber, 8 In. 5.00
Mineral Water, Champion Spouting Spring, Aqua, Pint 30.00
Mineral Water, Champion Spouting Spring, Dug, Aqua, Pint 22.00
Mineral Water, Clarke & Co., IP, Emerald Green, Pint 38.00
Mineral Water, Clarke & Co., Olive, Quart 39.00
Mineral Water, Clarke & Co., Potstone In Neck, Olive, Pint 30.00
Mineral Water, Clarke & White, C, N.Y., Olive Green, Pint .... 10.00 To 14.50
Mineral Water, Clarke & White, C, Quart 20.00
Mineral Water, Clarke & White, Dug, Pint 24.00
Mineral Water, Clarke & White, Emerald, Pint 17.00
Mineral Water, Clarke & White, N.Y., Bimal, Olive, 7 In. 15.00
Mineral Water, Clarke & White, N.Y., Olive Green, Pint 25.00
Mineral Water, Clarke & White, N.Y., Olive Green, Quart 22.00
Mineral Water, Clarke & White, N.Y., OP, Stain, Light Olive Green, Quart 45.00
Mineral Water, Clarke & White, Olive Green, Pint .... 22.00 To 23.00
Mineral Water, Clarke & White, Olive Green, Quart .... 20.00 To 40.00
Mineral Water, Clarke & White, Open Bubble On Base, Olive, Quart 14.00
Mineral Water, Clarke & White, Saratoga, N.Y., IP, Dug, Olive, Pint 26.00
Mineral Water, Clarke & White, Saratoga, N.Y., Olive Green, Pint .... 19.50 To 22.00
Mineral Water, Clarke & White, Saratoga, N.Y., Pontil, Yellow Green, Quart 47.00
Mineral Water, Clarke & White, Seed Bubbles, Olive Green, Pint 16.50
Mineral Water, Clysmik, Embossed On Bottom, Dark Green, 9 In.High 5.00
Mineral Water, Cold Indian Spring, Embossed, Aqua, 5 Pint 15.00
Mineral Water, Cold Spring Mineral Water Co., Blob Top, Aqua, 14 In. 12.00
Mineral Water, Congress & Empire Spring Co., Bubbles, Olive Green, Pint 16.50
Mineral Water, Congress & Empire Spring Co., C, Emerald Green, Pint 15.00
Mineral Water, Congress & Empire Spring Co., C, Emerald Green, Quart 17.50
Mineral Water, Congress & Empire Spring Co., C, Green, Pint 15.00
Mineral Water, Congress & Empire Spring Co., C, Olive Green, Quart 36.50
Mineral Water, Congress & Empire Spring Co., C, Pint 20.00
Mineral Water, Congress & Empire Spring Co., C, Quart 20.00
Mineral Water, Congress & Empire Spring Co., C, Whittled, Olive Green, Pint 37.00
Mineral Water, Congress & Empire Spring Co., E, Green, Quart 20.00
Mineral Water, Congress & Empire Spring Co., E, Olive Green, Quart 37.50
Mineral Water, Congress & Empire Spring Co., E, Pint 20.00
Mineral Water, Congress & Empire Spring Co., Emerald Green, Pint 20.00
Mineral Water, Congress & Empire Spring Co., Emerald Green, Quart 22.00
Mineral Water, Congress & Empire Spring Co., Hotchkiss, Green, Pint 25.00
Mineral Water, Congress & Empire Spring Co., Hotchkiss, Olive, 1/2 Pint 75.00
Mineral Water, Congress & Empire Spring Co., Hotchkiss, Yellow, Pint 28.00
Mineral Water, Congress & Empire Spring Co., Saratoga, N.Y., Amber, Quart 55.00
Mineral Water, Congress & Empire Spring Co., Saratoga, N.Y., C, Emerald, Pint ... 22.00
Mineral Water, Congress & Empire Spring Co., Saratoga, N.Y., C, Pint 20.00
Mineral Water, Congress & Empire Spring Co., Saratoga, N.Y., E, Emerald, Pint ... 22.00
Mineral Water, Congress & Empire Spring Co., Saratoga, N.Y., E, Pint 21.00
Mineral Water, Congress & Empire Spring Co., Saratoga, N.Y., Emerald, Pint 19.50
Mineral Water, Congress & Empire Spring Co., Saratoga, N.Y., Emerald, Quart 20.00
Mineral Water, Congress & Empire Spring Co., Saratoga, N.Y., Green, Pint 19.50
Mineral Water, Congress & Empire Spring Co., Whittled, Bubbles, Olive, Pint 28.00
Mineral Water, Congress & Empire Spring Co., Whittled, Quart 30.00
Mineral Water, Congress Spring Co., C, Pint 20.00
Mineral Water, Congress Spring Co., Emerald Green, Pint 20.00
Mineral Water, Congress Spring Co., Green, Pint 19.50
Mineral Water, Congress Spring Co., Saratoga, N.Y., C, Emerald Green, Quart 35.00
Mineral Water, Congress Spring Co., Saratoga, N.Y., C, Green, Quart 19.00
Mineral Water, Congress Spring Co., Saratoga, N.Y., Emerald Green, Quart 23.00
Mineral Water, Congress Spring Co., Saratoga, N.Y., Emerald Green, 8 In. 22.50
Mineral Water, Congress Spring Co., Saratoga, N.Y., Green, Pint 15.00
Mineral Water, Congress Spring Co., Saratoga, N.Y., Whittled, Pint 23.00
Mineral Water, Congress Spring, Great High Rock, Green, Pint 65.00
Mineral Water, Congress Springs Co., Hutchinson, Amber, Pint 45.00
Mineral Water, Congress Springs Co., S.S.N.Y. On Base, Emerald, 9 3/4 In. 15.00
Mineral Water, Cotton's Florida, Gold & Red Glass Label, Stain, 9 In. 17.50
Mineral Water, D.A.Knowlton, Green, Quart 25.00

Mineral Water, D.A.Knowlton, Olive Green, Quart .... 35.00 To 38.00
Mineral Water, Devonian, Lorain, O., Cylindrical, Amber, 8 3/4 In. 8.00
Mineral Water, Empire Spring Co., Saratoga, N.Y., Embossed, Emerald, Quart 33.00
Mineral Water, Everett Crystal Spring Water Co., Handled, Pottery, 5 Gallon 25.00
Mineral Water, Excelsior Springs, Syracuse, N.Y., Amber, Pint 38.00
Mineral Water, Excelsior Springs, Syracuse, N.Y., Emerald Green, Pint 28.00
Mineral Water, Excelsior Springs, Syracuse, N.Y., Green, Quart 35.00
Mineral Water, Excelsior Springs, Syracuse, N.Y., High Shoulder, Green, Quart 60.00
Mineral Water, Excelsior Springs, Syracuse, N.Y., Olive Green, Pint 28.00
Mineral Water, Florida Water, Label, 6 In. 5.00
Mineral Water, Florida Water, Murry S.Lannon, Druggist, N.Y., Aqua, 9 In. 2.00
Mineral Water, Florida Water, Solon Palmers, N.Y., Stain, Aqua, 8 3/4 In. 2.95
Mineral Water, G.W.Weston, Saratoga, N.Y., Dug, Pontil, Olive, Pint 40.00
Mineral Water, Gettysburg Katalysine, Emerald Green, Quart 45.00
Mineral Water, Gettysburg Katalysine, Emerald Green, 9 1/2 In. 28.50
Mineral Water, Gettysburg Katalysine, Green, Quart .... 30.00 To 45.00
Mineral Water, Geyser Spouting Spring, Aqua, Pint 24.00
Mineral Water, Geyser Spring, Aqua, Pint .... 14.50 To 26.00
Mineral Water, Geyser Spring, Aqua, Quart 29.50
Mineral Water, Gleason & Cole, IP, 7 1/2 In. .... Illus 250.00
Mineral Water, Gleason & Cole, Pittsburgh, Mold Blown, IP, Blue, 7 3/4 In. 175.00
Mineral Water, Glenn Springs, S.C., Bimal, C.1910, 12 Ozs. 8.00
Mineral Water, Great Radium Spring Water Co., Aqua, Quart 9.00
Mineral Water, Guilford Mineral & Spring, Vt., Green, Quart 31.00
Mineral Water, Guilford Mineral Spring, Vt., Deep Green, Quart .... 30.00 To 40.00
Mineral Water, Guilford Mineral Spring, Vt., Emerald Green, Quart 30.00
Mineral Water, Guilford Mineral Spring, Vt., Green, Quart .... Illus 35.00
Mineral Water, Guilford Mineral Spring, Vt., Quart 25.00
Mineral Water, Guilford Mineral Spring, Vt., Yellow Green, Quart 24.00
Mineral Water, H.H.Ricker & Co., Poland Water, Handled, Pottery, 3 Gallon 50.00
Mineral Water, H.W.Bostwick, Broadway, N.Y., Amber, 9 In. 22.50
Mineral Water, Hanbury Smith Kissengen, Olive Amber, Pint 35.00
Mineral Water, Hanbury Smith Kissengen, Olive Green, Pint 35.00

Mineral Water, Gleason & Cole, IP, 7 1/2 In.

Mineral Water, Guilford Spring, Dark Green, 9 1/2 In.

Mineral Water, Hanbury Smith Vichy, Blue Green, Pint 10.00
Mineral Water, Hanbury Smith Vichy, Olive, Pint 15.00
Mineral Water, Hathorn Springs, Saratoga, N.Y., Amber, Pint 23.00
Mineral Water, Hathorn Springs, Saratoga, N.Y., Amber, Quart .... 14.00 To 30.00
Mineral Water, Hathorn Springs, Saratoga, N.Y., Black Amethyst, Pint 21.00
Mineral Water, Hathorn Springs, Saratoga, N.Y., Black, Pint 22.50
Mineral Water, Hathorn Springs, Saratoga, N.Y., Bubbly, Green, Quart 25.00
Mineral Water, Hathorn Springs, Saratoga, N.Y., Dark Amber, Pint .... 21.00 To 28.00

Mineral Water, Hathorn Springs, Saratoga, N.Y., Emerald Green, Pint 35.00
Mineral Water, Hathorn Springs, Saratoga, N.Y., Emerald Green, Quart 19.00
Mineral Water, Hathorn Springs, Saratoga, N.Y., Green, Pint .... 22.50 To 30.00
Mineral Water, Hathorn Springs, Saratoga, N.Y., Olive Yellow, Pint 28.50
Mineral Water, Hathorn Springs, Saratoga, N.Y., Orange Amber, Pint 14.75
Mineral Water, Hathorn Springs, Saratoga, N.Y., Stain, Amber, Quart 12.00
Mineral Water, Hathorn Springs, Saratoga, N.Y., Yellow Olive, Pint 26.50
Mineral Water, High Rock, Congress Spring Co., Amber, Quart 60.00
Mineral Water, High Rock, Congress Spring Co., Saratoga, N.Y., Green, Pint 52.00
Mineral Water, High Rock, 1776, Congress Spring Co., Deep Amber, Quart 75.00
Mineral Water, J.Boardman & Co., Cobalt, 7 1/2 In. ....*Illus* 125.00
Mineral Water, John Clarke, N.Y., Whittled, Olive Green, Quart .... 60.00 To 72.00
Mineral Water, Lavator, Embossed, Lime Green, Quart 17.50
Mineral Water, Lavator, Lime Green, Quart 19.00
Mineral Water, Lincoln Spring, Saratoga, N.Y., Blob Top, Amber, Quart 7.00
Mineral Water, Lynch & Clarke, Whittled, Bubbly, Dug, IP, Pint 46.00
Mineral Water, Madden Co., Clarendon Springs, Round Bottom, Aqua, 7 In. 8.00
Mineral Water, Magnetic Springs, Henniker, N.H., Olive Amber, Quart 75.00
Mineral Water, Man-A-Cea, Manganese, Irondale Spring, Amber, 1/2 Gallon 25.00
Mineral Water, McDermott Co., Faywood Hot Springs, Aqua, 1/2 Gallon 16.00
Mineral Water, Mercy, Amber, 1/2 Gallon 12.00
Mineral Water, Middletown Healing Springs, Grays & Clark, Vt., Amber, Quart 25.00
Mineral Water, Middletown Mineral Spring Co., Round, Dark Green, 9 1/2 In. 40.00
Mineral Water, Middletown Springs, Gray & Clark, Amber, Quart 41.00
Mineral Water, Missisquoi A Spring, Green, Quart 32.50
Mineral Water, Missisquoi A Springs, Emerald Green, Quart 50.00
Mineral Water, Missisquoi A, Light Olive, Quart 35.00
Mineral Water, Mississippi Springs, Embossed A, Emerald Green, Quart 30.00
Mineral Water, Moses' Poland Water, 11 1/2 In. 20.00

Mineral Water, J.Boardman & Co., Cobalt, 7 1/2 In.

Mineral Water, Moses' Poland, Pint 9.50
Mineral Water, Moses' Poland, Stopper Top, Amber, Quart 17.00
Mineral Water, Mount Holyoke Lithia Spring, Blob Lip, Bimal, Aqua, Pint 25.00
Mineral Water, Oak Orchard, Acid Springs, Amber, Quart 55.00
Mineral Water, Oak Orchard, Acid Springs, G.W.Merchant, Green, Quart 30.00
Mineral Water, Oak Orchard, Acid Springs, G.W.Merchant, N.Y., Emerald, 9 In. 25.00
Mineral Water, Oak Orchard, Acid Springs, Lockport, N.Y., Emerald, Quart 35.00
Mineral Water, Oak Orchard, Acid Springs, Lockport, N.Y., Opaque, Amber, Quart 85.00
Mineral Water, Questover Springs Water Co., Blown In Mold, Aqua, 2 Quart 18.00
Mineral Water, Red Sulphur Springs, Monroe Co., W.Va., Amber, 9 In. 19.75
Mineral Water, Saratoga Red Spring, Green, Quart 35.00
Mineral Water, Saratoga Red Spring, Whittled, Green, Pint 30.00
Mineral Water, Saratoga Spouting Springs, Pint 22.00
Mineral Water, Saratoga Springs, Embossed Star, Amber, Quart .... 30.00 To 31.00
Mineral Water, Saratoga Springs, Embossed Star, Green, Quart .... 35.00 To 47.50
Mineral Water, Saratoga Type, Whitney Glass Works, N.J., Dug, Green, Pint 27.50
Mineral Water, Saratoga, N.Y., Pontil, Olive Green, Pint 18.50
Mineral Water, Star Spring, Saratoga, N.Y., Amber, Pint 35.00
Mineral Water, Stratford's Springs, Wheeling, W.Va., Blue, 9 3/4 In. 3.50
Mineral Water, Upper Blue Lick, Pierce, Ky., 9 In. ....*Color* 250.00

Mineral Water, **Vermont Springs,** Saxe & Co., Sheldon, Vt., Green, Quart 50.00
Mineral Water, **Veronica Medicinal Spring,** Santa Barbara, Amber, 11 In. 30.00
Mineral Water, **Vichy,** Green, 10 1/2 In. ....*Illus* 3.00
Mineral Water, **Vichy,** Saratoga, N.Y., Aqua, Quart 35.00
Mineral Water, **Victoria A Springs,** Frelighsburg, Canada, Blue Aqua, Quart 185.00
Mineral Water, **Virginia Bear Spring,** Shenandoah Valley, Blue Aqua, 5 Pint 16.00
Mineral Water, **Washington Spring,** Green, Pint 55.00
Mineral Water, **Weston & Co.,** C.W., Saratoga, N.Y., Dug, Olive Green, Pint 40.00
Mineral Water, **Weston,** C.W., Embossed Shoulder, Crude, Olive Green, Quart 43.00

Mineral Water, Vichy, Green, 10 1/2 In.

Mineral Water, **Weston,** C.W., Saratoga, N.Y., Crude, Olive Green, Pint 35.00
Mineral Water, **Weston,** Dug, Pontil, Olive Green, Pint 15.00
Mineral Water, **Whitney Glass Works,** N.J., Monogram, Hazy, Green, Pint 32.50
Mineral Water, **Witter Springs Water,** Amber, 9 1/2 In. 5.00
Miniature, **Abbey Wine,** Set Of 6 .... 35.00
Miniature, **Aidees Of Torquay,** Barrel Of Kindness Scotch 4.50
Miniature, **Aidees Of Torquay,** Bull 6.00
Miniature, **Aidees Of Torquay,** Chicken 4.50
Miniature, **Aidees Of Torquay,** Cries Of London Flask 4.50
Miniature, **Aidees Of Torquay,** Deacon Brodie Pub Handle 4.50
Miniature, **Aidees Of Torquay,** Devon Mead Jug 4.50
Miniature, **Aidees Of Torquay,** Doe Head 4.50
Miniature, **Aidees Of Torquay,** Dog, Glass 4.50
Miniature, **Aidees Of Torquay,** Dueling Pistol 5.00
Miniature, **Aidees Of Torquay,** Elf 4.50
Miniature, **Aidees Of Torquay,** Golf Ball 4.50
Miniature, **Aidees Of Torquay,** Lamp With Shade 4.50
Miniature, **Aidees Of Torquay,** Lighthouse 4.50
Miniature, **Aidees Of Torquay,** Little Sherry Butt 4.50
Miniature, **Aidees Of Torquay,** Rabbit 4.50
Miniature, **Aidees Of Torquay,** Robert Burns Bust 4.50
Miniature, **Aidees Of Torquay,** Scotch Barrel, Clear 4.50
Miniature, **Aidees Of Torquay,** Scotch Still 4.50
Miniature, **Aidees Of Torquay,** Scottie Dog 4.50
Miniature, **Aidees Of Torquay,** Ship's Lantern 4.00
Miniature, **Aidees Of Torquay,** Spirit Of Scotland Flask 4.50
Miniature, **Aidees Of Torquay,** Spirit Of Spain Book Flask 4.50
Miniature, **Aidees Of Torquay,** Tam-O-Shanter 4.50
Miniature, **Aidees Of Torquay,** Tennis Ball 4.50
Miniature, **Aidees Of Torquay,** Thistle, Clear Glass 4.00
Miniature, **Aidees Of Torquay,** Toby Jug 4.50
Miniature, **Aidees Of Torquay,** World Cup 4.50
Miniature, **All's Well That Ends Well,** 4 In. ....*Illus* 12.50
Miniature, **Alta,** Jug 3.50
Miniature, **Antique Bourbon** ....*Illus* 3.50
Miniature, **Ardo,** Gambia, 5 In. 3.50
Miniature, **Ardo,** Gondola, 6 In. 3.50
Miniature, **Ardo,** Nubian, 5 In. 3.50
Miniature, **Ardo,** Paestum, 4 1/2 In. 3.00
Miniature, **Argentine Gaucho** 15.00

Miniature, All's Well That Ends Well, 4 In.
(See Page 169)

Miniature, Antique Bourbon
(See Page 169)

Miniature, **Armagnac**, Shotgun Shell, Green	3.00
Miniature, **Armagnac**, Shotgun Shell, Red	5.00
Miniature, **Arrow Coffee Brandy**	1.00
Miniature, **Assumption Abbey**	1.00
Miniature, **Augustus Rex**, 5 3/4 In., Pair	250.00
Miniature, **Banker**	6.95
Miniature, **Bardinet**, Orange, Glass	15.00
Miniature, **Barsottini**, Cupid On Half Moon	35.00
Miniature, **Barsottini**, Dog On House	35.00
Miniature, **Barsottini**, Drunk On Lamppost	35.00
Miniature, **Barsottini**, Little Soldier	35.00
Miniature, **Barsottini**, Man Playing Guitar	35.00
Miniature, **Barsottini**, Nubian	35.00
Miniature, **Barsottini**, Soldier	25.00
Miniature, **Barsottini**, TV Screen	20.00
Miniature, **Battle Of Concord**	24.00
Miniature, **Beer**, Acme	2.50
Miniature, **Beer**, Ballantine's, Red Lettering	4.00
Miniature, **Beer**, Blatz	2.50
Miniature, **Beer**, Budweiser	2.50
Miniature, **Beer**, Drewry's Ale	1.75
Miniature, **Beer**, Eastside	5.00
Miniature, **Beer**, Edelweiss	6.00
Miniature, **Beer**, Fort Pitt	3.00
Miniature, **Beer**, Fort Pitt, Salt & Pepper, 3 & 4 In.	3.00
Miniature, **Beer**, Hamm's, Bear, Miniature, 1972	8.00
Miniature, **Beer**, Hamm's, Bear, 1973	8.00
Miniature, **Beer**, Jax-Beer	1.25
Miniature, **Beer**, Miller High Life	6.00
Miniature, **Beer**, Old Shay	7.00
Miniature, **Beer**, Pabst	3.00
Miniature, **Beer**, Piel's	6.00
Miniature, **Beer**, Prager	4.00
Miniature, **Beer**, Schaefer	7.00
Miniature, **Beer**, Schlitz	2.00 To 2.50
Miniature, **Beer**, Schmidt's	5.00
Miniature, **Bell's**, Bell Shape	1.00
Miniature, **Bellows Club Bourbon**	1.00
Miniature, **Beneagles**, Barrel, 2 In.	5.00
Miniature, **Beneagles**, Curling Stone, 2 1/2 In.	5.00
Miniature, **Beneagles**, Deer, 3 1/2 In.	4.00 To 6.00

Miniature, Beneagles, Eagle, 3 1/2 In.	5.00 To 6.00
Miniature, Beneagles, Edinburgh Castle	4.00
Miniature, Beneagles, Haggis	7.00
Miniature, Beneagles, Loch Ness Monster With Beret, 3 In.	5.00
Miniature, Beneagles, Pheasant	4.00 To 6.00
Miniature, Beneagles, Pike, 3 1/2 In.	4.00
Miniature, Beneagles, Robert Burns Cottage, 2 In.	4.00
Miniature, Beneagles, Sportsman Flask	6.00
Miniature, Beneagles, Tower Bridge	4.00
Miniature, Beneagles, Trout	4.00 To 6.00
Miniature, Benoit Series, Eiffel Tower	7.00
Miniature, Birds, Set Of 6, 1971	30.00
Miniature, Black Bull	4.95
Miniature, Black Velvet	1.00
Miniature, Bols, Farm Woman	25.00
Miniature, Bols, Gin Crock	3.00
Miniature, Bols, Lobster Claw & Creel	35.00
Miniature, Bols, Tulip, Hand Blown	30.00
Miniature, Borghini, Cat	5.00 To 8.00
Miniature, Borghini, Fruit Bowl, 7 In.	.49 To 8.00
Miniature, Borghini, Lantern, 6 In.	4.95 To 8.00
Miniature, Borghini, Man In Cask	8.00
Miniature, Borghini, Nubian	5.00
Miniature, Borghini, Old Man Cask, 6 In.	4.95
Miniature, Borghini, Penguin, 6 In.	3.25 To 5.00
Miniature, Brams, Guitarist	30.00
Miniature, Bresciani, Egyptian Urn, 5 In.	4.00
Miniature, Bronte, Jug No.1	5.00
Miniature, Bronte, Jug No.2	5.00
Miniature, Burro	15.00
Miniature, Buton, Amphora, Silver & Glass	15.00
Miniature, Cabin Still	.75
Miniature, Calvert	.75
Miniature, Canadian Goose	15.00
Miniature, Caravel, Sailor	8.00
Miniature, Casamari, Boot, 1 Oz.	14.00 To 15.00
Miniature, Castagnon, Joan Of Arc, Black Glass	110.00
Miniature, Caveman	12.00
Miniature, Cazalla, Tower Of Seville, Glass	8.00
Miniature, Cazanove, Seal With Ball	12.50
Miniature, Cazanove, Upside Down Woman	8.00
Miniature, Certosini, Monk, Large	20.00
Miniature, Certosini, Monk, Small	30.00
Miniature, Charles Jacquin Et Cie, 3 In. *Illus*	8.00
Miniature, Cherry Blossom	1.00
Miniature, Chivas Regal	1.25
Miniature, Clyde	12.50
Miniature, Columbus Monument, Spain, Milk Glass	50.00
Miniature, Condor	15.95
Miniature, Coronet	1.00
Miniature, Courvoisier	1.25
Miniature, Crown Distilleries	30.00
Miniature, Cuckenheimer, Square	2.50
Miniature, Cunnington Soda, Ginger Ale	2.50
Miniature, Cutty Sark	1.00
Miniature, Cyrus Nobel, The Miner, Bartender, & Assayer, Set Of 3, 6 In.	65.00
Miniature, Delatour, Vase	9.00
Miniature, Dewar's White Label	10.00
Miniature, Dickel, Golf Club	5.00
Miniature, Dickel, Powder Horn	3.00
Miniature, Dolfi, Glass Egg	20.00
Miniature, Dove	15.00
Miniature, Dr.Pepper	7.00
Miniature, Drioli, Bull, 1970	15.00
Miniature, Drioli, Cat	15.00

Miniature, Charles Jacquin Et Cie, 3 In.
(See Page 171)

Miniature, Drioli, Cat, Murano Glass, 5 In.	5.50
Miniature, Drioli, Dog	15.00
Miniature, Drioli, Dog, Murano Glass, 5 In.	5.50
Miniature, Drioli, Donkey, 1970	5.00
Miniature, Drioli, Duck	15.00
Miniature, Drioli, Duck, Murano Glass, 6 In.	5.50
Miniature, Drioli, Elephant, 1970	5.00
Miniature, Drioli, Hippies, Set Of 6, 1971	30.00
Miniature, Drioli, Indian Maiden	25.00
Miniature, Drioli, Limbo Dancer	12.00
Miniature, Drioli, Merchant Of Venus	5.00
Miniature, Drioli, Mouse	15.00
Miniature, Drioli, Mouse, Murano Glass, 5 1/2 In.	5.50
Miniature, Drioli, Natives, Set Of 6, 1971	20.00
Miniature, Drioli, Owl, 1970	15.00
Miniature, Drioli, Teardrop	15.00
Miniature, Drioli, Turkey, 1970	5.00
Miniature, Dubonnet Red	1.00
Miniature, Dubouchett, Coffee	1.00
Miniature, Dubouchett, Cylinder	5.00
Miniature, Duca D'Asti, Fish Bobbin, 4 1/2 In.	7.50
Miniature, Duca D'Asti, Soccer Ball	7.00
Miniature, Duca D'Asti, Soldier	7.50
Miniature, Dumont, Penguin	25.00
Miniature, El Lorito, Parrot	25.00
Miniature, Embros, Pitcher	7.00
Miniature, Escat, Fiddle & Drum	12.00
Miniature, Evelt, Light Bulb	5.50
Miniature, Famous Firsts, DeWitt Clinton Steam Engine	13.00
Miniature, Famous Firsts, French Telephone	12.00
Miniature, Famous Firsts, Lotus Indy Racer	13.00
Miniature, Famous Firsts, Marmon Wasp	13.00
Miniature, Famous Firsts, National 1912 Racer	13.00
Miniature, Famous Firsts, San Francisco Cable Car	13.00
Miniature, Famous Firsts, Sewing Machine	12.00
Miniature, Fanta	1.00
Miniature, Fleishmann	1.00
Miniature, Fockink, Cylinder	5.00
Miniature, For Pitt, Stubby	4.00
Miniature, Fox On Log	12.50
Miniature, Franzia Port	2.50
Miniature, Freemont Abbey Wine, Birds, Set Of 6, 5 In.	35.00
Miniature, Fulton Bourbon, 1906	9.00
Miniature, Fulton Rye, 1906	10.00
Miniature, Gagliano, Empress	25.00
Miniature, Gagliano, Gondolier	15.00
Miniature, Gagliano, Man With Shield	25.00
Miniature, Gagliano, Woman's Bust	25.00
Miniature, Galliano	1.50
Miniature, Galliano Soldier	6.00
Miniature, Garnier Abricotine	2.00
Miniature, Garnier, Bellboy	30.00

Miniature, Garnier, Butterflies, Set Of 6, 1971	30.00
Miniature, Garnier, Chessmen, Black, Set Of 6, 1972	36.00
Miniature, Garnier, Chessmen, White, Set Of 6, 1972	36.00
Miniature, Garnier, Dogs, Set Of 6, 1972	36.00
Miniature, Garnier, Elephant	25.00
Miniature, Garnier, Flowers, Set Of 6, 1972	30.00
Miniature, Garnier, Foreign Houses, Set Of 6, 1973	36.00
Miniature, Garnier, Hen & Chicks	25.00
Miniature, Garnier, Jack	6.50
Miniature, Garnier, King	6.50
Miniature, Garnier, Nurse	35.00
Miniature, Garnier, Pelican	35.00
Miniature, Garnier, Playing Cards, Set Of 6, 1971	30.00
Miniature, Garnier, Queen	6.50
Miniature, Garnier, Safari Animals, Set Of 6, 1973	36.00
Miniature, Garnier, Skittles, Set Of 6	175.00
Miniature, Garnier, Tropical Fish	36.00
Miniature, George Dickel	1.00
Miniature, Gettelman Rathskeller	3.50
Miniature, Gioiello, Tower Of Pisa	15.00
Miniature, Glass Animal, Camel, 4 In. .... *Illus*	7.00
Miniature, Glass Animal, Pelican, 4 In. .... *Illus*	6.00
Miniature, Glass Animal, Pig, 4 In. .... *Illus*	7.00
Miniature, Glen Garry	1.00
Miniature, Glen Grant Malt	2.50

Miniature, Glass Animal, Pelican, 4 In.   Miniature, Glass Animal, Camel, 4 In.   Miniature, Glass Animal, Pig, 4 In.

Miniature, His Masters Breath, 4 In.

Miniature, Goetz Country Club	4.00 To 6.00
Miniature, Goetz Super X	7.00
Miniature, Grand Canadian, Flask	2.50
Miniature, Grand Giffard, Coffeepot, 4 In.	7.50
Miniature, Grand Giffard, Pitcher, 4 In.	7.50
Miniature, Grand Giffard, Vase, 5 1/2 In.	7.50
Miniature, Grand Marnier	1.50
Miniature, Grenadier, Soldiers, Set Of 3, 5 1/2 In.	21.50
Miniature, H.H.Orange Bitters, 2 Oz.	2.00
Miniature, Haig & Haig, Pinch	1.25
Miniature, Harpy	15.00
Miniature, Hennessey	1.25
Miniature, Hiram Walker, Creme De Cacao	1.00
Miniature, His Masters Breath, Pottery, Japan .... *Illus*	10.00
Miniature, His Masters Breath, 4 In. .... *Illus*	15.00
Miniature, Hobo, Pottery, 5 In. .... *Illus*	45.00

Miniature, His Masters Breath, Pottery, Japan
(See Page 173)

Miniature, Hot Water Bottle

Miniature, Hobo, Pottery, 5 In.
(See Page 173)

Miniature, Horseshoe, Gold		6.50
Miniature, Horseshoe, Platinum		6.50
Miniature, Hot Water Bottle	*Illus*	22.00
Miniature, House Of Bottles, Elephant On A Drum		14.95
Miniature, House Of Koshu, Angel		5.00
Miniature, House Of Koshu, Beethoven		5.00
Miniature, House Of Koshu, Black Knight		5.00
Miniature, House Of Koshu, Cupid On Barrel		5.00
Miniature, House Of Koshu, Guitar		5.00
Miniature, House Of Koshu, Honey Apple		1.00
Miniature, House Of Koshu, Laurel Pitcher		5.00
Miniature, House Of Koshu, Plum		1.00
Miniature, House Of Koshu, Sailor		5.00
Miniature, Hudson's Bay, 2 Oz.		2.50
Miniature, Hulskamp, Airplane With Stand		35.00
Miniature, Hutique, Little Grass Shack, 3 1/2 In.		2.00
Miniature, IDA, Elephant, Pink		35.00
Miniature, IDA, Fish		25.00
Miniature, IDA, Robot		20.00
Miniature, Inca, Pisco, 4 1/2 In.		3.00
Miniature, Irish Mist, Soldier		7.00
Miniature, Isaiah, Accordionist, 5 In.		12.00
Miniature, Isaiah, Beetles, 4 1/2 In.		9.95
Miniature, Isaiah, Mermaid, 5 In.		12.00
Miniature, Isaiah, Tutankhamen, 4 1/2 In.		9.95
Miniature, Ivanoff, Drunk Russian		6.00
Miniature, J & B		1.00
Miniature, Jacquin, Washington Bust		9.00
Miniature, Jacquin's Blackberry Brandy		1.25
Miniature, Johnny Walker Black		1.25
Miniature, Jules Robin, Eiffel Tower		9.00
Miniature, Kangaroo		12.50
Miniature, King		2.50
Miniature, Kingsbury Pale		6.00
Miniature, Kiss Snookums, 5 1/4 In.	*Illus*	38.00
Miniature, Kord Kummel		2.00
Miniature, Kord, Horse's Head, Glass, 3 1/2 In.		2.00
Miniature, La Barracca, House		8.00
Miniature, Lady, Pottery, 5 In.	*Illus*	12.00

Miniature, Kiss Snookums, 5 1/4 In.
(See Page 174)

Miniature, Lamp, Rum, Carioca, 6 In.

Miniature, Lady,
Pottery, 5 In.
(See Page 174)

Miniature, Lady's Bust, 3 1/2 In.

Miniature, **Lady's Bust,** 3 1/2 In.	*Illus*	7.50
Miniature, **Lamp,** Rum, Carioca, 6 In.	*Illus*	10.00
Miniature, **Larsen's,** Viking Ship		12.00
Miniature, **Las Vegas**		5.00
Miniature, **Laurel & Hardy,** Each		9.00
Miniature, **Leroux,** Creme De Menthe		1.00
Miniature, **Leroux,** Ginger Brandy		1.00
Miniature, **Lindsfarne,** Cross		9.00
Miniature, **Lionstone,** Blue Crowned Chlorophonia, Tropical Bird Series		32.00
Miniature, **Lionstone,** Canary		25.50
Miriature, **Lionstone,** Cardinal, Fancy Bird Series	22.50 To	32.00
Miniature, **Lionstone,** Emerald Toucan, Tropical Bird Series		32.00
Miniature, **Lionstone,** Hummingbrid, Fancy Bird Series	22.50 To	32.00
Miniature, **Lionstone,** Leopold Lyon	9.50 To	32.00
Miniature, **Lionstone,** Lion	7.00 To	8.95
Miniature, **Lionstone,** Northern Flycatcher, Tropical Bird Series		32.00
Miniature, **Lionstone,** Oriental Woodpecker, Fancy Bird Series	22.50 To	32.00
Miniature, **Lionstone,** Painted Bunting, Tropical Bird Series		32.00
Miniature, **Lionstone,** Scarlet Macaw, Tropical Bird Series		32.00
Miniature, **Lionstone,** Tropical Birds, 1974, Set Of 6	60.00 To	67.50
Miniature, **Lionstone,** Western, Set Of 6		65.00
Miniature, **Lionstone,** Wild Canary, Fancy Bird Series		32.00
Miniature, **Lionstone,** Yellow Headed Amazon, Tropical Bird Series		32.00
Miniature, **Luxardo,** Amphora, Cinnamon & Rack		85.00
Miniature, **Luxardo,** Apothecary Jar		20.00
Miniature, **Luxardo,** Babies		30.00
Miniature, **Luxardo,** Bear		6.50
Miniature, **Luxardo,** Bison	6.50 To	7.50
Miniature, **Luxardo,** Black Cat, 1959		25.00
Miniature, **Luxardo,** Boar		7.50
Miniature, **Luxardo,** Bulldog, 1973	7.50 To	9.00
Miniature, **Luxardo,** Burma Ashtray, 1960		7.50
Miniature, **Luxardo,** Cat		7.50
Miniature, **Luxardo,** Chess Set, Set Of 6		450.00

Miniature, Luxardo, Dog	20.00
Miniature, Luxardo, Fish	42.50
Miniature, Luxardo, Frog, 1973	7.50 To 9.00
Miniature, Luxardo, Fruits, Set Of 6	250.00
Miniature, Luxardo, Gambia, 1973	7.50 To 9.00
Miniature, Luxardo, Gondola, 1968	7.50
Miniature, Luxardo, Gondolier, 1973	9.00
Miniature, Luxardo, Hippo	6.50 To 7.50
Miniature, Luxardo, Lion	6.50 To 7.50
Miniature, Luxardo, Mosaic Ashtray, 1959	7.50
Miniature, Luxardo, Mudbucket	12.00
Miniature, Luxardo, Nubian, 1973	7.50 To 9.00
Miniature, Luxardo, Owl, 1973	7.50 To 9.00
Miniature, Luxardo, Paestum, 1968	7.50
Miniature, Luxardo, Pig	6.50
Miniature, Luxardo, Rhino	6.50 To 7.50
Miniature, Luxardo, Turkey	40.00 To 50.00
Miniature, Luxardo, Venus De Milo, 1968	7.50
Miniature, Luxardo, Wild Animals, Set Of 6, 1972	48.00
Miniature, M.B.C., Banker	8.95
Miniature, M.B.C., Bar Scene, Set Of 6	75.00
Miniature, M.B.C., Battle Of Concord, Set Of 6	22.50
Miniature, M.B.C., Camel	8.95
Miniature, M.B.C., Foxes Pennsylvania Dutch, Pair	15.00
Miniature, M.B.C., Golden Horseshoe, 4 1/2 In.	9.00
Miniature, M.B.C., Golden Rooster, Black Base, 5 In.	9.00
Miniature, M.B.C., Golden Rooster, White Base, 5 In.	9.00
Miniature, M.B.C., Horseshoe	5.95 To 8.95
Miniature, M.B.C., Landmark Hotel	8.95
Miniature, M.B.C., Las Vegas, Dunes Hotel	8.95
Miniature, M.B.C., Las Vegas, Globe	8.95
Miniature, M.B.C., Las Vegas, Silver Horseshoe	5.95 To 9.00
Miniature, M.B.C., Laurel & Hardy, 6 In., Pair	16.00
Miniature, M.B.C., Peddler	8.95
Miniature, M.B.C., Reno, Gold Horseshoe	5.95 To 9.00
Miniature, M.B.C., Reno, Paul's Payless Slot	5.95 To 9.00
Miniature, M.B.C., Save Most Man	8.95
Miniature, M.B.C., Slot	8.95
Miniature, M.B.C., Stein, Blue	8.95
Miniature, M.B.C., Stein, Brown	8.95
Miniature, Manco, Capac Warrior	4.00
Miniature, Marie Brizard Apry	2.00
Miniature, Mattingly & Moore	.75
Miniature, McKelvy, Whiskey Jug, 1 3/4 Oz.	9.00
Miniature, McLecg, Dueling Pistols	8.50
Miniature, Mead, Koala Bear	4.00
Miniature, Meier's, Baseball	9.50
Miniature, Meier's, Football	9.50
Miniature, Metaxa, Vase	10.00
Miniature, Milshire Gin	3.00
Miniature, Mirinda, Orange	2.50
Miniature, Mirinda, Soda	2.50
Miniature, Mittenwalder, Bass Fiddle	15.00
Miniature, Mobana, Monkey	3.00 To 5.00
Miniature, Mogen David, Cannoneer, Set Of 6	24.95
Miniature, Mogen David, Revolutionary Soldiers, Set Of 6	25.00
Miniature, Motto Jug, Compliments, 2 1/2 In. *Color*	7.50
Miniature, Motto Jug, Detrick Distilling Co., Dayton, O., 1/2 Pint	17.75
Miniature, Motto Jug, Old Continental Whiskey, 3 1/2 In *Color*	17.50
Miniature, Motto Jug, 4 1/2 In. *Color*	18.00
Miniature, Mt.Eagle	16.95
Miniature, Nadwislanski, Mug	5.00
Miniature, Nassau, Royal Policeman	9.95
Miniature, Neuss, Lemon	2.50
Miniature, Old Crow	.75

Miniature, Old Scotch, Pottery, 4 1/2 In.

Miniature, One Of The Boys

Miniature, Old Grand-Dad	1.00
Miniature, Old Mr.Boston	1.00
Miniature, Old Mr.Boston Anisette	10.00
Miniature, Old Scotch, Pottery, 4 1/2 In. ....*Illus*	28.00
Miniature, One Of The Boys ....*Illus*	35.00
Miniature, Orange Crush	2.50 To 7.00
Miniature, Osprey	15.00
Miniature, Ouzo	1.50
Miniature, Paso De Los Toros	2.50
Miniature, Pastore, Cherry	2.50
Miniature, Pastore, Cola	2.50
Miniature, Pastore, Lemon	2.50
Miniature, Peddler	6.95 To 8.95
Miniature, Peppermint Schnapps	1.00
Miniature, Pepsi-Cola	2.50
Miniature, Peter Hagen Banana	1.50
Miniature, Peter Hagen Grasshopper	2.50
Miniature, Philip Blum, Barrel	35.00
Miniature, Pictorial Bottle Review, Antique Peddler	7.00
Miniature, Polmos Goldwasser	1.50
Miniature, Pritty, Orange	2.50
Miniature, Queen's Castle, Barrel, 3 In.	3.00
Miniature, R.E.Garner, Fine Liquors, Anniston, Ala., 3 In ....*Color*	15.00
Miniature, Remy Martin V.S.O.P.	1.25
Miniature, Riccadonna Dry Vermouth	1.00
Miniature, Riemerschmid Bavarian Monastery	2.00
Miniature, Riemerschmid China Coffeepot	2.50
Miniature, Ringmaster	13.00
Miniature, Rocher Freres, Admiral	25.00
Miniature, Rocher Freres, Aviator	20.00
Miniature, Rocher Freres, Guardsman	20.00
Miniature, Rocher Freres, Hindu	25.00
Miniature, Rocher Freres, Sailor	25.00
Miniature, Romantico	2.50
Miniature, Ron Carioca, Oxcarts, 1941	15.00
Miniature, Ron Carioca, Pirates, 1941	15.00
Miniature, Ron Rico Light	1.00
Miniature, Rooster, Black	5.00
Miniature, Rooster, White	5.00
Miniature, Royal Reserve M	.75
Miniature, Rutherford, Barrel	5.50
Miniature, Rutherford, Book, Black, Volume I	3.00
Miniature, Rutherford, Book, Blue, Volume III	3.00

Miniature, Rutherford, Book, Green, Volume II 3.00
Miniature, Rutherford, Book, Red, Volume IV 3.00
Miniature, Rutherford, Bull 6.00
Miniature, Rynbende, Baby 20.00
Miniature, Rynbende, Bulldog 20.00
Miniature, Rynbende, Delft Oil Lamp 5.00
Miniature, Rynbende, Delft Shoe 5.00
Miniature, Rynbende, Duck, Blown Glass 5.00
Miniature, Rynbende, Fox, Blown Glass 5.00
Miniature, Rynbende, Goose, Blown Glass 5.00
Miniature, Rynbende, Kangaroo, Blown Glass 5.00
Miniature, Rynbende, Lamp 30.00
Miniature, Rynbende, Owl, Blown Glass 5.00
Miniature, Rynbende, Pelican, Blown Glass 5.00
Miniature, Rynbende, Penguin, Blown Glass 5.00
Miniature, Rynbende, Sailor, Popeye Pipe, 5 In. 60.00
Miniature, Rynbende, Sea Lion, Blown Glass 5.00
Miniature, Rynbende, Swan, Blown Glass, 5 In. 5.00
Miniature, S.S.Pierce 2.50
Miniature, Samovar 1.50
Miniature, Sapins, Tree Trunk 7.50
Miniature, Scotch Whisky, Pottery, 7 In. .... *Illus* 50.00
Miniature, Seal Gin, HDB&c, Olive, 6 1/2 In. 60.00
Miniature, Serrandrea, Accordionist 15.00
Miniature, Serrandrea, David 8.00

Miniature, Scotch Whisky, Pottery, 7 In.

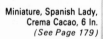

Miniature, Spanish Lady,
Crema Cacao, 6 In.
(See Page 179)

Miniature, Toreador,
Crema Cacao, 6 In.
(See Page 179)

Miniature, Serrandrea, Fisherman 15.00
Miniature, Serrandrea, Hunter Woman 15.00
Miniature, Serrandrea, Moses 8.00
Miniature, Serrandrea, Pieta 8.00
Miniature, Sicilian, Gold 9.00
Miniature, Sicilian, Gold Cremona 1.00
Miniature, Ski Country, Burro .... 13.00 To 15.00
Miniature, Ski Country, California Condo 10.00
Miniature, Ski Country, Canada Goose .... 11.00 To 13.95
Miniature, Ski Country, Caveman .... 11.00 To 12.50
Miniature, Ski Country, Clyde .... 11.00 To 13.00

Miniature, Ski Country, Condor .... 10.50 To 13.50
Miniature, Ski Country, Dove 11.00
Miniature, Ski Country, Eagle 20.00
Miniature, Ski Country, Eagle, Harpy 12.00
Miniature, Ski Country, Eagle, Majestic 25.00
Miniature, Ski Country, Elephant .... 14.00 To 20.00
Miniature, Ski Country, Fox On Log 11.00
Miniature, Ski Country, Gila Woodpecker 17.00
Miniature, Ski Country, Golden Eagle 13.00
Miniature, Ski Country, Goose 13.00
Miniature, Ski Country, Harpie 13.00
Miniature, Ski Country, Hawk .... 12.00 To 17.00
Miniature, Ski Country, Kangaroo .... 11.00 To 13.00
Miniature, Ski Country, Ladies Of Leadville, Pair .... 20.00 To 21.00
Miniature, Ski Country, Majestic Eagle 25.00
Miniature, Ski Country, Mallard Duck .... 12.50 To 13.75
Miniature, Ski Country, Mountain Eagle .... 10.00 To 13.50
Miniature, Ski Country, Mountain Lion 13.95
Miniature, Ski Country, Mountain Ram 10.00
Miniature, Ski Country, Osprey 15.00
Miniature, Ski Country, Peace Dove .... 13.00 To 14.00
Miniature, Ski Country, Peacock .... 12.00 To 17.00
Miniature, Ski Country, Ram 13.00
Miniature, Ski Country, Red Shouldered Hawk 10.00
Miniature, Ski Country, Red Tailed Fox 13.95
Miniature, Ski Country, Ringmaster .... 12.50 To 13.50
Miniature, Ski Country, Rocky Mountain Sheep 17.00
Miniature, Ski Country, Snowy Owl .... 11.95 To 25.00
Miniature, Ski Country, Woodpecker .... 12.00 To 15.00
Miniature, Smirnoff 100 .... 1.00
Miniature, Soda, Smile 5.00
Miniature, Spanish Lady, Crema Cacao, 6 In. .... *Illus* 18.00
Miniature, Sprite 1.00
Miniature, St.Glamer, Dog 20.00
Miniature, St.Glamer, Monkey 20.00
Miniature, Stock, Egg 45.00
Miniature, Stratton, Chick 35.00
Miniature, Tanqueray Martini 2.50
Miniature, Tavern Pale 5.00
Miniature, Teem 2.50
Miniature, Terma Naranja, Orange 2.50
Miniature, Terma Pomelo, Grapefruit 2.50
Miniature, The Greybeard, Crock, 3 In. .... *Illus* 10.00
Miniature, Toreador, Crema Cacao, 6 In. .... *Illus* 18.00
Miniature, Torras, King 7.00
Miniature, Torras, Queen 7.00
Miniature, Torras, Tower Of Columbus, Glass 13.00
Miniature, Toschi, Pharaoh & Egyptian Woman 35.00
Miniature, Vat 69, Green, 4 In. .... *Illus* 4.50

Miniature, The Greybeard, Crock, 3 In.

Miniature, Vat 69, Green, 4 In.

Miniature, Veille Cure, 86	2.50
Miniature, Vetter, German Santa Claus With Toys	13.00
Miniature, Whiskey, J.Rieger, Kansas	10.00
Miniature, Wild Turkey	.75
Miniature, Windsor	1.00
Miniature, Zubrowka	1.50
Miniature, 100 Pipers	1.00
Nailsea, Looped, 11 In. ....*Color*	140.00
Numano, Cherry Wine	1.00
Numano, Plum	.90
Numano, Saki	1.00

Nursing bottles were first used in the second half of the 19th century.
They are easily identified by the unique shape and the measuring units that
are often marked on the sides.

Nursing, Baby Bunting, Embossed Rabbit, ABM, 4 Oz.	5.00
Nursing, Baby Bunting, Rabbit, Wide Mouth, Graduated 8 Ozs.	12.50
Nursing, Bostonia In Slug Plate, Graduated 1-16 Tablespoons, 6 1/2 In.	12.00
Nursing, Bostonia, Flask Shape, 8 Oz.	4.00
Nursing, Cat & Kittens, Embossed	6.50
Nursing, Chestnut, Open Pontil, Light Apple Green, 9 In.	60.00
Nursing, Clapp's, Embossed, Amber, 4 Ozs.	2.50 To 4.00
Nursing, Cleaneasy Sanitary Sterilizer, Whitall Tatum, 10 Ozs.	9.00
Nursing, Cleaneasy Sanitary Sterilizer, Whitall Tatum, 12 Ozs.	9.00
Nursing, Dog, Embossed	6.50
Nursing, Double Ender, Clear, "Boots The Chemists Made In England"	35.00
Nursing, Embossed Baby, Oval, ABM, 7 In.	2.45
Nursing, Embossed Kittens	7.00
Nursing, Even-Flo, Nipple, Miniature	1.00
Nursing, Feed The Baby, 4 In. ....*Color*	125.00
Nursing, Graduated Nurser, The, Embossed	5.00
Nursing, Greetings To The New Baby, 4 3/4 In. ....*Color*	5.00
Nursing, Happy Baby, Embossed	5.50
Nursing, Kingwood Jersey's Sterilized Milk, 3 Mold, 8 Ozs.	12.00
Nursing, Madame Ling's Perfected, Embossed, Nipple & Stopper	15.00
Nursing, Mantua, 16 Ribs, Elongated, Yellow Green, 7 1/4 In.	45.00
Nursing, May's Sterile, Bimal	10.00
Nursing, Midwestern, Expanded 12 Diamonds, Pewter Nipple, Green, 6 1/2 In.	200.00
Nursing, Midwestern, Open Pontil, 14 Ribs, Aqua, 1/2 Pint	35.00
Nursing, Screw Top, Nipple, 2 1/2 In.High	4.00
Nursing, Sonny Boy, Embossed	8.50
Nursing, Soothing Nurser, The, Embossed, Turtle-Style	14.00
Nursing, Temp-Guard, 6 1/2 In. ....*Illus*	7.50
Nursing, The Hygienic	6.50
Nursing, The Little Papoose, 4 1/2 In. ....*Illus*	95.00
Nursing, Turtle Back, Lays Flat, Monogram, Stretched Neck, Bimal, 6 1/4 In.	11.00
Nursing, Turtle Shape, Diamond Embossed, 8 In. Center, 8 Ozs.	5.50
Nursing, Walker Gordon Laboratory's Modified, 8 Oz.	8.00
Nursing, Welfare, Twins, Nipple Openings Both Ends	23.00
Nursing, Wide Mouth, Embossed Graduated 8 Ozs.	2.50
Nursing, 12 Diamond, Light Blue Green, 6 1/2 In.	55.00
Obr, Balloon	6.50
Obr, Caboose	15.00
Obr, Covered Wagon	9.50
Obr, Pepsi-Cola St.Louis Blues Commemorative	5.00
Obr, Pierce Arrow	10.00
Obr, Pierce Arrow Sports Phaeton	25.00
Obr, River Queen	6.00
Obr, River Queen, Gold	18.00
Obr, Santa Monica Ship	20.00
Obr, Titanic	50.00
Obr, Train Engine	18.00
Ohio, Club Shape, 16 Vertical Ribs, Aqua, 9 1/2 In.	80.00
Ohio, Club, 24 Ribs Swirled To Right, Broken Swirl Base, Aqua, 8 1/2 In.	55.00
Ohio, Globular Club, 24 Ribs Swirled To Left, Broken Swirl Base, Aqua, 8 In.	50.00

Nursing, Temp-Guard, 6 1/2 In.
(See Page 180)

Nursing, The Little Papoose, 4 1/2 In.
(See Page 180)

Ohio, Globular, Folded-Down Lip, 3 1/2 In.	75.00
Ohio, Jug, Flat Globular, 24 Ribs Swirled To Left, Dark Amber, 8 In.	85.00
Ohio, Kent, Elongated Globular, 20 Ribs Swirled To Right, Aqua, 1/2 Pint	150.00
Ohio, see also Blown, Ohio	
Oil, Bear Oil, Blown, Aqua, 2 3/4 In.	17.50
Oil, Clock, Cobalt Blue	1.50
Oil, Hamilton, Aqua, 4 3/4 In.	2.00
Oil, Hamilton's Old English Black Oil, Paneled, 4 1/2 In.	2.00
Oil, Kendall, World War II, Embossed, Paper Label, Cap, ABM, Quart	5.00
Oil, Modoc, 25 Cent Size	1.00
Oil, Remington, U.M.L.	15.00
Oil, S.M.Kier, Petroleum, OP, Aqua, 7 In.	25.00
Oil, Shell Motor, Quart	5.00
Oil, Shell-Penn, Embossed, ABM, 14 In.	14.00
Oil, Sperm, Tester, Blue, 9 3/4 In.	34.00
Oil, Standard Oil, Test, Applied Lip, Cork, 7 In.	2.00
Oil, Thomas A.Edison Battery, 4 In.	1.75
Oil, Tiolene Motor, 18 In.	12.00
Oil, Vapo-Cresolene, Patent 1894, Aqua, 5 1/4 In.	3.75
Oil, 3 In 1, Triangular, Poison Ribs On 2 Sides, Emerald Green, 2 In.	7.00
Oil, 3 In 1, 3 3/4 In.	2.00
Old Crow, Bird	40.00
Old Crow, Bishop	12.50
Old Crow, Castle	12.50
Old Crow, Figurine, 1974	19.95
Old Crow, King	11.00
Old Crow, Knight	12.50
Old Crow, Queen	11.00
Old Fitzgerald, Blarney	7.00
Old Fitzgerald, California Bicentennial	11.00
Old Fitzgerald, Dog	6.50
Old Fitzgerald, Emerald	4.00
Old Fitzgerald, Flagship, Decanter	4.00 To 4.50
Old Fitzgerald, Fleur-De-Lis	10.00
Old Fitzgerald, Four Seasons	4.00
Old Fitzgerald, Gold Coaster	13.00
Old Fitzgerald, Gold Web	13.00
Old Fitzgerald, Hillbilly, Quart, 1954 .... *Illus*	45.00
Old Fitzgerald, Hillbilly, 1969 .... *Illus*	7.00

Old Fitzgerald, Hillbilly, Quart, 1954
(See Page 181)

Old Fitzgerald, Hillbilly, 1969
(See Page 181)

Old Fitzgerald, Illinois	12.00
Old Fitzgerald, Irish Counties	10.00
Old Fitzgerald, Irish Patriots	11.50
Old Fitzgerald, Leprechaun, "Plase God"	8.00 To 12.00
Old Fitzgerald, Leprechaun, Without God	8.00
Old Fitzgerald, Lexington	5.50
Old Fitzgerald, Man-O-War	6.00
Old Fitzgerald, Memphis	10.00
Old Fitzgerald, Monticello	4.00
Old Fitzgerald, Nebraska	18.00
Old Fitzgerald, Ohio University	15.00
Old Fitzgerald, Rip Van Winkle, 1971 .... *Illus*	16.00
Old Fitzgerald, Songs Of Ireland	10.00
Old Fitzgerald, Sons Of Erin	9.00
Old Fitzgerald, Vermont	14.00
Old Fitzgerald, 1962 .... *Illus*	7.00

Old Fitzgerald, Rip Van Winkle,
1971

Old Fitzgerald, 1962

Old Grand-Dad, see Whiskey, Old Grand-Dad	
Old Mr.Boston, Andretti Racing Car, Red, 1972	15.00
Old Mr.Boston, Andretti Racing Car, Yellow, 1973	18.00
Old Mr.Boston, Bookends	4.00
Old Mr.Boston, Dan Patch	17.50
Old Mr.Boston, Eagles, Boston, Mass.	20.00
Old Mr.Boston, Guitar .... 10.00 To	18.00
Old Mr.Boston, John L.Sullivan	35.00
Old Mr.Boston, Moose Club	15.00
Old Mr.Boston, Mooseheart	10.50
Old Mr.Boston, Paul Bunyan	8.00
Old Mr.Boston, Sailor	25.00
Old Mr.Boston, Venus De Milo	15.00
Old Mr.Boston, Wooden Ship Inside, C.1941, Quart	35.00
Old Taylor, see Whiskey, Old Taylor	
Omb, Bobwhite	5.00
Omb, Eagle Convention	11.50

Omb, Illinois State Capitol	8.00
Omb, Rider On Horse	12.00
Pacesetter, Unser, Olsonite Eagle No.8	22.50
Pacesetter, Vukovich, Sugaripe No.2	22.50
Pancho Villa, Mexican Gunfighter	23.50
Pepper Sauce, Blob Lip With Ring, Tapered Neck, Yellow Green, 7 3/4 In.	10.00
Pepper Sauce, Cathedral, Aqua, 8 3/4 In.	28.00

Pepper Sauce, Cathedral, Blue, 9 In.

Pepper Sauce, Cathedral, Blue, 9 In. ....*Illus*	55.00
Pepper Sauce, Cathedral, Deep Aqua, 8 1/2 In.	25.00
Pepper Sauce, Cathedral, Square, Whittled, OP, Stain, Aqua, 9 1/8 In.	35.00
Pepper Sauce, Cathedral, 6 Panel, Aqua, 9 In.	18.00
Pepper Sauce, Cathedral, 6 Panel, 3 Tier Windows, Aqua, 8 In.	22.00
Pepper Sauce, Emerald Green, 8 In.	7.50
Pepper Sauce, Flat, 8 Sided, Long Neck, Blob Lip, Aqua, 8 In.	7.00
Pepper Sauce, Fluted Neck, Blob Lip, Aqua, 9 In.	6.00
Pepper Sauce, Fluted Neck, Collared Lip, Blue Aqua, 9 In.	10.50
Pepper Sauce, Geo.Emerson, W.Somerville, Pear Shape, Ice Blue, 7 1/4 In. ..	20.00
Pepper Sauce, Geo.R.Emerson, West Somerville, Fluted Neck, Aqua, 7 1/4 In. .	28.00
Pepper Sauce, Gothic Arch, Square, Aqua, 8 1/4 In.	27.50
Pepper Sauce, Gothic Arch, Square, Light Blue, 10 In.	65.00
Pepper Sauce, Gothic Arch, 6 Sided, Aqua, 8 1/2 In.	20.00
Pepper Sauce, Gothic Arches & Windows, Burst Blister, Blue Green, 8 3/4 In.	25.00
Pepper Sauce, Hexagonal, Marked Pat.App.For S & P, Green Swirl, 8 In.	22.50
Pepper Sauce, S.& P.On Base, Swirled, 6 Sided, Emerald Green, 7 7/8 In. ...	25.00
Pepper Sauce, Spiral Ridges, Blue Green, 8 In.	22.00
Pepper Sauce, Spiral Ridges, Emerald Green, 8 In.	21.00
Pepper Sauce, Wm.Underwood, Boston, 18 Sided, Jagged Pontil, Green, 7 3/4 In.	110.00
Pepper Sauce, 4 Panels, 5 Embossed Stars In 3 Panels, Square, 6 1/2 In. ...	14.50
Pepper Sauce, 6 Sided, Straight Ribs, Turning, 8 1/4 In.	10.00
Pepper Sauce, 8 Columns Paneled Shoulder, Aqua, 9 1/4 In.	40.00
Pepper Sauce, 8 Panels, Aqua, 7 3/4 X 2 1/4 In.	30.00
Pepsi-Cola, St.Louis Blues	6.50
Pepsi-Cola, 75th Anniversary Bern Bottle, Clevenger	9.95
Perfume & Snuff, Sterling Caps, S.Mordan, Ruby, 4 3/4 In.	92.00
Perfume, A.A.Vantine Co., Oriental Orange Blossom, 3 3/4 In.	8.00
Perfume, Arched Design Front & Back, Fiery Opalescent, 2 3/4 In.	30.00
Perfume, Art Deco, Ground Stopper, Amethyst, 5 In.	6.25
Perfume, Art Deco, Ground Stopper, Golden Amber, 5 In.	6.25
Perfume, Atomizer, Czechoslovakia, Maltese Cross, Cobalt To Clear, 11 In. .	45.00
Perfume, Atomizer, Galle, Ovoid, Footed, Red Poppies, Metal Mounts, 8 3/4 In.	130.00
Perfume, Aurene, Gold Iridescence, 7 1/2 In.High	75.00
Perfume, Aurene, Iridescent, Signed, 4 1/4 In.	275.00
Perfume, Aurene, Signed, No.3294, Blue	265.00
Perfume, Baccarat, Amberina Swirl, 5 1/2 In.	24.00
Perfume, Baccarat, Atomizer, Amberina Swirl, 5 1/2 In.	30.00
Perfume, Baccarat, Faceted, Enamel Fish & Insects, Star Base, Crystal, 6 In.	70.00
Perfume, Baccarat, Green Faceted Stopper, 8 Sided Lip, 6 1/4 In.	35.00
Perfume, Baccarat, Stopper, Signed, 5 3/4 In.	17.50

Perfume, **Ball Shape,** Silver Stars, Flowers, & Base, Clear, 7 1/4 In.High 21.50
Perfume, **Banjo Shape,** Milk Glass, 3 1/2 In. 110.00
Perfume, **Blown,** Ribbed, 2 5/8 In. 15.00
Perfume, **Bohemian Glass,** Red Designs, 18K Gold Trim, 5 In.High 375.00
Perfume, **Brass Screw Cap,** Stopper, Miniature, Amethyst, 2 3/4 In.High 6.00
Perfume, **Bristol,** Blown, Stopper, Painting, Frosted, 9 3/4 In.High 18.50
Perfume, **Bulbous Base,** 3 Sided Neck, Stopper, Vaseline, 7 1/2 In. 45.00
Perfume, **Bulbous,** Gold & Blue Stopper, Light Green Opaque, 8 In.High 18.50
Perfume, **Buster Brown,** Buster In Black Hat, Frosted, 3 1/2 In. 12.00
Perfume, **Cat,** Germany, Painted, 2 In. 9.00
Perfume, **Charlie Ross,** 5 In. 22.00
Perfume, **Coalport,** Jeweled, 3 1/4 In.High 175.00
Perfume, **Cobalt,** Open Pontil, 5 X 2 In. 50.00
Perfume, **Coin Spot,** Bulb, Opalescent, 5 In. 22.00
Perfume, **Crystal,** Double, Silver Gilt Trim, Coral Beads, C.1867, 5 1/2 In. 275.00
Perfume, **Cut Crystal,** Smoky, 4 In.High 10.00
Perfume, **Cut Glass,** Cane, Hinged Silver Plate Cap With Leaf, 3 In. 21.00
Perfume, **Cut Glass,** Checko, Vaseline, 5 1/2 In. 20.00
Perfume, **Cut Glass,** Checko, 3 In. 10.00
Perfume, **Cut Glass,** Diamond Sides & Front, Stopper, 5 1/2 In.High 15.00
Perfume, **Cut Glass,** Etched Flowers & Leaves, Stopper, Signed Hawkes, 8 In. 95.00
Perfume, **Cut Glass,** French Ormolu Top With Paris Scene, Ruby, 3 1/4 In. 75.00
Perfume, **Cut Glass,** Hallmarked Sterling Cap, 3 In. 12.50
Perfume, **Cut Glass,** Hawkes, Sterling Top, Engraved Floral, 5 1/2 In. 39.00
Perfume, **Cut Glass,** Octagonal Diamond, Sterling Screw Cap, 5 1/4 In. 72.50
Perfume, **Cut Glass,** Ornate, Cranberry, 2 3/4 X 1 7/8 In. 36.50
Perfume, **Cut Glass,** Purse Size, Sterling Cap, 2 1/2 In. 15.00
Perfume, **Cut Glass,** Russian, Repousse Sterling Silver Top, 3 1/2 In.High 60.00
Perfume, **Cut Glass,** Star On Stopper, Hobstar, Block, & Bull's-Eye, 4 3/4 In. 50.00
Perfume, **Cut Glass,** Thumbprint & Engraved Carnation, Lapidary Top, 6 In. 77.75
Perfume, **Cut Smoky Crystal,** 4 In.High 10.00
Perfume, **D.Kerkoff,** Paris, Embossed, Paper Label, Ground Stopper, 3 1/2 In. 8.00
Perfume, **Danion & Baker,** Perfumers, Embossed, Metal Cap, Clear, 2 1/2 In.High 3.00
Perfume, **DeVilbiss,** Black Dragonflies On Lavender, 6 1/2 In. 22.00
Perfume, **DeVilbiss,** Gold Overlay, Opaque Rose, 6 1/2 In. 12.00
Perfume, **DeVilbiss,** Gold Wiggly Lines On Frosted, 4 1/2 In. 18.00
Perfume, **DeVilbiss,** Opalescent, 6 1/2 In. 8.00
Perfume, **DeVilbiss,** Paneled, Engraved Gold Collar, Cranberry, 6 1/2 In. 22.00
Perfume, **DeVilbiss,** Squat, Mercury Crackle, 3 In. 8.00
Perfume, **Dog,** Germany, Painted, 2 In. 9.00
Perfume, **Dresser,** Ornate Silver Overlay, Round, Green, 5 1/2 In. 26.00
Perfume, **E.Condray,** Paris Perfumeur, Aqua, 7 3/8 In. 4.00
Perfume, **E.W.Hoyt & Co.,** Lowell, Mass., Labeled, 3 1/2 In. 2.00
Perfume, **Eau De Cologne,** Shoe, 4 1/2 In.Long .... *Illus* 22.00
Perfume, **Enamel,** Viennese, 2 1/2 In.High 175.00
Perfume, **Figural,** High Boot, 3 1/2 In. 15.00
Perfume, **Figural,** Little Girl Holding Baby, 4 1/2 In. 32.00
Perfume, **Figural,** Reindeer, Blown, MUGU, 2 X 2 In. 100.00
Perfume, **Flacon,** Sterling Silver, Etched, Reserve, 2 In. 16.00
Perfume, **Flat Flame Design,** Ground Stopper, 3 In. 5.00
Perfume, **Florida Water,** Murray & Lanman, 9 In. .... *Illus* 5.00
Perfume, **Fountain With Lions,** 5 In. .... *Illus* 65.00
Perfume, **French Parfume,** Art Deco Knight, Smoky Stopper, 2 1/4 In. 5.00
Perfume, **French Porcelain,** Octagonal, Mushroom Top, White & Blue, 5 1/2 In. 27.00
Perfume, **G.W.Laird,** N.Y., Milk Glass, 4 1/2 In. 15.00
Perfume, **Galle,** Mountain Scene, Blue, Amethyst, Orange, Signed, 6 3/8 In. 235.00
Perfume, **Galle,** Orange Overlay On Robin's Egg Blue, 'etude, ' 6 1/2 In. 275.00
Perfume, **Germany,** Painted, Cat, 2 In. 9.00
Perfume, **Germany,** Painted, Dog, 2 In. 9.00
Perfume, **Gold Encrusted,** Colored Leaves, Cobalt Blue, 5 1/2 In. 35.00
Perfume, **Green,** 6 In. 5.00
Perfume, **Hand Blown,** Bubble Glass, 10 In. 7.50
Perfume, **Hand-Painted Cat,** Miniature 7.50
Perfume, **Hand-Painted Dog,** Miniature 7.50
Perfume, **Harrison's Columbian Perfumery,** Octagonal, 2 1/2 In. 18.50

Perfume, Eau De
Cologne, Shoe,
4 1/2 In.Long
(See Page 184)

Perfume, Florida Water,
Murray & Lanman, 9 In.
(See Page 184)

Perfume, Fountain
With Lions, 5 In.
(See Page 184)

Perfume, Jersey Joe Walcott, Plastic Base, 3 3/4 In.

Perfume, **Heisey,** Drip Stopper, Cut Design, Petaled Flowers, Ferns	22.50
Perfume, **Heisey,** Gold Embossed Stopper, Amber Flashed	38.00
Perfume, **Heisey,** Signed	32.50
Perfume, **Jersey Joe Walcott,** Plastic Base, 3 3/4 In. .... *Illus*	15.00
Perfume, **La Parfum Houbigant,** Gold Label, Baccarat, Ground Stopper, 3 1/4 In.	10.00
Perfume, **Lalique,** Disc Shape, Spirals Of Beading, 5 3/4 In.	62.00
Perfume, **Lalique,** Flat Swelling Shape, 'Martial Armand, ' Woman's Head	130.00
Perfume, **Lalique,** Sculptured Stopper Of 2 Frosted Birds In Flight, Signed	55.00
Perfume, **Lalique,** Spray, 4 Art Nouveau Seminude Figures	50.00
Perfume, **Lalique,** Two Overlapping Blossoms, Hobnail Centers, Signed	32.00
Perfume, **Larkin Co.,** American Beauty, Boxed	3.50
Perfume, **Lavender,** Applied Top, 4 1/2 In.	5.00
Perfume, **Lay Down,** Brass Collar & Hinged Cap, Cobalt Blue, 4 In.	30.00
Perfume, **Lay Down,** Engraved Silver Neck & Cap, Opalescent, 5 1/4 In.	45.00
Perfume, **Lead Crystal,** West Germany, Gold Sticker, 5 In.	2.50
Perfume, **Limoges,** Pedestal Shape, Enamel With Silver Gilt, 4 In.High	650.00
Perfume, **Lithyalin,** Reddish Browns, 4 3/4 In.High	245.00
Perfume, **Loetz,** Enameled Flowers, Blue Iridescent	55.00
Perfume, **Lutz,** Cap, Turquoise & White	40.00
Perfume, **Lutz,** Latticinio, Lay Down, 4 In.	35.00
Perfume, **Marble Glass,** Eggerman Type, Oriental Carvings People In Boat	125.00
Perfume, **Masonic,** Polar Star & 1913 In Silver Overlay, Green, 4 1/4 In.	65.00
Perfume, **Mellier's Quintuple Vogue,** Embossed, Glass Stopper, 8 1/4 In.	12.00
Perfume, **Midwestern,** 16 Vertical Ribs, Amethyst, 5 In.	450.00
Perfume, **Moon Mullins,** 2 In.	15.00
Perfume, **Moser,** Enameled Gold Filigree, Jeweled Flowers On Stopper, Signed	80.00
Perfume, **Moser,** Enameled, Applied Alligator & Turtle, Cut Stopper, Amber	75.00
Perfume, **Mouson & Co.,** Parfumeur, Jar, Embossed, Flared Lip, Amber, 2 1/2 In.	75.00
Perfume, **Mt.Washington,** Silver & Gold Floral, Green, 7 1/2 In.	95.00
Perfume, **Mugu,** Reindeer Shape, Blown, Cork In Nose, Gold Antlers, 2 X 2 In.	100.00

Perfume, Multicolor Coralene Beads In Random Pattern On Blue, 6 In. 155.00
Perfume, Nailsea, Flask, Gold & Orange Loopings, Blue, 2 1/2 In. 40.00
Perfume, Nash, Green & Blue Chintz On Aquamarine, Signed, 5 1/4 In. 250.00
Perfume, New England Glass Co., Clear 45.00
Perfume, Nudes, 7 3/4 In. ....*Color* XXXX.XX
Perfume, Opaline, Green, Gold Decoration 45.00
Perfume, Overlay, Embossed Screw Cap, Blue & Clear, 2 3/4 In. 175.00
Perfume, Overlay, Royal Blue & White Cut To Clear, Gold Tracery, Stopper 65.00
Perfume, Pairpoint, Controlled Bubbles, Stopper, Clear, 5 1/2 In. 35.00
Perfume, Pairpoint, Cornucopia, Petal Stopper, Cobalt & Crystal Paperweight 50.00
Perfume, Palmer Red Clover, Blob Stopper, Clear 4.00
Perfume, Palmer, 4 1/2 In. 6.00
Perfume, Pastel Coralene Beads, Transparent Blue, 6 In. 150.00
Perfume, Pencil Shape, Blue & Gold Stripes On Clear 15.00
Perfume, Phalon Perfumer, Open Pontil, 7 1/2 In. ....*Illus* 55.00

Perfume, Phalon Perfumer, Open Pontil, 7 1/2 In.

Perfume, Porcelain Egg, Tan & Brown Spots, Sterling Cap, 1885, 1 3/4 In. 45.00
Perfume, Pressed Glass, Designs, Atomizer, Dated 1890, 7 1/4 In. 16.00
Perfume, Pressed Glass, Star & Punty, Flint 68.00
Perfume, Purse, Daisy & Button, Tin Screw On Cap, Clear, 7 In.High 25.00
Perfume, Purse, Etched Flower On Clear, Silver Plate Stopper, 2 1/2 In. 9.50
Perfume, Purse, Silver, Crystal Flagon Inside, W.Comyns, 1901 .... 98.00
Perfume, R.S.Germany, Bulbous, Sunflowers, 5 In. 23.00
Perfume, R.S.Germany, Pink & White Roses On White To Green, 5 In.High 15.00
Perfume, Ribbed, Marked France, Amethyst, 4 In.High 10.00
Perfume, Richard Hudnut, 3 Flowers On Gold Label, Frosted, 8 Ozs., 5 3/4 In. 15.00
Perfume, Riker, N.Y., Scroll Shape, Ball Neck, Emerald Green, 2 3/4 In. 4.00
Perfume, Royal Sitzendorf Porcelain, Floral & Gilt, Crown Stopper 20.00
Perfume, Russian Enamel On Gilded Silver, Cathedrals, C.1900, 2 3/4 In. 1100.00
Perfume, Sandwich Glass, Canary, 6 In.High 95.00
Perfume, Satin Glass, Enameled, Flared Stopper, Pink, 5 In. 85.00
Perfume, Satin Glass, Leaf Motif, Cut Stopper, Pink 25.00
Perfume, Seely Perfumer, Detroit, Michigan, Boxed 10.00
Perfume, Shoe Shape, 3 3/4 In. 15.00
Perfume, Silver Deposit, Crystal Stopper With Silver Top, 2 1/2 In. 11.00
Perfume, Silver Deposit, Floral, Ground Stopper, 4 1/2 In.High 35.00
Perfume, Silver Deposit, Numbered Stopper, 3 1/4 In.High 19.50
Perfume, Silver Deposit, Slender, 3 1/2 In. 14.00
Perfume, Silver Deposit, Squatty, 3 1/4 In. 10.50
Perfume, Silver Deposit, 3 In. 9.00
Perfume, Silver Deposit, 3 7/8 In. 7.00
Perfume, Silver Overlay, Masonic Inscription, 1858-1908, Clear Crystal 14.50
Perfume, Silver Overlay, 3 1/2 In.High 15.00
Perfume, Silver Overlay, 3 3/4 In. 25.00
Perfume, Silver, Pink, Green, & Orange, Enameled Flowers & Crabs 40.00
Perfume, Souvenir, Sesquicentennial, 1776-1926, Bell Shape 18.75
Perfume, Sterling Overlay, Iris Decoration, Round Bottom, 5 In. 95.00
Perfume, Sterling Overlay, Lily Design, Alvin, 5 3/4 In.High 55.00
Perfume, Sterling Overlay, Poppies, 4 1/2 In. 30.00
Perfume, Sterling Scroll On Glass, Medium Size 20.00

Perfume, Sterling Silver, Round, Bright Cut, Monogram, 1 In.Diameter 15.00
Perfume, Steuben, Amber Teardrop Stopper, 6 1/2 In.High 90.00
Perfume, Steuben, Aurene, Gold Iridescent, Signed & Numbered, 4 1/2 In.High 275.00
Perfume, Steuben, Aurene, Signed, Blue, 3 1/2 In.High 575.00
Perfume, Steuben, Deep Amethyst, Signed, 6 3/4 In.High 125.00
Perfume, Steuben, Lavender Hollow Blown Stopper, 8 In.High 85.00
Perfume, Steuben, Mica Fleck & Pink Swirl Stopper, Amber, Blue Foot, Signed 425.00
Perfume, Steuben, Signed, Celeste Blue, 10 In. 95.00
Perfume, Steuben, Stopper, Signed & Numbered, Gold Aurene, 4 1/4 In., Pair 450.00
Perfume, Steuben, Verre De Soie, Cobalt Dipper, 3 1/2 In. 125.00
Perfume, Steuben, Verre De Soie, Florals, Sterling Cap, 4 In. 95.00
Perfume, Steuben, Verre De Soie, Rosaline Stopper, Carder, 8 In.High 150.00
Perfume, Stiegel Type, Checkered Diamond Pattern, 4 3/4 In. 150.00
Perfume, Stiegel Type, 20 Vertical Ribs, Bulbous, Amethyst, 5 1/2 In. 650.00
Perfume, Stiegel, Allover Ogivals, Amethystine Swirls, 4 1/2 In. 700.00
Perfume, Stiegel, Diamond Daisy Pattern, Amethyst, 4 3/4 In. 2500.00
Perfume, Stiegel, 12 Diamond Pattern, Amethyst, 4 1/2 In. 1100.00
Perfume, Stiegel, 16 Vertical Ribs, Dark Amethyst, 6 In. 550.00
Perfume, Swirl Cut, Pewter Dispenser Cap, McIlhenny, New Iberia, La. 5.00
Perfume, Teardrop Shape, Paneled, Sterling Cap, 3 1/2 In. 24.00
Perfume, Tortoiseshell Glass 38.00
Perfume, Tree Branch, Raised Bark & Stars, Frosted, 5 X 1/2 In. 2.00
Perfume, Turnip Shape, Blown, Flower Shape Stopper, Brass Pin, 1 In. 10.00
Perfume, Val St.Lambert, Cranberry Floral, Silver Plate Cap, Frosted, 6 In. 95.00
Perfume, Vantines, 7 In. .... *Illus*   2.00
Perfume, Verre De Soie, Bulbous, Melon Ribbed, Green Steeple Stopper 98.00
Perfume, Verre De Soie, Engraved, Enameled Sterling Stopper, Hawkes 48.00
Perfume, Verre De Soie, Melon Ribbed, 3 In. 38.00
Perfume, Verre De Soie, White, Pink Iridescence, 4 In.High 35.00
Perfume, Vial, Bird's Egg, Porcelain, Sterling Cap, 1885, 1 3/4 In.Long 40.00
Perfume, Vial, Chinese, Glass, Gold Paint 8.00
Perfume, Webb, Carved, White On Citron, 3 1/2 In. 300.00
Perfume, Webb, Laydown, Red Matte, Carved Floral Sprays In Cameo, Signed 575.00
Perfume, Webb, Sterling Top, White Winged Figure & Horn On Blue, Woodall 6500.00
Perfume, Webb, Turquoise Ground, Cut White Floral, Sterling Top 485.00
Perfume, White Enamel Florals, Stemmed, Amethyst, 6 1/4 In. 15.00
Perfume, White Frosted Intaglio Stopper, Flowers On Base, Rose Color 13.50
Perfume, Whittemore, Paperweight, Yellow Roses On Base & Stopper, 4 1/2 In. 300.00
Perfume, 2 Tiered, 6 Sided, Steeple Stopper, Vaseline, 5 1/2 In. 25.00
Perfume, 3 Mold, Ointment Barrel, Brass Lid, McKearin G I-19 .... 20.00
Perfume, 6 Sided, Bulbous Base, Steeple Stopper, Vaseline, 7 1/2 In. 22.50
Perfume, 12 Panels, Amethyst To Clear, 7 In. 23.00
   Perfume, see also Cologne, Scent
Pickle, Arrow Brand, J.J.Wilson, Amber, 9 1/2 In. .... *Illus* 100.00

Perfume, Vantines, 7 In.

Pickle, Arrow Brand, J.J.Wilson, Amber, 9 1/2 In.

Pickle, Barrel, 6 Rings, Emerald Green, 9 1/2 X 5 In. 25.00
Pickle, Bunker Hill, Amber, Pint .... 11.25 To 18.00
Pickle, Bunker Hill, Amber, Quart 25.00
Pickle, Bunker Hill, Amber, 3 Pints 18.00
Pickle, Bunker Hill, Embossed Tower & Barrels, Amber, Quart 17.00

Pickle, Cathedral, Blown-Out, Pontil, Aqua, 8 1/2 In.

Pickle, Cathedral, Deep Aqua, 11 1/2 In.

Pickle, Cathedral, 8 1/2 In.
(See Page 189)

Pickle, Bunker Hill, Honey Amber, Pint 80.00
Pickle, Bunker Hill, Round, Honey Amber, 7 1/2 In. 25.00
Pickle, Bunker Hill, Skilton Foote & Co., Aqua, 5 1/4 In. 6.50
Pickle, Bunker Hill, Stain, Aqua, 1/2 Pint 2.75
Pickle, Bunker Hill, Whittled, 5 1/4 In. 10.00
Pickle, Carnival Glass, Swirl, Smoke 18.00
Pickle, Cathedral, Applied Rolled Lip, Square, Deep Aqua, 11 In. .... 65.00 To 79.50
Pickle, Cathedral, Applied Rolled Lip, Square, IP, Dark Emerald, 11 In. 185.00
Pickle, Cathedral, Applied Rolled Lip, Square, IP, Light Aqua, 11 1/2 In. 124.50
Pickle, Cathedral, Aqua, 9 In. 48.00
Pickle, Cathedral, Aqua, 13 1/2 In. 50.00
Pickle, Cathedral, Blown-Out, Pontil, Aqua, 8 1/2 In. .... *Illus* 225.00
Pickle, Cathedral, Deep Aqua, 11 1/2 In. .... *Illus* 195.00
Pickle, Cathedral, Diamond Pattern Panel, Medium Green, 2 Quart 115.00
Pickle, Cathedral, Green, 1/2 Gallon .... 25.00 To 75.00
Pickle, Cathedral, IP, Aqua, 7 1/2 In. 42.50
Pickle, Cathedral, Light Green, 11 1/4 In. 95.00
Pickle, Cathedral, OP, Deep Aqua, 12 In. 125.00
Pickle, Cathedral, Square IP, Light Green, 12 In. 95.00
Pickle, Cathedral, Square, OP, Aqua, 1/2 Gallon 75.00
Pickle, Cathedral, 4 Sided, Aqua, 11 In. 45.00
Pickle, Cathedral, 4 Sided, Aqua, 11 1/2 In. 38.00
Pickle, Cathedral, 4 Sided, Embossed Flowers, Aqua, 13 1/2 In. 45.00
Pickle, Cathedral, 4 Sided, Embossed Lattice On 3 Panels, Aqua, 7 In. 55.00
Pickle, Cathedral, 4 Sided, Light Green, 12 In. 60.00
Pickle, Cathedral, 4 Sided, Medium Green, 1/2 Gallon 75.00
Pickle, Cathedral, 4 Sided, 7 In. .... 30.00 To 40.00
Pickle, Cathedral, 6 Sided, Aqua, Gallon .... 58.00 To 67.50
Pickle, Cathedral, 6 Sided, Aqua, 13 In. 35.00
Pickle, Cathedral, 6 Sided, Aqua, 13 1/2 In. .... 65.00 To 75.00

Pickle, Cathedral, 6 Sided, 13 1/2 In. 60.00
Pickle, Cathedral, 8 1/2 In. .... *Illus* 22.50
Pickle, Dodson & Hills Mfg.Co., St.Louis, 4 Sided, Aqua, 7 1/2 In.High 6.50
Pickle, East India, Aqua, 7 1/4 In. 15.00
Pickle, Embossed Roses & Trellis, Ground Lip, Pink, 5 X 15 In. 45.00
Pickle, Embossed Wreath Of Leaves, Whittled, Square, Light Aqua, 11 In. 85.00
Pickle, Goofus Glass, Embossed Gold Rose, Webb Ground, 14 In. 14.00
Pickle, Goofus Glass, Embossed Grapes & Leaves On Gold Lattice, 9 1/2 In. 8.00
Pickle, Goofus Glass, Embossed Statue Of Liberty & Eagle, Paint, 12 1/2 In. 40.00
Pickle, Goofus Glass, Embossed Statue Of Liberty & Eagle, 12 1/2 In. 49.50
Pickle, Gothic Arch, Rolled Collar, Hollow Ring Down 2 In., Aqua, 12 1/2 In. 40.00
Pickle, Gothic Arch, Square, Deep Green, 7 1/2 In. 65.00
Pickle, Gothic Arch, Square, Wide Mouth, Aqua, 7 1/4 In. 25.00
Pickle, Gothic Cathedral, OP, Aqua, 12 In. 85.00
Pickle, Grape Pattern, 15 In. 10.00
Pickle, Henry C.Kellogg, Philada., Embossed, Dug, Aqua, Pint 8.00
Pickle, Hyman Co., Louisville, Ky., Embossed, Yellow Green, 1 1/2 Quart 85.00
Pickle, Loetz, Threading, Silver Rim, Lid, & Handle, Blue & Purple, 7 In. 275.00
Pickle, Paneled, Square, Embossed Leaves, Whittled, Light Aqua, 11 In. 65.00
Pickle, Paneled, Square, IP, Light Aqua, 11 1/2 In. 100.00
Pickle, Patent Aug.20, 1901, Glass Lid, Metal Clamp, 12 In. 12.00
Pickle, Rowat & Co., Glascow, Square, Long Neck, Green, Quart, 9 1/4 In. 25.00
Pickle, Seville Packing Co., N.Y., Ribbed, Crown & Trademark, 10 3/8 In. 15.00
Pickle, Skilton Foote & Co., Bunker Hill Pickles, Honey Amber, 8 In. 15.00
Pickle, Skilton Foote & Co., Bunker Hill, Whittled, Bubbles, Aqua, 5 1/4 In. 9.00
Pickle, Skilton Foote & Co., Bunker Hill, Whittled, Yellow Green, 5 1/4 In. 9.00
Pickle, Whittled, Rolled Lip, Wide Mouth, Crooked, Blue Aqua, 4 3/4 In. 10.00
Pickle, 4 Paneled Sides, 16 Petals On Sloping Shoulder, 11 1/2 In. 28.00
Pickle, 4 Panels, Vertical Panels On Shoulder, Square, IP, Aqua, 11 In. 112.50
Pickle, 4 Sided, Amber, 7 In. 30.00
Pickle, 4 Sided, Petaled Neck, Aqua, Pint 23.50
Pickle, 4 Sided, Yellow, 8 1/2 In. 30.00
Pictorial Bottle Review, Antique Peddler .... 10.00 To 25.00
Pictorial Bottle Review, Bronc Buster .... *Illus* 29.95
Pictorial Bottle Review, Camel 45.00
Pictorial Bottle Review, Camel, Gold 75.00
Pictorial Bottle Review, Wrangler .... *Illus* 29.95

Pictorial Bottle Review, Bronc Buster

Pictorial Bottle Review, Wrangler

Poison bottles were usually made with raised designs so the user could feel the danger in the dark. The most interesting poison bottles were made from the 1870s to the 1930s.

Poison, Amber, 3 In.	2.00
Poison, Big Letters, Triangles, Ribbed Edges, Bimal, Amber, 8 In.	42.00
Poison, Bimal, Green, 6 Ozs.	36.00
Poison, Bimal, Light Cobalt, 3 1/2 In.	25.00
Poison, Bimal, Slight Haze, 6 1/2 In.	21.00
Poison, Carbolic Acid, Embossed, Coffin, Cobalt, 1/2 Oz.	8.00
Poison, Chestnut Shape, Cobalt Blue, 4 3/4 In.	150.00
Poison, Coffin Shape, Cobalt Blue, 3 3/4 In.	7.50
Poison, Coffin Shape, Embossed, Rectangular, Cobalt, 3 In.	9.50
Poison, Coffin Shape, Not To Be Taken, Blue, 1 Oz.	15.00
Poison, Coffin Shape, Not To Be Taken, Blue, 20 Ozs.	15.00
Poison, Coffin Shape, Not To Be Taken, Green, 1 Oz.	15.00
Poison, Coffin Shape, Not To Be Taken, Green, 20 Ozs.	15.00
Poison, Corrosive Sublimate, Triangular, Knobs On Corners, Amber, 2 3/4 In.	5.00
Poison, Diamond Shape, Amber, 2 3/4 In.High	2.95
Poison, Embossed Not To Be Taken, 6 Panels, Cobalt, 3 In.	6.50
Poison, Embossed Not To Be Taken, 6 Panels, Cobalt, 3 3/4 In.	6.50
Poison, Embossed Not To Be Taken, 6 Panels, Cobalt, 4 In.	7.00
Poison, Embossed Not To Be Taken, 6 Panels, Cobalt, 4 1/2 In.	7.50
Poison, Embossed Not To Be Taken, 6 Panels, Cobalt, 5 1/2 In.	8.00
Poison, Embossed Not To Be Taken, 6 Panels, Cobalt, 6 In.	9.00
Poison, Embossed Not To Be Taken, 6 Panels, Cobalt, 6 1/2 In.	10.00
Poison, Embossed On Shoulders, Paneled Front, Cobalt, 8 3/4 In.	40.00
Poison, Embossed On Shoulders, Paneled Front, Cobalt, 9 3/4 In.	65.00
Poison, Embossed Poison, Ground Stopper, Paneled, 1/2 Gallon	17.50
Poison, Flask, OP, Light Green, 1/2 Pint	75.00
Poison, Gift, German, Skull & Crossbones, 6 Panels, Aqua, 8 1/8 In.	8.95
Poison, Gift, German, Skull & Crossbones, 6 Panels, Bimal, Pint	15.00
Poison, Gift, German, Skull & Crossbones, 6 Panels, Flared Lip, 8 1/8 In.	8.95
Poison, Gift, German, Skull & Crossbones, 6 Panels, 8 1/8 In.	8.95
Poison, Knobs On Corners, Stain, Amber, 2 3/4 In.	3.00
Poison, Label, ABM, Light Cobalt, 3 1/2 In.	22.00
Poison, Lattice & Point, Stopper, Cobalt, 5 1/2 In.	10.00
Poison, Lewis & Whittly, Poisonous, Rectangular, Amber, 8 In.	22.00
Poison, Mercuric Chloride, Coffin Shape, Label, Cobalt Blue, 7 1/2 In.	125.00
Poison, Mercury Bichloride, Oval, Skull & Crossbones, Amber, 4 3/4 In.	20.00
Poison, Mercury Bichloride, Rectangular, Amber, 4 In.	10.00
Poison, Norwich On Base, Coffin, Hobnails, 2 Labels, Amber, 5 In.	135.00
Poison, Not To Be Taken, ABM, Emerald Green, 5 1/2 In.	15.00
Poison, Not To Be Taken, ABM, Emerald Green, 6 3/4 In.	20.00
Poison, Not To Be Taken, ABM, Emerald Green, 8 1/2 In.	30.00
Poison, Not To Be Taken, Cobalt, 6 3/4 In.	25.00
Poison, Not To Be Taken, Fluted Panels, Hexagonal, Amber, 2 1/4 In.	10.00
Poison, Not To Be Taken, Fluted Panels, Hexagonal, Amber, 2 3/4 In.	10.00
Poison, Not To Be Taken, Fluted Panels, Hexagonal, Amber, 3 In.	10.00
Poison, Not To Be Taken, Fluted Panels, Hexagonal, Amber, 4 In.	10.00
Poison, Not To Be Taken, Fluted Panels, Hexagonal, Amber, 6 1/2 In.	10.00
Poison, Not To Be Taken, Fluted Panels, Hexagonal, Cobalt, 2 1/4 In.	10.00
Poison, Not To Be Taken, Fluted Panels, Hexagonal, Cobalt, 2 3/4 In.	10.00
Poison, Not To Be Taken, Fluted Panels, Hexagonal, Cobalt, 3 In.	10.00
Poison, Not To Be Taken, Fluted Panels, Hexagonal, Cobalt, 4 In.	10.00
Poison, Not To Be Taken, Fluted Panels, Hexagonal, Cobalt, 6 1/2 In.	10.00
Poison, Not To Be Taken, Rectangular, Blue, 1/4 Oz.	8.00
Poison, Not To Be Taken, Rectangular, Green, 1/4 Oz.	8.00
Poison, Not To Be Taken, Rectangular, Green, 20 Ozs.	8.00
Poison, Not To Be Taken, 6 Sided, Blue, 1/4 Oz.	8.00
Poison, Not To Be Taken, 6 Sided, Blue, 20 Ozs.	8.00
Poison, Not To Be Taken, 6 Sided, Green, 1/4 Oz.	8.00
Poison, Not To Be Taken, 6 Sided, Green, 20 Ozs.	8.00
Poison, OK Is Absolutely Sure, Special Is King Of All, Aqua, 11 In.	50.00
Poison, Oval Back, Braille Corners, Label, Amber, 5 In.	10.00

Poison, Oval Triangle, Knobs On Corners, Amber, 2 3/4 In. 4.00
Poison, Owl, Triangular, Cobalt, Quart 100.00
Poison, Owl, Triangular, Cobalt, 3 1/2 In. 18.00
Poison, Owl, Triangular, Cobalt, 5 3/4 In. 35.00
Poison, Pat. Applied For, 4 In. ....*Color* 300.00
Poison, Poison On 2 Sides, Square, Amber, 2 1/2 In. 4.00

Poison, Quilted, Cobalt, 6 In.

Poison, Poison On 2 Sides, Square, Amber, 3 1/4 In. 3.50
Poison, Quilted, Cobalt, 3 1/2 In. 8.00
Poison, Quilted, Cobalt, 4 1/2 In. 15.00
Poison, Quilted, Cobalt, 6 In. ....*Illus* 22.00
Poison, Quilted, Label, Cobalt, 7 1/2 In. 42.00
Poison, Quilted, 4 1/2 In. 10.00
Poison, Rectangular, Blue, 20 Ozs. 8.00
Poison, Ribbed, Poison On Two Panels, 3 Sides, Amber, 3 1/2 In. 5.00
Poison, Round, Clear, 4 In. 2.50
Poison, Sharpe & Dohme, Baltimore, Md., 3 Sided, Cobalt Blue, 3 1/4 In. 5.00
Poison, Square, Ribbed Panels, Glass Stopper, Dark Cobalt, 8 Ozs. 20.00
Poison, Stiegel Type, Half Post Method, Dark Amethyst, 4 1/2 In. 125.00
Poison, Tincture Of Iodine, ABM, Light Amber, 3 3/8 In. 4.00
Poison, Tincture Of Iodine, Skull & Crossbones, ABM, Amber, 2 1/8 In. 4.00
Poison, Triloids, Cobalt, 3 Cornered 10.00
Poison, Vapo-Cresolene, Aqua, 4 In. ....*Illus* 2.50
Poison, Vertical Ribs, Embossed 16 Oz. & N, Square, Cobalt 30.00
Poison, Wyeth, Barrel Shape, ABM, Ring Lip, Cobalt, 2 1/8 In. 6.00
Poison, Wyeth, Quilted, Square Oval, Ring Lip, Cobalt Blue, 2 1/2 In. 5.50
Pomade, Ellipses, Plumes, & Diamonds, 9 Sided, Pewter Top, Fiery, 2 1/2 In. 35.00
Pomade, Sandwich, Raised Diamond Band, Pewter Cover, Opalescent, 2 1/2 In. 50.00
Pottery, A.P.Donaghho, Parkersburg, W.Va., Gallon 18.00
Pottery, A.P.Donaghho, 1/2 Gallon 15.00
Pottery, A.Phillips, Ginger Beer, Victoria V.I., 8 In. ....*Illus* 45.00
Pottery, Chris Morley's Ginger Beer, Canadian, 8 3/4 In. ....*Illus* 35.00
Pottery, Chris Morley's Ginger Beer, Doulton, 8 1/2 In. ....*Illus* 35.00
Pottery, Cooler, Water, D.W.Graves, Westmoreland, Handled, 5 Gallon 325.00
Pottery, E.A.Palmer & Bros., Cleveland, O., 1/2 Gallon 15.00
Pottery, English, Queen Victoria & Prince Albert, 8 In. 30.00
Pottery, F.Rober, Savannah, Ga., 7 In. 15.00
Pottery, Folkestone & District, L.V.Mineral Water, 7 In. ....*Illus* 4.00
Pottery, J.Kornahrens, Charleston, S.C., 8 In. 15.00
Pottery, Loyal Order Of Moose, 4 1/2 In. 27.50
Pottery, Myer's Made By E.H.Merrill Co., Akron, O., Incised, 10 1/2 In. 17.50
Pottery, Ottman Bros. 3 Co., Ft.Edward, N.Y., Blue Floral, Salt Glaze, Gallon 65.00
Pottery, T.Kerr & Co., Buffalo, N.Y., 8 In. ....*Color* 37.00
Pottery, Thomas Meager, 7 In. 10.00
Pottery, Thorpe & Co., Vancouver, 9 In. ....*Illus* 85.00
Pottery, Vincent Hathaway, Boston, Quart 17.00
Pottery, XXX Jug, F.H.Weeks, Akron, Ohio, Bail Handle, Cream, 1/2 Gallon 25.00
Pottery, Ye Olde Fashioned Ginger Beer, 7 1/2 In. ....*Illus* 20.00
Pottery, Ye Olde Fashioned Ginger Beer, Replace Stopper, 7 1/2 In. ....*Illus* 35.00
Raven, German 40.00
Royal Doulton, Sandeman Capeman 34.00

Poison, Vapo-Cresolene, Aqua, 4 In.
(See Page 191)

Pottery, Folkestone & District,
L.V.Mineral Water, 7 In.
(See Page 191)

Pottery, Chris Morley's Ginger Beer,
Canadian, 8 3/4 In.
(See Page 191)

Pottery, Chris Morley's
Ginger Beer, Doulton, 8 1/2 In.
(See Page 191)

Pottery, Thorpe & Co.,
Vancouver, 9 In.
(See Page 191)

Pottery, A.Phillips, Ginger Beer,
Victoria V.I., 8 In.
(See Page 191)

Pottery, Ye Olde Fashioned
Ginger Beer, 7 1/2 In.
(See Page 191)

Pottery, Ye Olde
Fashioned Ginger
Beer, Replace Stop-
per, 7 1/2 In.
(See Page 191)

Royal Doulton, Toby Mug, Walrus & Carpenter, Miniature	6.50
Rum, Caldwell's, Embossed Sailing Ship, Apple Green	3.00
Rum, Felton's, Boston, Labeled, Olive Green, Miniature	8.00
Rum, 3 Mold, Blob Lip With Skirt, Bubbles & Seeds, Black Amethyst, 10 In.	12.00
Saki, Satsuma, Panels On Men On Blue, 7 1/4 In.	95.00
Sandwich Glass, see Cologne, Perfume, Scent, Toilet Water	

Sarsaparilla bottles must be marked with the word sarsaparilla to be collected. Most date from 1840 to 1900.

Sarsaparilla, Ayer's Compound Extract, Aqua, 8 1/2 In.	6.00
Sarsaparilla, Ayer's Compound Extract, Lowell, Mass., 8 In.	5.00
Sarsaparilla, Ayer's Compound Extract, 4 Sunken Panels, Aqua, 8 1/2 In.	6.00
Sarsaparilla, Bristol's Genuine, Aqua, Quart	18.00
Sarsaparilla, Bristol's, Quart	15.00
Sarsaparilla, Dalton's, Nerve Tonic, Belfast Maine, Label, Bimal, 9 1/8 In.	8.95
Sarsaparilla, Dalton's, Nerve Tonic, Belfast, Maine, Bimal, 9 1/8 In.	7.45
Sarsaparilla, Dana's, Aqua	12.00
Sarsaparilla, Dr.Greene's, Label, Aqua, 9 In.	12.00
Sarsaparilla, Dr.Greene's, Sunken Panels, Rectangular, Bimal, Aqua, 9 1/4 In.	12.95
Sarsaparilla, Dr.Townsend's, Albany, N.Y., Square, Emerald Green, 9 1/4 In.	45.00
Sarsaparilla, Dr.Townsend's, Albany, N.Y., Stain, Emerald Green, 9 1/2 In.	45.00
Sarsaparilla, Dr.Townsend's, IP, Green, Quart	75.00
Sarsaparilla, Dr.Townsend's, N.Y., Bulge In 1 Side, Green, 9 1/4 In.	50.00
Sarsaparilla, Edward Wilder's, & Potash, Louisville, Ky., Windows, 8 In.	38.50
Sarsaparilla, Foley's, Label, Contents, Aqua	25.00
Sarsaparilla, G.E.M., George E.Mariner, Lacrosse, Wis., Aqua, 9 In.	75.00
Sarsaparilla, Guysott's, Oval, Spotty Cloud, Bluish Aqua	70.00
Sarsaparilla, Hobson's, Paper Label, Contents, Box, 8 In.	5.00
Sarsaparilla, Hood's, Aqua, 9 In.	4.00
Sarsaparilla, Hood's, Lowell, Mass., Bimal, 9 In.	3.15
Sarsaparilla, John Bull, Extract Of, Louisville, Ky., IP, Aqua, 8 3/4 In.	115.00
Sarsaparilla, Johnston's, Aqua, Quart	30.00
Sarsaparilla, Log Cabin, Rochester, N.Y., Flat Back, Amber, 9 In.	60.00
Sarsaparilla, Log Cabin, 9 In.	85.00
Sarsaparilla, Rush's, Stain	8.00
Sarsaparilla, Wynkoop's Atharismichonduras, N.Y., 10 In	*Color* XXXX.XX
Scent, Aventurine, 12 Sided, Silver Top Marked C.M., Cranberry, 9 In.	85.00
Scent, Bohemian Glass, Cut Grapes & Etched Leaves, Red Overlay, 8 In.	137.50
Scent, Elongated Egg Shape, Pewter, Cobalt Blue Glass, 2 In.Long	18.00
Scent, Flint, Stiegel Type, Swirled Ribs, McKearin 240, No.1	35.00
Scent, Flint, Stiegel Type, Swirled Ribs, McKearin 240, No.14	45.00
Scent, Galle, Mushroom Stopper, Lily Pads, C.1900, Purple On Yellow, 4 In.	275.00
Scent, Galle, Teardrop Stopper, Clematis, C.1900, Red On Yellow, 4 1/2 In.	250.00
Scent, Mold Blown, Flint, Shoe Shape, 3 1/2 In.	18.00
Scent, Sandwich, Egg Shape, Pewter Top Half, Cobalt Blue, 1 3/4 In.Long	35.00
Scent, Sandwich, Flint, Pewter Cap, McKearin 241, Amethyst	45.00
Scent, Sandwich, Flint, Pewter Cap, McKearin 241, Blue	40.00
Scent, Sandwich, Flint, Pewter Cap, McKearin 241, Fiery Opalescent	32.00
Scent, Sandwich, Flint, Pewter Cap, McKearin 241, Opalescent	26.00
Scent, Sandwich, McKearin 241, Amethyst	40.00 To 45.00
Scent, Sandwich, McKearin 241, Cobalt	40.00
Scent, Sandwich, McKearin 241, Fiery Opalescent	32.00
Scent, Sandwich, McKearin 241, Sapphire	40.00
Scent, Sandwich, Overlay, Triple Cut, Pink To White To Clear, 2 1/4 In.	80.00
Scent, Sandwich, Pewter Cap, McKearin 241, No.31, Amethyst To Cobalt, 3 In.	55.00
Scent, Sandwich, 1864, Pewter Screw Cap, McKearin 271, No.31, Opaque White	38.00
Scent, Silver Overlay, Stopper, 3 1/2 In.	22.50
Scent, St.Clair, Paperweight, Yellow Lilies, Green, 4 3/4 In.	25.00
Scent, Stiegel Type, Free-Blown, C.1760, Sapphire Blue, 3 In.	50.00
Scent, Straight Sided, Hinged Silver Cap, Cranberry, 2 3/4 In.	50.00
Scent, Webb Type Cameo Glass, Seagull's Head Form, White To Lemon, Silver	625.00
Scent, Webb Type Satin Glass, Rectangular, Gilt Prunus On Green, 7 In.	120.00
Scent, see also Cologne, Perfume, Toilet Water	
Schildt, Captain Meriwether Lewis	39.00

Schildt, Captain William Clark	34.00
Schildt, Sacajawea With Papoose	29.00
Schildt, York	24.00
Seal, D.B.D. & 8 Pointed Star, Bristol Glass Works, Olive Black, Quart	29.00
Seal, E.P.Middleton, Amber, 10 In. .... *Illus*	125.00
Seltzer, Dr.Pepper, 12 1/2 In. ....*Color*	15.00
Seltzer, Embossed, 12 Panels, Pewter Fittings, Emerald Green, 12 1/2 In.	6.95
Seltzer, Penn Bottling, Reading Penn., Etched, Clear	12.50
Seltzer, Saratoga Seltzer Water On Shoulder, Green, 1/2 Pint	60.00
Seltzer, 1i Panels, Embossed, Pewter Fittings, Emerald Green, 12 1/2 In.	6.95
Seltzer, see also Mineral Water	
Shoe Polish, Gilt Edge Dressing, 4 In. ....*Illus*	7.00
Shoe Polish, Mason's White Dressing, 4 In. ....*Illus*	5.00
Ski Country, Brown Bear	28.95
Ski Country, California Condor	29.95
Ski Country, California Condor, Miniature	11.95
Ski Country, Canadian Goose	35.00
Ski Country, Clyde	25.00
Ski Country, Colorado School Of Nimes Burro	25.00
Ski Country, Eagle, Decorated, Gallon	200.00
Ski Country, Elephant	35.00

Seal, E.P.Middleton, Amber, 10 In.

Shoe Polish, Gilt Edge Dressing, 4 In.

Shoe Polish, Mason's White Dressing, 4 In.

Ski Country, Elephant On A Drum	40.00
Ski Country, Fox On Log	28.50
Ski Country, Gila Woodpecker	49.50
Ski Country, Gila Woodpecker, Miniature	11.50
Ski Country, Gold Eagle	32.95
Ski Country, Gold Eagle, Miniature	11.95
Ski Country, Harpy	40.00
Ski Country, Harpy Eagle	14.00
Ski Country, Hawk	35.00 To 40.00
Ski Country, Hawk, Miniature	12.95
Ski Country, Holstein	28.50
Ski Country, Koala Bear	22.00
Ski Country, Ladies From Leadville, Miniature	17.95
Ski Country, Ladies Of Leadville	50.00
Ski Country, Majestic Eagle	125.00 To 150.00
Ski Country, Majestic Eagle, Gallon	200.00 To 225.00
Ski Country, Majestic Eagle, Miniature	18.50 To 20.00
Ski Country, Mallard Duck	13.75 To 36.50
Ski Country, Mountain Lion	14.00
Ski Country, Mountain Ram	34.50
Ski Country, Mountain Ram, Miniature	12.95
Ski Country, Oregon Caveman	21.85
Ski Country, Osprey Hawk	36.00 To 75.00
Ski Country, Peace Dove	32.00
Ski Country, Peacock	27.50
Ski Country, Peacock, Miniature	12.95
Ski Country, Ram	65.00
Ski Country, Red Shouldered Hawk	25.00
Ski Country, Red Shouldered Hawk, Miniature	11.50
Ski Country, Red Skier	14.00
Ski Country, Red Tailed Fox	13.95
Ski Country, Ringmaster	35.00
Ski Country, Rocky Mountain Sheep	70.00
Ski Country, Skier, Blue	35.00
Ski Country, Skier, Gold	49.95 To 100.00
Ski Country, Skier, Red	14.95 To 15.95
Ski Country, Snow Owl, Miniature	14.95
Ski Country, Snowy Owl	21.50 To 70.00
Ski Country, Woodpecker	65.00
Ski Country, Woodpecker, Miniature	12.95
Smelling Salts, Cut Glass Salts, Sterling Hinged Lid, 3 In.	20.00
Smelling Salts, Luscomb's Witch Liquid, Salem Witch 1692, Green, 2 1/4 In.	120.00
Smelling Salts, Pewter Top, Chemical Deposit, Canary Yellow, 2 3/8 In.	50.00
Smelling Salts, Pewter Top, McKearin 241-31, Fiery Opalescent, 2 1/4 In.	50.00
Smelling Salts, Violin Shape, Pewter Top, Amethyst, 2 5/8 In.	50.00
Smelling Salts, Violin Shape, Pewter Top, Cobalt Blue, 2 3/4 In.	52.00
Smelling Salts, Violin Shape, Pewter Top, Stain Inside, Emerald, 3 3/8 In.	50.00
Smelling Salts, 8 Concave Panels, Pewter Screw Top, Amethyst, 2 1/4 In.	40.00
Smelling Salts, 8 Concave Panels, Pewter Top, Amethyst, 2 3/8 In.	45.00
Smelling Salts, 8 Concave Panels, Pewter Top, Deep Amber, 2 3/8 In.	60.00

*Snuff bottles have been made since the eighteenth century. Glass, metal,
ceramic, ivory, and precious stones were all used to make plain or elaborate
snuff holders.*

Snuff, Agate, Chinese, Carved Animals & Foliage, Black & White, 2 1/2 In.	900.00
Snuff, Agate, Soochow, Chinese	1000.00
Snuff, Agate, Spider, Chinese	300.00
Snuff, Amethyst, Chinese, Carved, Deep Purple, 2 In.	200.00
Snuff, Aquamarine, Chinese, Carved, 2 1/2 In.	1000.00
Snuff, Best Virginia, Scotch Snuff, Sweetser Bros., Boston, Cork, 2 1/4 In.	38.00
Snuff, Blown, Aqua, 5 3/4 In.	15.00
Snuff, Blown, Olive Green	70.00
Snuff, Blown, Square, Flared Lip, Dark Olive Amber, 3 3/4 In.	12.50
Snuff, Bulbous, Dyed Blue Stone, Carved Ogre Mask, Ring Handles, Stopper	50.00
Snuff, Bulbous, Gray Agate, Carved Monkey, Peach, Horse, Amber Stopper, 1780	140.00

Snuff, Carnelian Agate, Chinese, Carved Eagle, Moth, & Floral, 2 1/2 In.	650.00
Snuff, Carved In Long Life Symbols, Animals, Agate, Brown, C.1821	245.00
Snuff, Carved Jadite, Turquoise & Coral In Silver Gilt Filigree Stopper	335.00
Snuff, Chinese Export, Blue Floral, Green Jade Stopper	38.00
Snuff, Chinese Export, Cylindrical, Famille Rose Enamels, Sages, C.1850	50.00
Snuff, Chinese Export, Flask, Famille Rose Enamels On White, Ch'ien Lung	60.00
Snuff, Chinese Export, Flask, Famille Rose Enamels, Cricket, Tao Kuang	170.00
Snuff, Chinese Export, Flask, Famille Rose Enamels, Sages & Boys, C.1850	150.00
Snuff, Chinese Export, Flask, Famille Rose Enamels, Tao Kuang Period	325.00
Snuff, Chinese Export, Flattened Flask, Famille Rose Enamels, Boy, C.1850	40.00
Snuff, Chinese Export, Flattened Flask, Famille Rose Enamels, C.1850	425.00
Snuff, Chinese Export, Flattened Flask, Famille Rose, Ch'ien Lung, C.1850	60.00
Snuff, Chinese Export, Flattened Ovate, Famille Rose Enamels, C.1850	30.00
Snuff, Chinese Export, Ovate Flask, Famille Rose Enamels, Tao Kuang Period	275.00
Snuff, Chinese Export, Ovate, Famille Rose Enamels, Riverscape, Chia Ch'ing	275.00
Snuff, Chinese Export, Ovate, Famille Rose, Dragon, Phoenix, Chia Ch'ing	275.00
Snuff, Chinese Export, Oviform, Famille Rose Enamels, Women, Boy, Tao Kuang	120.00
Snuff, Chinese Export, Oviform, Famille Rose, Riverscape, Chia Ch'ing	400.00
Snuff, Chinese Export, Quadrangular, Famille Rose, 8 Immortals, Chia Ch'ing	50.00
Snuff, Chinese, Black Koro Design On Clambroth, 3 In.High	65.00
Snuff, Chinese, Dragon & Phoenix Design, Carved Jadeite, Gold, 2 1/2 In.	475.00
Snuff, Chinese, Iron Red Foo Dogs On Both Sides, 3 In.High	75.00
Snuff, Chinese, Ivory, People, Trees	75.00
Snuff, Chinese, Silver, Carved Scene, 2 1/2 In.	320.00
Snuff, Cloisonne, Blue & Pink Floral On Beige	60.00
Snuff, Cloisonne, Blue Panels & Floral, White, 2 In.	100.00
Snuff, Cloisonne, Butterflies & Flowers	100.00
Snuff, Cloisonne, Floral, 2 1/2 In.	125.00
Snuff, Cloisonne, Flowering Trees On Dark Ground, Tan	75.00
Snuff, Cloisonne, Flowers, Yellow Butterflies On Light Ground	75.00
Snuff, Cloisonne, Metal With Coral Top, C.1850	90.00
Snuff, Cloisonne, Multicolored Dragon On Dark Ground, Brass Band, Signed	120.00
Snuff, Cloisonne, Multicolors On White Ground	75.00
Snuff, Cloisonne, Panda Bears On Bamboo & Blue Sky	100.00
Snuff, Cloisonne, Stag & Doe On Trees & Flowers Ground	120.00
Snuff, Cloisonne, Twin Gourd Shape, 2 1/2 In.	150.00
Snuff, Cobalt Blue, 2 X 2 In.	22.50
Snuff, Cobalt Blue, 4 X 2 In.	22.50
Snuff, Cobalt Blue, 4 X 2 1/4 In.	15.00
Snuff, Coral, Chinese, Twin, Carved, Deep Red, 2 In.	525.00
Snuff, Crystal, Chinese, Carved Fine Hairs, 2 1/2 In.	225.00
Snuff, Cylindrical, Blue & White, Peachbloom, Men, Boat, Agate Stopper, 1850	60.00
Snuff, Cylindrical, Iron & Gold On White, Dragon, Jade Stopper, Ch'ien Lung	70.00
Snuff, Cylindrical, Porcelain, White On Black, Dragons, Coral Stopper, C.1850	130.00
Snuff, Double Gourd, Green Gray Jade, Carved Branches, Bat, Coral Stopper	40.00
Snuff, Double Gourd, Rock Crystal, Carved Branches & Gourds, Coral Stopper	70.00
Snuff, Dr.Marshall's Catarrh, Emerald Green, 3 1/4 In.	6.00
Snuff, Dr.Marshall's, Aqua, 3 1/2 In.	13.00
Snuff, Drum Shape Flask, Fei-Ts'ui Jade, Carved Medallion, Figures, Stopper	225.00
Snuff, E.Room, Troy, N.Y., 4 1/2 In. ....Color	98.00
Snuff, Enameled People Fishing & Man In Pagoda On White	100.00
Snuff, Fish Form, Smoke Crystal, Carved Carp, Stopper	50.00
Snuff, Flat Cylindrical, Florals & Insects On White Opaque, 2 3/4 In.High	85.00
Snuff, Flattened Flask, Brown Agate, Carved Horses, Green Stopper, 1780-1800	625.00
Snuff, Flattened Flask, Brown Quartz, Mottled, Coral Stopper	30.00
Snuff, Flattened Flask, Cinnabar, Lacquer, Carved Woman, Ch'ien Lung	60.00
Snuff, Flattened Flask, Turquoise, Matrix, Fei-Ts'ui Jade Stopper	90.00
Snuff, Flattened Flask, White Jade, Coral Stopper	30.00
Snuff, Flattened Flask, White Jade, Pietra Dura Decoration, Mother-Of-Pearl	200.00
Snuff, Flattened Heart Shape, Blue Sodalite, Green Aventurine Stopper	30.00
Snuff, Flattened Ovate, Fei-Ts'ui Jade, Gray Green, Red Glass Stopper	50.00
Snuff, Flattened Ovate, Fei-Ts'ui Jade, Gray, Brown & Lavender Mottlings	225.00
Snuff, Flattened Ovate, Gray Agate, Carved Peonies, Insects, Stopper	60.00
Snuff, Flattened Ovate, Green Quartz, White & Black Mottlings, Stopper	50.00
Snuff, Flattened Ovate, Hair Crystal, Black Tourmaline Needle, 1800	150.00

Snuff, Flattened Ovate, Lapis Lazuli, Stopper	80.00
Snuff, Flattened Ovate, White Calcite, Carved Ogre Mask, Ring Handles	30.00
Snuff, Flattened Quadrangular Shield Shape, Mutton Fat Jade, Carved	40.00
Snuff, Flattened Quadrangular, Spinach Green Jade, Carved Panels, Stopper	160.00
Snuff, Flattened Shield Shape, Amethystine Quartz, Carved Birds	60.00
Snuff, Flattened Shield Shape, Cinnabar, Lacquer, Carved, Ch'ien Lung, C.1850	80.00
Snuff, Flattened Shield Shape, Fei-Ts'ui Jade, Lavender & Green, Stopper	100.00
Snuff, Flattened Shield Shape, Hair Crystal, Black Tourmaline Needles	50.00
Snuff, Flattened Shield Shape, Lacque-Burgaute, Mother-Of-Pearl Inlay	90.00
Snuff, Flattened Shield Shape, Lapis Lazuli, Green Aventurine Stopper	40.00
Snuff, Flattened Shield Shape, Spinach Green Jade, Gold Decorated	120.00
Snuff, Flattened Shield Shape, White & Brown Jade, Mottlings, Coral Stopper	40.00
Snuff, Flattened, Amber, Opaque Brown, Quartz Stopper, C.1850	80.00
Snuff, Flattened, Cinnabar, Lacquer, Pietra Dura Decoration, Stopper	80.00
Snuff, Flattened, Hair Crystal, Black Tourmaline Needles, Pine Tree, Agate	125.00
Snuff, Flattened, Mottled Brown Soapstone, Carved Deer & Crane, Stopper	30.00
Snuff, Flattened, Peking, Enamel Reserves On Pink, Gilded Metal Stopper	50.00
Snuff, Flattened, White & Brown Jade, Carved Deer, Mottlings, Jade Stopper	175.00
Snuff, Flattened, White Jade, Brown Mottlings, Incised, Orange Stopper	60.00
Snuff, Flattened, White Jade, Mottlings, Carved Elephant, Ruby Stopper	160.00
Snuff, Form Of Robed Woman On Elephant, Coral, Head Forms Stopper	300.00
Snuff, Green Crackled, Green Stone Top, C.1850	48.00
Snuff, Heart Shape, Cinnabar, Lacquer, Carved Deer, Ch'ien Lung, C.1850	70.00
Snuff, Helm's Railroad Mills, Glass Lid, Metal Band, Dated 1872, Amber, Quart	8.00
Snuff, Hornbill, Chinese, Carved Dragons, 3 1/2 In.	200.00
Snuff, Hornbill, Chinese, Carved, Natural Red Casque On Sides, 2 1/2 In.	600.00
Snuff, Imari, Cylindrical, Enamel, Dragon, Peonies, Coral Stopper, C.1850	80.00
Snuff, Indian Jade, Hand-Carved, 2 1/2 X 1 1/2 In.	10.00
Snuff, Ivory, Carved On Both Sides, Signed	60.00
Snuff, Ivory, Carved Tao T'uh Masks, C.1850	80.00
Snuff, Ivory, Flattened, Carved Catlike Animal & Crane On Pine Tree	60.00
Snuff, Ivory, Flattened, Japanese, Tinted, Carved Ladies, Ch'ien Lung	110.00
Snuff, Ivory, Japanese, Oval, Carved Equestrian Figures, Tinted, Ch'ien Lung	120.00
Snuff, Ivory, One Side Carved, Other Painted	24.50
Snuff, Ivory, Tapering Cylindrical, Etched, Mountain Landscape, Stopper	40.00
Snuff, J.M.Venable & Co., Petersburg, Va., Amber	40.00
Snuff, Jade, Chinese, Monkeys & Dogs, Red Skin Front, White, 2 5/8 In.	400.00
Snuff, Jade, Chinese, Silver Trim, Opens From Side, White, 3 In.	250.00
Snuff, Jadeite, Pendant, 14K Gold Dragon & Phoenix, Green, 2 1/2 In.	475.00
Snuff, King's Patent Tru Cephali, Pontil, Aqua, 3 In.High	25.00
Snuff, Lady's, Hinged Brass Lid With Chain, Gold Design, Round, Blue, 1 In.	35.00
Snuff, Lapis Lazuli, Carved	100.00
Snuff, Lapis Lazuli, Carved Birds, Malachite Stopper	95.00
Snuff, Lapis Lazuli, Chinese, Carved, 2 1/2 In.	125.00
Snuff, Lapis Lazuli, Flattened Ovate, Green Corundum Stopper	110.00
Snuff, Laque Burgaute, Chinese, 2 1/2 In.	95.00
Snuff, Lion Handles, Gold Hair Crystal, 2 1/2 In.	225.00
Snuff, MacCoboy, Amber, 4 1/2 In.	3.00
Snuff, Malachite, Chinese, Carved, 2 3/4 In.	200.00
Snuff, Marshall's, Aqua, 6 1/2 In.	13.00
Snuff, Marshall's, Quart	4.25
Snuff, Mei Ping Shape, Lacquer Burquate, Mother-Of-Pearl Landscape, 2 In.	95.00
Snuff, Melon Form, Carnelian Agate, Carved Dragonfly, Yellow Stopper	100.00
Snuff, Melon Form, White Jade, Carved Blossoms, Coral Stalk Stopper, C.1850	125.00
Snuff, Midwestern, 24 Ribs, Square, Cut Corners, Deep Aqua, 5 1/2 In.	250.00
Snuff, Milk White, Ovate, Famille Rose Enamels, Ku Yueh Hsuan, 1850	450.00
Snuff, Mother-Of-Pearl, Flattened Ovate, Applied Landscape Medallions	40.00
Snuff, Mother-Of-Pearl, Flattened Shield Shape, Carved Lady, Stopper	60.00
Snuff, Mother-Of-Pearl, Flattened, Carved Eighteen Lohan, Agate Stopper	60.00
Snuff, Nut Form, Gray & Brown Agate, Carved, Jade Stopper, 1780-1880	100.00
Snuff, Olive Green, 3 1/2 In.	3.00
Snuff, Opal Matrix, Chinese, Carved, Black, 2 1/2 In.	700.00
Snuff, Opal, Chinese, Carved Dragons & Phoenix, Red & Green Fire, 2 3/8 In.	500.00
Snuff, Opal, Chinese, Carved, Fire, 2 1/2 In.	350.00
Snuff, Opal, Chinese, Pendant, Carved Dragons, Red & Green Fire, 2 1/2 In.	750.00

Snuff, Ovate, Red & Opaque Yellow, Carved Fu Lions, C.1850	120.00
Snuff, Ovate, Red & Opaque Yellow, Coral Stopper, C.1850	50.00
Snuff, Oviform, Brown Quartz, Mottled, Red Glass Stopper	20.00
Snuff, Oviform, Fe-Ts'ui Jade, Gray White, Green & Lavender Mottlings	250.00
Snuff, Oviform, Lapis Blue Porcelain, Dragon & Phoenix, Chai Ch'ing Period	125.00
Snuff, Oviform, Peking, Enamel Reserves On Blue, Coral Stopper, Ch'ien Lung	60.00
Snuff, Oviform, Rock Crystal, Carved Basketry Design, Green Jade Stopper	120.00
Snuff, Oviform, Rock Crystal, Carved Toad, Green Glass Stopper, C.1800	60.00
Snuff, Oviform, White & Brown Jade, Carved Dragons, Metal Stopper	100.00
Snuff, Oviform, White Jade, Carved Dragons, Pursuit Of Jewel, Stopper	125.00
Snuff, Ovoid, Lacquer Burquate, Mother-Of-Pearl Floral, 2 In.	95.00
Snuff, P.Lorillard Co., Glass Lid, Wire Clamp, Dated 1872, Amber, Quart	8.00
Snuff, Painted Interior, Boy On Water Buffalo, Yeh Chung-San	250.00
Snuff, Pear Shape, Cloisonne, Lotus Blossoms On Turquoise, Metal Stopper	50.00
Snuff, Pebble Form, Gray Brown Agate, Carved Boys Holding Box	40.00
Snuff, Pebble Shape, Chinese, Matrix On 1 Side, Near White, 3 In.High	125.00
Snuff, Peking Glass, Blue Floral Overlay, Bronze Forms	65.00
Snuff, Peking Glass, Carved, Imperial Yellow, 2 3/4 In.	100.00
Snuff, Peking Glass, Carved, New York, 2 1/4 In.	30.00
Snuff, Peking Glass, Painted Inside, 3 3/4 In.	20.00
Snuff, Peking, Flattened Flask, Snowflake, Green Overlay, Stone Stopper	60.00
Snuff, Peking, Green & Red Floral Overlay On Yellow	240.00
Snuff, Peking, Horse Beneath Trees, Blue Overlay, 3 In.	85.00
Snuff, Peking, Ruby Red, Flask Form, Carved Horses, Ring Handles	25.00
Snuff, Porcelain, Baluster, Green, Bamboo Trellis, Jade Stopper, C.1850	260.00
Snuff, Porcelain, Flask, Iron & Green On White, Shou Figures, C.1850	60.00
Snuff, Porcelain, Flattened Hexagonal, Iron Dragon, Jade Stopper, Yung Cheng	60.00
Snuff, Porcelain, Flattened Pear, Lime Green, Landscape, Mountains, C.1850	180.00
Snuff, Porcelain, Flattened Quadrangular, Iron & White, Yung Cheng, C.1850	40.00
Snuff, Porcelain, Form Of Liu Han With Toad, Blue Gray, Quartz Stopper	40.00
Snuff, Porcelain, Hourglass Shape, Green Jade Cap, Ivory Spoon	18.00
Snuff, Porcelain, Jade Stopper	20.00
Snuff, Porcelain, Ju-I Shape Flask, Floral Medallion, White, C.1850	150.00
Snuff, Porcelain, Round, Lemon Yellow, Fu Lions, Obsidian Stopper, C.1890	70.00
Snuff, Porcelain, Twin, Cylindrical, Iron Red Dragons, C.1850	40.00
Snuff, Pratt, Jar, Blue, Gold, & Black, Marked 1856	18.00
Snuff, Pratt, Tan & Black Transfer Of Men & Animals On Blue, 4 In.High	18.00
Snuff, Pratt, Tan & Black Transfer Of Men & Animals, Blue, 4 In.	30.00
Snuff, Quadrangular, Smoke Crystal, Carved Blossoms, Bird, Pink Stopper	60.00
Snuff, Red Overlay, Clear & Frosted, Ivory Spoon, Inside Painted	25.00
Snuff, Round, Porcelain, Sepia Dragons On Yellow, Ch'ien Lung, C.1850	80.00
Snuff, S.B.I.O.H., Square, Aqua, 2 X 1 1/2 In.	15.00
Snuff, Sarreguemines, White Porcelain, Marked, 4 In.	9.00
Snuff, Silver, Chinese, Carved, 2 1/2 In.	325.00
Snuff, Similar To McKearin 227-13, Olive Green	30.00
Snuff, Sweetser Bros., Boston, Indian Smoking, Label, Bimal, Amber, 3 1/2 In.	25.00
Snuff, Swimming Goldfish Form, Carnelian Agate, Carved, Green Stopper	80.00
Snuff, Tapering Flask, Rock Crystal, Carved Ogre Mask, Handles, C.1800	60.00
Snuff, Tapering, Gray Agate, Chalcedony, Carved, Coral Stopper	180.00
Snuff, Tigereye, Chinese, Carved Fish In Skin, Blue, 2 1/2 In.	150.00
Snuff, Tigereye, India, Hand-Carved, 2 1/2 X 1 1/2 In.	10.00
Snuff, Toad Form, Malachite, Carved, Coral Stalk Stopper	60.00
Snuff, Toad Form, Mottled Green Jade, Carved, Coral Stalk Stopper	45.00
Snuff, Tortoise Form, Gray Agate, Carved, Green Glass Stopper	50.00
Snuff, Tortoiseshell, Chinese, 2 1/2 In.	200.00
Snuff, Tourmaline, Chinese, Carved Dragons, Watermelon, 2 In.	250.00
Snuff, Turquoise, Chinese, Carved, 2 3/8 In.	475.00
Snuff, Turquoise, Flattened Tapering, Carved Women, Twin Genii, Stopper	210.00
Snuff, Twin, Flattened Flask, Rock Crystal, Carved Peonies, Stoppers	60.00

Soda bottles held soda pop or Coca-Cola or other carbonated drinks.
Many soda bottles had a characteristic blob top. Hutchinson stoppers and
Coddball stoppers were also used.

Soda, A.L.Bert Von Harten-Savannah, Ga., Blue Green, Blob Top	20.00
Soda, American Soda Co., 1/2 Gallon	7.00

Soda, Bay City Soda Water, Medium Blue, 7 In.

Soda, Buffum's Sarsaparilla & Lemon, Cobalt, 7 1/2 In.

Soda, C.C.S.& M F 270 & 271, New Orleans,
Aqua, 7 1/2 In

Soda, B.F.Tatman, Owensboro, Ky., Blob, Embossed, Paneled, Dug, Aqua, 9 In.	4.50
Soda, Bay City Soda Water, Medium Blue, 7 In. ....*Illus*	65.00
Soda, Bryant's Root Beer, Amber, 4 1/2 In.	5.00
Soda, Buffum's Sarsaparilla & Lemon, Cobalt, 7 1/2 In. ....*Illus*	450.00
Soda, C.B.C.Co., Mass., Hutchinson, Blob Top, Aqua, 7 In.	9.00
Soda, C.C.S.& M F 270 & 271, New Orleans, Aqua, 7 1/2 In ....*Illus*	5.00
Soda, C.Cleminshaw, Troy, N.Y., Blob Lip, Whittled, Ice Blue, 7 In.	14.00
Soda, C.Cleminshaw, Troy, N.Y., Blob Lip, Whittled, Tapered Neck, Aqua, 7 In.	12.00
Soda, C.Cleminshaw, Troy, N.Y., Stubby, Whittled, Light Blue, 7 In.	13.00
Soda, C.H.Ramsdell & Co., Salem, Mass., Whittled, Blob Top, 9 1/4 In.	8.00
Soda, Canada Dry Ginger Ale, Carnival	.50
Soda, Casey Eagle Soda Works, Sac.City, Cobalt	26.00
Soda, Cawley, Dover, N.J., Hutchinson, Quart	14.00
Soda, Cedar Point Pleasure Resort, 5 1/2 In. ....*Color*	30.00
Soda, Cedar Point Pleasure Resort, 7 In. ....*Color*	70.00

Soda, Champagne Mead, Aqua, 7 1/2 In.

Soda, **Champagne Mead,** Aqua, 7 1/2 In. .... *Illus*	35.00
Soda, **Charles E.Tippett,** Chester, N.J., Blob Top, Bubbles, Aqua, 9 In.	6.00
Soda **Charles E.Tippett,** Chester, N.J., Blob Top, Bubbles, Ice Blue, 9 In.	8.00
Soda, **Chas.Umbach,** Eagle & Shield	3(.00
Soda, **Chero Cola,** Patent June 3, 1924, Checkered Diamonds, Aqua, 6 Ozs.	3.00
Soda, **Cherry Smash,** 5 Cents, Always Cherry, Black Lettering, 12 In.High	75.00

Soda, Craven, Union Glass Works,
Green, 7 In.

Soda, **Clicquot Club Celebrated,** Made In America, Clear, 10 In.High	3.00
Soda, **Clicquot Club,** Millis, Mass., Teal Blue	6.00
Soda, **Clysmic,** Embossed On Bottom, Dark Green, 9 In.	5.00
Soda, **Coffee,** Etched, Clear Swirling, Ground Bottom	65.00
Soda, **Colburn Lang & Co. Ginger Beer,** Stoneware, Jug, Quart	22.00
Soda, **Corbin Ice Co.,** Green, 8 1/2 In.	3.00
Soda, **Craven,** Union Glass Works, Green, 7 In. .... *Illus*	100.00
Soda, **Donald Duck Cola,** 7 Oz. .... 3.00 To 5.00
Soda, **Douglass Pineapple,** Black Lettering, 12 In.High	50.00
Soda, **Dr.Pepper,** Embossed	1.25
Soda, **Dr.Pepper,** Embossed 10-2-4 Clock, Miniature	6.00
Soda, **Dr.Pepper,** Embossed 10-2-4 Clock, 6 Oz.	3.00
Soda, **Dr.Pepper,** Miami Dolphins 1972 World Champions, 16 Ozs. .... 4.50 To 5.00
Soda, **Drewry,** Royal Canadian Mounted Police Effigy, 1920s, Green, 6 Ozs.	4.00
Soda, **Dyottville Glass Works,** Phila., Blob Top, IP, Green	45.00
Soda, **E Z E Beverages In Center,** Ribbed Top & Bottom, 1/2 Pint	2.75
Soda, **E.M.Heusits & Co.,** Charlestown, Mass., Porcelain Stopper, Bail, 9 In.	5.00
Soda, **E.Wagner,** Manchester, N.H., Embossed, Blob Top, Straw Yellow, 9 1/4 In.	18.00
Soda, **Eagle,** Light Green, Blop Top, Charleston, S.C., Pontil	145.00
Soda, **Ebberwein,** Ginger Ale, Tall Hutchinson Style	22.00
Soda, **Elliot & Ledlie,** Trenton, N.J., Aqua	12.00
Soda, **English Brewed Ginger Beer,** Pottery, 7 1/2 In. .... *Illus*	5.00
Soda, **Epping,** 8 1/2 In.	2.00
Soda, **Fowler's Cherry Smash,** Decal, Red, 12 In.High	50.00
Soda, **Francis Drake,** New Glascowns, Hutchinson, Aqua .... *Illus*	8.00

Soda, English Brewed Ginger Beer,
Pottery, 7 1/2 In.
(See Page 200)

Hutchinson, Francis Drake,
New Glascowns, Soda, Aqua
(See Page 200)

Soda, **Frank Nardorff,** Louisville, Ky., 7 1/2 In. ....*Color* XXXX.XX
Soda, **Geo.Gemenden,** Eagle & Shield, Iron Pontil 95.00
Soda, **Gilbert,** Minn., Hutchinson, Quart 15.00
Soda, **Glendale Spring Co.,** Everett, Mass., Hutchinson, Blob Top, Aqua, 7 In. 7.00
Soda, **Glendale Spring Co.,** Everett, Mass., Hutchinson, Blob Top, Blue, 7 In. 6.00
Soda, **Globe Bottling Works,** Savannah, Ga., 1/2 Quart 9.00
Soda, **Grape-Ola,** 4 Bunches Of Grapes, C.1928, 6 Ozs. 3.00
Soda, **H & Co.,** Blob Top, Bulged Neck, Deep Honey Amber, 9 1/2 In. 11.00
Soda, **H.Wetter,** St.Louis, Blob Top, Light Green 15.00
Soda, **Henry Kuck,** Savannah, Ga., Blob Top, Green, Quart 25.00
Soda, **Hoskin's Quality Soda,** 8 3/4 In. 4.00
Soda, **J.A.Lomax,** Charles Place, Chicago, Cobalt, 7 In. ....*Color* 40.00
Soda, **J.C.Parker,** Blob Top, Cloudy, Blue, 7 1/2 In. 14.00
Soda, **J.Chester Root Beer,** Embossed, Blob Top, Stoneware, Gray Glaze, 10 In. 100.00
Soda, **J.G.Schneider,** Albany, N.Y., Oval Slug Plate, Blob Top, , Aqua, 9 1/2 In. 6.00
Soda, **J.J.Campbell,** Boston, Mass., Whittled, Ice Blue, 9 In. 9.00
Soda, **J.Moran,** Burlington, Vt., Round, Embossed Flag With 13 Stars, Aqua 45.00
Soda, **Jackson Napa,** Aqua, 7 1/4 In. 8.00
Soda, **James Ray,** Ginger Ale, Cobalt 35.00
Soda, **John Imbesheid & Co.,** Mass., Blob Top, Whittled, Blue Aqua, 9 1/4 In. 6.00
Soda, **John Kuhlman Brewing Co.,** Ellenville, N.Y., Hutchinson, Aqua, 6 7/8 In. 3.95
Soda, **John Ryan 1866 Excelsior Soda Works,** Savannah, Ga., Cobalt, 7 In. 35.00
Soda, **John Ryan,** Porter & Ale, Savannah, IP 47.00
Soda, **John Ryan,** Savannah, Union Glass Works, IP 40.00
Soda, **John Ryan,** Savannah, 2 In. Letter, IP 46.00
Soda, **John Ryan,** Savannah, 1859, 1 In. Letters, Cobalt 35.00
Soda, **John Ryan,** Savannah, 1859, 2 In. Letters 40.00
Soda, **John Ryan,** 1852, Columbus, Georgia, Clear Blue 75.00
Soda, **John Wiebelt,** Ground Pontil 20.00
Soda, **Jumbo,** Embossed Elephant, ABM, 60 Ozs. 10.00
Soda, **Jumbo,** Enameled Elephants, Cap, Light Green, 1/2 Quart, 10 In. 4.00
Soda, **Knickerbocker,** Cobalt, 7 In. ....*Illus* 160.00
Soda, **Knickerbocker,** Saratoga Springs, Carpenter & Cobb, Blue Green, Pint 130.00
Soda, **Lancaster Glass Works,** Medium Blue, 7 1/2 In. ....*Illus* 75.00
Soda, **Lime,** Blown, Flint, Amelung Type, Case, 5 1/4 In. 35.00

Soda, Knickerbocker, Blue, 7 In.
(See Page 201)

Soda, Lancaster Glass Works,
Medium Blue, 7 1/2 In.
(See Page 201)

Soda, Milton Aerated Waterworks, Aqua, 8 In.

Soda, M.D., High Bridge, N.J., Oval Slug Plate, Blob Top, Whittled, Blue, 9 In.	9.00
Soda, M.Monju, Mobile, Iron Pontil	23.00
Soda, Mammy, Embossed Mammy, ABM, 60 Ozs.	10.00
Soda, Miguel Pons, Mobile, Iron Pontil	26.00
Soda, Milton Aerated Waterworks, Aqua, 8 In. ....*Illus*	10.00
Soda, Moxie, Aqua, 10 1/2 In.	4.00
Soda, Moxie, Drink Moxie, Printed ....*Illus*	9.00
Soda, Moxie, Embossed Licensed Only For Serving	12.00
Soda, Moxie, Label	10.00
Soda, Moxie, Label, Contents	15.00
Soda, Moxie, Porcelain, Wire Cap, Green, 11 3/4 In.High	12.50
Soda, Mu Icy, 9 In.	2.00

Soda, Moxie, Drink Moxie, Printed

Soda, Ohio Bottling Works,
Hutchinson, 5 1/2 In.

Soda, New Orleans, Eagle, S.Pablo, Blue-Aqua, Pontil 65.00
Soda, Nu Grape, 8 In. 3.00
Soda, O-T Cordial New Drinks Ltd., San Francisco, Embossed, Square, Quart 15.00
Soda, Ohio Bottling Works, Hutchinson, 5 1/2 In. .... *Illus* 15.00
Soda, Orange Crush, Amber, 9 1/2 In. 3.00
Soda, Orange Crush, July 20, 1920, Embossed, 6 Ozs. 1.50
Soda, Orange Crush, July 20, 1920, Embossed, 7 Ozs. 1.50
Soda, Orange Crush, 8 1/2 In. 3.00
Soda, Pepsi Cola, Amber, 16 Ozs. .... 4.00 To 5.00
Soda, Pepsi Cola, Salt & Pepper, Plastic Top, 4 1/2 In., Pair 4.00
Soda, Pepsi Cola, 75th Anniversary Commemorative, 12 Ozs. 3.00
Soda, Pepsi, Non Returnable, Amber, 16 Oz. 5.00
Soda, Philadelphia Glass Works, Blue Green, 7 1/2 In. .... *Illus* 40.00
Soda, Premium Soda, Albany, N.Y., W.W.Lappus, Blue .... *Illus* 200.00
Soda, Raspberry, Etched, Cruet Shape, 7 In.High 12.00
Soda, Razorback Hog, Emerald Green, 6 Oz. 8.00
Soda, Root Beer, Etched 35.00
Soda, Round Bottom, Green 7.50
Soda, Royal Crown, Copyright 1936, 12 Ozs. 3.00
Soda, Sach's Prudent Famous Ginger Ale, Footed, 6 1/2 In. 10.00
Soda, Schmuck's Ginger Ale, Hutchinson Type, 12 Sided, Stain, Aqua, 8 In. 20.00
Soda, Schmuck's Ginger Ale, Hutchinson, 8 In. .... *Illus* 20.00
Soda, Seven Up, Mexican Writing, Painted Crown Top, Emerald Green, 9 1/2 In. 1.50

Soda, Philadelphia Glass Works,
Blue Green, 7 1/2 In.

Soda, Premium Soda, Albany, N.Y.,
W.W.Lappus, Blue

Soda, Sherbert-Jade, Recessed Label, Metal Top, Red, 12 In.High 35.00
Soda, Soda & Mineral Water Co., Warren, Pa., 7 In. .... *Illus* 10.00
Soda, Sprite, Full & Capped, 3 In. .... .50 To 1.50
Soda, Sprite, Miniature, Hobnail, Emblem, Capped & Filled, Green .... .50
Soda, Sunken & Pinched Neck, Marble Stopper Inside, Aqua 6.00
Soda, Superior, Charleston, Embossed Eagle, Umbrella Top, Dark Green, 7 In. 145.00
Soda, Tall One, 9 1/2 In. 1.00
Soda, Thos.Maher, Green 25.00
Soda, Trayder's Belfast, Blob Top, Squat, Puce Amber 13.50
Soda, Umbach, Eagle, Savannah, Green 75.00
Soda, W.H.Buck, Cobalt Blue, 7 1/2 In. .... *Illus* 140.00
Soda, W.L.Rose & Co., Wheeling, W.Va., Hutchinson, Aqua, 7 In. 8.75
Soda, Wainscott's, 9 In. 2.00
Soda, Wm.A.Kearney, Shamokin, Pa., Hutchinson, Amber, Quart 90.00
   Soda, see also Mineral Water, Pottery
Souvenir, Chicago, Century Of Progress, 1933 .... 5.00
Souvenir, World's Fair, 1939, Milk Glass, 9 In. 9.50
Spice, Chinese, Underglaze Blue Decoration, Calligraphy, C.1750, 9 1/4 In. 95.00
Stiegel Type, Case, Etched Star & Flower, Half Post Neck & Collar, 6 In. 20.00
Stiegel Type, Case, Hexagonal, Etched Star & Flower, 8 1/4 In. 7.50
Stiegel Type, Enamel Decoration, Pewter Neck, 5 1/2 In. 150.00
Stiegel Type, Enameled Floral, 6 In.High 150.00
Stiegel Type, Etched Design, OP, Pint 5.00
Stiegel Type, Flagon, Wine, Etched Vine & Flowers, Applied Handle, 12 In. 30.00
Stiegel Type, 18 Broken Swirled Ribs, Deep Amethyst, 7 1/4 In. 625.00
   Stoneware, see Pottery
Toilet Water, Blown, 3 Mold, McKearin G I-7 .... 45.00
Toilet Water, Blown, 3 Mold, McKearin G I-11 .... 45.00
Toilet Water, Blown, 3 Mold, Tam-O'-Shanter Stopper, Deep Blue, 1/2 Pint 170.00
Toilet Water, Jar, Dresden, Floral, Square, Marriage Stopper, 5 In.High 10.00
Toilet Water, Lilac Mauve, Brass Crown Dobber, Camphor Glass, Miniature 5.00
Toilet Water, Milk Glass, Bulbous, Stopper, 10 In.High 30.00
Toilet Water, Milk Glass, 6 In., Pair .... *Illus* 42.00
Toilet Water, Sandwich, 3 Mold, Fine Swirl, McKearin G I-3, Sapphire Blue 85.00
Toilet Water, Sandwich, 12 Sided, Ring at Neck, Flared Lip, Cobalt, 6 In. 85.00
Toilet Water, 14 Vertical Ribs, Tam-O'-Shanter Stopper, Cobalt, 5 1/2 In. 225.00
Toilet Water, 16 Vertical Ribs, Pale Amethyst, 6 In. 40.00
   Toilet Water, see also Cologne, Perfume, Scent

Soda, Schmuck's Ginger Ale, Hutchinson, 8 In.
(See Page 203)

Soda, W.H.Buck, Cobalt Blue, 7 1/2 In.

Soda, Soda & Mineral Water Co.,
Warren, Pa., 7 In.

Viarengo, Clown Playing Drum 18.00
Viarengo, Gondola 18.50
Vinegar, Champion's, Light Green, 14 1/2 In. 20.00
Vinegar, Champion's, Paneled, Stain, 15 In. 16.00
Vinegar, Cottell's Malt, 4 1/2 In. 6.00
Vinegar, Dated '23, Pouring Spout, Embossed, Pint 1.50
Vinegar, F.C.P. Piegaro, Molded, Green, 8 1/2 In. 5.00
Vinegar, McKearin G I-7, Type 4, Three Mold, Sandwich, Stopper, Cobalt Blue 170.00
Vinegar, White House, Aqua, Pint .... 5.00 To 10.00
Vinegar, White House, Embossed, 1/2 Pint 9.00
Vinegar, White House, Embossed, Pint 4.00
Vinegar, White House, Embossed, Quart .... 4.00 To 15.00
Vinegar, White House, Embossed, 1/2 Gallon 5.00
Vinegar, White House, Embossed, Gallon 10.95
Vinegar, White House, Jug, 7 In. 4.00
Vinegar, White House, Picture, 1/2 Gallon 6.50
Vinegar, White House, Writing, 1/2 Gallon 6.50
    Water, Mineral, see Mineral Water
    Water, Moses, see Mineral Water, Moses'

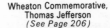

Wheaton Commemorative,
Thomas Jefferson
(See Page 206)

Toilet Water, Milk Glass, 6 In., Pair
(See Page 204)

Wheaton Company was established in 1888. The firm made hand-blown and pressed glassware. In 1938 automatic equipment was added and many molded glass items were made. Wheaton Commemorative now makes all types of containers for pharmaceuticals and cosmetics, and foods, as well as gift shop antique-style bottles.

Wheaton Commemorative, Abraham Lincoln .... 3.75 To 8.00
Wheaton Commemorative, Alexander Bell .... 4.25 To 5.00
Wheaton Commemorative, Andrew Jackson .... 3.75 To 4.25
Wheaton Commemorative, Apollo 11 .... 11.00 To 12.00
Wheaton Commemorative, Apollo 12 .... 47.00 To 50.00
Wheaton Commemorative, Apollo 13 .... 3.75 To 6.00
Wheaton Commemorative, Apollo 14 .... 3.75 To 6.00
Wheaton Commemorative, Apollo 15 .... 3.75 To 6.00
Wheaton Commemorative, Apollo 16 .... 3.75 To 4.25
Wheaton Commemorative, Apollo 17 .... 20.00
Wheaton Commemorative, Benjamin Franklin .... 3.75 To 4.25
Wheaton Commemorative, Betsy Ross .... 3.75 To 4.75
Wheaton Commemorative, Billy Graham .... 3.75 To 6.00
Wheaton Commemorative, Charles Evans Hughes .... 3.75 To 5.00
Wheaton Commemorative, Charles Lindbergh .... 3.75 To 4.25
Wheaton Commemorative, Christmas, 1971 .... 12.00 To 18.00
Wheaton Commemorative, Christmas, 1972 .... 6.00
Wheaton Commemorative, Christmas, 1973, Ruby 6.00
Wheaton Commemorative, Christmas, 1974 .... 6.00 To 7.00
Wheaton Commemorative, Clark Gable .... 4.25 To 6.00

Wheaton Commemorative, Democrat, McGovern, 1972 .... 5.00 To 12.00
Wheaton Commemorative, Democrat, 1968 .... 6.00 To 16.00
Wheaton Commemorative, Democratic, Eagleton, 1972 .... 20.00
Wheaton Commemorative, Douglas MacArthur .... 3.75 To 4.25
Wheaton Commemorative, Dwight D.Eisenhower .... 3.75 To 4.25
Wheaton Commemorative, Franklin Roosevelt .... 3.75 To 8.00
Wheaton Commemorative, General Eisenhower .... 3.75 To 8.00
Wheaton Commemorative, General Patton .... 3.75 To 4.25
Wheaton Commemorative, George Washington .... 3.75 To 8.00
Wheaton Commemorative, Harry Truman 6.00
Wheaton Commemorative, Helen Keller .... *Illus* 5.00
Wheaton Commemorative, Helen Keller, Born 1880, Died 1968, 1972 Issue 45.00
Wheaton Commemorative, Herbert Hoover 3.75
Wheaton Commemorative, Humphrey & Muskie, 1968 .... 3.50 To 8.00
Wheaton Commemorative, Humphrey Bogart .... 3.75 To 4.75
Wheaton Commemorative, Jean Harlow .... 3.75 To 4.75
Wheaton Commemorative, John Adams 7.00
Wheaton Commemorative, John F.Kennedy .... 22.50 To 35.00
Wheaton Commemorative, John Paul Jones .... 3.75 To 6.00
Wheaton Commemorative, Lee W.Mintoin, 1971 .... 10.00
Wheaton Commemorative, Lyndon B.Johnson 6.00
Wheaton Commemorative, Mark Twain .... 4.00 To 4.50
Wheaton Commemorative, Martin Luther King .... 3.75 To 6.00
Wheaton Commemorative, McGovern & Shriver, 1972 .... 5.00 To 12.00
Wheaton Commemorative, Mini Set, President, Nos.1, 2, & 3, Each .... 8.00 To 12.50
Wheaton Commemorative, Nixon & Agnew, 1968 .... 5.00 To 16.00
Wheaton Commemorative, Nixon & Agnew, 1972 .... 5.00 To 6.00
Wheaton Commemorative, Paul Revere .... 4.25 To 6.00
Wheaton Commemorative, Pope Paul IV 6.00
Wheaton Commemorative, Republican, 1968 .... 5.00 To 16.00
Wheaton Commemorative, Republican, 1972 .... 5.00 To 6.00
Wheaton Commemorative, Robert E.Lee .... 3.75 To 4.25
Wheaton Commemorative, Robert F.Kennedy .... 4.00 To 8.00
Wheaton Commemorative, Sheriff's Assoc., 1971 .... 12.00 To 15.00
Wheaton Commemorative, Skylab I 6.00
Wheaton Commemorative, Skylab II 6.00
Wheaton Commemorative, Theodore Roosevelt .... 3.75 To 8.00
Wheaton Commemorative, Thomas Edison 5.00
Wheaton Commemorative, Thomas Jefferson .... *Illus* 10.00
Wheaton Commemorative, Ulysses S.Grant .... 3.75 To 8.00
Wheaton Commemorative, Vietnam Memorial 10.00
Wheaton Commemorative, W.C.Fields .... 4.75 To 7.00
Wheaton Commemorative, Will Rogers .... 3.75 To 4.25
Wheaton Commemorative, Woodrow Wilson .... 3.75 To 8.00

Whiskey bottles came in assorted sizes and shapes through the years. Any
container for whiskey is included in this category.

Whiskey, A.Bauer & Co., Chicago, Tapered Gin Shape, Amber, 6 1/4 In. 20.00
Whiskey, A.C.Kerr & Co., Buffalo, N.Y. In Gold, Jug, Handled, Porcelain, Quart 23.75
Whiskey, A.G.Marshuetz & Co., N.Y., Embossed, Bimal, Amber, 32 Ozs., 12 In. 10.00
Whiskey, A.Graf Distilling Co., St.Louis.Mo., 3 Mold, Amber, Quart 20.00
Whiskey, Acker, Merrall & Condit, N.Y., 8 1/2 In. .... *Illus* 20.00
Whiskey, Adolph Harris & Co., Inside Screw, Rectangular, Amber, Quart 15.00
Whiskey, Anderson's, Bimal, Quart 2.50
Whiskey, Antique, 1929, Amber, 1/2 Pint 20.00
Whiskey, Aquinas Pure Malt Whiskey, Quart 6.00
Whiskey, Armour & Company, Mini, Amber 6.00
Whiskey, Ashland, Stoll & Co. Lexington, Bimal, Quart 4.50
Whiskey, Ball Glass, 1951, Pint 3.00
Whiskey, Ball Glass, 4/5 .... 5.00
Whiskey, Balsamic Schnapps, Square, Beveled Corners, Olive Green, Quart 30.00
Whiskey, Banded Flask, Embossed Eagle, Sun Colored Amethyst, Quart 4.00
Whiskey, Bar, Dyottville, Amber, 11 In. .... *Illus* 95.00
Whiskey, Bell Scotch, Bell, 1970, Regal .... *Illus* 15.00
Whiskey, Bell Scotch, Bellringer .... *Illus* 16.00

Wheaton Commemorative,
Helen Keller
(See Page 206)

Whiskey, Bar, Dyottville,
Amber, 11 In.
(See Page 206)

Whiskey, Acker, Merrall
& Condit, N.Y., 8 1/2 In.
(See Page 206)

Whiskey, Bell Scotch,
Bell, 1970, Regal
(See Page 206)

Whiskey, Bell Scotch, Bellringer
(See Page 206)

Whiskey, Bell's Scotch Whiskey, Royal Doulton, Brown & Gold, 9 In.	35.00
Whiskey, Bell's Scotch, Royal Doulton, Brown & Gold, 9 In.	35.00
Whiskey, Bernheim Bros. & Uri, Louisville, Applied Seal, Squatty, Fifth	24.00
Whiskey, Big Squaw, Amber, Quart	75.00
Whiskey, Bininger, see Bininger	
Whiskey, Black & White Rye, Alameda Co., Label, Blob Lip, Flask, 1/2 Pint	9.00
Whiskey, Blake's Kentucky, Light Amber, Quart	55.00
Whiskey, Bluthenthal & Bickart B & B Fine Old, 6 In.	4.00
Whiskey, Bott & Cannon Co., O., Bail Handle, Turning Amethyst, Gallon	24.00
Whiskey, Brook Hill, Compliments Railway Exchange Buffet, Jug, 1/4 Pint	16.00
Whiskey, C.A.Richards, Boston, Quart	8.00
Whiskey, C.A.Richards, 99 Washington St.Boston, Amber, Quart	15.00
Whiskey, C.A.Richards, 99 Washington St.Boston, Olive Amber	20.00
Whiskey, C.Berry & Co., Boston, Flask, Strap Sided, Sun Color, 1/2 Pint	12.00
Whiskey, C.Berry & Co., Boston, Flask, Union Oval, Strap Sided, 1/2 Pint	10.00
Whiskey, C.H.Eddy & Co. Jamaica Ginger, Vt., Embossed Pumpkinseed, 4 In.	18.50
Whiskey, C.Jevne, Chicago, Round, Amber, 11 In.	15.00
Whiskey, C.Koepper, Indianapolis, Drum Shape, Porcelain, Footed, Quart	35.00
Whiskey, C.Krause & Co., Wheeling, W.Va., Jug, Handled, Porcelain, Quart	22.50
Whiskey, C.Oppel & Co., Olive Green, 8 1/2 In.	7.50
Whiskey, Cabin, Roehling & Schutz, Inc., Chicago, Amber	75.00
Whiskey, Cahn Belt & Co., Baltimore, Md., Flask, 1/2 Pint	2.00
Whiskey, Canada Malt Rye, Flask, Amber, Pint	28.00
Whiskey, Canadian Club, Marigold, Fifth	9.00
Whiskey, Canadian Club, Marigold, Pint	6.00
Whiskey, Canteen, 26th Annual, GAR, June 12-13-14, 1900, Pottery, 1/4 Pint	40.00

Whiskey, Coffin, Clear

Whiskey, Cedar Valley Rye,
C.K.Bowman, 12 1/2 In.

Whiskey, **Carhart & Brothers,** Wide Mouth, Handled Jug, Amber, Quart	100.00
Whiskey, **Carnival Glass,** 1/2 Pint	15.00
Whiskey, **Cartan McCarthy Co.,** Monogram, Rectangular, Amber, Quart	16.00
Whiskey, **Case,** Stiegel Type, Blown, Decorated, Pewter Top, 7 1/2 In.	55.00
Whiskey, **Casper's,** Cobalt, Quart	140.00
Whiskey, **Castle,** F.Chevalier Co., San Francisco, Castle Shape, Amber, Quart	30.00
Whiskey, **Cedar Valley Rye,** C.K.Bowman, 12 1/2 In. .... *Illus*	20.00
Whiskey, **Cerrutti Mercantile,** San Francisco, Lady's Leg Neck, Amber, Fifth	18.00
Whiskey, **Chapman & Core,** Inside Screw Thread, Honey Amber, Fifth	15.00
Whiskey, **Cherry,** Dark Cobalt Blue, Miniature	15.00
Whiskey, **Chevalier's Old Castle,** San Francisco, Inside Screw, Quart	20.00
Whiskey, **Chickencock Pure Rye,** Embossed Rooster, Honeycombed, Pint	6.00
Whiskey, **Chickencock,** For Medicinal Use, Tax Stamp 1917-1929, Miniature	15.00
Whiskey, **Cigar Shape,** Amber, Sample Size	20.00
Whiskey, **City Liquor Store,** Tacoma, Wash., Amber, 1/2 Pint	20.00
Whiskey, **Clock,** Pumpkinseed Flask, 6 3/4 In.	20.00
Whiskey, **Club House,** St.Louis, Lady's Leg Neck, Bimal, Amber, 1/2 Pint	15.00
Whiskey, **Coales Gh,** Script, Irish, Haze, Aqua, Fifth	7.00
Whiskey, **Coffin,** Clear .... *Illus*	1.50
Whiskey, **Compliments Of H.B.Mitchell,** Bull & Best St., Jug, 1/4 Pint	15.94
Whiskey, **Compliments Of Henry Schroder,** 401 Broughton St., Jug, 1/4 Pint	15.95
Whiskey, **Compliments Of Hirsch Bros. & Co.,** Ky., Incised, Jug, 1/4 Pint	13.50
Whiskey, **Compliments Of J. & O.,** Jug, 1/4 Pint	15.00
Whiskey, **Compliments Of John Schmitt,** 836 Michigan Ave., Jug, 1/4 Pint	15.98
Whiskey, **Compliments Of Pomona Co-Op Union,** Cal., Jug, 1/4 Pint	15.00
Whiskey, **Compliments Of T.W.Chafee,** Pontiac, Mich., Jug, 1/4 Pint	16.99
Whiskey, **Compliments Of Wm.Ellebrecht,** St.Louis, Mo., Incised, Jug, 1/4 Pint	17.50
Whiskey, **Cook & Bernheimer,** Squatty, Mt.Vernon Pure Rye, Amber	15.00
Whiskey, **Cork Bar Type,** Silver Overlay & Fluted, Wicker Holder, 11 1/2 In.	25.00
Whiskey, **Cork,** Amber, 11 3/4 In.	3.50
Whiskey, **Cottage Brand Embossed,** Cabin Shape, Aqua	95.00
Whiskey, **Crabfelder,** Square, Amber, Pint	4.00
Whiskey, **Crown Distilleries,** Amber, Pint, Inside Threads	40.00
Whiskey, **Crown Distilleries,** 6 3/4 In.	22.50
Whiskey, **Crown,** Cylindrical, Amber, Fifth	20.00
Whiskey, **Cunningham & Ihmsen,** Pittsburgh, Pa., 3 Mold, Honey Amber, Quart	20.00
Whiskey, **Cutter Old Bourbon,** A.P.Hotaling & Co., Amber, Quart	17.95
Whiskey, **Cutty Sark,** Scotch	.80
Whiskey, **Cylinder,** Three Mold, Honey Amber, 11 1/2 In.	6.00
Whiskey, **Cylindrical,** Collared Lip With Ring, Bubbles, Green, 4 1/2 In.	6.00
Whiskey, **Cylindrical,** Free-Blown, Aqua, Sample Size	8.00

Whiskey, Cylindrical, 3 Part Mold, IP, Quart 15.00
Whiskey, D.H.Chambers, Pittsburgh, Pa. On Base, Whittled, Amber, Fifth 13.75
Whiskey, Dallemand & Co., Chicago, Fluted Shoulder, Amber 12.00
Whiskey, Dallemand, Basket Weave, Bimal, 1/2 Pint 6.00
Whiskey, Decorated, 1951, 4/5 .... 3.00
Whiskey, Deep Springs, Amber 12.00
Whiskey, Deep Springs, Round, Amber, Quart 14.00
Whiskey, Detrick Distilling Co., O., Jug, Handled, Motto, Stoneware, 1/2 Pint 17.75
Whiskey, Dew Drop, Hotchkiss, Fenner & Bennett, 8 1/2 In ....*Color* 150.00
Whiskey, Dewar's, Embossed Scene, Doulton Lambeth, Green & Brown, 6 1/4 In. 45.00
Whiskey, Dewar's, Raised Cameo Figures, Royal Doulton, Quart 30.00
Whiskey, Dickel Powder Horn, Amber, Leather Carrying Strap, Dickel, Tenn. 24.00
Whiskey, Dome Shape, Embossed, 1/2 Pint 6.00
Whiskey, Donnelly Rye, Full Quart, Inside Screw, Rectangular, Amber, Quart 18.00
Whiskey, Dore 15 Cent Special, Dobe Harley, N.Y., Pumpkinseed Flask, Pint 12.00
Whiskey, Duffy's Malt, Bimal, Sample Size 17.75
Whiskey, Duffy's Malt, Honey Amber, Pint 20.00
Whiskey, Duffy's Malt, Miniature .... 17.00 To 35.00
Whiskey, Duffy's Malt, Rochester, N.Y., Aug.24, 1886, ABM, Amber, 11 1/4 In. 3.15
Whiskey, Duffy's Malt, Yellow, Miniature 30.00
Whiskey, Duffy's Malt, Yellow, 3 7/8 In. 22.50
Whiskey, Duffy's Malt, 3 7/8 In. 15.00
Whiskey, Duffy's, Bimal, Quart 2.50

Whiskey, E.G.Booz, Old Mr.Boston, 1959, 8 1/2 In.

Whiskey, E.B.Hartman Pure Rye, Figural, Dog, 9 1/2 In.

Whiskey, Durham, 11 1/2 In. ....*Color* 800.00
Whiskey, E.B.Hartman Pure Rye, Figural, Dog, 9 1/2 In. ....*Illus* 75.00
Whiskey, E.G.Booz, Old Cabin, McKearin G VII-3, Amber 200.00
Whiskey, E.G.Booz, Old Mr.Boston, 1959, 8 1/2 In. ....*Illus* 17.00
Whiskey, E.G.Booz, 2 Story House, Beveled Roof, Amethyst, Quart 1100.00
Whiskey, E.R.Betterton & Co. Distillers, Chattanooga, Tenn., Amber 12.00
Whiskey, E.R.Betterton Dist., Chattanooga, Tenn., Amber, Pint 10.00
Whiskey, East Liverpool, O., Medicinal, Green Letters, Porcelain, Quart 55.00
Whiskey, Elk's, Ear Of Corn, 5 In. 75.00
Whiskey, Ellenville Glass Works, Green, Quart 22.00
Whiskey, Embossed Club Within Diamond, Lockport Green 300.00
Whiskey, Embossed Dancing Girl, Machine Made, Amber, Fifth 30.00
Whiskey, Embossed Shoulder, Patent 3 Mold, Amber, Quart 5.65
Whiskey, English, Squat, 1750, 6 1/2 In. ....*Illus* 250.00
Whiskey, Envoy Club, Embossed Mesh, Flask, Amber, Pint 20.00
Whiskey, F.Chevalier Old Castle, Embossed Castle, Screw Cap, Fifth 20.00
Whiskey, Finest Old Sour Mash, Brand & Co., Jug, Handled, Stoneware, Quart 45.00
Whiskey, Fleishmann's Medicinal, Flask, Pint 20.00
Whiskey, Fluted Neck & Shoulders, Quart 2.00
Whiskey, Four Roses, Back Bar, Miniature 10.50
Whiskey, Four Roses, Embossed, ABM, Dug, Amber, Miniature 3.50
Whiskey, Four Roses, Embossed, Labels, Amber, Pint 5.00

Whiskey, English, Squat, 1750, 6 1/2 In.
(See Page 209)

Whiskey, Fred Rashen, Monogram, Sacramento, Cal., Bimal, Amber, Fifth	19.00
Whiskey, Freiberg Bros., Cincinnati, O., 1879 Old Jug, Crockery, 10 1/2 In.	60.00
Whiskey, G.O.Blake's Kentucky, Embossed Barrel, Label, Honey Amber, Quart	45.00
Whiskey, G.O.Blake's Rye & Bourbon, Barrel, Embossed, Quart	6.00
Whiskey, G.O.Taylor Pure Rye, 1885, Embossed Base, 3 Mold, Amber, Quart	32.50
Whiskey, George S.Ladd, Stockton, Cal., Bimal, Amber, Fifth	22.00
Whiskey, George W.Torrey, Amber, Sample Size	8.00
Whiskey, Germania Peppermint Schnapps, 6 Sided, 11 In.	15.00
Whiskey, Gilka, Amber	12.00
Whiskey, Gilka, Green	18.00
Whiskey, Glasner & Barzen Distillers, Kansas City, Rectangular, Sample Size	5.50
Whiskey, Golden Heart Fire Copper, Prestonville, Ky., Amber, Fifth	35.00
Whiskey, Golden Rule XXXX, Braunshweiger Co., San Francisco, Amber, Fifth	55.00
Whiskey, Golden Treasure, Barrel, 5 In.	55.00
Whiskey, Golden Wedding, Carnival Glass, Light Marigold, Pint	10.00
Whiskey, Golden Wedding, Carnival Glass, Marigold, Pint	10.00
Whiskey, Golden Wedding, Carnival Glass, Pint	10.00 To 15.00
Whiskey, Golden Wedding, Carnival Glass, Quart	4.00 To 15.00
Whiskey, Golden Wedding, Embossed Bells, Tin Closure, 7 1/4 In.	3.00
Whiskey, Golden Wedding, Fifth	9.00
Whiskey, Golden Wedding, Screw Top, Carnival, 1/10 Pint	16.50
Whiskey, Goldie Klenert Co., Stockton, Cal., Bimal, 1/6 Gallon	15.00
Whiskey, Good Old Bourbon In A Hogs–, Figural Pig, Embossed, 7 In.	50.00
Whiskey, Gorden's, Bimal, Quart	2.50
Whiskey, Grannymede, Square, Amber, Pint	4.00
Whiskey, Green Mountain Club Straight, Offsided Neck, Purpled, 6 3/4 In.	25.00
Whiskey, Green River, Paper Label, 6 In.	12.00
Whiskey, Green River, 2 Labels Of Negro & Horse, Quart	9.00
Whiskey, Greenbrier, Bimal, Quart	3.50
Whiskey, Grommes & Ullrich National Club Bourbon, Jug, Handle, Quart	28.50
Whiskey, Grover Rye, Bimal, Pint	3.50
Whiskey, H F & B, N.Y., 9 1/2 In. ....*Color*	800.00
Whiskey, H.B.Kirk, Embossed Indians, Amber, Fifth	12.00
Whiskey, H.J.Wollacott, Los Angeles, Cylinder, Amber, 11 3/4 In.	35.00
Whiskey, H.W.Huguley & Co., Boston, Square, Paneled, Quart	12.00
Whiskey, H.W.Huguley, 134 Canal St., Boston, Amber, Quart	8.00
Whiskey, H.W.Huguley's, Sample Size	6.00
Whiskey, Half Barrel, Embossed Rooster & Girl, Pint	50.00
Whiskey, Handled Jug, Red Amber, Pint	14.50
Whiskey, Hapner, Bimal, Quart	3.50
Whiskey, Hathorn Spring, Coffee Black	22.50
Whiskey, Hathorn Spring, Yellow Olive, Fifth	26.00
Whiskey, Hayner Distilling Co., Quart	3.00
Whiskey, Hayner, ABM, Pint	8.50
Whiskey, Hayner, Amber, Quart	19.00
Whiskey, Hayner's Distillers, Troy, O., Patent Nov.30, 1897, Quart	9.00
Whiskey, Hayner's, Bimal, Turning Purple, Quart	7.00

Whiskey, Hayner's, Dayton & St.Louis, Quart 14.00
Whiskey, Hayner's, Dayton, O., Amber, Quart 15.00
Whiskey, Hayner's, Fancy Design, Oval, Hazy, Amber, Pint 50.00
Whiskey, Hayner's, Fancy, Oval, Amber, Pint 45.00
Whiskey, Hayner's, Quilted, Bimal, 1/2 Pint 6.00
Whiskey, Hayner's, Stain, Amber, Quart 13.75
Whiskey, Hayner's, Troy, Bimal, Pint 3.50
Whiskey, Hayner's, Troy, O., Nov.30, 1897, Stain, 11 1/2 In. 2.00
Whiskey, Hayner's, 4 Cities, Fluted, Stain, Quart 5.00
Whiskey, Hellman Dist.Co., St.Louis, Pint 8.00
Whiskey, Helme's Railroad Mills, Glass Cap, Ground Mouth, Amber, Quart 8.00
Whiskey, Hig Scotch .... .80
Whiskey, Hildebrandt Posner, San Francisco, Inside Screw, Bimal, Amber, Fifth 18.00
Whiskey, Holiday Chimes, 1903-1904, 4 1/2 In. ....*Color* 60.00
Whiskey, Hoyt Brother's Liquors, Mass., Union Oval, Strap Sided, Pint 6.00
Whiskey, Hoyt Brothers, Mass., Union Oval Strap Sided Flask, Pint 9.00
Whiskey, Hub Punch, C.H.Graves & Sons, Boston, 9 In. ....*Color* 30.00
Whiskey, J.A.Gilka In Script, Octagonal, Amber, 10 In. 12.00
Whiskey, J.A.Gilka, Berlin, Amber, 9 1/2 In. .... *Illus* 22.00
Whiskey, J.A.Gilka, Berlin, Schutzen Str. No.9, Deep Red Amber, 9 3/4 In. 5.00
Whiskey, J.H.Cutter Bourbon, Flask, Guaranteed Full 1/2 Pint 6.00
Whiskey, J.H.Cutter Old Bourbon, A.P.Hotaling & Co., Amber, Quart 17.95
Whiskey, J.H.Cutter Old Bourbon, Crown, Amber, Quart, 11 3/4 In. 18.00
Whiskey, J.H.Cutter UFO Rye, Louisville, Ky., Label, Miniature 6.00
Whiskey, J.J.Kelly, Seattle, Wash., Flask, Quart 20.00
Whiskey, J.Rieger & Co., Kansas City, Fluted, Round, Sample Size 5.00
Whiskey, J.Rieger & Co., Kansas City, Quart 9.00
Whiskey, J.Rieger & Co., Round, Fluted Shoulder, Quart 18.00
Whiskey, JM & Co., Boston, Long Neck, Tapered Collar, 4 1/2 In. 8.00

Whiskey, J.A.Gilka, Berlin, Amber, 9 1/2 In.

Whiskey, Jacob & Wolford, Brown, 8 1/2 In. .... *Illus* 325.00
Whiskey, James Dingley & Co., 99 Washington St., Boston, Mass., Amber 15.00
Whiskey, Jenever, Blankenheym & Nolet, Green, 11 In. .... *Illus* 25.00
Whiskey, Jesse Moore & Co., Louisville, Ky., Sole Agent, Amber, Quart 23.95
Whiskey, Jesse Moore Hunt Co., San Francisco, Cal., Amber, Quart .... 9.95 To 23.95
Whiskey, Jesse Moore Pure Rye, Covered Wagon & Horses, Amber, Pint 3.95
Whiskey, Jimmie Durkins, Spokane, Wash., Amber, Bulb Neck, Quart 25.00
Whiskey, Jimmie Durkins, Spokane, Wash., Bulb Neck, Embossed, Amber, Quart 25.00
Whiskey, Jno Wyeth & Bro., Phila., Malt, Amber, 9 In.High 4.50
Whiskey, Jos.A.Magnus & Co., Cincinnati, O., Dragon, Flask, 1/2 Pint 2.00
Whiskey, Judge's Favorite, Embossed Squares, Flask, Amber, Pint 20.00
Whiskey, Jug, Sailboat Inside, Miniature, 3/4 In. 6.50
Whiskey, Julius Kessler Bourbon Co., Quart 8.00
Whiskey, Kahn Bros., Distillers, N.Y., Squat, Quart 5.00
Whiskey, Kellerstraus Belle Of Missouri Rye, Bar, Enameled, Quart 30.00
Whiskey, Kellerstraus Distilling, St.Louis, Mo., Quart 16.00
Whiskey, Kellstraus Distilling Co., St.Louis, Mo., Sun Color Amethyst 7.00

Whiskey, Jacob & Wolford, Brown, 8 1/2 In.
(See Page 211)

Whiskey, Jenever, Blankenheym & Nolet, Green, 11 In.
(See Page 211)

Whiskey, **Kentucky Dew,** D.Meschendorf, Louisville, Ky., Amber, Pint	12.50
Whiskey, **Keystone Club,** Embossed Stars, Flask, Pint	20.00
Whiskey, **Kingsbury Bourbon,** Ginter Co., Boston, Straight Sided, 1/2 Pint	8.00
Whiskey, **Kit Cars. n,** Wood, Pollard & Co., Boston, Label, Pint	4.75
Whiskey, **Klein Bros. & Hyman Cincinnati Keystone Rye,** Gold Script, Quart	11.00
Whiskey, **Klein Bros. & Hyman Keystone In Gold,** Jug, Handled, China, Quart	22.50
Whiskey, **Kuhl's,** San Francisco, Bimal, Amber, Fifth	18.00
Whiskey, **Lady's Leg,** Turn Mold, Amber, Quart	6.00
Whiskey, **Lawton Rye,** Roth & Co., Inside Screw, Rectangular, Amber, Quart	16.00
Whiskey, **Levaggi Co.,** San Francisco, Cal., Rectangular, Amber, Quart	15.00
Whiskey, **Lincoln Inn,** Embossed Men & Horses, Flask, Pint	10.00
Whiskey, **Liqueur Of The Devil,** 3 Devils' Heads, Barrel, Amber	125.00
Whiskey, **Livingston & Co.,** S.L.F., Old Bourbon Livingston & Co., Amber	45.00
Whiskey, **Lord Calvert,** 1948, Label, 1/2 Gallon	7.00
Whiskey, **Lotus Club Handmade Sour Mash,** Gold Script, Quart	16.50 To 24.50
Whiskey, **Lotus Club Handmade Sour Mash,** Pottery, 8 In. ....*Color*	32.00
Whiskey, **Louis Taussig & Co.,** San Francisco & N.Y., Square, Fifth	12.00
Whiskey, **M.C.Russel & Son,** Maysville, Ky., Spiral Neck, Pint	8.50
Whiskey, **M.E.Woodward Palace Saloon,** 6 In. ....*Illus*	4.50
Whiskey, **M.M.Uri & Co.,** Inc., Louisville, Ky., Amber, 4 3/4 In.	25.00

Whiskey, **M.Salzman Purity Above All,** Swirled Neck, Amber, Fifth 16.50
Whiskey, **MacKinlay's Very Old Scotch,** Stoneware, Royal Doulton, Blue 55.00
Whiskey, **Mailbox Rye,** Small Size 125.00
Whiskey, **Maryland,** Flask, Pint 18.00
Whiskey, **McCleod O'Donnell Co.,** Rectangular, Aqua, Quart 13.00
Whiskey, **McDonald Cohn,** San Francisco, Inside Screw, Stain, Green, Quart 15.00
Whiskey, **McLeod,** Hatie Co., San Francisco, Amber 15.00
Whiskey, **McPhelemy,** New Place, Danbury, Conn., Flask, Aqua, 6 In. 25.00
Whiskey, **Meredith's Diamond Club Pure Rye,** O., Jug, Handled, K.T.K., 1/2 Pint 65.00
Whiskey, **Meredith's Diamond Club Pure Rye,** O., Jug, Handled, K.T.K., Pint 65.00
Whiskey, **Meredith's Diamond Club Pure Rye,** O., Jug, Handled, K.T.K., Quart 69.50
Whiskey, **Meredith's Diamond Club Pure Rye,** O., Jug, K.T.K., 1 1/2 Quart 25.00
Whiskey, **Meredith's Diamond Club,** Pittsburgh, Pa., 3 Mold, Quart 30.00
Whiskey, **Merry Christmas & Happy New Year,** 1 1/2 In. ....*Color* 35.00
Whiskey, **Mill Creek,** Embossed Cabin & Waterwheel, Flask, Pint 20.00
Whiskey, **Millbrook,** Bimal, Pint 2.50
Whiskey, **Miller's Game Cock,** Boston, Oval Flask, Bubbles, Seeds, Aqua, Pint 7.00
Whiskey, **Miller's Game Cock,** Ring Lip, Embossed, Haze, Sun Colored, Quart 12.50
Whiskey, **Mold Blown,** Massachusetts Pattern, 3 1/2 X 11 In. 25.00
Whiskey, **Monk's Old Bourbon,** Wilson & Fairbanks, IP, Square, Olive, Quart 135.00

Whiskey, M.E.Woodward Palace Saloon, 6 In.
(See Page 212)

Whiskey, **Monks Loin,** Brown ....*Illus* 85.00
Whiskey, **Monongahela Rye,** Flask, Amber, Pint 14.00
Whiskey, **Montezuma Rye,** James Maguire, Phila., 12 In. ....*Color* 69.00
Whiskey, **Moonshine,** Jug, Stoneware, Brown, Gallon 5.00
Whiskey, **Moore Old Bourbon & Rye,** Jesse Moore, Amber, Quart, 11 3/4 In. 24.00
Whiskey, **Mt.Vernon,** Embossed, Label, Bimal, Amber, Miniature 12.00
Whiskey, **Mt.Vernon,** Medicinal, Flask, Pint 20.00
Whiskey, **Mt.Vernon,** Square, Amber, Quart 10.00
Whiskey, **Mum's Rye,** Uri & Co., Louisville, Ky., Embossed, Amber, Miniature 12.00
Whiskey, **Myers & Co. Pure Fulton,** Covington, Ky., Jug, Aqua, 9 X 7 In. 12.50
Whiskey, **N.Muri & Co.,** 3 1/2 In. 12.50
Whiskey, **O.F.A.Taylor,** Jug, Pottery, 8 In. ....*Illus* 20.00
Whiskey, **Oak Lawn,** Flask, Amber, Pint 14.00
Whiskey, **Old Belle Of Anderson,** Milk Glass, Pint 140.00
Whiskey, **Old Blue House,** Sample, Brown & White Glaze, 4 In. 18.00
Whiskey, **Old Bourbon Whiskey,** For Medicinal Purposes, Square, Aqua, 10 In. 52.00
Whiskey, **Old Bushmills Distillery Co.,** Square, Aqua, 9 3/4 In. 12.00
Whiskey, **Old Charter,** Bimal, Amber, Quart 6.50
Whiskey, **Old Club House 1860,** Macy & Jenkins, Handled, 9 1/2 In. 20.00
Whiskey, **Old Dexter Distilling Co.,** Ky., 1891, 7 1/2 In. ....*Color* 62.50
Whiskey, **Old Elk,** Lexington, Ky., Embossed Elk's Head, Quart 13.50
Whiskey, **Old Grand-Dad,** Label, Glass Stopper, Tax Stamp 1911-1918, Miniature 6.00
Whiskey, **Old Grand-Dad,** Label, Unbroken Seal, Bottled In 1923, Quart 200.00
Whiskey, **Old Grand-Dad,** Labels, Sealed, 1933, Quart 125.00
Whiskey, **Old Irish American,** 1934, Less Than 1 Month Old, Flask, Pint 20.00
Whiskey, **Old Jefferson County,** Enameled, Cylindrical, Quart 23.50
Whiskey, **Old Joe Anderson,** Blown In Mold, Quart 3.00

Whiskey, Monks Loin, Brown
(See Page 213)

Whiskey, O.F.A.Taylor,
Jug, Pottery, 8 In.
(See Page 213)

Whiskey, **Old Joe Gideon,** Flask, Stain, Amber, 1/2 Pint	2.00
Whiskey, **Old Joe Perkins,** Paper Label, Miniature	6.50
Whiskey, **Old Kentucky Bourbon,** Bininger Barrel, Small Size	145.00
Whiskey, **Old Kentucky Bourbon,** 1849, Bininger, 8 1/2 In. ....*Color*	200.00
Whiskey, **Old Kentucky Distilling Co.,** Covington, Ky., Quart	10.00
Whiskey, **Old Lewis Hunter Rye,** Quart ....*Illus*	11.00
Whiskey, **Old Lexington,** Bimal, Quart	4.00
Whiskey, **Old Log Cabin,** Embossed Cabins & Trees, Flask, Pint	20.00
Whiskey, **Old Maryland,** Jug, Gold, Porcelain, Quart	48.00
Whiskey, **Old Monarch,** Flask, Amber, Pint	14.00
Whiskey, **Old Overholt,** Medicinal, 1912, Flask, Amber, Pint	14.00
Whiskey, **Old Pirate,** 1934, Flask, Amber, Pint	14.00
Whiskey, **Old Plantation Distilling Co.,** Los Angeles, Embossed, Amber, Gallon	50.00
Whiskey, **Old Polk 100 Proof,** 1934, Medicinal, Flask, Pint	20.00
Whiskey, **Old Prentice,** J.T.S.Brown & Son, Bimal, Quart	6.50
Whiskey, **Old Quaker,** Quart ....*Illus*	.50
Whiskey, **Old R.B.Grainger,** Blown In Mold, Quart	3.00
Whiskey, **Old Rye,** A.D.H.C., Union & Clasped Hands, Aqua, Quart	42.00
Whiskey, **Old Rye,** Pike's Peak & Prospector & Eagle & Pittsburgh, Aqua, Pint	60.00
Whiskey, **Old Rye,** Union & Eagle, Pittsburgh, Alorc On Pennant, Aqua, Quart	50.00
Whiskey, **Old Smuggler Gaelic Whisky** ....*Illus*	10.00
Whiskey, **Old Stony Brook Rye,** Medicinal, 1931, Flask, Pint	20.00
Whiskey, **Old Taylor,** Castle, 1967 ....*Illus*	4.00
Whiskey, **Old Taylor,** Label, Unbroken Seal, Bottled In 1923, Pint	150.00
Whiskey, **Old Taylor,** Labels, Sealed, 1933, Pint	95.00
Whiskey, **Old Taylor,** Medicinal, Flask, Pint	18.00
Whiskey, **Old Times,** 1st Prize, World's Fair, Dug, Miniature	4.50
Whiskey, **Old Times,** 1st Prize, World's Fair 1893, Clear	10.00
Whiskey, **Old 81,** Bimal, Quart	2.50
Whiskey, **Olde Campe Rye,** Embossed On Neck, Whittled, Red Amber, Fifth	10.00
Whiskey, **Otto Wagner & Bros.,** Tiffin, O., Jug, 1/2 Gallon	25.00
Whiskey, **P.G.Co. On Bottom,** 3 Mold, Collared Lip With Ring, Blue, 32 Ozs.	6.00
Whiskey, **P.J.Kennedy & Co.,** Boston, Quart	10.00
Whiskey, **P.M.,** 1/2 Pint	2.00

Whiskey, Old Lewis Hunter Rye, Quart
(See Page 214)

Whiskey, Old Smuggler Gaelic Whisky
(See Page 214)

Whiskey, Old Quaker, Quart
(See Page 214)

Whiskey, Old Taylor, Castle, 1967
(See Page 214)

Whiskey, **Patent On Shoulder,** Amber, Quart 11.00
Whiskey, **Paul Jones & Co.,** Rectangular, Off Center Neck, 1/2 Pint 30.00
Whiskey, **Paul Jones Pure Rye,** 9 1/2 In. ....*Color* 15.00
Whiskey, **Paul Jones,** Blob Seal, Amber, Quart 6.00
Whiskey, **Paul Jones,** Blob Seal, Miniature 13.00
Whiskey, **Paul Jones,** Blob Seal, Quart 9.00
Whiskey, **Paul Jones,** Embossed Ships, Medicinal Purposes, Flask, Amber, Pint 22.00
Whiskey, **Paul Jones,** Flask, Embossed Ships, Bimal, Amber, Pint 4.00
Whiskey, **Paul Jones,** Label, Amber, 3 1/2 In. 5.00
Whiskey, **Paul Jones,** Louisville, Ky., Glass Seal On Shoulder, Amber, 9 In. 5.00
Whiskey, **Paul Jones,** Miniature .... 5.00 To 8.00
Whiskey, **Paul Jones,** Paper Sticker, 1/2 Pint 6.50
Whiskey, **Paul Jones,** 1/2 Pint 2.50
Whiskey, **Paul Jones,** Pint 2.50
Whiskey, **Paul Jones,** Sample Size 9.00
Whiskey, **Pebble Ford Bourbon,** Blown In Mold, Quart 3.50
Whiskey, **Peru Brewery One Quart,** Blown, Amber, 9 3/4 In. 15.00
Whiskey, **Peter Dawson Distilleries,** Blown In Mold, Olive Green, Quart 10.00
Whiskey, **Petts Bald Eagle,** Quart 4.00
Whiskey, **Peychaud's Bitter Cordial,** Cylindrical, Amber, Fifth 12.00
Whiskey, **Pfeffer Brothers,** Quart 6.00
Whiskey, **Piper & Company Bourbon,** Syracuse, N.Y., Wicker, Amber, Quart 138.00
Whiskey, **Pretoria Rye Is Better,** Scharff Distilling, Mo., Amber, Pint 18.00
Whiskey, **Pure Fulton,** Myers & Co., Aqua, Gallon 15.00
Whiskey, **Pure Malt Whiskey Bourbon Co.,** Ky., Jug, Handled, OP, Amber, Quart 45.00
Whiskey, **Pushed Up Base,** Jug, Handled, Red Amber, Pint 16.75
Whiskey, **Q On Bottom,** Collared Lip With Skirt, Olive Green, 10 1/2 In. 7.00
Whiskey, **Quinine Co.,** Ky., Lady's Leg, Stain, Amber, 1/2 Pint 20.00
Whiskey, **R.B.Cutter,** Louisville, Ky., 9 In. ....*Color* 275.00
Whiskey, **Red Top,** Uneven Base, Amber, 1/2 Pint 3.00
Whiskey, **Reefer's Green Mountain,** Quart 8.00
Whiskey, **Rey Del Rey,** Clear 6.00
Whiskey, **Rosenblatt Co.,** San Francisco, Square, Whittled, Light Amber, Fifth 30.00
Whiskey, **Rosskam Gerstley & Co.Fine Old,** Phila., Squat, Amethyst, 4 1/2 In. 22.50
Whiskey, **Rosskam Gerstley Old Saratoga Extra Fine Whiskey,** Clear, Fifth 19.00
Whiskey, **Roth & Co.,** Guaranteed Full Quart, Rectangular, Amber, Quart 14.00
Whiskey, **Roth & Co.,** San Francisco, Amber 18.00
Whiskey, **Russ's Aromatic Schnapps,** New York, Dull Olive, 8 1/4 In. 75.00
Whiskey, **Rutherford McRae's Whisky Punch,** Jug, Porcelain, White, 4 In. 6.50
Whiskey, **Rutherford McRae's Whisky Punch,** Porcelain, Scotchman, 4 In. 6.50
Whiskey, **Rutherford Scotch Whisky Pot,** 1970, Thistle, Porcelain, 3 1/2 In. 6.50
Whiskey, **Rutherford Scotch,** Barrel, Porcelain, 2 Piece, Brown, 2 1/2 In. 5.50
Whiskey, **Rutherford Scotch,** Jug, Porcelain, Brown & White, 3 3/8 In. 6.00
Whiskey, **Rutherford Scotch,** Porcelain, Thistles, Basket Weave, 3 3/8 In. 6.00
Whiskey, **Rutherford Scotch,** Pot, Porcelain, 1970, Thistle Shape, 3 1/2 In. 6.50
Whiskey, **S.F.Petts & Co.,** Purity Guaranteed, Boston, Amber, Quart 12.50
Whiskey, **S.Hyde,** Seattle, Wash., Bimal, Amber, Fifth 20.00
Whiskey, **S.S.P.On Base,** Strap Side, Olive Green, Quart 8.00
Whiskey, **Salzman & Siegleman Pure Old Rye,** Crockery, Brown, White, 7 In. 25.00
Whiskey, **Salzman's,** Embossed, Label, Quart 7.00
Whiskey, **Samuel Westheimer,** Pint 1.00
Whiskey, **Schnapps,** Citron 10.00
Whiskey, **Schwaske,** San Francisco, Bimal, Amber, Fifth 18.00
Whiskey, **Scotch,** Monarch, Stoneware, Handled, Brown & Tan, 3 3/4 In. 6.00
Whiskey, **Security,** Bimal, Quart 3.50
Whiskey, **Sheen & Nelson,** Cork, Paper Label, Amber, 5 3/4 In. 5.00
Whiskey, **Sherman Rye,** Hildebrandt Posner, Inside Screw, Amber, Quart 18.00
Whiskey, **Shoe Fly,** Clear ....*Illus* 2.00
Whiskey, **Shortell & Timmins,** Boston, Bimal, Sun Colored Amethyst, Quart 12.00
Whiskey, **South Carolina Dispensary,** Strap Sided Flask, Embossed Tree, Fifth 27.00
Whiskey, **South Carolina Dispensary,** Union Flask, Amber, Quart 325.00
Whiskey, **Special Highland,** Royal Doulton, Norse Ship On Browns, Handle 50.00
Whiskey, **Spring Lake Handmade Sour Mash Bourbon,** Jug, Handled, K.T.K., Quart 49.75
Whiskey, **Sprinkle,** Embossed, Quart 4.50
Whiskey, **St.Jacobs Malt,** Cincinnati, Duffy Shaped, Fifth 16.00

Whiskey, Shoe Fly, Clear
(See Page 216)

Whiskey, Sterling Overlay	95.00
Whiskey, Straight Neck, Collared Lip With Ring, Olive Green, 4 1/4 In.	5.50
Whiskey, Straight Sided, Collared Lip With Ring, Amber, 3 3/4 In.	4.50
Whiskey, Straus Bros. Kenwood Sour Mash In Gold, Jug, Handled, China, Quart	26.75
Whiskey, Strauss Bros., Chicago, Old Crow, Gold Script, Flowers, Quart	55.00
Whiskey, Strauss Bros., Chicago, Pint	1.00
Whiskey, Strickland's, Flask, Amber	50.00
Whiskey, Strickland's, Flask, Aqua	50.00
Whiskey, Sunset Reserve Bourbon, Quart *Illus*	9.00
Whiskey, Sweet Home Rye, Altshul Distilling Co., O., Barrel, Label, Quart	8.20
Whiskey, Sweet Home Rye, Altshul Distilling Co., O., Barrel, Quart	3.90
Whiskey, Taylor & Williams, Embossed, ABM, Jug, Miniature	5.00
Whiskey, Taylor & Williams, Pint	1.00

Whiskey, Sunset Reserve Bourbon, Quart

Whiskey, Taylor & Williams, Quart	1.00
Whiskey, Taylor & Williams, 1/2 Pint	1.00
Whiskey, Taylor, Base Cloudy, Amber, Miniature	7.00
Whiskey, Telusky Bros. Fine, N.Y., Strap Sided Flask, 1/2 Pint	5.00
Whiskey, The Campus, Gossler Bros., Amber, Embossed	100.00
Whiskey, The Campus, Gossler Bros., N.Y., Applied Handle, Amber, 9 1/4 In.	40.00
Whiskey, The Old Bush Hill's Distilling Co., Aqua	10.00
Whiskey, The Old Mill, Whitlock & Co., Handled Jug, Amber, Pint	575.00
Whiskey, Theo, Blauth & Son, Sacramento, Cal., Bimal, Amber, Fifth	24.00
Whiskey, Tracer, Embossed, Amber, Quart	5.00
Whiskey, Tracer, Embossed, Amber, 1/2 Pint	7.50
Whiskey, Trager & Co., Cincinnati, O., Red Amber, Quart	5.00
Whiskey, Umpire Bourbon, Kelly Steinmetz Co., Jug, Handled, Quart	14.75
Whiskey, Uri & Co., Louisville, Ky., Stain, Amber, 4 3/4 In.	6.00

Whiskey, Van Arsdell Sour Mash, Mercer Co., Ky., Dark Amber, 10 In. 5.00
Whiskey, Van Dunck, Light Golden Amber 95.00
Whiskey, W.H.Holt, Limited, Pinch, Bimal, Amber, Quart 10.00
Whiskey, W.H.Jones & Co., Boston, Mass., Aqua, Rectangular 8.00
Whiskey, W.H.Kirby, Bimal, Quart 4.50
Whiskey, W.J.Van Schuyver, Portland, Ore., Amber, Fifth 20.00
Whiskey, W.J.Van Schuyver, Portland, Ore., Inside Screw, Bimal, Amber, Fifth 18.00
Whiskey, W.L.Weller & Sons Distillers, Louisville, Ky., 10 In. 7.00
Whiskey, W.P.G.Co. On Bottom, Flask, Diamond Pattern, 5 In. 8.00
Whiskey, Walker's Kilmarnock, Cork, Bubbles, Dug, Aqua, 10 In. 20.00
Whiskey, Weeks & Gilson, Stoddard, N.H., Olive Amber, Quart 80.00
Whiskey, Wellington Hotel, Clayton Le Moores, Coffin Flask, Aqua, Pint 7.95
Whiskey, Wellington Hotel, Clayton Le Moores, Coffin Flask, 1/2 Pint 7.50
Whiskey, Westheimer, Square, Amber, Pint 4.00
Whiskey, Weston's Special Reserve, Oval, Amber, Quart 10.00
Whiskey, Wharton's, 1850, Chestnut Grove, Jug, Whitney, N.J., Amber, 10 In. 155.00
Whiskey, Wharton's, 1850, Chestnut Grove, Pocket Flask, Amber, 5 In. 95.00
Whiskey, Wharton's, 1850, Chestnut Grove, Pocket Flask, Sapphire Blue, 5 In. 115.00
Whiskey, Wheat, Seal, Mineral Water Shape, Amber, Quart 80.00
Whiskey, White Horse Scotch, Amber, Miniature 5.00
Whiskey, White House, Flask, Bimal, Dug, Stain, 1/2 Pint 3.50
Whiskey, Winedale Co., Monogram, Oakland, Cal., Bimal, Amber, Fifth 25.00
Whiskey, Wise's Old Irish In Black, Jug, Handled, Porcelain, Quart 20.00
Whiskey, Wolf Creek, Embossed Trees, Flask, Amber, Pint 20.00
Whiskey, Wright & Taylor Distillers, Louisville, Ky., Amber, 9 1/2 In. 5.95
Whiskey, Wriglet And Taylor Distillers, Amber, Quart 8.50
Whiskey, 2 Mold, Stain, Light Blue, Fifth 115.00
Whiskey, 3 Mold, Collared Lip With Ring, Whittled Shoulder, Gold, 11 1/4 In. 7.00
Whiskey, 3 Mold, Cylindrical, Pontil, Aqua, 10 In. 4.00
Whiskey, 3 Mold, Green, 12 In. 15.00
Whiskey, 3 Mold, IP, Deep Green, Quart 10.00
Whiskey, 3 Mold, Whittled, Honey Amber, Quart 4.50
Whiskey, 3 Mold, Whittled, IP, Deep Green, Quart 10.00
Whiskey, 3 Mold, Whittled, IP, Green, Quart 10.00
Whiskey, 100 Pipers Scotch 8.00
Whiskey, 999 Straight, 1934, Flask, Pint 18.00
    Whiskey, see also Ballantine, Beam, Bininger, Dant, Ezra Brooks
Wild Turkey, Standing With Baby, 1974 .... 24.50
Wild Turkey, Tom Turkey In The Straw, 1971 .... Illus   65.00
Wild Turkey, Turkey On A Log, 1972 .... Illus   28.50
Wild Turkey, Turkey On The Wing, 1973 .... Illus   26.50
Wine, Celadon, Pyriform, 3 Stylized Branches, Black, Green, C.1250 .... 175.00
Wine, Cobalt Blue, 12 In. 40.00
Wine, Cohodua Vineyards, Inc., Geneva, O., Figural Hound Pup, 4 In. 12.00
Wine, Duff Gordon Sherry, U.S.A. Medical Department, Amber, 10 In. 135.00
Wine, Face Under Glass, 14 In. .... Color   250.00
Wine, French, Billiard Balls & Cues, Pontil, Depose, 16 3/8 In. .... 100.00 To 110.00
Wine, George Drewry, Crockery Jug, Gray & Blue, Gallon 25.00
Wine, Goldberg Bowen Merchants, San Francisco, Coffin Flask, Stain, Pint 25.00
Wine, Hock, Applied Collar, Red Amber, 15 In. 3.85
Wine, Hock, Bimal, Emerald Green, 14 In. 9.00
Wine, Hock, Bimal, Teal Blue, 16 In. 9.00
Wine, Hock, Deep Emerald Green, 14 1/2 In. 12.00
Wine, Hock, Dug, OP, Aqua, 11 1/2 In. 8.50
Wine, Hock, Red Amber, 11 1/2 In. 5.00
Wine, L.Jacobs, San Francisco, Hock Type, Amber, 13 In. 95.00
Wine, Mary Gregory, Crystal, White Boy, Teardrop Stopper 45.00
Wine, Mary Gregory, Crystal, White Girl, Teardrop Stopper 45.00
Wine, Mary Gregory, Girl, Tinted Face, Teardrop Stopper, Crystal, 10 In. 50.00
Wine, Pinch, Pewter Stopper & Grapes & Leaves, Olive Green, 9 1/2 In., Pair 100.00
Wine, Punch'ong, Korean, White, White Slip, Kerong-San Kilns, C.1450 .... 300.00
Wine, Schlesinger & Bender, In.C.Cal., Amber, 25 Ozs. 22.00
Wine, Sherry, Sandman, Wedgwood, Prince Of Wales, July, 1969 .... 15.00
Wine, Sherry, Zorro, Royal Doulton, Marked A 25.00
Wine, Stoneware, Double Gourd Shape, Gray, Pierced On Each Side, C.1150 .... 375.00

Wild Turkey,
Tom Turkey In The Straw,
1971
(See Page 218)

Wild Turkey,
Turkey On The Wing,
1973
(See Page 218)

Wild Turkey,
Turkey On A Log,
1972
(See Page 218)

Zanesville, Globular, 24 Ribs Swirled To Right, Aqua
(See Page 220)

Wine, Tester, Green, 7 1/4 In.	25.00
Wine, Trumpet Mouth, Free Blown, 6 Sided, OP, Aqua, Quart	45.00
Wine, Vino Rosso, Cat, Amber, 13 In.	4.50
Wine, Vino Rosso, Cat, Green, 7 In.	5.00
Wine, Vino Rosso, Cat, Green, 13 In.	5.00
Wine, W.H.Clark In Raised Print, Flat Flask, Light Green, 5 1/4 In.High	60.00
Wine, Wm.Steinmeyer, Wine Merchants, Milwaukee, Wis., Gallon	9.00
Zanesville, Club Shape, 24 Broken Swirled Ribs, Citron, 7 3/4 In.	500.00
Zanesville, Club Shape, 24 Broken Swirled Ribs, Sapphire Blue, 7 3/4 In.	1200.00
Zanesville, Club Shape, 24 Slightly Swirled Ribs, Deep Aqua, 7 1/2 In.	70.00
Zanesville, Club Shape, 24 Swirled Ribs, Aqua, 8 1/2 In.	55.00
Zanesville, Club Shape, 24 Swirled Ribs, Deep Aqua, 7 3/4 In.	65.00
Zanesville, Club Shape, 24 Vertical & 24 Swirled Ribs, Aqua, 8 3/4 In.	45.00
Zanesville, Club Shape, 24 Vertical Ribs, Deep Aqua, 8 1/4 In.	65.00
Zanesville, Flattened Globular, 24 Swirled Ribs, Aqua, 9 In.	95.00
Zanesville, Globular, Aqua, 8 1/2 In.	55.00
Zanesville, Globular, Blue Green, 10 In.	90.00
Zanesville, Globular, Tightly Swirled Ribs, Dark Golden Amber, 8 1/2 In.	150.00
Zanesville, Globular, 24 Broken Swirled Ribs, Golden Amber, 7 3/4 In.	2500.00
Zanesville, Globular, 24 Ribs Slightly Swirled To Left, Amber, 8 In.	400.00

Zanesville, Globular, 24 Ribs Swirled To Left, Dark Amber, 7 1/2 In. 300.00
Zanesville, Globular, 24 Ribs Swirled To Left, Deep Aqua, 6 Quart, 12 In. 300.00
Zanesville, Globular, 24 Ribs Swirled To Left, Long Neck, Amber, 8 3/4 In. 650.00
Zanesville, Globular, 24 Ribs Swirled To Right, Amber, 3 Quart 450.00
Zanesville, Globular, 24 Ribs Swirled To Right, Aqua .... *Illus* 110.00
Zanesville, Globular, 24 Ribs Swirled To Right, Golden Amber, 7 1/2 In. 375.00
Zanesville, Globular, 24 Swirled Ribs, Amber, 7 In. 250.00
Zanesville, Globular, 24 Swirled Ribs, Amber, 8 In. 275.00
Zanesville, Globular, 24 Swirled Ribs, Aqua, 7 1/2 In. .... 70.00 To 100.00
Zanesville, Globular, 24 Swirled Ribs, Aqua, 8 1/4 In. 140.00
Zanesville, Globular, 24 Swirled Ribs, Citron, 7 1/2 In. 1000.00
Zanesville, Globular, 24 Swirled Ribs, Citron, 8 In. 900.00
Zanesville, Globular, 24 Swirled Ribs, Dark Red Amber, 8 In. 275.00
Zanesville, Globular, 24 Swirled Ribs, Golden Amber, 8 In. 350.00
Zanesville, Globular, 24 Swirled Ribs, Light Blue, 7 1/2 In. 150.00
Zanesville, Globular, 24 Swirled Ribs, Red Amber, 2 Quart, 9 1/2 In. 425.00
Zanesville, Shepherd & Eagle, Neck Lip, Dark Amber, 6 1/2 In. 450.00
Zanesville, Shepherd & Eagle, Neck Lip, Light Amber, 6 1/2 In. 400.00
Zanesville, Swirled, Domed Bottom, Aqua, Quart 60.00
    Zanesville, see also Flask, Chestnut, Flask